A FIGHT FOR GOD

Henri Daniel-Rops: *History of the Church of Christ:*

1. *The Church of Apostles and Martyrs* (A.D. 30–397)
2. *The Church in the Dark Ages* (397–1050)
3. *Cathedral and Crusade* (1050–1350)
4. *The Protestant Reformation* (1350–1564)
5. *The Catholic Reformation* (1500–1622)
6. *The Church in the Seventeenth Century*
7. *The Church in the Eighteenth Century*
8. *The Church in an Age of Revolution* (1789–1870)
9. *A Fight for God* (1870–1939)

A FIGHT FOR GOD

1870–1939

by

H. DANIEL-ROPS

TRANSLATED FROM THE FRENCH BY
JOHN WARRINGTON

LONDON: J. M. DENT & SONS LTD
NEW YORK: E. P. DUTTON & CO. INC.

Made in Great Britain
at the
Aldine Press · Letchworth · Herts
for
J. M. DENT & SONS LTD
Aldine House · Bedford Street · London
First published 1966

With the approval of the author, some sections of this English version of *Un Combat pour Dieu* have been condensed.

H. Daniel-Rops: *L'Église des Révolutions: Un Combat pour Dieu*, first published in France by Librairie Arthème Fayard, 1964

Nihil obstat: Joannes M. T. Barton, S.T.D., L.S.S., *Censor deputatus.*

Imprimatur: ✠ Patritius J. Casey, *Vic. Gen.*

Westmonasterii, die 13*a Aprilis*, 1966.

The *Nihil obstat* and *Imprimatur* are a declaration that a book or pamphlet is considered to be free from doctrinal or moral error. It is not implied that those who have granted the *Nihil obstat* and *Imprimatur* agree with the contents, opinions or statements expressed.

TRANSLATOR'S NOTE

This volume is translated from *Un Combat pour Dieu*, the second part of *L'Église des Révolutions*, which latter forms the sixth volume of M. Daniel-Rops's *Histoire de l'Église du Christ*.

CONTENTS

*

CHAPTER I

'GOD IS DEAD!'

1. The Challenge

On 25th August 1900, in a small house at Weimar where friends had sheltered his loneliness and his insanity, Friedrich Nietzsche lay dying; a writer whose books had awakened few echoes among his contemporaries, but who would be seen fifty years later as the prophet of humanity's abyss. His strange autobiography, with its faintly blasphemous title *Ecce Homo*, which he had written just before sickness struck him down, contained these dreadful words combining anguish with satanic pride:

'Where is God? I will tell you: we have slain him, you and I! Yes, we are all his murderers! But how were we able to do that? How have we managed to empty the sea? Is not the magnitude of that deed too great for us? For there has never been a mightier achievement, and that is why our successor on earth will be part of a history loftier than all history. God is dead! God is dead! and it is we that have killed him!'

Just as the author was departing from the scene, a very old man, himself close to the Great Threshold, twice made solemn utterance to give mankind the most trenchant parts of his message. On 25th May 1899 Pope Leo XIII had published his Encyclical *Annum Sacrum*, which consecrated the entire human race to the Sacred Heart of Jesus, symbol of the God-Man's love for all, even for those who knew Him not, even for those who fought against Him, even for those many who denied Him. Then, on 1st November 1900, another Encyclical appeared: *Tametsi futura*, in which the redemptive sacrifice of Christ was shown as the ultimate explanation of all that happens upon earth, the alpha and omega of man and of his destiny.

2. A World on New Foundations

On 20th September 1870, when the Piedmontese artillery thundering at Porta Pia ended the temporal power of the popes, eighty years had rolled by since other guns, firing on the walls of the Bastille, had overthrown the Old Regime of France. Although this was not at first apparent, the two events were closely linked as cause and effect. One cannonade echoed the other.

The Revolution which for ten long years had kept France in turmoil had not concerned France alone. The doctrines which had produced it, the ideals which its adherents had served, had claimed worldwide significance. They had penetrated deep into the minds of men, so deep that all the efforts of their opponents to eradicate them had proved futile. Victorious armies, as well as literature, had spread them among whole peoples. During eighty years they had been seen at work, arraying 'liberals' against authoritarian regimes, 'nationals' against foreign domination, culminating everywhere in violent crises, giving the Old World a very different appearance from that to which so many generations had been accustomed. 'Revolution has been accomplished in Europe and it must follow its course,' Napoleon Bonaparte had said. It had indeed followed its course.

Such was the first element that had transformed society; but there was another, less noticeable at the outset but soon to reveal itself as even more decisive. Simultaneously with the intellectual and political revolution there had taken place a scientific and technical revolution. The steam-engine, almost contemporary with the Declaration of the Rights of Man, had done as much as the latter to bring about a change of values and of principles. The rhythm of work had quickly altered, together with its environment. The birth of large-scale industry had had two corollaries: the growth of capitalism, that inhuman reign of anonymous wealth, and the emergence of a proletariat with its enormous masses devoid of hope. The result was a profound disequilibrium, favourable to subversive movements and socialist doctrines. Since 1848 the stream of social revolution had joined that of political revolution, rendering it more violent, more effective. 'The world is changing its foundations,' wrote Eugène Pottier in 1871;[1] and he was not mistaken.

Seventy years were destined to pass during which new transformations were achieved in political, social and moral life, transformations so thorough that we can in all truth speak of 'changed foundations'. Writing the preface to his *Histoire du XIXe siècle* in 1872, Michelet observes: 'One of the gravest but least noted facts is the complete alteration in the character of the age. It has somehow doubled its rate.' His remark is much more applicable to the following period, when that 'acceleration of history'[2] became truly apparent. Within a few years the balance of world forces was radically altered: new relations tended to become established between races and classes; ways unknown to previous generations imposed themselves and transformed the practical life of men together with the meaning they gave that life. All the phenomena we have seen foreshadowed by the French Revolution,

[1] *L'Internationale,* the revolutionary hymn, set to music by Degeyter.

[2] Daniel Halévy, *Essai sur l'accélération de l'histoire,* Paris, 1947; reprinted 1961.

and then assuming concrete form, reached their fulfilment. There is a greater difference between the world of 1939 and that of 1789 than between the latter and the age of St Louis.

There were changes on every front. In politics the most spectacular seemed to be those produced by the 1914–18 war. Prepared by long years of diplomatic play, it broke out as a trifling dispute for hegemony, but soon developed into a global tragedy which caused a complete revision of the world situation. Under pressure of the forces unleashed, centuries-old empires collapsed, leaving behind them only dust and debris, foundations too unstable to support a solid future. Governmental systems suffered a like fate; others arose, formidable regimes of unknown type in which the European spirit, based upon a certain scale of values, was no longer discernible. Old Europe tottered; the very continent which had created that spirit now felt herself menaced both in her supremacy and in her vital strength. Oswald Spengler prophesied 'the Decline of the West', the physiologically unavoidable end of one of those 'mortal civilizations' spoken of by Paul Valéry, a civilization which had ruled the Continent for a thousand years. In the far west the prodigious advance of the United States, due to the world war, seemed to crown the abasement of Europe, but at the same time partly to ensure the safety of European values, although these had been fundamentally modified by their transference to the New World. Meanwhile in the East, in the very heart of Asia, another phenomenon appeared, of which the sudden entry upon the scene of Japan, with her victory over czarist Russia in 1905, was only the first sign. I refer, of course, to the revolt of coloured peoples against the white race which for three hundred years had claimed exclusive control of the planet and whose triumphant colonialist expansion had everywhere sown the seeds of that rebellion. The world was face to face with something comparable to a biological mutation, which the Second World War was to precipitate, closing that page of history—and with it a long chapter of more than one thousand years—prior to inaugurating a dramatically new era for mankind.

Even so, these enormous changes were hardly on a level with those which caused the irruption of science and technique into social structures and ways of life, an irruption which also partially accounts for the political transformation. The progress achieved in the scientific and technical domains during the first third of the nineteenth century, great though it was, is nothing in comparison with that which followed, particularly in the last thirty years of that century and the beginning of the twentieth. It was an astonishing and in many respects admirable age, witnessing a forward surge of man's intelligence such as history had never yet experienced. Almost every one of those years was marked by a discovery pregnant with significance for the future; and

when the Americans came to draw up a graph of 'decisive inventions', the line was found to move upwards to a near-vertical position as if the power of human creativeness were stretching out to infinity.

All was change, all was regeneration—in man's vision of the universe no less than in the most transient circumstances of his life. Pure science opened the mind to dizzy prospects, wherein matter, energy, time and light became identified. From largest to smallest—from limitless space where galaxies swam by millions, down to the atom with its dance of electrons round a nucleus—a world was revealed which the mid nineteenth century could not have imagined. Of capital importance was the fact that the highest of these speculations nearly always had practical consequences, assuming concrete shape in the altered lives of men. Hertz laboured to perfect a theory of waves, and so laid the foundations of 'radio' which was destined to revolutionize the transmission of thought. X-rays were discovered by Röntgen in 1895, radium by Pierre and Marie Curie in 1900. Both of these revolutionized the domain of therapeutics, while the work of Lorenz, Perrin and Thomson resulted in electronics and atomism, which, for better *and* for worse, heralded other fundamental changes in man's way of life.

Applied science and technology were the sovereign agents of advancement. Dates speak for themselves; all the great practical inventions which rule our lives today date from those years: 1875, Graham Bell's telephone; 1888, the internal combustion engine perfected by Forest; 1889, the hydro-electricity of Gramme and others; about 1890, the motor-car; 1894, Lumière's 'cinematograph'; 1895, the 'wireless telegraphy' of Hertz, Branly, Lodge and Marconi; about 1900, the aeroplane. The list might be prolonged to cover every science: metallurgy, where new minerals came into use; the chemistry of dyes and solvents; textiles and materials for every purpose; medicine and pharmacy, which so many, from Pasteur to Fleming, laboured to regenerate.

All those inventions revealed themselves in ever more varied and ever more efficient machinery, which revolutionized the means of transport and communication, as well as those that transmit thought and information, altering the physiognomy of the world perhaps more rapidly and more profoundly than all other discoveries. Machinery also, ever more enormous, ever more costly and ever more indispensable, reigned supreme in the production of goods. Practically speaking, all that modern society consumes is turned out by machines, including to a large extent the fruits of the earth, since agriculture has been mechanized and is in all the new countries only one industry among many. Between machinery and man links have been forged which nothing can now break.

The many consequences of this event were seen in the daily lives of individuals as well as in the very structure of society. In countries of advanced technical civilization, of which the United States is the prototype and symbol, the standard of living rose and comfort became an ideal. But while it is true that machinery could produce consumer goods in vast quantities, the world's economic system was not yet geared to its rhythm; crises occurred, notably that of 1929, after which several countries witnessed the burning of food in order to counterbalance over-production while Chinese and Indians died of hunger by hundreds of thousands.

Perhaps even that was not the most serious result of all, for the irruption of technology affected man in every way. We recall the dreadful effects upon the life of the workers brought about by the advent of machinery. Those conditions gradually improved, but another danger soon became apparent. In theory the machine should reduce the workers' toil; but in fact man himself was often reduced to the role of slave to the machine, which he had to feed and tend. About 1900 F. W. Taylor introduced his famous system of production founded on the three principles of 'identity, repetition and rapidity'; twenty years later Henry Ford included 'taylorism' in a general concept not only of production and exchange, but of all working-class life, in which each one must obey the rules of the standard. There was great danger that man would become no more than a cog in a giant machine, good only for manufacture and consumption.

To this phenomenon of the technical order, the triumph of machinery, another was correlative, and largely dependent on it: the monstrous enlargement of towns, the concentration of human masses. Between 1870 and 1914 the population of all the great capitals increased twofold, while the countryside was deserted. The old social structures were broken up. Men lost the natural framework of their fulfilment; they found themselves part of enormous, anonymous and interchangeable masses, subject to all the increasing pressure of collectivity. A gregarious society was in course of formation. The process was world wide, wherever large-scale modern industry grew up.

To describe fittingly the stupendous changes accomplished during those seventy years we can find no other word than revolution. The results are indeed very different from those envisaged by the French Constituent Assembly in 1789; its individualism would scarcely have harmonized with mass civilization, and the Rights of Man appeared to be in grave danger one hundred and fifty years after their proclamation. It is none the less true that the forces which continued to shake the foundations of the world, which accompanied that 'vertical ascent of the barbarians' in western society as described by Ortega y Gasset, and which roused Asia and Africa against the colonialists, were forces

that had been unleashed by the French Revolution. The irruption of technical science, by multiplying the causes of imbalance, had given them fresh fields of activity. Revolution, social or political, was still at work; and the Church, which had to carry Christ's message among men, was still the Church in an Age of Revolution.

3. The Reign of the Secular Spirit

All those events which wrought fundamental changes in human society seemed far removed from the spiritual preoccupations of the Church and from her sphere of work. In fact they concerned her directly. It has always been recognized, and theology repeats, that the Church, though supernatural in her essence and transcending earth in respect of her goal, is nevertheless composed of men, creatures of flesh and blood, and therefore involved in temporal affairs. The problem of her grafting into successive forms of civilization is as old as her own existence, and it was about to be raised in a manner more urgent than ever before. Man's salvation, which had been entrusted to her, was at stake. God Himself was menaced by those obscure and terrible powers which wrought the transformations we have seen. In her relations with secular governments, with social classes and with various races, the authority of Holy Church was at issue, and her chances of being able to preach the Word were put in hazard; her very existence was threatened by a host of determined foes.

The seventy years whose importance in profane history we have just outlined were equally momentous in the domain of religious history. They coincide with an enormous increase of enemies whom we have long watched rising up against Christianity and endeavouring to undermine its bases. On all sides and at every level a vast assault was mounted against the Christian faith, against Christian morality and against the Church. The question now was whether that extraordinary mutation within the womb of history would mark the end of religion. Would the world, by changing its foundations, get rid of God?

Three French words cover all the forms assumed by hostility towards religion from the beginning of our period, three words that became current or received a new meaning: [1] *laïc*, *laïcisme*, *laïcité*. The term

[1] It was about 1875 that these words took on the sense we give them here. At that date Renan spoke of *laïcité* in a speech to the Académie Française; but the 1878 edition of the *Dictionnaire de l'Académie* ignores the word and defines *laïc* in the old sense. In 1871 Littré had defined *laïcisme* as 'the body, or character of *laïcs*'. In 1935 the Académie defined the term thus: 'doctrine which tends to give institutions a non-religious character'. In reality it is more than a 'doctrine'; it is a general attitude of mind.

Translator's Note. The author's references here to French dictionaries make it desirable to leave the three words untranslated in the text on this their first occurrence. But 'laicity' and 'laicism' are not normal English words, and even 'lay' (or 'laic') is often clumsy and unpleasing to the ear. Throughout the remainder of this volume, therefore, I shall translate them as 'secular', 'secularism' and 'secularity'.

laïc, which originally denoted a man who was not a cleric, had henceforward a more polemical sense; it meant 'that which is separated from all religious reality'—'separated from', and very soon 'hostile to'.[1] *Laïcisme* is the attitude of mind which, both in theory and in practice, rejects faith and all that proceeds therefrom. It includes all manifestations of the struggle against Christianity. Its purpose, in short, is the complete unhallowing of life and of the world. That is why Pius XI, by no means a narrow-minded pope, described secularism as 'the plague of our time, containing the worst elements of all our errors'.[2]

The secular spirit was at work throughout the period with which we are concerned, undermining all parts of the Christian edifice. It was active first at the political level, inspiring governments and infiltrating regimes. It demanded total separation of Church and State under pretext of preventing encroachment of one upon the other, but really in order to free all human institutions from the sway of religion. Adopting once again the methods employed by so many governments in the past, but with a more radical intention, it launched an attack on religious congregations, on the recruitment of the clergy and on the ties that bound Catholics to the Roman See. Its first object was to dismember the framework within which the Church operated, and to do so by means of a process it had learned from the Regalists, the Gallicans, the Josephists and, more recently, the French Conventionals. This undertaking could be carried out in many ways: usually by means of laws, as was done in Bismarck's Germany and in France under the Third Republic; but it sometimes happened that governments, in their struggle against the faith, had recourse to violent persecution, as in Mexico and Spain. Later, the totalitarian regimes combined both methods, using terror and the legislative arsenal to bring about the triumph of irreligion.

The secular spirit possessed a secret army wherewith to influence those in power: freemasonry. Without falling into the extravagance of certain polemists who, like Leo Taxil, see freemasons everywhere, it must be acknowledged that the sect played an important part in the grand assault upon religion. There had been some discussion regarding its activity in preparing the French Revolution, the conclusion being that while some of its members had distinguished themselves in the movement of ideas which led to the revolutionary explosion and its

[1] Since the terms *laïc* (secular), *laïcisme* (secularism) and *laïcité* (secularity) are equivocal, it is fair to remark that there have been and still are in the most 'secular' camp noble and upright minds which have never sought to overthrow the Church or to uproot the morality of the Gospel. But the 'secular saints' themselves, by their very presence, reject the supernatural and help to undermine the bases of faith. The respect due to some of them is not sufficient to belie the lesson of facts.

[2] Encyclical *Quas primas*, 1925.

antichristian trend, freemasonry could not in fact be held entirely responsible.[1] Moreover the Revolution, so far from encouraging it, had abolished most of the lodges in France. Reorganized under the Empire, when Joseph Bonaparte and Cambacérès had been placed at its head, it had included in its ranks marshals of the army, senior magistrates and notabilities in all walks of life. The Restoration, in spite of difficult beginnings, had not been unfavourable to freemasonry, which was protected by the Duc de Berry and the minister Decazes, two 'brothers' haloed in the glory of La Fayette. But it was chiefly under Napoleon III that France and other lands witnessed its full flowering. The one-time *carbonaro*, though he viewed it with mistrust, had allowed it to grow; but he had endeavoured to control it through Lucien Murat, Maréchal Magnan and 'Brother' Morny. Meanwhile in Italy (where Cavour and Garibaldi were members) and in Germany it had shared directly in the anti-Roman nationalist and liberal movements.

The period which opened in 1871 marked its apogee. The part taken by certain of its members in the Commune might have rendered it suspect, but it immediately occupied a position of great though secret importance under the Third Republic. 'Masonry', wrote 'Brother' Gadaud,[2] 'is the Republic under cover, just as the Republic is Masonry unveiled.' Leading members of the government were masons or fellow travellers. But that was not true of France alone: masons were active in Bismarck's empire, as they were in Italy; they wielded power in many South American republics, as well as in Portugal; in Spain the revolution which overthrew the monarchy was prepared in the lodges and led by nominees of the general assemblies. Masonry grew continuously more prosperous until the eve of the Second World War, when it counted almost two million members.

At the same time a change became apparent. Straightforward deism, more or less clearly formulated, which had inspired freemasonry in the years before 1789 and which Joseph de Maistre supported during the Restoration, had gradually disappeared. After 1848 many lodges had erased the name of God from their ritual. Only a minority of masons continued to respect the 'Great Architect'; the majority was rationalistic and atheist. Passionate anticlericalism underlay the propaganda disseminated by the lodges in the name of liberty and justice. Hatred of the Church became the principal motive of their action. 'Let us not forget we are the counter-Church', exclaimed one. To which another added: 'We freemasons must strive for the complete destruction of Catholicism.' And yet another declared: 'What must be destroyed is

[1] *The Church in the Eighteenth Century*, Chapter I, section 17.
[2] *Convent du Grand Orient*, 1894, p. 389.

the instrument used by the clergy to subjugate the masses, that is to say religion itself.'[1]

Animated by such principles, freemasons in high places did their best to establish the reign of the secular spirit. With this end in view a systematic campaign was undertaken at every level. The offensive launched by Strauss, Renan and others was resumed and stepped up. Critical work on the Sacred Books, not all of which was worthless—e.g. that of Harnack and that of the *Formegeschichte Method*[2]—was carefully directed against the scriptural bases of faith, which were presented as a mass of improbabilities. Doubt was cast upon the figure of Christ. The Old Testament, upon which Wellhausen concentrated, was treated even worse and its miracles made matter for derision. Archaeology too was invoked: publication of such documents as the Babylonian Code of Hammurabi and the Egyptian 'Book of the Dead', together with the study of Iranian dualism, made it possible to show the Judaeo-Christian message as a hotchpotch of oriental religions. Furthermore, when the science of Comparative Religion was born in England, its professors abandoned themselves to the joyous pursuit of analogies and prefigurations of the Holy Trinity in the Capitoline triad of the Romans and that of Brahma, Vishnu and Siva venerated in India; while 'sacred royalty', dear to the Upsala school, 'explained' the messiahship of Jesus. Likewise the study of primitive religions, inaugurated by Edward Burnett Taylor and developed by Sir J. G. Frazer in his *Golden Bough*, authorized 'truly free' minds to see the origin of all religions, Christianity included, in obscure practices, and to account for everything by means of 'totem', 'taboo', the 'eating of God' and 'magic rites'.[3] History, of course, was not excluded from this game: it was invoked to reveal the 'scandals of the Church' and her monstrous iniquities—even those least capable of proof, such as the alleged 'Pope Joan'; while the Inquisition, the trial of the Templars and the affair of Galileo were all fine subjects of polemic. Teaching of this kind was spread abroad by the popular press as well as by text-books destined for use in primary schools.

The moral as well as the intellectual bases of Christianity were

[1] These three quotations are taken from official records of masonic meetings, in the following order: Regional Congress of Belfast, May 1911; General Assembly of the Grand Orient, 1895; International Congress at Paris, 1900.

[2] See Chapter VI.

[3] Salomon Reinach, author of *Orpheus*, a manual of the history of religions, won fame by using and abusing these comparisons. The early Christians employed the anagram *Ichthus* to symbolize Jesus Christ—clear proof, according to Reinach, that they worshipped a 'fish-god'. He regarded the Eucharist as a magic rite analogous to primitive anthropophagy; even now, he proclaimed, there are tribes which eat the liver of their victim in order to make its strength their own! It is sad to think that during the first thirty years of the twentieth century *Orpheus* was looked upon in many university circles as worthy of belief.

undermined; secular laws sought to ruin the Christian edifice by abrogating the rules of morality laid down by the Church. It is significant that divorce, condemned by Catholics as 'a return to paganism and naturalism', was immediately introduced by governments committed to anti-religious strife, for example in France (1884) and in six or seven other countries. It is also significant that in Brazil, Argentina, Spain, Hungary and other States, where matrimonial law had been subject exclusively to religious jurisdiction, civil marriage was sanctioned by law. Finally, it is significant that anticlerical regimes took care, among other provisions, to authorize cremation of the dead, because the Church was hostile to that practice.

One of the most important features of the secular spirit was its anxiety to obtain control of youth. Here undoubtedly the ambiguity of terms was most in evidence. There was a demand for 'neutrality' of 'secular' schools, that is, the right to educate children apart from any sort of religious influence; in fact the ultimate purpose was to drive God from the schools and from the consciousness of children. 'The war between us is not in the streets but in the schools,' Clemenceau told his adversaries.[1] And Viviani acknowledged that 'neutrality is always a lie'.[2] Ferdinand Buisson, one of the ringleaders of secularism, made the following avowal in a book entitled frankly *La foi laïque*: 'Schools must be secular in their teaching', that is to say, not only in fact. Thus in every country where the religious problem was a major issue the most serious discussion turned upon the schools and the training of youth; this was true not only in the pre-1914 democracies, but also in Mussolini's Italy and Hitler's Germany.

Such was the paramount theme of the whole world's evolution during the period under consideration. The secular spirit reigned ever more supreme; and this state of affairs was so constant that it spread far beyond the so-called liberal democracies of pre-war days, which had served it so well. The totalitarian regimes that emerged after the conflict were no less 'secular', no less fundamentally opposed to the Church and to all religion, than the democracies they had destroyed or which they set at defiance. Lenin, Stalin and Hitler were just as 'secular' as the ministers of Combes or Crispi. The very methods employed by those regimes to instil secularism into the mind and conscience of their subjects were identical: interference with family life, influence on youth and critical polemics. The ultimate aim of the entire process of secularization was well known; the adherents of secularism made no attempt to conceal it. The Church, her institutions, her members—and indeed religion itself, no matter what form it may take—aspire to a certain concept of life which is based upon faith. 'The

[1] Speech in the Senate, 15th April 1901.
[2] Quoted in *L'Humanité*, 4th October 1904.

secular idea', says an historian of secularism,[1] 'includes a philosophical notion which rests upon the independence and capacity of reason.' When he embarked on his struggle against the Church, Bismarck gave it a highly significant name: *Kulturkampf*, 'struggle for civilization', pointing thereby to a collision between two concepts of civilization. The Marxists, as we know, adopt a similar attitude.

4. 'Belief and Unbelief'

Thus in the vast offensive launched against Christianity there was far more than commonplace anticlericalism or even hatred of the Church as an institution. At the root of the movement which seemed to carry the world against religion there was a concept of man essentially opposed to that offered by Christianity. Leo XIII understood as much and pointed it out in the first and one of the most important of his Encyclicals, *Inscrutabile Dei*: 'A close look at the critical circumstances of our time shows that there is only one cause of the evils which threaten us—the philosophical errors with which certain schools have imbued so many minds.'

This philosophical poison was no new thing. The 'battle between belief and unbelief' in Christian Europe, which Goethe had long ago described as 'the most profound, the only true and the one unique theme of world history', was joined as soon as man started to dispute the laws of the Church and to oppose the certitudes given by faith with the more immediate certitudes of reason. The intellectual revolt, dating from the Renaissance and encouraged by the triumph of Cartesianism, had never ceased to work upon the consciousness of Europe, even when the latter appeared to be established on unshakable foundations.[2] It had burst into the light of day during the eighteenth century. Appealing to other 'lights' than those of faith, the human mind had pretended to discard it like a bandage impeding sight. The French Revolution had marked the climax of that process; though it was not the direct outcome of the intellectual rebellion, it had received and disseminated its doctrine, and had been its most striking and most terrible manifestation. In its bloody glare, moreover, the consequences of that rebellion had begun to reveal themselves.

The first seventy years of the nineteenth century had witnessed a third stage in the satanic revolt, a third *Aufklärung* as it has been called, more radical than those of the Renaissance and the Age of Enlightenment. In the first stage the principal object of attack had been the structure of the Church; hence the Protestant Reformation

[1] G. Weil, *Histoire de l'idée laïque en France.*
[2] See Paul Hazard, *La Crise de la Conscience européenne.*

following immediately upon the Renaissance. During the Age of Enlightenment faith in Christ had been challenged. But the age of Kant, Hegel, Auguste Comte, Renan, Taine and Marx had gone much further. The various but in fact convergent efforts of all those minds led to the rejection of any faith whatsoever in a transcendent Being. It was truly a 'conflict between belief and unbelief'. The God of Christian revelation now found Himself disputed—some said finally abolished.

The period which opened in 1871 added nothing to this result. All its antichristian teaching proceeded directly from those of the early nineteenth century; all, that is to say, except one, which, though different, gave off a sound so dramatically new that very few minds were able to catch its echo. The others did no more than reproduce Auguste Comte or Feuerbach and Marx, and draw the consequences of ideas propounded by those great men. One of the most curious features of the contemporary intellectual crisis was a sort of sterilization of doctrinal irreligion, its lack of creative sap, at the very moment when it seemed on the verge of triumph.

The three earlier streams of irreligion then reappeared. One was positivism, the child of Auguste Comte. Positivists, unlike materialists, are ready to concede the existence of spiritual as distinct from material substances. But according to them the sole reality that truly counts is that which affects the senses and is perceived by the human intellect. 'Positive' knowledge is therefore the most complete; to it modern man attains, now that science has enabled him to escape first from the 'theological' and then from the 'metaphysical' age. On his death in 1867 Comte left numerous disciples.[1] In France, Littré, author of the famous dictionary, posed as the master's zealous propagandist before returning to Christianity on his deathbed. Hippolyte Taine (1828–93) applied Positivism to many historical and aesthetic subjects, even after his views on Comtian metaphysics had changed. In England the positivist current joined another springing from John Stuart Mill and continued by his disciple Alexander Bain. In Italy Positivism enjoyed great prestige with Roberto Ardigo (1828–1920), 'the philosopher of facts' and founder of *Rivista di filosofia scientifica*, as also with the anthropologist physician Mantegazza. In German-speaking countries, where Ernst Lass and Friedrich Jodl appointed themselves Comte's thurifers, the positivist theories assumed a rather different colour with the empiricism of Richard Avenarius and Ernst Mach, who reduced knowledge to sensation and subjected all phenomena to physico-chemical laws; that empiricism which Lenin described as 'a bastard doctrine, incredibly chaotic and reactionary'. In various guises

[1] Most of them dropped the famous Religion of Humanity which, for Comte, was the crown of his thought. Pierre Laffitte in France, Congreve in England and a few thinkers and politicians in South America remained faithful to it.

Comtian Positivism exerted a profound influence. Minds as different as Charles Maurras and Lévy-Bruhl made use of it. Its apparently objective and substantial nature delighted academic circles. It continued to inspire large fields of thought until it yielded pride of place to materialism, which had been revived and systematized by Karl Marx.

Materialism is, in a sense, more logical. It rejects outright the existence of any spiritual entity independent of matter, and maintains that all intellectual or moral activity proceeds from the functioning of the body—theories which had been upheld in the seventeenth century by Thomas Hobbes, and in the eighteenth by La Mettrie and some of the Encyclopaedists. During the nineteenth century the influence of materialistic monism steadily increased. Was not the sole reality that from which science derived? Ludwig Büchner's work *Force and Matter* (1855), which was reprinted twenty times in half a century, spread such theories far and wide. Germany was the privileged land of this doctrine, with the physiologist Moleschoff (who used to become frantic with rage at the very word 'spirit'), Carl Vogt and Ernst Haeckel, a second-rate thinker but a great vulgarizer. Even so brilliant a scientist as Wilhelm Ostwald (1853–1932), who received a Nobel prize for chemistry, did not avoid the shallowest materialism in his notion of the world as an agglomerate of atoms governed by the laws of an incomprehensible system of dynamics. This materialistic current was propagated everywhere. It drove the Italian psychiatrist Cesare Lombroso to his theory of genius as a form of madness. In France it was responsible for the eminence of Félix Le Dantec (1869–1917), according to whom 'consciousness is nothing but a by-product' and all thoughts mere consequences of 'sociological determinism'. Finally, it prepared the ground for another form of materialism, a form infinitely more structural and more active—the materialism propounded by Marx.

Positivism and materialism, which incidentally were often near neighbours and hard to distinguish, seemed willing to share the field of thought. We find them associated more or less closely with all the new scientific disciplines: with sociology, for example, which arose from Auguste Comte's teaching that mankind's development is subject to laws whose principles can be established by scientific methods; which was systematized by Durkheim (1858–1917); and whose application was extended to the sphere of morals by Lévy-Bruhl (1857–1929). Sociologists, observes their faithful interpreter Albert Bayet, hold that one must 'consider social phenomena as things' and discard all transcendent and teleological explanations. It is human society that makes man, without any ulterior purpose. 'There can be no theoretical morality,' says Lévy-Bruhl; the only reality is that which society

imposes. J. M. Guyau, in a book now forgotten but which caused a great stir in its day (1885),[1] had already spoken of a 'morality without obligation or sanction'.

Outside the vast domain where the violent waves of Positivism and Materialism broke ever closer upon one another's heels, it appeared that there were only small islets threatened with destruction. Persistent affirmations by those who stood for spiritual reality—Bergson and such Christian thinkers as Blondel or Maritain—were regarded by many as whimsical and absurd, as curiosities comparable with the preservation of mammoths in polar ice. The only philosophical trend was idealism, which soothed the conscience of intellectuals when they rejected the platitude of mechanism and vulgar materialism. Offspring of Hegel, it saw in the 'Idea', that is to say in the Spirit, Universal Being from which every individual being proceeds. Its heralds were: in England, Bradley and Pringle-Pattison; in Italy, Benedetto Croce (1866–1952) and Giovanni Gentile (1875–1944); in France, Léon Brunschvicg (1869–1944). Their teaching was not without nobility; for it preserved a sense of the true hierarchies, although it was rebuked for taking too little account of the real and having no grasp of it. Lenin was to remind idealists that the earth existed before man, that is to say before the idea, and Péguy hurled at them this sarcasm: 'Idealism has clean hands, but it has no hands.'

All those doctrines moved in the same direction; even Idealism, which, by centring everything upon the thinking self, necessarily eliminated absolute Spirit, creative and pre-existent, and whose adherents one and all were determined foes of Christianity either in the sanctimonious fashion of Brunschvicg or in the more violent manner of Gentile and Croce. Hostility towards religion was clearly marked among the rest, whether positivists or materialists, who were allies in this respect. Since the supernatural, by definition, escapes sensible experience and, being without matter, cannot be grasped, the whole of metaphysics is absurd. 'To speak of faith', says Mach, 'is to speak of wind.' Even the more moderate, such as Herbert Spencer, reduce God to an Unknown, of which there can never be any science and of which it is therefore best to take no account. For Haeckel neither the existence of God nor the immortality of the soul nor free will have any meaning; 'God', he says, 'is only a gaseous vertebrate animal.' The sociologists, even more influential, based everything on 'collective consciousness imposing itself upon the individual'; from which they concluded that belief in God is nothing but illusion, and their morality, as we have seen, is the exact antithesis of Christian morality, which presupposes obligations ordained by an authority superior to that of earth and admits eternal punishment. From whatever side one approaches it, this

[1] See the end of section 5 below.

immense flow of modern thought seems directed to a single objective: elimination of the sacred, and negation of God. There you have the creed embraced by all those who believe themselves to be moving with history and working for the progress of the human mind—a veritable faith turned inside out, whose premises are often no less gratuitous than those which grace established in the Christian conscience.

5. The Religion of Science and the Myth of Progress

The doctrines we have been outlining were not relegated to the limbo of pure thought; they penetrated into the consciousness—and even into the subconscious—of modern man. Powerful currents bore them along, currents which did not belong to one or another system of thought, but which were admitted or presupposed by all.

'Science is a religion.' Those words were written in 1848 by Renan in his *Avenir de la Science*, a book which he long let lie in manuscript, but which he decided to publish in 1890, two years before his death. That new faith, born during the nineteenth century, continued to unfold. An epoch which beheld the most prodigious flowering of pure and applied science ever known could not but stand amazed. The intellect is proud of itself; that is something quite legitimate, and Christianity makes no objection, recognizing in man's superiority an ineffable likeness. But as progress makes greater and greater strides, the deformation we have described as scientism becomes more and more prominent. Intoxicated with its triumphs, man makes science an idol, around which there grows up the 'religion' of which Renan speaks, with its own dogmas, its own ministers and its own morality. To science men look for a blissful future; science alone is capable of revealing truth in its entirety; science alone teaches man how to behave; science alone is the basis of wisdom. Why seek other explanations? 'We no longer believe in the philosophers,' jeered Nietzsche; 'nor in priests.' But trust in the scientists was absolute.

Today, in the blinding light of events, many have turned their backs on such illusions. We have learnt that science is worth what men are worth, and Rabelais's celebrated maxim has never seemed more pertinent: 'Knowledge without conscience is but a soulless ruin.' Half a century ago there were very few who resisted the scientific flood: Henri Poincaré, for instance, establishing the anatomy of scientific knowledge and of metaphysical knowledge; William James, whose 'pragmatism' beheld in science nothing but a convenient instrument; Henri Bergson proving science a construction of the intellect, incapable

of grasping reality, and at once demanding 'a supplementary soul' to exorcize the scientistic peril; Tolstoy denouncing 'modern superstitions'; or Brunetière in rather too much of a hurry to proclaim the 'downfall of Science'. The great majority of influential minds at that date were scientistic by conviction: savants such as Marcellin Berthelot, Claude Bernard and T. H. Huxley, as well as writers such as Flaubert, Zola or the Dane Brandes. Scientism had its own theologians: Wundt, a German who claimed to have effected a synthesis of all the sciences, and his fellow countryman Dilthey, who tried to create an 'anti-metaphysic'.

To that faith the masses clung in ever greater numbers—an easy gesture, since no constraint was involved. And everything helped to spread that faith. The press and literature alike were full of it. Universal exhibitions, held in the largest cities of the western world, contributed much to its expansion. The golden book of the Eiffel Tower, a souvenir left in the heart of Paris by the exhibition of 1889, is full of aphorisms on the theme: 'Whither will man not ascend now that he has raised the Tower?' The romances of Jules Verne, of Robida and later of H. G. Wells, in which imagination took its stand on scientific reality, helped to propagate the belief that all things were now possible to man. Even strongly conservative minds such as Melchior de Vogüe and Paul Bourget abandoned themselves to the triumphant mood.

This current was joined and strengthened by that of evolutionism. We have already described the beginnings of the evolutionary theory during the first part of the nineteenth century,[1] following upon the emergence of prehistory as a science, and after Lamarck and Darwin, each in his own way, had put forward the hypothesis of transformism. Many discoveries appeared to support the transformists; for example, those of *Pithecanthropus* in Java (1890) and Neanderthal man had some bearing upon human origins. As regards the mechanism of evolution, there was no agreement after Darwin contradicted Lamarck, and in 1901 the Dutch botanist Hugo de Vries advanced a new hypothesis called Mutationism. But the fundamentals of the theory did not alter; it even assumed a more general and absolute character.

That indeed was a fact of capital importance. Evolutionism tended more and more to become not merely a scientific hypothesis, but an explanation of the world. Huxley and Spencer applied it to the moral and social structure of mankind. Haeckel spread it far and wide through his book *The Enigma of the Universe* (1899), of which 400,000 copies were sold. Evolution was now considered as 'the law of the cosmos', 'not only one theory, one system, one hypothesis, but a general condition to which all theories, all hypotheses, all systems must bow and conform in order to be true and tenable'. Thus wrote a young

[1] *The Church in an Age of Revolution*, Chapter VI, section 3.

palaeontologist, Father Teilhard de Chardin,[1] who in 1913 contributed some new elements to the knowledge of fossil man. Haeckel went so far as to say that the intelligence of a people could be measured by its faith in evolution. The evolutionist concept invaded all the sciences, anatomy as well as genetics, geology as well as anthropology and sociology. Psychology and morality did not escape it, and Marx applied it to economic facts. Ferdinand Brunetière, the same who announced 'the downfall of science', spoke of 'the evolution of literary *genres*'!

The religion of science and the doctrine of evolution combined to produce the Myth of Progress. The human mind pretended to understand the whole history of our race, from its remotest origins to its furthest future. The idea was simple, and appealed at once to the masses. Just as it was known that man had steadily advanced towards a more perfect type, towards better organized forms of civilization, so also it was believed that, thanks to science and the increasingly powerful means at his disposal, he would become still greater until he had mastered the whole world and life itself. The triumphal ascent of man was a certitude. Everything must be directed to Progress;[2] the myth obtained a hold on the mind, and very few escaped its grasp. Even after the terrible warning of the gas-chambers and Hiroshima, it seems to fill the consciousness of millions today.

It need hardly be said that those dominants of the modern mentality all tend to reject faith and deny God. Not that Christianity is fundamentally hostile to science and progress; in our own day the apologetic of Father Teilhard de Chardin has attempted to base itself on both. But that stage had not yet been reached at the time when Haeckel and Le Dantec flourished. Evolution and scientism did much more than propagate the ridiculous axiom 'Man descends from monkey' or provide critical weapons for use against the miracles of the Bible. What they proposed was an entire concept of the world and of man essentially antagonistic to that held by Christianity. The very idea of an intentional origin of the world and that of finality were equally unacceptable: God the Creator was no less absurd than Providence. Why should man, demiurge of the world of tomorrow, feel himself dependent on a superior Being to whom he owes worship and obedience? 'The laboratory supersedes the oratory.' Nor was there any sense in the Christian image of man, wounded by sin but redeemed, if an inevitable process of evolution was leading mankind to a state of superior perfection. The opposition was irreducible. Baudelaire had seen it clearly when he wrote: 'True progress does not consist in gaslight or steam, but in obliterating the traces of original sin.'

[1] *Le Milieu divin*, Paris, 1955.

[2] Between 1880 and 1914 the word became fashionable on café signs, on the flag of positivist Bolivia and as watchword of the Young Turks.

Thus man's forward march towards a future illuminated by science and technology appeared to lead of necessity to one only goal—the ruin of faith. In the world of tomorrow religion would no longer have a place.

6. 'Homo Homini Deus'

There is yet another aspect of modern thought to be considered if we would understand the mechanism of the 'death of God' proclaimed by Nietzsche. All those negations we have been discussing had their corresponding affirmations, which are equally decisive in the workings of irreligion. It was not just a matter of atheism in various forms, but of 'atheistic humanism'.[1] Man's need of belief was so great that the void left by faith in God was filled by another faith, faith in another absolute which was none other than man himself. Thus was accomplished that replacement of religion, whose complete destruction could be ensured only by such means.

But atheistic humanism itself was no more a novelty than were the doctrines of irreligion. It came into being and grew with the intellectual rebellion. The French Revolution had formulated its teaching and introduced aberrant forms of it. Thereafter it had never ceased to make headway, thanks to the writings of Hegel, Feuerbach, Marx and Comte. All trends of thought which rejected faith adhered to it. Béranger's refrain, heard on all sides at the beginning of the nineteenth century, expressed a conviction that was becoming more and more general: 'Mankind, reign! This is your age—which is vainly denied by the voice of pious echoes.' And Feuerbach gave it a motto with the words *Homo homini deus*: 'Man is man's god.'

Auguste Comte had dreamed of erecting on this foundation a whole new religious system. Renan had talked of 'divine humanity'. Berthelot had unceasingly proclaimed that the ultimate goal of scientific effort was the revelation and glorification of man. This aim was henceforward, so to speak, a presupposition of anti-faith, something accepted without demur. It was occasionally expressed in a manner so uncouth as to merit laughter. Haeckel, for instance, wrote: 'The secret of theology is anthropology. God is man adoring himself. The Trinity is the human family deified.' We find the same idea among the scientists and the fanatics of progress, who looked into the future and beheld man as absolute master of the world; we find it, too, among the idealists, for whom the thought of man included that world itself and called it into being. Man as the measure of all things, as the sole *raison d'être* of all:

[1] The phrase was coined by Father de Lubac, *Le Drame de l'humanisme athée*, Paris, 1945; reprinted 1960.

such was the image offered to itself by the mind detached from God, and such was the image welcomed ever more readily by the masses.

Its falsehood became steadily clearer as years passed and events along the line of man's forward march grew more catastrophic. Paradoxically the glorification of man went cheek by jowl with his inner degradation and, before long, with his utter negation. If the human being is nothing but an aggregate of molecules controlled in its behaviour by blind forces, it is hard to see upon what his 'greatness' can be founded. If there is any truth in the theories of Charcot and Janet, who explained mystical states as mental aberration, or in those of Lombroso, who attributed the highest creative gifts to the same cause, then it is the superior types of humanity—the geniuses, the heroes, the saints, in a word those who alone could justify man's glorification—that collapse in ruin. If the human person is the measure of all things, what becomes of it in the system established by technology, where the worker, dependent on the automatism of machinery, is reduced more and more to a standard, while in the rest of its experience it is subject to heavier and heavier pressures all of which tend to destroy its freedom? The age of triumphant atheistic humanism was also that during which there rose on the world's horizon fearful totalitarian monsters with their infallible methods of reducing the individual to collective slavery and annihilating that which makes man truly man—the opportunity and the right to fulfil a personal destiny. That twofold evolution is noticeable throughout the period with which we are concerned. After 1918 it accelerated at a terrifying speed; the day would come when these bitter words would flow from the pen of one who was among the most reliable witnesses of his age: 'They say that God is dead; maybe man died with him.' [1]

Meanwhile, before history smote this inordinate pride, before humanity began to experience increasing doubt as to the reality of its deification, a change became noticeable within the very vitals of atheistic humanism and eventually uncovered its satanic nature. The various philosophies that nurtured irreligion led to atheism as the term of speculative reason. They declared that God does not exist, since He is not reducible to experience; that He is not a material fact but only an hypothesis, because possession of the idea of an object does not demonstrate its reality. Twentieth-century atheistic humanism went much further. It was not content to say that God does not exist and that all religion is absurd; it wanted to make sure that such would be the case. Proudhon was already talking of 'anti-theism'. In order that man might be God, it was necessary that there should be no other God: the conclusion was one of imperious logic. God felt as the decisive obstacle to man's fulfilment, as an enclave that must be smashed before

[1] André Malraux in a personal letter to the author.

man could be himself and truly free—such was the aim of all brands of positivism, materialism, evolutionism and scientism. Therein lay the originality of twentieth-century irreligion, the furthest point of its progress. Two great systems of thought determined that final evolution; they were very different from each other but complementary in the last resort: that of Karl Marx and that of Friedrich Nietzsche.

7. Nietzsche, Prophet of Darkness

Friedrich Nietzsche . . . I cannot speak without affection of this man, whom the atheistic world acknowledged as one of its guides. He loved nature, animals and flowers; delighted in the thought of Italy and Greece; found in music the satisfaction of a vital need; and was among the greatest German poets, disciple and rival of Heine and of Hölderlin. Though he believed himself to hate goodness and mercy, he was good, compassionate towards the humble and the poor, so gentle in behaviour that his neighbours at Geneva used to call him 'little saint'. But above all—and this is why no Christian can look upon him with indifference—he committed himself entirely to that battle with the Angel, which every man must fight, regardless of risk, knowing that he endangered more even than his life, face to face with mystery in an almost Pascalian agony, bearing witness to our worst temptations.

Let us watch him [1] as he stands beneath the rock of Surlei in the Engadine, looking out across the cold blue lake of Sils-Maria, finding himself 'six thousand five hundred feet above sea level but far higher above all human things', overwhelmed by a flood of wellnigh unutterable intuition, yet experiencing to the point of delirium a longing to proclaim his revelation. Hegel and Feuerbach, Comte and Renan, Spencer and Stuart Mill, all those doctrinaires of unbelief, were dreary intellectuals, logicians, teachers. Nietzsche was otherwise; he rejected them all with contempt: rationalists and positivists, materialists and idealists, and socialists as well. He wanted nothing to do with logical demonstration. What he had to give the world was an existential certitude that had suddenly taken shape within him, in a moment of miracle and anguish. And he knew that a terrible secret had been entrusted to him. 'I would rather be a lecturer at Basel than be God,'

[1] The life of Nietzsche was uneventful, with nothing—not even his short and disappointing love affair with Lou Andreas Salome—to rouse idle curiosity. Born at Roecken in Prussia, in 1844, he worked for some time as a schoolmaster and made friends with Richard Wagner, with whom he subsequently quarrelled. In 1879 he gave up teaching and thereafter led the wandering life of a penurious invalid, writing books which no publisher seemed to want, dividing his time between the Engadine and various parts of Italy. Finally he fell victim to insanity in a Turin street (1889), and died at Weimar in 1900.

he cried; 'but I am too much of an egoist to refrain from creating the world!' He had the look of an inspired prophet; with his enormous brow, huge moustache and deep-set feverish eyes, he might have been painted by Michelangelo on the walls of the Sistine. Did he not call himself 'prophet of a darkness hitherto unknown'? Modern irreligion was to have no more pathetic voice.

Can we, with reference to Nietzsche, speak of a doctrine? He was subject to so many influences: those of Heine and Dostoyevsky, which he accepted; those of Strauss and Feuerbach, which he rejected; that of Richard Wagner, which he likewise scorned. In him there was something of Mani, something of Buddha, something even of Christ, many of whose sayings were twisted by Nietzsche into aphorisms of his own. Nothing is further from a systematic approach than the way in which he expresses himself through strings of lyrical maxims and lapidary phrases, all of which are in shameless contradiction one with another. It is easy to quote him in support of every thesis, even of those which form a traditional part of Christian apologetics. Where for him do paradox and irony begin; or where the need to cry the most scandalous of truths? And yet from that teeming medley there emerges a true philosophy, if we accept 'philosophy' as meaning an attitude towards life. If there is no Nietzschean system, there is certainly such a thing as Nietzschism.

The fundamental principle adopted by this Thuringian pastor's son was radical unbelief. 'For me', he wrote in *Ecce Homo*, 'atheism is not a result of something, still less an event in my private life; it is of course instinctive.' Small matter that one sometimes suspects this avowal of being forced, arbitrary, and that the God whom he pretends so serenely to dismiss remains for him an opponent, terribly real and close. It is from this assumption that all his theories derive: there is no God, heaven is empty, thus saith Zarathustra.

The first consequence of such an axiom is that there can be no religion. According to Nietzsche religion comes of man's 'doubling' himself. Among the strongest there comes about an awareness of human grandeur; but this dare not give expression to itself, and ends by conferring the attributes of man upon a supernatural being. These attributes of divinity are such as the weak and second-rate can never possess. Religion is thus in every respect an 'alienation of personality', 'a negation of man's greatness'. It prevents him from being 'faithful to the earth', i.e. from realizing all his potentialities. God is nothing but the symbol beneath which man's cowardice and feeble will take shelter, and if so many cherish the myth, they do so merely because it is more convenient not to be than to will to be, because the majority refuse the heroic effort necessary in order to 'become what one is'.

It was mainly against Christianity that Nietzsche directed the barb

of his criticism: Christianity is the religion that carries the derangement and degradation of man to the furthest possible extreme. It is 'an eternal blot upon humanity'. By laying down as principle that 'all good, all greatness and all truth are gifts of grace', Christianity deprives man of the chance to be himself. Christian faith destroys 'faith in life'. Christian morality, too, is the direct opposite of all that makes a true man. Supremacy of the simple-minded, of the pure of heart, of the needy, of the failures—is that the true hierarchy of values? In 'faith, purity, simplicity, patience, love of the neighbour and resignation' Nietzsche saw 'a repudiation of one's proper Self'; and that is quite correct, except that he interpreted it as an outrage against man. All the sentiments which Christianity recognizes as virtues he regarded as absurd and despicable. 'Pity is a squandering, a harmful parasite on moral health. A true man should take as his motto: "Be hard".' Is not that, in practice, the advice followed by great men, the conquerors, the geniuses, who subject events to their own measure—the Caesars and Napoleons? This inevitable conclusion, then, falls from the prophet's contemptuous lips: 'It is not decent to be a Christian.'

For here is the ultimate message Friedrich Nietzsche thought himself called to give the world. A capital event has come to pass, which has escaped the notice of mankind: *the day of religions is over; God is dead.* The certainty of 'the death of God', which he had received from Heine,[1] is the basis of his message; but not a somehow static certainty, a discovery like that made by historians. The famous words in which he announces this event [2] likewise declare an act of choice. 'We are all the murderers of God', and we continue to murder Him every day. In 'deciding against Christianity, not by reasoning but by inclination', we commit that crime of crimes. 'The death of God is not only a terrible fact for man; it is willed by him. Why? Surely, to put an end to his alienation and abasement'. To slay God is to assert man. Nietzschean atheism is not only negative; it claims to offer each one the grandiose adventure of 'the difficult and dangerous conquest' of true manhood instead of the cowardly facilities given, as he said, by religion. 'Since there is no longer a God, solitude has become intolerable; the superior man must go into action.'

Such is the tone of Friedrich Nietzsche's atheistic humanism. It acknowledges that the death of God is an event of fearful import, even though the majority of living men are not as yet aware of it. Among those who are, many stand as if stricken with amazement in presence

[1] This fact was little known until it was pointed out by Father de Lubac. In 1834, half a century before Nietzsche, Heinrich Heine had written an article in the *Revue des Deux Mondes* entitled 'Germany since Luther', which contained these words: 'Do you not hear the bells? Down on your knees! They are taking the sacraments to a dying God.'

[2] See the opening of section 1 above.

of that murder. 'How have we been able to do it? How have we managed to empty the sea?' And they give way to fears which were to be confirmed by historical events: 'Shall we not now be continually falling? Shall we not wander in infinite nothingness? Do we not feel the wind of emptiness upon our face? Does it not grow colder and colder, darker and darker?' Prophet of a world swallowed up in night, Nietzsche knew better than anyone that mankind, having murdered God, had entered upon an immense cycle of catastrophe. Unlike the various brands of socialism, he offered no paradise on earth: his 'exhilarating science' was devoid of optimism. It is not easy to make a God of man.

What do we find, at last, is the term of that choice? Nothing other than man; not weak and cowardly man wallowing in the mud of religion, but man who truly brought about the death of God and realized all its consequences; man who, like Wagner's Siegfried, lives human life to the full, without fear of death; man who is conscious of the infinite powers that lift him up and who gives them play; in a word, Superman. It is a Messianic view, but devoid of God, regarding Superman both as saviour and saved. Associated with the 'morality of life', which can be inferred from the invective hurled against Christian morality, Nietzsche's concept led to the justification of violence, cruelty, the worst inequality of human conditions, and even slavery; for it is right that the race of Superman should be served by the second-rate and cowardly. 'It may be', says Nietzsche, 'that all this fills us with terror, but there is something terrible about nature too.' It is 'beyond Good and Evil' that man will stand erect, a God wonderful in his perfection, wholly dedicated to the achievement not of virtue nor indeed of pleasure, but of nobility and grandeur.

Such is the atheistic humanism of Friedrich Nietzsche, than whom, it must be said, there has been in our age no more complete embodiment of the satanic rebellion. Aristocratic in the highest degree and accessible to very few minds, Nietzsche's message went almost totally unheard during his lifetime. That writer whom none read convinced nobody when he assured his neighbours at table: 'Forty years from now I shall be famous in Europe.' And yet, without inaugurating a worldwide movement such as that inspired by the thought of Karl Marx, the author of *Will to Power* and *Antichrist* was destined to nourish the minds of those who would later believe themselves called to the vocation of supermen. A whole river flowed from Nietzsche, visible in literature. Mussolini and Hitler, those monsters who imposed their tyranny upon millions, were his readers and disciples. Only the concentration camps and gas-chambers could teach humanity the logical significance of Nietzsche's lyrical aphorisms on the morality of Superman and the crushing of inferior races.

As for the prophet himself, the prophet of abysmal night, he had long been dead, having lived for ten years insane—an existence worse even than death. He had been the most vehement herald of man in rebellion against God; but no one else had given so clear a warning of the risks involved. A Christian cannot speak without emotion of that tragic, that broken witness of the Void.

8. The Rise of Marxism

Nietzsche was an isolated romantic; he spoke not to the crowds, and he was guided more often by passion than by reason. Shortly before the utterance of his gloomy forebodings another man of genius, living as an exile in London, was elaborating a doctrine altogether different in tone from the paradoxical wisdom of Nietzsche, a logical doctrine and difficult to penetrate, yet capable of stirring the masses. That doctrine was soon to flourish exceedingly, emerging from the medley of antichristian philosophies and embracing them all. A day was near upon which the leading witness and most effective agent of the 'death of God', proclaimed by Nietzsche, would be found beyond dispute in the person of Karl Marx.

A German Jew, disciple of Hegel, but rejecting his master's idealism in order to follow the road opened by Feuerbach towards a radically determinist materialism, then passing from speculative philosophy to the study of economic and social facts, Karl Marx had just accomplished an enormous synthesis in which he claimed to include and arrange the whole of reality—to express, in the words of his disciple Plekhanov, 'a total concept of man and of life'. At the same time he had joined the revolutionary movement, to which he had contributed the daring propositions of the Communist Party Manifesto in 1848. The first volume of *Das Kapital* had appeared in 1867 bearing a misleading subtitle ('Development and Production of Capital') which took no account either of its breadth of design or of the richness of the theories it expounded. This first volume had not gone unnoticed; the intelligentsia of Germany and France had read it. Nevertheless when Marx died in 1883 his ideas were less than celebrated. He himself, though convinced of having inaugurated a new epoch of history, felt some anxiety and sadness on learning that his influence was small and on seeing the *Workers' International*, of which he had been the principal founder, lose support and finally expire at the Congress of Philadelphia in 1876.

Marxism, however, made steady progress year by year. There were many reasons for its success. Most obvious was the fact that all the themes we have recognized as common denominators of the modern

outlook were tapped by it and channelled into a system of rigorous precision. Scientism, the myth of progress and inevitable evolution were all assumed and extrapolated in Marxism. There the Luciferian optimism of Godless man reached its fulfilment. There also materialism was carried to its furthest extreme. According to Marx, indeed, material reality alone existed, it alone was knowable; but while so many thinkers derived only shallow forms of determinism from those affirmations, he claimed to answer the existential anguish of man by showing him why he is on earth and the purpose of his life. Marx's method, dialectic, which he had borrowed from Hegel but 'put back on its feet', derived everything from matter and not from the Idea, i.e. not from mind. It thus became 'materialist dialectic', offered a general explanation of all reality—notably of human reality, which translates itself into history—and gave 'dialectical materialism' an inner vitality which no other philosophic teaching possessed to the same degree. Finally, and above all, Marxism presented itself not as a mere ideology, a speculative truth, but as a *praxis*, a doctrine for action, 'effecting the unity of theory and practice'. None of the positivist or materialist philosophers, not even Auguste Comte, dreamed of concrete means for translating into human reality the consequences of the notions they put forward; nor did the prophet Nietzsche. Revolutionary Marxism, on the other hand, declared its resolve not 'to comment upon the world, but to transform it'. By revealing to the oppressed and suffering masses the means of their liberation this doctrine, based upon figures and dry analysis, stirred up resentments and hopes, that is, all the elementary instincts of man from the very worst to the best. Small wonder that it disturbed and called to its own service those 'telluric forces' of which Keyserling was to speak.

The system of thought presented in the first volume of *Kapital* was elaborated by the posthumous publication of three others, based upon notes and rough drafts. Volumes II and III were written by Marx's closest friend, Engels, who spent ten years at the task; Volume IV is the work of Kautsky. All three were published between 1904 and 1910. This monumental whole was quickly translated into all the chief western languages.

The mere recording of those publications is enough to show the important place occupied by Marxism during the thirty years after its founder's death. As Marx himself had wished, its ascendancy was continuous on the two planes of doctrine and action. Whereas Nietzsche left no one to propagate his teaching, a veritable school of Marxism existed and made rapid headway. In England the American Henry George, in his book *Progress and Poverty*, made an impressive application of Marxist theories to the lamentable state of the country. In France, Jules Guesde, a self-educated hothead, drew upon them for

arguments when he sought to revive the old collectivism; and Georges Sorel, a middle-class sociologist at loggerheads with capitalist society and author of *Réflexions sur la violence*, flirted for a while with Marxism. But it was chiefly among the Russian intellectuals who had been driven from their homeland by the czarist police that Karl Marx found his most zealous heirs. In 1883 Plekhanov and Akselrod formed a Marxist group which soon recruited many adherents from the exiled intelligentsia. A Marxist press also came into being, more or less clandestinely: *Iskra* ('The Spark') in London, and *Pravda* ('Truth') in Vienna, both founded by Lev Trotsky. Above all there was Vladimir Ulyanov, called Lenin, who spent long periods as a refugee at Paris or Geneva, but sometimes profited by a lull in czarist persecution to re-enter Russia and pursue his work there in secret. A prolific writer and vitriolic journalist, who made *Pravda* the most important organ of the movement, he proved himself the leading continuator of Marx. Lenin played St Paul to the new Messiah, brilliantly adapting his master's thought to the practical circumstances of revolutionary work; and so penetrating was his thought, so fruitful his endeavour, that the Communist doctrine became known henceforth as Marxism-Leninism.

The immediate consequence of Marxism's progress was the disappearance of those various socialist systems which had been elaborated during the first part of the nineteenth century. What could the humanitarian ideologies of older socialism avail against the new doctrine with its stern logic, its appeal to class warfare and to the dictatorship of the proletariat? Within the ranks of Marxism itself an evolution took place which was destined to have important consequences. Two tendencies became manifest. The partisans of one hoped to achieve the victory of socialism by legal, parliamentary means; those of the other, while firmly rejecting anarchist views, saw their only chance in the subversion of liberal capitalist society. Politically this opposition between those two tendencies was plain for all to see. At the Congress of London, in 1903, Russian socialism split into two: by a very small majority, the advocates of 'revolution at all costs', led by Lenin and known thereafter as *Bolsheviks* (majority men), defeated the reformist minority, who were called *Mensheviks* (minority men). Fourteen years later the Bolsheviks seized power and established Communism in Russia.

Here undoubtedly was the salient fact in the modern history of ideas: atheistic humanism in its most systematic and unyielding form, offering itself as the sole solution of all human problems, made ready to prove itself capable of founding a human society. This rise of Marxism was a grave threat to Christianity and to the Church. Christians would now find themselves face to face with the most resolute and best armed opponents they had ever met. There were many weaknesses

in the irreligion of the socialist Proudhon, as well as in the anti-christian teaching of the positivist Auguste Comte; the ordinary run of materialists were unable to erect a system on their over-simple assertions, and the 'secular' ministers of France and Italy had little or no doctrine to offer. Henceforward it was a doctrine, a total and positive system of thought that confronted faith, firmly resolved upon its destruction.

The opposition of Marxism is not accidental; it belongs to the very essence of Marx's philosophical and social thought. His atheism is the necessary counterpart of his idea of man: it is at the root of his definition of liberty. To be free is to derive one's being from oneself alone; to believe in God the Creator is to agree to be a slave. The impulse that drove atheistic humanism in all its forms to reject God as an obstacle to the development of man found its term in Marxism. 'Religion', said Marx, 'is the opium of the people.' 'Not even opium', declared Lenin, 'but a sort of bad spiritual vodka in which the slaves of capitalism drown their human existence.' In order to perfect man, in order to enable him to build a world of his own stature, religion must disappear and the very idea of God become incomprehensible. That task was to be accomplished by the whole of society on its forward march. Atheism had never shown itself so radical and so complete.

It must also be noticed that while Marxism operated on the minds of men with a view to their embracing materialism and atheism, there was another influence at work in the practical sphere. In the ultimate Marxist perspective there is no specific requirement that man should make himself 'the murderer of God', as Nietzsche desired. Since religion is a superstructure of capitalist society, it will disappear along therewith in accordance with the dialectical movement of history. Meanwhile, however, since we are as yet in the transitory phase, where capitalist society is all powerful, religion, an important element of the established order, must be considered as an ally of the capitalist regime, that is, as an enemy to be annihilated. And so, just as Marxist dialectical materialism collected and absorbed all the old formulae of atheism, Marxist policies were likewise able to use all the means employed by opponents of the faith, even though the latters' thought was fundamentally bourgeois. Thus we shall see the Marxists taking over the arguments of the most traditional secularism, e.g. in the fields of biblical criticism, sociology and morals. We shall also find them adopting the methods used by secularists to make war upon the Church, her clergy and her institutions, but doing so more violently and systematically. Was atheistic humanism of the Marxist brand, that compendium of irreligion, destined to polarize in its activity as well as in its doctrine all the forces which for many years had been conducting the great offensive against God?

9. The Totalitarian Menace

The period which opened with the end of the First World War marks a new stage in that offensive. It was not that other doctrines arose to teach men new ways of 'killing God'; those which did appear were only variants of or substitutes for the various types of positivism and materialism that had long been at work. It was in the realm of events and institutions that the danger was more immediate and more pressing. It was a question not only of theory, but also of practical application. Whole peoples were summoned to achieve the 'death of God' in their own lives.

On 6th and 7th November 1917[1] a handful of Marxists, led by Lenin and Trotsky, overthrew with one thrust the fragile edifice which Kerensky's reformist socialists were attempting to build on the ruins of the czarist empire. Despite countless difficulties the Bolsheviks brought order from chaos by means of merciless severity, repelled the attacks of domestic and foreign enemies, and thus came to dominate the whole of Russia. Four years later, in 1921, it was perfectly clear that this small minority of revolutionaries, whose downfall was prophesied daily by the bourgeois press, had so firmly established its power with support from the 'soviets' of soldiers and workers that it would not be ousted. A new destiny lay before Holy Russia. The Bolshevik revolution was of capital importance not only in the political field, but also in the history of ideas and in that of religion.

There now existed a state founded on the most absolute and determined Marxism. Lenin (1870–1924), that 'little bourgeois' with the face of a Kalmuk, to whom the success of the October Revolution was mainly due, re-thought his master's teaching, adapted it more closely to contemporary needs, gave it a language simpler, more accessible to the masses and more polemical in tone, and thus rendered it more effective, that is to say more formidable to Christian faith. Like Marx, Lenin and his associates were violently hostile to religion; they spoke of it with even greater contempt than their master had done. The Russian Church was linked traditionally with the autocratic and plutocratic regime which Bolshevism had overthrown. The young Marxist state would therefore seek its destruction at any price, not excluding bloody persecution, and would devote all its strength to the uprooting of faith everywhere, in order to build the 'Godless society'.

Such was the capital fact: for the first time in the history of human

[1] Because of the time-lag in the Russian calendar the event is known as the 'October Revolution'.

society there existed an apparently durable regime which rejected all reference to God or to supernatural forces, resolved to strive for a civilization stripped of all that is sacred. Never before had such an attempt been made, an attempt that was literally satanic because it substituted man for God. Even in the darkest days of the French Revolution, the most vicious leaders of the campaign against religion had never appealed to such principles; or at least the whole-hearted atheists had never been able to use the apparatus of government to impose their ideas. Henceforward those who made it their aim to annihilate religion would have this pattern before their very eyes. The Communist parties which sprang up in an increasing number of countries embodied the determination to build a Godless world; and the Third International, founded in 1919 by Lenin, who federated all Communist movements and parties under the control of the Komintern, acted as something akin to an atheistic 'Church', a counter-Church endeavouring like the Church of Christ to direct the whole human race.

Lenin and the Bolsheviks did more than prove to the world that a Godless regime is possible; they devised an instrument that would force men to accept irreligion. In one of his principal works, *State and Revolution*, Lenin expressly declared that 'the State, as an organ of compulsion, must be placed entirely at the service of revolutionary principles'. All the means at its disposal must co-operate in establishing the Marxist society and in producing the Marxist man. Thus with the triumph of Russian Bolshevism there was born the first of modern totalitarian regimes.[1] In such a regime all depends upon, proceeds from and tends towards the State, which animates and controls economic life as well as that of the intellect. There is no individual freedom outside the framework appointed by the State. Nor is there such a thing as justice or morality. The supreme law, the one and only law, is that dictated by the interests of the regime. Properly speaking, there is no longer such a thing as free man answerable to his conscience alone; only the collective exists, expressed in abstract fashion by the regime, by the State.

There undoubtedly lay the brilliant intuition of Lenin: he foresaw that the evolution of the world under the influence of technical progress would lead inevitably to primacy of the collective over the individual. At a time when everything tended to uniformity, both in the commercial system and in the daily life of the rootless urban masses, totalitarianism seemed to harmonize with that evolution. A certain concept of man and of society was about to find itself outmoded,

[1] Modern because others had existed in the ancient world, e.g. Egypt under the Pharaohs and Peru under the Incas. But the ultimate aim of those regimes was very different from that of the Soviet State.

together with the more or less liberal democratic regimes which claimed to be based upon it. Despite the cries of alarm from writers and philosophers,[1] an increasing number of men began to look upon totalitarianism as necessary or inevitable; so much so that this type of regime was not limited to Soviet Russia which gave it birth. During the twenty inter-war years it emerged at several points of the globe, nor was it always at the service of Marxist doctrine. It even happened, as in Italy and Germany, that totalitarianism was considered the only effective obstacle to Bolshevism. But the principles and methods of government were exactly the same; there was not much difference between the Russian O.G.P.U. and the German Gestapo, and in all totalitarian states the same pressure was exerted to orientate opinion and mould the intellect as to control the entire life of man. For Mussolini and Hitler, as for the Bolsheviks, the State alone must decide what should be thought, believed, said and done. 'The totalitarian and integral education of every Italian', said the Duce, 'belongs exclusively to the State as one of its primordial functions, or rather as *the* primordial function of the State'; and a German professor, voicing the thought of the National Socialist regime, exclaimed: 'Now that the era of political authority has opened, the neutrality of the State disappears: law, art, religion, economy, science, culture, education and discipline must all be regulated by the State.'[2]

Such was the new menace with which Christianity was confronted. The rise of totalitarianism was its direct concern. True, there were great differences of purpose and of emphasis between the various regimes. While Russian Bolshevism, by virtue of being Marxist, is expressly based upon the negation of God and of all religion, such was clearly not the case with Fascism, which intended as far as possible to respect the Christian convictions of the Italian people; but the 'pagan statolatry'[3] of Mussolini's regime, its repeated assertion that 'the individual is nothing, the collectivity is all', and its constant use of official propaganda to exalt force and violence, were essentially antichristian, just as was the intransigent nationalism to which Fascist policy appealed. The same is true of the regime which Hitler and his Brownshirts set up in Germany; in this case the above-mentioned errors were all included in a veritable heresy—that of racism, to which the Church opposes her great principle of the fraternal equality of all men, whatever their nationality, their class or the level of their civilization.

Against these new enemies therefore Christianity was compelled

[1] e.g. Georges Duhamel in *Scènes de la vie future*, Aldous Huxley in *Brave New World.*

[2] The totalitarian dictatorships will be studied in Chapter VIII.

[3] These words were used by Pius XI.

to fight.[1] They were much more formidable than earlier opponents; while totalitarian governments did not disdain to employ the methods of democratic secularism, they possessed weapons far more powerful than those wielded by the pre-war masonic democracies to achieve a Godless society. And perhaps no less dangerous than the pressure they could exert in order to impose their principles on their subjects, were the positive elements of the ideals to which they appealed: the sense of grandeur, of creative enthusiasm and of solidarity within the party, all of which seemed to challenge the virtues which Christians are obliged to practise. It is those elements that seem to have established most completely the worship of man, which, as we have remarked, is the principal characteristic of modern thought. That which made the totalitarian regimes particularly formidable to Christianity was, perhaps, not so much their barbarian atrocities as the poison they spread abroad, from which very few peoples have been entirely preserved.

The rise of totalitarianism, however, had one unexpected result. Democracies of the old liberal type, feeling themselves threatened, drew closer to the Church. Proof of this is to be found in the number of concordats signed on the morrow of the First World War. The Church stood forth ever more clearly as the champion of true liberty, and her authority was greatly enhanced. Freemasonry itself, whose traditional antipathy towards the Christian faith had revealed itself at the time of the Peace Treaty (1919) and the foundation of the League of Nations,[2] continued to obey its old principles, but with this difference, that some of its members saw the totalitarian menace directed against themselves no less than against the Church, and advocated a cessation of anticlericalism.[3] Nevertheless this slackening of hatred did not suffice to render the Church's peril any the less grave. Atheistic humanism in the mid twentieth century was to find its most redoubtable incarnation in those systems which reduce man to slavery in order to annihilate God.

10. The Great Drift

We have now considered the many forces leagued against religion; but that is not the end of the story. In order to grasp the direction and

[1] Note that the Church's opposition to statism is not occasional. It was not in order to withstand totalitarianism that she adopted this attitude. The thirty-ninth proposition of the *Syllabus* (1864), which formulated the doctrine condemned by the Church, ran as follows: 'The State is the origin and fount of all rights, and enjoys unlimited authority.'

[2] e.g. in the destruction of Catholic Austria-Hungary and the refusal to admit the Vatican to the deliberations at Geneva.

[3] In January 1937 Albert Lantoine, member of the supreme council of Scottish freemasonry, addressed an 'Open Letter to the Sovereign Pontiff' on those lines. It was answered in a series of articles by Father Berteloot in *Revue de Paris*, and afterwards in a lengthy book by the same author.

significance of this gigantic assault, we shall have to estimate the effect of all those influences upon human behaviour; we must try to see whether they accomplished what they set out to do, whether the world really ceased to be Christian.

It is not easy to give an answer; in such matters one must be cautious of hasty generalizations. There has been too much talk of 'missionary lands' with reference to countries where the Church, though admittedly impaired and reduced in numbers, was none the less firmly rooted and had every chance of revival. To speak of a 'soulless world' in respect of western society, without defining the exact connotation of that phrase, is to liken the almost entirely faithful peasants of Ireland or Poland to the almost wholly paganized industrial proletariat of the great cities. Again, if it is true that quality counts for more than quantity in the sphere of religion, the presence of many saintly figures in an age commonly dismissed as atheist gives the lie to certain pessimistic utterances.

Nevertheless our period, taken as a whole, witnessed a grave fall in Christian standards. Or one might say there was a vast drift which appeared to sweep men irresistibly away from religion. The phenomenon was nothing new; there had been many signs of it, perhaps since the eighteenth century and at all events since the beginning of the nineteenth, with intervals of slowing down and then of acceleration. It became stronger throughout our period, closely linked as it was with technical and sociological progress, with the triumph of mechanical industrialism and with the monstrous growth of large towns. The process might well lead to a situation in which a majority of hitherto Christian peoples looked upon God no longer as a vital need, but as a myth, a deceit, even an enemy, and religion as intolerable slavery.

The phenomenon of dechristianization took concrete form. Two facts were particularly noticeable: the abandonment of religious practices and the breakdown of the Christian structure of society. A religion is not a philosophy, but a dedication of one's whole self, an attitude of life, and at the same time membership of a group which requires the individual to obey certain rules of earthly existence with a view to supernatural fulfilment. Now all those fundamental elements of Christian life were more and more imperilled.

The decline of religious practice was remarkable. The sight of near-empty churches, where Sunday Mass was attended by a handful of old women and children, was eloquent of the facts; and that sight was becoming ever more frequent. It could, however, be misleading; in order to form a just opinion one must set it against the enormous crowds that filled the esplanade at Lourdes and the serried ranks of those attending eucharistic congresses. Fifty years ago it was necessary to rely on simple comparisons of that kind. Today the science known

as religious sociology, which, though not altogether new, has been highly developed and systematized, enables us to estimate with some degree of precision the abandonment of religious practice. But the detailed inquiries it necessitates were little more than projects in 1939, sometimes no more than individual experiments without sequel.[1] Even now they are far from being undertaken in all Christian countries.

Nevertheless, without having recourse to scientific documentation, one can safely say that during the seventy-five years which concern us the drift from religious practice was a definite fact. It took place always and everywhere in the same way.[2] First men neglected their Easter duties; then they stopped hearing Mass on Sundays, attending only on major feasts in accordance with immemorial custom; and once even that custom had been abandoned they were well on the way to godlessness.

This phenomenon was most apparent in the working class. It had been noted towards the middle of the nineteenth century and provoked bold reaction on the part of 'social Catholicism'.[3] Crushed as they were by the inhuman conditions of labour, how could the proletariat of the giant workshops lead religious lives? How could they remain loyal to a Church that seemed indifferent to their fate, if not the sworn ally of those who exploited them? But even when technical advances and the intervention of faith had improved the material life of the factory worker, the drift away from God continued. The working class, indeed, was far less Christian in 1924 than in 1874. Must we blame modern technology, which seemed to reduce a man to the status of an automaton? Or the mounting influence of scientism and the myth of progress? Or the break-up of natural social structures brought about by the monstrous agglomeration of human beings in the great cities? All three factors were responsible. When it became possible to make an exact assessment of the paganization of the working class, the figures were appalling. In 1943 an inquiry carried out by the Abbés Godin and Daniel[4] revealed that the number of working-class French Catholics who practised their religion hardly exceeded 2 per cent. Things were a little better in Germany and Italy, but there too the decline was evident. On the eve of the Spanish Civil War all travellers in the land of St Teresa and St John of the Cross noticed that the working masses seldom went to church. For those millions of human

[1] The true father of religious sociology, Gabriel Le Bras, did not begin publishing the results of his labours until about the time of the Second World War. He had had a few predecessors inspired more or less by Le Play, e.g. Tristran de Athayde in 1934 and Roger Bastide in 1935.

[2] The analysis which follows owes much to the remarkable labours of Canon Boulard.

[3] Cf. *The Church in an Age of Revolution*, Chapter VI, section 10; and Chapter IV, section 1, of the present volume.

[4] *France, pays de mission*, 1943; reprinted 1952.

beings who formed the industrial proletariat, God seemed to have been blotted out. Such was the 'great scandal' to which Pius XI referred in an interview with the Abbé Cardijn.[1] The Church had lost the working class.

Modern factories are all situated in towns, and chiefly in the very large towns. Hence dechristianization seemed to be mainly an urban phenomenon; but the countryside was not spared. Towards the middle of the nineteenth century, immediately after the Christian revival that followed the revolutionary crisis, the rural masses constituted solid bastions of faith and practice. But as improved means of communication brought the cities nearer to the countryside; as country life became assimilated to that of townsfolk; and as secular education and compulsory military service also took their toll, the decline became more and more apparent. Moreover there were enormous differences not only between one country and another, but also between areas of the same country. In France, for historical as well as psychological reasons, Brittany remained true to the faith while in Haute-Marne and Corrèze the churches were empty. True 'missionary zones' existed also in Spain, Portugal, Italy and even more notably among the Catholic nations of South America.

The ebb of Christianity, however, was not confined to factory workers and peasants, though the middle classes offer a more complicated picture. Since the beginning of the nineteenth century there had been in progress among the middle classes a return to the faith which cannot be explained solely by panic fear of the Revolution or by a desire to establish the reign of moral order and the world. But while numerous middle-class folk resumed to some extent the practice of their religion, an even greater number, won over to scientistic and materialistic theories, had abandoned the Church altogether. Every western country possessed a violently antichristian bourgeoisie, whose vehemence was proved by several happenings in Italy and France. Besides, many of the self-styled Christian bourgeoisie retained little more of Christianity than a measure of conformism. There was also a 'practical atheism', which, says Jules Lagneau, consisted 'not in denying the truth of God's existence, but of refusing to show forth God in one's actions'.[2] Finally, there was the unbelief of those who claimed to believe; it consisted in failure to give one's pretended faith reality in everyday circumstances and social relations. This dichotomy of life into two parts, in one of which some sop was offered to religion while in the other there was a total disregard of Christian law, became more and more widespread among the middle classes. It too revealed the general drift away from God.

[1] See Chapter VIII, section 8.

[2] *Célèbres leçons et arguments*, p. 229.

No less evident was the disruption of Christian society, the second factor which marked the process of dechristianization. The collapse of Christian social structures was both cause and consequence of that process. It was not by chance that in all countries one of the first aims of anticlerical governments had been to secure the passing of laws to legalize divorce. Indeed one of the most flagrant signs whereby the ebb of religion might be recognized was the progress of divorce. It gained ground wherever it was made legal. At the same time there was a marked increase in the number of purely civil marriages.

While ecclesiastical law was thus flouted, Christian morality itself was undermined. This becomes clear when one looks at the sexual life of countries which still called themselves Christian. The strict principles of the Church were openly defied. The number of children born outside marriage steadily increased; at Paris it rose from 22 per cent in 1877 to 39 per cent in 1937. The situation was no better in Spain and Germany. But even that was not the most serious feature; abortion was common, and adultery, fostered by a certain type of literature, was frequent among the middle classes. The whole western world was gliding towards that obsession with sex which is so characteristic of our age; and the cinema from its very beginning contributed largely to encourage such an outlook.

Nor was sexual morality alone at stake; all the principles taught by the Gospel were gradually abandoned and betrayed, charity more than any other. The world to which Renan had promised paradise through science was discovering that science also increased the means of destruction. It was a long step from the modest bloodshed of 1870 to the hecatombs of 1914–18; but the horrors of Verdun and Le Chemin des Dames paled before those of the Second World War with its concentration camps, its gas-chambers and the nuclear bombing of Hiroshima. Social relations provide still further evidence of that irresistible tide of violence. Class-hatred grew and, when unleashed, was responsible for hideous atrocities, as in Mexico and Spain. The world which had lost its consciousness of God was also a world in which, to quote St Francis of Assisi, 'Love was not loved'.

Recalling the symptoms of that crisis which affected man and cut him off from his own soul, this chapter might have ended on a note of despair. Nietzsche seemed to be right and the 'death of God' to be an inescapable fact. But it was not so, and half a century later the Church of Christ was not only intact, but appeared stronger, more youthful and more sure of her future.

CHAPTER II

UPON THIS ROCK . . . MY CHURCH

1. The Fight for God

The spread of irreligion during the nineteenth and twentieth centuries is an undeniable fact, but it certainly does not represent the whole climate of the period. While it is true that vast and increasing numbers of men looked upon God as dead and gone, there were still many for whom He remained 'the way, the truth, the life'. Far from having vanished for ever, the religious phenomenon continued to claim the attention of objective historians.[1] 'The Churches [2] have by no means renounced their task; despite opposition from the "secular spirit" they labour untiringly, often with success and always in the unshakable certainty of being able one day to regain the upper hand. Not the least curious feature of this period is the evidence of that ceaseless religious activity concurrent with the continual efforts of a society which appears at first sight to be concerned only with material progress and strictly human problems.'

The history of the Church during the period we are about to study is nothing other than the history of that tireless activity, inspired by the conviction that the gates of hell will never prevail against the word of Christ. Christianity, which Berthelot described as 'well and truly dead', showed surprising vitality; and the Catholic Church, which so many declared to be worn out with age and incapable of meeting the attacks of her enemies with anything but lamentations and sermons, faced the peril with increasing vigour and determination. She did not confine herself to defensive warfare, as she had been perhaps too prone to do in the first two-thirds of the nineteenth century, when she answered threats with little more than condemnations and anathemas. Henceforward we shall see her working to recover lost ground and proclaim her universal presence. She was engaged in a counter-offensive which was crowned with success in many sectors.

The Church would have to fight this battle on all fronts—intellectual, political, moral, social and others as well. She would have to confront doctrines and philosophies which sought to undermine her

[1] See M. Baumont in Halphen and Sagnac, *Histoire générale*, vol. xviii, p. 505.

[2] Baumont's plural includes the Catholic Church and the Protestant Churches. The work of these latter will be studied in the next volume of this series.

foundations; and the enemy had more or less willing allies within her fold. She would have to withstand earthly governments which, in more or less violent forms, mobilized against her the apparatus of laws and police regulations. She would have to fight, even among the ranks of the baptized, a kind of spiritual torpor or creeping debility which, depriving the soul of all religious sense, ultimately destroys the sacred element in life. And she would have to conduct that campaign without any relaxation of her effort to bear witness before men, a duty she had always considered paramount and which was all the more necessary now that the world was expanding.

For the rapid changes in society and in the conditions of life obliged the Church to renew and adapt herself. She has always been faced with a dilemma which her sanctity alone has enabled her to overcome. On the one hand she must defend the immutable deposit of truth, which can suffer no compromise. In this respect she is an altogether conservative force; she is faithful to the past, and tradition plays a decisive role in her thought. But at the same time, because she is composed of living beings involved in history, she cannot escape from the flow of events; otherwise she will be a mere sacred fossil devoid of links with the actual life of men. She must therefore renew her manner of expressing truth, and adapt her structure to conditions imposed by the age. This dilemma had become more and more dramatic since the close of the Middle Ages, when the Church ceased to inspire and control all human institutions. It dominated the whole nineteenth century, requiring Christians to make a choice for or against the Revolution, for or against the modern world. It assumed a more serious aspect in the period now under discussion. All the circumstances in which man has to fulfil his destiny, and human nature itself, were now at issue. The Church must accordingly understand the formidable change that was taking place and adopt a corresponding attitude. Once again she was called upon to accomplish what she had so often achieved in the course of centuries: the visible incarnation of the spiritual, the grafting of an eternal message upon a transitory form of civilization.

It would be an exaggeration to say that between 1871 and 1939 the Church always saw clearly in the often complex situations in which she found herself, that she always acted in her own best interests, that she did not overlook certain aspects of the problems confronting her. The infallibility recognized by the first Vatican Council as residing in Peter's successor, though plenary and without appeal in the dogmatic sphere, did not extend to temporal undertakings. However, an objective view of events leads us to conclude that on the whole mistakes were fewer than wise decisions, failures than positive results.

2. Four Guides

Throughout the struggle she was called upon to wage, the Church was fortunate in having at her head four successive popes who, undeniably, but each in a different way, proved themselves outstanding leaders. For more than sixty years St Peter's barque was steered with a firm hand amid many a storm and many a dangerous reef. Not one of those four men seems to have lacked the qualifications needed for his overwhelming responsibility. Each was qualified in the first place by spiritual stature—by his virtues. Ever since the Council of Trent, indeed, the Church had been accustomed to find the Vicar of Christ not only above suspicion, but often setting a magnificent example. The four who governed her during the period under review were all morally admirable, and one of them has since been canonized. But they were also qualified by their human gifts of intelligence, strength of character and courage, to rule the Catholic world; in the case of one at least, the sum total of his powers was such that we can fairly use the word 'genius'. None showed himself unequal to the heavy task that Providence had laid upon him.

Those facts are of supreme importance. Since the middle of the nineteenth century the Pope's authority in the Church had steadily increased, mainly through the achievement of Pius IX. Gone for ever were the days when certain nations treated Rome with contempt. The proclamation of the dogma of papal infallibility, linked with the abolition of the temporal power, had marked the culmination of a movement that tended to clothe the Apostle's successor with undisputed spiritual authority. The immediate result was to place the fortunes of the Church more than ever before in the hands of a single person, who was able by his sole will to orientate the Catholic world—and to some extent the entire world—in one direction or another. We shall have occasion to notice more than one example of this autonomy in deciding the course of events. We shall see Leo XIII resolving on his sole initiative to make a radical change of policy and to impose it notwithstanding the repugnance of the national Church which it concerned.[1] We shall see Pius X halting a trend of thought which seemed destined to engulf the whole Catholic intellect.[2] We shall see Pius XI condemning a political regime and thereby taking upon himself the risk of catastrophe for the Church in Germany.[3] The part played by the popes during those years was so important that the most logical way to describe their events would be to deal with the four pontificates one after another. It will be best, however, to embark

[1] Chapter III, section 8. [2] Chapter VI, section 7.
[3] Chapter IX, section 5.

on the study of our period with a preliminary consideration of those four men whom we shall find always present and always active in every field to which the Church's influence extends. Seldom has the pun used by Our Lord to designate Peter as head of the *ekklesia* and guardian of His message been more aptly applied to Peter's successors: each of them was indeed the Rock upon which the Church of Jesus Christ is founded.

Those popes have not always been justly judged. The holiest of their number has been dismissed by one illustrious Catholic with the contemptuous phrase 'This saint is not my cup of tea'! Another, criticized with equal vehemence by the nationalists of both camps during and after the First World War, bequeathed to history a sadly disfigured image of his true self. Yet another was dragged in the mud by a political clique for having exercised the right of admonition enjoyed by all spiritual leaders. A more precise view of events shows that each fulfilled what was his duty and, on the whole, in the best interests of the Church. Particular decisions which at the time caused alarm or indignation are now seen to have been beneficial and are no longer disputed.

It need hardly be said that those four popes were very different from one another, and commentators enjoy the game of comparing them. Ecclesiastical history has long borne witness to the fact that the pontifical succession obeys as it were a law of alternation, setting the tiara upon the head of a statesman after that of a mystic. But this alternation has limits: an objective view of the facts disproves the summary opinion that each pope will be the absolute opposite of his predecessor and will be disavowed by his successor. The truth is not so simple. Just as we are led to recognize the 'liberal' Pope Leo XIII as one of those who inspired the reactionary *Syllabus* of Pius IX, so also we shall discover a perfect identity of principles between him and his successor Pius X, whom some represent as the grave-digger of his work. And we shall find the vigorous Pius XI a continuator, in large measure, of Benedict XV who is so often regarded as a nonentity.

Nevertheless it would be altogether futile to deny the very real differences between the four pontiffs: differences of style and attitude, and even more profound differences bearing upon the guidance of Christendom. They derived from many causes, human and historical. First, of course, there was a difference of temperament: the popes who followed one another had no more the same character than the same physique. Secondly, there was a difference of origin: the Church has always been proud of choosing her leaders irrespective of their social standing, and the son of a peasant will not react to circumstances in the same way as the heir of a long aristocratic tradition. Thirdly, there was a difference of training: a man who has risen from the

humbler ranks of the parochial clergy will not have the same view of the world as a product of the Pontifical Academy of Ecclesiastical Noblemen or as a distinguished intellectual. Yet, when all is said and done, such dissimilarities are useful in allowing the Church a variety of outlook. The efforts of those four men appear complementary, applied by differing temperaments to likewise differing circumstances.

3. Genius of Leo XIII

On 20th February 1878 a crowd stood waiting in the Piazza di San Pietro for the white smoke that would rise above the Sistine Chapel and mark the election of a new pope. When Cardinal Caterini announced the choice of 'the Most Eminent Lord Cardinal Joachim Pecci' there were murmurs of surprise; to the great majority of Romans this name meant nothing. Rumour quickly spread that His Holiness would break with custom and not appear on the outside loggia of the basilica, in order to protest from the very start against the odious attack upon the Temporal Power, signified by the presence in Rome of the victorious 'Piedmontese'. The piazza emptied in the twinkling of an eye as the human tide surged into St Peter's.

Two hours later there came forth upon the inside balcony a tall, slender figure dressed in the white cassock, about whose features there was something hieratic, something supernatural. His gaze moved slowly over the vast congregation as it knelt in silence. Then Peter's new successor raised his voice, strong and sonorous, with the nasal tone of an aristocrat. Thrice the long white arm moved in blessing, and the answering roar of acclamation swept upward to the dome of Michelangelo. The pontificate of Leo XIII was beginning.

Though the Roman masses hardly knew Mgr Pecci, the Sacred College had shown little hesitation in electing him. Three days had sufficed for the sixty cardinals present—thirty-seven Italians and twenty-three foreigners—to make their choice. After Cardinal Bilio, a friend of Pius IX, had declared his intention of refusing the tiara—an avowal which saved Cardinal de Bonnechose from having to pronounce against him a veto [1] in the name of France, as he had been instructed—Mgr Pecci advanced, scrutiny by scrutiny, from eighteen to forty-four votes, that is to say four more than the necessary two-thirds. This event gave the lie to an old saying that 'a Camerlengo always leaves the Conclave Camerlengo'; for the newly elect had indeed been Cardinal Camerlengo, entrusted as such with administration of the Church during the vacancy of the See.

Joachim Pecci was not a young man; he was on the threshold of

[1] See section 4 below.

his sixty-eighth year, but while his health was not robust his vigour of mind and character was intact, and he was fully capable of shouldering the burdens of a pontificate that was clearly going to be difficult. His previous life had been a long preparation for this final task. Rapid advancement in a brilliant career had been followed by a halt and apparent stagnation for more than thirty years; but he had made good use of the interval, and it does much to account for the greatness of his reign.

Born in 1810 at Carpineto, near Rome, Joachim Pecci was destined by his father, a colonel of militia, for the papal administration. But the influence of his devout mother, family tradition (two Pecci had been beatified) and, above all, his education at a Jesuit school, inspired him to become something more than just another of those cassocked officials, few of whom had risen above the sub-diaconate and who swarmed throughout the Papal States. Ordained priest at the age of twenty-seven, and holding a doctorate of theology, he thought for some while of becoming a missionary. Such, however, was not his destiny; he entered the Palazzo Severoli on the Piazza Minerva, where the Academy of Ecclesiastical Noblemen trained future pontifical diplomats and administrators.

The esteem in which his superiors held him may be judged by the difficult undertakings with which he was soon entrusted. As delegate of the Pope at Benevento, an enclave in the territory of the Two Sicilies, he brought brigands and *carbonari* to heel with smiling firmness. Transferred to Spoleto, in Umbria, and then to Perugia, he was equally successful, proving himself a shrewd administrator, an able reformer of ministries and tribunals, as well as a builder and surveyor of roads.[1]

In 1843 he was sent as Apostolic Nuncio to Belgium; but there things ran less smoothly. It was an awkward situation. The schools question was beginning to array Catholics against liberals; whatever may have been his private view, the nuncio was obliged to support the bishops, and thereby offended the left as well as King Leopold. Next, the young prelate found himself involved in a dispute between the Society of Jesus and the professors of Louvain. Complaints reached the Vatican; he was invited to abandon diplomacy and return to Perugia, this time as archbishop. He accepted.

Mgr Pecci occupied the archiepiscopal see of Perugia for thirty-two years. Why so long? The answer lies in a single word: Antonelli. It may be that Pius IX's secretary of state, while mistrusting Pecci, also feared him as a rival; or he may have considered his ideas unsafe. At all events, so long as Antonelli lived, the archbishop remained in his

[1] The Via Gregoriana was his work, named after Gregory XVI.

diocese, deriving small comfort from a red hat which the Pope had not dared refuse him.

Those thirty-two years of episcopate were by no means unfruitful. Not only did the archbishop behave on many occasions as a true leader, defying even Garibaldi and sheltering under his own roof young refugee seminarists; he also gave his diocese an intellectual thrust such as was most uncommon in papal Italy. Personally in touch with all that was being thought and written, including the works of Rosmini and La Mennais, he gathered around himself men interested in philosophy, in criticism and in exegesis; he also established a Thomist Academy under the presidency of his brother, where the great Dominican's theories were discussed. The results of these efforts did not go unobserved, for the archbishop's pastoral letters bore witness to a breadth of view and an audacity of mind rarely met with in documents of that sort; while at the provincial synods, which he summoned with unfailing regularity, the bishops of Umbria more than once obeyed his wishes by passing the most unaccustomed resolutions.

Although Joachim Pecci was a virtual stranger to the Roman people, he was far from unknown in ecclesiastical circles. When Antonelli died Pius IX no longer remained deaf to the appeals of those who expressed astonishment that such gifts should be held at arm's length. He summoned the archbishop to Rome, learned to esteem him, and appointed him Cardinal Camerlengo in order, as some said, to mark him out as a likely successor, or, as others maintained, to make sure of excluding him from the Apostolic Throne.

From beginning to end of his pontificate Leo XIII made a deep impression upon all who met him. Capable in turn of affability and aloofness, of familiarity and majesty, he had a wonderful way of profiting by his own radiance, by his commanding appearance, by the strength that emanated from his fragile form. His emaciated body seemed ready to fall apart, his face had the pallor of wax; but there was something lordly in the carriage of his head, in his gait and in the rapid movement of his arms; while the drawn features, the lofty furrowed brow and the prominent chin were clear signs of an unyielding determination. Here manifestly was a creature in whom the spirit had completely subjugated the flesh. But that strength of soul was never brutal: the brilliant eyes and the wide, thin-lipped mouth were often lit up with a smile that was sometimes tinged with gentle irony.

Leo XIII was a natural leader of men. Like Richelieu and Bismarck, he might have described himself as 'devoid of all sentiment and of all resentment', utterly detached from personal preferences, as soon as the Church's interests were at stake. Despite a certain volubility, he did not lack that aridity of heart without which good government of

the human species is quite impossible. But the greatest of all his gifts were an eagle-eyed view of men and events, absolute freedom from gullibility, an unfailing recognition of what could and what could not be done and, lastly, the power to carry out his decisions with extraordinary tact, skill and subtlety. Those gifts made him the archetypal diplomat and statesman.

The Romans, always slightly ironical about their popes, have a saying that all can be ranked in one or another of three categories: *i dotti, i zelanti, i politici*; and it was, of course, in the third that they placed Mgr Pecci. But they were wrong; for that great statesman was also a distinguished intellectual, a master of Latin and several other languages, endowed with true culture, able to take an interest in the loftiest theological speculation as well as in current literary theories, and holding strong personal views on many subjects. Above all, he whom Gambetta had described on his accession as 'more diplomat than priest' was in fact a deeply religious soul, a priest in the fullest sense of the word. He who, as Pope, would publish no fewer than twenty-seven Encyclicals on purely spiritual topics was the very opposite of that 'white-cassocked Talleyrand' whom some were pleased to imagine.

The situation confronting Leo XIII on his elevation to the papal throne was in many ways disquieting.[1] None could doubt that Pius IX had been a very great Pope. He had been first the join battle with the heresies of the modern world. Thanks to him the papacy was now acknowledged to possess, along with infallibility, a degree of spiritual authority such as it had never before wielded; and his long pontificate had been marked by countless signs of a spiritual revival. In the temporal sphere, however, results had been less satisfactory. It often seemed as if the traumatic experience of that violent check to his 'liberal' inclinations at the beginning of his reign [1] had caused him to foster towards all, even the most legitimate, innovations a distrust which had ended by cutting him off from the problems and realities of his age.

The loss of his temporal power and territorial possessions, to the enjoyment of which he had undoubtedly shown too much attachment, had been a dreadful blow. It appeared that the capture of Rome had extinguished some central fire within him, and the last eight years of the pontificate had been a disappointment. Cradling himself in illusion, deriving consolation from enthusiastic tributes from the entire Catholic world, the 'prisoner of the Vatican' had allowed those last years of his life to flow away without the least effort to grapple with events, to adapt the papacy to new conditions or to profit by the increase of his spiritual authority as compensation for material losses. The picture of 'stagnation' brought back by Cardinal Manning from a visit to Rome

[1] See Chapter III, section 1.

was only too well justified. Meanwhile a huge offensive against the Church was mounted in many lands. The French Commune, Bismarck's Germany, Switzerland, Mexico under Juarez, even Austria and Spain, each with a greater or less degree of violence attacked the Christian bases. Indignant protests from Rome fell upon deaf ears. At a time when she ought to have rallied all her strength against her enemies, the Church, like her visible head, appeared senile, incapable of effort and hopelessly outstripped by events.

A change was therefore indispensable. That much had been realized by Pius himself, whose melancholy thoughts have been preserved in the memoirs of Cardinal Ferrata: 'My successor will have to draw inspiration from my attachment to the Church and from my desire to do good. For the rest, everything has changed around me; my system and my policies have had their day; but I am too old to think and do otherwise—that must be the work of my successor.' It was indeed upon this urgent need for change that Leo XIII had pondered during his long isolation at Perugia. Listening to the voices of his age and wide awake to contemporary thought, Joachim Pecci had had the intelligence and the leisure to count the problems facing the Church and even to think out possible solutions. He had drawn up for himself a complete programme of government, whose main features had been suggested in more than one of his episcopal pronouncements, increasing the mistrust of Antonelli. On assuming the tiara, therefore, he knew exactly in what direction he was going to orientate the activities of Holy Church. His first Encyclical, *Inscrutabili Dei consilio*, left no doubt on that point. Like all first Encyclicals, it set out the aims of the new pontificate; but it did so, only a few weeks after the coronation, with a breadth of vision and a wealth of detail that at once excluded any idea of improvisation.[1]

What now was the change contemplated by Leo XIII? It would not affect the basic principles which must always underlie government of the Church. In this respect the first Encyclical left no room for equivocation. With as much vigour as his predecessor Leo denounced the weakening of the Church's authority, the abandonment of Christian rules, 'the excesses of unbridled and perverted liberty', all of which were responsible for the human tragedy. Regarding modern civilization, riddled with immorality and atheism, he went so far as to declare: 'It is but a phantom of civilization; the word stands for no reality.' Historians who insist on opposing one pope to another are consequently mistaken when they treat Leo XIII as a 'liberal' pontiff in the sense given to that word by *Quanta Cura* and the *Syllabus*, that is to say as a man ready to stretch the principles of order and authority with a view to achieving an illusory reconciliation with his enemies.

[1] See Chapter III, section 6.

Indeed he himself was among those who had instigated the *Syllabus*. In 1849, as Archbishop of Perugia, he had persuaded his provincial synod to pass a resolution asking the Pope to 'draw up a list of the most widespread crucial errors, in order to make it possible to recognize them at a glance and condemn them with due formality'. Cardinal Pie was not far from the truth in writing that 'Leo XIII is animated by a spirit none other than that of Pius IX'.

Nevertheless the means adopted for the furtherance of God's cause and that of the Church were different from those employed by his predecessor with the same end in view. First there was a noticeable change of general behaviour, dictated by a difference of temperament. Pius IX, so open to innovation in his early days, had wrapped himself in an aura of refusal and anathema after the revolution of 1848. He had considered the Church as a besieged fortress which must be defended by murderous attacks on its assailants. The result had been tension and open conflict between himself and civilian society, a result which in the long run had favoured the enemy's designs. Leo XIII, diplomat and statesman, thought it his duty to give the Church of Christ a new look, to yield in small matters in order to safeguard fundamentals, not to be harsh until all other means had failed. He believed that shutting up Catholics as though in a battlemented castle was no way to bring back the Gospel to mankind; he must go among men with an open mind, get close to their thoughts and troubles, show them that concern for eternal values was not incompatible with a Christian policy of contact and welcome.

This change of attitude went hand in hand with a modification of principle in respect of a problem which had faced the Church since the days of the Renaissance: that of her relations with the modern world. Should it be accepted or rejected? For centuries a majority of the popes had opted for the second choice; and the violent upheavals of the Revolution had confirmed their nineteenth-century successors in that idea of the modern world as something wholly unacceptable. They had therefore followed a line of political reaction in the strictest sense, condemning even such perfectly legitimate innovations as technical progress along with attempts at subversion. Leo XIII intended to break with folly of that kind. 'Can it be true', he asked, 'that civilization can bear no fruit in a society that lives by the spirit of Jesus Christ? Can man develop physically, socially and politically only upon condition of his repudiating the Catholic Church? That is what We call the great and crucial question, realizing that if it is answered to the detriment of the Church there can no longer be any means of halting the apostasy of her children.' And so the papacy under Leo XIII would plan the avenues which were to lead to the Rock from all points of the globe.

He had twenty-five years in which to carry out that programme, nor was his exceptional longevity unconnected with his success and the glory that surrounded him. Another advantage he enjoyed was the collaboration, from 1887, of Cardinal Mariano Rampolla del Tindaro (1843–1913), whom he appointed secretary of state. Seldom have two men so fully understood and complemented each other. In that young Sicilian aristocrat, a former pupil of the Jesuits, a one-time member of the Noble Academy and an ex-nuncio, Leo XIII recognized himself. Though never prone to excessive admiration of any man, he admired the vast intelligence, the deep-seated virtues, the broad-mindedness and the firmness of his junior. We know how powerful an influence a secretary of state can exert upon a pope. Every morning for sixteen years, while the Sovereign Pontiff was finishing his breakfast,[1] Rampolla entered the study carrying a portfolio and sat down at the opposite side of the table, where they spent two hours dealing with all sorts of business. Their association was so intimate, so complete, that in considering the great achievements of Leo XIII it is impossible to draw a hard and fast line between Leo's personal contribution and that of Cardinal Rampolla.

Leo XIII's programme of renovation and enlargement was made to operate in every field and at every level. The *Acta* of his pontificate show that not a single contemporary problem was ignored. Each is handled in at least one of those *motu proprio* whose more rapid style he preferred to that of the long Encyclicals favoured by Pius X, and which he himself used to write or revise in faultless Latin.

It was in his dealings with foreign powers that Leo achieved his most notable successes. He desired, in conformity with his plan, to establish 'peace and harmony' with sovereign States, even with those whose constitutions offended the principles of the *Syllabus*, even with those upon which Pius IX had not unreasonably looked as hostile. By insisting that the Church teaches obedience to the civil power, and by repeatedly declaring Christianity to be the sole effective barrier against subversive doctrines, he showed that an understanding with such governments was still possible. In return for his goodwill he demanded at least freedom of activity for the Church, and, wherever feasible, legislation favourable to Catholic interests. Thus he renewed contacts whose abandonment had done nothing but harm. In Germany, the end of Bismarck's *Kulturkampf* and the resumption of cordial relations evidenced by three visits to the Vatican by Wilhelm II; in Switzerland, an end to the *klein Kulturkampf*; in Spain, the liberal government's revocation of anticlerical measures—all were manifest achievements of the new policy. But that same policy was no less

[1] It consisted of the yolk of an egg beaten into a cup of goat's milk.

beneficial in dealings with Russia, which re-established diplomatic relations with the Vatican; with Gladstone's Britain, which was grateful for the counsels of moderation given to the Irish and sent an official representative to the Holy See; with the United States, where Leo XIII, by refusing the claims of immigrants to bishops of their own nationalities and thereby helping the fusion of Catholics into a homogeneous mass, joined hands with the federal government and was allowed to send an apostolic delegate to Washington; even with Norway and several South American States. This wide-reaching policy attained its fullest extent in France. There above all one sees the audacity of Leo XIII's views. Whereas his predecessors, including Pius IX, had considered successive French regimes as heirs of the Revolution and therefore suspect, he thought, as Cardinal Rampolla noted, that 'it was not right to allow certain political realities . . . to be presented to the masses as an incarnation of certain antichristian ideas, as associated with the reign of a philosophy hostile to the Church'. The application of this new concept was the *Ralliement*,[1] the urging upon Catholics not to persist in blind opposition to the Republic.

It was not only with foreign States that Leo sought to forge new links; he wished also to make contact once again with those social classes which the evolution of the modern world had torn from the Church, particularly with that proletariat of the workshops and factories whose unhappy condition was well known to him and to whom his archiepiscopal pronouncements had often referred. The key document in this field was his instructive Encyclical *Rerum Novarum* (1891), which expounded and adopted the main theses of the 'social Catholics', and led the Church back to the very heart of that social scene from which she had been too long absent.[2] His audacity went so far as to denounce the economic liberalism which likened human labour to raw materials, a form of liberalism he held responsible for the unjust misery of the workers and for the resultant class hatred. Thereby he deprived socialism of the arguments it was using for its own ends, placed the Church in a better position to recover the working class for Christ, and made the first constructive moves in the struggle against atheism.

Leo XIII took similar steps in many other fields. During long hours of meditation in his Umbrian retreat he had given a great deal of thought to the inner causes of the tragedy with which mankind was wrestling; and he had concluded that an intellectual crisis lay at the root of all the prevailing disorder. He deplored particularly the mistake of which the Church had so often been guilty in turning her back upon the methods of modern thought, that is to say upon science. Surely,

[1] See Chapter III, section 8. [2] See Chapter IV, section 8.

in order to conquer error, she must take her stand on the same ground, and employ the same weapons, as her adversary. Hence the enormous task which he fulfilled in the sphere of learning. Christian philosophy had languished. Joachim Pecci had made an exhaustive study of St Thomas's *Summa* at Perugia; and so it was that one of his first Encyclicals, *Aeterni Patris*, was devoted to Thomism, which he proposed as the basic philosophy of Christianity, as one that would make possible the solution of that greatest of all contemporary problems, the relations between faith and reason. Catholic historiography, in particular religious historiography with its adjunct exegesis, was dying: it purposely ignored the methods of science, for fear of the imagined perils to which they would subject faith. Leo XIII took a diametrically opposite position. 'The Church', he declared, 'has nothing to fear from truth', a maxim which he often repeated and which he elaborated in an eloquent letter to the learned Cardinals Pitra, De Luca and Hergenröther. The practical result was the opening of the Vatican archives to historians. At the same time biblical exegesis was encouraged, in order to refute Strauss and Renan by fighting them with equal arms. The Encyclical *Providentissimus* laid down its principles and was the starting-point of that biblical revival which was to be one of the capital events in modern Catholic history, a revival whose most notable landmarks were Father Lagrange's foundation of the Biblical School at Jerusalem and, later, the setting up of the Biblical Commission in Rome. Restoration of Catholic thought, however, would be futile unless the information acquired by scholars were spread abroad among the masses. Measures were therefore adopted to improve the teaching in seminaries; encouragement was given to the founding of Catholic institutes and universities in Germany, France, Belgium, Italy and Switzerland; while messages of goodwill were sent to Catholic scientific congresses, which had hitherto been objects of such profound mistrust.

In the reign of Leo XIII the missionary movement started by Gregory XVI and Pius XI went from strength to strength. The Pope took a keen personal interest in this work, presiding over the committees which appointed vicars-apostolic, following closely the achievements of the Oblates of Mary Immaculate in the Far North, encouraging Cardinal Lavigerie and his White Fathers, stressing the need for native clergies and the fostering of coloured churches. Within the Church herself he gave effect to the same principles, striving to forge anew the links between Rome and the Catholic Churches of the East, towards whom his predecessors had sometimes shown a lack of courtesy. He did even more. As champion of 'peace and harmony' he dreamed of re-establishing them wherever their ruin was worst, by reconciling all Christians. First of the great modern popes to work

for oecumenical unity, he witnessed the earliest renewal of contact with the Anglicans, and wrote a sensational letter that revealed his interest in the dialogue between the Lazarist Father Portal and Lord Halifax. He was also the first pope to show on many occasions a sincere sympathy for Holy Russia, her noble liturgy and her spiritual heritage.

All that manifold and intense activity compels us to enlarge the portrait of Leo XIII and to see him as something more than a mere statesman and diplomat. The goal of his numerous undertakings was man's return to the Christian way of life, a return whose principles he set out in the Encyclical *Exeunte iam anno*, and the means to which he made clear in countless documents such as the Encyclicals *Tametsi futura* on Christ the Redeemer and master of the world, *Mirae Caritatis* on the Eucharist and *Divinum illud* on grace. The Pope who so often dwelt upon the need for devotion to Our Lady, who instituted the feast of the Holy Family in its present form, who dedicated the month of March to St Joseph and who wrote more forcefully perhaps than any of his predecessors on the Holy Ghost, was assuredly no mere political pontiff; in him political endeavour merged with his spiritual purpose. This will become clear to anyone who reads his great Encyclical *Annum sacrum*, wherein towards the end of his life, as a spiritual testament and in reply to his adversaries, he consecrated the entire human race to the Sacred Heart.

This last and exclusively spiritual aspect of Leo XIII's vast and multiform endeavour proves also how mistaken it would be to think of him as an indulgent pope, weak on principles, as some have represented him. In the doctrinal sphere he showed a degree of firmness, almost of rigidity, no less obvious than his flexibility in other fields. Pius IX had refrained from condemning the theories of Rosmini; it was Leo XIII who censured them. Memorable too was the promptness with which he called a halt to the deviation known as Americanism.[1] Earlier, in December 1878, his second Encyclical had struck like a thunderbolt at Socialism, Communism and Nihilism. As regards the strictly political field, it is false to imagine that he was always compromising, cautious, meek and mild. His attitude towards the new Italy was just as harsh as that of his predecessor, his energy not a whit less in claiming his rights. It was he who forced the retractation of Father Curci, author of a pamphlet on the 'Royal Vatican', which Pius IX had been unwilling to denounce. Again, the most severe condemnation ever fulminated by the Church against freemasonry was Leo's Encyclical *Humanum Genus* (1884), which described the members of that sect as 'the real abettors of evil in our age'. Whatever methods he employed, his aim was always identical with those popes who had

[1] See Chapter XI, section 3.

gone before him and those were yet to come; he was waging war for God.

Considering the extent and importance of the work accomplished by Leo XIII it is difficult to refrain from admiration, not only because he succeeded in restoring the papacy to the concert of nations, but also in view of his having taken options on the future whereby we continue to profit. The Church's evolution during the twentieth century derives in several respects from the initiatives of Leo XIII, which were thought by many at the time to be too venturesome and most alarming. It seems that the word 'genius' applied to him is no exaggeration; and the world at large bore witness to the greatness of his achievement. Every year a host of pilgrims came to applaud him in public audiences and at liturgical ceremonies in St Peter's; the workers' pilgrimages organized by Léon Harmel [1] caused a sensation far beyond the confines of Rome. The celebration of Holy Year in 1900, the first since 1825, was marked by countless tributes of honour and respect. Visits by ruling sovereigns—notably those of King Edward VII and Kaiser Wilhelm II, both non-Catholics—were rightly considered as acknowledging the prestige newly acquired by the Vicar of Christ; and certain governments invited him to arbitrate on their disputes.[2]

Nevertheless his closing years were sad. While he might have recalled his many services to the Church, he experienced a sense of failure. Often, when walking in the Vatican gardens with a member of his household, he would state the reasons of his anxiety and even hint at his feeling of having made mistakes. He was worried above all by events in France—by the insulting attitude adopted by Combes, which seemed to have frustrated his generous policies. In Italy itself the Catholic adherents of Popular Action gave cause for much concern; their activities showed symptoms of deviation, and the Encyclical *Graves de communi*, on Christian Democracy, betrayed the Pope's disquiet. Omens of even worse doctrinal errors were apparent in a strange and widespread intellectual ferment in the realms of philosophy and exegesis: Americanism, then Modernism and so forth. Catholics, to whom the paths of science had been opened, were surely going too far; and the aged pontiff wondered whether he had laid sufficient emphasis on essentials—moral reform, the rebuilding of faith.

His anxiety steadily increased, but to the very end he preserved intact the energy and vigour of mind which had served his genius so well. Though he no longer ate anything but clear soup and the yolks of eggs, he continued to attend the numerous ceremonies of canonization and beatification in St Peter's; but all who saw him were struck by the mortal pallor of his countenance, in which the eyes alone shone—those eyes which had lost nothing of their youthfulness. He often

[1] See Chapter IV, section 8. [2] See Chapter III, section 11.

used to joke about his great age, saying, for example, to a nun who expressed a hope that he would live to see his centenary: 'My daughter, why set a term to the bounty of Providence?' And on the eve of his death (5th July 1903) he murmured with a smile: 'What a crazy stir there'll be here tomorrow!' Some days earlier he had written in the purest classical Latin a poem which formed his spiritual testament. It was an appeal to divine mercy, but also a mystic hymn of hope and of gratitude to Christ.[1]

4. Sanctity of Pius X

'We have today in Leo XIII a Pope who, with his deep understanding, his far-sightedness and his ability, has raised the Church's position in the world to a point beyond all expectation. But when Leo XIII dies the Church may have need of a supreme head who will lead her back by narrower paths to the evangelical virtues of apostolic times, to goodness, charity, the spirit of poverty and meekness, in order to exert a more widespread influence on the masses at large.' Those words were written about 1900 by Contardo Ferrini, an eminent jurist who has since been beatified. Later Cardinal Mathieu,[2] describing the conclave which elected Leo's successor, summed up the views of his colleagues as follows: 'We wanted a pope who had never engaged in politics, whose name would signify peace and concord, who had grown old in the care of souls, who would concern himself with the government of the Church in detail, who would be above all a father and shepherd.' The man chosen was Cardinal Giuseppe Sarto, Patriarch of Venice, who, not thinking for a moment that he himself could be the object of such desires, had said one day to a visitor: 'The wisdom with which Leo XIII illuminates the world makes one hope that a great pontiff may be called to succeed him.' [3] A 'father and shepherd', one who would lead back the Church by narrower paths to the evangelical virtues—such exactly was Giuseppe Sarto, whom the Church canonized in 1954, forty years after his death.

[1] While the vast majority of comments on Leo XIII were couched in terms of admiration, there were a few discordant notes, particularly in circles that were later called 'integrist'. The famous Abbé Barbier, author of *Les Progrès du libéralisme catholique sous Léon XIII*, dared to attribute to Pius IX these words: 'Dying is a small matter; what worries me is that I shall have as my successor Cardinal Pecci, who would ruin the Church, if that were possible, by his statesmanship and diplomacy.' To which a certain Mgr Fèrre added: 'To hope to win by inertia and meekness is a frivolity of mind unworthy of the least respect . . . a confidence which presupposes treason rather than ignorance.'

[2] In an indiscreet article in *Revue des Deux Mondes*, 15th March 1904. It was signed 'Un témoin', but the author's identity was so quickly apparent that nothing was done to conceal it.

[3] Quoted in L. Ferrari's *Life of Pius X*, Turin, 1924.

The unwonted speed with which the cause was handled in Rome [1] is sufficient evidence of the prestige which had continued to halo this man of God, a prestige deriving from affection quite as much as from respect. Catholics admired Leo XIII and Pius XI; but they loved Pius X, his luminous smile, his invariable kindliness and his unbounded charity. A golden legend grew up around him during his lifetime, including even stories of miracles. The clamour of such popular applause can be safely muted; one can admire Giuseppe Sarto without believing that his family was so poor that he had to walk four miles to school barefooted every day. But while some aspects of his life have been overplayed, there are sufficient grounds for considering him as a most remarkable personality.

Sarto came from the humblest ranks of society. Excepting him, every pope from the time of the French Revolution until the election of Angelo Roncalli in 1958 belonged to the nobility or to the middle and professional classes. At Riese, the little sub-Alpine village where he was born, Giuseppe Sarto's parents were certainly not people of rank; his father was a postman, his mother a sempstress who worked hard to bring up her numerous family. But the faith was deep rooted in their home. Margherita Sarto, pictures of whom show that air of natural dignity common among the old peasant women of Italy, was a sensible and saintly woman. When Giuseppe received Holy Orders she would no longer address him in the second person singular and forbade her other children to do so. But after his episcopal consecration, when he showed her his amethyst ring: 'It's a fine ring you have, Giuseppe, but don't forget you wear it because I first wore this'—and she touched her own simple wedding-ring.

That upbringing proved decisive. A son of the poor, Giuseppe Sarto retained the spirit of poverty throughout his life, refusing after his accession to the papacy to confer on his relations honours and prebends that would have been quite legitimate. He never lost interest in the condition of the poor, and his heart was wrung by their misfortunes. He remained the little boy who would have been unable to pursue his studies but for the support of his parish priest, the financial aid of a few kind people and a seminary scholarship granted him by the Patriarch of Venice; the same whose dinner was often a mere hunk of bread and a piece of Parmesan. Austerity in youth had formed his mind as well as his character; he had been a model and gifted pupil at school, college and seminary.

Sarto's career had been unhurried, with a kind of rhythmic harmony. 'I studied for nine years at the seminary,' he used to say; 'I spent nine years as curate of Tombolo, nine years as a canon at Treviso, nine years at Bishop of Mantua. . . . You will see I shall be nine years

[1] No pope had been canonized since Pius V.

Patriarch of Venice; and if one day I become Pope, it will be for nine years, because I'm made of the stuff that's used in every sauce.' It was a long period of training. Just like Leo XIII, it was not until his sixty-eighth year that he was raised to the apostolic throne. His exclusively sacerdotal and episcopal formation was very different from that received in various nunciatures by his predecessor and successor; its principal advantage lay in the fact that it acquainted him with the concrete spiritual problems of his time.

Don Sarto revealed the same qualities in every post he held. His zeal and generosity were admired no less than his faith. At Tombolo, where he almost killed himself with overwork, doing duty for an aged parish priest, he was found one day digging a grave in place of the sexton, who was ill. In the large market town of Salzano, whose citizens had welcomed him without enthusiasm, he made himself so well loved that when he had to leave for Treviso his flock protested officially against the move. Much in demand as a fine preacher, he would work far into the night preparing his sermons and retreats, after labouring from dawn to dusk at his appointed tasks. Many stories, of course, were told about his charity: how he permitted a charge of theft against the cat rather than say he had himself given the roast chicken to a tramp; and how his sisters, who kept house for him, had to employ all sorts of tricks to get him to order a new cassock. There was something of St Vincent de Paul and the Curé d'Ars about Don Sarto. At the same time, however, like M. Vincent, he was a man of order and achievement, a builder and an organizer. The diocese of Mantua, at that time a very second-rate see, was shaken from top to bottom by its indefatigable bishop; and at Venice Mgr Sarto, a favourite with the gondoliers, also took in hand the diocesan Catholic press and successfully resisted the freemasons of the city council. A sort of halo already shone round about him, and he was talked of even in Rome. Leo XIII, who liked him and sought his advice, often spoke of him as his own successor. But so far was Giuseppe Sarto from desiring or expecting such an event that when he left Venice for the conclave he took a return railway ticket.

His election, however, was by no means a foregone conclusion; at the first of the seven scrutinies he obtained only five votes. The most likely candidate was Cardinal Rampolla, the late pontiff's close collaborator and confidant; but it is open to doubt whether he would have received more than the thirty votes cast for him at the fourth scrutiny. If Mathieu's account is true, Rampolla does not seem to have been the pope wanted by many of the Sacred College.[1] In any case, his chances were not long at issue. Before the third scrutiny Cardinal

[1] Besides the article in *Revue des Deux Mondes* see the memoirs of Mgr Landrieux, Cardinal Langenieux's conclavist.

Puzina, Prince-Bishop of Cracow, announced that the Austrian Government was using its right of veto against Rampolla in accordance with the ancient privilege recognized by tradition as belonging to the sovereigns of France, Spain and Austria. A dignified protest by the former secretary of state and the many marks of sympathy he received were of no avail;[1] and at the morning scrutiny on 4th August 1903 Cardinal Sarto obtained fifty out of sixty-four votes.[2] When asked what name he wished to take, he answered: 'Pius, in memory of those holy pontiffs who fought bravely during the last century against a swarm of errors.' That same evening he admitted to his friends: 'I have accepted this burden as though I were climbing Calvary. It is a cross which they have laid on my back.'

Few popes have been the object of such contradictory judgments as Pius X. Some have described him as a hero, fearless and without reproach, in that war which Holy Church must ever wage to defend the rights of God: a vigilant guardian of orthodoxy, a successful reviver of faith and devotion. Others have called him a harsh intransigent, always ready to condemn or to reject, guilty of innumerable blunders. This second view was expressed with more wit than respect by Mgr Duchesne, director of the École Française at Rome: 'The Holy Father steers St Peter's barque with an unskilled hand.' It is with particular reference to Pius X that many historians invoke the so-called law of alternation, according to which a pope is always the direct opposite of his predecessor. They fail, however, to notice that Pius in many ways continued the work of Leo XIII. Nor do they stop to ask themselves whether, in the circumstances of that period, when the Church was threatened from without by the violent hostility of secular governments and from within by suspect doctrines, there was not some need for reaction, and whether it was not perhaps desirable to build as it were a landing from which another flight might be carried on later. It would of course be ingenuous to deny the differences of temperament and manner between the Pope and his predecessor; but it is at least probable that if Leo XIII had lived another ten years he would have acted as did Pius X.[3]

Moreover it has often been said that the man really responsible for the 'reactionary' policy of Pius X was his lifelong collaborator, Cardinal Merry del Val (1865–1930). Mgr Merry del Val was a Spaniard of noble birth—a grandee if ever there was one. Son of a diplomat, and himself a diplomat whom Leo XIII had employed in many a delicate undertaking, he was also a fine linguist with a splendid intellectual equipment; and there can be no doubt of the influence he exerted on

[1] One of the first acts of Pius X was to suppress the right of veto.

[2] Thrity-eight Italian, twenty-six foreign.

[3] Especially in the affair of Modernism (see Chapter VI).

the Holy Father, a former parish priest who was fluent only in Italian. During the conclave, of which he was secretary, he showed himself remarkably skilful, and that is why Pius X gave him the red hat and appointed him secretary of state at the early age of thirty-eight. Had he, as one witness declared,[1] 'a notion of authority such as one might have cherished in Spain three centuries earlier', hiding 'steel beneath the velvet of great natural benevolence and exquisite politeness'? He cannot be blamed for adopting 'an extremely hierarchic view of the Church's organization, regarding Catholics as subject in all things to the bishops, and the latter as taking their cue from Rome'. That idea has been entertained by all popes since the time of the French Revolution. The truth is that Cardinal Merry del Val found himself in complete and spontaneous agreement with the Pope, whom he served without hesitation or reticence, and that the policies which distinguished the pontificate were, like those of Leo XIII and Rampolla, their common achievement. Those policies, moreover, represented an evolution marked by changes of personnel. At first the secretary of state retained the services of Cardinal Rampolla's immediate collaborator, Mgr Della Chiesa (the future Pope Benedict XV); but as soon as the latter was appointed Archbishop of Bologna others became influential at the Vatican, among them the disturbing figure of Mgr Benigni. Then began, despite the Pope's kindliness and the extreme courtesy of Cardinal Merry del Val, that 'serene and stubborn intransigence' which some came to regard as characteristic of the pontificate.

Whereas Leo XIII had decided on a programme of government some time before his election, Pius X came to the apostolic throne with nothing more than a rule of conduct upon which he had long based all his actions, a maxim of life which was to be that of his entire reign and which he very often repeated: *Omnia instaurare in Christo*—a mystic phrase re-echoing St Paul's famous words: 'It is no longer I that lives, but Christ who liveth in me.' To place Christ at the centre of all life, to rest everything upon His message, must be the aim of every Christian and *a fortiori* of a pope. It was the purpose that dictated all the great decisions of Pius X in the spiritual sphere; but it would be false to believe that the same principle failed to inspire his conduct in matters other than those of frequent communion and liturgical reform. He himself took care to explain his ideas on this point.[2] 'To restore all things in Christ is to strengthen not only what belongs strictly to the divine mission of the Church, but also what derives from that mission; it is to promote a Christian society in all those fields.'

[1] An Italian prelate reported by the Abbé Desbranges in his *Carnets intimes* (i. 103), a mine of detailed information on this period.

[2] In the Encyclical *Il fermo proposito*, 1905.

When, therefore, an historian compares the 'non-political' Pius X with his 'political' predecessor Leo XIII, he must be clear as to the meaning and connotation of the words. No doubt the future saint intended to be a 'non-political' pope, above all else a religious pope. But besides the fact that a resolution to eschew politics is already a policy, it is certain that the Pope who wished 'to bring back all men to the paths of Jesus Christ' did not exclude politics as a means to achieving that end. We shall see [1] that he considered politics as subject to religion—as indeed had Leo XIII—adding that 'it is impossible to separate them from the magisterium exercised by the Pope in the realm of faith and morals'. And so wherever the interests of the Church and of her members were at stake no political consideration must predominate; but in his day those interests were threatened, and hence the often seemingly apparent rigour of his decisions. No pontiff ever saw more clearly than Pius X that he was waging war for God.

These facts account for the stresses, strains and shocks of his pontificate. Before accusing him of intransigence one must know whether the various conflicts were started by him or by his adversaries, and ask oneself whether some of his decisions which appeared churlish at the time did not achieve better results than any which might have followed from a more flexible but weaker attitude. True, in his dealings with secular governments he did not seek to avoid risks of conflict, and that once such conflicts had broken out he did nothing to mitigate their consequences. But the positions which he took up were justified by events, as well as bearing witness to a keen perception of the Church's real interests and to a degree of foresight which the activity of the Holy Ghost alone can explain. Thus we find him fencing for Ireland against England, for Poland against Russia, long before those two noble Catholic nations recovered control of their own destinies. So too in French affairs we see him boldly confronting the repeated assaults of anticlericalism, defending with serene intransigence the rights and dignity of the Apostolic See. Then, when the rupture has been completed by his adversaries and France turns with anguish to a new chapter of her history, we see the Pope refusing any sort of compromise, accepting a difficult situation as if he knew for certain that great good would come from this ordeal, a fuller 'restoration in Christ'.

The same wish to subject all things to the law of Christ and to the authority of the Church, which interprets and applies that law, underlay the harshness of the censures fulminated by Pius X. Some of them affected Catholic politicians, especially those of the left. Not that he was basically hostile to democratic regimes; he declared more than

[1] Chapter V, section 1.

once that he respected them, even those which behaved as enemies. But he was troubled by the sight of so many Christian democrats accepting the secularist doctrine of the people's absolute sovereignty; indignant, too, on discovering that the spirit of discipline and respect for hierarchic principles was not the leading virtue in such circles. Hence the condemnation of two otherwise unimpeachable Catholic movements, Opera dei Congressi in Italy and Sillon in France.[1] To attribute it, however, to political motives would be to misunderstand the holy pontiff's thought. There, as in every other field, his purpose was to defend spiritual interests; and there too one may ask whether, by adopting so firm an attitude and forestalling possible deviations, he did not prepare the ground for more fruitful labour.

This conclusion is the more inescapable when we consider the unflinching severity with which Pius X handled the Modernist affair. He was no longer dealing with mere political vagaries alone—although the Catholic political thinkers whom he condemned were not untainted by Modernism—but with an extremely grave doctrinal error which did nothing less than dispute the very foundations of Christian faith while claiming to renovate the methods of philosophy, of exegesis, of religious history and even of morality. Leo XIII, towards the end of his life, had already suspected the danger; Pius X's merit lies in his having seen it clearly and checked it with all the strength at his command. Had the Church allowed the Modernist current to develop along the lines it was following at the time of Cardinal Sarto's election, Catholicism would have lost its spiritual substance and would have become a sort of humanist doctrine, more or less rationalistic, as was liberal Protestantism at that date. *Omnia instaurare in Christo*: in order that man's thinking and all else might be 'restored in Christ' it was necessary to get rid of the subtle heresy, which was particularly strong and disquieting because it appealed to the most up-to-date intellectual methods. That is what Pius X did by means of the Decree *Lamentabili sane exitu* and the Encyclical *Pascendi*. True, he sensed the danger as it were instinctively and made no attempt to oppose the error with positive facts. The Church's hour of affirmation and reconstruction was to come later, after that of prohibition and condemnation; but that positive achievement would surely have been impossible if Pius X had not cleared the ground and fixed the boundaries which must not be overstepped, if he had not put Catholics on their guard against the temptation to lay down their arms in face of the enemy and against the illusion of compromise.[2]

It is this aspect of the work of Pius X, an aspect which may be called defensive, that has engaged the attention of most historians,

[1] See Chapter V, section 6.

[2] On the Modernist affair see the whole of Chapter VI.

no doubt because of its sensational character. But it is not the most important. A great deal of constructive effort too was in progress during his pontificate; from it the Church later derived much benefit, and by it perhaps the saintly Pope earned the words of praise uttered by Pius XII, on the day of his beatification: 'He saw exactly what ought to be done, the mission of the Church and her place in the world such as it then was.'

From this great principle, *omnia instaurare in Christo*, to which we must constantly return, there resulted a whole programme whose purpose was to make the best use of the forces of the Church, to increase her influence and, above all, to renew and deepen the spiritual life in souls. There the former parish priest and diocesan bishop felt most at home. Few popes have been able to pride themselves on forty years of pastoral ministry. After his elevation to Peter's throne Don Sarto remembered them and managed to ally the sense of practical achievement with the highest spiritual aims.

Practical achievement. 'The spiritual is itself carnal,' wrote Péguy at about that time; and Pius X thought that, in order to succeed, the spiritual had need of institutions. Here we have one of the most remarkable aspects of his personality. Cardinal Merry del Val's memoirs show Pius X working month after month on the apostolic constitution *Sapienti Consilio* (1908), a massive document of eighty close-written pages together with two appendices, which reorganized at one stroke the entire central administration of the Church, and reorganized it so thoroughly that Pius X has been described as 'the second founder of the Roman Curia'. The latter was based in theory on Sixtus V's famous letter *Immensa* (1588); but after three centuries and more the machine was no longer running smoothly. Pius found himself in a jungle of departments, often at loggerheads with one another; a confused mass of governmental offices, many of which (e.g. the ten supposed to deal with the City of Rome and the Papal States) had become useless. The reform of Pius X had a threefold aim: to suppress unwanted organisms,[1] to separate the executive from the judiciary, and to establish the jurisdiction of the several tribunals. It is upon the bases laid down by Pius X that the Holy See continues to function.[2]

Another of his undertakings roused fewer protests but was equally decisive: the revision of Canon Law, which was represented at that date by a tangled web of laws, decrees and decisions heaped together in the course of centuries, and in volumes that were often inaccessible, without any attempt to eliminate their contradictions or adapt them to

[1] The number of Roman Congregations was reduced from twenty to eleven.

[2] At the time of writing (September 1964) other reforms are projected by Pope Paul VI.—TRANSLATOR.

new circumstances. Mgr Sarto had a logical mind, and while serving as a diocesan bishop he had frequently expressed his disapproval of such disorder. Immediately after his accession to the papacy, therefore, he inaugurated a reform of Canon Law. Throughout his pontificate he took a keen personal interest in the task, fixing *motu proprio* its object and methods; appointing fifty 'consultors' who were to carry out the work in Rome, assisted by 'collaborators' chosen from among the best diocesan and university canonists; and discussing their progress with Mgr Pietro Gasparri, a senior official of the secretariat of state who had been teaching Canon Law for twenty years at the Institut Catholique in Paris. 'Hurry up!' he would often say; 'I'm getting old and I'd like to see this job finished before I die.' In fact it was not until three years after his death that the gigantic labour was completed: 2,500 canons in five books, covering every juridical subject. When promulgating the new Code on Whitsunday 1917, Benedict XV likened its true author to Innocent III, Honorius III and Gregory IX, each of whom in his own day had erected as it were a milestone on the road of Canon Law.[1]

At the time of the Council of Trent it was often said that the reform needed by the Church should be carried out *in capite et in membris*. Anxious though he was to put the Church's house in order as regards the head, Pius X was not without concern for the members. Many decisions taken during his pontificate show him eager to inject more abundant life into the whole vast organism of the Church. The episcopate was the object of his particular attention. He reorganized the procedure governing appointments (excepting those in missionary lands) by entrusting them to the Consistorial Congregation. The powers of this body were enlarged, but it also received detailed instructions on the manner of preparing candidates' dossiers, which were studied by the Pope himself before any decision was reached. In order to strengthen Rome's control over the episcopate, visits *ad limina*, which had been obligatory since the reign of Pius IX, were now to operate according to a strict rotation, so that every bishop would go to the Vatican once in five years; and they were supplemented by

[1] This enormous twofold enterprise of Pius X in the administrative field was crowned by certain measures of which one at least deserves special notice. Strange as it may appear, there existed no official means of promulgating a papal decision. Once an Encyclical had been signed by the Pope it was sent to the bishops, who might or might not have it read from the pulpit; but it was not issued in any form that would give it force of law. Father Pietro Avanzini had for some years been publishing his *Acta Sanctu Sedis*, but the father's publication was a private (or at most a semi-official) journal. As Patriarch of Venice, Mgr Giuseppe Sarto had already expressed a desire that this publication should become official. On becoming Pope he looked into the matter, and in 1908 gave orders for the foundation of *Acta Apostolicae Sedis*, in which would appear 'the papal constitutions, the laws, decrees and all ordinances of the Roman pontiffs, as well as the decisions of the Sacred Congregations and Tribunals'. This official organ of the Holy See continues to appear in its original large quarto format.

a report on the state of his diocese which every bishop had to submit to the Consistorial Congregation.

The Pope's chief concern, however, was for the rank and file of the clergy, which is really an emanation of the episcopate. It was not by chance that he kept a statue of the Curé d'Ars on his desk. In his very first Encyclical he revealed his idea of a true priest: while describing as 'praiseworthy' those who devote themselves to useful studies, he admitted that his preference lay with priests 'who dedicate themselves exclusively to the welfare of souls . . .' As Bishop of Mantua and later of Venice he had preached by example, attending personally to the training of his seminarists and to the spiritual life of his priests, sharing their retreats, hearing the confessions of those who wished, reproving backsliders with gentle firmness. At the same time, however, he was thoroughly practical, and took some long-needed steps for the benefit of priests, e.g. amalgamation of the seminaries of dioceses too small to provide a satisfactory training on their own.

The same direct experience of pastoral life that enabled him to explain so clearly to his priests the conditions they must fulfil in order to carry out their task as men of God, led him also to make what one might in his day have called a new discovery: the role of the laity. He more than once proclaimed the urgent need for laymen capable of breathing life into the parishes. Here was an altogether original note; and his Encyclical *Il fermo proposito* on the Italian Unione Popolare can now be seen as foreshadowing Catholic Action.[1]

The work of Pius X affords many examples of such farsightedness in respect of what the Church should do to make her apostolate more fruitful. When we consider that pontificate, so often held to have been traditionalist and reactionary, it is amazing to find how much benefit we still derive from measures adopted sixty years ago. Sarto, the one-time country priest, declared over and over again that if Catholicism was to be revivified Catholics must be given a truly Christian culture. Throughout his life he gave religious instruction to children and adults; even as Pope he used to welcome all who chose to gather on Sunday afternoon in the courtyard of San Damaso and hear him speak on the gospel for that day or on some point of doctrine. His Encyclical *Acerbo nimis* (1905) solemnly reminded parish priests of their grave obligation to teach the catechism. He also tried to improve the sermon, a form of instruction that had fallen on hard times. As a bishop he used often to tell his priests: 'I don't want a lot of sentimental rubbish; I want you to teach the Gospel.' As Pope he said the same, and also

[1] The work of Pius X in the missionary sphere was less original than in other fields. But he showed active sympathy with the missionary congregations, beatified several of their martyrs, and created forty vicariates and thirty-eight prefectures apostolic.

objected to the precocious style affected by 'bogus Bossuets' in their academical tirades.

Steps were taken to rejuvenate the teaching in seminaries, particularly that of Holy Scripture. Pius, who is generally credited with few intellectual gifts, realized that a sound training in Christian philosophy was indispensable both for clerics and for educated laymen. Leo XIII's instructions on the revival of Thomism had been largely ignored. 'The majority of professors', says Desgranges, 'were affected by distortions of Kantianism'; Pius X called them to order, notably in a sensational letter to the papal Academy of St Thomas. Towards the end of his pontificate the theologians of his *entourage* actually drew up a list of twenty-four fundamental Thomist theses, with a view to their being made canonically binding on all professors of Catholic philosophy, a measure which some considered too dictatorial. Pius X likewise adopted the views of his predecessor in the matter of biblical studies. The Biblical Commission was reorganized and established as a sort of tribunal; its decisions were recognized as possessing the same authority as decrees of the Roman Congregations, and it was granted the right of conferring academic degrees. In 1909 there was founded the Biblical Institute, which the Pope desired to see 'endowed with all the resources of modern scientific progress'; and its creation was a decisive step towards the biblical revival witnessed by the mid twentieth century. Moreover, in order to establish the text of Holy Scripture, Pius X entrusted the Benedictines with the work of revising the Latin Vulgate, an enormous undertaking whose first-fruits appeared in 1926 with the publication of Genesis.

That huge constructive task, at once pastoral, apostolic and educational, culminated in a final and exclusively spiritual set of achievements which constitute the very keystone of the pontificate. *Omnia instaurare in Christo* . . . The first and most essential aim of Pius X was to give souls an ever more abundant spiritual life. The Christian world cannot be rebuilt unless Christ is present in the hearts of men, unless His example regulates their conduct, unless His doctrine inspires their thought. Hence the numerous documents in which the saintly Pope, exercising to the full his mission as father and pastor, emphasized the need to live in Christ. And because he was realistic, because his experience at the parochial and diocesan levels had shown him the real needs of the faithful, he took active steps to foster that spiritual life by placing at the disposal of Catholics the supreme sacrament of life, the Eucharist. His decisions on frequent communion and the communion of children, by putting an end to much debate, gave reception of the Holy Sacrament so strong an impulse that it continues to be felt in our own day. The eucharistic revival, so characteristic of twentieth-century Catholicism, remains the work of Pius X.

So too does the liturgical revival. Making his own the results achieved by Dom Guéranger and the monks of Solesmes,[1] Pius X took important steps quite early in his pontificate to restore to the liturgy its true significance and to re-establish as far as possible the the long-severed link between it and the Christian people. At the same time he sought to bring back the pristine dignity of sacred music by the revival of Gregorian chant.

If we recall that Pius X reigned for little more than eleven years, and study the work he accomplished in order both to defend the Church and to strengthen her foundations, it is difficult to withhold admiration. 'I'm only a country priest,' he used to declare with unfeigned humility. But hear now what Aristide Briand thought of him: 'Many Catholics as well as others used to dismiss him as a mere peasant. He was indeed a peasant; that is why we admired him and why he dominated all of us. Do you know how I always thought of Pius X? Wearing big hobnailed shoes beneath his white soutane, heavy shoes that gave him his slow gait and attached him to the soil. He had both feet on the ground: he was a man of common sense, of common sense that verged on genius. And perhaps he *was* a genius after all.'

The truth is that Pius X was a complete man. Pius XII spoke of his 'clear, profound and wide intelligence'. Émile Olliver has described him as endowed with 'a penetrating insight into human nature and the forces that control the world'. He was also a wonderful listener, grasping immediately the subject under discussion. Above all, he possessed a keen understanding of what was possible and what impossible, together with an unfailing recognition of the limitations imposed by circumstance. Prudent and slow in counsel, never taking a hurried decision but inflexible once he had made up his mind, he also proved himself a leader of men both in the kindliness of his welcome and in the magnetic force of his personal charm. His handsome countenance, which old age crowned with white hair but left almost unwrinkled, along with those bright hazel eyes, delighted his visitors, who were attracted no less by his conversation—simple, direct, full of happy phrases alive with peasant wit. Less courtly in manner than Leo XIII, he could nevertheless behave with immense dignity when the situation so required, particularly on ceremonial occasions. Yet all those characteristics were only the human manifestation of something superhuman. The priest who prolonged his daily Mass, often interrupting it to contemplate the Host he had just consecrated; the mystic who so often told his *entourage* to 'remember that we are always in the presence of God'; the man of prayer who often spent hours at a time

[1] *The Church in an Age of Revolution*, Chapter VIII, section 12.

in his private chapel, and who on the night before he condemned the French Law of Separation went down to St Peter's and prayed for two hours prostrate before the Confession—all those facts help to explain the Pope of great political conflicts, author of *Pascendi*, and a mighty herald of the future.

All those facts, too, were recalled by Pius XII at his canonization in 1954. Forty years had passed since his death (20th August 1914) in the early days of the First World War, which he had clearly foretold and which he had done his utmost to prevent. But Catholics were not alone in acknowledging his greatness, and even his sanctity, before he vanished from the scene. On the morrow of his death a Parisian newspaper paid this tribute to his memory: 'The Pope is dead, and he must be recognized as a great pope. His policy was very simple: it consisted in restoring the values of the Faith with apostolic firmness. He followed that purpose without flinching. His simplicity of soul and the sincerity of his virtues, which cannot be questioned from any point of view, oblige us to say that he was a great pope.' The newspaper was none other than *l'Humanité*, founded by the socialist Jean Jaurès.

5. Benedict XV

'It's Rampolla's revenge!' cried the 'Black' drawing-rooms of Rome on the evening of 3rd September 1914, when it was learned that Cardinal Giacomo della Chiesa had been elected to the papal throne. The conclave had lasted for only two days, and appears to have been uneventful. I say 'appears to have been', because strict silence had been imposed for the first time and was faithfully observed. On account of the war, only fifty-two cardinals were present—twenty-eight Italians, twenty-four foreigners—and they found no difficulty in agreeing as to who should bear the crushing responsibility of steering Peter's barque through the cyclone that swept the planet. He had not wept, like his saintly predecessor, on hearing himself proclaimed; he had offered no objection. He had welcomed the result of the final scrutiny with that simplicity, nay humility, which characterized his every action.

The new Pope was a puny little figure, slightly deformed; with one shoulder higher than the other, and a limping gait, he was not likely to impress the crowds. But his irregular features radiated intelligence, and the bespectacled eyes gazed steadily upon those with whom he talked.[1] He whom the Romans had nicknamed *il piccoletto* (the little

[1] Benedict XV had a somewhat acid sense of humour. Receiving a prelate who had once been accused of Modernism he remarked: 'I hope you are now sure of Our orthodoxy: We are infallible.'

fellow) during his time at the secretariat of state showed in his normal bearing a vivacity and spontaneity that contrasted with the majesty of Leo XIII and the bright serenity of Pius X. One might have said that he derived from his external appearance yet another motive for practising the celebrated precept of the *Imitation*: 'Love to be unknown and accounted as nothing.'

But beneath that unprepossessing exterior there lurked a soul strong as steel, a mind open to all the great problems and very far from obsequious, a splendid intellect served by familiarity with Italian, French and Spanish culture and by an unlimited capacity for work. On the whole he was the exact opposite of a timid and vacillating nonentity, blown about by every wind, as one historian has described him. Giacomo della Chiesa would undoubtedly have been capable of great things had not Providence subjected him to two misfortunes: that of being Pope during a world war, and that of dying after a pontificate of only seven years and four months at the age of sixty-eight—the very age at which Leo XIII and Pius X had begun their labours. Descended on both sides from ancient noble families of Liguria, and related to those of the dukes of Spoleto and Pope Calixtus II, the Marchese della Chiesa's son was bidden by his father to study law before heeding the summons he had heard in boyhood. Not until he had taken his doctorate was he allowed to enter the Collegio Capranica and study at the Gregorian University, with a view to membership of the Diplomatic Academy in the Piazza Minerva. Soon after joining the secretariat of state he was noticed by Mgr Rampolla, who took him to the nunciature at Madrid. This sojourn in Spain largely determined his future. His initiation by Rampolla into the secrets of diplomacy was particularly thorough, because just at that time the nunciature at Madrid had the duty of preparing a dossier on the Hispano-Germanic affair of the Carolines, in which Leo XIII had agreed to arbitrate.[1] Brought back to the Vatican by his patron on the latter's appointment as secretary of state, given the rank of Deputy and entrusted with two delicate missions in Vienna, little Mgr della Chiesa became so precious a cog in the higher administration of the Church that Pius X and Cardinal Merry del Val were content to leave him at his post.

In 1907 a new chapter of his career began and a new feature of his character emerged when he undertook the care of souls. 'New', perhaps, is hardly the right word; for even in Rome he had often left the Vatican offices to visit the poor, hear confessions in the parishes and preach to his friends the Franciscan Tertiaries. At Bologna, however, he spent himself to the utmost, and the inspiring efforts of his seven years as archbishop of that enormous diocese have never

[1] See Chapter III, section 11.

been forgotten. Strangely enough—whether through oversight or through the petty vindictiveness of certain anti-Rampolla circles in Rome is uncertain—the red hat was slow to alight upon his head; it was not until the spring of 1914 that Pius X, in the last consistory he held, raised him to the purple. Three months later he was elected to the papacy.

By virtue of his training therefore, no less than of his personality, the new Pope seemed likely to effect a synthesis of the lessons taught by his two predecessors. Like Joachim Pecci he was a diplomat, inclined like him to view the Church as a great supranational institution, and resolved like him to extend the arm of his influence to every field of life. At the same time he was no less generous and zealous a pastor than Pius X, an apostle in whose eyes the duty of bearing witness to Christ and spreading His message took precedence of every other. In assuming the regnal name taken by Cardinal Lambertini, an earlier Archbishop of Bologna who, as Benedict XIV, had been praised by Voltaire, Président de Brosses and the Protestant Walpole, Della Chiesa may have wished to signify that he too would be at once broad-minded, prudent and bold, that he would be in fact, like him, a *dotto*, a *politico* and a *zelante*. But on the very day of his coronation the French and German armies confronted one another in a terrible ordeal upon the Marne.

Benedict XV's short pontificate was dominated directly or indirectly by the appalling conflict in which he was involved from the moment of his accession: directly throughout the period of hostilities, indirectly when it came to rebuilding Europe amid the spiritual and material chaos left by the war. Like his two predecessors, he was fortunate to have the assistance of a most able secretary of state [1] in Cardinal Gasparri (1852–1934), an ex-nuncio, a distinguished canon lawyer and a vigorous personality, whose outward and rather heavy calm concealed an ardent spirit which nothing could quench.

The war placed the Vicar of Christ in a tragic situation. He could not accept that atrocious violation of the great law of love given to men by Jesus Christ, let alone resign himself to the spectacle of Catholics ranged against one another in a bloody duel. A pope is in his element when he obeys so manifest a duty of his calling as to speak of and strive for peace. Yet Benedict XV was blamed for doing just that, not only by politicians of the two camps, but also by many Catholics. His action, considered today after the passage of half a century, seems neither extravagant in its aims nor even clumsy in its methods. Unfortunately, however, it anticipated events and clashed head-on with those primitive passions that are roused in the hearts of men at moments

[1] His first secretary of state, Cardinal Ferrata, died after holding office for a month and left valuable memoirs.

of grave peril. And so all that Benedict XV strove to do during the war in the cause of peace not only proved ineffective but actually assisted in making him the slighted figure he remains. Not even his charitable work, indisputably admirable though it was, failed to win just appreciation. It is alarming to discover with what ingratitude and unfairness many historians, some of them Catholics, still pass judgment on him.[1]

That injustice became manifest after the return of peace; it powerfully assisted those who, like the anticlerical rulers of Italy, were apprehensive at the prospect of the Holy See appearing once again in the diplomatic concert which was going to decide the fate of the world. Thus the papacy was not only excluded from the negotiation of the peace treaties, but was also denied a place in the League of Nations although it had been the first to put forward the grand idea of obligatory international arbitration. It seems then that every circumstance was directed to an eclipse of the Apostolic See at a moment when it was more than ever necessary that the Church's disinterested voice should be heard appealing for a true, equitable and brotherly settlement—which the Treaty of Versailles most certainly was not.

Nevertheless, despite his unwelcome situation, Benedict XV continued to do his best for the interests of God and of the Church. It was indeed during the last three years of his pontificate, which coincided with the establishment of an uneasy peace, that he proved as never before his diplomatic gifts and his breadth of view. He managed to introduce the Church into places whence she was officially banned—e.g. Versailles, where his private representative Mgr Cerretti showed the utmost skill; he knew when to abandon too rigid attitudes and to take account of circumstances in order to regain a footing where it had seemed that all was lost; and he was thus able to inaugurate a policy of concordats which was afterwards continued by Pius XI. His greatest triumph was the resumption of diplomatic relations with France and the settlement of questions that had been outstanding since the early years of the century. Benedict XV's policies were no less fruitful in other fields, particularly in Italy, where he took the first steps towards the *conciliazione* accomplished by Pius XI, and where, by allowing Catholics to try a new political experiment, he opened up paths whose safety did not become apparent until after the cataclysm of a second world war.[2]

It must, however, be repeated that at the time none of this activity was understood or appreciated as it should have been by anyone with an eye to the future. A disordered world was soon to feel with mounting intensity that the great moral force represented by the Pope was

[1] For the work of Benedict XV during the war see below, Chapter VII, section 2.
[2] On Benedict XV and the democratic parties see Chapter VII, section 5.

indispensable. Meanwhile the increasing prestige of the Holy See under Benedict XV, despite the injustice and violence of his critics, may be judged from the fact that the number of States seeking representation at the Vatican rose from fifteen to twenty-seven.

A policy so perfectly coherent and so firmly pursued shows clearly how false is the commonly accepted image of Benedict XV as a 'caretaker pope', crushed by his closeness in time to two illustrious pontiffs, a colourless figure buffeted by events. Far from allowing himself to be paralysed by the enormous difficulties confronting him, the frail Giacomo della Chiesa pursued throughout the war and immediate post-war years the work begun by Leo XIII and Pius X. No matter how tragic the circumstances, they could not prevent the Church from leading her own life, nor the papacy from its activity in realms remote from politics.

Finding the Church still shaken by the tempest of Modernism, realizing that that 'manifold heresy', as he called it, had not yet been everywhere eliminated, he repeated in his first Encyclical (November 1914) the condemnations fulminated by his predecessor. Equally aware, however, that towards the end of Pius X's pontificate the anti-Modernist reaction had displayed some quite odious features, he resolved to issue a warning against certain abuses and certain proceedings, as well as against certain men who were posing as 'masters in the Church'. He tried thereby to ward off the danger afterwards called 'integrism', pointing to the *via media* which the Church sought now to follow.[1] He also did justice to certain victims of the integrist reaction, among them Father Anizan.

Still, those were merely restrictive measures. The steps that Benedict XV took in several other fields were obvious attempts to carry forward what he considered as the most important and necessary undertakings of the two preceding pontificates. The Code of Canon Law, begun in 1904 by order of Pius X and completed in 1917, was proclaimed on 15th September, at a time when it might have been thought that the Pope was preoccupied with other objectives; and a commission was set up to interpret this new document, with authority to answer all questions raised by diocesan bishops or the Roman tribunals. The reorganization of those tribunals, inaugurated by Pius X was completed. The Congregation of the Index disappeared, its duties being transferred to the Holy Office. A new Congregation of Seminaries and Universities was created, which, though entrusted officially with the supervision of ecclesiastical education, particularly in theology, was intended primarily to give it new life and vigour. The appointment of Cardinal Mercier, Archbishop of Malines and a distinguished Thomist, as first prefect of this Congregation was

[1] See Chapter VI, section 8.

sufficient evidence of the direction in which the Pope desired that it should move.

A second new organism was the Congregation for Oriental Churches. Founded in 1917, it was another sign of that desire for a wider outlook we have noticed in other fields; and such importance did Benedict XV attach to it that he himself assumed the office of prefect, a cardinal taking his place as secretary. Too long regarded as a negligible factor in the Church, and sometimes offended by lack of courtesy,[1] Catholics of the Eastern rites now saw that their interests and traditions would be defended in Rome. A Pontifical Institute of Higher Oriental Studies was opened to them, as well as to clergy of the Latin rite who wished to serve in the East, and even to Orthodox priests. This admission of the Orthodox to the new Institute was only one aspect of Benedict XV's attitude towards his 'separated brethren'. He more than once reminded the oriental Christians that the Church entertained no less admiration than themselves for their beloved Greek Fathers; and he proclaimed the Syrian St Ephrem a Doctor of the Church, which title had long since been conferred upon him by the Orient. Though he declined to be represented at the World Conference organized by the Episcopalian Church of America, he sent his good wishes to the promoters; in 1916 he ordered a novena of prayers for the reunion of Christendom; and in 1921, when Lord Halifax and Cardinal Mercier began their talks at Malines with a view to reconciliation of the Church of England with Rome, he sent a note of encouragement.

As a man of wide culture, Benedict XV inevitably adopted the views of his predecessors in the intellectual field. His Encyclical *Saeculo sexto exeunte* (1921), published to commemorate the sixth centenary of the death of Dante and addressed to the professors and students of Catholic universities and institutes, is among the finest papal documents on the significance of culture as well as upon the relation between things divine and the beauties which adorn the human spirit. The same purpose which moved the Pope to create the Congregation of Seminaries and Universities made him the protector of all those universities and higher institutes which were then in process of foundation or development. Thomism was given fresh impulse: it became the official basis of theological studies in seminaries and the scholasticates of religious orders; while the Institut Léon XIII was established at Louvain, linked with the University and intended to promote higher studies on the *Summa*.

In the biblical sphere Benedict XV's activity was even more closely akin to that of Leo XIII. Very soon after the signing of the armistice in 1918 he invited Catholics to celebrate the twenty-fifth anniversary

[1] e.g. during the Vatican Council. See *The Church in an Age of Revolution*, Chapter V, section 17.

of *Providentissimus Deus*; in 1920 the Encyclical *Spiritus Paraclitus*, published on the fifteenth centenary of St Jerome's death, repeated its central themes, carefully marking out the frame of scriptural studies but urging a more widespread reading of the Bible. The Pious Society of St Jerome, over which Mgr della Chiesa had once presided and which had the propagation of Bible-reading as its aim, received encouragement and financial assistance. A popular edition of the New Testament was published by the Vatican Press; and some have found reason to credit Benedict XV with the inauguration of that biblical revival which is one of the most striking features of the Church today.

Nor shall we be far wrong in acknowledging the same Pope as having played some part in the genesis of that great movement which, under Pius XI, was to become what is known as Catholic Action; for the *Unione Popolare*, founded by the Conte Dalla Torre and the Marchese Patrizzi, had interested Benedict during his residence at Bologna, and he continued to support it after his accession to the papacy.[1] Above all, he was passionately concerned for the welfare of the missions. His Encyclical *Maximum illud* (1919) laid down the principles that were applied so successfully by the next Pope, particularly as regards the building up of native clergies and the foundation of coloured Churches.[2]

Thus death, which struck him down on 22nd January 1922 after a three days' illness, found Benedict XV busily engaged in a constructive task; not, of course, having completed all he had set out to do, but having done more than pioneer the road for his successor. More fairly judged today, even in respect of his attitude during the war, he is seen as the first in a line of popes who have shown that in times of mortal danger the Church can fulfil the task appointed by Christ only if she upholds her standards and at the same time progresses, only if she remains both present to God and present to the world.

On the morrow of his death one panegyrist declared: 'Never has the prestige of the Holy See been greater than it is today; we should have to go back several hundred years in order to find its like.' One might be inclined to treat such enthusiasm as mere pulpit oratory. But the man who spoke those words was soon to learn whether or not his opinion was justified; for he was none other than the Cardinal Archbishop of Milan, Achille Ratti.

6. Strength of Pius XI

If the word 'genius' is appropriate to Leo XIII, and 'sanctity' to Pius X, there is surely no better term than 'strength' with which to

[1] He appointed Dalla Torre director of the *Osservatore Romano*.
[2] See Chapter XI, section 8.

describe Pius XI; strength, that is to say, in its theological sense,[1] a divine attribute and one of the four cardinal virtues of man, distinct from natural energy of temperament but completing it and raising it to the summit of its efficacy, a potentiality derived from God. According to St Thomas,[2] strength sublimates and places at the service of divine causes 'the irascible', i.e. the appetite for struggle and domination which is part of man's nature; and that, of course, explains why possession of this virtue goes together with an imperious and even peremptory character. It presupposes the spirit of decision, the breadth of purpose, which the schoolmen call 'magnanimity'—courage, invincible faith in a cause, backed by patience and constancy. These scholastic definitions paint so good a psychological portrait of Achille Ratti that no more need be said. Seldom had it been so unnecessary to recall that the Holy Ghost, alighting upon a man to make him head of the Church, endows him with that 'strength from on high', *virtus Dei*, which filled the souls of the Apostles on the first Christian Pentecost.

Those virtues, however, are not such as might normally be expected of a librarian, in which post the future pontiff spent thirty years of his life after teaching in a seminary and serving as chaplain to a convent—none of them duties ordinarily requiring heroism or conducive to pugnacity. In 1918 Mgr Achille Ratti was in his sixty-first year; he had been working four years as prefect of the Vatican Library, having already served as sub-prefect, and before that (from 1888) as an assistant in the Ambrosian at Milan. His career had been uneventful. He was born in 1857 at Brianza, son of the manager of a spinning-mill at Desio in Lombardy. At the age of ten he entered the junior, and at eighteen the senior seminary. Proceeding to Rome, he took a doctorate in canon law at the Gregorian University, a doctorate in theology at the Sapienza and another at the new Academy of St Thomas. From boyhood upwards he had given proof of such outstanding gifts of intellect and assiduity that the phrase 'an excellent pupil' might have been coined for him. He had also shown himself so extremely serious, so extremely industrious, that his archbishop nicknamed him *mio giovane vecchio*.

There was, however, something besides the model student in the seminary professor at Milan, in the conscientious employee of the Ambrosian Library, in the scholar whose reputation spread quickly throughout the learned world. While teaching Hebrew and theology, or compiling card indexes, Don Achille Ratti was at the same time an ardent apostle who taught catechism in the poorer quarters; a generous

[1] The English translation of *fortitudo* as 'fortitude' belies the sense of the theological term, since 'fortitude' has come to denote mere passive endurance.—TRANSLATOR.

[2] III *Sent.*, disp. xxiii, q. 1; *Sum. Theol.* I. IIae, qq. lix, lx.

soul who one hard winter sheltered fifteen little Tyrolean chimney-sweeps whom he found adrift in Milan; the priest who displayed nothing less than heroism during the tragic events of 1893 brought about by a grave crisis of unemployment in that city; and lastly the skilled Alpinist who climbed the eastern face of Monte Rosa, where some of his forerunners had lost their lives. In a word, he combined the gifts of a pure intellectual with those of a man for whom the external world, its realities and exigencies, are of deep significance. The success of his pontificate was largely due to his remarkable personality.

In 1918 his forceful character was called upon unexpectedly to deal with political factors and the problem of human leadership. Sent by Benedict XV as apostolic visitor to Poland, he had to face a more than delicate situation in a country where ecclesiastical organization had been systematically destroyed by the occupying Russians, whose problems of jurisidiction appeared to be insoluble because certain dioceses had been placed under German bishops, and whose very existence was imperilled by the invasion of Bolshevik armies. Those three years in Poland were not without disappointments and setbacks for Mgr Ratti, but they completed his training as a man of action, a statesman and a diplomat. One episode in particular revealed the calm and clear-headed courage of which his later career furnished so many proofs. When Tukhachevsky's cavalry approached Warsaw all the ambassadors of the great Powers prudently fled; but the Nuncio, representing the least armed Power on earth, remained.

That heroic gesture counted for much in Benedict XV's decision to give him the red hat and entrust him with the archdiocese of Milan in succession to Cardinal Ferrari. Cardinal Ratti, however, did not long enjoy the pleasure of governing the illustrious See. Five months after his entry into the city the Pope died, and the subsequent conclave—fifty-three members of the Sacred College, of whom twenty-nine were Italians—gave the Archbishop of Milan forty-two votes, many more than the two-thirds required, after four days of indecision and thirteen scrutinies. To the canonical question 'Do you accept election to the supreme pontificate?' he replied in these words, which were no mere formality: 'Despite my unworthiness, of which I am well aware, I accept, because I do not want it said that I shirked a heavy burden.'

The new Pope was of medium height and stocky, with massive square shoulders—more like a mountaineer than a scholar. The fresh and almost unlined countenance proclaimed a sturdy constitution. He wore glasses, but his eyes were bright and clear, and his penetrating gaze was that of a man who is not deceived by appearances. Accustomed by long experience to the study of documents and conflicting interpretations, he added to his natural prudence the cautiousness of an historian. But once he had pondered and taken a decision on any

matter nothing could make him change his mind; he went forward with unshakable resolution, fists clenched and eyes aglow. All the same, though intransigent to the point of violence where essentials were at stake—his table-thumping was notorious!—he was indulgent and conciliatory in matters that seemed to him of secondary importance. Remembering his career as a diplomat, he was no less capable of handling an affair with patience and flexibility than of breaking his adversary or launching an anathema. This explains the two very different aspects of his policy—one of negotiation, the other of condemnation.

Those qualities, which somehow combined many of the characteristics of his three predecessors, were at the service of a very lofty idea of his duty. For Pius XI, as for Leo XIII and Pius X, nothing counted but the glory of God and the establishment of His reign. Curiously enough, this twentieth-century Pope, in many respects so 'modern', had an even more imperious concept of the reign of God than had his predecessors, a concept which some have judged medieval and which found expression above all in the Encyclical *Quas primas* (1925) instituting the feast of Christ the King. It would be foolish to suppose that a mere desire to increase the number of liturgical celebrations of Our Lord's prerogatives moved him to consecrate the last Sunday of October to this new devotion. Such a demonstration would have been pointless, had it done nothing but re-echo Epiphany, Easter and Ascension. We have to place a literal interpretation on the Encyclical's statement that 'Christ reigns', that He is the sole master of mankind. This intransigent declaration, directly opposed to those of contemporary atheistic humanism, is valid first and foremost in the spiritual order. Nevertheless that Messianic kingship is wielded over all men and over all things upon earth. 'States, princes and governments are rulers in their own domains, and Christ, whose kingdom is not of this world, has no wish that His Church should interfere therein; but she must remind them of the spiritual and moral principles to which their labours should conform, and declare repeatedly that they too are bound to promote the kingdom of God.' Here we have a theocratic notion of the Church's activity, just as imperious as that held by Innocent III, but radically different inasmuch as it transcends all politics and lifts the Pope's function into a strictly spiritual field, the field to which it was dedicated by two major events of 1870—the proclamation of papal infallibility and the loss of temporal power. There the Vicar of Christ is unassailable and invincible. All the decisions of Pius XI are explicable by this basic concept, which his successors have inherited.

Such an attitude might have restricted the Pope to doctrinal affirmations or condemnations and to the exposition of moral principles. But

Pius XI, we have seen, was not the sort of man to limit himself to the realm of pure ideas. As an historian he had learned from the past that 'in history the living tissue of events is a compound both of human and of divine thoughts and actions, the two elements alternately mingling, contradicting each other and colliding so as to fulfil the plan of Providence'. In other words, he thought that God had need of men in order to promote His reign. He was therefore deeply concerned with the material needs and troubles of his age, going so far as to declare: 'We intend to speak as head of the Catholic Church, but also and above all as a man of our time, that is to say as a witness of and a participant in the events which menace our contemporaries. From one point of view we are preoccupied rather with purely human institutions, social and governmental, than with the Catholic Church herself.' [1] In order to establish the reign of Christ it was necessary that He and His Church should be present everywhere. The activity of Pius XI, during the seventeen years of his pontificate, had no other end in view.

In the solemn silence of the Sistine Chapel, when all the canopies but that of Cardinal Ratti had been lowered, the newly elect made two decisions that indicated the direction his pontificate would take. Asked for his regnal name, he answered 'Pius'; not only, he explained, because he was born under Pius IX and ordained under Pius X, but also because 'the name Pius signifies peace, and peace will be my principal concern', an idea which he repeated in his motto *Pax Christi in regno Christi*. Then came the unexpected announcement that he would impart his first blessing *Urbi et Orbi* from the outside balcony of St Peter's, showing that he rejected the attitude of his three predecessors.[2] Here was another declaration of peaceful intentions, of a desire to make new contacts with the world and to manifest the Church's presence to mankind.

In this latter policy, to which he clung throughout his reign, Pius XI was ably supported by Cardinal Gasparri, his secretary of state until 1930. He continued the post-war efforts of Benedict XV to establish or re-establish relations with the secular Powers and to lead the Church back into the concert of nations. Unlike his predecessor he made no attempt to associate the Apostolic See with the League; he encouraged and helped it, but regarded it privately as unstable and of little use. On the other hand he continued and enlarged Benedict's policy of agreements. The twenty-five concordats or treaties of *modus vivendi* into which he entered were remarkable not only for their number, but also for the great variety of countries and regimes with which they were signed, as well as for the novel characteristics which many of them

[1] Quoted by Marc Bonnet, *La Papauté contemporaine*, p. 110.

[2] See Chapter IV, section 7.

assumed. In order to restore the Church's presence, Pius XI did not hesitate to negotiate with such notoriously hostile governments as those of Czechoslovakia, Mexico and the Third Reich. Had it been possible, he would have negotiated with Red Russia. In each of those agreements, however, his aim was to secure not only recognition of the institutional rights of the Church, but also the acceptance of the Christian principles of morality and justice, by virtue of that spiritual primacy which he had so much at heart. This policy reached its climax in 1929 with the Lateran Treaties,[1] which put an end to the thorny 'Roman Question'. By agreeing that the temporal power should be restricted to an area of about 350 acres—a domain so small that it could be considered as merely symbolic—Pius XI emphasized the true, spiritual and worldwide significance of papal authority.

But diplomatic relations between the Church and secular governments was of little consequence so long as men continued lukewarm in the profession of their faith. Hence the Pope's unceasing effort to make Christ present once again in every sphere of life. Leo XIII had pioneered the way on the social and intellectual fronts. Pius XI followed the same paths, and indeed went a great deal further,[2] e.g. in 1931 when his Encyclical *Quadragesimo anno* commemorated the fortieth anniversary of *Rerum novarum.* He did more than simply recall the great principles of Christian brotherhood and denounce the evils of social inequality; he condemned not only Communism, but also the economic liberalism which 'leads to Communism', protesting against the 'undeserved misery' of so many workers and the 'degradation of man' brought about by modern industry, and formulating with unequalled clarity the distinction between the obligation of justice and that of charity, charity being in his eyes 'mere falsehood and hypocrisy' so long as the former duty remains unfulfilled. His constant and effective backing of social Catholicism and Christian trade unionism was a step in the same direction.

In the intellectual order too Leo XIII had made a serious attempt to lead the Church back wheresoever she belonged; and Pius X had not hindered the development of that trend. The necessity for a renewed effort was plain, especially after the crisis of Modernism. Strict limits had been defined beyond which, it was claimed, innovation would amount to rashness; but it was most desirable that Catholics should adopt the methods of their adversaries in order to meet them on equal terms. No one was better qualified to give a lead in this respect than Achille Ratti, who once remarked: 'Our motto will always be "Know in order to live".' Thus his entire pontificate was marked by an extraordinary upsurge of the Catholic intellect in the realms of science, philosophy and literature. Of this there is abundant

[1] See Chapter IX, section 8. [2] See Chapter X, section 4.

evidence: growth of the Pontifical Biblical Institute in Rome, of the Biblical School at Jerusalem, and of the Benedictine abbey of St Jerome where the Vulgate was in process of revision; foundation of the Pontifical Academy of Sciences, which was opened to non-Catholics; and an increase in the number of scientific, literary and juridical congresses organized by Catholics. Even the most recent means of self-expression were used by Pius XI to manifest the Church's presence. A friend of Marconi, he himself inaugurated the Vatican radio station; and among his titles to fame are two Encyclicals in which he showed the importance of the cinema and suggested how it could serve the faith.

At the root of all that effort lay the apostolic purpose indicated in the Encyclical *Quas primas* on Christ the King: to promote the reign of Christ wherever it had been undermined. Such was the aim of a new enterprise, born spontaneously in several countries but most clearly conceived and fostered in Belgium under the Abbé Cardijn: specialized Catholic Action. It is to the credit of Pius XI that he immediately recognized the importance of this movement, welcomed it whole-heartedly and generalized its methods. Two innovations were thereby accomplished: first, the direct association of the laity with the Church's apostolate; secondly, specialization of the forms and methods of that work according to the environment of those who were to be won back to (or kept within) the Christian fold. The years from 1925 onwards, which saw the beginning of Catholic Action, mark a turning point in the history of the Church, as well as in that of the pontificate.[1]

It was not only to the members of Catholic Action that Pius XI commended this variation upon a theme of St Paul: 'Become a worker among the workers, a peasant among the peasants.' He saw clearly that in order to make the Church's presence felt among peoples known at that time as 'colonial', it was necessary to modify and enlarge the traditional concept of the missions. Reviving the ideas of Father Matteo Ricci and Father de Nobili,[2] as well as developing and systematizing in *Rerum Ecclesiae* the proposals of Benedict XV's *Maximum illud*, he laid the foundations of those 'coloured Churches' which have since appeared as the Church's only hope in Asia and Africa.[3] This decisive orientation was manifested with great splendour in 1926 at the consecration by the Pope himself of some bishops of the yellow race. And Pius XI even dreamed of playing a similar role in the tragedy of Christian disunion. None of his predecessors had overlooked that unhappy problem, but he approached it with more determination. His Encyclical *Mortalium animos* (1928) set out fully

[1] See Chapter VIII, section 6. [2] *The Catholic Reformation*, see Index.
[3] See Chapter XI, section 8.

the doctrine of the Catholic Church on this matter; and if concrete results were few, an effort had at any rate been made to re-establish contact both with Anglicans and Protestants. Moreover many opportunities were taken to show towards the separated brethren of the East a sympathy and interest which, in default of other merits, had at least that of preparing a new climate.[1]

A pope who had achieved nothing more than we have seen accomplished by Pius XI would undoubtedly be considered great. But that represents only half of his work. Though he believed it indispensable to make the Church present to the world, such an aim was but a means to a higher end. His ultimate purpose was to render the Church present to God: *adveniat regnum tuum*. Hence the gigantic threefold effort he undertook (in the spirit of Pius X rather than of Leo XIII) to defend the faith, to bring back mankind to the observance of Christian principles, and to lift humanity towards spiritual truths. This threefold plan inspired the whole of his pontificate; but it seemed to become more urgent after 1930, when the overthrow of the old order by the economic crisis of 1929, the rise of totalitarian regimes and the gradual disappearance of international institutions convinced him of the imminent menace to Christendom and to the entire human race. He felt himself bound to raise his voice; and in doing so he displayed exemplary courage and strength.

In that second part of his pontificate, in the hour of his decisive battles, Pius XI had at his side a representative of the younger generations, a man whose whole experience had fixed his attention on contemporary problems, and who, while serving the Pope with unwavering devotion, encouraged him in his attitude. That man was the secretary of state, chosen in 1930 to succeed Cardinal Gasparri: Mgr Eugenio Pacelli (1876–1958).

The new secretary, a born diplomat whose career in the nunciatures had strengthened him in the conviction that every means of settlement must be tried before permitting a rupture, was also a man of iron beneath the appearances of exquisite refinement and tremendous dignity, one whom the habit of strict personal discipline had endowed with absolute self-mastery, a mystic who lived only in and through the supernatural. Those two men, outwardly so different, were destined to be the perfect complement of each other. The cardinal, with his supple intelligence, was accustomed to handling innumerable matters without an intermediary, thanks to his extraordinary command of languages; and he was able thus to forestall or to remove misunderstandings due to the Pope's frequent abruptness of manner. But in all essentials the understanding between them was complete; and in 1939, when Eugenio Pacelli was elected to succeed Pius XI, he did not

[1] See the next volume of this series.

hesitate for a moment to choose as his regnal name that of the great captain whose work he meant to continue.

The struggle for the faith assumed for Pius XI two aspects, one defensive and the other constructive. Seeing it attacked by ever more virulent forms of materialism and atheistic humanism, he struck out on both fronts. In the early days of his pontificate he had denounced 'positivist naturalism', which formed the philosophic basis of the doctrine of Charles Maurras.[1] But his tone was less compromising when he came face to face with the idols that claimed allegiance from mankind: first the State-king proclaimed by all totalitarian regimes, absorbing all liberties, determined to control every human activity from the cradle to the grave; and secondly the deified race, that pagan monstrosity which Adolf Hitler's National Socialism sought to impose on Germany. His great Encyclicals *Non abbiamo bisogno*, against Fascist 'statolatry', and *Mit brennender Sorge*, against Hitlerian racism, marked the reaction of the Christian conscience against the threat to humanity at a moment when the weakness and pusillanimity of statesmen encouraged the enterprises of tyranny. Pius XI, looking beyond the immediate horizon of politics, meant to save the principles of Christianity, defending at the same time those which make man truly man and appointing himself the advocate of a Christian humanism that appeared more and more as the sole chance of salvation for a world threatened with death. Here again a climax was reached when, in 1937, he tackled Communism in *Divini Redemptoris*, the finest Encyclical of his pontificate, a full and penetrating analysis of Marxist philosophy, of dialectical materialism and its consequences. This was indeed a magisterial document, written without any political aim but precluding any future confusion or tactical compromise, an irrevocable condemnation of a system which recapitulates all the dreams of rebellious man and his yearning to 'kill God'.[2]

It was not sufficient, however, to condemn the principles that were endeavouring to overthrow Christian society. Pius XI realized that, in order to rescue the twentieth century from the ghastly peril to which it was exposed, he must also reinvigorate it with Christianity. To rechristianize morals, mental attitudes and institutions, while taking account of contemporary situations, was the second aspect of his struggle for the faith. Opposing that dichotomic form of religion which, as we have seen, confines itself to imposing outward conformism while disregarding the fundamentals of human existence, Pius XI, faithful to his notion of Christ's sovereignty, reminded men that faith must penetrate and regulate all the activities of life, social as well as economic, professional as well as family. This thought recurs frequently in his messages, letters and Encyclicals. Two documents are

[1] See Chapter IX, section 2. [2] See Chapter IX.

of special significance: *Divini illius magistri* (1929), on education, and *Casti connubii* (1930), on marriage and the family. Every word of them is valid and valuable today as it was thirty years ago.

All that effort culminated in a final and purely spiritual aspect of his work. It is in the hearts of men that Christ must reign first if His dominion is to be established upon earth. And so more than two hundred documents published by Pius XI had an exclusively supernatural aim; and to them he devoted the utmost care. Such Encyclicals as *Caritate Christi* on the Sacred Heart, *Miserentissimus Redemptor* on the reparation due to divine love for the sins of men, *Ingravescentibus malis* on the rosary, and another two dealing with the message of St Francis of Assisi, reveal some of his inner purposes; so do his forty beatifications and twenty-seven canonizations. It is not without significance that the Pope who fulminated anathemas against every form of materialism had a great devotion to the Carmelite St Teresa of Lisieux, whom he declared patroness of the missions.

The last years of Pius XI were darkened by those clouds which all could see gathering on the horizon. From 1934 onwards his every utterance was mingled with sorrowful warnings of the impending cataclysm. Sometimes he spoke with vehemence: more than once he told the warmongers of the doom which Providence held in store for them—annihilation. His diplomacy endeavoured time and time again to discover possible grounds for settlement between the hostile camps; he never hesitated to intervene, even in circumstances [1] where his own position was particularly difficult and occasionally misunderstood, for fear that local conflict might degenerate into a European war.

Pius XI died on 10th February 1939, at the age of eighty-two. His pontificate, like that of Pius X, ended on the threshold of a world war; but the hostilities which broke out six months after the great Pope's death proved infinitely more tragic and more terrible in their consequences than those which began in 1914 and caused the Holy Father to die of grief. A completely new chapter was about to open in the history of the world and likewise in that of the Church, a chapter which has since been written in blood and tears. On the morrow of the Lateran Treaties, Benito Mussolini spoke more truly than he could have imagined when he referred to Pius XI as 'the man of destiny'.

7. Grandeur and Power of Rome

The death of Pius XI afforded an opportunity to measure the prestige surrounding the person of the Pope and the Apostolic See. It

[1] e.g. on the occasion of Italy's invasion of Ethiopia.

was recognized by the whole press as an event of worldwide significance, even in totalitarian States; and if one recalls the almost complete indifference which had greeted the death of Pius IX sixty years earlier, it is hard not to be impressed by the change.

The truth is that never in the course of centuries had the papacy been so powerful and commanded so much respect as at the moment when Pius XI went to his last resting place in the Vatican crypt. Nor had the person of the Sovereign Pontiff ever been haloed with such glory, so admired and loved. By the dignity of their lives, their virtues and their saintliness, the last four popes had earned the whole-hearted veneration of their children. It is the man himself that Catholics cherish in the Pope. The Holy Years draw hundreds of thousands of pilgrims to Rome. Every night a little group stands in the piazza of St Peter's, gazing up at a lighted window in the huge dark façade of the palace. No scientific or professional congress of Catholics meets without asking for a message from the Sovereign Pontiff. At eucharistic congresses he is represented by a legate, who is received with all the honours ordained by protocol.

The Pope is now sovereign of a territory smaller than the Bois de Boulogne, consisting only of a group of palaces, churches and gardens; but who would think of ranking its master with the Prince of Liechtenstein, or comparing his government to that of Andorra or San Marino? Though he is free and sovereign in the Vatican City, the true city which he rules is that of souls; and it is because he has profited by the events of 1870 and conceived his role as exclusively spiritual that he wields such influence today. Here indeed is a most remarkable paradox: the more materialistic the world becomes, the greater seems to grow the sole exclusively spiritual power. Amid general chaos the Church, personified in the eyes of the masses by the Pope, appears with increasing brilliance as a rare element of stability and hope. Over against the process of dehumanization, which seems to have an irresistible hold upon the twentieth century, the Pope stands ever more clearly as representing those higher principles without which man is no longer man.

This increase of spiritual authority, however, is not without repercussions in the political and diplomatic field. The Encyclical *Mit brennender Sorge* did more than Hitler imagined to undermine the edifice of the Third Reich; and *Divini Redemptoris*, by cutting short the policy of 'the outstretched hand', put paid to a Communist manœuvre. Secular governments, too, acknowledge the worldwide importance of the Holy See: in 1870 there were two ambassadors, ten ministers plenipotentiary and three *chargés d'affaires* at Rome—fifteen diplomatic representatives in all. In 1939 there were thirty-eight heads of missions (thirteen ambassadors and twenty-five ministers)

accredited to the Pope. Likewise in 1870 papal representation throughout the world included only nine nuncios or internuncios, one *chargé d'affaires* and five apostolic delegates—a total of fifteen diplomats. In 1939 there were thirty-eight nunciatures and twenty-three apostolic delegations.

This outward prestige went hand in hand with a considerable strengthening of the Pope's authority over the Church. Papal infallibility in respect of faith and morals was no longer disputed by anyone who mattered. There was no more talk of resuming the Vatican Council, which had been suspended but not closed; Pius XI declared that he had thought of doing so, but was waiting for God 'to reveal His will more clearly'.[1] With the Roman Congregations reorganized and increased by Pius X and Benedict XV, the government of the Church now functioned in a way that might well have been envied by many secular administrations. The episcopate was controlled as never before: appointment of bishops by the Pope alone; [2] compulsory visits *ad limina*; obligatory quinquennial reports on the state of each diocese. Religious orders, congregations and institutes, all of which had a cardinal-protector appointed by the Pope, gradually adopted the custom of establishing their headquarters in Rome, as also did such great missionary undertakings as the Propagation de la Foi. The strengthening of papal authority was noticeable everywhere and in every field, primarily in that of dogma but also in the realm of discipline. Nor was it accidental that the new-born Catholic Action won the strong support of Pius XI: by making this widespread movement their own, subsequent popes have been able to guide and exert a more direct influence upon the mass of the faithful, even though the public at large are not given to the close study of Encyclicals.

It may be asked whether this reinforcement of papal authority over the whole Church did not arouse misgivings and even resistance. There were some perhaps who disapproved of 'Romanization' to the extent of obliging all priests to pronounce Latin in the Italian fashion and forbidding the wearing of clerical neck-bands; some countries, even Catholic Ireland, rebelled against having to wear the cassock out of doors; and there was some opposition to the spread of Gregorian chant. More serious were a number of comments on the danger of excessive centralization, of an imposition of uniformity that might weaken the living forces of the Church, render her less adaptable to circumstances, and even cause a revolt of minorities; nor was Pius XI insensible to apprehensions of that kind, as is clear from his benevolent attitude towards the oriental Churches. But such criticism proved of

[1] See Daniel-Rops, *Vatican II*, p. 60.

[2] Except in countries where the secretariat of state negotiated such appointments with the Government under the terms of a concordat.

small weight against the enormous increase of power and prestige enjoyed by Peter's successor.

On the other hand, this strengthening of papal power would have counted for little had it not been the corollary and consequence of a development still more important and significant: that of the Church's own situation. During those four pontificates she too witnessed an enormous increase in her power and in the strength of her position. In a period of sixty years she had freed herself from the tutelage of secular States and at the same time managed to re-establish her presence among them; she had taken her stand upon more solid doctrinal foundations, but without neglecting those intellectual bases which she recognized as indispensable; she had fortified her internal organization; she had steadily enlarged her sphere of activity, making herself co-extensive with the world; she was more keenly aware of the dangers that threatened her, and had created organisms capable of resisting the mounting tide of irreligion. Meanwhile, faithful to what is always her most urgent duty, the duty of leading souls to a Good transcending all earthly goods, she had given birth to a cohort of saints equal in all respects to those she had produced in the most splendid epochs of her past. Associated with all that manifold enterprise, whose results are still with us, were the four white-robed men in the Vatican whom Christ had appointed to lead His Church. They must never be forgotten by an historian who would follow the several stages of that combat for God waged by the Church under their direction.

CHAPTER III

LEO XIII: OPTIONS ON THE FUTURE

1. A Firing Squad

At about seven o'clock in the evening of Thursday, 24th May 1871, six men were taken from their cells in the Parisian jail of La Roquette, lined up against a wall and shot. They included a layman, Bonjean, president of the appeal court, and five priests: Clerc and Decoudray of the Society of Jesus; Allard, a former military chaplain; Deguerry, rector of the Madeleine; and the Archbishop of Paris, Mgr Darboy. All behaved with exemplary courage in presence of the firing squad; Darboy once again blessed his executioners and their victims, and a second bullet was necessary before his arm, raised in absolution, fell.

That happened during the Week of Blood which ended the short and tragic venture known as the Paris Commune. Sprayed with petrol, the Tuileries, the Palais de la Cour des Comptes and other monuments went up in flames. The Seine ran between two curtains of fire. Four days earlier Government troops from Versailles had entered the capital through an unguarded breach in the ramparts. But instead of wiping out all centres of insurrection within twenty-four hours, the 'Versaillais' advanced slowly, with dreadful caution, as if Thiers, carrying out the plan he had commended to Louis-Philippe in 1848, was permitting excesses with a view to justifying harsh reprisals. The Communards thus had time to take vengeance on their enemies by murdering innocent men whom they had seized as hostages.

This measure had been decided by the Insurrectional Committee six weeks earlier by way of revenge for the execution of some of their own partisans who had been taken prisoner during an abortive counter-attack. On 5th April a decree had been signed, stipulating that for every Communard condemned to death three friends of Versailles would be shot. Preparatory to this monstrous deed, hundreds of unfortunates had been thrown into jail without discrimination: policemen and tradesmen, army officers and magistrates, and a hundred and twenty priests. Negotiations for an exchange of prisoners had come to nothing—thanks to the evasions of Thiers, which may have been intentional. On the day when the Versaillais launched their attack the prisons of Paris were emptied of hostages, among them the six victims of La Roquette. The excuse put forward for their

execution was that Communard prisoners had been shot on the Place de la Madeleine by order of General de Galiffet.

It is hard to say whether priests were included among the hostages as victims of an anticlerical purpose, or as presumed supporters of the Government. Mgr Darboy was asked the question by one of his fellow captives, and he replied as follows: 'They are not killing us because I am Monsieur Darboy and you are Monsieur X, but because I am Archbishop of Paris and you are a priest; it is on account of our sacred orders that they are going to immolate us, and our death is therefore martyrdom.'[1] The religious policy of the Commune, like all its activity, was in fact hopelessly inconsistent. True, many churches remained open, Lent was preached as usual at Notre-Dame, and one leader of the Commune was actually seen taking his children to a catechism class; but from the very start the insurrection had an anti-religious character which became more pronounced as the increasing peril exasperated public opinion.

An onlooker might have believed himself back in the days of the Convention. Speakers were heard to declare that 'real human progress would not begin until there was no longer one priest alive or one church standing'. Immediate steps had been taken, first to separate Church from State, and then to requisition churches, chapels and religious houses for the manufacture or storage of munitions. In many quarters of Paris the police and the *Garde républicaine* had stood by and allowed a saturnalia of impiety. On 29th April, in the Place du Carrousel, ten thousand freemasons had gathered to acclaim the Commune and echo Voltaire's cry: 'Écrasez l'infâme.' Moreover, when the Abbé Amodru identified himself as 'a priest, curate of Notre-Dame des Victoires', a clerk, no doubt remembering Fouquier-Tinville, answered: 'That's a criminal offence.'[2]

The sudden outburst of hatred, however inexcusable, is nevertheless explicable. 'Religion', observes Cardinal Ferrata in his memoirs, 'was looked upon by the masses as a political weapon, as a monopoly of the aristocracy, as a relic of the *ancien régime*.' The price was paid for two mistakes: too close an alliance of the clergy with the Empire, and the indifference on the part of most Catholics to the unhappy social problem.[3] It was none the less tragic that the inhabitants of Paris, confusing the Church with those whom they considered responsible for their misfortunes, seized the first opportunity to blame the clergy. The mob continued to howl around the prisons where the hostages were detained even while the salvoes of the Versaillais crushed the insurrection street by street. On 25th May the Dominicans of the École Saint-Albert d'Areueil, having been allowed to escape, were shot down

[1] Émile Ollivier, *L'Église et l'État au Concile du Vatican*, vol. i, pp. 416–22.
[2] Fabre. [3] See Chapter IV.

like rabbits on the Avenue d'Italie. On the 26th ten priests, among them three Jesuits and two Picpucians, were massacred in the Rue Haxo. Father Plauchat too was shot, despite his labours on behalf of the poorest workers. Altogether fifty-four members of the clergy perished in the course of those fearful days; and the final scene of that appalling drama is the firing of Notre-Dame, which was saved in the nick of time, as though by a miracle.

Such was the first challenge to meet the Church on the threshold of a period that began with the conclusion of the Franco-Prussian War. The bloody glare of those events revealed a truth which twenty years and more of bourgeois tranquillity had concealed from Catholic eyes: the age of revolution had not ended. The rampant forces of secularism, which had been trying for almost a century to overthrow the Church, were still intact and formidable; we shall see them at work throughout the next seventy years, sometimes with a violence equal to that of the Commune, sometimes in more secret ways, but always with determination.

2. Glory in Eclipse

The closing years of Pius IX's pontificate provided those hostile forces with a set of circumstances more than favourable to their designs. The octogenarian Pope seemed worn out, morally as well as physically. Since 20th September 1870, when the 'Piedmontese' cannon opened a breach in the city wall, he had felt that all his work had failed. The occupation of Rome appeared to crown the triumph of Evil, of that hundred-headed monster with which he had so often done battle. It was the modern world, the atheist world, that had entered the Eternal City with Victor Emmanuel's troops; the world he had denounced in *Quanta Cura* and the *Syllabus*, the world of Renan and godless socialism, the world of the great betrayal. Shut away in the Vatican palace, which he had chosen to make his prison, and spurning the accommodation offered him by the Law of Guarantees, he deplored with unrelenting bitterness the outrage inflicted not only upon his own person and his rights, but also, he believed, upon the Church of Christ and her message. Nothing consoled him, not even the touching marks of veneration poured forth at his feet by countless pilgrims. True, he retained a lively wit and a gift of repartee, which often supplied him with hard words wherewith to denounce the Attilas and Genserics, the new barbarians, seated upon the ruins of faithful Europe. But what was the good of those anathemas? More and more convinced that there was no recourse but heaven, praying day and night to the Blessed Virgin, offering to God with sublime constancy

the physical sufferings laid upon him by old age, he met every threat with blank refusal, never with a planned counter-attack or with positive argument. His decisions appeared to be dictated exclusively by a reactionary extremism, which did not spare even his closest friends when they questioned his line of conduct.

Papal policy amounted to a categorical *non possumus* charged with nostalgia; but that was of little use against the hostility which Pius IX had roused in the days of his greatness. The great doctrinal condemnations of *Quanta Cura* and the *Syllabus* had shown the enemy that no reconciliation was possible between Christianity and the principles upon which it was proposed to build a society without God; all the various devotees of atheistic humanism were affected by the blow, and their indignant protests against the papal admonitions acknowledged that plain fact. In 1870 the proclamation of the dogma of papal infallibility had completed his work and at the same time provoked still greater fury. Was not the Vicar of Christ giving the Church new vigour by fortifying his own authority? Further, were not the principles to which he appealed diametrically opposed to those of his adversaries? 'If a community', wrote one of them, 'had just established itself in accordance with the dogmatic principles laid down by the Catholic Church at the Vatican Council, we would undoubtedly consider that the State had a duty to crush and annihilate it by force.'[1] There was indeed no equivocation. Far from having failed in his task, Pius IX had made the Church more conscious of the dangers that beset her, and had strengthened her defences. It was but natural that the enemy should react.

Thus the last eight years of the great pontificate were marked by numerous manifestations of that hatred which had assumed such hideous guise in the events of 1871. The anguish of the dying pontiff was only too well justified.[2]

3. KULTURKAMPF

The author of the words quoted above, on the duty of atheist States to oppose the dogma of papal infallibility and its consequences, was Professor Friedberg, a high official in the Prussian ministry of cults. And it was in Germany that the conflict started, straightway imperilling the very existence of the Church. The name under which that conflict was destined to remain celebrated is significant: *Kulturkampf*, 'struggle for civilization'. In the eyes of those who were about to give battle

[1] J. Rovan, *Le Catholicisme politique en Allemagne*, Paris, 1956.

[2] On the end of Pius IX's pontificate see *The Church in an Age of Revolution*, Chapter V, section 19.

there was indeed a clash between two concepts of civilization: the true concept was that of the future, inspired by the theories both of the Protestant revolution and of free thought; the other, retrograde, was that of an obscurantist and tyrannical past. Accordingly the grand assault was led by a combination of atheist philosophers, rationalist exegetes, liberal politicians, advocates of Prussian predominance and freemasons. The import of the battle was clearly explained by the philosopher Robert von Hartmann in a masonic journal: 'Here we have the last, desperate struggle of the Christian idea before its final disappearance from the scene of history, a mortal conflict waged against it by modern civilization in defence of the mighty achievements of our age.'

Why did Bismarck, a cautious and able statesman, embark upon a venture that jeopardized the moral unity of Germany? Strange as it may seem, his most compelling reason was fear that the Pope, having made himself 'a more absolute monarch than any ruler on earth', would claim to rule civil societies. But other, more immediate apprehensions may have prompted him. He was not unaware that many Catholics, patriots though they were and advocates of German unity, would have preferred Austria as its nucleus. Mgr von Ketteler, the famous Archbishop of Mainz, had gone so far as to declare in public that the Prussian victory at Sedan was a German defeat. Now ten years earlier the Catholics had formed themselves into a party under the leadership of Windthorst, Savigny and Mallinckrodt. This party, the *Zentrum*, had only about sixty members in the Reichstag and the Prussian Landtag; but it was very strong in the Rhineland, thanks to the traditional antipathy of southern Germans towards the Prussians, and attracted to itself malcontents of every kind. When it is added that Bismarck, a resolute conservative, disliked the social tendencies which were spreading among German Catholics,[1] and that in the international field his anxiety to prevent a Franco-Italian alliance led him naturally to espouse Italy's quarrel with the Pope, it is clear that the Chancellor had many reasons for undertaking the *Kulturkampf*, apart from his own ardent Protestantism and his marriage to a devout Lutheran—two personal factors which caused him to detest Catholicism and its head.

Battle was joined in the month of December 1870, when the Prussian Government, followed by several others, forbade preachers to read the decisions of the Council. But since those decisions were available in the newspapers, the ban remained a dead letter. The affair of the Old Catholics, however, 'set fire to the sacristies'. It will be remembered[2] that after the proclamation of papal infallibility Döllinger,

[1] *The Church in an Age of Revolution,* Chapter VI, section 19.
[2] *The Church in an Age of Revolution,* Chapter V, section 17.

one of its most vigorous opponents, refused to submit and accused Pius IX of having fabricated a 'new Church'. A number of small groups going a stage further, set up an independent Church, which claimed to be alone faithful to authentic tradition. As it happened, the 'Old Catholic' movement made little headway, even when it obtained its own bishop, Reinkens, who was consecrated by a Dutch Jansenist bishop. But Bismarck, in order to embarrass Rome, did his best to support it. When the bishops forbade Old Catholics to teach theology in the universities, the Prussian Government came down firmly on the side of its excommunicated subjects. Rome protested and diplomatic relations were broken off.

The appointment of Dr Falk as minister of cults in January 1872 marked the beginning of 'war'. He secured the passage, both for Prussia and for the Reich, of definitely anti-Catholic laws. One threatened with penal sanctions any priest who 'endangered public order' from the pulpit; another excluded members of religious congregations from the schools; and a Bill was drafted to banish the Jesuits and all kindred orders. 'Germany is now in a state of war with Rome, as in the days of the struggle between the priesthood and the Empire,' declare the Pomeranian deputy Wagener. 'But we shall not go to Canossa!' added Bismarck; and a committee was straightway formed to erect a granite block upon which were graven those immortal words.

Catholics accepted the challenge, and in Ludwig Windthorst (1812–91) they had a first-rate leader. A Saxon by birth, but from 1848 a deputy in the parliament of Hanover and then minister of that kingdom, Windthorst was a tiny little man with an abnormally large skull, dark twinkling eyes and a mouth so wide that the least hint of a smile appeared to cut his face in two. He was not much to look at beside Bismarck, 'the white dragoon'. In fact, however, 'His Little Excellency', who became true leader of the *Zentrum* as soon as the conflict began, resisted 'His Big Excellency' with such firmness that the latter was compelled at last to bite the dust. Windthorst replied to each of the Chancellor's legislative moves with speeches of such scathing wit that on several occasions Bismarck lost control of his temper.

The crisis was reached in 1873, and lasted for three years. Every twelve months, in May, a new legislative salvo was fired against the Catholics; hence the term 'May Laws' applied to those instruments of persecution. The law against the Jesuits had been passed (May 1872). But that was a mere trifle; there were fewer than two hundred Jesuits in the whole of Germany. The May Laws of 1873 were far more ambitious: their purpose was to remove the entire clergy from Roman influence and imbue it with sound convictions. Junior seminaries were closed; future priests were obliged to attend courses in the State

secondary schools for six half-yearly terms, to do their theology in the universities and to pass an examination in Germanic culture! Bishops were ordered to present all candidates for sacerdotal office to the *Oberpraesident*, the prefect of the province, who might set them aside on grounds of 'hostility to the State'. Finally, every priest was given the right of appeal to a State tribunal against disciplinary penalties inflicted by his bishop. The May Laws of 1874 were concerned mainly with civilian status; this was laicized, so as to make civil marriage the only legal form. But since there had been widespread resistance to last year's measures, an additional law was passed to punish refractory priests with banishment and loss of German nationality. The May Laws of 1875 expelled all religious congregations, excepting those which cared for the sick, and entrusted management of ecclesiastical property to a council of laymen. Bismarck believed that with such an arsenal he was in a position to shatter 'the vast organization established by the Vatican in Germany'. He was slowly disillusioned. One after another the May Laws were declared unacceptable by the bishops and condemned by the Vatican. The bishops, rather than see them applied in their dioceses, preferred to be haled before the courts and risk imprisonment or exile. Mgr Ledochowski, Archbishop of Posen, was actually detained and expelled from Germany; he went to Rome and was immediately created cardinal by Pius IX. The archbishops of Paderborn and Munster were jailed. Mgr Melchers of Cologne just managed to escape arrest. Six out of twelve bishops were deposed according to law; four hundred parishes were deprived of their priests, whom the Government sought in vain to replace with Old Catholics. In February 1875 an Encyclical encouraged the faithful to resist.

Although a few governments, notably those of Bavaria, Baden and Hesse, had followed the movement, the southern states manifested extreme reluctance. Steps were taken everywhere to organize a 'Church in the desert'. The *Katholikentag*, founded on a small scale in 1848, assumed the appearance of mass demonstrations against persecution. An attempt was even made upon the Chancellor's life as he drove through the streets of Bad Kissingen. This enabled the authorities to increase their pressure, but it did not further the Government's plans. Pius IX had referred to Bismarck as the 'boa constrictor', the 'grand sorcerer', 'Satan in a helmet', and his words were repeated on all sides. Day by day it became more and more apparent that Bismarck would never defeat the Catholic resistance. He must have realized as much by 1877. At the elections held in that year the *Zentrum* won many seats, not only in the Reich as a whole but even in Prussia itself. Canossa seemed to loom on the horizon; it appeared not unlikely that the Chancellor would follow in the footsteps of Henry IV and go to ask pardon of Pius IX.

Meanwhile his ambassadors had invited all foreign powers to reach an understanding with a view to the approaching vacancy of the Roman See. The plan was to secure the election of a more accommodating pope, or to summon a new assembly that would annul the proceedings of the Vatican Council; and such proposals found willing ears, for the Iron Chancellor enjoyed great prestige.

Thus during the last seven years of Pius IX we see half a dozen States, including even France, following in Bismarck's footsteps. The *Kulturkampf*, originally an internal struggle between the Catholic party and the centralizing policies of Prussia, was developing into a conflict of ideas in which all peoples and all governments might become involved.

4. Assaults and Ruptures

Italy was of course the first power tempted to join the 'champions of civilization'. After the fall of Rome and the collapse of his temporal authority, Pius IX had adopted an unyielding attitude of proud and mournful negation. On 15th May 1871 he had declared that he 'did not and never would accept' the immunities and indemnities offered him by the 'subalpine government' in its Law of Guarantees: recognition of his sovereignty; affirmation of his rights over the Vatican, the Lateran and Castel Gandolfo; a promise to respect his freedom of correspondence with all bishops; payment of an annuity, and so on.[1] He had accounted all that as nothing, and had consummated the rupture by excommunicating the despoilers.

The adversaries of the Church were therefore in a strong position from which to launch their attack. Italy was swept by a wave of anti-clericalism. The remnants of Ghibellinism, Jansenism and Jacobinism deployed their forces under the leadership of freemasonry. Even before Parliament had passed a law against the congregations, the Collegio Romano was taken from the Jesuits and eight large convents were expropriated; in 1873 Rome contained seventy religious houses whose communities had been dispersed. In 1877 a Bill was drafted to provide for the prosecution of priests who 'had insulted the institutions of the State'. Further, Protestants were authorized to build churches in the Eternal City. Encouragement was given to the ridiculous little 'Old Catholic' movement, which had been started in Naples and Girgenti,[2] as well as to a 'Society for the Emancipation of the Clergy', which demanded election of parish priests by the faithful, as was done in France during the Revolution. Pius IX protested, but in vain.

[1] *The Church in an Age of Revolution,* Chapter V, section 18.

[2] Now Agrigento, in Sicily.—Translator.

At the same time Victor Emmanuel made approaches to Germany, alleging that the Comte de Chambord, pretender to the French throne, whose early return was expected by many, had allowed it to be said that he would restore the Pope's temporal power. He sent private envoys to Bismarck, and soon afterwards received a visitor in the person of Friedrich Karl, the German crown prince, who was welcomed in Rome with ostentatious cordiality. 'We are behind you,' declared His Royal Highness; 'if Italy is attacked by France, Germany will go at once to her assistance.' Thus was laid the first stone of the Triple Alliance.

What attitude could Catholics adopt to counter this offensive? They might, like the German *Zentrum*, have joined battle in the parliamentary field; but Pius IX would allow no such course. When asked by some of the faithful what they should do at elections, he stood firm by his principle of completely ignoring the monarchy, and directed the sacred penitentiary to tell them 'it is not fitting' that they should take part therein. This formula, *non expedit*, imposed upon Italian Catholics a rule of conduct; they must not vote at political elections; and in fact when balloting took place in 1871 more than half the population of Italy abstained. They were advised, however, to take a hand in municipal and other local elections, in order to sway public opinion. For more than half a century, at least in theory, *non expedit* remained the rule, imprisoning Catholics in a sullen opposition to all that the government of their country might do. But this categorical rejection of any official share in political life had one fortunate result. Catholics became organized with a view to exerting their influence; what they might not cry aloud in Parliament they would proclaim elsewhere. Thus in 1871 Carlo Cazzani, a young journalist, put forward the idea of holding Catholic congresses like those which had been held by Belgian Catholics at Malines. Meetings of this kind were held at Venice in 1874, at Florence in 1875, at Bologna in 1876; and Pius IX gave them his warm approval, though they provoked counter-demonstrations from the left. Such was the beginning of the Opera dei Congressi, which was to occupy so prominent a place during the next pontificate.

On the death of Pius IX, therefore, the situation in Italy was strained. The prime minister Minghetti, an 'enlightened conservative', had been succeeded by the cynical Depretis. It is true that the Pope, on learning that Victor Emmanuel lay at the point of death, sent a prelate to absolve him *in extremis*; for he had always been fond of the king, had refused to name him in the decree of excommunication, and had even corresponded with him privately through Don Bosco. But his final gesture, though inspired by charity, was cleverly timed, since it obliged Crispi to announce that his sovereign had died fortified

with the rites of the Church. Tension between the two powers remained acute, and it was difficult to see how Vatican and Quirinal could cease to look upon each another as enemies.

Italy was not the only Catholic land whose rulers turned against the Church. Austria did likewise. The government of Francis Joseph had been at loggerheads with Rome since 1869, because of an educational law which had subjected Catholic schools and junior seminaries to State control. The proclamation of papal infallibility aggravated the conflict, and Chancellor von Beust, a friend of Bismarck, shared the views of his Prussian colleague on the 'popish peril'. During the Council the emperor had protested violently against the forthcoming dogma, and had congratulated the Austrian bishops who opposed it. Once the dogma was promulgated the Government at Vienna not only forbade its announcement from the pulpit, but also declared that the Sovereign Pontiff as defined by the Council was no longer the same pontiff who had signed the concordat of 1855, which it therefore considered as null and void. This was the signal for a minor war in which the Catholic king-emperor, once champion of all struggles against heresy, took up the rusted arms of Josephism and began tilting at the Church. The Old Catholic movement was fostered to the point of being granted places of worship. An attempt was made to suppress two bishoprics in Dalmatia under pretext of reorganizing ecclesiastical administration. All universities were secularized. A series of 'confessional laws' completely remodelled civil legislation in such a way as to destroy religious influence. In Bohemia the police actually allowed a mob to burn an effigy of the Pope. Meanwhile Francis Joseph, officially recognizing the Government of new Italy, appointed an ambassador with instructions to call at the Quirinal and leave a gift that was no less magnificent than unexpected.

In the twofold case of Italy and Austria it was still possible to believe that the hostility of both governments towards the Church was dictated by circumstance and also, since they aligned themselves with Germany, by diplomatic motives. The outburst of anticlericalism in Switzerland was, in a way, more serious. There it was possible to detect the ancient Protestant hatred of papists envenomed by the antipathy of masonic radicals. A regular 'little *Kulturkampf*' developed in several cantons with a violence worthy of Bismarck's operation.

It began in the diocese of Basel, which covered twelve of the Helvetic cantons. In seven of them there was a current of protest against the dogma of papal infallibility, and this enabled local radicals to stir up the *Vorort* (diocesan council), which, by the terms of the concordat, shared in ecclesiastical administration. The Bishop, Mgr

Lachat, was called upon to forbid promulgation of the dogma. When he ignored this ultimatum, and even suspended two anti-infallibilist priests, he was 'deposed' and expelled from his residence at Soleure. Neither the Federal Council nor the Chambers would hear his appeal.

Catholic resistance was now organized. It was particularly strong in the Bernese Jura where the priests, on being told to have nothing more to do with Mgr Lachat, answered with a solemn protest, while the cities conferred their freedom on the proscribed bishops. The Government at Berne then barred all signatories of the protest from the exercise of their ministry; on appeal, the court directed that the worst offenders should be expelled from their parishes. A law was passed entrusting the choice of parish priests to the civil authorities, and its initial application resulted in suppression of three-quarters of the parishes. Such was the ensuing explosion of popular fury that the Bernese Government had to occupy the Jura with troops. As in the days of the Terror in France, the clergy fulfilled their ministry in secret, celebrating Mass in barns while the churches, to which more accommodating French and Belgian priests had been appointed, remained empty. The situation became so grave that the Federal Government took charge of the affair in hopes of putting an end to it.

At Geneva the assault upon Catholicism was still more violent. The city of Calvin had already distinguished itself (1848) by its treatment of Mgr Marilley, who had been imprisoned for eight years.[1] The atmosphere remained bad, and it deteriorated still further with the appearance on the scene of Mgr Mermillod (1824–92), an enterprising young man whom Pius IX had appointed bishop auxiliary to Mgr Marilley with residence at Geneva; for a rumour spread that the Pope, when raising him to the episcopate, had declared: 'You are the man who will convert the Protestant Rome.' Mgr Mermillod's strong personality crystallized Calvinist and masonic hates; and the cantonal president Carteret, a determined anti-papist, took the first opportunity to create trouble.

Mgr Mermillod having appointed a country priest, the Genevese authorities informed him that they refused to accept his choice because the only bishop they acknowledged was Mgr Marilley, not his auxiliary. The latter replied that the Pope had formally entrusted him with Geneva, part of Mgr Marilley's diocese. Thereupon he was told he would have to withdraw from all episcopal duties, while the Council expressly forbade hierarchical relations between him and his priests (August 1872). Mgr Mermillod's answer was both clever and courageous: he invited Rome to appoint him vicar-apostolic, as if to some missionary outpost among the Redskins or Kaffirs (January 1873). President Carteret repeated the order of suspension. Mermillod refused

[1] *The Church in an Age of Revolution,* Chapter V, section 10.

and was therefore banished, despite the fact that as a native of Carouge he was a perfectly true Genevese citizen. Settling at Ferney, in French territory, he continued to manage his diocese and received every day hundreds of the faithful who crossed the border in defiance of Carteret's police.

This was open war. The Grand Council of Geneva, like the German Parliament, hurriedly passed a 'Law for the Reorganization of the Catholic Church', under which parish priests were to be elected by the faithful, the right to create and suppress parishes would belong exclusively to the cantonal authorities, and no papal or episcopal document might be published without an official *placet*. It was tantamount to setting up a National Catholic Church; but the only result was to provoke such agitation that about thirty priests were arrested or exiled.

In order to replace them, Carteret thought of appealing to the Old Catholics, who enjoyed some support in various cantons and who had recently been joined by the celebrated Père Hyacinthe Loison, once a Carmelite and preacher at Notre-Dame, now married and a vehement anti-infallibilist.[1] One E. Herzog, an Old Catholic, was appointed bishop and sent to Germany for consecration at the hands of 'Bishop' Reinkens. Geneva presented this new church with buildings it had stolen from the Catholics (1876).

The undertaking had, of course, no chance whatever of success. The Catholics resisted with all their strength. Tares had been sown early among the Old Catholics, and Hyancinthe Loison, after playing priest for three years, had left the 'liberal Catholic Church', declaring it to be neither liberal nor Catholic. The cantonal government showed itself daily more and more embarrassed.

Switzerland's *Kulturkampf*, then, had not ended in 1878; but it had already had two consequences—one good and one bad: first the growth of *Piusverein*, a Catholic league of action; but secondly (1874) the introduction into the Federal constitution of articles, which are still in force, against religious congregations (even the Sisters of Charity and Little Sisters of the Poor) and the establishment of new religious houses in the country.

Without appearing quite so systematic, this war upon the Church was waged during the same period in Spain, where political upheavals afforded a convenient starting-point. After the revolution of 1868, which overthrew Isabella II,[2] the Cortes had passed a law proclaiming freedom of worship, establishing civil marriage and taking other steps most unwelcome to the clergy, many of whom had been arrested or

[1] *The Church in an Age of Revolution,* Chapter V, section 17.
[2] *The Church in an Age of Revolution,* Chapter V, section 10.

deprived of their salaries. Having looked in vain for a sovereign among the Hohenzollerns,[1] the Spaniards chose Amedeo I, second son of the King of Italy, who was quickly taken in hand by a small group of atheist liberals. Measures hostile to the Church were adopted, including a ban on the publication of Encyclicals without a royal *placet*, obligatory civil marriage and revision of ecclesiastical salaries. The abdication of the little Italian prince at the end of two years, and the creation of a markedly left-wing republic (1873), aggravated an uneasy situation. In the Cortes there were violent clashes between Catholics and Voltairean democrats. Worse things came to pass when the republic foundered. Persecution followed on the heels of a civil war between the adherents of Don Carlos and the partisans of Isabella's son. At Barcelona, Valladolid and Madrid priests were beaten up, arrested or insulted, and in Andalusia convents were burned. The Restoration of 1876 and the enthronement of Alfonso XII brought back tranquillity. The young king forgot his rancour against the clergy, who had been Carlist almost to a man, and wisely heeded the voice of those more reasonable Catholics who had abandoned Don Carlos and rallied to his side. He restored ecclesiastical property confiscated by the Republic, reopened the Catholic schools and resumed diplomatic relations with Rome. The constitution of 1876, while recognizing 'the existence of non-Catholic cults', proclaimed Catholicism as the official religion of Spain.

Religious peace, however, remained uncertain: a left-wing opposition was still active and strongly hostile to the Church, hoping for an opportunity to pass laws that would reinstate the governmental *placet* for publication of papal documents, oblige priests to do military service, and dispense institutions from the duty of seeing that their pupils heard Mass. The tension between intransigent Catholics and liberals had by no means disappeared.

5. 'Clericalism, there is the Enemy!'

In France that same tension was increasing day by day. There too political conditions account for the unfolding of events. The National Assembly which met at Bordeaux in February 1871 conferred power on Adolphe Thiers. His task was to make peace, maintain order against the Commune and reinvigorate the country; but when he showed republican sympathies the monarchist majority ousted him (May 1873) in favour of Maréchal de MacMahon, whose 'government of moral order' was directed to prepare the restoration of the

[1] This was one of the causes of the Franco-Prussian War.

monarchy. When that restoration failed, it was decided to establish 'a republic without republicans', whose president, elected for seven years, could easily yield place to a king. But the left, which had been dismantled by the defeat of the Commune, now reorganized, and the elections of 1876 and 1877 brought into the Chambers a growing number of its partisans. A left-wing electoral victory in 1879, together with the resignation of MacMahon, finally restored the Republic to the republicans.

Now the Church found herself involved willy-nilly in this political conflict. Horrified by the bloody events of the Commune, the Catholics closed their ranks around the party of order without realizing the disaster which might result from Catholicism's apparent identification of her cause with that of a regime that based its power on terrible reprisals and was not accepted by the people. The governments of Thiers and MacMahon were naturally favourable towards the Church. High above Paris, in accordance with a vow made during the siege, rose the basilica of the Sacré-Cœur, bearing witness to the gratitude of 'France penitent and devout'. A law proclaimed full freedom of higher education; students of the Catholic universities were to be examined by mixed boards consisting in equal numbers of State and Catholic teachers. Pilgrimages enjoyed a popularity they had not known for centuries; led jointly by bishops and members of parliament, enormous crowds gathered at Chartres, Paray-le-Monial, Lourdes and Saint-Martin-de-Tours, singing the famous hymn 'Sauvez Rome et la France, au nom de Sacré-Cœur'. The political intentions were only too clear. At Chartres, in the presence of forty thousand pilgrims, Mgr Pie, Bishop of Poitiers, declared from the pulpit: 'France awaits a leader, France calls for a master.' As usually happens in periods of official conformism, espionage and the informer's trade flourished exceedingly: civil servants, officers and mayors suspected of irreligion were dismissed; and the people beheld once again, as in the great days of the Second Empire, troops marching to church in column of fours.[1]

This alliance between the great majority of Catholics and the parties of the right inevitably entailed a counter-blow. The republicans had a fine time denouncing the political interference of the clergy, and showing that agitation on behalf of the Pope's temporal power would lead straight to war with Italy and Germany. The more far-sighted bishops, among them Dupanloup, were alarmed at the approach of anti-Catholic reaction, believing that attacks on the political activity of Catholics were to be directed sooner or later against religion itself.

[1] Only one bishop, Mgr Guilbert of Gap, dared say: 'To wish to link or identify religion with any form of government whatever is surely to compromise the Church and the clergy, as well as to commit a glaring mistake.'

It was the republican press that gave the signal for a virulent anticlerical campaign: *République française, Dix-neuvième siècle* and *Rappel* denounced what they called the abuse of authority on the part of priests, while Jean Macé's 'Ligue d'Enseignement' gathered schoolteachers into a vast wave of irreligion. And Gambetta, starting on his bid for power, uttered this famous battle-cry: 'I am only expressing the inmost thoughts of the French people when I say—Clericalism, there is the enemy!'

After the elections which marked the first republican successes it was plain that if they became masters of France they would make Catholicism pay for the folly of her sons. Bills were drafted for the suppression of mixed boards of examiners, for the authorization of divorce, for the abolition of ecclesiastical subsidies, and even for the separation of Church and State. Catholic committees formed to organize petitions on behalf of the Pope were declared illegal and dissolved. On 30th May 1878, in accordance with a proposal emanating from the freemasons of the Grand Orient, the centenary of Voltaire's death was celebrated with a national subscription and the printing of thousands of copies of his most impious works. The stage was set for a grave crisis in France, and Bismarck's representative at Paris informed his chief that the republicans would lend their earnest support to 'a common policy of Germany and France against Rome'.

The Latin American countries also were hotbeds of anticlericalism. In Mexico the democrats had seized power after the execution of Maximilian, and in 1875 had proclaimed the separation of Church and State. In Columbia and Venezuela feeling ran high against the priests. In Chile the hierarchy had been obliged to excommunicate their rulers. In Brazil the prime minister, Rio Branco, had won over the Emperor Pedro II to his anticlerical views. Two countries alone remained loyal to the Church: Peru and Ecuador; but Garcia Moreno,[1] president of the latter, had been assassinated in 1875. The only lands where relations between the Government and the Church were good proved to be those where heresy predominated. Britain, for example, continued to maintain a diplomatic representative at the Holy See notwithstanding the agitation of Catholic Ireland; in Holland the Catholic party was steadily gaining ground; while in the United States President Grant officially thanked Pius IX for the honour done to his country by the first creation of an American cardinal. Those exceptions, however, due mainly to governmental indifference towards the Church, served to emphasize the prevailing hostility to Catholicism and the rising tide of anticlericalism.

When Pius IX died in 1878 the position of the Church appeared unstable. The considerable achievements of that long pontificate

[1] *The Church in an Age of Revolution,* Chapter VII, section 4.

had been eclipsed by spectacular defeats, and it was difficult to see how lost ground could be recovered or even how the enemy's offensive could be halted.

6. The Christian Policies of Leo XIII

Twenty-five years later all had changed. Once again Rome spoke aloud, and her voice was heeded. Catholicism, whose influence had seemed exhausted, was once again a political force which secular governments recognized and took into account. The Church was present once again in every field, and whatever position she chose to adopt could affect the solution of many a problem. True, not every conflict had been settled; grave difficulties remained and others were on the horizon, but no one would have ventured to describe the papacy as vanquished.

That striking reversal was due to Pope Leo XIII. Seldom is it so easy to detect at what point history is made by men rather than by mere economic pressures at the caprice of blind Fortune. The presence on the apostolic throne of a remarkable personality, open to the winds of life and capable of welcoming without prejudice the new ideas, sufficed to transform the Church's situation and restore opportunities which most men believed to have been lost for ever.

On the morrow of his election, Leo told Cardinal Franci, his first secretary of state: 'I mean to carry out a grand design of statesmanship.'[1] Those words must evidently be understood in their widest possible sense, as covering the entire programme devised by the former Archbishop of Perugia with a view to resolving the difficult problem of relations between the Church and the modern world.[2] But they must undoubtedly be taken in the first place as referring to the papacy's own relations with the secular powers, a domain in which the genius of Leo XIII is most apparent and in which he obtained the most spectacular results. To it he brought a brilliance of intellect and strength of character which enabled him to lead the Church from more than one blind alley without abandoning the principles which must always guide the activities of a pope.

It is necessary to insist upon Leo's fidelity to principle and the close connection of those principles with tradition. It would be wholly false to represent him as a 'statesman' in the ordinary sense of that word, let alone as a politician—a clever man capable of winning a game with no trump cards and of escaping from any tight corner.

[1] Recorded by the Pope's friend Conte Conestabile, in an article on the papal election (*Correspondant*, 25th October 1878).

[2] See Chapter II, section 3.

Leo XIII was neither a Mazarin nor a Talleyrand, still less a Machiavelli. His statesmanship was something far different from a scaffolding of ingenuity; it was the application of ancient principles rooted in profound theological beliefs. It was in fact the contrary of opportunism.

The Encyclical *Immortale Dei* (1885) forms the most detailed exposition of the great Pope's political ideas.[1] Written at the height of a violent antichristian offensive in Italy and France, this document has an undeniably polemic character. The first part is devoted entirely to an analysis of the situation in which the Church had been placed by the attacks to which she was then subject. At the same time it is a penetrating criticism of the dangers arising from the totalitarian monism of the State, which identifies itself with society and claims to be the most perfect social form, upon which all other human associations must depend. Finally, it is an indictment of the modern State, which has almost everywhere apostatized and endeavours to set up 'the parasite of philosophy' in place of religion.

Even more important is the second part, in which Leo explains 'the Christian constitution of society'. Notice, however, that he introduces nothing new. What he says is substantially the same as what Pope Gelasius I had said long ago in the fifth century: [2] 'There are two powers that govern the world: the sacred authority of the pontiffs and the royal dominion,' adding, however, that the first is superior to the second because it derives directly and uniquely from God. That is almost exactly what Leo XIII wrote: 'God has divided the government of mankind between two powers: the ecclesiastical and the civil, the former placed over things divine, the latter over human affairs.'

But Leo went on to develop this notion: 'Each is sovereign in its own field. Each is confined within boundaries that are well determined and marked out in accordance with the nature and end of each. There is therefore, so to speak, a limited sphere in which each of them exercises its function *jure proprio*.' That is the doctrine of Gelasius, rendered more precise by the Encyclical on two important points: the difference between the State and society, and man's twofold character as Christian and citizen. Nor does *Immortale Dei* fail to remind us of another truth proclaimed by the fifth-century pontiff: 'Since the Church's end is the noblest of all, her power extends over all other powers, and can in no way be subjected to the civil authority or considered inferior thereto.'

Such words, expressing a theocratic view of relations between the

[1] Other relevant documents are *Arcanum* (1880), *Nobilissima Gallorum gens* (1884), *Officio Sanctissimo* (1887), *Sapientiae christianae* (1890), *Praeclara gratulationis* (1894) and *Pervenuti* (1902).

[2] *The Church in the Dark Ages*, pp. 108, 153.

Church and civil society, will doubtless amaze those who like to think of Leo XIII as a 'political' and even 'liberal' pope. For him, as for Pius IX, God is the source of all law, of all power; and failure to recognize as much will lead to a subversion of principles that will necessarily entail the overthrow of institutions. Against such a background the theory which serves as the foundation of democracy, i.e. sovereignty of the people, seems absurd and almost blasphemous. On the other hand, if we leave the field of principle for that of practice, Leo XIII's doctrine opens a door to a supple and conciliatory approach. 'It is clear that rulers are free in the exercise of their own powers. The Church, so far from refusing to acknowledge that freedom, backs it with all her strength. . . . But upon one condition: speaking in the name of God, the Church has a right to ask the State not to oppose religion.'

Such were the principal ideas that were to guide the policies of Leo XIII. He would not intrude upon the affairs of secular governments so long as the latter confined themselves to their own functions and did not have recourse to usurpation or persecution. He stated clearly time and again that the Church teaches respect for the civil power, that Catholics must obey Caesar provided Caesar does not overstep his rights. An understanding with secular governments would always be possible if they themselves placed no obstacle thereto by attacking the rights and institutions of religion. Moreover Catholics would enjoy complete liberty to choose whatever political regime they wished, upon the sole condition that their political activity included care for the common good and readiness to live in accordance with the dictates of their faith.

This was a new attitude, no matter how ancient were the principles from which it flowed. Holy Church accepted the *de facto* situation and declared herself ready to collaborate with regimes deriving from the Revolution; but at the same time, as guardian of eternal truths, she set her face against all subversive doctrines.[1]

7. An End of Conflict

The most notable success was obtained in Germany. At the time of Leo's accession the *Kulturkampf* had already lost some of its violence, and there were grounds for thinking that Bismarck had abandoned all hope of triumph. Nevertheless the situation was bad: many ecclesiastics, among them several bishops, were in prison; many priests had been driven from their parishes; the religious orders had been expelled; and

[1] On the political ideas of Leo XIII see J. C. Murray, 'L'Église et la démocratie totalitaire', in *Vie intellectuelle*, April 1953.

the May Laws provided the Government with well-furbished arms for use against the Catholics. The situation in fact was so explosive that the slightest incident could precipitate disaster.

Immediately after his election, and notwithstanding the suspension of diplomatic relations between the Vatican and Berlin, Leo XIII sent the Emperor Wilhelm a personal message informing him of his accession to the Apostolic See and at the same time expressing his anxiety over the protracted conflict. 'I appeal to the magnanimity of your heart', he wrote, 'that Catholics may be restored to peace and tranquillity.' Meanwhile 'they will not fail, as their faith requires, to show themselves, with the most conscientious devotion, Your Majesty's respectful and loyal subjects'. It was a skilful letter, to which the Emperor replied with some reserve but on a markedly deferential note. Contact had been re-established. Bismarck was wide awake to the necessity of terminating the conflict, but he hesitated. During the eighteen months of negotiations, conducted through intermediaries, the Chancellor tried to limit himself to purely formal concessions,[1] while the Pope demanded guarantees. But the political climate of Germany was altering; the Social-Democratic party was making rapid strides in the industrial centres, to Bismarck's grave disquiet, and the Liberal-Nationals disapproved of his customs policy. The Chancellor was therefore compelled to seek help from the best organized party—the *Zentrum*; and two Socialist attempts on the Emperor's life hastened his conversion to the idea of a *détente*. 'I'm quite ready to do a little Canossa,' he told the nuncio at Munich, and he arranged a meeting with Windthorst in order to learn upon what conditions the *Zentrum* would support his policy. An initial gesture of appeasement was made in July 1879 when Falk, a leading light of the *Kulturkampf*, who had boasted of having secularized and rationalized education, was asked to resign.

Henceforward the two powers moved steadily towards reconciliation. Progress, however, was slow: Bismarck haggling for the lowest price and at the same time forced to take account of furious indignation of those whom he had set to wage the *Kulturkampf*; Leo XIII determined to make no easy sacrifice of the results obtained by the courageous attitude of the bishops and the political strength of the *Zentrum*. Meanwhile the German Catholics themselves proved so cautious that Bismarck rebuked them for sluggishness in their obedience to the Pope. At length, however, in 1881, the Chancellor informed the Reichstag that he was going to re-establish diplomatic relations with the Holy See not only in the name of Prussia but in that of the Empire as well. In 1882 orders were given to resume payment of ecclesiastical salaries in Prussia, and State examinations for priests were abolished.

[1] e.g. that the May Laws should become abeyant with no undertaking as to their repeal.

In 1883 it was decided that bishops need no longer submit appointments of parish priests for approval or rejection by the civil authorities.

The whole apparatus of the May Laws was thus dismantled. But Leo did not parade his victory; he was too sagacious to risk provoking the Chancellor's uncertain temper, and so perhaps undoing all that had been accomplished. He had obtained what was essential. The May Laws were to be 'revised', a process which began in the spring of 1886. The fifteen hundred priests who had been driven from their parishes returned. The religious orders were readmitted—excepting the Jesuits, who were not allowed back until 1903. Lastly, as a gesture of goodwill and reconciliation, Wilhelm I appointed Mgr Kopf, Bishop of Fulda, to the House of Peers. There remained only the somewhat embarrassing problem of certain bishops, including Ledochowski of Posen and Melchers of Cologne, who had resisted Bismarck with more violence than their colleagues, sometimes in terms that could not be readily forgotten. So far from demanding their reinstatement, Leo took thought for the higher interests of the Church and asked them to resign.

By 1888 the *Kulturkampf* had ended. In the same year a new chapter of German history opened with the death of Wilhelm I, that of his son Friedrich III three months later, and the accession of his grandson Wilhelm II, who dismissed the illustrious chancellor in 1891.[1] Though Catholics represented less than one-quarter of the electoral body, the *Zentrum* was now the hinge of every government. It became more and more closely linked with official policies, a situation which led to great social achievements,[2] but which boded ill for the future.

Bismarck's Germany was not the only land where the Church stood at bay in the year of Leo's accession. Her plight in Switzerland was perhaps more painful still. Mgr Lachat and Mgr Mermillod had been expelled from their dioceses, as had scores of priests from their parishes. Violence stalked the Jura, where Catholics lurked in the forests ready to do battle. The Old Catholic priests installed here and there by the authorities had practically no congregations, and the Federal Government could no longer hide its embarrassment.

Leo XIII was anxious to reach a settlement in this 'little *Kulturkampf*'; and the Federal Council itself provided him with an opportunity to intervene when it planned a law that would have saddled every canton with so-called neutral schools. A large number of Protestants resisted the project with no less vigour than the entire Catholic population; a referendum was held and the scheme rejected. Leo

[1] The Kaiser paid three visits to the Pope (1888, 1893 and 1913), revealing on each occasion his notorious lack of discretion and good taste.

[2] See Chapter IV, section 14.

immediately informed the government of the canton of Basel that he was ready to collaborate in the search for some means of ending conflict in the Bernese Jura. Mgr Lachat agreed not to return to his diocese but to go instead to Lugano as apostolic administrator of Ticino, which was separated for that purpose from the Italian diocese of Como. Then, turning to Geneva and profiting by the vacancy of the See of Lausanne, Leo offered to abolish the famous vicariat-apostolic which had so offended the Genevese, upon the condition that Mgr Mermillod was recognized as bishop of the reconstituted diocese of Fribourg-Lausanne-Geneva. Carteret agreed in 1883, though with some reluctance. The causes of friction between the Church and the Swiss authorities had been thus removed, and Catholics began to play an important part in the affairs of the cantons through the conservative Catholic Party. After some hesitation Leo approved this body, and in 1891 it secured the election of one of its members to the Federal Council, which had hitherto been entirely in the hands of Protestants and radicals. Meanwhile the foundation of Fribourg University by Georges Python in 1889 furnished ample proof of the new authority enjoyed by Catholics.

Belgium, where he had been nuncio, retained a special place in Leo's heart; but the young kingdom gave him much cause for anxiety. The liberal and authoritarian prime minister, Frère-Orban, was a prominent freemason. In 1879 he secured the passage of an educational law creating 'neutral' schools, and he did this for the avowed purpose of destroying Catholic influence. When the Belgian bishops protested, Frère-Orban told the Pope that if he supported them diplomatic relations between Brussels and the Vatican would be terminated. Leo XIII, striving for religious peace, gave the episcopate counsels of moderation. But when the prime minister boasted in Parliament of having obtained from the Holy See an express disavowal of the bishops' attitude towards this problem, the answer was rapid and forthright: a papal Brief congratulated Cardinal Déchamps upon the perfect unanimity of both clergy and laity. Frère-Orban returned the nuncio's passport. There seemed no way out of this impasse, but the Pope's courage in refusing to yield on matters of principle was handsomely rewarded. United in the *Fédération des cercles* and led by the *Comité central catholique*, Catholics stood firm and triumphed at the elections of 1884. Seventy of them won seats in the Chamber against fifty-two liberals, and they were destined to hold power for thirty years. Diplomatic relations with the Vatican were promptly resumed and a new educational law was passed.

The Spanish Crown was on excellent terms with the Vatican; but religious feeling still ran high in Spain, and the liberals did their best to clip the wings of the Church. In 1887, after various measures of

little consequence, a Law of Associations exempted only three congregations from the formalities it imposed; other orders, which unlike those three had not been expressly designated in the Concordat of 1851, were obliged to present their statutes and submit to control by civil servants. These provisions remained for a long while ineffective; but after the Spanish reversals in South America the republicans used the religious question as a battering-ram against the Crown. A violent secularist campaign was launched by Canalejas, and in 1901 the Liberal minister Sagasta decided to apply strictly the law of 1887. Leo protested vigorously, threatening at the same time to recall his nuncio; and this caused such a disturbance in the peninsula that the Government preferred to yield and grant legal existence to all congregations.

In Portugal Leo XIII scored yet another diplomatic victory (1886), by ending fifty years of dispute over the delicate question, half political and half religious, known as the Schism of Goa.[1] King Louis I renounced his ancient privilege of 'patronate' over all the churches of India and the East Indies.

But the Pope's diplomatic successes were not limited to Catholic countries. Links were forged even with nations whose predominant religion was hostile towards Rome: with Russia, for example, which renewed diplomatic relations with the Vatican; with Norway, where religious liberty was restored to the Catholics;[2] with Gladstone's Britain, which, grateful for the counsels of moderation addressed to the Irish, and flattered by the Pope's congratulations on Queen Victoria's golden jubilee, sent an official representative to the Holy See; and lastly with the United States, where, by refusing to give the immigrants bishops of their own nationalities, and thereby contributing to the fusion of Catholics into a homogeneous mass, Leo XIII supported the views of the Federal Government and was allowed to send an apostolic delegate to Washington.

8. In France: the 'Ralliement'[3]

The most astonishing political decision of Leo XIII's pontificate was taken in the matter of France, a land for which he felt particular concern. His culture was French, and he admired the French Catholics. He was grateful to the French Government for having done its best to defend the Holy Father's rights over Rome at the time of his accession; and a French warship still lay at Civitavecchia to assure the Sovereign

[1] *The Church in an Age of Revolution*, Chapter VII, section 11.

[2] See Chapter X, section 2.

[3] 'Rallying'. The word was first used in this context not by Leo XIII, but by Abbé Garmier. Some have considered it ill chosen.

Pontiff's escape if need arose. Maréchal MacMahon therefore, with the Austrian Emperor and the King of Spain, was one of the first heads of state to whom he notified his election. Throughout his pontificate he manifested towards 'the noble French nation' a remarkable degree of patience and generosity, though it cannot be said that the rulers of the Third Republic showed much gratitude.

On his accession to the apostolic throne he found the religious situation of France in process of rapid deterioration, due both to the Catholics themselves and to their adversaries. A great majority of the former, with the bishops at their head, had exhibited strong repugnance towards the new regime; and some of them, notably Cardinal Pie, had paraded aggressively monarchist sentiments. There had even been instances of what can only be compared to a miniature White Terror: school-teachers rebuked by priests for singing the *Marseillaise*; tradesmen denounced by name from the pulpit as republicans and punished with savage boycott of their goods. Such conduct gave grounds for a hostility that could not be long restrained.

The existence of such hostility, let it be remembered, is beyond all possible doubt. As was later observed by Cardinal Matthieu, one of those prelates who 'rallied' most sincerely to the Republic, the subsequent violence against the Church was due entirely to the tactlessness of Catholics. Different though they were from one another—radicals like Clemenceau, opportunists like Gambetta or Jules Ferry—all republicans looked upon themselves as spiritual heirs of the French Revolution, secularist and anticlerical. Many were freemasons or sympathetic towards the lodges. Anticlericalism was a basic article of the 'Ligue d'Enseignement', to which all school-teachers belonged. One cannot therefore attribute the forthcoming crisis to mere isolated occurrences. In 1871, when Gambetta insulted the Archbishop of Tours in his own palace, the Sixteenth of May was still some years ahead....

The trial of strength named after that date gave the signal for some unpleasant events. When MacMahon fell, together with his 'ministry of 16th May' (1877), and the republican party came to power, it was foreseeable that the Church would have to meet the cost of the operation. Despite the ministerial instability which characterized the new regime, the general direction of republican policy remained single, orientated towards anticlericalism. The first attack was launched in the scholastic field, whence it moved inevitably to that of the religious congregations. It was led by one man, Jules Ferry (1832–93), minister of public instruction, an icy doctrinaire, an atheist freemason, but withal a first-class administrator. He it was who organized primary and compulsory education, and who introduced secondary education for girls.

These innovations were not likely to please the Church, who viewed them as rivalling her own schools, particularly those in which 'girls were brought up on their knees'. She was likewise offended in the realm of higher education by a measure which reserved to State teachers the right of conferring degrees, and also by the passing of a law which removed the bishops from the Superior Council of Public Instruction. Those acts did not in themselves constitute an open declaration of hostilities; but the original draft of the law on higher education included a certain Article 7, the effect of which was to bar all members of unauthorized congregations from the direction of any public or private educational establishment. Now this article covered the most powerful congregations, including the Jesuits, whom indeed its author had chiefly in mind. While claiming to observe the terms of the concordat, and even 'to revive a tradition', Ferry declared that he wanted to 'rescue the soul of the youth of France' from the Society of Jesus, a formation 'prohibited by all our history'.

The Senate threw out Article 7; but the Government hit back with two decrees, one purporting to dissolve the Society and the other giving all unauthorized congregations three months within which to regularize their position. Eight thousand male and nearly one hundred thousand female religious were affected. There were many protests, from the nuncio, from the bishops, and from four hundred magistrates who resigned rather than apply the decrees; but all were fruitless. The Jesuits were expelled first. A few superiors tried to avoid the worst by signing a declaration of republican loyalty; but that did not prevent the dispersal of five thousand members of various congregations. There followed a series of 'republican laws': one to laicize the whole teaching personnel, another to conscript seminarians for military service, another to bar priests from municipal schools committees, and yet another to reintroduce divorce. Additional steps were taken to abolish theological faculties, as well as chaplaincies in teachers' training colleges; to exclude nursing sisters from certain hospitals; and to reduce subsidies for public worship.

It need hardly be said that those measures provoked a great deal of unrest. The majority of Catholics viewed them as outright persecution, and adopted an attitude of intransigent anti-republicanism. Such an attitude, however, was bad strategy; negotiation would have been a more enlightened course. The republicans, divided among themselves, evidently had no intention of carrying their offensive to extremes: no drastic steps were taken to prevent the congregations, including the Jesuits, from remaining quietly in France; and a great many free schools were opened between 1880 and 1885. In short, the bridges had not been broken.

Leo XIII therefore behaved with more moderation. At the height

of the crisis he remained in touch with the republican leaders through his nuncio Mgr Czacki; persuaded Gambetta that the Church's support would be useful in the pursuit of the worldwide influence he was planning for France; and even wrote a personal letter to President Grévy, assuring him that although doctrinal considerations compelled the Church to defend her rights, none of those considerations prevented her from recognizing the Republic. Going still further, on 8th February 1884 he published the Encyclical *Nobilissima Gallorum gens*, in which, while observing with sorrow that France, an ancient Catholic country, was turning her back upon the Church and that religious peace was threatened within her borders, he nevertheless bade the clergy and faithful to obey their 'legitimate superiors'; and next year *Immortale Dei* opened the door to an understanding with the republican as with all other regimes. Both documents were welcomed by almost the entire left-wing press, and were praised by the Protestant Pressensé in the Senate; but many Catholics read them with unconcealed horror.

Events quickly justified Leo's approach. The Republic, whose imminent collapse was foretold, not only survived but went from strength to strength with the passing of each year. Surely then it was only sensible to profit by the lesson of inescapable fact and put an end to the sterile opposition of Catholics to the regime. Large numbers had thrown themselves headlong into the abortive Boulangist conspiracy (1887–9), and it was greatly to be feared that the victorious left would make the Church pay for the error of so many of her children.

In the mind of Leo XIII, therefore, the policy known as the *Ralliement* harmonized with a firmly based doctrinal concept and also with equally sound tactical considerations. Its purpose was to lead Catholics to accept the republican regime, so that they might work from within for some modification of its anti-religious laws. In 1890 the situation appeared to favour such a move, for the republican opportunists were alarmed by the rising tide of Socialism and showed themselves in a mood for conciliation.

Leo seized his opportunity, and the Encyclical *Sapientiae christianae* (January 1890) contained these significant words: 'To draw the Church towards one party, or to seek her as an ally against one's political foes, is an abuse of religion.' Throughout that year it was rumoured that the Holy See was preparing to make a surprise move; for Cardinal Lavigerie, founder of the White Fathers and one of the most celebrated churchmen, had several private interviews with the Pope. Twenty years earlier Lavigerie had been a monarchist; but he now believed that the royal cause could never be revived, and at Leo's request he agreed to take the initiative. In November 1890 the French Mediterranean Fleet put in at Algiers, and the archbishop welcomed

its officers, together with representatives of the army and the civil administration. At the end of dinner he rose to give the usual toast, and his guests were astonished to hear him say: 'When the will of a people has been clearly expressed, when there is no means of saving one's country from disaster except by whole-hearted support of a particular form of government, it is time to declare an end to resistance. . . . That is what I teach those around me; that is the example I wish to see followed in France by all our clergy, and in saying so I am certain that no one in authority will deny my words.' The orchestra then struck up the *Marseillaise*.

Catholics hostile to the Republic learned of this event with transports of indignation. The right-wing press thundered against 'the African', who received dozens of insulting letters, some of them defiled with ordure. It was declared that the Pope had had nothing to do with these 'Carthaginian fantasies'. Mgr Freppel, the turbulent Alsatian Keller and Mgr d'Hulst, rector of the Institut Catholique in Paris, went to Rome and protested, while the Comte de Paris sent a message to the same effect. Hurried attempts were made to set up the 'Catholic Party' of which Albert de Mun had dreamed. And of course the few bishops who congratulated Cardinal Lavigerie were publicly vowed to destruction.

Leo watched the tumult with close attention, but found no reason to go back upon his plan. In June 1891 he appointed as nuncio in Paris Mgr Domenico Ferrata, a prelate of rare penetration and one of the men who understood most fully his own thought. Ferrata had served on Mgr Czacki's staff; he was well known in the capital, and proceeded to make contact with the republican rulers; whereupon the five French cardinals published a joint letter in which, while admitting that 'it is the duty of Catholics to allay political dissension by taking a firm stand on constitutional ground', they set forth the Republic's anti-religious activity during the previous ten years; and this account so closely resembled an indictment that there was reason to ask whether their eminences' purpose was merely to guard against the future. But the Pope held his course, and the Encyclical *Au milieu des sollicitudes* (20th February 1892) declared that 'acceptance of the new regime is not only permitted, but demanded, and even imposed by the necessity of the social tie which has created and maintains it. Such an attitude is the surest and most salutary line of conduct for all Frenchmen in their civil relations with the Republic, which is the present government of their nation.'

The welcome extended to Leo's Encyclical varied according to circumstances. Truly loyal Catholics, those who placed obedience to the Holy Father in the front rank of Christian virtues, submitted, though in some cases not without anguish of mind. So too did the

great majority of bishops, but clearly with little enthusiasm. The right indulged in an orgy of wrath. *La Gazette de France* talked about 'a coalition of Rome and the Grand Orient'; in *Libre Parole*, Drumont asked what French knight 'still had the iron gauntlet with which Nogaret struck Boniface VIII'. Many priests and laymen, without going to such extremes, remained hostile to the new policy and made no secret of their views. As the elections of 1893 approached, an appeal went out to Catholics asking them to vote against the *ralliés* even if that meant choosing a masonic radical. Ten years later, shortly before his death, Leo XIII said to the Abbé Frémont: 'By their disobedience to my programme in 1892 the French clergy rendered me powerless to save them.' Nor was his bold decision understood in certain parts of the opposing camp. While some republicans recognized a 'new spirit' activated by tolerance, many others had no wish to bring about a reconciliation; and measures either clumsy or intentionally hostile to Catholicism were very soon taken, e.g. the establishment of a 'subscription' to replace the tax on the increase of property owned by religious congregations, and the abolition of Good Friday mourning in the French Navy.

Thus, for the time being, Leo's courageous attempt to get rid of antagonism between the French Republic and the Church did not produce the results upon which he had counted. Through the fault of Catholics as well as of anticlericals the *Ralliement* failed to prevent the grave crisis which followed the Dreyfus affair and led to the separation of Church and State. Not until later did the fruitfulness of his idea become apparent, when circumstances permitted an honest relationship between the Church and the Republic for the benefit of both sides. In this case, as in so many others, Leo XIII had taken an option on the future.

9. Under the Double Eagle

Another such option was taken in Austria-Hungary, an option so bold and so far-sighted that no historian seems yet to have understood its significance. The Hapsburg Empire, ruled by His Apostolic Majesty Francis Joseph, prided itself as one of the bastions of Catholicism in Europe. Its ministers constantly referred to the Pope's situation in Rome and to the necessity of guaranteeing him full independence. But the court of Vienna was riddled with antichristian or at any rate anti-Roman influences: Josephism continued to enjoy some measure of support; freemasonry was gaining ground there as elsewhere; banking and big business were in the hands of Jews hostile to the Church; and Bismarck had countless admirers. Accordingly Leo XIII

failed in his efforts to revive the Concordat; nor was he able in 1894 to prevent the passing of a law which made civil marriage obligatory and sufficient, and imposed a fine upon any priest who ventured to bless future spouses before the civil registration of their union.

To this minor war waged by the Austrian Government against Catholicism Leo XIII replied with an appeal to the Catholic conscience, asking the faithful to be true believers, not to be content—as was too often the case—with a façade of religion, and to insist that their rights should be respected. Not without hesitation, he approved the birth of a Social-Christian party founded by Prince Aloys of Liechtenstein and Dr Lüger, Burgomaster of Vienna; and he even defended it against the complaints of some conservative aristocrats.[1]

But he did something else besides. Playing a most daring card, he made a public show of his particular interest in those racial elements of the Empire which were not of Germanic stock. Throughout his reign he conducted a pro-Slav and pro-Hungarian policy which appears to have derived from a deep-rooted conviction. Led by Mgr Strossmayer,[2] the southern Slavs, Croats and Slovenes organized and strengthened themselves; while their pilgrimages went to Rome to acclaim the Pope and thank him for having ordered the celebration by the universal Church of the feast of SS. Cyril and Methodius, apostles of the Slavs. A deep impression was made also by the papal directive that Slav priests were to teach the catechism in their own language.

A similar attitude was adopted towards Hungary, upon which Leo XIII lavished favours and advice, recalling—especially in 1886, the bicentenary of the deliverance of Buda—the part long played by the Hungarians in the defence of Christendom against the Turks. Here too catechism was to be taught in the vernacular, and no longer in German according to long-established custom. It may well be that Leo had foreseen the day when the nationalities then grouped under the Hapsburg monarchy would find themselves independent.

10. Vatican and Quirinal

There was, however, one sector in which Leo XIII's usual breadth of view appears to have been at fault. I refer to the Italian sector, wherein, as we can see today, flexibility was altogether indispensable. It would seem that the great diplomat's whole Italian policy was dominated by the Roman Question, which he would not (and perhaps could not) approach with his familiar daring. The position as he found it was absolutely clear, and none could see any hope of a solution. The

[1] See Chapter V, section 6.

[2] *The Church in an Age of Revolution*, Index.

papacy still considered itself the victim of unwarrantable brigandage; the power that occupied Rome was illegitimate. Negotiation was impossible, since to negotiate would be to recognize the Italian Government. In the Pope's view there was no Italian Government, only a 'Piedmontese' or 'Subalpine' Government which had usurped the Sovereign Pontiff's rights in Rome; and the Vicar of Christ, a voluntary prisoner in the Vatican palace, could have no relations with it. As for Italian Catholics, they had been required to express their refusal to accept the usurper by abstaining from all political activity.

Many had wondered whether Leo would continue in the rigid attitude adopted by his predecessor. During the conclave this question had been on all lips, and at one time it had been thought likely to determine the outcome of the election. It had also been discussed in the Council of Ministers, who had decided that if the new Pope came out on to the loggia of St Peter's to bless the crowds, and thereby showed that he no longer considered himself a prisoner in the Vatican, the troops would present arms. Leo, however, did not appear; he gave his first blessing from a balcony inside the basilica, thus letting it be known that his attitude would be that of Pius IX.

Intransigence on the Roman Question was in fact the rule, at least officially, throughout Leo's pontificate. His first Encyclical (April 1878) 'renewed and confirmed' Pius IX's declarations and protests against the violation of the rights of the Church in respect both of the temporal power and of the occupation of Rome. Nine years later a sensational letter addressed to the new secretary of state, Cardinal Rampolla, likewise claimed an 'effective sovereignty' as guarantee of independence; and in 1902 the aged pontiff repeated his demands. There were members of his *entourage*, some of them very close to him, who urged a more accommodating policy; but all who ventured to air such views in public were straightway called to order. These latter included not only Father Curci, an ex-Jesuit and founder of *Civiltà cattolica*, whose pamphlets on 'the Royal Vatican' were little better than lampoons, but also a number of quite reasonable and moderate priests: the Benedictine Dom Torti, sub-archivist of the Holy See and author of a booklet whose title, *Conciliazione*, was later to re-echo round the world; and Mgr Bonomelli of Cremona, whose article in *Rassegna nazionale*, advising a more realistic acceptance of hard facts, was immediately placed on the Index.

Thus during the twenty-five years of Leo's pontificate the only official relations between Vatican and Quirinal were those of sterile antagonism. In the Eternal City society was divided into 'Blacks' and 'Whites', the former devoted to the Pope, the latter faithful to the Crown. It was an unpleasant situation for everyone: Leo himself

always felt handicapped by his 'captivity'; the new Italy 'was never quite at home in her capital';[1] and those Italians who desired to remain loyal to the Pope and at the same time to live as patriotic citizens were placed in a most awkward dilemma.

It has frequently been asked how Leo XIII, broad-minded and clear-sighted as he was in other respects, came to imprison himself within such narrow confines. The answer may lie in his own earlier career: he was born in the Papal States and grew grey in the service of a pope who rejected all thought of compromise. It is also probable that he had to take account of such intransigents as Cardinal Pitra and the Spanish leader Nocedal, both of whom accused him of liberalism, both of whom he had occasion to rebuke, and both of whom would have welcomed an opportunity to attack him left, right and centre had he pardoned the despoiler. At all events, his unyielding attitude combined with the open hostility of Italian anticlericals to foster a disagreeable state of tension from beginning to end of the pontificate.

Trouble began very soon after his election. The municipality of Rome decided that religious instruction should no longer be obligatory in schools under their authority. Leo protested against this measure and also against the encouragement of Protestant propaganda in the Eternal City, while the liberal press and liberal congresses raged against the Vatican. Two incidents caused an even greater uproar. In July 1881 the transfer of Pius IX's remains to San Lorenzo fuori le Muri was the occasion of riotous scenes. By agreement with the Government this operation was arranged to take place at night, but the secret was not well kept. A crowd of a hundred thousand Catholics followed the hearse and were attacked by counter-demonstrators who rushed upon the cortège yelling 'To the Tiber with the blackguard!' The garrison of the Castel Sant' Angelo took three hours to restore order. The following year, 1882, was the sixth centenary of the Sicilian Vespers, and an acrobatic interpretation of history afforded an opportunity for anti-papal demonstrations.[2] No chance indeed was lost of pouring oil upon the fire. A Vatican architect, one Martinucci, became involved in a dispute with his employees, and the secular courts were only too pleased to declare themselves competent to try the case. Next, real property owned by the Congregation of Propaganda was confiscated and paid for with Government stock. Again, the exequatur was refused to bishops, so that twenty sees were left vacant. And finally, under pretext that the King of Italy was heir to the monarch of the Two Sicilies, who used to appoint the bishops of his realm by virtue of a concordat, the Archbishop of Chiesi appointed by the Holy See was denied entry to his diocese.

[1] Ernest Lavisse, *Vue générale de l'Histoire politique*, pp. 210–12.

[2] Because Pope Martin IV had sided with Charles of Anjou and the French.

In point of fact several members of the Italian Government viewed this petty warfare as ridiculous, mere socialist agitation; and Leo XIII himself took every opportunity to lament 'the fatal discord'. About 1887 there was talk of reconciliation, and a number of solutions were considered, e.g. temporary reinstatement of Florence as the Italian capital or recognition of papal sovereignty over the Leonine City. Nothing, however, was achieved; the attempt was sabotaged by anticlericals who clamoured that the Pope was at last going to renounce temporal power, with the result that Leo wrote his sensational letter to Cardinal Rampolla insisting upon all his rights.

The advent to power of Crispi, an anticlerical fanatic, marked the beginning of fresh hostilities. The new code provided stern punishment for any priest who ventured 'to make a public attack on State institutions or governmental decisions'; and one decree abolished the catechism in all primary schools. There was also a revival of absurd or obnoxious incidents. Thus in 1888, the year of Leo's sacerdotal jubilee, which brought many pilgrims to Rome, the Government saw fit to erect a statue of Giordano Bruno [1] on the Campo dei Fiori, where that unfrocked Dominican, a professor of atheism and immorality, had been burned in 1600. Renan sent a congratulatory telegram, and one Roman newspaper declared that the Church was now dead beyond recall. Year by year vexations continued. Most of the property belonging to religious confraternities was requisitioned for the benefit of State charities. In 1895 the twenty-fifth anniversary of the capture of Rome was celebrated with great pomp; the date (20th September) was declared an obligatory national holiday, and an equestrian statue of Garibaldi was erected on the Janiculum overlooking the Vatican itself. The quarrel with the Church had become so well established that, even when Crispi's ministry was overthrown after the disaster of Adowa (1896), the moderate Marchese Di Rudini dared not abandon its anticlerical policies. In 1898, after a series of almost revolutionary strikes, hundreds of Catholic social and economic undertakings were suppressed on the grounds that they were Socialist. To the very end of the pontificate less violent but repeated incidents revealed the same tension between Quirinal and Vatican.

Leo XIII, on the other hand, never resigned himself to that deplorable situation. Whenever the rights of the Church were violated, or religion insulted, he raised his voice in strong but unruffled protest. More than once, when tension was abnormally acute, he was heard to say that he might leave Rome and take refuge in Spain, Malta or Austria, though it is uncertain whether his words expressed a serious intention or merely a diplomatic threat. He was nevertheless always prepared to welcome any move towards reconciliation, and even

[1] *The Catholic Reformation*, Index.

displayed a measure of forbearance which some Catholics thought excessive. Thus, in 1900, when King Umberto I was assassinated, the Pope authorized his burial in the Pantheon, the church of Santa Maria dei Martiri. But he was well aware of the danger in which the situation placed the Church, and of the countless difficulties it raised. For example, when a foreign head of state visited Rome the Sovereign Pontiff was obliged to refuse him audience if he called first at the Quirinal; whence innumerable complicated questions of protocol. More serious was the fact that continued hostility between the Holy See and the Kingdom of Italy helped to drive the latter into the Triple Alliance with Germany and Austria, a manœuvre that worried Leo to such an extent that he began to wish for a Franco-Russian *rapprochement* in order to counterbalance its effect.

Common sense clearly dictated a search for some *modus vivendi*, and secret negotiations were in fact more or less continuous. The intermediaries were Cardinal Hohenlohe, a Franciscan friend of the royal family, the Calabrian deputy Fazzari, and Don Bosco's Salesians. The extent and details of those negotiations will not be known until the Vatican archives on this period are made available. In any case, nothing was achieved: neither camp would yield sufficient ground. A few minor points were settled, among them the exequatur for bishops; but the Roman Question remained unsolved, maybe because the time was not yet ripe.

The Pope's intransigence, however, which was approved by a large majority of Catholics throughout the world, did much to vitalize Italian Catholicism. The *non expedit* laid down by Pius IX and upheld by Leo XIII excluded Catholics from political activity, and thereby reduced the strength of conservative parties. But so long as Catholics were forbidden to vote or to stand for election they sought other means of exerting their influence. They gave much attention to municipal affairs, as the Pope himself urged them to do; and the Roman Union, led by Mgr Jacobini, became a central organism for the encouragement and direction of this kind of work. Among prominent groups that might be described as quasi-political were the Pian Federation, created under Pius IX to defend the rights of the Pope; the Society of Italian Catholic Youth, which remained active until the First World War; and the Pious Union of Catholic Women. At the same time Catholics interested themselves in social undertakings, friendly societies and co-operatives.

One venture soon eclipsed all other such movements, and from the beginning of Leo's reign onwards provided a unique and general framework for Catholic activity. The *Opera dei Congressi* was formed under Pius IX. Officially approved in 1876 and encouraged by Leo XIII, its aim was 'to unite all the Catholic associations of Italy' with a

view to 'common and concerted action in defence of the Holy See's rights and of the religious and social interests of all Italians, under the impulse of the Sovereign Pontiff and the direction of the bishops and clergy'. It therefore tended to organize itself in such a way as to overlook nothing that concerned Italian Catholicism. The society's activity was distributed among five sections: the first and second were concerned with general and social work respectively; the third with instruction and education; the fourth with newspapers; the fifth with Christian art. The whole was directed by a central committee, elected by provincial committees and headed by a general president. Some first-rate men devoted themselves heart and soul to this undertaking: the Marchese Salviati, Baron Vito d'Ondes, Professor Toniolo, the great orator Paganuzzi, the future statesman Filippo Meda, and Don Romolo Murri. It would indeed be disingenuous to suppose that the society's work was fruitful in every sphere; there were sometimes a great many more words than deeds. But we shall have occasion to show[1] that in the field of social endeavour it accomplished great things under the leadership of Giuseppe Toniolo.

11. Arbiter of Nations

The 'Christian policy' of Leo XIII as defined in *Immortale Dei* involved more than establishing harmony between Church and State. He had recalled that the Vicar of Christ, by virtue of an authority transcending that of secular governments, had the right to counsel human societies, to remind them of their duties imposed by Christian faith and, in a word, to act as their guide and arbiter. Leo XIII endeavoured to revive the Church's influence and his own in this respect.

The Pope's function as arbiter between man and man is to quieten inflamed spirits and bring about the reign of justice. Leo undertook that role in two spheres. In the social sphere his intervention was so unprecedented, so daring, that it opened a new chapter in the history of Christianity and calls for separate consideration.[2] But the appeal of *Rerum Novarum* for a more just and brotherly society did much to enhance its author's prestige and confirm his influence. By posing as arbiter between social groups Leo XIII performed an act of statesmanship in the highest sense of that word.

In the diplomatic field the Church carried little or no weight. For more than a hundred and fifty years the papacy had been excluded from international discussions that determined the fortunes of mankind. Even Consalvi, despite the friendship and esteem of many

[1] Chapter IV, section 14. [2] See Chapter IV.

foreign diplomats, had failed to win representation for the Holy See in the counsels of Europe. It seemed more than unlikely that the Pope would ever again be invited to regulate the conduct of governments and put an end to their differences. Yet that is exactly what Leo XIII was called upon to do in 1885, and by none other than the Prince von Bismarck.

Germany and Spain were disputing ownership of the Caroline Islands. War appeared imminent when Bismarck announced on behalf of his emperor that he was ready to submit the case to arbitration by the Pope, whom he regarded as the only man possessing unquestioned moral authority. He wrote a personal letter to the Pope addressing him as 'Sire'; and if this word was intended to avoid such expressions as 'Most Holy Father' or 'Your Holiness', it was none the less a polite allusion to the Pontiff's sovereignty. The Spanish Government could not refuse this offer. An official Berlin newspaper, *Die Post*, said that the Pope would be expected not merely to act as conciliator, but 'to let the world know the reasons for his judgment' and thereby to strengthen 'the foundations of international law'. The world, it added, 'was expecting a sentence that would harmonize modern civilization with the laws of Christianity'. Could more have been said? Who would have thought that the *Kulturkampf* was not yet officially ended? Of course the Protestant journalists accused the chancellor of leading the world back to medieval theocracy. And Crispi exclaimed: 'If someone had said fifteen years ago that the Pope might be asked to serve as an international mediator, he would have been sent straight to a madhouse.'

Leo made no attempt to act as an international lawgiver. He confined himself to proposing an agreement that recognized the older rights of Spain but allowed Germany particular advantages. Both governments accepted the compromise; Leo wrote to congratulate Bismarck on his moderation and conferred on him the Order of Christ.

Other opportunities arose of proving that the Pope was ready to intervene whenever justice, charity and peace were at stake. He gave energetic support to campaigns for the abolition of slavery in Africa; [1] after the catastrophe at Adowa it was he who concerned himself with the fate of Italian prisoners and wrote to the Negus urging their release; and the British Government asked him on several occasions to use his influence in Ireland. When Wilhelm II decided to summon an international conference at Berlin, to study means 'of improving the workers' condition', he informed the Pope of his programme, asked for his 'gracious approval', and invited him to send a representative. Leo, however, declined this last proposal, knowing the political motives that underlay the magnanimity affected by the Kaiser. In

[1] See Chapter X, section 12.

1889, before the first international peace conference at The Hague, the Queen of the Netherlands sent the Pope official notification of its agenda and asked for his 'moral support'. To this Leo replied: 'It is a very special part of Our function to lend not only moral support but also effective co-operation to the work of ensuring peace.' But when Cardinal Rampolla let it be known that the Holy See would gladly accept an invitation to be represented, the Italian Government took fright, thinking that the Pope's envoy would raise the Roman Question. The Quirinal therefore imposed a formal veto to the invitation, and the great powers dared not ignore it. From one point of view, however, this renewed gesture of sectarian hate may be said to have furnished additional proof of the Papacy's recovered influence and prestige.

12. France: the Dreyfus Affair Leads to Persecution

The closing years of the pontificate of Leo XIII were darkened by grave anxieties. His chief preoccupation was France, where a crisis of appalling magnitude gave him reason to fear that Catholics would have to pay a heavy price for their mistakes.

The Dreyfus affair began in 1898 as a trifling matter of espionage. Four years earlier, in the autumn of 1894, Captain Alfred Dreyfus, an artillery officer on the general staff, had been accused of having sold military secrets to Germany. Tried by court-martial, he had been convicted and condemned to dismissal from the army and imprisonment for life, although he had never ceased to deny his guilt. The judges had had before them a document which, contrary to law, had not been communicated to the defendant or his counsel. Dreyfus was sent to Devil's Island off the coast of Guiana; but his brother Matthieu and his friend Bernard Lazare began at once to make inquiries with a view to establishing his innocence.

The affair began in earnest not long after the appointment of Colonel Picquart as head of the Deuxième Bureau, the French intelligence service. Picquart came to the conclusion that the guilty man was not Dreyfus but Esterhazy, an officer of dubious reputation. His superiors ordered him to remain silent and not to raise the question; but certain politicians, Scheurer-Kestner and Clemenceau, got wind of this conspiracy and intervened—Clemenceau, with his usual violence, in the newspaper *L'Aurore*.

Common sense and elementary justice said: 'If Dreyfus is indeed guilty, he deserves his punishment; but if there is any suspicion of a judicial error his case must be reopened.' Dreyfus, however, was a

Jew, and some people regarded that as a presumption of guilt so strong as to amount to certainty. It mattered little that the means employed to condemn him had been illegal; the Jew Dreyfus could not be innocent, and it would not be right to disavow the findings of a military tribunal in order to debate the facts. On the other hand, all those who were soon to become known as 'Dreyfusards' considered that responsibility for the injustice done to Dreyfus lay with the entire general staff, with the whole army, and also with the Government, which consisted at that time of moderate republicans. Both arguments were inadmissible. 'The Affair' moved on to the political plane.

Sensational events followed one upon another. Commandant Esterhazy was acquitted. Zola was prosecuted for having libelled the army in his article *J'accuse*. Colonel Henry, convicted of having inserted a forged document among the Dreyfus papers, committed suicide. The judgment of the first court-martial was annulled, and a second delivered a more lenient but ridiculous verdict which gave the accused benefit of extenuating circumstances. Meanwhile France was split from top to bottom. Dreyfusards and anti-Dreyfusards fought in press and Parliament, in high society and in family circles. Violence knew no bounds: Dreyfus's counsel was lucky to escape assassination, while an anti-Dreyfusard assaulted the President of the Republic. Dreyfus himself had passed into virtual oblivion; men were now for or against the army, for or against State policy, for or against the regime. In this affair pathetic struggles of conscience were mingled with sordid intrigue. Not only was the Government overthrown, swept away by the storm; the national unity, even the very existence of France herself, was at stake.

What was the attitude of Catholics in this drama? It must be confessed that very few of them faced the question of justice and reasoned calmly. Paul Viollet, Père Maumus and others formed a Catholic Committee for the Defence of Right; but they were a mere handful, overwhelmed with hatred and contempt. A vast majority of Catholics had been brought up to admire and venerate the army, most of whose officers were Catholics. It appeared almost blasphemous to suggest that certain military leaders had perpetrated or cloaked a denial of justice, as the Dreyfusards claimed. 'Free inquiry is not permitted in these matters,' wrote Père Vincent-de-Paul Bailly in *La Croix*. Albert de Mun, for all his goodness, haughtily declined an interview with Matthieu Dreyfus, while Cardinal Richard told the condemned man's brother: 'The Church has no reason to interfere.' Among the masses, imbued with anti-Semitism, passion went much further. The Catholic press served its readers with scorching *anti-dreyfusisme*. 'Christian and anti-Jewish—the two terms are inseparable,' proclaimed *La Croix*, whose first page was adorned with a

picture of the crucified Jew! Thousands of Catholics joined the anti-Dreyfusard 'League of Patriots'; thousands contributed money for the erection of a memorial to Colonel Henry. And then, as if to give this movement an unassailable warrant, *Civiltà cattolica*, the Roman Jesuit review, published an article in which occurred these words: 'The Jew was created by God to act the traitor everywhere.'

Sorrow filled the heart of Leo XIII as he watched that outburst of rage among his sons. In 1899 he informed the directors of *La Croix* that he deplored 'the spirit and tone of their newspaper', and in the following year he ordered the Assumptionists to quit that journal.[1] He was not deceived as to the true significance which some attached to the affair. 'Surely,' he said on more than one occasion, 'the real defendant is the French Republic.' In an interview granted to Boyer d'Agen, a correspondent of *Figaro*, he exclaimed: 'Happy the victim whom God considers so just as to liken his cause to that of His own sacrificed Son'.[2] Yet, when those words were reported, some ladies in the Faubourg Saint-Germain made novenas praying that God would speedily recall unto Himself the heretical Pope.

Leo was well aware that a counter-blow was inevitable and that the Church would have a dreadful price to pay; for passion was no less violent among the Dreyfusards. If the general staff was anti-Semite, they argued, it was because the officers came from Jesuit schools. The Jesuits, therefore, must suffer for the Affair; and, of course, not only the Jesuits, not only the Assumptionists, but all the congregations and indeed every priest. *La Lanterne* carried a headline: 'Cassocked Monsters.' 'All is permissible against the priest,' wrote *La Raison*; 'he is a mad dog whom every passer-by has a right to destroy.' Without going to such extremes, the left-wing republicans saw an opportunity to launch a new offensive against 'clericalism' and, through it, against the Church. There were in the Dreyfusard camp upright minds, hearts in love with justice, men such as Charles Péguy, who later recalled the Affair in *Notre Jeunesse*. But, as Péguy himself observed, 'everything begins with a lofty ideal and ends in politics'; the struggle for truth soon took on the appearance of a radical and socialist campaign against Christ and His faithful. The more far-sighted anticlericals knew what they were about in playing this game. Clemenceau, raising the question of principle, wrote that conciliation between the Republic and the Church was impossible until such time as the papacy disavowed the *Syllabus*. Catholics had provided their adversaries with a splendid chance.[3]

[1] It was taken over by the great industrialist Paul Féron-Vrau.

[2] *Figaro*, 15th March 1899.

[3] 'It cannot be doubted', writes the historian Debidour, 'that the Dreyfus affair was the decisive cause of the anticlerical movement which resulted in the laws of 1901 on associations and those of 1905 on separation' (*L'Église et l'État en France*, vol. ii, p. 169).

The collapse of the moderates made way for a 'ministry of republican defence' under Waldeck-Rousseau. This man was not a freemason, and had no intention of backing the extreme left. A typical politician, he planned to satisfy the anticlericals by attacking 'the leaguer monks and political priests', but without breaking with the Church, and above all without endangering the concordat, which he regarded as 'the only practical and effective means of holding clericalism in check'.

Having dealt with the nationalists and anti-Semites, he instituted proceedings against the Assumptionists, i.e. the Augustinians of the Assumption, a congregation founded in 1850 by Père d'Alzon for the express purpose of an apostolate through the medium of the printed word. Their publishing house, known as La Bonne Presse, together with the newspaper *La Croix*, had considerable influence in Catholic circles. This congregation, however, had not been authorized, and twelve of its leaders—including the superior-general, Père Picard, and the editor of *La Croix*, Père Vincent-de-Paul Bailly—were accordingly prosecuted by virtue of Article 291 of the Penal Code. They were fined, and the congregation was dissolved. Cardinal Richard called at their house in the Rue François-Ier, to offer his sympathy; but Leo XIII, as we have seen, bade them have nothing more to do with *La Croix*.

Throwing the Assumptionists to the wolves along with the Jesuits and, for good measure, the Brothers of the Christian Schools,[1] did not suffice to calm the howling pack. Having started on the road of anticlericalism, Waldeck-Rousseau found himself led further than he had ever meant to go. The steps he had just taken had earned him a marked increase of his parliamentary majority: could he hesitate to proceed and make still heavier sacrifices? 'The Revolution forms a single bloc!' Clemenceau had cried; the 'left-wing bloc' had formed; Waldeck-Rousseau was its prisoner, and so he declared war upon all religious congregations.

The point of attack against the Church was well chosen. The essential duty of the great congregations, from the centre of Catholic unity and under direct control of the Holy See, is to guard that unity and do battle with all that is likely to imperil it. To strike them down was to wound Catholicity in a vital centre. Such was the true purpose of the Law of Associations (2nd July 1901). Complete freedom was allowed to all associations, excepting religious associations or congregations. These latter were subjected to special rules: none might

[1] Albert de Mun had shown that in fact none of Dreyfus's accusers had been educated by the Jesuits. The attack on the Brothers arose from a charge of murder brought against one of their members, Bro. Flaminian, in circumstances even more revolting than the prosecution of Dreyfus.

be founded without statutory permission, and even in the case of those already authorized, no new house might be opened without a governmental warrant. Furthermore every congregation had to be able to present the civil authorities with a complete list of its members and a detailed inventory of its goods.

Waldeck-Rousseau already considered that Parliament and its committees had gone a little too far; but he was now leader of the anticlericals, and had to follow his troops. He desired at least that the law of 1901 should be applied with moderation, that account should be taken of services rendered by the congregations, that 'intrigue but not charity should be excluded'. And he even wrote to the Pope, to reassure him. But he was already outmanœuvred. The elections of 1902 took place in an atmosphere of incredible agitation. The barons and retainers of masonic anticlericalism were mobilized. In the other camp a preacher declared that there were only two candidates: Jesus and Barabbas. And several bishops published their directions for battle. The left-wing bloc won the day with 368 deputies, among whom the radicals were most numerous. Waldeck-Rousseau, old and tired, resigned, advising the President to send for Émile Combes.

Thus began the political reign of one destined to be considered as the incarnation of anticlericalism at its worst. Combes was a renegade priest who had obtained his D.Litt. with theses on St Bernard and St Thomas Aquinas. He had taught in the junior seminary at Albi, and then, having lost the Christian faith—though remaining ostensibly a deist and spiritualist [1]—had studied medicine. Finally, at one and the same time, he had entered freemasonry and politics, in both of which he had quickly displayed his hostility towards a Church that had cradled his youth. 'Little Daddy Combes', a kind of dictatorial and cross-grained pedagogue, his undersized frame draped in conventional frock-coat, declared war upon the Church as soon as he had taken office.

His immediate policy was to apply the law of 1901 in all its rigour. Certain quite lawful congregations had opened establishments without seeking authorization; and these, one hundred and twenty-five schools opened since 1st July 1901, were promptly closed. Three thousand which had been opened before that date were ordered to close within eight days, because authorization had not been sought in time. Some bishops protested, and their complaint was reported to the Council of State. The Government then considered the requests for authorization submitted by congregations of men. Only five were granted: those of the Trappists, the Brothers of St John of God, the Cistercians of Lérins, the African Missions and the White Fathers; all others were

[1] *Spiritualiste.* The word here denotes one who admits the existence of spirit as substantial reality.—TRANSLATOR.

refused. Fifteen hundred establishments were closed, though not without numerous incidents, demonstrations and still more violent acts of resistance, which in Brittany led even to bloodshed. Female congregations suffered the same fate. Minor measures completed the picture: crucifixes were removed from all court rooms; priests were forbidden to sit for competitive examinations; and the colonial minister, Doumergue, went so far as to expel the nuns from their hospitals in Indo-China, Senegal and Madagascar. When Leo XIII died, on 20th July 1903, Combes was preparing an assault on the authorized congregations, in order to 'smash the formidable educational machine erected in the name of a freedom inimical to freedom', and was picking a trumpery quarrel with the Vatican over the appointment of bishops.

Leo had followed events with bitter grief. After reading the text of the law of 1901, he had tried to make the best of it by ordering sixty male and four hundred and ten female congregations to seek authorization. But this final attempt at appeasement had clashed with the stubborn determination of little Homais.[1]

The Pope continued to receive news of what seemed to him very like the prelude to persecution. In private he railed against 'that devilish Monsieur Combès',[2] and on more than one occasion he assured his *entourage*: 'I was deceived when they told me that the Law of Associations was an unimportant formality, decieved when they told me it would be applied broadly and with goodwill, deceived yet again when they told me that the sacrifice of the Assumptionists would save the other congregations.' Nine days before his death Cardinal Mathieu said to him: 'France is not hostile to religion; only a small number of men are persecuting her.' To which His Holiness replied: 'No doubt, but they are the masters and are allowed to do so.'

It seemed, from the human standpoint, that his policy of *Ralliement* had failed. Far from showing gratitude for the confidence placed in her by the Pope, the Republic set herself up as an adversary not only of the Church but even of the Christian faith. Leo XIII might well be sorrowful; but he had in fact looked into the future. A day would come when the republican regime in France would be found reconciled with the Church. That option too, taken by the great pontiff, would be justified.

[1] The author likens Combes to the atheist chemist Homais in Flaubert's *Madame Bovary*.—TRANSLATOR.

[2] Leo invariably accentuated the final e in 'Combès'.

13. Catholics and Politics: the Problem of Christian Democracy

The serious difficulties which he encountered in France were certainly not without influence upon the attitude adopted by Leo XIII in his closing years towards the delicate question of what part Catholics could and ought to play in politics. Some historians have written of a radical change in the line followed hitherto by the Pope, and have even held that he retracted his earlier decision. Their view is altogether exaggerated. But various particular cases—e.g. that of the French Catholics during the Boulangist crisis and the Dreyfus affair, or that of the Italian Catholics—led him to state more precisely his thought on this point, which he had outlined at the start of his pontificate.

Except in the isolated case of Italy, there was certainly no question of banning Catholics from political activity: *Immortale Dei*, preceded and followed by the other documents, was perfectly clear in that respect. Provided the regime 'did not violate personal rights and left those of the Church intact', every Catholic might help to run it. But when a Catholic takes part in politics, does he act *qua* citizen or *qua* Catholic?

It is always difficult, as Leo XIII found on several occasions, to distinguish between the politics of Catholics and Catholic politics. His thought appears to have been based on the principle that Catholics as such ought to refrain from political commitment, in order not to jeopardize the Church herself, with whom public opinion is likely to identify them. In Italy, while strict insistence on the *non expedit* simplified the problem, Leo encouraged Catholics to take a hand in municipal affairs, and thereby showed that he agreed to their participation in public but not in political life. In France, Albert de Mun was highly esteemed by the Pope for his social activity; but when he sided openly with the monarchist cause, in a speech delivered during a Catholic congress, he was called to order. And even when he tried, in 1885, to set up a Catholic Party with a programme that included social ideas that were afterwards voiced by Leo himself, the Pope, who had recently honoured him with the Grand Cross of St Albert the Great, expressly disapproved his scheme on the grounds that it was likely to divide French Catholics.

In certain countries, however, where the regime was not in question, Leo XIII accepted the existence of self-styled Catholic parties. In Germany, for example, he found the *Zentrum* already powerfully organized, and the decisive aid he received from that Catholic party in his struggle with Bismarck inevitably earned his goodwill. In Switzerland, after the 'little *Kulturkampf*', he did not oppose the formation

of a Catholic party, though it was far from winning the support of all Catholics. So too in Belgium, where it would have been folly not to uphold a great political party that had enabled Catholics to drive the Liberals from power. In Austria the passing of 'antichristian' laws, notably one allowing divorce, was followed by a public message from Leo XIII, who bade Catholics unite in opposition. Accordingly the Pope offered no objection when some disciples of Vogelsang, among them Prince Aloys of Liechtenstein and Dr Lüger, created a Social Catholic Party whose aim was to carry on the struggle and promote the ideas of *Rerum Novarum*.

These undertakings, on the other hand, gave rise to numerous difficulties. In Germany the *Zentrum*, which had become the ruling party after the *Kulturkampf*, concerned itself less and less with the defence of Catholic interests, and more and more with that of the political interests of the Empire. Elsewhere the intervention of Catholics in politics had the immediate result of splitting Catholic society from top to bottom. This was particularly so in France, where the virtual failure of the *Ralliement* was due to such a cleavage. In Spain, notwithstanding the victory of Alfonso XII, Catholic 'Alfonsists' and 'Carlists' remained so bitterly hostile to one another that Leo XIII was obliged to issue his Encyclical *Cum multa*, in which he declared that 'while it is an error to separate religion completely from secular affairs, it is no less an error to identify religion with a political party', and an even worse error 'to say that those who belong to another party have virtually disowned the name of Catholics'. In Austria the birth of the Social Catholic Party had very similar consequences, partly because of attacks by its orators upon Catholics (including priests and bishops) whom they considered lukewarm, together with their violent anti-Semitism, and partly because of Conservative protests against a social policy that was deemed much too bold. Leo XIII had to decide this conflict, which he did with his customary prudence, supporting the Social Catholics in their efforts for the under-privileged, but requesting them to abstain from violence in any form.[1]

The question, however, which soon preoccupied the mind of Leo XIII as regards the political attitude of Catholics was that of Christian Democracy. This, in its noblest sense, is 'an attempt to introduce into public life the spirit of the Gospel and the moral principles propagated by the Catholic Church';[2] Its origins are well known: it derives from Lamennais and *L'Avenir*, from Lacordaire, from Ozanam and *L'Ère Nouvelle*,[3] all of whom attempted to rebuild society on genuinely Christian foundations. But the words 'Christian

[1] See Chapter IV, section 5.
[2] Maurice Vaussard, *Histoire de la démocratie chrétienne*, 1956.
[3] *The Church in an Age of Revolution*, Chapter IV, sections 5 and 6.

democracy' are a mere mask of generous intentions; they denote in fact a definite political system. Democracy, according to Littré,[1] is a form of government 'in which the people exercises sovereignty', or a 'free and above all egalitarian society in which the popular element has the preponderating influence', or again 'a political regime in which the interests of the masses are favoured or supposedly favoured'. To what extent can the Church accept such a regime, such a form of government, such a society? Leo XIII was no more opposed in principle to democracy than to any other regime. 'The greater or less participation of the people is not in itself reprehensible', says *Immortale Dei*; 'indeed at certain periods, and under the rule of certain laws, that participation may be the duty of citizens as well as to their advantage.' A later Encyclical, *Sapientiae christianae*, declared once again that the Church by no means rejected a constitution 'based on the popular element'. But was there not in the very principle of democracy something harmful to the Church? To recognize authority as residing exclusively in the people was surely to jeopardize the hierarchical system of the Church, in which authority is founded upon God and comes from above, not from below. Was the complete liberty sought by the democrats compatible with ecclesiastical discipline? Was egalitarianism, which Littré made the principal characteristic of a democratic society, compatible with the Christian acceptance of natural inequalities willed by God? Democracy was daughter of the Revolution; for Catholics, therefore, to accept or reject it was to settle the awkward problem of relations between the Church and the Revolution.

It was after 1891 that the Christian Democratic movement began to make astonishing headway. But, though deep-rooted and lofty-minded, it was also composite and confused. Encouraged by the Pope's Encyclical *Rerum Novarum*, it sometimes failed to distinguish the sphere of politics from that of social endeavour. For a very long time there was complete confusion between the 'Christian democrats' and the 'social Catholics'. Was it necessary, in order to promote the interests of the masses, to become active in the field of politics? Was political democracy essential to the inauguration of a more just and more Christian social system? The question was not raised in so many words, but it could not be left unanswered.

Meanwhile there was a notable increase of Catholic formations under the banner of democracy. In Belgium, from the Christian-Democrat movement, started by Gustave de Jaer in 1871, and from the Federation of Catholic Workers' Societies, there emerged the Belgian Democratic League founded by Verhaegen and the Abbé Poltier. Originally a social group, it soon embodied the tendency towards

[1] Author of the great *Dictionnaire de la langue française*.—TRANSLATOR.

political democracy in the Belgian Catholic Party. In France the Democratic Unions which arose in the Ardennes, the Nord, and then in Paris, professed to be mainly social, as did the 'democrat' Léon Harmel.[1] The trend, however, was much more political in the works of Père Maumus (e.g. *L'Église et la démocratie*), of the Abbés Klein and Calippe, of the Abbé Six in the periodical *La démocratie chrétienne*, but above all in the activities of a team of enthusiastic though unruly priests who became known, somewhat pejoratively, as 'the *abbés* Démocrates'. In Italy the young people of the *Opera dei Congressi* proclaimed themselves democrats. Throughout the Catholic world, wherever men were anxious to 'introduce the spirit of the Gospel into public life', there was found this inclination towards political activity, bringing with it the consequences we have noticed—insubordination and demagogy.

Leo XIII was not slow to perceive the danger. Serious incidents up and down Europe caused him to intervene. In Belgium the impetuous Abbé Daens, deputy of Alost, regarding the social activity of the Catholic Party as insufficiently democratic, started on a course of relentless demagogic propaganda, in which he made free use of the socialist vocabulary of class warfare, and then formed a Flemish Christian Democratic Party which distinguished itself by the violence of its language and by its rebellious attitude towards all episcopal and even papal authority. Expelled from the Democratic League and punished with ecclesiastical censures, Daens left the Church and allied himself with the Liberals and Socialists. A very similar episode occurred in Austria. Father Stojalowski, of the diocese of Lwow (Leopold) in Galacia, was a sincere Christian Democrat and social worker; but he was also an intemperate demagogue. His superiors tried in vain to control him, and he was eventually excommunicated. Unlike Daens, however, he ended by retracting and submitting to the Church.

The peril of deviation was everywhere. In Italy, in the very bosom of the *Opera dei Congressi*, while young Filippo Meda extolled a form of political activity that respected the decisions of the Holy See, the writings and speeches of Don Romolo Murri, one of the movement's leaders and a fervent democrat, sounded a disturbing note of independence and doctrinal rashness. The immediate consequence was described by the secretary of state as 'a tidal wave of protest and denunciation', and Murri's attitude led ultimately to his break with the Church.[2]

In France the *abbés démocrates* were likewise a source of grave anxiety. It is true that as journalists, as lecturers, as speakers at public meetings, and even as members of Parliament, they displayed extraordinary fervour and devotion in serving the cause of Christian truth

[1] See Chapter IV, section 2. [2] See Chapter V, section 7.

and social justice. But their conduct on the whole was not that expected of priests: in polemics the majority went too far, not disdaining to employ the coarsest demagogic methods; nor was obedience their outstanding virtue. Some fell without hesitation into the most deplorable excesses. Among these was the Abbé Dabry of Avignon, founder of *La Vie catholique*; his extremist ideas, together with his violent abuse of other priests and even of certain bishops, resulted in his condemnation by Rome. He refused to submit, preferring the isolation of hopeless rebellion. The majority did not proceed to such lengths. It included the Abbé Naudet, director of *Le Monde*; the Abbé Fesch, an excellent journalist; the Abbé Gayraud, author of doctrinal works on Christian democracy; the Abbé Lemire (1853–1928), most famous of them all, who was destined to a long and difficult career in politics; and—somewhat apart, because of his unwillingness to be classified with the others—the Abbé Théodore Garnier, founder of the newspaper *Le peuple français*, a remarkable propagandist and formidable polemist. All these *abbés démocrates* accomplished a task whose social importance none can dispute; but it is not hard to appreciate the concern felt in high places by those who heard them speak of 'the consecration of King People' or 'the anointing and coronation of Democracy'—an unsurpassable admixture of the religious with the political, to the grave damage of the former.

It was in order to put an end to such deviations that Leo XIII published his Encyclical *Graves de Communi* (18th January 1901), in which he proposed to define the correct meaning of Christian democracy. 'The expression', he said, 'offends many virtuous people, who consider it to have an equivocal and dangerous significance. They fear that it may indicate a preference for popular government over other forms of government, that it may restrict the virtue of Christian religion to the interests of the people alone, and lastly that it may hide an intention to disparage all authority, both civil and religious.' The criticism was not unjustified. In what sense ought the phrase to be understood? 'The expression "Christian democracy"', Leo continued, 'must not be understood in a political sense. Etymologically, of course, "democracy" denotes the popular regime; but in the present circumstances its use must exclude all political meaning and must endow it with no signification other than that of a benevolent Christian activity with regard to the people.' Professor Giuseppe Toniolo, an authorized commentator on papal thought, added the following interpretation: Christian democracy must be defined as 'that arrangement of civil society in which all social forces, juridical and economic, in the plenitude of their hierarchical development, co-operate proportionally for the common good, finally achieving an increase of advantages for the lower classes'.

This definition, in fact, brought Christian democracy within the limits of Social Catholicism and subjected the political order to that of charity—a conclusion whose importance must be emphasized. Towards the end of his long pontificate the Pope who is considered to have been more 'political' than any other of the nineteenth century withdrew Catholics from the political arena so that they might become active in truly religious, apostolic and charitable work; a proof, if such be needed, that his entire policy had been Christian and nothing else. At every step, in the realm of diplomacy as elsewhere, Leo XIII, the Pope of bold options, had done nothing but serve what his successor Pius X would one day call 'the interests of God'.

CHAPTER IV

THE TRIUMPHANT MARCH OF SOCIAL CATHOLICISM

1. The Decisive Date

'THEN, on 15th May 1891, rang out the voice so long awaited, a voice which had not been daunted by difficulties or enfeebled by age, but which, with vigorous daring, set the footsteps of mankind on a new road in the social field.' Thus, in *Quadragesimo Anno*, Pius XI celebrated the fortieth anniversary of Leo XIII's Encyclical *Rerum Novarum*. In 1961 the voice of another pope was raised to mark the importance of that same document. 'Rarely', said John XXIII in *Mater et Magistra*, 'have the words of a pope aroused so universal an echo. . . . A new path of activity opened before the Church. The supreme Pastor, making his own the sufferings, complaints and aspirations of the humble and oppressed, once again stood forward as the champion of their rights.'

That tribute paid to the first 'social' pope by two of his successors has been ratified by history. Of all the options taken by Leo XIII, this was to prove the most fruitful. The principles, of course, were already there, contained in Scripture and Tradition; and many Christians were running their factories accordingly. But the time had come when those principles must be applied to circumstances and expounded in a single body of doctrine. That was accomplished in 1891.

It is not suggested that *Rerum Novarum* marked the historical beginning of that great movement which was later called Social Catholicism. For more than half a century Christians with no official mandate had had the courage to raise certain problems and even to propose solutions. The question now was whether the infallible Magisterium would grapple with those problems. By taking upon himself the preparatory work, and by adopting its results, Leo XIII gave the weight of his supreme authority to what was as yet a more or less vague aspiration and subject of discussion. That is why 1891 is recognized as a decisive date and *Rerum Novarum* as a document of capital importance.

The social problem had been raised long since, in the first thirty years of the nineteenth century,[1] by Chateaubriand and Lamennais. Others had protested against the conditions to which the workers were

[1] *The Church in an Age of Revolution*, Chapter VI, which is briefly summarized here.

subjected by the growth of large-scale industry, and emphasized the peril confronting faith among the proletarian masses. They had believed the gospel and the teaching of the Church capable of solving those urgent problems.

France had produced the forerunners of Social Catholicism. Some, such as the Vicomte Alban de Villeneuve-Bargemont and the Comte Armand de Melun, were aristocrats anxious to stem the tide of revolution. Others were disciples of Lamennais, among them Charles de Coux and the Abbé Gerbet, or Christian revolutionaries like Buchez. The two groups were linked by Frédéric Ozanam.

Those early strivings of Social Catholicism in France were interrupted by the terrible June Days which followed the revolution of 1848. The left-wing tendency had been annihilated; the other, urged by subsidies from Napoleon III and by the theories of Le Play, had moved in the direction of 'paternalism'. All that remained of any significance were the achievements of Maurice Maignen on behalf of young workers. The torch, however, had been relit elsewhere: in Spain by Balmes, in Italy by Father Taparelli d'Azeglio, but above all in Germany by Mgr von Ketteler, Kolping, Schorlemer and Baron von Vogelsang.

Unfortunately Catholic opinion had remained indifferent to their efforts. Nobler souls clung to standard forms of charity; the rest, as Albert de Mun observed, were 'a little worse than worthless' in the field of social endeavour.[1] About 1870 there were scarcely a dozen socially minded bishops. Pius IX, while condemning liberalism, had said nothing about economic liberalism, which resulted in the exploitation of man by man.

2. The Founders

The twenty years following the Franco-Prussian War were of capital importance. The movement gained strength and impetus. An ever-increasing number of men, in many lands and from all walks of life, became aware of these problems, to which some devoted the remainder of their lives. The principles of Christian social teaching were debated in such a way that some official pronouncement by the Church seemed indispensable.

To what must those developments be attributed? To the progress

[1] In this respect they were on a footing with the least Christian elements of the ruling classes—disciples of Renan and Taine; anticlericals like Gambetta, who in 1872 declared: 'There is no social question.' In the same year the French Chamber appointed a commission of inquiry into the social situation, and its report, drawn up by the Duc d'Audiffret-Pasquier, concluded that all was perfectly normal, that the working class had no reason to complain of its lot, and, moreover, was not complaining!

of ideas of justice in the human conscience? To the result of so much generous striving? Not entirely. External factors played a part. First there were heavy clouds on the social horizon, many signs that the working class had nearly reached a point at which its wrath could no longer be contained. The violence of the Commune had been in some respects indicative of social revolution. The economic crisis, whose effects became apparent from 1884 onwards, brought proletarian reactions in its wake: strikes became more and more frequent in the United States, in Belgium, in Britain, in Germany and in France.

These events threw the social problem into strong relief. Sincere Catholics experienced something more than natural fear: conscience bade them grapple not only with the forces of revolution, which precipitated such disturbances, but also with the more fundamental evils which provided an excuse for such unrest. The period 1871–91 witnessed a notable expansion of Socialism; not of the old French school as expounded by Fourier or Proudhon, which, apart from its anticlerical tirades, was by no means antichristian in its social teaching, but Marxism—atheist and materialist. Those were the years during which *Das Kapital* appeared,[1] and it was largely by way of counter-attack that the Social Catholics set to work. Several contemporary documents gave warning that unless the Church managed to reach the working class, the enemy would do so. Thus in 1878, long before *Rerum Novarum*, Leo XIII, alarmed by attempts upon the lives of the German, Spanish and Italian sovereigns, issued his Encyclical *Quod Apostolici*, condemning 'that sect of men who call themselves by such near-barbaric names as socialists, communists and nihilists, and who strive to overthrow the foundations of civil society'. It was not enough to condemn men and doctrines; they must be opposed with effective barriers.

Such were the circumstances in which, during those twenty years, Social Catholicism made a memorable advance. Amid the intense activity we are about to describe, three basic factors should be noted. First, Catholics became more aware of the existence of a social duty, a duty distinct from and prior to that of charity. Second, they realized that the Gospel and ecclesiastical Tradition contained the data of a social morality or, rather, of a 'doctrine' in the theological sense, namely an object of instruction. Third, they considered that 'while the exposition of new principles in the social field was the business of qualified theologians, the application of those principles was the duty of laymen . . .'[2]

[1] See Chapter I, section 8.

[2] J. Folliet. See bibliographical notes.

3. The Triumvirate of Social Catholics in France

In this undertaking Frenchmen again led the way, elaborating the doctrines and taking the initiatives that were to serve as a pattern. While the representatives of earlier teams continued their efforts, a new generation came upon the stage, three members of which played such important parts that even today Social Catholicism remembers its indebtedness to them.

One day in May 1871, while the Versaillais were besieging Paris, Général Ladmirault was inspecting his outposts, accompanied by one of his orderly officers, Lieutenant Albert de Mun. A party of soldiers came along, carrying a man covered in blood. 'Who is he?' asked the general. 'A rebel,' they answered. Then, sitting up with a final effort and pointing an accusing finger at the two officers: 'You are the rebels!' cried the dying man.

Those words stuck like an arrow in the young lieutenant's mind, but the problem was not altogether new to him. As prisoners of war in 1870 he and a fellow officer, René de la Tour du Pin, had become interested in questions to which they had never previously given a thought. Ernest Keller's book, *L'Encyclique du 3 décembre et les principes de 1789*, had convinced them that 'the French Revolution, by substituting for Christian society a new order based on purely human principles, had been the cause and origin of the many evils which had subsequently overwhelmed France and the rest of Europe'. They had also heard much about Mgr Ketteler and Kolping. The tragedy of the Commune completed their enlightenment. 'A secret summons', wrote Albert de Mun, 'revealed to us the goal to which those events were going to direct our lives.' For him, as for La Tour du Pin, that secret summons was a vocation.

The first opportunity towards fulfilment of that vocation was afforded by one man. After the Commune, La Tour du Pin and De Mun were asked by Ladmirault, now Governor of Paris, to conduct an inquiry into the origins of the insurrection. They were given an office in the Louvre, and there they received many persons capable of supplying the necessary information. Among these was Maurice Maignen,[1] who had conceived the idea of forming an association in which adult workers would labour for the betterment and rechristianization of the proletariat. The *Cercle Montparnasse* was his first achievement.

The meeting of these three men was decisive. Standing at a window, pointing at the calcined shreds of the Tuileries, Maignen exclaimed: 'Yes, it's horrible. . . . But who is responsible? Not the people, the

[1] *The Church in an Age of Revolution*, Index.

real people, those who work and suffer. They are not the criminals who have burned Paris. . . . It is *you* who are responsible, you the rich, the great, the happy, who have spent so much time amusing yourselves within those shattered walls; you who pass by the people without seeing them, without recognizing them; you who know nothing of their souls, of their needs, of their sufferings. I live with them, and I tell you on their behalf: they do not hate you, but they ignore you as you ignore them; go to them with an open heart, offer them your hand, and you'll see that they will understand you. . . . I am alone: what can I do? If you come with me, we will conquer France and lay her at the feet of our God.'[1] On the following Sunday, Albert de Mun, dressed in the full uniform of a light cavalry officer, went to address the *Cercle Montparnasse*.

Thus was born that 'social vocation' which was to govern the whole existence of those two men. One of them, Albert de Mun (1841–1914), whose eloquence and commanding figure made a deep impression on the masses, was to be spokesman of the movement at congresses and in Parliament. The other, René de la Tour du Pin (1834–1925), more reserved but better equipped intellectually, became its thinker and doctrinaire. Long united by friendship, they never disagreed except upon one important point—the *Ralliement*, which Mun accepted in obedience to Leo XIII, but which La Tour du Pin rejected because of his royalist allegiance. Their origins, their temperaments and their reading explain the trends of their social activity and account for their limitations. Maignen had told them it was their business to reconcile the governing class with the people, by making it heedful of their suffering and fraternal. Was that generous design sufficient?

At about the same time, in another sphere, a third man awoke to a social vocation no less exacting, but which he interpreted in a very different way. Léon Harmel (1829–1915) owned a textile factory which his father had established in the valley of the Suippe, not far from Rheims, a site whose rural charm had earned for it the name Val-des-Bois. Harmel had proved himself a competent industrialist and a kindly employer. His father too had lived among his own workers; in 1840 he had introduced 'collective pay' and founded a savings bank, which was followed in 1846 by a mutual benefit society. About 1870 Léon himself inaugurated further means of social improvement and thought out the elements of his Christian Corporation. None of the problems raised by technical requirements escaped his notice or left him indifferent to their solution. Moreover, with a view to strengthening Christian ties between his workmen, he had built a chapel in the factory and organized retreats. Then, in 1869, he had founded the

[1] De Mun, *Ma vocation sociale*, p. 62.

Association Intime, a confraternity of men and women who dedicated themselves by vow to the rechristianization of the working class.

Harmel possessed those conjoint virtues which Bergson discovers in the mystics: a sense of mundane reality and an irresistible urge towards 'the things that are above'. This admirable Christian, a devout Franciscan tertiary and stern ascetic, was at the same time an unusually competent man of affairs. He radiated charm, and his goodness was manifest, even though his candour was sometimes abrupt. He strove for fifty years, with all his vast energy, to establish that 'Christian social order' of which, like his friends De Mun and La Tour du Pin, he dreamed.

Nevertheless between him and them there were marked differences of outlook. Léon Harmel, grandson of a worker, saw no need 'to go to the people'. He did not believe that the one thing necessary was to rouse the fortunate of this world. What he desired was to bring about the social advancement of the masses. Far removed from paternalism, of which he is often accused, he managed to give French Social Catholicism a slant that proved to be that of the future. One phrase sums up his attitude: 'The good of the worker through the worker, and with him, never without him, and *a fortiori* never in spite of him.'

4. Social Endeavour in France Before the Encyclical

The most notable achievement of French Social Catholics was the *Œuvre des Cercles catholiques d'ouvriers,* originally an extension of the *Cercle Montparnasse*. When De Mun and La Tour du Pin answered Maignen's appeal, the *Cercle Montparnasse* was released from its somewhat narrow confines; and De Mun had no difficulty in winning the support of numerous friends: Brissac, La Bégassière, Récamier, Marolles, Benoit d'Azy, Clermont-Tonnerre. Some famous names appeared on the committee lists of the *Œuvre des Cercles*.

Branches were soon established in the provinces, as well as in several districts of the capital; the episcopate as a whole favoured the movement, and by 1884 there were as many as four hundred circles with fifty thousand members.[1] Realizing that success depended upon something more than just hoisting the flag, the Central Committee appointed a Council of Studies. A militant newspaper, *Association catholique*, was founded, and the *Œuvre des Cercles* believed that the gulf between the classes had been crossed.[2]

[1] Each circle was governed by a committee, which was represented in turn on a regional committee, while a Central Committee directed the work as a whole.

[2] Armand de Melun, the most illustrious representative of the preceding generation, agreed to encourage the new undertaking, though he considered Albert de Mun as too systematically anti-revolutionary and insufficiently liberal.

In fact, however, such hopes were largely chimerical. While Léon Harmel, as secretary-general of the *Œuvre*, had done much to orientate it towards the true working class (that of the industrial labourers), there were very few proletarians in the circles, which consisted mainly of artisans and servants. Moreover, though such people as Père Forbes, S.J., Mgr Freppel, Henri Joly and Claudio Januet considered the undertaking subversive, it was in fact little more than plain paternalism, and its boasted corporatism was falsified by the desire of its upper- and middle-class directors to 'control' the workers for their own good. There were other reasons that gave grounds for suspecting that the work would fail to make headway. Albert de Mun and his friends presented the movement as an organ of the counter-revolution—a fact which disturbed Léon Harmel—and even of the royalist cause, which was hardly calculated to attract the workers. Again, the ruling classes whom it sought to influence remained virtually inactive; the clergy were lukewarm; and the approval of many bishops was purely verbal. The *Œuvre des Cercles*, however, continued on its way until 1891; and if its progress was not destined to endure, it must at least be recognized as having exposed the social problem to numerous Catholics.

Associated with the *Œuvre* through his desire to collaborate in an enterprise whose purpose he admired without always approving its means, Léon Harmel, while trying to breathe a new spirit into the work, preached by example. The Val-des-Bois witnessed a series of innovations which in those days appeared quite astonishing. The principle was that 'benefits conferred by employers are ineffectual if they are not based upon a workers' association'. The result was a close network of religious and secular institutions which enveloped the lives of the workers from the cradle to the grave, while a council consisting of the employer and elected workers' delegates met every fortnight to regulate the entire system.

Now Harmel was unwilling that the light that shone in his own factory should be hidden beneath a bushel. He set out his principles in a *Manuel de la corporation*, and when the law of 1884 authorized syndicates he advocated the setting up of autonomous trade unions. At the same time, together with Robert (a locksmith and former socialist) and the parish priest of Saint-Rémy, he founded at Rheims the first Circle of Social Studies. Turning then to his fellow employers, he appealed to them for a united social effort and begged them to cease thinking of themselves as little autocrats in their factories. But his words, alas, woke very few echoes. Indefatigable, he travelled all over France to spread his ideas. To Rome he led a party of one hundred Christian employers, and subsequently (1887–91) three huge workers' pilgrimages. It is hard to imagine the vigour with which he alone, the

saintly master of Val-des-Bois, endowed Social Catholicism during that period of growth.

Meanwhile Social Catholicism made progress also in the field of legislation, thanks again to Albert de Mun. Elected deputy for Pontivy in 1881, he accomplished a twofold task: on the one hand he expounded the hitherto unfamiliar principles of Social Catholicism, refuting the objections of Conservatives and Liberals; on the other he tabled or supported laws intended to improve the workers' lot. Catholics thus contributed a great deal to the passing of those social laws which did honour to the French Chamber between 1884 and 1898: a law on syndicates; another on accidents sustained in course of employment; another on female and child labour, which limited their working day to eleven hours; and yet another on arbitration in labour disputes, which De Mun proposed to make obligatory.

These measures bore fruit. In the Nord employers combined to ameliorate the workers' life, their first move being the introduction of Sunday rest. Elsewhere the *Cercles chrétiens d'études sociales*, derived from Harmel's foundation at Rheims, gradually became distinct from the *Œuvre des Cercles*, inasmuch as the workers, instead of being mere listeners, were invited to contribute the results of their experience; in some circles they alone deliberated and voted. In 1882 Christian syndicalism erected its first landmarks in the agricultural world, where Hyacinthe de Gailhard-Bancel, a landowner of Allex in Bas-Dauphiné, instituted the first agricultural syndicates.[1]

Over and above such concrete achievements, the most important result of these efforts was the formation within the Catholic Church of a militant wing determined upon action. A series of congresses brought together the most active elements, who were often joined by delegates from Belgium, Italy and Germany.

The movement, however, could not fail to provoke adverse criticism. Even the paternalist *Œuvre des Cercles* itself was violently attacked. A succession of articles by Henri Joly in *Le Correspondant* ranked Albert de Mun and his friends with the Socialists. In the *Revue des Deux-Mondes* (1885) Comte d'Haussonville wrote: 'Why seek to involve the Church in questions that are none of her concern?'[2] Père Forbes treated Léon Harmel as a 'Utopian', while the Liberals insisted that wages corresponded not to a man's needs but to his work. Distinguished members of the clergy, too, were opposed to Social Catholicism, among them such advanced thinkers as Mgr Dupanloup and *a fortiori* the more conservative Mgr Freppel, Bishop of Angers. The latter was fully awake to the social problem and joined De Mun

[1] They were of the so-called mixed type, including both employers and workers.

[2] Between 1885 and 1891, under Brunetière's influence, the *Revue* changed its attitude towards the social problem.

in backing the social laws; but he considered that the Social Catholics were going too far. It is not certain whether Freppel was thinking of them or of the Socialists when, in a sermon at La Madeleine, he attacked 'the demagogues who are exploiting the terrible problem of suffering'. At all events, shortly before publication of the Encyclical, he went to Rome and begged Leo XIII 'not to speak on the social question'.[1] But the very liveliness of the opposition says much for the importance of the Social Catholic movement in France.

5. From Mgr von Ketteler to Mgr Doutreloux

In Germany the impetus had been so strong that it continued to produce results. Mgr von Ketteler died in 1877, but he left disciples who followed his programme; and the social laws passed in 1878 and subsequent years became known as Ketteler's Laws. Canon Christoph von Moufang, a pupil of the great archbishop, founded an Association for the Wellbeing of Workers. Father Hitze and others organized the German Catholic People's Association, which in 1890 became the *Volksverein*. Kolping's *Gesselvereinen*, with their well-kept houses, their orderly meetings, their youth centres and their newspapers, were so firmly established that fifty years later Adolf Hitler himself was unable to destroy them. Meanwhile Schorlemer's *Bauernvereinen* counted their membership in tens of thousands; Brandt formed a union of Catholic employers; and Father Darbach of Trier founded the first 'social bank'. These efforts were supported by the *Zentrum*,[2] which exerted considerable influence in the passing of social laws, in obtaining the Imperial Rescripts of 1880 and in the International Labour Conference convoked by Wilhelm II at Berlin in 1890.

These German Social Catholics were men of action rather than theorists. But Karl von Vogelsang continued his doctrinal work in Austria. Hostile to economic liberalism, he developed his corporative theses by demanding that a State-controlled organization should safeguard the workers' rights. His disciples went still further: Belcrede wanted an obligatory system of guilds, Kufstein the application of socialism in Christian form.

Their teaching was re-echoed throughout the Catholic cantons of Switzerland. Though mistrustful of revolutionary ideas, that small country was the meeting point of liberal, radical and socialist exiles; and there the Workers' International had first seen the light of day. A Swiss Socialist Party was born in 1888. But the forces of revolution were already opposed by three Social Catholic movements: the

[1] F. Hayward, *Léon XIII*, p. 229.

[2] See Chapter III, section 7.

Piusverein, the *Fédération ouvrière romande* and the German Federation, which in 1887 was amalgamated with the *Fédération générale ouvrière*.

Two outstanding personalities emerged in the realm of Swiss Social Catholicism. One was Gaspard Decurtins (1855–1916), who was for many years the life and soul of the Swiss workers' movement. He had come to Social Christianity by way of Socialism, which he abandoned after reading St Thomas, and he joined Python and others in forming a group determined upon rousing the Catholic conscience. Thanks to him Swiss syndicalism, then in its infancy, adopted a fundamentally Christian outlook; and it was he too that asked the National Council of Berne to take the initiative of suggesting to all countries an international control of labour.

The second notable figure, whose influence later spread far beyond the framework of the cantons, was Mgr Mermillod (1824–92), whom we have seen at grips with the civil authorities during the 'little *Kulturkampf*'.[1] Together with Manning, Langénieux and Gibbons he was one of the first four 'social cardinals'.[2] It was through the influence of Decurtins and Mermillod that Fribourg became a centre of doctrinal studies, where in 1885 began those international meetings of Social Catholics known to history as the *Union de Fribourg*.[3]

Belgium had awakened to the social problem long before 1871. Traditionally linked with the French movements, she had taken part in the birth of Social Catholicism. *L'Avenir* and then *L'Ère nouvelle* had had readers there. The University of Louvain had been the first to create a chair of social studies, with Charles de Coux as its first occupant. It was in Belgium too, in 1893, that Edouard Ducpétiaux, one of the founders of sociology, began his great study of pauperism. By about 1870 the Belgian Social Catholic movement appeared to be torn between two sympathies: Charles Perrin, successor of De Coux at Louvain, inclined towards authoritarian corporatism, while the philosopher François Huet and the journalist Adolphe Bartels, founder of *Débat social*, preferred a democratic tendency.

In the years immediately following 1871 Social Catholicism was extraordinarily vigorous in that small country, where economic life was intense and Socialism was making progress. A number of young men from the upper classes (Verhaegen, Carton de Wiart, Mabille, Helleputte) became interested in social problems, as did the Belgian clergy, whose influence was still great. The social movement profited by this new impetus. Looking back to her past, Belgium found an example of highly successful trade associations in the Flemish guilds, which now became her inspiration. Mutual benefit societies and

[1] See Chapter III, section 4. [2] Mermillod was raised to the purple in 1890.
[3] See section 7 of the present chapter.

'Catholic workers' houses' sprang up on all sides. The movement was corporative, more or less paternalist; but within the *Fédération des Œuvres ouvrières catholiques*, founded in 1868, there was a tendency to let the workers play a more active part, a tendency that became more pronounced after 1891 in Helleputte and Verhaegen's *Ligue démocratique belge*. The *Boerenbund*, a union of peasants formed in 1890, proposed 'to work for the religious, intellectual and social progress of its members'. Both *Ligue* and *Boerenbund* were copied in the Netherlands. One final undertaking, crowned with success, will show how prominent a place Social Catholicism occupied in Belgium. This was the *Congrès des Œuvres sociales*, attended by delegates representing every shade of opinion. Its moving spirit was Mgr Doutreloux, Bishop of Liège, friend of the miners and other industrial workers, as well as one of the most attractive figures of that period.

6. New Awakenings: Italy, Britain and America

Thus in the twenty years preceding the Encyclical, Social Catholicism enjoyed a brilliant career. Spain alone of the great Christian nations lagged behind; not because the question was irrelevant, but because anything suggestive of the Revolution was heartily detested in that country, where trouble among the miners and peasants in 1873 shocked public opinion and led to Serrano's dictatorship. Consequently there was not much activity on the part of Social Catholics.

In Italy the situation was more encouraging. Only a few Catholics, among whom were Archbishop Joachim Pecci of Perugia and a small group headed by Father Taparelli d'Azeglio (*d.* 1862), had as yet begun to take an interest in the social question. Heroic charity was practised by men such as Don Bosco and Giuseppe Cottolengo, but social work was virtually non-existent; earlier institutions, e.g. the famous 'people's banks', which had been of great assistance to farmers and small tradesmen from the fifteenth to the eighteenth century, had vanished. The year 1871, however, marked a turning-point. Various groups applied themselves to the study of those problems, which took a rather different form in a country where industrialization was less advanced than elsewhere. It was by way of reaction against Socialism that Social Catholicism first reared its head. Costa and Berni, former Garibaldians who had fought with the communards in Paris, started a campaign of popular agitation, especially among agricultural labourers, to whom they promised partition of land. The Catholic answer came from Mgr Bonomelli, Bishop of Cremona, whose pastoral letter on *Property and Socialism* denounced those really responsible for the Costa-Berni propaganda—the great landowners who ignored the

needs of their workers, subjected them to iniquitous contracts, and, being themselves unbelievers, were quite incapable of setting a true Christian example.

Bonomelli's philippic marked the entry of Social Catholicism upon the Italian stage. The movement, however, was destined to remain predominantly speculative until 1891: its chief concern was to study the problems and discover doctrinal solutions rather than to provide concrete remedies. This effort was indeed somewhat confused; but it should not be underestimated, for it helped to supply the materials of *Rerum Novarum*. A leading part was played by Taparelli's disciples—Fathers Liberatore and Zigliara, Professor Niccolò Rezzara of Bergamo, and Mgr (afterwards Cardinal) Jacobini in Rome—but above all by Giuseppe Toniolo.[1] The *Opera dei Congressi*[2] assigned one of its five sections to the study of social problems. The *Circolo di San Pietro*, encouraged by the Pope and directed by Mgr Jacobini, was a group of aristocrats and intellectuals dedicated to the same task. At Bologna, two years before the Encyclical, Toniolo assembled a committee of ten persons whose duty it would be to draw up a programme. The result of that meeting was the *Unione cattolica di studi sociali*, which later did much to propagate the teaching of *Rerum Novarum*; its members included Contardo Ferrini and Giuseppe Sarto.

Practical achievements were neither numerous nor highly original, but they were better than nothing at all. The principal concern of Social Catholics was to relieve the misery of rural populations by means of farmers' unions, sick funds, penny banks and suchlike. At Rome the *Circolo di San Pietro* founded night shelters and established mutual benefit societies. Meanwhile at Schio, the 'Manchester of Italy', Alessandro Rossi, owner of a large textile factory, turned his business into a 'Christian corporation'.

The social problem was likewise considered urgent in Britain and the U.S.A., where the Church, being a minority, might well have declined to lead the way. In both countries, however, Catholics took advantage of a violent crisis to declare their views on this grave matter. On 13th August 1889 the London dockers went on strike against excessive hours and insufficient wages; other trades were affected, and two hundred and fifty thousand workers were soon idle. Cardinal Manning, Archbishop of Westminster, intervened. Some of his pastorals had already deplored the miserable state of Ireland's peasantry, had flayed the system of female and child labour in the factories and had even criticized the omnipotence of capitalism 'against which the wage-earner is helpless'. 'The purpose of life', said Manning, 'is not simply to produce endless yards of cotton', and 'freedom of the home is far more important than free trade'.

[1] See section 12 of the present chapter. [2] See Chapter III, section 10.

When the dockers' strike paralysed the Port of London he called a meeting of employers and workers' delegates. The latter hesitated, regarding the employers' concessions as inadequate. Whereupon Manning declared: 'I myself will go and talk to the strikers; twenty-five thousand of them are my sons, they will listen to me.' And it was indeed by the Cardinal's arbitration that the strike was ended. *The Times* was sternly critical, and one employer roared: 'Your Eminence's conduct is plain Socialism.' 'In your eyes maybe,' answered Manning; 'in mine it is just Christianity.'

A similar attitude was adopted by the leaders of the American episcopate: they too headed the social movement hitherto non-existent in the United States. Two names are outstanding: Cardinal Gibbons, Archbishop of Baltimore, and Mgr Ireland, Archbishop of St Paul, Minnesota. Gibbons had first-hand experience of the world of labour, having belonged to it; Ireland had received a more intellectual training, but he possessed a fiery temper. Both were remarkable for a characteristic which continues to distinguish the majority of American bishops, who consider themselves as trainers of men rather than as administrators.

One curious affair showed the United States that the Catholic Church, though still more or less despised, was capable of vigorous action in the social field. About 1885 the economic situation was deteriorating, and the working-class problem had become urgent. Wages fell and the cost of living rose, while the rapid acquisition of huge fortunes opened a yet wider breach between the classes. A workers' association was formed, and it soon had seven hundred and fifty thousand members. Calling themselves Knights of Labor, they had adopted some harmless esoteric rites in the manner of secret societies; and when they tried to establish themselves in Canada, the episcopate denounced them to Rome as freemasons. The bishops of the United States, however, did not share that view. Powderly, who had founded the association, was a Catholic, as also were a majority of its officials and more than half the Knights. Was it not an admirable means of bringing the working class into contact with Catholicism? The ten principal archbishops pronounced in favour of the association, and Cardinal Gibbons sent to Rome a detailed memorandum. The movement was perhaps open to criticism in some respects; but its leaders were prepared to correct anything that might be judged reprehensible, 'on condition that they were allowed to struggle against avarice and opression'. 'Let the Church', concluded His Eminence, 'take care not to rebuff the working classes when they try to improve their lot. She must never allow herself to be suspected of indifference to their progress, of contempt for sentiments of justice, of rigour and severity towards their proceedings. To lose influence over the

people would be to lose the future.' [1] He won the day. His warning summarized the aims of Social Catholicism, which were likewise those proclaimed by Leo XIII soon afterwards.

7. La Tour du Pin and the 'Union de Fribourg'

In many countries, then, Catholics had become attentive to the social problem. Did that mean that they held a common doctrine? No doubt their ultimate aims were identical: to bring about the reign of justice, to give the labourer his due, to prevent class warfare. But when it came to working out a concept of social order there were substantial differences of opinion.

One man's influence, however, was almost universal—that of Frédéric Le Play.[2] His method, the study of particular social case-histories in a series of monographs, with a view to drawing up rules of conduct, had been extremely popular during the last years of Napoleon III. But it was possible to quote Le Play in support of many and widely divergent theories. Violently hostile to the 'false dogma of providential equality', derived from the Revolution, he also had some hard things to say about 'the rich who fail in their duty to the poor', about 'manufacturers who sweep together hosts of underprivileged people into hideous depravity'. He thought that society should be conceived as some huge family of the ancient type, whose *paterfamilias* would be represented by the 'governing classes', conscious of their obligations and determined to make the 'lower classes' happy. That was the principle of 'paternalism', which was not necessarily Christian but to which many employers adhered.

A great many Social Catholics, on the other hand, regarded paternalism as inadequate. Instead of relying on the goodwill of the governing classes, was it not better, as Buchez had maintained, to found the social order upon the basis of inter-class collaboration, by creating or re-creating institutions that would make it obligatory? About 1880 the idea of association had begun to prove the most acceptable, and it had become fashionable to use the word 'corporation' as denoting the system that would ensure organic collaboration of the classes. But the term itself was ambiguous. What was it meant to signify in the context? The guild of the *ancien régime*? Or the State organism advocated by Vogelsang? Or Léon Harmel's great family, which was at the same time a confraternity? From this tangle

[1] This was the occasion on which Cardinal Gibbons spoke some words which are often quoted: 'Yesterday it was with dynasties that the Church had to deal; today it is with the people.'

[2] *The Church in an Age of Revolution*, Chapter VI, section 18.

of dispute one man emerged and made his mark by the very power of his thought: René de la Tour du Pin. He alone among Christians stated the social problem in its entirety and was thereby destined to wield an enormous influence which continues to be felt. Immediately after the Commune he had studied Le Play; then, as military attaché at Vienna, he had pondered the teaching of Vogelsang. Finally Léon Harmel, whom he met through the *Œuvre des Cercles*, had told him of his own experiment at Val-des-Bois. It was in fact through the articles modestly entitled 'Avis', which he wrote for the *Œuvre*'s journal *Association catholique*, that La Tour du Pin first presented his doctrine, before expounding it much later and more fully in two books *Vers un Ordre social chrétien* (1907) and *Aphorismes de politique sociale* (1909).

La Tour du Pin was a bold critic, of whom Karl Marx might have approved. He described as 'barbarous' the law of supply and demand in the field of labour. Of capitalism he said: 'It is the exploitation of the work of all for the sole profit of a few.' He foretold that 'the employers would one day see the popular wave gradually tear from them all that they would not willingly concede'. He claimed for the worker not only a living wage, but also a 'natural wage' to cover risks of accident, sickness and old age. At the same time he declared that those measures of strict justice still seemed to him inadequate, for they would enable the workers to achieve 'neither economic progress nor social advancement'. What he desired was a remoulding of society within the framework of the corporative regime. That would mean discarding both the 'anarchic freedom' which leaves the worker defenceless against his employer, and also the revolutionary idea that authority and freedom are mutually antagonistic. The social order must rest upon institutions in which authority is an expression of the free will of all.

In practice, the corporative regime would operate as follows. In every locality all those, whether employers or workers, who belonged to the same trade would form a *corps d'État*, and might, if they wished form themselves into a 'professional association', the equivalent of a modern trade union. At higher levels (provincial, then national) the 'corporation' would combine, without confusing, all the elements which enable a given trade to function. It would organize the conditions of labour, fix remuneration, control the engagement and dismissal of workmen. It would have its tribunals: a corporative council to prevent disputes between employer and employed, a disciplinary council to settle private litigation. A common fund, to which all would subscribe, would finance trade schools and a system of assurance. The employers would stand at the head of these institutions, but they would so so within the framework and under the control of the workers. Since the corporation would enjoy judicial prerogatives,

and since its decisions would be legally binding, no abuse of power would be possible. Moreover the 'corporative State', the supreme authority emanating from the will of the corporations, would see that their decisions were applied.

La Tour du Pin was convinced that 'historical evolution' would ensure the triumph of a system whose purpose was to abolish social injustice through obligatory collaboration of the classes. To what extent did the guiding principle, which was to substitute association of persons for that of stocks and shares, take account of the typical phenomenon of capitalism—the concentration of capital, which tends to place entire responsibility for a business in the hands of a few persons? At the time when La Tour du Pin wrote, the phenomenon was far from being as apparent as it is today.

In the years before the Encyclical the corporation, firmly constructed and regulated by a supreme authority, seemed to many Catholics to offer some chance of remoulding society according to the principles of Christian justice.

That, however, does not imply agreement among Social Catholics as to the means. The school of Angers opposed the school of Liège, thus providing yet one more example of the old opposition between Catholics of the right and Catholics of the left. The school of Angers, so called because Mgr Freppel used to hold meetings of its supporters in his episcopal city, was hostile to any form of intervention by the State, which should confine itself to making sure that each class was free to organize itself within the professional framework. It believed also that the Church ought not to interfere as such in social problems, but only to remind her children of the requirements of justice. The principal 'Angevins' were Père Forbes, S.J., Comte d'Haussonville, Professors Henri Joly and Claudio Jannet, the Capuchin Ludovic de Besse, Mgr d'Hulst and the Belgian disciples of Charles Perrin.

The school of Liège derived its name from the city of which another great prelate, Mgr Doutreloux, was bishop. With a view to promoting indispensable reforms, the 'Liègois' advocated reliance on governmental support, and thought that the urgent duty of the Church was to formulate solutions of the social problem by recommending Christian institutions. Among those who belonged to the school were Albert de Mun and the *Œuvres des Cercles*, Giuseppe Toniolo, Gaspard Decurtins, as well as Cardinal Manning and the leaders of the München-Gladbach movement.

La Tour du Pin, alarmed by doctrinal squabbles and convinced that his corporatist theory would render agreement possible, launched the idea of confrontation, an idea which took concrete form in the *Union de Fribourg*. Mgr Mermillod heard about the scheme and gave it his enthusiastic support. The result was a seven-year series of annual

study sessions in that delightful city on the banks of the Sarine: they were attended by delegates from all countries, and an enormous doctrinal task was accomplished. An organization was set up, with a control council and national sections. It was arranged that each year, before separating, the members of the *Union* would share among themselves the next questions to be studied; and in the following year each would make known the fruit of his investigations in the shape of a written report, from which the Assembly, after full discussion, would extract brief, compact formulae.

Between 1884 and 1891 the sessions accumulated a huge mass of information on all subjects relevant to the social problem, and in many cases proposed solutions that were later adopted by the Church.

The *Union de Fribourg* played a fourfold part: its meetings brought men together; it was the crucible in which various theses combined; it helped to spread social ideas; and it exerted considerable influence on the mind of Leo XIII. True, the Pope did not accept all its conclusions; but the men of Fribourg recognized the Encyclical as the fulfilment of their efforts, and after its publication they never met again.

8. The Social Teaching of Leo XIII Before 1891

When *Rerum Novarum* appeared, on 15th May 1891, the Church was well prepared to listen. There is no doubt that in drafting the Encyclical the Pope and his collaborators made use of existing material, doing their best to find the common denominator between theories that were often contradictory.

It had long been known that Mgr Pecci, Archbishop of Perugia, was one of the more socially minded prelates. How had such a preoccupation entered the mind of that aristocrat, who had had little or no contact with the working class? He probably made his first social discoveries as nuncio in Belgium (1843–6), where he had first-hand evidence of the deplorable state of the proletariat. But his interest in those problems was strengthened, during his long episcopate in Umbria, by the works of such thinkers as La Mennais, Ozanam, Balmes and Ketteler. Another influence was his familiarity with St Thomas Aquinas, who declares that 'the workman's labour is the unique source of all a State's wealth' and that 'the use of material goods should be directed to the common welfare'.

In 1887, a year before his accession to the apostolic throne, the Archbishop of Perugia had published a Lenten pastoral which had created no little stir among Italians. He had flayed 'the unworthy abuse of the poor and weak by those who sought to exploit them for the sake of profit', and had denounced 'the excessive hours of labour'.

Using even the vocabulary of Socialism, he had spoken of the 'brazen law' by virtue of which employers, having hired the physical strength of a man, ignored that man and his real needs. He had actually implied that the religious and moral crisis, which grieved so many good Catholics, had no other cause than undeserved misery.

The conclusions of the pastoral, however, might have seemed inadequate. While demanding, in a few words, legislation that would 'curb this inhuman traffic', Mgr Pecci had emphasized the necessity of a return to Christian principles 'which temper the stern law of labour', and of having confidence in the Church which, 'by restoring dignity to labour, reconciles the harsh law thereof with the freedom of man'.

As Pope, Leo XIII continued to take a keen interest in the social problem. That interest became more marked when he thanked Cardinal Manning for his arbitration in the London dock strike and refused to condemn the American Knights of Labor. A report sent in 1888 by the *Union de Fribourg*, as well as some conversations with Giuseppe Toniolo and others, at length convinced him that a Christian social order could be established only by institutional reforms, and that the Church had no more urgent duty than to prepare them.

Why did he choose to publish an Encyclical in 1891? For several reasons. That year occupied a unique place in the nineteenth-century economic movement. It ended a seven-year phase during which prices had fallen, and a new periodic crisis was in sight. From the social point of view, therefore, the situation was bad. The strikes of German miners and British dockers were still of recent occurrence; there had lately been bloodshed at Fourmies in France; and Leo feared that Socialism might profit by those events. Again, fully aware of wrangling within the Social Catholic movements themselves, he saw that it was time to give them all a body of incontestable doctrine. Moreover he had been deeply impressed by the workers' pilgrimage organized by Léon Harmel in 1887.

It was apparently after receiving the memorandum drawn up by the *Union de Fribourg* early in 1889 that the decision was taken to promulgate an Encyclical. Its preparation was entrusted to Cardinal Zigliara, Mgr Borchali, Father Matteo Liberatore, editor of *Civiltà cattolica*, and Cardinal Mazzella, secretary of the *Accademia di San Tommaso*. From July 1890 onwards they submitted a number of schemata to the Pope, who studied them in person. Careful analysis shows that between the report of the *Union*, the initial draft of the schema and the text of the Encyclical the difference was often considerable; and it was no doubt under the Pope's direct influence that agreement was ultimately reached.

9. 'Rerum Novarum'

The Encyclical *Rerum Novarum*, as it came from the printers in May 1891, is an admirable document, showing a remarkable unity of thought and of language. It gives a striking impression of broad-mindedness and bold thinking. It approaches the social problem with equal strength and serenity.

The Encyclical consists of a preamble and two parts. Why this publication? asks the short introduction. Because the fever of innovation—*rerum novarum*—which agitates society has extended from the political to the social field, owing to the growth of industry. 'Relations between employers and workers have altered. Wealth has poured into the hands of a few, leaving the masses in poverty.' The result is a distressing conflict. The Pope therefore considers it his duty to discuss this problem, which is not, he makes clear, the *entire* social question, for the latter includes everything relative to the Christian organization of society. He will deal only with 'the condition of the workers'. Even thus restricted, 'the problem is not easy to solve nor exempt from danger'.

The first part of the document states that problem in vigorous terms. There exists a social evil: 'Members of the lower classes are for the most part in a situation of misfortune and undeserved misery. The guilds which once protected the humble have been destroyed, religion has been banished from institutions and from laws. Thus the workers, isolated and defenceless, have gradually found themselves delivered to the mercy of inhuman masters and to the cupidity of atrocious competition. The evil has been made still worse by the advent of ravenous usury. . . . The concentration of industry and commerce in the hands of a few lays an almost servile yoke upon the boundless multitudes of proletarians.'

Such phrases sound very much like Socialism. Must the solutions put forward by Socialists be accepted? No. The Encyclical goes on to demolish their theories. 'They urge the poor to jealous hatred of the well-to-do,' which is against charity. 'They argue that all private property should be abolished' and converted to public ownership, whereas 'private and personal property is, for man, part of natural law', the legitimate and desirable basis of the family. One can indeed say that by tilling the earth man 'leaves upon it a certain imprint of his personality, so that in all justice that property will be possessed henceforward as his own'. Finally the Socialists give too prominent a position to the State, whereas domestic society has a logical priority and a real primacy over civil society. Socialism is therefore pernicious; its triumph would be harmful, even to the workers.

Having dismissed economic liberalism and Socialism, Leo proceeds

in the second part of his Encyclical to call upon three spheres of authority for a transformation of the social situation. First there is the moral law, for there is a problem of justice which falls within the scope of moral theology. In nature there are undoubtedly, between man and man, many differences which give rise to social inequalities. But those inequalities ought to serve the welfare of society. It is a capital error to believe that the classes are 'born enemies', as though nature had armed rich and poor for a duel to death. On the contrary, they must be united and balanced. The worker is bound loyally to fulfil his contract of labour, to respect the person and goods of his employer, and to repudiate violence. The employer is equally bound not to treat his workmen as slaves, not to impose tasks beyond their strength, and to pay them a just wage.

The second sphere of authority to which Leo appeals is the State. Its duty is to promote the common welfare. It is obliged, in the first place, to preserve public order, but also to guarantee distributive justice. It must, especially, protect the weak, 'safeguard the lives and interests of the working class'; and in failing to do so it 'violates strict justice'. Turning to details, the Encyclical lays down that the State should intervene to control conditions of work, moral and material, as well as to ensure the 'just wage'. Rejecting the liberal theory that 'the employer fulfils all his undertakings by paying the freely agreed wage', it declares the worker's right to receive 'the wherewithal to procure necessities', and thereby defines wages in terms of a man's needs, not of an economic calculation.

The third and final authority invoked is that of the interested parties themselves, employers and workers. They should combine to solve these difficult problems. Trade associations are lawful; they are of natural right. They should be private, i.e. not obligatory, but protected and controlled by the State. Many Catholics, to whom Leo pays tribute, have already laboured to organize such associations, and important results have been achieved by mutual benefit societies. Those associations ought to go further: they should inspire and regulate professional life, and eliminate grounds of dispute. Prophetically, as if foreseeing the growth of an apostolate to the workers and the development of Christian trade unionism, Leo XIII, realizing that workers' associations are often hostile to religion, invites Christian workers to 'organize themselves and join forces in order to be able to fling off so unjust and so intolerable a yoke'.

The document ends with an appeal to all Catholics—priests and layfolk, employers and workers—to take such steps as will bring about the triumph of those principles which the Encyclical has laid down: 'It is from an abundant outpouring of charity that we must hope for success.'

Thus *Rerum Novarum* placed the social attitude of the Church above the differences of conflicting schools; it invited Catholics to fight on two fronts—against social injustice and against the pernicious doctrines of class hatred. That is still the position of the Church. Unlike the famous pastoral of 1877, Leo's Encyclical did not confine itself to protesting against an economic system whose injustice was apparent only to a few. It carried out a constructive task; it brought to the social crisis, which appeared to be governed by irreducible contradictions, a wise and humane solution founded upon principle. In certain material respects—the notion of a just wage, the recognition of the workers' right of association, the right of the peasant over the land—it showed itself so advanced that sixty years have not sufficed to invalidate its principles. From it, substantially, derives the grand ideal of our own century: the economy must be at the service of man.

Admittedly *Rerum Novarum* formulated the social problem in contemporary terms, without pretending to offer ready-made answers to questions that would not arise until long afterwards, questions turning upon the 'second Industrial Revolution', 'technological' unemployment and the subjection of man to the machine. But the text of an Encyclical is never definitive and unalterable, a fact well known to the popes who supplemented *Rerum Novarum* with *Quadragesimo anno* and *Mater et Magistra* in order to adapt an ever-moving current of thought to historical circumstances. One might even say that it overlooked some points (perhaps intentionally), and that in other respects it had already been outstripped by events. For instance, the Encyclical said nothing about the need for international regulation of labour, although *Osservatore Romano* carried a long article on that subject in the very issue that summarized the contents of the papal text. But Leo may well have chosen to sidestep a question which had proved highly controversial at the Congress of Berlin in 1890. Again, his criticism of Socialism is directed against various French brands rather than against Marxism. But the significance of Marxism, a doctrine at that time unknown to the vast majority of Catholics, had been grasped by a mere handful of obscure individuals. It is none the less certain that a major advance had been accomplished, the importance of which is perhaps not fully realized now that the ideas of *Rerum Novarum* have become part and parcel of Catholicism.

10. Opinions of 'Rerum Novarum'

How was the Encyclical welcomed by the world at large? One cannot truthfully say that it was recognized unanimously as a document of prime importance. Yet even men who did not share the Pope's

convictions understood it as a measure of 'high policy', and that the Vicar of Christ was proposing to arbitrate between social classes, as he had already done between nations. In Germany the Socialist newspaper *Vorwärtz* congratulated Leo XIII for having 'stolen a march on secular governments'. In England the *Guardian*, noted for its links with the High Church, declared the Encyclical to be 'the work of a sage'. In France, Émile Spueller, a colleague of Gambetta, remarked: 'It is a great event in the history of modern society.' Anatole Leroy-Beaulieu, a distinguished advocate of liberalism, spoke in the *Revue des Deux Mondes* of his profound admiration for the Pope's courage, and concluded: 'It is a sign of the times that lie ahead.' Émile Ollivier exclaimed: 'The Pope has surpassed himself.' And Maurice Barrès, not perhaps without some exaggeration: 'After the Encyclical, anticlericalism seems quite unthinkable.'

Such tributes, however, must not mislead us. We must not imagine that the papal message succeeded overnight in setting all Catholics to work on the site of social reconstruction. Encyclicals commonly go unread by the majority of Catholics, and *Rerum Novarum* was no exception. Although the Social Catholics tried to spread its message in the form of tracts, most newspapers virtually ignored it. In Italy the royalist journals passed it over in silence. In France the only two Catholic dailies, *L'Univers* and *La Croix*, were reserved, and the neutral press even more so. 'Why does the Church come meddling at this moment, and what's the social question got to do with the Pope and his priests?' That opinion, expressed by an old man and reported in the *Revue des Deux Mondes*, was fairly widespread.

Among the clergy themselves, even in the ranks of the episcopate, assent was far from unanimous. No doubt there were enthusiasts, such as Cardinals Langénieux, Lécot and Manning, the American Bishop Ireland, Cardinal Monescillio, Primate of Spain, and some others. But the episcopate as a whole remained undemonstrative, and the clergy, overwhelmingly conservative, reacted in the same way. In 1897, addressing a sacerdotal congress at Fiesole, Mgr Radini-Tedeschi, a confidant of the Pope, was moved to utter this solemn warning: 'If priests do not fulfil their social duty, a catastrophe is inevitable.'[1]

It was, of course, among Social Catholics that the Encyclical received its warmest welcome. Albert de Mun, Toniolo and Decurtins wrote numerous articles and lectured tirelessly. Decurtins even persuaded a workers' congress, most of whose members were Protestant and Socialist, to congratulate Leo XIII in a formal address.

[1] Radini-Tedeschi formed a link between the three 'social' popes. He enjoyed the friendship and for some time the collaboration of Don Achille Ratti, afterwards Pope Pius XI; and as Bishop of Bergamo he had among his seminarians Angelo Roncalli, the future John XXIII.

Hardly a single working-men's club, hardly a single study group failed to devote at least one of its meetings to a discussion of the papal text. Georges Goyau's *Le Pape, les catholiques et les questions sociales* [1] made a deep impression, and Canon Perriot wrote a book [2] to prove that *Rerum Novarum* was an *ex cathedra* document.

11. A New Climate

Although its immediate influence was limited, the Encyclical created a new climate. During the years following its publication there was an extraordinary ferment of social generosity. The problem of the working class, hitherto ignored, became one of the chief concerns of those who meant to live their religion. Institutes directly concerned with that branch of the apostolate flourished as never before. Some surprising ideas, too, emerged, which our age wrongly believes itself to have discovered. For example, there was talk of establishing 'worker-priests' who would earn their living by manual labour, so as to be closer to the proletariat; and there actually came into being an Association of Worker-Priests, which had four hundred members in France. In Italy the Neapolitan Aviolo demanded 'a proletarian clergy holding all its property in common', while in Belgium a number of priests went to live among the miners and factory workers. It was now possible to say that the militant wing of the Church would be 'social'. The social section of the Italian *Opera dei Congressi* made such progress that Pius X left it intact when he suppressed the *Opera* itself. In Germany the *Volksverein*, founded as a mere mustering of Catholics for the defence, if necessary, of their rights, became a social movement. Nothing is more significant than the evolution of the *Association catholique de la jeunesse française*, founded in 1886 [3] as an aristocratic nursery that would produce the leaders of that 'Catholic Party' of which De Mun was dreaming. From 1892 onwards it reached out to the lower orders, particularly to the peasant youth, and concerned itself with the social problem. Its new president, Henri Bazire, made it more and more a centre of social training; and it was during one of the association's congresses that Albert de Mun spoke his famous words: 'The Church is not a policeman in the service of upper-class society.' No movement hoping to attract young Catholics could now refrain from becoming 'social'.

This social preoccupation gradually extended to wider fields. Readers of *Gaulois* and *Echo de Paris* found such problems discussed

[1] He wrote under the pseudonym Léon Grégoire.

[2] *L'Encyclique Rerum novarum et son enseignement*, Paris, 1898.

[3] By Robert de Roquefeuil with the help of Albert de Mun.

by Albert de Mun, Maurice Barrès, Georges Goyau and Costa de Beauregard. In *Ouest-Éclair*, Emmanuel Desgrées strove long and resolutely for the ideas of *Rerum Novarum*. Literature followed suit: social writers included Jacques Debout (the Abbé Rollet), Yves de Querdée (Georges Fonsegrive) and even successful novelists, among whom were Foggazzaro, René Bazin, Paul Bourget and young Henri Bordeaux.

12. 'Social because Catholic'

Social Catholicism profited by the initiative of Leo XIII. The highest authority was sanctioning ideas and doctrines which had hitherto been judged subversive. Yesterday the small teams of Social Catholics had seemed like irregulars whom the authorities could disown at a moment's notice. Today they could feel sure of being on the straight road desired by the Church, able to fight unhampered.

Better still, Social Catholics now recognized themselves as depositories of a message; they considered that their campaign alone could save the Church from the perils that threatened her. They were even convinced that the only true form of Christianity was their own. 'Social Catholics have these social ideas', declared Henri Bazire, 'because they are Catholics. They are social not *as well as being* Catholics: they are social *because* Catholic.'

In the service of that ideal groups of men would continue the work they had begun, and their ranks would swell. Not that Social Catholics had ever been very numerous; they had always suffered, and continued to suffer, from a twofold mistrust. Their faith rendered them suspect to men who shared their ideas of social justice but were unbelievers. Their exacting charity, however, was a source of no less disquiet among certain of their co-religionists, maybe because it stood as a reproach; and there was violent criticism. Despite these difficulties, they made progress year by year until, on the eve of the First World War, they had inaugurated a movement which was to count for much both in the Church and elsewhere.

The main centres of Social Catholicism were those towns or districts where its doctrine was elaborated and its active work prepared: in France, Lyons and Lille, as well as Paris; in Italy, Milan and Brescia and Venice; in Germany, the Lower Rhineland. A Catholic press was born, consisting chiefly of reviews such as *La Chronique sociale* in France, *Cultura sociale* in Italy, *Paz sozial* in Spain, all of which strove to apply the papal teaching to concrete cases.

Much effort and much generosity was expended, and perhaps even

something more. For there emerged from among those who proclaimed themselves 'social because Catholic' several men of such exemplary virtue that one is inclined to think of them as embodiments of modern sanctity. They were what Ozanam had been in the preceding period, men who viewed social activity as nothing but a means of serving the charity of Christ, and who devoted their whole lives to that task. Léon Harmel was one; Toniolo and Gonin were two more.

Giuseppe Toniolo (1845–1918), professor of political economy at the University of Pisa, was an aristocrat by birth, great-grandson of Joseph de Maistre. He seemed in no way predestined to any but a purely academic life; but his craving for self-sacrifice was such as could not be satisfied with the conscientious fulfilment of his professional duties. The words of the *Pater* haunted him: 'Thy kingdom come'; what could he do to bring about God's reign on earth? Social Catholicism appeared to answer that question. The turning-point was his study of the economic life of medieval Florence and his reading of St Thomas: he had believed in economic liberalism, now he rejected it. With his friend Count Medolago-Albani he discovered the writings of French and German Social Catholics, and made contact with the *Union de Fribourg*. Thenceforward he was the champion of their cause, through the *Opera dei Congressi* as well as through the *Unione cattolica di studi sociali* and the *Rivista internazionale di scienze sociale*, both of which he himself founded. His life was now consumed by the apostolate in which he had engaged. On the morrow of the Encyclical, to which he had made no small contribution, he laboured unceasingly with voice and pen to spread abroad its teaching. At first he thought that the best means of promoting Social Catholicism would be Christian democracy; but when Leo XIII, and later Pius X, warned the Church against certain misleading theories, he looked to the *Unione cattolica italiana* and then to the *Unione popolare*. In 1910, at the age of sixty-five, he founded a Social Catholic school for the training of young men who would one day take over the apostolate. All his activity went hand in hand with an inexhaustible kindness of heart, an unbounded devotion to his fellow men, a Christian faith lived to the full.

Very different from Toniolo was Marius Gonin (1872–1937), son of a Lyons coachman and a dressmaker. He needed no instruction in the social problem, having experienced it at first hand. Educating himself, climbing the steps that led to the editorial chair of a daily newspaper, he made acquaintance with the works of Social Catholics—Lacordaire, De Mun, La Tour du Pin. He was eighteen when the Encyclical appeared and it filled him with enthusiasm. He recognized in the Pope's words the ideal of his life, and the whole of his life was to be dedicated to the service of that ideal—a typical representative of the new generation which, having reached the age of manhood in the

atmosphere engendered by *Rerum Novarum*, would enable Social Catholicism to complete another stage of its journey.[1]

13. New Men and New Problems

The development of Social Catholicism, however, was hindered by difficulties arising from the evolution of ideas, from the emergence of new men, and from certain political involvements which the leaders of the movement failed to avoid. *Rerum Novarum* had laid down the principles of social action, but had not suggested how its ends were to be achieved. It was natural, therefore, that Catholics, starting from the papal directives, should seek to accomplish the work of social justice according to methods dictated by their tastes and temperaments. Since the middle of the nineteenth century those who sincerely wished to improve the working man's lot tended to follow one or other of two roads: paternalism, which hoped to make the ruling classes generous but firm guides of a docile proletariat; or corporatism, which sought to establish obligatory collaboration between employers and wage-earners. Very few followed Harmel in his belief that the right course was 'to promote the betterment of the working class by restoring initiative and responsibility'.

In 1891 a third tendency became manifest: the resurgence of left-wing Social Catholicism, which had been in eclipse since 1848. It intended to make the working class responsible for its own future and so the active force of social evolution. Certain passages in the Encyclical appeared to allow such an interpretation. Ostensibly it was a democratic idea; but it appeared to link up with those political movements which, in the name of Christian principles, advocated governments by the the people for the people, in other words Christian democracy.[2] Verbal confusion added to the difficulty, as also did the fact that *Rerum Novarum* was followed a few months later by the Encyclical *Au Milieu des Sollicitudes*, which bade the Catholics of France rally to the democratic Republic.

The situation became critical with the entry upon the scene of those young men who looked at the problem in a different way from that of their elders. They had not been brought up in the shadow of the *Syllabus* or in the hatred of everything that recalled the Revolution, however faintly. A democratic regime appeared to them as the best possible means of accomplishing social reforms. They looked upon their elders as too timid, too theoretical and too paternalist. None could fail to observe a great gulf set between the generations, in respect of principles no less than of methods.

[1] See Lives by Crétinon (1938) and Folliet (1960). [2] See Chapter III, section 13.

The Church could not allow the identification of Social Catholicism with a political movement. The problem raised in the political had repercussions in the social sphere. The Church could no more permit her fortunes to be associated with those of a single class than she could permit herself to become tied to the democratic system under pretext of breaking her links with the *Ancien Régime.*

Leo XIII himself realized the danger when he saw how his social teaching was exploited by certain Christian democrats in France, Italy, Belgium and Austria. Such was the cause of a reaction manifested in 1901 by the Encyclical *Graves de Communi*: 'The precepts of nature and of the Gospel', declared His Holiness, 'are above all human vicissitudes, and it is therefore necessary that they should not depend on any form of civil government.' His words were a timely warning, but perhaps insufficiently explicit. For instead of putting an end to the ambiguity of terms, the Pope continued to speak of 'democracy', trying to empty the word of its political substance and confine its meaning to that of 'a beneficent Christian activity among the people'.

The situation, equivocal and thwarting, could not but last under Pius X, a pope inclined to worry less about temporal problems than about greater spiritual concerns. As early as 1902 Cardinal Sarto had expressed in a pastoral his belief that it was 'most reprehensible to divert the generosity of Catholics into political channels'. Towards the end of 1903, soon after his election to the papacy, he established a 'fundamental regulation of Christian popular action'; but the Pope who encouraged the Social Weeks [1] and Christian syndicalism scarcely deserves the charge of reaction and extreme conservatism so often levelled against him. While it is true that his condemnation of the *Opera dei Congressi* in Italy and of *Le Sillon* in France affected movements that had done good work in the social field, they were not suppressed *qua* social, but for quite different (mainly political) reasons.[2]

The lessons of Pius X did much to determine the position of true Social Catholics. A path had to be found between the hazardous road followed by the more advanced elements of Christian democracy and the traditional route of more or less corporatist paternalism. That path, though not easy to discern, was the only one that could lead to the end appointed by the Church; a *via media* which has led to Social Catholicism as we know it today.

[1] See section 15 of the present chapter.

[2] It has been said that Pius X struck a blow at 'social modernism'. The expression is perhaps exaggerated, and in any case was not current during the Modernist crisis. It must however, be acknowledged that the principles upon which some elements of Christian democracy took their stand, notably that of the people's sovereignty, were closely akin to certain modernist theories. Again, many Christian democrats showed themselves not unfavourable to the theological and exegetical theses of the modernists. See Chapter VI.

14. Social Catholicism after the Encyclical

A quarter of a century was to elapse between the publication of *Rerum Novarum* and the First World War, which effected a radical change in the conditions of social life. There was no great Christian country that did not witness considerable achievements.

In France the paternalist current vanished. *L'Œuvre des Cercles* was doomed, mainly because of its inability to associate the working class with its activity. Corporatism enjoyed a longer life; though it was no longer regarded as the sole solution, it nourished a right-wing brand of Social Catholicism.

Corporatist Social Catholicism was by no means ineffectual, and later supplied *Action française* with the elements of its social doctrine. But the current that assumed real importance was left-wing Social Catholicism, which reared its head first in the *Cercles ouvriers d'études sociales*. The latter gave rise to a series of Workers' Congresses, and with them recruited the active members of democratic Catholic Socialism.

Several teams followed one another at the head of the movement. First there was the group called by its enemies *les abbés démocrates*.[1] Those daring young priests, who saw frank adhesion to the democratic regime as the Church's best opportunity, were all convinced 'socials'. They followed enthusiastically the advice given by Leo XIII to the clergy: 'Don't shut yourselves away in your presbyteries, but go among the people and take a whole-hearted interest in the worker.' Men such as the Abbé Six were true guides of the working-class world, and remained so even after the Encyclical *Graves de Communi* had expressed the Pope's anxiety, not on account of the young priests' social activity, but because of the ambiguous political attitude adopted by some.

Social Catholicism was thus on the crest of a new wave, that of the generation whose civic life began about 1901. It seemed at the outset that one group, *Le Sillon*, was going to monopolize all sources of energy. In its luminous childhood Marc Sangnier's creation laboured magnificently on the scaffolding of social endeavour. Pius X himself, in the letter which eventually condemned *Le Sillon*, spoke of it as having in those early years 'raised the standard of Jesus Christ among the working classes, and nourished its social activity at the well-springs of grace'. Its study circles, its People's Institutes, its press and its books imbued an ardent youth with social ideas. Its condemnation by Pius X in 1910 put an end to its social and other undertakings. Meanwhile, however, other teams had set to work; and the outbreak of war

[1] See Chapter III, section 13; Chapter V, section 8.

in 1914 found French Social Catholicism on the flood-tide of success, backed by stable organizations which had managed to take the *via media*, away from the controversies in which political aims had involved the *abbés démocrates* and the *Sillonistes*.

In Italy the Encyclical gave rise to some notable activity. Savings banks, co-operative societies and trade combines sprang up in many places throughout the peninsula. The progress of Socialism, too, made such efforts indispensable, as was openly acknowledged by a Catholic congress held at Geneva in 1892. After 1895, when the *Opera dei Congressi* attained its fullest expansion, social Catholic activity became centred in its Second Section. As in France, the advent of a new generation raised problems. The ideas and vocabulary of Toniolo and his friends were no longer acceptable to Don Romolo Murri. The *Opera dei Congressi* was gradually transformed, adopting standpoints that became more and more political, until Pius X was obliged to intervene;[1] but it continued its social work with vigour during its last ten years.

In Germany firm foundations were laid by Social Catholicism. Its leaders were the men of München-Gladbach, an industrial centre in the Lower Rhineland, where the ideas of Mgr von Ketteler had long been making practical headway. Still there were problems, one of which we have already noticed in France and elsewhere: disagreement within the movement as to means of action. The München-Gladbach group, considered as too democratic, was opposed by the 'corporatives', who were supported in turn by Baron von Loë's peasant associations. A crisis broke out over the confessional allegiance of syndicates,[2] but it was merely the pretext which revealed doctrinal antagonism. Another problem was specifically German, deriving from the circumstances in which political life had developed within the Reich.[3] The Catholic party known as the *Zentrum*, victorious in the *Kulturkampf*, had obtained a footing in the counsels of government; and it retained that footing, except for a period of two years (1907–9), until the First World War. It was thus able to exert considerable influence in the field of social legislation, a field in which Germany was ahead of all other nations; but the result was a tendency towards state control more marked than anywhere else.

The situation was quite different in Belgium, although Catholics enjoyed a virtually uninterrupted run of power. For while the Belgian Catholic Party had conservative leanings, and its leaders were paternalist, the Belgian Democratic League (formed in 1891)[4] was otherwise

[1] See Chapter V, section 7. [2] Ibid., section 9 *ad fin.*

[3] See Chapter III, section 7.

[4] It sprang from the remains of the old *Fédération des Œuvres ouvrières catholiques* led by Helleputte and Verhaegen.

inclined. The party restricted its activity and prevented it from becoming too independent; but its influence was undeniable. The social programme drawn up by the League for the electoral campaign of 1894 was taken into consideration; it became the charter of the party in power, so much so that many of the laws passed were inspired by the ideal of Christian justice. Moreover—and this is important—the Belgian Catholic State did not seek to impose uniformity by means of authoritarian discipline; it endeavoured rather to animate and foster the social cells.

The impulse given by the Encyclical was thus felt in all countries that had witnessed the birth of Social Catholicism. Switzerland alone, which had formerly led the way with its *Union de Fribourg*, gives an impression of lassitude. The conservatives managed to get rid of Decurtins, and thus left the initiative to Socialism during the next fifty years. On the other hand, countries which had hitherto ignored the Social Catholic trend now awoke to it. In Holland a Catholic Democratic League issued a manifesto in which it adopted the teachings of Leo XIII as its programme. In Spain the Cardinal Primate, Archbishop Monescillio of Toledo, assumed leadership of the movement, and in 1895 denounced the tyranny of money. The dean of Oviedo, Arboleya Martinez, devoted himself to the welfare of the miners in Asturias; much good work was done among the gipsies by Father Andres Manjon, professor of canon law in the University of Granada; while a Catholic congress at Tarragona voiced the grievances both of industrial workers and of peasants.

Outside Europe, Social Catholicism flourished mainly in the United States. The influence of Mgr Ireland was considerable: in countless speeches he demanded for the working class not so much charitable assistance as the right to control its own destiny and 'to shake off the yoke of inhuman economic forces'. The American Federation of Catholic Societies,[2] founded in 1901 under the direction of Mgr McFaul, Bishop of Trenton, and Mgr Messmer, Archbishop of Milwaukee, studied the directives of Leo XIII at its annual congresses. Under the influence of Fathers John Ryan and Dielz a committee of social service was formed. The Federation expressed its sympathy with the workers who were trying to improve their lot; it upheld the principle of collective agreements, as well as demanding the abolition of Sunday labour, limitation of the working day, adequate wages, hygienic conditions and indemnity in case of accident. From 1910 onwards the National Conference of Welfare Organizations set up a regular social service, and later, in 1917, the Catholic War-time Committee published a programme of social reconstruction which included several measures of the highest importance: insurance

[1] It had three million members in 1912.

against sickness and unemployment, recognition of trade union rights, State action against capitalist monopolies, and so on. That programme was lulled to sleep by the intoxication of post-war prosperity, but some of its elements reappeared in Roosevelt's 'New Deal'.

15. Social Weeks

The seed whence was to spring what is called the today the Social Week took shape in Germany. In 1892 Father Hitze and the industrialist Brandt, leaders of the *Volksverein*, conceived the idea of inaugurating 'practical social courses'. These were to be held each year, now in one city, now in another; and distinguished representatives of the movement would attend to give theoretical and practical instruction. Among those who attended the first meetings were Canon Cetty of Mulhouse and the journalist Max Turmann, both friends of Marius Gonin. They told him how successful had been the courses at München-Gladbach, and asked whether it would not be a good thing to copy them in France.

Later, in 1901, M. Savatier, editor of *L'Association catholique*, founded the *Union des catholiques sociaux* as a centre both of study and of propaganda. Among its earliest members were Adéodat Boissard, a professor of law at Lille, and Henri Lorin, a business man who had come to Social Catholicism by way of Le Play and had attended the meetings at Fribourg.

In 1902 it was proposed to organize a meeting at which the heads of the *Union* would compare their points of view; but the project failed. Marius Gonin, however, had been kept informed. After discussing the German achievement and the French plan, he and some of his friends thought of combining the two. They would rent a house on the shores of Lake Annecy, where the leaders of Social Catholicism would give lectures and hold discussions with anyone interested in the problem. In the spring of 1904 Gonin submitted his plan to Boissard, who accepted it on behalf of his colleagues. The meeting was to take place at Lyons early in August, and last for eight days. Such was the beginning of the Social Weeks.

That first Week was a success: an audience of two hundred was expected; four hundred and fifty-eight attended. Cardinal Coullié agreed to open the session, and some very distinguished men came to speak. Procedure was settled without delay: 'No debates, no opposition, no voting'; solid and clear instruction would be provided through authoritative discourses and lectures to the general public. Until 1913 no one thought of concentrating the Week upon a single theme; a new subject was taken each day. The result was in no way sensational:

the press as a whole gave the scheme a cold shoulder or confined itself to a summary criticism; but Cardinal Merry del Val sent a telegram conveying the Pope's blessing.

The inauguration of Social Weeks was thus due to two men, Marius Gonin and Adéodat Boissard. But the scheme might not have proved so successful if a third man had not come upon the scene next year at Orleans. This was Henri Lorin (1869–1915), who assumed the presidency and held it until the outbreak of the First World War. His opening speeches at the nine Weeks over which he presided were as clear in exposition as they were rich in substance. From 1905 to 1914 he was virtually the doctrinaire of the Social Weeks, and, through them, of a large part of Social Catholicism.

The success of the Lyons Week was decisive. Ever since that date the Social Catholics of France have continued (with two interruptions caused by the world wars) to hold a Week in the summer of each year. Those gatherings have contributed enormously to the advancement of social science, as well as to the spread of Leo XIII's teaching among Catholics at large. The bishops almost without exception—if not without private misgivings—supported the movement, and it became customary for Rome to send a papal message appointing the framework within which the assembly would perform its task. As for attendance, it rose from 458 at Lyons in 1904 to 1,433 at Rouen in 1910, and during most of that period the clergy supplied at least half the numbers.

The Weeks prior to 1914 appear to have aimed at a more exact statement of the Church's doctrine, which accounts for the predominance of philosophers and theologians at those gatherings. The subjects dealt with were general: property, the family and work; sometimes even highly abstract, e.g. the idea of responsibility; more rarely practical, e.g. syndicates and contracts of labour.

It would have been surprising if such a work had managed to avoid the obstacles encountered by all human undertakings, and those Catholics who did not whole-heartedly approve the social orientation of the Church were forthright in their criticism of the Weeks. Some even of Henri Lorin's writings, which appeared to suggest that the right of property lapsed as soon as property ceased to fulfil its social function, were rebuked by Cardinal Merry del Val. Such storms, however, were not serious. The French example was followed, and between 1906 and 1913 similar gatherings were held in Spain, Belgium, Holland, Italy and Switzerland. By 1914 the brave leaders of the Weeks had won the day against those who accused them of temerity as well as against those who maintained that their work was futile.

16. Birth of Christian Syndicalism

During the years that followed *Rerum Novarum* the threefold object of Social Catholicism was to formulate doctrine, build up a social *élite* and improve the workers' lot. At the same time, and within a very different framework, other steps were taken that were destined to have portentous results. Catholics were to become associated with the powerful movement that uplifted the working class and revealed itself in the birth of syndicalism. Many Catholics, on the other hand, even Social Catholics, would remain outside and even distrustful of this movement. According to the corporatist doctrine, workers' groups might indeed exist, but only within the confines of the corporation; and that notion was so firmly entrenched that Albert de Mun waited until 1912 before abandoning the idea that mixed syndicalism was the only Christian means of organizing labour.

In the peasant world it was this formula that prevailed until 1914; circumstances were not the same in agriculture as in industry, and the problem of rural workers had not yet attracted attention. Nevertheless agriculture was threatened by crises, competition and natural disasters; landowners, unskilled labourers and journeymen were all alike anxious to defend their livelihood. Agricultural syndicalism was therefore quite naturally 'corporative', and more concerned with the price of fertilizers and the sale of produce than with social defence. But that did not necessarily exclude agricultural syndicalism, or rather agricultural corporatism, from the field of Social Catholicism, where some genuinely social activity was accomplished and social institutions of great interest were established, making this movement one of the most conclusive examples of what corporatism could give.

In France agricultural syndicalism began to make progress after 1884, following the passing of a law which made syndicates legal. Seventy-four of these were created, and then combined to form a Central Union in which members of the aristocracy rubbed shoulders with minor landowners. True, small farmers and labourers were not well represented; but the movement had been started, and it eventually spread.

The evolution of agricultural syndicalism in the direction of human rather than of economic concerns was the achievement of men who had been won over to Christian social ideas, men such as the Abbé Farel, Gailhard-Bancel and Louis Milcent. At their instigation, then in imitation of their work, sick funds, mutual benefit funds, superannuation funds and even agricultural assurance funds were established. The *Fédération du Sud-Est* performed a similar task under Émile

Duport, Louis Durant and Marius Gonin; in particular it provided for the education of agricultural workers.

In Germany the strongly corporatist *Bauerverein*, which had existed for half a century,[1] organized various social institutions without ceasing to concern itself with the defence of professional interests. In Belgium the *Boerenbund*, an association of employers and workers, set up numerous co-operative and mutual benefit societies. In Italy, where the rural movement was essentially the work of small landed proprietors, 'rural banks' were the most effective means of mutual aid.

But were all the problems of the agricultural world solved thereby? Theoretically yes, in practice no. There were others in addition to those of buying and selling, problems of credit and mutuality. Had farmers and agricultural labourers the same interests as landowners? This question was raised in the Workers' Congress at Lyons (1897) by the Abbé Trochu, a young Breton curate. 'Are leasing and hiring always just?' he asked. Ought one not to recognize the right of those who tilled the land to defend their interests by forming distinct groups? Before long agricultural syndicates of wage earners and of farmers would come to be regarded as necessities.

In industry this development was much more rapid. Among the proletariat, whose numbers continually increased, the syndical movement began during the last quarter of the nineteenth century to make strides that have never slackened. The law, however, was against it. In France Le Chapelier's law (1791) had made 'coalition' a crime; a law of 1864 had abolished the crime, but continued to forbid association for the common defence of interests. It was not until 1884 that Waldeck-Rousseau's law permitted the formation of syndicates. All the same, though in violation of the law, groups of workers had arisen, modelled upon foreign institutions. Recognized since 1871, the British trade unions included 1,500,000 members in 1895. In Germany, Belgium, the Netherlands and Switzerland syndicalism was in full flood. In the United States the Federation of Labor was demanding 'a just wage for a fair day's work'. Labour exchanges were springing up on all sides like fortresses for the worker's defence.

Among French Social Catholics there existed a current favourable to working-class syndicalism. 'Corporatist' though he claimed to be, Léon Harmel never ceased to strive for what he called 'the ascent of the people through the restoration of initiative and responsibility', showing clearly that in a mixed syndicate the worker was always subject to a certain amount of pressure, even if unintended, on the part of his employer. Was the magisterium of the Church opposed to workers' associations? Apparently not, in the light of *Rerum Novarum*, which acknowledged their right to exist. Moreover Pius X, in *Singulari*

[1] *The Church in an Age of Revolution*, Index.

quadam (1912), so far from condemning them, actually encouraged those which 'have the Catholic faith as the basis of their activity and follow the directives of the Church'. It seemed therefore that syndicates of labourers were perfectly acceptable provided they remained strictly Catholic in character.

The first French Christian syndicate appears to have been founded by a few silk-weavers at Lyons in 1884. Other small groups were formed in 1885 and 1886 in the department of Nord. But the first achievement of any real size was the *Syndicat des Employés du Commerce et de l'Industrie* at Paris in 1887. It owed its existence to the Brothers of the Christian Schools, who, having lost the right to teach in municipal schools, devoted themselves to the organization of technical schools and continuation classes.

The movement thus started continued, and year by year Christian syndicates (some of them expressly for women) were established in all trades. Born spontaneously, in accordance with the needs of life, they tended to coalesce. While the primary purpose of all was the defence of their members' rights, they had also definitely religious aims, which were indicated by the presence of a chaplain. The movement was approved by the most far-sighted Social Catholics, such as Henri Lorin, who declared that the true expression of the idea of brotherhood should be the syndical link. But the enemies of Christian syndicalism were numerous. Employers were indignant that the Church should back the workers' claims, and numerous protests against the syndical leaders reached the Holy See. Among Social Catholics themselves, members of *Le Sillon* were hostile to Christian syndicalism; they would have preferred to see Catholics join the *Confédération générale des travailleurs* (C.G.T.) and work from within. Inevitably, too, non-Christian workers seized the opportunity to accuse Catholics of disrupting the proletarian forces. Nevertheless, on the eve of the First World War Christian syndicalism was firmly established in France. It included about 120,000 members, a very small figure in comparison with the entire French proletariat, but considerable when one recalls that the C.G.T. numbered at most 350,000.

France, however, was by no means the only country to witness the rise of Christian syndicalism. It appeared wherever there was religious tension, that is to say wherever Catholics might hesitate to join non-Christian syndical organizations. In Belgium it arose with support from the Democratic League. In Holland the first syndical association was founded in 1889 by Mgr Ariens, and was one of the elements used by Mgr Schaepman in building the Catholic Party. In Germany the syndical movement began as early as 1875 and spread quickly, especially when the *Volksverein* declared in its favour. Before long, however, it was the occasion of a bitter quarrel which brought to a head

the opposition between the two tendencies of German Catholicism.[1] The pretext was that of confessionality. München-Gladbach favoured a single syndicate, which would admit Protestants and non-Christians. In the Rhineland, where Catholics were extremely numerous, this plan was acceptable; but at Berlin, where they formed a minority, it would have been dangerous. Those who wished to see in a corporative and rather feudal organization the basis of social order were gravely alarmed by the peril of interconfessionality. In 1906 the affair was taken to Rome, where the adversaries of München-Gladbach accused the movement of doctrinal deviation. The sequel was confused. Pius X told a party of syndicalists that he approved of collaboration with the Protestants, and then allowed himself to be contradicted: Canon Pieper published an article in *Osservatore Romano* favourable to München-Gladbach, and was then disowned though honoured with a prelacy. Tension increased until 1912, when the syndicalists themselves were wise enough to settle matters by declaring that they all submitted unreservedly to the authority of their bishops. This was one way of solving the confessional problem, and in the same year the Encyclical *Singulari quadam* approved syndicalism on condition of its remaining Catholic. Meanwhile it had not ceased to grow, and in spite of the crisis numbered about four hundred thousand members.

In Italy it was the *Opera dei Congressi* that launched the syndical idea, in 1899. The bloody agitation caused at that date in Sicily by the *Fasci dei Lavatori* made it desirable that Catholics should back the workers' claims without delay. Accordingly the 'white syndicates' movement began with numerous small local 'leagues', which gradually combined and whose Catholic character was strongly marked. But, as in France, those organisms were always numerically weak. In 1914 the total number of Christian syndicalists in Italian industry and agriculture reached the figure of only 104,000.

Lastly, there were even some countries in which social action had been almost unknown before *Rerum Novarum* but which now witnessed the birth of Christian syndicalism. The most curious example was Spain, where on the eve of the First World War the movement was strong enough to rouse the suspicion of the anarcho-syndicalists, so powerful at that time.

Thus the Christian syndicalist movement, though non-existent when the Encyclical was published, appeared a quarter of a century later as a power in full process of development. In the new conditions created by the war, it was to prove, like all the elements of the Social Catholic movement, capable of playing an important role.

[1] See Chapter V, section 9.

17. On the Eve of the First World War

On the outbreak of that conflict which was to lay the old Europe in ruins Social Catholicism had made decisive progress in less than fifty years. Once an *avant-garde* school more or less suspected by the majority of Catholics, it now enjoyed the benefit of the authority conferred upon its theories by papal approbation. In all Christian countries teams of men, steadily increasing in number, appealed to its teaching, and they included at any rate the most active members of the clergy. A doctrinal effort had been undertaken, in order to establish the movement more securely and to enlarge its field of activity. It was no mere sentimental reaction in face of proletarian misery, but a clear resolve to think of society from the Christian standpoint. Finally, at the practical level, the social undertakings inspired by Catholics were innumerable, and the progress achieved by legislation in various countries bears their stamp.

Does all this mean that the picture included no shadows?[1] Three facts are undeniable: (1) Despite the emergence and growth of Christian syndicalism, Social Catholicism remained a movement of intellectuals and upper-class people, a movement to which few workers belonged. (2) Even at its own level it suffered from a certain weakness: while 'right-wing' Social Catholicism rested on the solid foundations of La Tour du Pin's thought, that of the 'left' had little structure; its attitudes derived from moral rather than from theological considerations; they did not rely upon an economic and sociological analysis of the situation such as that of which Marxism enjoys the benefit. Lastly (3), though supported by the highest authority, Social Catholicism was far from commanding the enthusiasm of all the faithful. It was still subject to plentiful criticism, and still more so to indifference. One might well have asked with Canon Leclercq whether the Sovereign Pontiff had not been followed only 'by those who were already walking in that direction'.[2]

It was to solve these three problems that Social Catholics would labour after the conflict. The circumstances brought about by that great upheaval, by altering relations between the classes, would render Catholics more attentive to these questions. In the light of another great Encyclical an effort would be made to give Social Catholic thought stronger foundations. At the same time, the discovery of new methods of apostolate, notably among the workers,

[1] Some have reproached Social Catholicism with laying too much emphasis on temporal engagements to the detriment of strictly spiritual values. In Chapter VIII we shall see how the leaders of specialized Catholic Action, notably the Abbé (now Cardinal) Cardijn, insist on the necessity of reconciling the two sets of values.

[2] *Les Droits et les devoirs individuels*, p. 369.

would provide the Church with hope of being able to re-establish contact with the proletariat. But that new stage would not have been possible if the other had not been cleared; if believers, in conditions that were often unfruitful, had not striven to make social justice Christian; if the mighty voice of Leo XIII had not been heard.

CHAPTER V

PIUS X AND 'THE INTERESTS OF GOD'

1. The Politics of a Saint

Pope Pius X is credited with a surprising maxim, written in the straightforward style which he never hesitated to use but none the less demanding some explanation: 'The policy of the Church is to take no part in politics.' Clear as the purpose of these words may be, they will hardly bear a literal interpretation. Apart from the fact that 'to take no part in politics' is in itself to follow a policy, the very nature of the Church, both human and superhuman, inevitably involves her in politics. Even when circumstances do not oblige her, for her own safety, to keep a watch on the intentions of States and of political parties, so many legitimate Christian interests are at stake in the realm of politics, and so many dangers threaten them, that the Holy Father cannot remain unconcerned without betraying the duties of his office.

Indeed, throughout the eleven years of his pontificate, this Pope who liked to call himself a country priest was repeatedly called upon to solve problems that were strictly political and often extremely difficult; nor did he devote to a single one of those problems any less attention and care than to matters which concerned the life of souls, matters to which his heart and thoughts were more naturally inclined. A number of his decisions, too, had important political consequences. On this point, as on all others, the repeatedly alleged opposition between Leo XIII and his successor cannot command unqualified assent.

Moreover the principles on which Pius X took his stand are exactly the same as those formulated by his predecessor. Like him he believed that the Sovereign Pontiff should intervene, and even play a decisive part, on the political stage. To be convinced of that one need only peruse his first Encyclical, which, according to tradition, declares the aims of the new pope and indicates the general spirit of his pontificate: 'The Soverign Pontiff cannot separate politics from the magisterium he exercises over faith and morals,' we read in *E supremi apostolatus*. That is precisely the doctrine of Leo XIII, inherited from Pope Gelasius in the Dark Ages; [1] and Pius X never missed an opportunity of citing *Immortale Dei*, the great Encyclical in which his predecessor had shown why the Vicar of Christ has a right and even a duty to

[1] See Chapter III, section 6.

exercise his control in the political field. Both meant to serve what Pius loved to call 'the interests of God', though they sometimes had recourse to different means.

How did the 'political' activity of Pius X vary from that of Leo XIII? In order to appreciate its originality one must consider it within the general framework of Sarto's purpose—*omnia instaurare in Christo*—and thus refer to what is known of his character.[1] All the evidence goes to show that Pius X considered political activity as only one element in an immeasurably larger whole, one aspect of an enormous enterprise which was nothing less than the repair and strengthening of the Church's foundations so that she might more successfully repel the attacks of her adversaries. By checking the least move towards disobedience or doctrinal error he tried on all occasions to enhance the authority of the Holy See and to tighten its discipline. It was with the same end in view that he carried out the administrative reform of the Curia and took steps to obtain fuller control of the episcopate. In order to determine his attitude towards the involvement of Catholics in the politics of their countries he adopted first this criterion: Whatever is subject to the hierarchy is lawful; whatever is likely to diminish its power is unlawful. And even in his relations with secular governments, for example with that of France, his desire to strengthen links between a national Church and the Apostolic See was occasionally at the root of what appeared as narrow intransigence.

Moreover Pius X desired that the work of restoration to which he had dedicated himself should proceed *in Christo*, in other words that the bases upon which it was to rest should be first and foremost spiritual. Several consequences flowed from this conviction, which the Pope's entire attitude made manifest. First, in his eyes political action is only secondary; he considered it much more essential to provide for the training of a zealous clergy or bring back souls to frequentation of the sacraments than to succeed in negotiations with a foreign government; on more than one occasion, for instance, he showed that he attached far more importance to the meeting of a eucharistic congress than to some political matter. Hence a certain contempt for political affairs, such as could never have been attributed to the diplomat Leo XIII; a contempt, however, that was nothing more than a profound sense of the true scale of values. The 'interests of God', after all, take precedence over human concerns, and—here is a second consequence—the two must never be confused, for example, by allowing Catholics to compromise the Church by committing themselves as such to political parties. And if it happened that the interests of God were in opposition to those of the faithful, even to the temporal interests of the Church, Pius X never hesitated to sacrifice the latter to the former, no

[1] See Chapter II, section 4.

matter how grave the material loss might be. This fact explains certain displays of apparent harshness, certain decisions which at first glance seemed disastrous; they transcended the interests ordinarily served by politics—they were not, as Pascal would have said, of the same order.

This most unusual concept of politics agrees fully with the character of the man who gave it practical expression. Giuseppe Sarto remained priest and pastor even when crowned with the tiara, anxious in the highest degree for the welfare of souls. A mystic, he lived naturally in the supernatural. That fact did not prevent his having a keen sense of the real, but it made his realism the contrary of Machiavelli's. Absorbed in the awareness of God's abiding presence and of his duty to follow the divine will in all things, he was incapable, not of suppleness and even adroitness—as we shall see in the affairs of Italy and Germany—but of evasion or of appearing to forget essentials. When he thought the interests of God were threatened, this wonderfully good and kindly man became hard as rock. At such times, says Cardinal Merry del Val in his memoirs,[1] 'after days of anxious reflection and many sleepless nights he would lay his arm on his desk, slowly clench his fist and then, raising his head, with his ordinarily calm and gentle gaze now stern, deliver his judgment in a few well-weighed words, after which there was nothing more to do or say'. Have the saints ever behaved otherwise when engaged in politics? One thinks of St Gregory the Great, St Bernard, St Louis, St Joan of Arc, St Pius V.... St Pius X was of the same breed, like them inexplicable by the standards of human wisdom, like them a mystic even in the realm of politics, like them rigorous through love and bellicose through loyalty.

2. Separation of Church and State in France

No chapter in the history of Pius X's pontificate makes us feel the quasi-supernatural and, by the same token, disconcerting character of his 'politics' as does that of his relations with the French Republic at a time of violent crisis. On his accession to the papal throne Pius X found the Church in France seriously endangered. Anticlerical and even antichristian measures were following one upon another under pretext of 'republican defence'.

The Pope's first reaction was by no means drastic. He tried to reduce the violence of the conflict by writing personally to the President of the French Republic a firm but most courteous letter, telling him that he was alarmed by the plan of dechristianization which the Government appeared to be following and by the prospect of disturbances to which it could lead. To this Émile Loubet replied, with his usual moderation,

[1] *Pius X: Impressions and Memories.*

that since he was 'constitutionally irresponsible' he could not intervene; but he quite rightly took the opportunity to complain of the abusive language employed by certain Catholics.[1] Despite the failure of this initial approach, and when he learned that new measures against the teaching congregations were imminent, Pius X became more outspoken and protested in advance. His protest, however, did not prevent the Chamber from passing a law (7th July 1904) which barred all members of religious congregations from teaching and resulted in the immediate closure of two thousand schools.

The field was as yet that of French legislation, where the Pope's intervention laid him open to a charge of meddling in the internal affairs of a sovereign State. But the enemies of the Church, who held power in Paris, were following a more comprehensive plan and were determined to provoke a conflict with the papacy itself. Three incidents, whose gravity seemed out of all proportion to that of the decisions in which they resulted, were systematically exploited by Combes with a view to rupture.

The first ground of dispute, which had originated during the pontificate of Leo XIII, was that of the *nobis nominavit*, the formula traditionally employed by the Roman Curia since 1804 in confirming a candidate for a bishopric proposed by the Government. Its subtle Latin implied that the bishop had not been *appointed* by the Government, but only *named* to the Pope, to whom alone belonged the right of actual appointment. When Combes made the formula a new *casus belli*, Pius X yielded over a mere matter of words and abandoned the *nobis*.

Fundamentally, however, he did not yield. Combes claimed that the Government had a right to choose the bishops on its own; but Pius X, like Leo XIII, demanded retention of the 'earlier agreement', to which the president replied by notifying the Holy See of several appointments about which it had not been consulted. The Pope refused canonical institution to the bishops concerned. Following the example of Louis XIV in the matter of the *Régale*,[2] Combes retorted with a declaration that he would leave without a pastor any diocese that became vacant. Such was the position in March 1904, and a half-compromise was under consideration when a more serious dispute broke out and caused a great sensation.

After the visit of King Edward VII to Paris there had been talk of an exchange of official visits between the President of the French Republic and young King Victor Emmanuel of Italy. Cardinal Rampolla, Leo XIII's secretary of state, had warned Delcassé, the

[1] During a reception Mme Loubet had complained to the nuncio, with justifiable indignation, that some Catholic journalists were referring to her husband by the insulting nickname of 'Panama I'.

[2] *The Church in the Seventeenth Century*, Chapter IV.

French minister of foreign affairs, that serious consequences would result from the arrival in Rome of M. Loubet to visit a sovereign whom the Apostolic See regarded as a despoiler. It would be looked upon as an insult both to the rights of the Holy See and also to the august person of the Pope. Nevertheless the project was carried out in April 1904, Paris considering a *rapprochement* with Italy useful for international reasons—in order to forestall an Italo-German alliance. It was the first time that the head of a Catholic State had crossed the threshold of the Quirinal since 1870. Embittered less by the event itself than by the insulting manner towards himself in which the freemasons, the anticlerical press and even the Italian Government treated the visit, the 'rigorist' Pius X could hardly do less than the 'diplomat' Leo XIII. He refused to receive the French president, and then sent to all Catholic heads of state a note of protest against this outrage. The note was in theory secret; but the Prince of Monaco, a convinced anticlerical, passed it on to the Socialist newspaper *L'Humanité*, which printed it. The published text contained a sentence which did not occur in the note sent to France: 'That the papal nuncio has remained in Paris is due solely to very grave reasons of an order and of a nature in all respects peculiar,' which was simply another way of saying: '. . . because everyone knows that Combes's government is about to fall'. Combes reacted by recalling the ambassador to the Holy See and leaving a mere *chargé d'affaires*. 'We have decided to have done', he declared, 'with the outmoded fiction of a temporal power which vanished thirty-four years ago.'

One final step would lead to the breaking off of diplomatic relations, and this was taken on 30th July 1904 in consequence of a third incident. The Holy Office had summoned to Rome two bishops, Mgr Le Nordez of Dijon and Mgr Geay of Laval, who were known for their republican sympathies and better still as being at loggerheads with their diocesans. Geay, an impulsive neurasthenic, had closed the chapel of the free college and forbidden the Jesuits to preach; his relations with the mother superior of Carmel, too, were causing a good deal of tittle-tattle. Le Nordez, an ambitious prelate who dreamed of the archiepiscopal see of Paris, was considered to be so hand in glove with the civil authority that the archpriest of his cathedral had denounced him to Rome as a freemason, his seminarists refused to be ordained by him and parents objected to his confirming their children. The French Government protested: it maintained that these summonses, made without reference to itself, were violations of the Concordat—that in fact they disobeyed the Organic Articles! Pius X would not give way; the two bishops, threatened with suspension, betook themselves to Rome and made their submission. Here was a splendid opportunity for Combes and his *légistes*. 'The pleasure of the Holy See', they said,

'makes diplomatic relations between France and the Vatican altogether futile.' The French *chargé d'affaires* left Rome and the nuncio took leave of Paris. That situation, so prejudicial to both parties, was to last for seventeen years.

Combes, who would none the less have preferred to keep the Concordat as a means of keeping an eye upon the Church, was now obliged to prepare a Bill for its abrogation. This Bill, in fact, envisaged a kind of national Church under strict control; but before it came up for debate the Government, as foreseen, was driven from office.

What would the new ministry do? Neither Rouvier, who headed it, nor Bienvenu-Martin, who held the portfolio of cults, cherished the same cross-grained temper towards the Church as had Combes. They left the Chamber to settle religious affairs, and for this purpose a commission was set up under the chairmanship of Aristide Briand (1862–1932). This militant Socialist, an extreme left-wing journalist who had also appeared as counsel for strikers and anarchists, was possessed of an intelligence far above the stupidities of anticlericalism. A diplomat naturally more inclined to solution by compromise than to rupture, Briand nevertheless realized that most people considered separation as inevitable, and therefore turned his thoughts to bringing it about. But he wanted so he said, a 'straightforward, fair and moderate' law, which would not be 'a pistol aimed against the Church' but would guarantee her 'what she had the right to demand, namely full freedom to become organized, to live and to develop according to her own rules and by her own means, without any other restriction than respect for the law of the land and public order'. He made inquiries of certain bishops, notably Mgr Fuzet of Rouen, and would have liked to negotiate with Rome. Feeling, however, ran so high that this broad-minded policy could not succeed. Bitterly attacked by Clemenceau and the extreme left, as well as by the majority of Catholics, Briand came into collision also with the intransigence of Pius X, an intransigence the motives of which he did not understand until later.

The Law of Separation of Church and State was passed in July and promulgated in December 1905. Its three main provisions were: (1) the Napoleonic Concordat and Organic Articles were repealed; (2) the Republic would neither recognize nor subsidize any form of religious cult; (3) the goods of the Church were and would remain the property of the State, but churches, chapels etc., would be gratuitously entrusted to *associations cultuelles* elected by the faithful, while other buildings, such as bishops' palaces and seminaries, would be left at the disposition of the clergy for only a few years. Numerous less important clauses made provision for the livelihood of aged priests, ordered that the police be notified of all religious gatherings and even regulated the ringing of bells.

There was some disagreement as to whether such a law was in itself acceptable to the Church. Mgr d'Hulst, among others, had argued several years earlier that separation of Church and State might prove beneficial. Passed in an atmosphere of calm it could have been used by Catholics to further their own interests. The regime for which Briand had hoped was similar to that which existed in the Anglo-Saxon countries, based on liberal tolerance without legal restrictions other than those of the common law; in the United States, for example, such a system worked very well. But in France the anticlericals interpreted separation in quite a different way: it meant total rupture between the French Republic and the Church, an end of age-old relations between the two powers. Some indeed went further, regarding it as a decisive victory for freethinking and secularism, the prelude of victories yet to come. 'What must be understood', wrote Ranc, a freemason, 'is that for us the separation is only a means; our goal is complete secularization of the State, and an end to the influence of the Church.' Ferdinand Buisson was more explicit: 'Democracy, impelled by a wonderful instinct of its needs and of its immediate duty, is preparing to detach the nation, families and individuals from the Church.' Such aims, which were clear as daylight to the Pope, explain why he reacted with such firmness. As for the Catholics of France, aggrieved by the anticlerical measures of Combes, they could hardly have looked upon the Law of Separation as anything but a weapon of war directed against themselves.

In order therefore that the law might be accepted by Catholics it was essential that the Holy See should, if not recognize it, at least tolerate its application. Pius X quickly made known what he thought of it. In February 1906 there appeared an Encyclical whose title, *Vehementer nos*, gave the key to the Pope's attitude. Taking his stand upon Leo XIII's *Immortale Dei*, he declared that the very principle of separation constituted an 'insult to God', that its application would be 'an injustice to the Church', since it did not allow her full and complete freedom but subjected her to control by the civil authority, and also a trespass upon her canonical laws, since the conduct of worship would in effect be entrusted to the 'citizens' instead of to the hierarchy, which is alone responsible. This amounted to pure and simple rejection of the law, as Pius X emphasized a few days later in a consistory. It was, he said, 'an iniquitous law, concocted for the ruin of Catholicism', and every Catholic had a duty to fight against it. Shortly afterwards, taking advantage of the freedom just restored to him by the denunciation of the Concordat, the Pope appointed *motu proprio* bishops to fourteen vacant diocesan sees, giving to these appointments the character of a manifesto. The new bishops were solemnly consecrated by himself in St Peter's, and he handed to each personally the cross and ring. Then,

receiving them in audience on the following day, he declared with emotion that he appreciated 'the sacrifice they were making by exposing themselves to poverty, privation and perhaps persecution', and added that he 'would like to be departing with them to share the sufferings and privation which the Church in France was about to endure'. At the same time he announced that he was going to beatify the Curé d'Ars.

Application of the law did in fact open the road to a veritable persecution. Article III had prescribed an inventory of the goods of the Church, which were to be handed over to the *associations cultuelles*. The legislators thought of this as a conservative measure—many Catholic deputies had voted for it—but in the passionate climate of the moment it was represented by the anticlerical left as a means of exposing the scandalous wealth of the Church, and by many Catholics as nothing less than sacrilege, a seizure of religious buildings by way of prelude to a nationalization on the model of 1790. It was said that the agents of the Republic would profane the sacred Host and drink altar wine from ciboria. A resistance movement was organized, not without political undertones, and battalions of volunteers, most of them quite young, were formed to resist by force the taking of inventories. Eventually, at Bolschepe in the department of Nord, a demonstrator was killed by the son of a government official who believed his father's life to be in danger, a tragic incident which had an unexpected political result. Attacked by a coalition of Catholics and the extreme left, Rouvier's ministry was overthrown and succeeded by that of Sarrien, in which Clemenceau received the portfolio of the Interior and Briand that of cults.

A delicate problem remained to be settled: Should the Church accept the *associations cultuelles* in the form laid down by the law, or reject them and thereby reduce to penury not only the clergy but all religious institutions as well? Since Pius X had condemned the entire law, the question of principle was already decided, but was it not possible to reach some kind of arrangement? The Pope himself certainly gave the matter some thought, for he asked the bishops of France to meet in full assembly and tender him their advice. A very large majority of the French episcopate was unfavourable to the *cultuelles*, but did not want total rupture. Mgr Fuzet, Archbishop of Rouen and a personal friend of Briand, urged a compromise solution, which Mgr Fulbert-Petit, Archbishop of Besançon, professed to discover in what he called 'canonico-legal associations' within the framework of the law but under the control of the hierarchy. A group of influential laymen published a manifesto counselling moderation, thus earning for themselves, from those who regarded them as 'scuttlers', the delightful nickname of 'green cardinals'.

The final decision lay with Pius X; it cost him some painful qualms of conscience and long hours of prayer. He knew full well that by rejecting the *cultuelles* he was condemning the Church in France to extreme material difficulties, to poverty and even to destitution. When his secretary of state provided figures to show him of how many millions of francs he was going to deprive the French clergy, he answered in one noble sentence: 'It is not the goods of the Church that I am defending, but the Good.' And when a cardinal asked him how the Archbishop of Paris could fulfil his duties without a palace, without a budget and without material means, he replied with some vehemence: 'If he cannot do so, I will appoint a Franciscan in his place—a man who will have taken a vow of poverty.'

On 10th August 1906 the Encyclical *Gravissimo officii* made known the Holy Father's decision. The *associations cultuelles* were forbidden, even in the suggested 'canonico-legal' form. They were declared unacceptable 'so long as the divine constitution of the Church, the unalterable rights of the Roman Pontiff and the bishops, as well as their authority over sacred goods and buildings, were not irrevocably guaranteed'. Thus was the Church of France driven out into the unknown.

As it happened the situation did not deteriorate. While the French bishops unanimously and solemnly proclaimed their acceptance of the papal decision, thereby setting a magnificent example alike of discipline and of self-sacrifice, the politicians whose business it was to apply the new law tried openly not to press their advantage to the point at which serious trouble might be expected. Clemenceau, having succeeded Sarrien in October 1906, retained Briand at the ministry of cults, and the latter continued his policy of conciliation. The inventories were suspended. 'We're not going to have men killed for the sake of counting church candlesticks,' said Clemenceau with a laugh. A series of decrees and circulars left Catholics the right and the means to carry on without having to set up those *cultuelles* which Protestants and Jews had not hesitated to establish. Nor was public notice of religious gatherings any longer required. Buildings intended for worship would be placed freely at the disposal of priests by the communes, their legal owners.

These measures, it is true, involved storm and stress. Briand's repeated approaches to the Holy See were misinterpreted. It even appears that Cardinal Merry del Val failed to understand Briand's purpose and thought he was dealing with another Combes. Clemenceau in turn, following some petty dispute, indulged his fury to the extent of ordering Mgr Montagnini [1] to leave Paris and of defying all diplomatic custom by ordering seizure of the nuncio's archives in

[1] Secretary to the papal nunciature, who had remained for the time being at his post.

order to provide material for the left-wing press. By 1909, however, despite this and other incidents,[1] it could be said that a *modus vivendi* had been established, which allowed the Catholics of France to practise their religion. Briand would have liked to go further; he secured the passage of a law assigning to 'ecclesiastical benefit societies', which were as yet non-existent, the clergy's superannuation funds and the property of ancient religious establishments bound by pious obligations. But this solution also was rejected by Rome, since it took no account of the hierachy.

Thus at the end of that grave crisis the Church in France found herself despoiled of all her goods, without receipt or compensation. All buildings dependent on the clergy had been seized—bishops' palaces, schools, church halls and all funds, including superannuation funds to which priests had contributed sou by sou, and also capital given or bequeathed for foundation masses. In order to live, therefore, priests had to commit themselves to Providence and rely upon the generosity of the faithful. Threatened at every moment by the whims of a prefect or the ill humour of a mayor, they might find themselves driven from their presbyteries, just as the Archbishop of Paris had been expelled from his residence.

And yet, however painful the situation might appear, it had its brighter side. In the first place, from the Church's standpoint, it marked the end of Gallican tendencies, which was a notable contribution towards Pius X's effort to strengthen the hierarchy and centralize ecclesiastical government. Henceforward there would be no intermediary between the Pope on the one hand and the clergy and Christian people of France on the other. The bishops would be chosen exclusively by Rome, the records of candidates being drawn up by the nuncio and then examined by the Consistorial Congregation. A page of history had been turned for ever; and some have thought that consideration of this advantage had something to do with the rigour subsequently displayed by the Curia.

But even for the Church of France the situation brought with it blessings that became apparent with the passing of years. The French clergy, subjected to the stern school of poverty, underwent a severe crisis of vocations. But that very fact excluded from its fold those who would otherwise have become priests for motives far from spiritual. It was about to receive an impulse that would make it one of the best in the world, and certainly the least subservient to material interests and secular authority. More united, more homogeneous, more disciplined and more heroic, it would prove itself increasingly apostolic, while the faithful in turn would understand better the real ties that

[1] e.g. forcible seizure of bishops' palaces and seminaries, and conscription of young ecclesiastics for the army.

bound them to their priests. The Separation, whereby the anticlericals had expected to accomplish the total ruin of Catholicism in France, was on the contrary the starting-point of an extraordinary revival within the very bosom of the Church.

Thus Pius X's intransigence, which had not always been understood, was destined to prove serviceable in 'the interests of God'. In it we can surely see the guiding hand of the Holy Ghost. Aristide Briand, his opponent in that unhappy dispute and whose exact aims the Pope had failed to discern, afterwards paid him this tribute: 'Pius X was the winner from every point of view, and he well deserved to be. . . . Marvellous, that's what the Pope was! I did not always fully understand him. It's only now, looking back, that I can see the whole thing in focus. He was the only one who saw clearly. Often and often in the Chamber, when I had to face up to both sides, left and right, I longed to tell them that they were all a poor lot, that there was only one man who saw clearly, who had a consistent policy and was working for the future—the Pope. He didn't want to die slowly, peacefully. He wanted the Church to live, and life is adventure. . . . His sacrifice was necessary: it has borne its fruits.' [1]

3. The Cause of Justice and of Faith

The same determination to serve 'the interests of God', regardless of immediate consequences, is revealed in many other circumstances. Pius X, for example, showed in a more active way than Leo XIII had done his fatherly affection and support for Catholic peoples subject to the yoke of great foreign States. He did so without stopping to ask whether the interests of the Holy See did not require him to remain on good terms with those powers, and going to the point of open rupture when he judged it necessary to serve the cause of justice.

Poland at that time was partitioned among three masters, and subject in the Russian zone to what Ladislas Reymont later described as 'the apostolate of the knout'; nor were other Catholic communities in the czarist empire, Ruthenians and Uniates, more fortunate. Leo XIII had made vain attempts to improve their lot; Alexander III had continued the policy of Russianization; Vincent Vanutelli, sent as legate to the czar's coronation, had obtained nothing. However, the Russo-Japanese War (1904–5) and the crushing defeat sustained by Nicholas II appeared to bring about a change of policy in the religious

[1] Reported by the Abbé Ferdinand Renaud in *Ecclesia* (Paris), March 1951. Renaud was closely concerned in the renewal of relations between France and the Holy See after the First World War (see Chapter VII, section 5), at which time he had numerous meetings with Briand.

as in every other field. Catholics were allowed religious freedom, and this measure was followed by a tide of conversions which rose to the number of about two hundred thousand souls. The Orthodox Church reacted at once, supported by the imperial authorities, who saw therein a danger to Holy Russia. A systematic campaign of defamation was launched against Rome, and outright persecution was resumed, especially in Poland. Pius X vented his furious indignation by denouncing the czar's perfidy, caring not a jot for the serious difficulties in which he might become involved with the Government at St Petersburg. At about the same time, when the German emperor ventured to imitate his Russian colleague, the Pope lent his firm support to the Archbishop of Posen, who was protesting against the 'Prussianization of the Poles'. It was all done as if Pius X foresaw that the partition of Poland was temporary and that one day the heroic Catholic nation would again be free and united. In this policy on behalf of God the Pope went so far as to make a public scene at an audience for ambassadors who had come to offer him their good wishes on New Year's Day, 1911. When the Russian's turn came, Pius told him he could not accept the compliments of a perjurer; then, cutting short excuses, he showed him the door, through which the diplomat departed pale as death.

Another unfortunate Catholic people were the Irish. Leo XIII had not been insensible to their protests against British rule; but having established good relations with the Government in London, he had tried to play the part of a mediator whose good offices would prevent the situation from becoming explosive. He had even, in 1881, approved a letter signed by all but three of the Irish bishops, condemning the revolutionary violence of the Fenians. The independence movement, however, gained ground year by year. A. G. Parnell inaugurated a new technique of resistance, of which Captain Boycott was to be the first and symbolic victim. The temperature mounted, and the Fenians assassinated Lord Cavendish, secretary of state for Ireland. Despite the Redemption Act (1903), a first step towards a solution of the agrarian question, it was certain that the 'sister-isle' would not much longer endure the tutelage of her elder. Pius X decided that he ought to come down on the side of a free Ireland, as he had done in the case of Poland, and he showed his active sympathy towards the Irish on every possible occasion. Without associating himself officially with the Home Rule campaign, he let it be known that he hoped that the independence of Ireland would be recognized in the near future. He even sent a legate [1] to represent him at an Irish eucharistic congress—a gesture that did not please His Majesty's Government. In England

[1] Mgr Vincent Vanutelli, whom he had previously entrusted with a delicate mission in Russia.

itself, at about the same time, Pius X encouraged Catholics to resist the new educational laws whereby Parliament proposed to transfer Catholic schools to local authorities, which would thus be able to interfere in the education that parents intended to give their children. The English hierarchy, led by Mgr Bourne, Archbishop of Westminster, objected. Pius X gave them his whole-hearted support, and but for Cardinal Merry del Val's personal friendship with members of the British aristocracy a situation akin to that between Rome and St Petersburg would undoubtedly have resulted.

On another occasion it was not justice that Pius X sought to defend, as he had felt obliged to do on behalf of the Poles and the Irish, but the cause of Catholicity in face of aggressive Protestantism. That occasion was a visit to Rome by Theodore Roosevelt in 1910, a visit which provoked an incident which has often been misunderstood. On his arrival in the Eternal City the ex-President of the United States expressed a wish to call upon the Pope as well as the King of Italy. Since the United States was not an officially Catholic country, and since Roosevelt was no longer in office, the problem that had attended Loubet's visit in 1904 did not arise, and the secretariat of state replied that an audience would be granted. But the left-wing press announced with much ado that the illustrious visitor would give a talk in the Methodist chapel. Cardinal Merry del Val promptly made known that if the ex-president really meant to give this talk the papal audience would be refused. Roosevelt replied that if he had to make a choice he would keep his appointment with the Methodists and forgo, not without great regret, the honour of seeing the Pope.

'Sectarianism! Fanaticism!' howled the Roman press. In fact, however, Pius X had grave reasons for not behaving more liberally in an affair which, though it seemed trifling, could have had serious repercussions. At that date, even in Rome, the various Protestant sects, and particularly the Methodists, encouraged by the freemason mayor Ernesto Nathan, were indulging in well-organized propaganda, opening chapels and holding numerous spectacular gatherings. Furthermore, the Methodists were offering a warm welcome not only to Catholic laymen but even to priests who were abandoning the Roman Church on account of Modernism.[1] Finally, and here beyond all doubt was the principal reason, American Catholics were again in a state of thinly veiled war with Protestantism: the Ku Klux Klan had given pride of place in its programme to the anti-Catholic as well as to the anti-Negro campaign. Might it not have seemed to American Catholics that the Sovereign Pontiff was lending the mantle of his authority to the workings of Protestant propaganda in the shape of Roosevelt's discourse to the Methodists? It was not simply the Pope's legitimate

[1] See the following chapter for an account of Modernism.

pride and his desire to enforce respect for the Apostolic See that were opposed to a gesture of indulgent politeness; it was nothing less than the higher interests of the Church.

4. Tragedy in Portugal and Spain

It must, however, be noted that in several instances the troubles that occurred during the pontificate of Pius X cannot be fairly attributed to the drastic features of his policy. Attacks were launched, the malignant violence of which leaves no doubt as to the ultimate goal of those who directed them. We have seen what purpose inspired the most far-sighted and most determined secularizers in France; 'to organize a godless society' was not the aim of Jules Ferry alone. Elsewhere too the very existence of the Church was threatened; and if Pius X was led too frequently to fulminate indignant protests and condemnations, it was because he had no other means of defending religion.

The most striking example is afforded by Portugal, where the separation of Church and State was brought about under conditions far worse than those prevailing in France, conditions which made it impossible for the Pope to intervene in any way other than by protest. The steps taken by Lisbon, modelled on those of Paris, during the last days of Leo XIII had been more or less ineffectual; and during the first years of Pius X the monarchy had even drawn closer to the Church, thanks to the influence of Queen Amelia, a member of the house of Orleans. The result was to exasperate the anticlericalism of Portuguese republicans, who were supported by revolutionary refugees from Brazil. The situation quickly deteriorated when, on 2nd February 1908, King Carlos and his elder son were assassinated in the heart of the capital. The 'progressive' dictatorship of Franco collapsed, and two years later young Manuel, who had succeeded his father on the throne, was ousted by a military revolution which established the Republic.

The republicans, many of whom were freemasons or members of Protestant sects, immediately set to work with a view to overthrowing the Church, and anticlerical decrees followed rapidly one upon another. The congregations were expelled and education was laicized; but the Portuguese anticlericals proved their inventiveness by having recourse also to less conventional measures. For example, one-third of the total sum collected to defray the cost of public worship would be confiscated for the benefit of secular charities; wearing of the cassock in the streets would be treated as a crime; associations equivalent to the French *cultuelles* were established, and all priests barred from membership; religious buildings, whether existing or to be built later, would become

secularized after a certain period of time; seminarists would be obliged to pass through the State schools, and, for good measure, teachers, books and curricula of seminaries would depend on Government approval. Furthermore legal indemnities and subsidies would be granted to the families of married priests. Combes himself had not gone that far.

The application of these measures naturally provoked resistance. While excited mobs attacked churches and convents, while the police confiscated diocesan archives and even those of the nunciature, Catholics reacted under the leadership of Mgr Bella, Patriarch of Lisbon, and clashes occurred in various parts of the country. Six thousand priests and laymen were thrown into prison. Confronted with such a situation, Pius X could do nothing but voice his indignation. He did so in May 1911 through the Encyclical *Jamdudum in Lusitania*, which went straight to the heart of the problem and denounced the Portuguese Law of Separation as evidence of a determination 'to despise God, to repudiate the Catholic faith, to insult the Roman Pontiff and to dismember the Church'. Twice again he repeated his protest, but twice again to no effect. It was not until 1917 that the Lusitanian *Kulturkampf* ended with the overthrow of the sectaries and the accession to power of Machado-Santos, a liberal, and the Catholic Felicien da Costa. But that attempt at dechristianization was to have serious consequences for the land which later witnessed the apparitions of Fatima.

Things were not carried to such lengths in Spain; but the Church there too had cause for grave anxiety. The firmness of Leo XIII had restored peace and enabled Spanish Catholics to devote themselves to those social works which had just taken root in their country. But the left-wing movements, in which the influence of Socialists and Anarchists led by Pablo Iglesias was steadily gaining ground, were violently anticlerical; nor in this respect did Canalejar and his liberals lag far behind. Supported by the young King Alfonso XIII, the moderate minister Maura tried to settle fairly the problem of religious congregations; but his replacement by liberals was followed by the passing of a law against them—a law, however, which no one dared apply.

The real trouble began in 1909. During the summer, at Barcelona, a general strike quickly developed into rioting, at the instigation of syndicalo-anarchists who were very active among the workers. Soon the whole of Catalonia was prey to a veritable red terror which directed its fury against the Church. One hundred and thirty-eight priests and religious were massacred; twenty convents and as many churches were burnt. One man was considered as inspiring the whole movement: Francisco Ferrer, an atheist freemason and anarchist,

founder of a secularist society calling itself the Modern School. He was arrested and, after a trial which, it is true, was little better than a mockery, he and six of his partisans were shot. A wave of wrath swept the working class of Spain. It brought to power Canalejas and a team of liberals hostile to the Church. Their attack was immediate: a Bill was laid before the Cortes which would deprive non-recognized congregations of the right of association. Pius X recalled his nuncio, but (and this must be emphasized) he avoided any violent official declaration which might have created an irreparable situation. At the very moment when the anticlerical law was passed there was held at Madrid an enormous eucharistic congress, an extraordinary demonstration of faith. For the saintly Pontiff that was a more important and more decisive event than all the measures of the sectaries. Speaking in his turn, he declared that Spain, resolutely Catholic, would never agree to become separated from the Church. But in fact the situation was far from being clarified; even the assassination of Canalejas in 1912 left the question unanswered. Relations between Church and State in Catholic Spain had not been defined in any stable fashion; many a collision lay ahead, to culminate in the most serious of all, the civil war twenty-five years later.[1]

5. Quirinal and Vatican: Signs of a New Policy

However categorical may appear Pius X's attitude towards many States, to describe it as 'unyielding', 'clumsy' or 'churlish', as many historians, and even Catholic historians, have done, is to take too summary a view of events. The 'fruitful intransigence' admired by Albert de Mun was not the only means employed by the saintly Pope; when he thought that the interests of God would be better served by gentler methods he was always ready to employ them, though not without a reminder that in the circumstances those interests were not identical with other more temporal interests. And on one point at least this Pontiff, who has been so often represented as rigid within the bounds of a narrow conservatism, proved himself far in advance of his time. I refer to relations between the Apostolic See and the new Italy.

The situation which he inherited at his accession was as simple as it was rigorous. Refusing to recognize the capture of Rome by the 'Piedmontese' monarchy, the Pope continued to ignore the new regime, considered himself as a prisoner in the Vatican, brushed aside

[1] On the eve of the First World War persecution struck the Church in Mexico; the news which Pius X received of it did much to increase the sorrow and anguish which the international situation caused him.

with contempt the offers made to him by the Law of Guarantees and, in the celebrated formula *non expedit*, forbade Italian Catholics to share in the political life of Italy. That attitude, which had been strictly observed by the diplomat Leo XIII, seemed in all respects likely to satisfy Pius X. His own, nevertheless, was much more finely shaded.

Giuseppe Sarto had personal reasons for judging the new Italy otherwise than his last two predecessors had done. In his twenties he had, like all young people of his age, been enthusiastic for the cause of Italian unity. A most affectionate son of the Venetian lands, he never forgot that it was due to the action of the Piedmontese monarchy that his little fatherland had been delivered from the Austrian yoke. He felt sympathy with the royal family, and showed that sympathy on many occasions. Like so many Italians who were both Catholics and patriots, he was saddened by the break between the two powers.

There was yet another reason why his sentiments were not altogether the same as those of his predecessors. Joachim Pecci, formed by French culture and a reader of books by French liberal Catholics, had thought of relying upon France in order to withstand the despoiler that was Italy; but his hopes had been disappointed, and at his death the Republic was evidently moving towards virulent anticlericalism. Sarto, who spoke very bad French and was not well acquainted with French thought, felt no confidence in republican France, and on several occasions during his episcopate he had voiced the disquiet with which she inspired him. He was therefore inclined to bring about a sort of 'reversal of alliances'.

An incident immediately after his election revealed his inmost feelings. The question arose as to where and how he would give the blessing 'Urbi et Orbi'. If he appeared on the outside balcony, it would show that he was breaking with the rigidity of his predecessors. He sought advice from the master of ceremonies, and when the latter could not make up his mind, he questioned the secretary of the conclave as to the opinion of the Sacred College in this matter. It was only when Cardinal Merry del Val told him that their eminences thought the blessing should be given inside the basilica that he abandoned the idea of showing himself above the Piazza of St Peter's.

Officially, therefore, Pius X did not break with the tradition established by his predecessors as regards the Roman Question. He never left the Vatican, always declined to benefit by the advantages offered in the Law of Guarantees and continued, as a matter of principle, to claim his rights. But on this last point one has a feeling that his protests did not express a very strong conviction. There is no recorded case of his having used the phrase 'temporal power', 'Papal States' or

'domain of St Peter'. Though always intransigent whenever the dignity of the Apostolic See appeared to be at stake, he never went out of his way to demand the ownership of land. Moreover when Count Della Torre, president of the Italian Catholic Union, wrote that 'territorial possessions are not the only means of safeguarding the spiritual independence of the Holy See', his bold words went unrebuked.

The change of attitude was still more pronounced as regards the participation of Catholics in the politics of their country. At the time of Pius X's accession the question of the *non expedit* was already in the air. The young generations understood less and less the reasons for that measure. On the other hand Socialism was making progress, especially in the north of Italy, and the enforced abstention of Catholics was likely to bring about the collapse of the moderates. Before the parliamentary elections of 1904 a number of prominent Catholics, among whom were Mgr Bonomelli, Bishop of Cremona, and Professor Nicolo Rezzara, one of the leaders of the social movement, asked the Pope for his instructions at the forthcoming polls. The answers were significant. To the bishop Pius X declared officially that the traditional ban remained in full force. But to the lawyer Bonomi, who had been granted a private audience for the purpose of submitting a petition from the Catholics of Bergamo, the Pope said twice: 'Do what your conscience tells you.' Then he added: 'Pass on this reply to Rezzara and assure him that the Pope will keep quiet.' The door was thus set ajar. Bergamo elected a Catholic deputy, and in Italy as a whole the participation of Catholics in the elections reduced the number of abstentions from 50 per cent to 37 per cent.

The following year another advance was made with the Encyclical *Il fermo proposito*, which reorganized the Catholic movement after the suppression of the *Opera dei Congressi*.[1] Having parried all danger of deviation, crushed the extremists of Christian democracy and placed the whole Catholic movement under the exclusive control of the hierarchy, Pius X decided that since the interests of God required that anticlerical Socialism be prevented from invading Italy, it would be fitting to throw the weight of Catholicism into the political scales. Bishops were authorized, whenever there were 'particularly grave reasons', to seek dispensation from the *non expedit* on behalf of their flocks. At the elections of 1909 a large number of them had the ban lifted. Some twenty deputies who declared themselves Catholics were elected; more significant, however, was the fact that, by voting for the moderates, Catholics contributed much towards their victory over the revolutionary left. A Catholic Electoral Union was formed, and its president, Count Gentiloni, was quickly recognized as an important political figure. On the morrow of the elections in 1913 the success of

[1] See Section 7 of the present chapter.

this new attitude was crowned by the signing of the Gentiloni Pact between the Government and the Catholics, to secure religious guarantees.

We must not indeed exaggerate the importance of the change thus brought about. Ever mistrustful of anything that might commit the Church in the field of politics, and fearing that a political party might elude episcopal authority, Pius X was careful to insist that there were no 'Catholic candidates', no 'Catholic deputies', but only Catholics who took a share in the political life of their country and were elected to the Chamber. His enemies, on the other hand, made no mistake as to the significance of the event. Refusing to admit the distinction between Catholic deputies and Catholics who happened to be deputies, they were incensed by what appeared to them as interference by the Church in politics. Their wrath found expression in a number of incidents, particularly in Rome, where the fortieth anniversary of the capture of the city was the occasion of anticlerical demonstrations, during which the mayor, Ernesto Nathan, delivered a speech of uncommon violence. It was none the less evident that a new orientation had been given to relations between Vatican and Quirinal, between the Church and the new Italy, and that a solution of the Roman Question was no longer inconceivable. This manifestation of Pius X as herald of Pius XI's *Conciliazione* is not the least surprising aspect of his strict pontificate.

6. Catholics in Politics and the Question of Democracy

The remarks of Pius X on 'Catholic candidates' and 'Catholic deputies' quoted above reveal some of his most clearly defined ways of thought: his mistrust of any commitment of Catholics as such in the realm of politics and, above all, of their belonging to political groups. There lies the real meaning of his declaration that the policy of the Church 'is to take no part in politics'. We have seen that this attitude resulted from his lofty conception of the task laid upon him, from his firm resolve to serve 'the interests of God' in every respect, without allowing them to become identified with those of men, and from his determination to strengthen the Church by tightening her hierarchic links. It must not, however, be inferred that his attitude never varied, that he confined himself to summary condemnations.

There can be no doubt that he had a horror of what might be called a 'Catholic party'. He was fundamentally opposed to the formation of any such group in Italy; and in France he did nothing to encourage

Catholics to band themselves together in such a way with a view to fighting their enemies politically. He once remarked of the *Zentrum*, the famous German party which was professedly Catholic and as such had brought Bismarck to Canossa: 'I do not like it, because it is a Catholic party.' Nevertheless there were cases, e.g. in Belgium and Austria, where he not only refrained from acrimony against parties officially described as Catholic, but even approved their activity.

The explanation of these differences of attitude is simple, if we remember the principles on which Pius X relied, principles of order and discipline. However unfavourable he may have been towards the existence of a Catholic party in a country, he was unwilling to condemn or even to thwart it when he saw clearly that its disappearance or enfeeblement would profit the enemy. But in every instance he required that that party should accept the more or less direct control of the hierarchy, and that it should regulate its conduct in accordance with papal directives. Pius X's main objection to the *Zentrum* was that even in certain grave matters it fulfilled those conditions only when it chose to do so.

This is the viewpoint from which the events of the pontificate must be considered if we seek a correct estimate of the Pope's attitude towards democracy, its system and the parties which, even among Catholics, took their stand upon its theories. He has often been represented as a born foe of all democratic regimes and of the very idea of democracy. It must, however, be noted that, in cases of conflict between the Holy See and democratic regimes such as those of France and Portugal, Rome was not the aggressor, and that while Pius X showed severity towards the governments of those two countries he had good reason to do so. But that does not mean that he was hostile to the regimes themselves. He frequently declared that the Church 'could and should accommodate herself to all regimes', provided they respected the rights of God and worked together with her for the common good. 'Nowhere', wrote Cardinal Gasparri later, 'did Pius X suggest that the defence of religion should be conducted on ground other than that of existing institutions.' And in 1907, after the harsh ordeal to which the French democracy had recently subjected the Church, the Pope upheld the same doctrine: 'The rulers of France', he said in his Easter message, 'hope eventually to convince the people that when We defend the rights of the Church We are opposed to the popular regime; and yet We have always accepted and always respected that regime.'

Such words, on the other hand, must not be taken as indicating that Pius X *approved* of that regime. The very principle of democracy could not win his approbation. To hold that all power emanates from the people was in direct opposition to the Christian idea, which derives

it from God; nor was Pius X disposed to admit that the 'voice of the people' is the 'voice of God'. The contradiction between the two theories was obvious, and led to a veritable antinomy in those Catholic political groups which adopted democratic principles. If they claimed to introduce democratic ideas into the very bosom of the Church or to base their conduct upon those ideas, without regard to the instructions and interests of the Church, the rupture would be fatal; for Pius X was not the man to accept such breaches of his own principles. It is precisely there, and not in a political resolve to impose on Catholics one regime rather than another, that we must see the cause of the severity which he displayed in a number of sensational episodes.

7. The End of the 'Opera dei Congressi'

The first of those episodes occurred in Italy; it concerned the *Opera dei Congressi.* This Catholic movement had flourished uninterruptedly during the pontificate of Leo XIII until it seemed to polarize the whole activity of the Church in Italy.[1] But its character had undergone a gradual change. Having started as a body of religious thought, somewhat restricted and controlled by the Holy See through the bishops, the *Opera* had developed into a huge organization which professed to cover the whole field of activity—political, social, economic and cultural, as well as religious—in which Catholics might assert themselves. Founded at a date when Catholics, excluded from politics, envisaged a close life among themselves, the *Opera* now found itself linked with all the ardent forces of the nation and, by the same token, involved in affairs at every level. Finally, by the very fact of its having lasted, a new generation had appeared within its fold, a generation of enormous enterprise and increasing influence. Unlike the 'old men', who were politically conservative and socially paternalists, the 'young' held more advanced ideas. Without our having to admit that the whole of this new generation embraced the theories of 'Christian democracy', which, as we have seen,[2] had been on the flood-tide of expansion since 1896, it is certain that the more energetic wing of the *Opera dei Congressi* welcomed those ideas. The 'young' had their weekly newspaper, *Il Domani d'Italia*, which printed forty thousand copies—a very large figure in a country two-fifths of whose population were unable to read. They formed themselves into a 'cultural society', which proclaimed itself Christian Democrat and had no fewer than three hundred sections.

The man who embodied this tendency, and whom most of the younger people considered as their leader, was an energetic and

[1] See Chapter II, section 10. [2] Ibid., section 13.

enthusiastic priest, Don Romolo Murri (1870–1943), a fascinating and yet a forbidding character. Some of his ideas have left traces in our own day and he is in some respects reminiscent of Lamennais, to whom he once likened himself. A brilliant intellect, a powerful orator, capable above all and in the highest degree of invigorating whatever he took in hand, labouring incessantly to stir up men and ideas, this young cleric soon enjoyed in the *Opera dei Congressi* a prestige out of all proportion to his age. At twenty-three he had already laid the foundations of the Catholic University Federation, and given it its own review, *Vita nuova*. At twenty-six, passionately devoted to the social aims of *Rerum Novarum*, he had launched *Cultura sociale* as a means of giving effect to the teaching of Leo XIII. Like Lamennais in his youth, Murri proclaimed his unshakable attachment to the Church and to the Roman See. Time after time he declared on the strength of the *Syllabus* that Catholics could never in any circumstances accept the materialist and pagan concept of modern society; and if anyone talked in his presence of looking for a conciliatory solution of the Roman Question, he exploded. If the Church would only unite and rally round her head, she would assume the new look awaited by mankind, and victory would be certain. So cried Murri; but it need hardly be added that for him, as for Lamennais and Gioberti, the new look would be one of his own devising. Pride, which has ever been the making of heresiarchs and schismatics, was not absent from that fiery soul.

During the last five years of the pontificate of Leo XIII the propensity of this hothead to act according to his own whims became more and more apparent, especially after the measures adopted by the Government in 1898 against a certain number of economic and social institutions dependent on the *Opera dei Congressi*. Murri and his friends wanted to meet force with force and, with that end in view, to organize the Catholics on a political basis. The formula 'Christian democracy' became the *leit-motiv* of this movement. Taking open control of the *Opera dei Congressi*, the 'young' went so far as to denounce what they called its congenital vice—the fact of its being a religious organism dependent on the hierarchy, in which laymen found themselves hampered at every turn. Leo XIII's *Graves de Communi*,[1] which had clarified the meaning of 'Christian democracy', did not embarrass Murri and his comrades. When the 'old men' claimed victory the 'young' retorted that the Encyclical, by identifying democracy with a 'beneficent social activity', left them an open field; and Count Grosoli's appointment as president of the *Opera* seemed destined to mitigate the conflict, since he was a prudent man well respected by both camps.

It is not unlikely that Leo XIII perceived the danger and feared a

[1] See Chapter II, section 13.

possible spread of Romolo Murri's anti-hierarchical tendencies. At all events, shortly before his death the secretary of state published a new regulation stipulating that all sections of the 'young democrats' must remain affiliated to the *Opera dei Congressi* and consequently subject to the control of its directors. Murri had bridled at once. *Il Domani d'Italia* had replied to the instructions with a *non possumus* that already savoured of revolt. In April 1902, speaking in the Republic of San Marino on the subject of Liberty and Christianity, the impetuous orator had proclaimed the necessity not only of throwing off the hierarchical yoke, but also—this was a well-worn theme in Italy, used later by Fogazzaro in his novel *Il Santo*—of reforming the Church by freeing her from squalid routine and so restoring her pristine purity. At the same time he had made some tactless and unseasonable references to the critical works of certain exegetes and philosophers, such as Loisy and Tyrrell, whose activities were causing the Holy Office grave anxiety. However, when rebuked in a stern note from the Cardinal Vicar, Romolo Murri had submitted; he had withdrawn from circulation all unsold copies of his incendiary discourse, and had even asked for and obtained an audience with the Pope, at which he begged the papal blessing.

Pius X thus found a situation which, despite appearances, was explosive; and of course Don Murri's attitude was more than likely to displease him. How genuine was the young adventurer's submission? At the Congress of Bologna in 1903 the tremendous ovation with which he was received proved that a vast majority of the eighteen hundred participants was firmly on his side. The 'old men', who still controlled the Directing Committee, retorted with a vigorous address to the Pope demanding separation of the *Opera dei Congressi* from the democratic agitation that had more than once been reprobated by the Holy See.

Pius X did not react as the 'old men' would have liked. He answered with an appeal for reconciliation and the union of all Catholics, a hope that was not fulfilled. He then published an instruction which recalled the definition of Christian Democracy in *Graves de Communi*, repeated the ban forbidding Catholics to take part in politics, and ended once again by insisting that all Catholic activities must be subject to the control of the hierarchy. This appeal also was fruitless. Murri and his friends, believing that they had won the day at Bologna, brought pressure to bear on Count Grosoli, hitherto regarded as an arbitrator between the factions, and persuaded him to draw up a new programme inspired, so he said, by papal directives, but in which the influence of the militant wing was only too aparent. Disowned by the secretary of state, the president of *Opera dei Congressi* resigned.

Pius X now realized that it was no longer possible to keep the

association under control of the hierarchy and that, notwithstanding its change of direction, it would be torn between the two tendencies. He must therefore go back to a properly religious undertaking, Catholic in the strictest sense of the word and entirely obedient. That required a preliminary step, and he took it: on 20th July 1904 he suppressed the *Opera dei Congressi*—not without some anguish of heart, for he knew how much it had done for the Church in Italy.

Romolo Murri and his followers would not acknowledge defeat. They founded an Italian Democratic League with the intention of rallying 'free men' and 'true democrats'. The Pope forbade clerics to join the league, and it withered away in four years. *La Rivista di Cultura*, the movement's journal, which also showed itself extremely favourable to Modernist doctrines, was placed on the Index together with several of Murri's works. He himself was first suspended *a divinis*, and then excommunicated in 1909 immediately after his election to the Chamber, in which he was about to take his seat as a radical—'Chaplain of the left', said Giolitti with a laugh.[1]

Pius X, however, was fully aware of the void that would result from suppression of the *Opera dei Congressi*. Accordingly, on 11th June 1905, the Encyclical *Il fermo proposito* established a new organization to be known as the Italian Catholic Movement. The Catholic forces were arrayed in four groups: a Popular Union, modelled more or less on the *Volksverein*; an Economic and Social Union to carry on the work of the second section of the *Opera dei Congressi*, whose social activity had exposed it to no criticism;[2] a Society of Italian Youth, to which was attached later a Catholic Women's Union; and the Catholic Electoral Union, which we have already noticed.[3] The formation of this last was particularly important and significant: coinciding with the permission that henceforward allowed Catholics to work in the political field,[4] it was charged with the guidance of that work. Its president, Count Gentiloni, was joined soon afterwards in the task of supervision by a distinguished journalist who had edited the Brescia *Cittadino*, Giorgio Montini, father of Pope Paul VI.

All these groups were placed under the control of the hierarchy—of the bishops at diocesan level, of the Holy See at national level. Romolo Murri's Christian democracy, autonomous and more or less anarchic, gradually disappeared; but in a new and perhaps near perspective it was possible to observe another type of Christian democracy taking shape and developing under the eye of the Pope himself, a type that would resolve the contradiction between submission to hierarchical

[1] Murri went through a form of civil marriage, and continued his career as a political writer and journalist for more than thirty years. But on his deathbed he asked pardon of the Church, and Pius XII granted his request.

[2] See Chapter IV, section 10. [3] Section 5 above. [4] Ibid.

discipline and the necessary independence of Catholics in political life. Moreover, in the general secretariat of the 'directoral Junta' of the movement's five groups there appeared a man who, after the First World War, was to found the Italian Popular Party, the party of Christian democracy recognized and encouraged by the Holy See, Don Luigi Sturzo.

8. In France: the 'Abbés democrates' and 'Le Sillon'

The situation in France was obviously different from its Italian counterpart. No *non expedit* forbade Catholics to take a hand in politics, and they took full advantage of their freedom. Since about 1895 a movement had been spreading among them which derived from the principles of democracy. Fostered by the new climate resulting from Leo XIII's policy of *ralliement* and by the social teaching of *Rerum novarum*, it was led by a few young members of the clergy who had seen in those two events the sign of a new orientation of the Church and who were called by their enemies 'les abbés démocrates'.[1] No one had ever denied the generosity, devotion or courage of these young priests; their press campaigns and public meetings had helped to spread the social theories of the Encyclical, and when the Church of France was attacked they had been in the front rank of her defenders. Rome itself had thanked them. But they clearly tended to confuse the religious with the political order, and to see in the democratic regime the necessary means of all Catholic action. 'Religion, science and democracy are the three foundations of modern social order,' declared *La Concorde*, one of their newspapers. It was to a large extent the hazardous position adopted by the 'abbés démocrates' that had moved Leo XIII to publish *Graves de Communi*.

There was no evidence that the Encyclical had had much effect on those whom it had in view. Leo's definition of Christian democratic action as 'a beneficent social activity' seemed to them, from a distance, inadequate. They continued to proclaim the necessity of securing the triumph of democracy, which they regarded as the sole means of establishing social justice. 'The advent of democracy', said one of them, the Abbé Gayraud, 'is the term of that social evolution which was begun in the world by the proclamation of the dogma of divine brotherhood.' Elsewhere it was written that 'no one has embodied the republican idea in so perfect a manner as did Jesus Christ'. Elsewhere

[1] See Chapter III, section 13.

again, that 'the Church is essentially democratic', a statement which entailed the corollary that her institutions must be remodelled on democratic lines.

Tension increased steadily between the Church of France and the 'abbés démocrates'. Too responsive to the pressures and plaudits of the radical and socialist left, they adopted towards all subjects an attitude of the greatest daring and closely akin to that of the enemy. In the social field they were opposed to corporatism, and in the matter of syndicalism they rejected 'mixed' syndicates. Carried away by their own hot-headed enthusiasm, they came to describe as 'execrable' those Catholics who did not share their ideas, and to voice in public their bitter disappointment when one of the latter was victorious at an election. More dangerous still, because of their anxiety to be in the vanguard, they allowed themselves to be drawn into the Modernist affair,[1] as their Italian rival Murri had done. While proclaiming that they had nothing to do with Modernism, they lent the support of their journals to suspect theses, notably to those of the Abbé Loisy. One Christian democrat paper declared that 'those who condemned it did not understand it', which was indeed to prepare a rod for their own backs. Those bishops in whose dioceses these rash men were at work repeatedly called them to order and issued solemn warnings; but the 'abbés démocrates' disregarded their superiors, stated in black and white that 'the hierarchy is not the whole Church', and even suggested a democratic reform of the Church which would empower 'the ordinary faithful to make their views heard'.

Remembering the principles upon which Pius X relied one easily understands that such behaviour was ill calculated to please him. The only surprising thing is that he waited so long before taking action. No doubt he recoiled from censuring priests who had fought bravely during the painful events of the Separation, even though they were too ready to blame their Catholic brethren for what they held to be political mistakes. But in the heavy atmosphere of the Modernist crisis evasion was no longer tolerable in any field, and Pius X resolved to strike.

On 13th February 1908 a decree of the Holy Office condemned the two most notorious Christian Democrat journals—the Abbé Naudet's *Justice sociale* and the Abbé Dabry's *Vie catholique*; both priests were 'expressly required, under pain of suspension *a divinis*, not to publish in future either those journals or other writings of that nature'. The Abbé Naudet submitted without hesitation; he was on his way back from saying Mass when he read the decree in a newspaper. 'Let us kneel down', he murmured, 'and say a prayer.' He died an admirable death. The Abbé Dabry, a more excitable character, began by

[1] See Chapter VI.

submitting; then, two years later and without even warning his friends, he left the Church and sank deeper and deeper into gloom, despair and destitution until death overtook him at Marseilles in 1916.[1] All the 'abbés démocrates' acknowledged the blow. Most of them bowed to the Pope's will. One case, however, remained outstanding, that of the Abbé Lemire, deputy mayor of Hazebrouck, whose political attitudes led to violent dispute with the Bishop of Cambrai and then with the Bishop of Lille. In 1913 a decree of the Consistorial Congregation forbade members of the clergy to offer themselves for election without leave of their bishop. Lemire refused to obey and was suspended; only the First World War put an end to that painful conflict.

The affair of *Le Sillon* caused an even greater commotion than that of the 'abbés démocrates'. Because the Holy See had expected a great deal from this movement, and had shown it extraordinary favour from the outset, its condemnation had much wider echoes. It was born and grew to maturity during the last ten years of Leo XIII's pontificate; Pius X found it already well established and full of vigour, but none the less heavily criticized. At Paris, in 1894, Marc Sangnier, Paul Renaudin, Étienne Isabelle and a few kindred spirits used to meet every Friday in the crypt of the Collège Stanislas, where they discussed the future of Christianity and the difficulties confronting the Church. They had seen religious communities expelled from their convents, Christian schools closed and their teachers lose heart. They themselves, however, were by no means despondent. Why, they asked, had Christ so many foes? Because His message had been betrayed or misunderstood. To live according to the Gospel, and at the same time to carry it to those who knew it not, was the only possible solution of the problem. And so there went out from the Stanislas crypt a militant Christian company, utterly devoid of prejudice, determined to make their faith penetrate the surrounding world of indifference and hostility, and calling itself *Le Sillon* after a small review founded by Paul Renaudin.

Marc Sangnier (1873–1950) had quickly outstripped his companions and emerged as their sole leader. In appearance he was rather an insignificant little man; but his warm-heartedness, his oratorical gifts and his unfailing intuition of young people's aspirations had earned him an extraordinary measure of prestige. When he addressed a large assembly, a mysterious force seemed to lift him above himself: a medley of subjects and quotations flowed from his lips—the Church and the Republic, the Canticles and the *Marseillaise*, Ibsen and the

[1] 'I have reason to believe', writes the Abbé Brugerette, 'that before his death Pierre Dabry had made contact with his former superior M. Delbidos and other priest friends with a view to reconciliation with the Church.'

Gospel. But his manner was unique; at the end of a discourse on Christ for ever persecuted, he would shed real tears, choke with sobs and convulse the whole audience. Wonderful, moreover, in his contact with individual souls, Marc became the guide, inspiration and supreme friend of all those who had discovered through *Le Sillon* the meaning of life. He might, however, have laboured more successfully had he possessed a surer sense of the possible and the impossible; and, great Christian though he was, he lacked that humility of heart to which the Kingdom of Heaven has been promised.

Le Sillon had quickly proved a notable success; many young men, among them the cream of Catholic France, had joined its ranks, and the number of student circles had increased. Those who sought enlightenment from its teaching learned from Marc Sangnier that in order to serve Christ they must go to the people, seek to understand and love the people before trying to instruct them in the knowledge and love of Jesus. Popular Institutes were founded, with a view to accomplishing the brotherly alliance of all men. A guard of young men was formed, at once a mystical militia and a body of shock-troops; wearing a black and white uniform, they sold *Silloniste* publications at church doors and kept order at public meetings. The Church looked favourably upon all those activities: Oratorians, Marianists and Brothers of the Christian Schools supported the movement, and young workers were beginning to join the upper-class students in their study circles. Some bishops publicly declared their esteem and confidence, and Leo XIII showed his kindly interest by conferring upon Sangnier the Order of St Gregory the Great. Surely, thanks to these young men, the grand design of *Rerum Novarum* was about to become a living reality. In September 1903, very soon after his accession, Pius X received a pilgrimage of *Sillonistes* in solemn audience. The movement had now reached its apogee.

Some far-sighted observers, however, had already begun to ask disturbing questions about *Le Sillon*. Was not the leader so self-centred and domineering that he was making it increasingly difficult for the more able of his companions to collaborate with him? Again, here was a body of young men who had undertaken nothing less than the rebuilding of Christendom; but were they sufficiently trained in theology, sociology and political economy to ensure the safety of their foundations? Finally, was it not clear that the further the movement advanced the more suspect its purpose became, that it was increasingly concerned with politics, and that the originally religious character of *Le Sillon* was steadily yielding pride of place to a democratic activism which was not always discreet? Those questions became more frequent year by year and were asked in an ever-widening circle. Hostile to Marc's totalitarian ascendancy, men of great worth and influence

parted company with him, while thirty-one bishops forbade their priests and seminarists to have anything to do with *Le Sillon.*

Seven years passed, during which the disquieting transformation of the movement proceeded more and more rapidly. Then, on 25th August 1910, Pius X addressed to the French episcopate a letter which, though fatherly in tone, pronounced a sentence of condemnation from which there was no appeal.

The chief grounds of the censure were four. (1) Though continuing to recruit its members from church youth clubs, Catholic action groups and seminaries, *Le Sillon* had practically ceased to be a religious movement and had become a political organization; at the very least it identified religious with political activity in a way that the Church could not allow. This development led it beyond the control of ecclesiastical authority, to rejection of guidance by the Church in matters upon which she has the right to counsel her children.

(2) The polity extolled by *Le Sillon* was that of democracy, this latter word being expressly understood not in the sense given it by *Graves de Communi,* but in a political sense: 'The aim of *Le Sillon*', Marc Sangnier had written, 'is to bring about the democratic Republic in France.' Political democracy was declared 'alone capable of inaugurating the reign of perfect justice', 'the form of government most advantageous to the Church'. Therein lay the confusion of politics and religion which Pius X was determined to avoid at all costs. One might add that this exaltation of the democratic system occasionally manifested itself in some very strange formulae: the Holy Trinity was proposed as the archetype of democratic equality, and the mystery of the Eucharist as the image of democratic brotherhood!

(3) The social ideas of *Le Sillon* had more recently taken a course of which Pius X disapproved. In the name of the equality of God's creatures, *Le Sillon* was striving for social egalitarianism, 'advocating Socialism with its gaze fixed on a chimera', and, as Marc Sangnier had expressly stated, moving away from Leo XIII's doctrine on the lawfulness of ownership, on social hierarchies and on natural inequalities.

Lastly (4), *Le Sillon* tended in the name of fraternity to include within its ranks all sorts of non-Catholic and even non-Christian elements; it regarded fraternity as consisting in respect for the opinions of others, no matter how false those opinions might be, and as based upon the simple notion of humanity independent of all religion. That view was described by Pius X, perhaps with some exaggeration, as the 'new Gospel' of the *Sillonistes.* Here again some curious formulae were current within the movement: it was said that the revolutionary theories of Danton and Robespierre were 'of the substance of the Gospel', that all democrats should look back to the 'great ancestors of

the Revolution', that the 'mystic-souled Russian anarchists' were just as much witnesses of Christ.

There were also four secondary causes underlying the papal condemnation. (1) As happens in the case of every great orator, Marc Sangnier sometimes used ill-considered phrases. He declared, for example, that *Le Sillon* was 'not properly speaking and directly a Catholic work', and that a certain bishop (whom he named) had 'committed a blunder and understood nothing about political or social questions'. (2) Increasingly anxious not to be enfeoffed to the hierarchy, he too often neglected to defend the Church against the many attacks made upon her at that period; for instance, at the time of the Law of Separation his attitude was by no means firm. Again (3), he refused to help the Catholic syndicates, preferring, as he said, to operate within the C.G.T., which at that date was anarchical. Lastly (4), without maintaining such close relations with the Modernists as the 'abbés démocrates' had done, he had embraced some of their views; and, moreover, his tendency to radical criticism of ecclesiastical institutions, together with a certain proneness to cry up the worth of material activity on every possible occasion, rendered him more or less suspect of Americanism and Modernism.

All those factors had presented a wide-open flank to his enemies, who had made full use of their advantage. A number of bishops had tried to defend *Le Sillon*, denouncing the attacks launched against it as inspired by political motives—by a secret design to strike at the Republic, its regime and the *ralliement* desired by Leo XIII; but Pius X judged that the errors of the movement were too serious and too flagrant.

The reaction of Marc Sangnier and his associates was that of true Catholics. He himself wrote the Pope an utterly noble letter of submission, and all his friends behaved with equal humility. Pius X suggested that 'Catholic *Sillons*' be formed in the dioceses, without interconnection, without political aims, but as organs of Catholic action controlled by the bishops. This scheme of 'do-goodery' was hardly calculated to attract the young enthusiasts who had supported Marc. He himself tried to follow a strictly political line in a new movement, the *Jeune République*; but the electorate took little notice of his plan. After the Second World War the most sensible and most powerful concepts launched by *Le Sillon* were effectively revived by M.R.P. (*Mouvement Républicain populaire*) in a religious, political and social context quite different from that of 1910; and Marc himself, now patriarch of Christian democracy, sat quietly in the first Assemblies of the Fourth Republic. But what movement would ever rekindle the flame of *Le Sillon* in its early years? [1]

[1] The severity of Pius X in dealing with the 'abbés démocrates' and *Le Sillon* has often been contrasted with his indulgence towards Charles Maurras and the royalist movement of

9. Some Catholic Parties

The intransigence manifested by Pius X towards Catholic movements such as the *Opera dei Congressi* and *Le Sillon* was by no means his unvarying attitude. In other cases he showed himself not only conciliatory, but also favourable to strictly political groups which sometimes appealed to democratic principles and whose main virtue, on occasion, was anything but docility. The truth is that certain situations seemed to require decisions which might seem to contradict his principles but which were in fact inspired only by his deep sense of the 'interests of God'.

The most striking example occurred in Belgium. Not that that country was causing the Church any grave concern; on the contrary, it was the one Catholic nation of the West in which Pius X encountered no obstacle. At first, however, the situation might well have alarmed the Pope, who, as we have seen, was hostile to 'Catholic parties' and mistrustful of democratic ideas. Belgian Catholics had been solidly organized as a party ever since their victory in the matter of the schools. That party was no less solidly established in power, and was destined to remain so until the First World War. It was on the whole middle class and moderate; but it felt the growing influence within itself of the Democratic League formed by Verhaegen and Helleputte, and the conservative elements were being supplanted by more daring men. In 1911 Michel Levic joined the government,[1] and his advent marked the climate of that process. Finally, among the democratic members of the Belgian Catholic Party there was an undeniable tendency to make common cause with those non-Catholics who shared their idea of social justice.

All this seemed unlikely to please Pius X. In fact, however, no serious incident or even a moment of tension occurred between the

---

Action française. After the Holy Office had condemned four works by Maurras and the movement's bi-monthly review, Pius X, while confirming that those works should be considered then and there as prohibited, reserved the right to decide exactly when the decree should be published. He died without having done so, and publication was delayed until 1926. Many reasons account for his attitude, the most important of which was undoubtedly the fact that the royalists had always supported the Church against republican persecution, and had been almost unanimously hostile to the Modernist thinkers whom Pius X had condemned. Again, those very members of *Action française* who later rebelled when condemned were at the date in question representing themselves as champions of order and discipline, emphasizing that aspect of the Church which they called the 'power of order and tradition', and thereby pleasing the Pope. Nor did any of them talk of reforming the Church. Finally, it should be observed that nationalism, the harmful results of which would be better appreciated in 1926, did not appear in 1914 in the same perspective as on the morrow of the First World War.

[1] Levic, a barrister by profession, was considered by all *bien-pensants* as a dangerous revolutionary.

Roman See and the Belgian Catholics during the whole pontificate. Pius was fully aware of the irreplaceable role played by the Catholic Party, and he realized that if the latter were weakened to the point, perhaps, of dissolution, the anticlericals alone would benefit. Besides, the party maintained contact with the hierarchy, though not enfeoffed to it as its enemies complained; and most of its leaders had been trained by the Church in the University of Louvain, which was becoming more and more prominent in the nation's life.

The Belgian Catholic Party, therefore, enjoyed the unshaken confidence of Pius X, all the more so because the Pope regarded Catholic Belgium as possessing an utterly reliable chief in the person of one of his dearest friends. This was Mgr Mercier (1851–1926), Archbishop of Malines, to whom the University of Louvain owed much of its prestige and who was created cardinal in 1907.

In Austria the situation was less eirenic, but the attitude of Pius X was even more clearly defined. Notwithstanding the *de facto* termination of the Concordat by the 'confessional' laws of 1867–8, and despite an unchristian trend during the pontificate of Leo XIII, the Emperor Franz Josef continued officially to uphold the Catholic cause. Nor did a campaign of *Los vom Rom*, resumed at intervals by the liberals and freemasons who were powerful even at Court, prevent good relations between Vienna and the Vatican throughout the reign of Pius X. Furthermore the Pope knew well that in Austria his authority could rely upon an entirely docile episcopate, on many loyal religious congregations, on extremely powerful Catholic associations such as the *Piusverein* and *Leogesellschaft*, and even more securely upon the traditional faith of the masses. Of this last the Eucharistic Congress at Vienna, in 1912, gave such eloquent proof that the Pope declared he saw therein a sign from heaven.

Accordingly he took a benevolent view of the political organism through which the Austrian Catholics operated within the framework of the State. That organism was the Social-Christian Party, which had been founded by the Prince of Lichtenstein and Dr Karl Lueger to put in practice Vogelsang's ideas,[1] and which was growing steadily year by year. In the field of social improvement its members had taken a most unconventional line: hostility towards financial concentration, towards monopolies, towards abuses of capitalism, almost towards capitalism itself, and a demand for extension of workers' rights over their contracts. Owing to the rather peculiar situation of Austria they had increased the number of their watchwords with others of a more questionable nature. As it happened, the Jews were extremely numerous and powerful in the Empire of the Double Eagle, occupying three-quarters of the liberal professions and, above all, controlling the

[1] See Chapter IV. section 5.

central banks and through them big business. The struggle against Jewish capitalism had led the Social-Christian Party into general anti-Semitism, the verbal violence of which delighted the masses and was later to be remembered by Adolf Hitler, who had experienced it as a youth.

Reaction had not been long delayed. Leo XIII had already been alerted, and Pius X received formal denunciations. Adversaries of the Social Christians lost no time in reminding the Pope that the party's anti-Semitism was intolerable, and the government itself intervened. But the Nuncio, Mgr Agliardi, worked in Rome on behalf of Lueger and his companions. No doubt, he urged, there were excesses in the party's anti-Semite campaign; but was the attempt to get rid of the Social Christians really due to their anti-Semitism and not rather to the fact that they embarrassed the Jewish bankers? It was certain that Jewish elements close to the seat of power had been behind the *Los vom Rom* campaigns and the secularizing laws. To sacrifice the Social Christians would be to play into the enemy's hands. Pius X understood the argument. Though anti-Semitism is incompatible with Christian charity, ought the struggle against Jewish influence to be forbidden in the political field? He advised the party's leaders to moderate their language, but he would not condemn their line of action. Supported by a large majority of the bishops, the Social Christians became the strongest party in the Austrian parliament, and their triumph was crowned by the election of Lueger as Burgomaster of Vienna. Devoted to the papal teaching, that party was destined to be the country's sure shield after the First World War and until the Nazi invasion.

In Germany the situation was not so simple, and events were rather confused. But there also Pius X showed a degree of moderation and diplomatic versatility far removed from the intransigence ordinarily attributed to him. He was confronted with a major political fact: the existence of the *Zentrum*, which had continued to play a notable part in German affairs ever since its victory in the *Kulturkampf*. The Pope disliked it, and did not hesitate to say so. This was not because it was a political party, but because German Catholics as a whole were less willing than their French and Belgian counterparts to follow papal directives. Since its earliest days the great Catholic association of the *Volksverein* had conducted its affairs with a large measure of independence.[1] The *Zentrum* behaved likewise; no matter how respectful it might appear towards the Pope and the Apostolic See, in practice its leaders did very much as they saw fit.

[1] Later, during the Modernist affair, Pius X himself was obliged to take account of that sentiment, which was fairly common in the Germanic clergy and universities, and refrained from applying to them the Draconian measures imposed in France and Italy. See Chapter VI, section 7.

On two important points the party adopted an attitude that was bound to alarm Pius X. Ernst Lieber, Windhorst's successor, died in 1902. Peter Spahn and Hertling, who took his place and were not such strong personalities, gradually forsook the tradition of the pan-German and democratic *Zentrum* in favour of a governmental party, which rallied little by little to Wilhelm II's *Weltpolitik*, naïvely believing it to be defensive, and, like most other Germans, failing to calculate its tragic international consequences. This nationalist orientation of the Catholic Party disturbed Pius X, as he more than once informed its leaders. But the *Zentrum*, for fear of appearing *undeutsch*, continued its way down that slippery slope, voting (perhaps reluctantly) military funds and not dissociating itself from the least acceptable of the Kaiser's views. Moreover the party showed an increasing tendency to enlarge its own framework by admitting non-Catholics to membership and by establishing friendly relations with the Liberal and even Socialist parties. The problem, indeed, was met at every level, e.g. in the sphere of syndicalism.[1]

There is no doubt that his personal feelings inclined Pius X to reject a policy too cordial towards non-Catholics, especially as the active elements of Protestantism had once more become aggressive, instigating in university circles a full-scale offensive against the Catholics. But a curious incident showed the Pope that he could not just ignore the reality of Protestantism and keep Catholics shut up in an ivory tower. In 1910, to commemorate the tricentenary of the canonization of St Charles Borromeo, he published an Encyclical which painted a merciless picture of the Reformation in Germany, and minced no words in portraying some of the reformers. This provoked a very strong reaction on the part of Protestant journalists. The Pope was insulting German patriotism! *Katholik, undeutsch!* Catholics felt embarrassed. A number of bishops forbade distribution of the Encyclical, while some Catholic papers spoke of an 'inopportune publication'. Pius lulled the storm by declaring officially that he had never meant to give offence in Germany, towards which he entertained sentiments of great benevolence; but the incident taught him a lesson. Although the Encyclical on St Charles Borromeo had seemed to favour the 'integrals', he took the opportunity afforded by the syndicalists themselves to present a very different face. The Brief *Singulari quadam* of 1912, which authorized interconfessionalism in the syndicates, had a more general significance. Since the majority of Catholics in the *Zentrum* advocated a broad, outward-looking policy, the Pope came down on the side of this moderate tendency, knowing well that the great Catholic Party represented a vast reserve of organized strength in Germany. Besides, the policy of the *Zentrum* as a

[1] See Chapter IV, section 16.

'governmental party' was beneficial, as might be seen from the help it gave to Catholic social undertakings, as well as from the support given by the imperial government to German missions. Later, it would become clear that peril lurked therein. But Pius X had strengthened the party by agreeing to its unification around the moderate tendency. He was to be proved right some years later by the role of the former *Zentrum* in the post-war revolutionary crisis.

10. Isolation? Eclipse?

A careful survey of his policy will show how inaccurate is the traditional image of Pius X. He has been described as a pious pontiff more anxious to improve the liturgical chant and lay down rules for the first communion of children than to ensure the presence of the Church among the nations; an incompetent saint incapable of handling a diplomatic venture with a minimum of skill. The truth is quite different. Anyone who keeps in view his self-appointed goal, and the principles according to which he meant to act, will realize that, throughout a number of crises (some of them disastrous) and at the cost of delicate negotiations, Pius X always had his eye upon that goal and that he was largely successful. The 'coherent policy' for which he was praised by Aristide Briand reappears in every situation capable of analysis.

Must one even accept the familiar view that he 'placed the Holy See in a position of isolation and eclipse which would prevent it from playing any serious part in the world conflict'? [1] Note first that it is curious to talk about 'eclipse' of the head of the Church at the very moment when that Church was giving so many proofs of her presence and activity in so many fields, both intellectual and social; at the very moment also when she was flowering in missionary lands and making a stupendous advance in the United States. It is hard to see how such progress could run parallel with a diminution of strength in the head of Catholicism.

As regards the international level, 'isolation' is a relative term. Though it is true that the saintly Pope was less popular in diplomatic, political and journalistic circles than the skilled tactician who preceded him—and in any case he never tried to win public favour—many facts reveal how great were his moral authority and personal radiance. The part played by Leo XIII as arbiter between sovereign states was filled on at least one occasion by Pius X. Brazil, Bolivia and Peru were disputing ownership of territories watered by the Acre, a sub-tributary of the Amazon, and two treaties had failed to end the litigation. The governments of those three Catholic States had recourse to the Pope's

[1] Marc-Bonnet, *La Papauté contemporaine*, p. 91.

arbitration, and his decision was applied. In 1911, when the Carnegie Foundation for International Peace was established, he gladly accepted membership, was represented at the inaugural ceremonies and took the opportunity to publish an important letter on the problem of war and peace. All this was not the doing of a man politically insignificant and regarded by the world as such. Cardinal Merry del Val related that when Pius X died several ambassadors declared that they would ask to be transferred, so deeply had they been impressed by the Pontiff to whom they were accredited.

One might go further and suggest that Pius X's apparent 'anti-diplomacy' was in fact the working out of a very great diplomatic scheme. Certain historians (the same who accuse him of having placed the Church in 'isolation' and 'eclipse') describe him in a truly remarkable phrase: 'Pope of the Triple Alliance.' According to them Pius X was the artificer of, or at any rate one of those who inspired, the great diplomatic formation which united the Central Empires and Italy, as against France, Britain and Russia, in a confrontation pregnant with far-reaching consequences. It must be frankly acknowledged that the theory rests upon evidence which makes it not unacceptable. The three powers of the Entente were all on bad terms with the Apostolic See, France and Russia having broken off relations, while Britain held coldly aloof. Meanwhile the two empires of Germany and Austria-Hungary, where Catholics played a prominent part, showed on every occasion their respectful attachment to the Pope, and the Vatican's relations with Italy were improving. It is not impossible, indeed it is even probable, that in the depths of his heart Pius considered Austria and Germany as elements of order and equilibrium. Nevertheless that he helped to form the Triple Alliance is mere hypothesis the grounds of which cannot be verified until such time as historians have access to the Vatican archives of that period. And even though that hypothesis be one day confirmed, any suggestion that he was at all responsible, directly or indirectly, for the sequence of events that led to the outbreak of war in 1914 is belied by his attitude when the conflict seemed imminent, and particularly by his disapproval of the aggressive decisions of the Central Empires.[1] It is strange to reproach him with not having prevented the explosion. No man on earth could have done so in a Europe where there was hardly a single government that did not regard war as the only possible escape from an international situation that was becoming more and more inextricable. It is unlikely that Leo XIII himself could have done better; and twenty-five years later, as the Second World War approached, Pius XI was to find himself utterly helpless in face of human madness. Yet no historian has ever said of either Pope that he 'isolated' his See from the concert of nations.

[1] See Chapter VII, section 1.

It is, however, above all in considering the 'internal' policy of Pius X that one sees that he fulfilled his purpose. And there it is even more absurd to talk of eclipse. In almost every Catholic country the Sovereign Pontiff saw his authority enhanced, his influence more firmly established, discipline strengthened and rebellion crushed. What he laboured to accomplish was good order within the Church, and he was largely successful. His pontificate marked one of those stages from which it is possible to go further in the task of construction, as another Pius would do after the tragedy of the First World War. This must be our standpoint if we hope not only to appreciate the political work of Pius X, but also to measure the importance of the decisions he took in quite a different field, in the most momentous affair of his pontificate—the affair of Modernism.

CHAPTER VI

MODERNISM: A SPIRITUAL AND INTELLECTUAL CRISIS

1. AN INTERNAL DANGER

WHILE Pius X was resisting the attacks of secularism and endeavouring quietly but resolutely to restore the threatened foundations of the Catholic world, the Church was confronted with another peril, this time to the sacred deposit of truth. The roots of this internal crisis are traceable to a state of mind which, in itself, was altogether praiseworthy. Some even of the most fervent Christians had become aware that their religion was labouring at an intellectual disadvantage which caused them grave disquiet. 'Is the whole of modern knowledge, then, a contradiction of our faith?' asks young Jean Barois in Roger Martin du Gard's novel. Such indeed was the conviction which the champions of atheistic humanism were endeavouring to propagate. Nor was it science alone that seemed at variance with faith, but also the vision of the world which it offered and which an increasing number of men appeared to accept. The gulf between modern thought and Christian thought was widening, and might become impassable.

Those who understood the problem wondered whether it had been rightly handled. One must admit, as all historians today recognize, that during the early years of the nineteenth century the Church had lagged behind in every branch of thought, even in those of the greatest consequence to herself. That retardation was due to many causes. On the morrow of the French Revolution it had seemed more necessary to provide a sound moral and spiritual training for priests, whose duty it would be to rebuild a Christian society, than to prepare them for intellectual strife. The prevailing idea was that of the supernatural priest—*sacerdos alter Christus*—deeply pious and standing aloof from the world. M. Tronson's 'method of prayer' and 'particular examination' were believed to be worth a world of study, and current theories were looked upon as hostile to the faith. To erect a barrier between them and the Catholic mind seemed the most indispensable task: science was so full of snares and temptations! Moreover there lacked the means of preparing Catholics for the struggle; before 1870 very few people grasped the need for Catholic higher education.

The argument from authority appeared adequate for the solution of the new problems: *Quanta Cura* and the *Syllabus*, not always properly interpreted, were considered as ample confirmation of that view. Even long after 1871 the preference was for a militant apologetic of deplorable weakness. Too often associated, openly or not, with political prejudice, it worked on the assumption that anathemas would suffice to vanquish the enemy. Such books as *La divinité de Jésus-Christ vengée des attaques du rationalisme* (1888), by the Belgian Dominican Père Portmans, embarrass by the feebleness of their arguments. So too with the works of Mgr Bougaud, full of romantic sentimentality, and the Abbé Picard's *Chrétien ou agnostique* (1896), where bluster goes hand in hand with failure to grasp the real issues.

Those very sciences which we today look upon as fundamental for the training of priests were intellectually bankrupt. Exegesis was the poor relation of the seminaries. In one of them the following couplet might be read carved on a wooden desk:

C'est ici que l'on fait la classe d'exégèse
Où chacun rit et cause et n'en prend qu'à son aise.[1]

Such childish humour is understandable if one thinks of the incredible fatuity of what was then called exegesis. Most textbooks were inspired by 'concordism': scientific concordism, which identified the 'days' of creation with the geological periods, or explained the Hebrew cosmogony in terms of fashionable theories while remaining free to alter the interpretation when those theories changed; and historical or ethnographical concordism, which discovered in the early chapters of Genesis the equivalent of the palaeolithic or neolithic age. . . . Some idea of the inadequacy (to say the least) of the so-called exegetical science may be obtained from a glance through *Les livres saints et la Science, leur accord parfait*, by the Abbés Dessailly and Moigns. This book, widely used in seminaries, purported to explain scientifically (!) 'the fact of Jonas living and praying in the belly of the whale' by comparing his situation 'to that of a child which lives in its mother's womb', or again 'to that of toads which, after being entombed in very hard rocks, have been seen to emerge alive after hundreds and even thousands of years'.

All other sciences were in much the same plight. Church history was seldom if ever taught in the seminaries before the 1880's. The books that claimed to deal with it were often so feeble that *La Croix* itself acknowledged that one written by the Abbé Maron, besides containing errors of fact, did not show 'the healthy impartiality required in this matter'. So also with Barthelemy's best seller, *Erreurs*

[1] J. Hébert, *Sous le joug des Césars*, Paris, 1924.

et mensonges historiques, which sought to make good its lack of solid substance with sarcasm and sallies of wit. 'That book', wrote the great Bollandist Père de Smedt, 'is a scandal and a peril to Catholic learning which must be fought at all costs.'

Even those disciplines without which it seems impossible to establish religious thought on firm foundations were in an equally ruinous state. It is remarkable that the danger of Hegelianism, which had been denounced by the Protestant Kierkegaard and clearly perceived by Rosmini in Italy and Staudenmaier in Germany, was practically ignored by all orthodox Catholic writers until well into the present century. The same is true *a fortiori* of the doctrines of Karl Marx and Nietzsche. No truly Catholic philosophy found favour. A vague eclecticism, in the form of debased scholasticism, was current almost everywhere, inclining sometimes to a spirituality of Cartesian origin, sometimes to an idealism derived more or less from Kant but hopelessly degenerate. This latter, says Fonsegrive, was 'almost as destructive of dogma as were materialist negations; more dangerous, perhaps, because more subtle, more seductive'. Even the attempts made during the first three-quarters of the nineteenth century to establish a Christian philosophy in accord with modern needs had ended almost invariably in a mere claim to impose rash theories—the fideist traditionalism of Bonald and Lamennais, the ontologism of Ubaghs and Rosmini, the critical system of Gunther and Hermes; and the reaction of the Roman authorities to those deviations helped to convince the prudent that they would do best by lying low.

Theology itself was therefore feeble. 'Theology is an end-product. In order to flourish it needs well-developed skills that enable it to read aright its inspired sources. It needs also a general system of thought in which to discover the radiance of the revealed deposit.' [1] Not so had it been considered, but in its most external form, that of apologetic; and even apologetic, though it had possessed fertile thinkers in Frayssinous, Gratry and Cardinal Deschamps, confined itself too narrowly to the secondary aspects of faith—beauty, social value—when it was not lured by immediate preoccupations to stress the ideas of order and social peace, the importance of religion as a bastion against the Revolution.

What has been said above does not mean that everything in Catholic intellectual life was insignificant or futile. In every discipline a few men had preserved the right spirit and, while remaining within the framework of orthodoxy, had signposted new roads. In the sphere of exegesis there had been the Abbé (later Cardinal) Meignan and the great Sulpician Le Hir; in that of religious history, the pioneer Bollandists at Brussels, then Hergenröther, Stolberg and Hefele; in

[1] Père Vicaire, *Histoire illustrée de l'Église*, II, p. 313.

that of philosophy, Ravaisson; in that of apologetic, Cardinal Newman. And while speculative theology was virtually ignored in the seminaries, it must not be forgotten that a revival of Thomism had been inaugurated by Leo XIII in the middle of the nineteenth century. Yet, when all is said, very few men understood the importance of the problem; and fewer still were those determined to solve it. In 1891, at the Congress of Malines, Mgr (later Cardinal) Mercier publicly regretted that Catholics had 'thought too little about the need to fashion and bring together the materials which should serve to create the new synthesis of science and faith'.

Nor indeed was it at the intellectual level alone that Catholics seemed powerless to prepare that synthesis. A gulf was forming not only between Christian thought and modern thought; it was apparent also in morals, laws and ways of life. The entire modern world seemed resolved upon acting as the 'murderer of God'.

Some Catholics, however, were not prepared to accept that situation; they would not admit that divorce between the modern world and their religion was unavoidable. On the contrary, they asked whether it were not the duty of Christianity to re-establish contact with its foes. This was no recent question; it had confronted the Christian conscience ever since the dismemberment of Christendom, but it had become more urgent since the unleashing of hostile forces by the French Revolution. During the first part of the nineteenth century it had preoccupied the minds of many Christians: it had disturbed such men as Lamennais, Balmes, Rosmini and Gioberti. Since it was evident that the forward march of modern thought could not be halted, Christianity must be either reconciled with or destroyed by it.

Reconciled—how? Vincenzo Gioberti had declared: 'We must accomplish in the field of today's Catholic Christianity what the prophets did in that of Judaism six centuries before our era, by reforming positive religion and harmonizing it with science and civilization.' That opinion was to be shared by an increasing number of educated Catholics. If Catholics were equipped in such a way that they could meet the enemy on equal terms; if Christianity were rid of all that was fossilized and outmoded, so as to nullify the arguments of positivists and rationalists; if all that might be acceptable and useful in the thought and methods of the enemy were taken over; then, and only then, would religion be associated once more with the advance of humanity and resume its place in the swiftly flowing stream of history. As was later said by Alfred Loisy, one of the most clear-sighted leaders of the movement, it was necessary 'to adapt the Catholic religion to the intellectual, social and moral needs of the present'.

In itself that aim was praiseworthy; it could in a certain way be traced to the designs of Leo XIII. It was dictated by an apologetical and apostolic urge. To bring back the best of modern thinkers into the fold of Christ was a plan of which none could disapprove. Nor was the method proposed objectionable in theory. Christianity has more than once erected its defences in hostile territory—did it not absorb pagan philosophy?—and it has never been suggested that the intellectual, social and moral framework within which Christians live must remain for ever unalterable. But the fundamental deposit of faith must never be impugned; and it would be so impugned if innovation and rejuvenation proceeded without caution—if, under pretext of maintaining contact with the enemy, Catholics allowed themselves to be contaminated by him. What had become of Lamennais's vaunted loyalty to the Church when he slid into compromise with modern thought? What had happened to Renan's faith through the continuous employment of rationalist criticism? In 1887 Mgr Sarto, at that time Bishop of Mantua, had denounced with prophetic accuracy a 'modern Christianity', which, he said, 'claimed to adapt the dogmas of faith to the requirements of the new philosophy'. To adapt the dogmas, that is to say bend unalterable truth to suit modern thought, whether the latter expressed itself by way of metaphysical, moral or critical theories, would be an unpardonable error. If the Church tolerated that, she would imperil her sacred charge.

Such precisely was the internal threat to which she was subject during the last ten years of the nineteenth century and the first ten of the twentieth. A current of thought initially apologetic and apostolic in purpose, but quickly vitiated in its choice of means, led men to claim that dogmas could change, that the mysteries of faith could be interpreted in an entirely human fashion, that it was permissible to regard as no longer true all that one read in the Bible, that one could empty religion of all its spiritual demands and reduce it to little more than a code of practical morality. That current, that body of doctrinal errors, is known to history as Modernism, a word little used until it was adopted by Pius X's Encyclical *Pascendi*.

The crisis which disturbed the Church for twenty years was one of the most severe that she has ever experienced. The theological battle of which Modernism was the occasion has been compared in respect of its intensity to that of Jansenism; in many ways it was more serious, because it was more concerned with the essentials of faith. It was in any case more serious than any of the political conflicts of that time, the Church can more readily endure an assault by unbelievers on her temporal institutions than see her own sons strip Christ of His divinity or deny the attributes of God. The crisis of Modernism appeared for

the moment to shake the very foundations of Catholicism, and one suspects that it continues to lie heavily upon us.[1]

2. Prelude to the Crisis: Americanism

The average Catholic first became aware that a curious unrest was abroad in the Church when, about 1893, there began to be much talk in Europe of American Catholicism. In the United States, as we have seen,[2] the Church had been growing prodigiously for a hundred years. From a despised and humiliated minority it had become a power that counted in the life of the Union. The 30,000 Catholics of 1789 had increased to 4,500,000 by 1870, and the number was still growing. Orestes Brownson had taught them to realize their strength and to proclaim that they represented the hope of young America as against the swarm of Protestant sects. In 1875 Pius IX had recognized their achievement by conferring the red hat upon Mgr MacClosky, Archbishop of New York.

But the Church had not developed in America in the same way as it had done much earlier in Europe. The apostolate conducted by American Catholics had been conceived according to the methods of democracy. Associated from their beginnings with the Revolution, American Catholics had no reason to mistrust or oppose it. They felt themselves sons of that liberty for which their forefathers had shed their blood. Theories such as the necessary separation of Church and State, which roused horror in Italy and France, were taken for granted in America, for the simple reason that a State Church there would have inevitably been Protestant. Thus there was no opposition between religion and the modern world, with which indeed American Catholics quite naturally tended to seek contact. In 1888 Mgr Spalding, Bishop of Peoria, exalted 'the marvellous political, social, moral and intellectual achievements which give the nineteenth century its character'. The great majority of bishops shared his views, particularly Ireland, Gibbons and Keane. What was emerging was a liberal form of Catholicism, youthful, enterprising, perfectly adapted to a race of pioneers.

[1] Modernism was not an exclusively Catholic phenomenon. Among the Churches descended from the Reformation we find something analogous in 'Christianity with dogmas', of which Dreyer speaks, of which Ritschl posed as theorist and Harnack as protagonist. In the Anglican Church it inspired the reformism of the Churchmen's Union for the Advancement of Liberal Thought and the writings of the Rev. R. J. Campbell. In the Orthodox Russian Church one may consider as Modernism the humanitarian Christianity of Tolstoy. There has even been talk of Jewish Modernism, of Modernism in Islam, of Modernism in Buddhism. This phenomenon in its various forms was universal. See the next volume of this series (*Frère Séparés*).

[2] *The Church in an Age of Revolution*, pp. 362–9.

An observer might well have asked whether this enthusiastic apostolate and boyish determination to move with the times were not going too far. 'The religion we need today', cried Mgr Ireland, Archbishop of St Paul, 'does not consist in singing beautiful anthems in cathedral choir-stalls, vested in cloth of gold, while the nave and aisles are empty of people, and the world outside is dying of spiritual starvation.' And Mgr Spalding said: 'Jesus Christ did not teach the world philosophy; He founded not an Academy, but a Church.' Surely those ideas, carried to their extremes, would lead to rejection of the liturgy as well as of Christian philosophy. Certain gestures on the part of the American episcopate, in the same large-hearted spirit of apostleship, savoured likewise of imprudence. In 1893, when a World Exposition was held at Chicago, some of its directors conceived the idea of summoning an International Congress of religions, at which representatives of each would explain what it was doing for the good of mankind. Cardinal Gibbons accepted on behalf of the Catholic Church, and for seventeen days priests were to be seen in conference with Protestant ministers, a few archimandrites and even delegates of Brahmanism and Buddhism, their aim being to 'reach agreement on common moral and religious principles with a vew to concerted action against common foes'.

The whole of this movement had found its hero and its thinker in Father Isaac Hecker, a somewhat extraordinary character who died in 1888, but whose memory was still fresh in the United States. As a baker's labourer he was converted at the age of twenty and became a Redemptorist. But he left that order to found the Missionaries of St Paul (or Paulists), a new congregation without vows, similar to the Oratorians or Sulpicians but intended solely for the apostolate, especially among Protestants. A strong personality, whom some regarded as a superman and saint even during his lifetime, Father Hecker was hostile to book-learning, almost impervious to logical argument, but of uncommon energy and generosity. He was, moreover, a mystic, believed himself to be guided directly by the Holy Ghost, and was therefore little inclined to attach much importance to tradition and hierarchical institutions. 'He knew', says his biographer, 'that the American non-Catholic sought to deal directly with God, with a minimum of external aid. He longed to tell his compatriots that the Catholic Church offers a flight to God much more direct than any of which they had ever dreamed.' This form of spirituality, favourable to conversions, aimed at building up a race of apostles rich in active virtues, well equipped to conquer the modern world; but in such a context what would become of the Christian virtues of obedience, sacrifice and humility?

So long as those ideas were confined to America, Rome did nothing.

They were recognized as agreeing with the transatlantic temperament, and the amazing vigour of the Church in the United States proved them effective in that country. Everything changed when they were imported into Europe. As early as 1892 Mgr Ireland, while staying in Paris, accepted an invitation from a number of French Catholics to give a series of lectures; these made perfectly clear the views of the American Church: 'An intimate union of the Church and the age is desirable for both. It is better to study works on social economy than those of Bourdaloue.' The phrases of this frock-coated prelate, so unlike a bishop in appearance, surprised and thrilled his hearers. Some young priests thought that his message supplied an answer to contemporary problems: 'The words of life and of the future come to us today from the United States,' exclaimed one of them, the Abbé Félix Klein. Many at Saint-Sulpice were fascinated by this new-style Catechism. Some laymen, e.g. Henry Bérenger, Paul Desjardins (who had just founded the *Union pour l'Action morale*) and Paul Bourget thought that they saw here the bases of a 'neo-Catholicism' which would fully satisfy contemporary needs.

Could the Church allow herself to be led by such paths? Certain expressions of Mgr Ireland lay open to criticism; still more so did those of the neo-Catholics. Eugène Melchior de Vogüé, a contributor to the *Revue des Deux Mondes* and a future member of the Académie Française, declared that transatlantic Catholicism represented the triumph, after three centuries, of 'all that was legitimate and necessary' in the Protestant Reformation. Would Rome allow the spread of this rather equivocal doctrine, which its own partisans called 'Americanism'?

The situation grew more serious in 1897, when Félix Klein published his translation of Father Elliott's *Life of Father Hecker*, preceded by his own elaborate preface. This young professor at the Institut Catholique presented Hecker as the apostle of the new age, who had 'found and realized in himself the ideal priest of the future'. But what could be tolerated in America—because everything there was still more or less in a state of flux, swept along by the current of apostolic activity with ideas holding a far less important place than practical achievements—appeared infinitely more grave when re-thought by a French mind and clearly expounded in a systematic way. The book, praised by many members of the hierarchy with Cardinal Richard, Archbishop of Paris, at their head, provoked violent reaction. Mgr Turinaz, Bishop of Nancy, Canon Delassus of Cambrai and the *Vérité française* undertook to demolish the so-called saint of America. The most determined offensive was led by the young Abbé Charles Maignen, nephew of Maurice, who wrote a regular lampoon against the American: *Le Père Hecker, est-il un saint?* When the Archbishop of Paris refused him an *imprimatur*, because he had directed his shafts

at certain American bishops by name, he sought and obtained one from Mgr Lepidi, master of the Sacred Palace. The American episcopate protested in vain to the cardinal secretary of state.

Just then Rome was disturbed by another affair: some groups of 'neo-Catholic' laymen and of priests with 'Americanist' tendencies proposed to repeat the Congress of Religions—there was even talk of a 'Parliament of Religions'—at the World Exhibition in Paris (1900). *La Revue de Paris* printed an article on the subject by the Abbé Charbonnel. The French bishops immediately voiced their disapproval. Leo XIII was informed, but in order not to appear to condemn what the American hierarchy had done at Chicago, he simply wrote a letter to Mgr Satolli, his Apostolic Delegate at Washington, advising Catholics to 'hold their congress separately'. The Parliament of Religions was still-born.

Soon afterwards it was learned that the Congregation of the Index had condemned the *Life of Father Hecker*. Did that censure apply to the whole of Americanism? And anyhow, in what exactly did Americanism consist, and what errors did it contain that were liable to condemnation? Urged by many of his closest collaborators, Leo XIII decided to speak. But, anxious as before to avoid hurting the American episcopate, he did not have recourse to the 'big guns' of an Encyclical. Instead he wrote to Cardinal Gibbons a very restrained but none the less firm letter, *Testem benevolentiae* (1899), according to which it was necessary to distinguish two meanings of the word 'Americanism'. If that word denoted 'the gifts of the spirit which do honour to the American people', the apostolic virtues of Catholics, their generosity and their courage, it signified nothing reprehensible. But it might also refer to errors, which the Pope went on to enumerate: the wish to change everything in Catholicism—'Christ does not alter with the ages,' he said; the desires to 'leave in the shade certain doctrinal elements regarded as of small importance'; excessive love of freedom, which ran the risk of endangering authority within the Church; exaltation of merely natural and active virtues to the detriment of passive, purely spiritual virtues which are fundamental to Christianity; disdain for monastic vows, which were claimed to be unsuitable for modern man. Leo's letter clearly had in mind the 'Americanists', if not American Catholics as a whole. These latter replied, through Mgr Ireland, that they joined the Pope in condemning all such errors, but assured His Holiness that they had never taught anything of the kind.

Was Americanism a phantom heresy which existed only in the writings of the Abbé Maignen? Whatever the answer, the papal document brought about no change in the behaviour of American Catholics, who were later to discover the importance of the passive virtues and contemplative standards. Leo XIII no doubt intended his condemnation

of Americanism to serve also as a warning to certain European Catholics whose tendencies were causing him concern. No doubt he recognized, in the current of thought which he denounced, the prelude to what was to become Modernism.

3. First Signs in France

When the papal warning revealed the peril of Americanism, shrewd observers of Catholicism in Europe had long since noticed the premonitory signs of a far graver crisis. During the first years of Leo XIII's pontificate it had been possible to detect in Catholic intellectual circles, and especially among the professional bodies of the recently founded Catholic Institutes, novel views which had caused a good deal of surprise. Those views were held by sincere believers, often by priests deserving of the highest esteem. Not all of them were destined to lead their holders into the error later known as Modernism; but they were its heralds, and in one fashion or another pioneered its road.

In 1877 the Abbé Louis Duchesne (1843–1922) had attracted attention with a doctoral thesis on the *Liber Pontificalis*, in which he employed the strictest methods of historical criticism and thereby opened the way to a revival of Christian history. His boldness, however, had proved unacceptable in high places. It had horrified Mgr Freppel, who talked of having it placed on the Index. Duchesne's subsequent teaching, his articles in the *Bulletin Critique*, which he edited, and above all his book *Les Fastes épiscopaux dans l'ancienne Gaule*, had created an even greater sensation and caused still more alarm. In the hands of this *dénicheur des saints*, what became of the venerable traditions honoured in so many churches? Arles had not been evangelized by St Trophimus, Clermont by St Austremonius, Limoges by St Martialis, or Toulouse by St Saturninus. It was no longer possible to believe that those holy men, supposedly the first bishops of those dioceses, were direct disciples of the Apostles. Duchesne's criticism, though perfectly well founded, gave offence by its sneering tone, and he was obliged for a time to suspend his lectures at the Institut Catholique. In 1895 the government appointed him director of the French School at Rome, a post which he retained until his death, continuing his scholarly labours, amusing the 'black' world and the embassies with his witticisms, possessing many friends among the Modernists, but taking care not to become a member of their troupe. It is none the less certain that he helped to set in motion the first stones of the landslide.

Much more serious was an episode involving the Abbé Marcel Hébert (1851–1916), director of the École Fénelon, a young and highly

gifted priest who tried to 'modernize' Christianity by reconciling it with philosophy. Steeped in Kant and Hegel, he found no better means of forging a link between idealism and faith than the interpretation of dogmas by symbols. His reviews in Duchesne's *Bulletin critique*, his memoirs and two books, *Profession de foi du Vicaire Savoyard* and *Wagner*, all led back to this form of interpretation. God was merely 'the great idealizing law of universal activity'; Christ, an image of the perfection of which man can dream; faith, a representation of conscience. In *Souvenirs d'Assise* (1899) he expressed those ideas with such clarity and violence as to leave no room for ambiguity. The work, printed only for the author's friends, fell into the hands of the Archbishop of Paris. The cardinal ordered Hébert to repudiate his errors or resign, and Hébert chose the second alternative. Shortly afterwards, in a sensational article in the *Revue de métaphysique et de morale*, he crowned his rupture with the Church by describing the God of faith as the 'ultimate idol'.

In 1893, at the Sorbonne, Maurice Blondel (1861–1949) sustained a thesis on the unusual subject of 'Action', by which word he meant that impulse which drives the whole man (intellect, will and sensibility) to spiritual self-realization. According to him this movement leads inevitably to God. That was the starting-point of a new Christian philosophy, capable of answering the anxious questions of modern man; it was the foundation of a new apologetic. Since modern man, swayed by positivism and rationalism, refuses to accept revealed religion, because it transcends what the senses can grasp, why not take a stand in the immanent, in that which is clear-cut and tangible, in order to show him that the immanent itself postulates God, the spiritual, the supernatural. Such was the 'method of immanence', which must be carefully distinguished from 'immanentism'.[1] It considerably surprised the masters of the Sorbonne and the secular authorities, who made the young teacher wait a long time for the chair of philosophy which his talent deserved. But it came as very little less of a shock to the religious authorities, particularly when its originator expounded his method in *Lettre sur les exigences de la pensée contemporaine en matière d'apologétique* (1896), insisting that the roots of the supernatural must be sought in the inmost tendencies of man, in his need to believe. Maurice Blondel certainly did not pose as a 'modernizer' of Christianity; that admirable Catholic, of the stock of the great mystics, had none of the Modernist spirit. Again, he never joined the Modernist troupe, though he had numerous friends there, and he even

[1] Immanentism is a pantheistic doctrine which considers God as immanent in the world, i.e. identical with the substance of the world; whereas in Christian doctrine God transcends the world and is therefore distinct from it. Blondel often asserted that his 'method of immanence' had 'nothing to do with the doctrine of immanence'.

showed extreme severity in his criticism of some of the most notorious Modernists, such as Edouard Le Roy.[1]

But from his philosophy, more or less clearly understood, it was possible to derive more disturbing theories, subjectivist and fideist, to which he himself would never have subscribed: that, for example, according to which Truth does not exist in itself, apart from man, but is his work. Unwillingly and unwittingly Blondel too had prepared the way for Modernism.

4. Alfred Loisy and Biblical Criticism

Of all the premonitory signs of the crisis, the most flagrant appeared in a sector where the Church has always been vigilant—that of Holy Scripture. It will be remembered [2] that in the mid nineteenth century Baur, Strauss and Renan had attacked the figure of Jesus Christ as presented by the Gospel. That attack had continued without pause; it had even enlarged its front and was more powerfully equipped.

Renan died in 1892 at the height of his renown, restored since 1870 to his chair at the Collège de France (from which he had been removed by order of Napoleon III on account of his *Vie de Jésus*), a member of the Académie Française, an official personage already sure of a place in the Panthéon. 'Something great, something of ourselves is perishing,' cried Anatole France at his tomb. His influence was enormous. All 'free' criticism followed in the footsteps of him who had boasted of having 'forced Jesus to resign His divinity'. His thought was minted in articles and school textbooks. The works of his old age on the history of Israel and on the origins of the Church were no less disquieting: they too emptied history of the supernatural and the finality which believers had thought it to possess.

Renanism is even now a constant of rationalist criticism, but it is not the only one. More radical still, there had developed a liberal school. Born in the field of Protestantism, where it was destined to exercise a profound influence until the theological reaction of Karl Barth, it had also reached other circles. According to this school Jesus was clearly not God, but simply a man, stripped even of the kind of halo which Renan allowed Him. It was agreed, in Middleton Murry's words, that he was a 'brilliant man'. Stress was laid (to good purpose) on the human aspects of His nature; but everything which, in the eyes of Christians, guarantees His divinity, e.g. His miracles and resurrection, was categorically rejected. Germany had been the first to welcome

[1] In 1945 Pius XII paid official tribute to Maurice Blondel, to his perfect good faith and orthodoxy, in a letter to the secretariat of state.

[2] See 'Renan' in the Index to *The Church in an Age of Revolution*.

those theories, which were propounded by Bernard Weiss, Beyschlag and, above all, Adolf Harnack (1851–1930), the illustrious professor of the Germanic University, who was ennobled by Wilhelm II and whose book *Wesen des Christentums* (*Essence of Christianity*)[1] applied Hegelian analysis to scriptural criticism. Renan himself had thought that the liberal school went too far: 'They make Christ a professor of secular morality,' he used to say.

Another school, which went further still, was that of the so-called *Formgeschichte Method*, headed by Bertram Bultmann, Dibelius and K. L. Schmidt. Relying on formal criticism of the documents—whereby, as is now recognized, it did good service—it left very little of the objective evidence for the existence of Jesus Christ. The school claimed to see in the New Testament the work of the first Christian communities, among whom grew up traditions, more or less legendary stories, doctrinal lessons, a whole complex to which the gospels did no more than give an historic framework. The person and teaching of Jesus were so completely demolished that one might well ask if he had really existed. Of Christian belief in inspiration and scripture, nothing whatever remained.

A few learned Catholics followed the labours of these various schools with the purpose not only of refuting them, but also of using for their own ends the scientific methods of which 'free' exegesis and 'free' criticism claimed to have a monopoly. Among them, and towering above them in many ways, stood the remarkable figure of Alfred Loisy (1857–1949). This man, one of the most dangerous adversaries whom the Church has ever encountered, was a priest. His private life was absolutely irreproachable. The seminary at Châlons remembered his exemplary piety, and the association which he had formed among his fellow students in order to keep alive the flame of their apostolic zeal in after years. But in him was staged the drama of *homo duplex*. Did Alfred Loisy at the age of thirty still sincerely belong to that religion to which he appeared outwardly loyal?

Possessed of a mind both acute and profound, capable of handling a subject with scholarly thoroughness, and at the same time of expounding it with tremendous verve, young Loisy was noticed by his bishop, who sent him to complete his training at the Séminaire des Carmes at Paris. Ordained priest at the age of twenty-three, he was offered by Mgr d'Hulst first the mastership of lectures and then the professorial chair of Hebrew and Holy Scripture at the Institut Catholique. As a teacher he sparkled with a mordant and sarcastic eloquence that took pleasure in catching out an opponent, full of an irreverant zest when speaking of the traditionalist exegetes and even, sometimes, of the Sacred Books. 'He seemed', says Mgr Baudrillart,

[1] To be distinguished from Feuerbach's book of the same name.

'to experience a kind of glee on discovering the sacred text to be at fault. One felt that passion and courage lay behind all he said. He was convinced that biblical criticism must be given new life at any cost.' [1]

To revivify biblical criticism had been Loisy's aim since the early days of his career. As we have seen, it was an altogether praiseworthy and perfectly loyal design; the resurrection of exegesis and biblical criticism was quite clearly an absolute necessity. But it was essential to avoid two mistakes: routine which passes as tradition, and novelty for its own sake which passes as truth. 'O my God,' he prayed, 'give me twenty years of health, of patience and of work, together with that spirit of discernment, of sincerity and of humility which enables Christian science to accomplish, without danger to the scholar, the edification of the Church and the confusion of her enemies.' 'My ambition', he added, 'was one day to defeat Renan with his own weapons, by means of the critical method I was learning in his school.' Such indeed was the typical attitude of all Modernists at the outset: their sole purpose was to serve the Church and her truth, to conquer her adversaries.

Meanwhile those dangers of which Loisy spoke in his prayer as threatening the scholar became all too clear in his own case. In 1885, that is to say at the age of twenty-eight, he felt no longer conscious of 'the supernatural character of religion'. A sense of 'relativity' had taken possession of his mind. Overwhelmed by this evidence he could not escape the fact that he was 'outside the stream of Catholic thought'. But was that stream the stream of truth? Was it not imperative to 'rid the Church of that narrow and outdated gnosis which Rome frankly opposed to a world in constant progress'? In 1890, at the Institut Catholique, he sustained a thesis on the canon of the Old Testament, in which he played fast and loose with traditional teaching on the inspiration of the Scriptures. It startled many theologians and exegetes; but the Abbé Loisy continued fearlessly on his way, founding a review, *Enseignement biblique*, for the benefit of young priests who desired 'to complete the necessarily imperfect introduction to this subject which they have received in the seminaries'. He also attacked the most difficult parts of the Old Testament, especially the account of Creation and of the Deluge. Those 'grandiose tales' he compared to the Chaldaean myths, proposing to consider them 'as magnificent theological and moral lessons' rather than as historical documents upon 'particular facts, precise and strictly accurate in every detail'. When one thinks of what is read today in work after work, it is hard to imagine that view unleashing thunderbolts; but in 1892 it was scandalous, and what it provoked was indeed a scandal.

When the schools reopened in October 1892, M. Icard, superior

[1] *Vie de Mgr d'Hulst*, tome I, p. 475.

general of Saint-Sulpice, forbade his students to attend Loisy's course. The abbé, exasperated, retorted in his opening lecture by proclaiming the rights of critical thought. The affair caused a sensation in Catholic intellectual circles, and Loisy looked around for support. The aged Cardinal Meignan, his former bishop, was non-committal, backing him in principle but advising caution. Mgr d'Hulst, rector of the Institut Catholique, who was more directly implicated in the affair, upheld his professor, though perhaps with more ardour than skill. On 25th October, in *Le Correspondant*, he published an article on Renan, lately dead, the indulgence of which caused astonishment and roused strong resentment among the die-hards. Worse still, on 25th January 1893 there appeared another article by d'Hulst on the 'Biblical Question'. This study contained a number of perfectly sound observations; but having been hurriedly written by a man who was less than a specialist, and published without consultation with Loisy, who was the person most concerned, it clumsily propounded the theories of what it called the 'broad school', going so far as to say that 'there are serious difficulties in the way of maintaining absolute inerrancy as the necessary concomitant of Inspiration'. That article, printed over such a name, provoked a battle royal in which the great secular newspapers *Matin*, *Figaro* and *Univers* took part. Mgr d'Hulst hurried to Rome. There he became convinced that neither he nor anyone else would be condemned for the time being, but that he would do well to get rid of some ballast. This he did by cancelling the abbé's appointment to teach exegesis and confining him to Hebrew, Chaldaean and Assyrian.

Loisy, however, was not the man to bow before petty administrative scheming. His reply was an explosive article in *L'Enseignement biblique*. 'The presence of error in the holy book is manifest,' he said, 'but it is compatible with over-all inspiration and with a truly Catholic theology.' Such words at such a moment seemed mere bravado. Asked to resign, he did so with good grace, and, leaving the Institut Catholique, took a humble post as chaplain to a girls' school run by Dominican nuns at Neuilly.

On 18th November 1893 there appeared the Encyclical *Providentissimus Deus*. Gently, but with great firmness, Leo XIII drew attention to the peril of rationalism, condemning those who 'in order to escape scientific and historical difficulties in biblical exegesis, do not fear to hold that divine inspiration applies to matters of faith and morals, but to nothing else'. The Abbé Loisy at once made a formal act of submission, suppressed his review, resigned his appointment at Neuilly and retired to Bellevue 'in order to spend a while in meditation and silent work'.

Unfortunately that 'silent work' ended by setting him outside the Catholic fold. In 1898 there began to appear a long series of articles so

strangely alike in thought and style that the use of more than half a dozen pseudonyms did not long conceal the single mind and hand of Loisy. The Pentateuch, he said, was not Mosaic; inspiration is incomprehensible and indefinable, not being a matter of experience; the thought of the authors of the Bible had evolved, and the form in which they express it bears the mark of their age, an age when there was no such thing as scientific knowledge.

Such ideas began to spread among the younger members of the clergy and to alarm the bishops. The Pope was disturbed and decided to call a halt. 'Liberal' though he was in many respects, he was not so careless of doctrinal integrity and fidelity to tradition as to tolerate certain kinds of rashness. His warnings took the form of a letter to the minister-general of the Franciscans and then an Encyclical (*Depuis le jour*, 1899) addressed to the clergy of France, both very firm in tone.

Loisy, however, was now beyond recall. We know from his memoirs that he had long since lost all his Catholic convictions. Why then had he remained in the Church? Was it because he saw her as 'a great spiritual force, alone capable of imposing itself upon the world'? Was it through loyalty to his priestly obligations? Why moreover did he solicit in turn the bishoprics of Monaco and Maurienne? Was it merely in order to work better for the 'renovation of the Church'? The motives of that complex soul are hard to discern. In October 1900, in the *Revue du Clergé français*, he set out the fundamentals of his exegesis and apologetic, explaining particularly that in order to forestall the objections of modern criticism he threw overboard the book of Genesis and various other features of the Bible. This was too much. 'Even among priests', wrote a contemporary,[1] 'faith in the divine authority of the Bible has been shaken. . . .' The crisis was now plain for all to see.

Cardinal Richard forbade the *Revue du Clergé français* to continue publication of the articles on the religion of Israel, and again warned their author of the risk he was running. The answer was immediate: Alfred Loisy asked the Ministry of Public Instruction for a post at the École Pratique des Haute Études, where he could resume his lectures on exegesis. Thanks to the famous scholar Gaston Paris, his request was granted, and he took as the subject of his first course 'Genesis and the Babylonian myths'.[2]

[1] Abbé Gayraud, *La Crise de la foi.*

[2] Loisy's influence continued to be felt after he had left the Church. Recognized as one of the leaders of rationalist criticism, he had many pupils, of whom the most notorious was Charles Guignebert. From him, too, derived the eschatological school, so called because it saw in the idea of the glorious return of Christ the basic element of original Christianity.

5. 'The Crossroads of all the Heresies'

At the beginning of the twentieth century, therefore, the crisis, which had long been hatching, had fully matured. It is difficult to imagine the excitement which these 'Modernist' theories caused among the clergy and in intellectual circles concerned with matters of faith. New reviews were founded in order to spread them; others gave them an unexpected welcome. They were found in *La Quinzaine*, edited by Georges Fonsegrive; in the *Bulletin de la Semaine* which took its place, as well as in *Demain*, a magazine founded by some Catholics at Lyons; in the *Annales de philosophie chrétienne*, doyen of Catholic reviews; and in the *Revue du Clergé français*. The *Revue d'histoire et de littérature religieuse* was wholly devoted to the Abbé Loisy. The Modernist doctrines were opposed with equal vigour by traditionalist reviews and newspapers ranging from *Civiltà cattolica* to *Vérité française*. Religious weeklies in several dioceses were full of admonitions, episcopal letters and articles. The agitation was not without a certain grandeur, for the ultimate subject-matter of those violent disputes was something that concerns the world most deeply; nevertheless, inasmuch as it shook the foundations of the Church and compromised Catholic unity, it amply justified the stern intervention of the Holy See.

Before attempting to give an idea of the movement's numerical strength, one must be able to state exactly what is meant by 'Modernism'. As with Jansenism in the seventeenth century, we must be careful not to represent it as a kind of sect whose ranks men joined in an explicit and formal manner. There were many shades of opinion between complete adherence to the theories of a Loisy and the qualified approval given to certain untraditional views. It is therefore useless to quote figures, upon which the Modernists themselves did not always agree. Tyrrell declared his belief that there were forty thousand Modernist priests in the Church as a whole, and Houtin told Salomon Reinach that in France alone one could count fifteen thousand. 'Nonsense!' said Loisy; 'fifteen hundred at the most.'

The truth is that the movement was led by a very small number of men; far fewer than might be inferred from the many signed articles in journals and reviews, all the authors of which adopted pseudonyms, some making use of thirteen or fourteen. Always in close contact with one another, they collated their ideas, their written theses and also, it must be said, their attacks upon their enemies. Did they really constitute that 'secret society' of which Pius X spoke in *Pascendi* and of which he said later, in 1914, that it had continued 'to recruit new members'. Strictly speaking, no one has ever proved that the Modernists

were a disciplined organization like freemasonry. But they undoubtedly hung together and acted in concert; moreover the influence of those small groups was felt throughout fairly large areas of the clergy and the Catholic intelligentsia. One must be careful, however, not to include in the Modernist ranks those men who, though keenly aware that the Church needed refurbishing, never professed the basic error of wishing to alter her dogmas, or those who, because they had friends among the Modernists and even shared their views at the outset, were placed on the same footing as them by adversaries more vigilant than fair and well informed.

In France the spearhead of Modernism consisted of no more than half a dozen men. The most outstanding, beyond question, was the Abbé Loisy, because of the boldness of his thought and his vigour in controversy, and also on account of the notoriety he earned. Many sincere believers regarded him as embodying the whole of Modernism. Second comes the Abbé Albert Houtin of Angers, another biblical critic and ecclesiastical historian. He once boasted of building up a 'munitions dump' for the battle; but he quickly broke away from the reforming Modernists, having made up his mind that 'there is not and has never been such a thing as revealed religion'. He was to be the first historian of the affair. In the realm of philosophy and dogma, apart from Marcel Hébert, who had already left the Church and was teaching in the Masonic University at Brussels, there were two striking personalities: Père Laberthonnière (1860–1932) and Édouard Le Roy (1870–1954). The former was an Oratorian, remarkable alike for his piety and for his learning. A disciple and friend of Maurice Blondel, he made rash use of the doctrine of immanence in his *Annales de la philosophic chrétienne*. Le Roy, a brilliant mathematician who had turned to philosophy, was Bergson's successor at the Collège de France and then in the Académie Française. He attempted a bold synthesis of the Catholic faith with idealism, Bergsonianism and evolutionism. In a class by himself stood the Abbé Joseph Turmel, who was quickly suspected of 'playing a double game, writing simultaneously as an orthodox thinker under his own name and as an unbeliever under false names'.[1] His aim was no longer to renovate religion but to destroy it.

In England, George Tyrrell (1861–1909) represented a variety of the movement which was not unlike that of Édouard Le Roy. A convert from Anglicanism at about the age of eighteen, he had joined the Society of Jesus. He too dreamed of reconciling science and faith by insisting on internal devotion, feeling and intuition of heart as justifications of dogma. Expelled from the Society in 1906, he incurred excommunication in 1907 and died two years later. By the clarity of

[1] He was not finally exposed until 1928.

his thought and the grace of his literary style, as well as by his close relations with all the leaders of the movement, George Tyrrell exerted an undeniable influence. His friend, Baron von Hügel, a man of vast erudition and deep piety, acted as a sort of link between the great Modernists, placing his influence at the service of what he called 'progressist Catholicism', but remaining unshakably loyal to the Roman Church.

Italy too had its handful of Modernists, outstanding among whom were two priests: Salvatore Minocchi, editor of *Studi Religiosi*, and Ernesto Buonaiuti, who was to become the doctrinaire of the movement. Their influence was felt by all who yearned to reanimate the Church in other fields, such as Romolo Murri, whose political and social activities we have already noticed. The most famous, however, was Antonio Fogazzaro (1842–1911), a lofty soul and great novelist, all of whose works exalt the Christian virtues, but who was led into error by his longing to cleanse Catholicism of all mere routine and to reconcile dogma with Darwinism.

Germany, though less affected by the crisis, had its Modernists, most of whom were principally concerned to 'renovate' the Church from the political rather than from the dogmatic standpoint. At least two, however, ventured into the field of theology. Hermann Schell, a professor at Würzburg, attacked the mysteries of the Trinity, the Incarnation and original sin, while Dr Josef Muller sought to build up a *Reform-Katholizismus*.

The men responsible for this crisis were not isolated. They were in constant correspondence. As had happened in the days of Jansenism, they were continually exchanging visits and letters, sometimes using nicknames to designate either their adversaries or themselves. But one must not infer from these numerous contacts any hard and fast agreement upon doctrine. Within the Modernist clique there was a good deal of acrimonious debate, and certain men whom we range together under a single flag would be more than surprised to find themselves in such company. Each national brand of Modernism had its own characteristics, according to the circumstances in which it had developed. In France the influence of Lamennais, Gratry and Ollé-Laprune, strengthened by that of Blondel, directed Modernism towards that *théologie du sensible* of which Édouard Le Roy became the spokesman, while the action of Renan was felt, both positively and dialectically, among exegetes and historians. In Germany, where Döllinger was a leading figure, the Modernism of Friedrich Kraus and particularly of Dr Muller, though steeped in a virulent anti-Romanism, affected the basic principles of faith no more than superficially. In Italy the influence of Rosmini was chiefly philosophical, while that of Gioberti looked rather to institutional initiative. It was largely because of the delicate situation

of Italian Catholics in the political field that demands for religious reforms predominated. Meanwhile in England the Modernism of Tyrrell and Baron von Hügel was saturated with mysticism, linked, at any rate in some respects, with the thought of Cardinal Newman and his apologetic of 'assent'.

Differences, however, were no less marked within the national movements themselves: differences of temperament, together in some cases with great differences of age. There were also differences of fundamental attitude: perfectly orthodox Catholics such as Père Laberthonnière, Le Roy and Fogazzaro had nothing in common with those priests who, like Loisy, performed all the outward gestures of faith but were tormented by doubt.

We must not, therefore, represent the Modernist crisis as a perfectly simple and straightforward conflict, in which the Church had to face a clearly defined enemy. Modernism cannot be considered as a heresy, if it is true that a heresy is a formal deviation on a particular point of orthodox doctrine. Viewed from outside, it looks like a sort of patchwork flag flying above a phalanx of men utterly dissimilar in respect of both character and fields of study. It was Pius X's Encyclical *Pascendi* that gave it its name and the appearance of a doctrinal coherence which it never had. Considered from within, it appears as a general orientation of Catholic thought, a stream deflecting that thought far from its traditional course, far even from basic certitudes. Herein lay the peril; while it made no special attack on any point of dogma, it subjected dogma as a whole to a purely human concept of history and metaphysics. In this sense it was justly described by Pius X as 'the crossroad of all heresies'.

6. Three Aspects of Modernism

The Modernist crisis thus endangered all that constitutes the Church, everything whereby she lives, her hierarchic institutions and her liturgy, her morality and her dogmas. It even affected her relations with secular society. Dogmatic, scriptural, literary and other forms of Modernism have been distinguished. Some historians use the phrase 'political Modernism' with reference to certain deviations that occurred in such apostolic undertakings as the *Opera dei Congressi* and *Le Sillon*. But they do so with little or no justification. For (*a*) while it is true that the leaders of Christian democracy wished, like the Modernists, to renovate the Church, they never dreamed of undermining her foundations by claiming, for example, that the people should assume all the rights of God; the basic error of the Modernist was his desire to change dogmas. And (*b*) young men such as Romolo

Murri, the Abbé Naudet or Marc Sangnier could never have followed the exegesis of Loisy or the philosophical theories of Le Roy or Laberthonnière. Still more incorrectly the term 'social Modernism' has been employed to stigmatize the enterprise of social Catholics who were completely loyal to the Church. The confusion was undoubtedly made easier by the fact that Christian democracy and *Le Sillon*, because of their desire to be always in the lead, were often excessively indulgent towards the most temerarious Modernist theories upon dogma and Holy Scripture.

In order to obtain an over-all picture of the crisis which rocked the Church during the first seven or eight years of the twentieth century, one must consider it in its three fundamental aspects.

1. *Scriptural Modernism.* At the end of November 1902 Alfred Loisy, whose candidature for the episcopate had been set aside by Rome, published *L'Évangile et l'Église*, which soon became generally known as the 'little red book'. It was a vigorous reply to Adolf Harnack's *Wesen des Christentums* (*Essence of Christianity*), which sought to prove that the Kingdom of God, preached by Jesus, was wholly interior and that it had nothing to do with a Church which, though claiming descent from Him, betrayed his message. Loisy was successful in proving that the Church and her dogmas proceed directly from Christ's message, and indeed that Catholicism preserves 'the essence of Christianity'. *L'Évangile et l'Église* was thus a polemical work, and might have won for its author unanimous applause.

As we have seen, however, Loisy's convictions were at that time already far removed from implicit faith, and he took the opportunity to slip into his book, in somewhat Machiavellian fashion, the theories to which he was attached. Applying his critical methods to the Gospel, he rejected the traditional belief that the Church and the sacraments were instituted by Christ, adding that Jesus was mistaken as to the course events would take after His death, the core of His message being the proclamation of an earthly Kingdom of God which was to be inaugurated after the approaching end of the world. This 'eschatological' thesis was the very negation of Christianity; for if Christ were mistaken He could not be God, and it was therefore necessary to admit that He had been 'deified' by the first Christian generations. Shrewd theologians were not deceived by the anti-Protestant apologetic of Loisy; controversy broke out, and his theories were refuted successively by the Abbé Gayraud in *Univers*, by the editors of *Verité française* and by such exegetes as Père Lagrange and Père de Grandmaison. On 19th January 1903 Cardinal Richard condemned the little red book as 'calculated seriously to disturb the faith of Catholics'. The author at once submitted, or at any rate appeared to submit, while Mgr Mignot declared in *Le Correspondant* that the priest's intentions

were pure. Just then, however, Loisy published his own defence in the shape of another 'little red book', entitled *Autour d'un petit livre*, in which, not content with an apologia for his own theses, he put forward others still more audacious on biblical criticism, the historicity of the gospels and the foundation of the Church, contrasting 'the Christ of history' with 'the Christ of faith'. This provoked a new and more vigorous counter-offensive, in which the *Ami du clergé*, the Institut Catholique de Toulouse, Père Prat, Père Fontaine, Mgr Legendre and Mgr Le Camus all took part. At about the same time there appeared *Le Quatrième Évangile*, in which Loisy maintained that the Fourth Gospel was not written by the apostle John, that it was not reliable evidence but a piece of mere theological speculation, the 'product of Christian faith' and not one of its foundation stones.

Loisy, however, was not alone in his attack upon the scriptural bases of Christianity. The uneasiness caused by rationalist criticism was brought into the full light of day by the Abbé Houtin's *La Question biblique au XIXe siècle* and E. Lefranc's *Conflits de la science et de la Bible*. Even in circles where doctrinal stability might have been taken for granted, some curious statements were heard. Mgr Mignot did not hesitate to say: 'Scripture, so admirably divine as regards the religious spirit that breathes through it, contains a certain number of facts and accounts that are humanly speaking improbable, and would cause a profane book which related them to be considered as mere legend.' Elsewhere he declared that 'the modern intellect feels ill at ease in presence of a miracle. Even among those who are not scared by the supernatural one perceives an embarrassment, a hesitation, an uncertainty, a "why", a "perhaps".' And he concluded with some more than cautious words: 'If we believe the Bible it is because we believe the Church'—which left the whole problem unsolved.

2. *Dogmatic Modernism.* On 16th April 1905 there appeared in *Quinzaine* a sensational article 'Qu'est-ce qu'un *dogme*?' by Édouard Le Roy. A sincere believer, resolved to satisfy the rational demands of modern positivist and Cartesian mind, he raised the question of the philosophic value of dogmas and proposed a solution. If scholars and philosophers were repelled by dogmas, was it not because the formulation of dogmas was indefinite and their content unverifiable? Does there not come between revealed (and therefore unalterable) truth and the critical intellect a merely human mode of expression—concepts, abstractions? In order to recover the living truth of a dogma, one need only view it in the light of God's own purpose, which is to provide man with a shield against false notions and a rule of life. It was upon this 'practical' sense of dogma that Le Roy insisted: Live dogma in order to believe it, and leave its intellectual contents as problematical. By re-creating the dogma in your life you will prove it. For example,

though you do not *comprehend* the dogma that 'God is a Person', because God is strictly incomprehensible, behave in your relations with God as with a person, and the dogma will become for you a vital experience. And if you find the dogma of the Resurrection a stumbling block, try to be towards the risen Christ as you would have been towards Him in His lifetime, as you would be towards a contemporary.

It is clear that such a philosophy, derived from the method of immanence carried to extremes, emptied dogma of its substance and reduced faith to mere subjectivism.

Teaching similar to that of Édouard Le Roy is found among other Modernists. 'What are dogmas for us?' wrote George Tyrrell. 'Necessary symbols no doubt, but inadequate, transitory, our only means of drawing near to God and God's only means of approaching us. A truth is simply and solely practical.' Whither would such theories lead? Even Laberthonnière, so different from Le Roy, whom he criticized openly and whose spiritual attitude was diametrically opposed to that of the learned philosopher,[1] was driven by 'realism' to ignore the distinction between nature and grace. He had written that 'truth, the very law of our being', is carried by us 'in the depths of ourselves', that all religious belief is 'an affair of the soul', that consequently one should not attribute to a dogma 'a static, purely objective and extrinsic character', still less propound it 'as a doctrinal norm, definitive and complete'. The theologians who replied to the Modernists had little difficulty in showing that this pragmatist concept of religious beliefs meant abandoning the objective truth of dogmas. Loisy himself wrote to Le Roy: 'Let us take care that we do not, by calling it a philosophy of action, construct a new metaphysic less logically deduced and more absurd than the old.'

3. *Literary Modernism.* The question of Scripture and that of the value of dogmas were thus the twin poles of the Modernist crisis. But what decided Pius X to speak *ex cathedra* and launch a systematic and decisive condemnation was the publication in 1905 of Fogazzaro's *Il Santo*, the third part of a novel in four volumes the first two of which had been in no way open to criticism. Its hero, Piero Maironi, now a gardener at Subiaco, was leading a life so exemplary that the community and indeed the whole neighbourhood regarded him as a saint. But Fogazzaro put into the mouth of this character pronouncements on all kinds of subjects, all directed to a single end. He declared, for example, that the teaching of the Church should adapt itself to the doctrine of evolution, particularly to Darwinism; that dogmas should

[1] As Mgr Nédoncelle observed, 'external nature was of no interest to Laberthonnière apart from spiritual destiny, whereas for Le Roy Christianity had no meaning if it lost contact with the evolution of the world and of mankind' (*Cinquante ans de pensée catholique française*, 1959).

be modified to suit present-day needs; that faith has no meaning unless it is lived. The direct influence of the author's friend Tyrrell was manifest. But to this compendium of current errors, to this 'Divine Comedy of Modernism', as it was called, the novelist had added elements familiar in Italy since the medieval indictments of Christian morals and the Church by John of Flora, the Spirituali and Savonarola. In one of the principal scenes Maironi stands before the Pope and denounces the four evil spirits that have invaded the Church: the spirit of falsehood, which closes men's eyes to the light of modern science and arraigns the ablest champions of truth; the spirit of domination, which transforms paternal authority into an exercise of a frightful dictatorship; the spirit of avarice, which despises evangelical poverty and fills the rulers of the Church with greed for gold; and lastly the spirit of obstructionism, breeding fear of all progress, the same spirit which drove the Jews to reject and condemn Jesus. It was clear that the author was expressing his own thoughts. Another of his characters explained that social activity and the apostolate were worth much more than dogmas and blind obedience to discipline. Never had that 'spontaneous anarchism', as Mgr Baudrillart later described Modernism, revealed itself more flagrantly.[1]

7. Pius X Condemns Modernism

The Church could not, of course, stand by and watch the spread of such ideas. 'I cannot bring myself to believe', said Mgr Duchesne, 'that the Church, that Christianity could accept a certain form of biblical and doctrinal exegesis. When one is allowed to say that Jesus Christ is the son of Joseph and that He did not rise from the dead, it will mean that no one is left to defend Christian tradition.' Even some non-Catholics thought a reaction inevitable. 'Catholicism', remarked Giovanni Gentile, 'can never become the negation of itself, as Tyrrell and Loisy would like.'

If only those rash doctrines had been confined to a few intellectual circles; if only their discussion had been limited to ecclesiastical dinner tables.... But they were penetrating every stratum of society. 'A pestilential atmosphere has sprung up on all sides,' said Pius X. The seminarists were 'passionately for or against Loisy' wrote Mgr Cristiani

[1] It is worth noting that Modernism supplied material for a number of other novels: Roger Martin du Gard's *Jean Barois*; Paul Bourget's *Démon de Midi*, in which, however, it was largely misunderstood and presented in summary fashion; J. Malègue's *Augustin ou le maître est là*, which provides a masterly analysis of the intellectual crisis unleashed by Modernism in the soul of many a believer; and Joseph Wilbois's *L'homme qui ressuscite d'entre les vivants*, where the author makes use of some precious memories.

in his diary;[1] they used to carry the little red books on their walks, and discuss them sentence by sentence. The trouble was so obvious that the press became interested. Articles in *La Quinzaine* were echoed in Sunday sermons and Lenten conferences. The whole body of the faithful was in danger of contamination. 'The duty of the Church is to protect the faith of simple folk', wrote a far-sighted witness of the drama; 'a policing of ideas is as necessary in the Church as is supervision in the education of individuals'. That far-sighted witness was Alfred Loisy.

A counter-attack, moreover, had been launched against the Modernist offensive at many points. Among those who had joined in the fray were a number of bishops, such as the famous Mgr Turinaz of Nancy, whose customary extravagance of language did not always serve the good cause; theologians such as Père (later Cardinal) Billot; exegetes and historians such as Père Lagrange and Mgr Battifol; above all, polemists such as the ex-Jesuit Barbier and the vehement Canon Delassus. At Rome the *Civiltà cattolica* was heavily engaged—more heavily than its rather coy French counterpart *Les Études*—while at the Vatican a mounting tide of opinion urged an out-and-out condemnation of all the fashionable errors. So long as Leo XIII lived no decisive step was taken. He had indeed uttered warnings against the perils threatening faith, and his Encyclicals had clearly shown what course should be steered in order to avoid the reefs; but he had not, perhaps, taken sufficient care to see that his instructions were followed. 'In the failing hands of the aged Pontiff', writes Père de Grandmaison, 'the reins grew a little slack towards the end.'

There was a complete change when Pius X ascended the throne of Peter in 1903. Giuseppe Sarto was no intellectual, and he never found it easy to follow an exegetical or philosophical debate; but he had an innate sense of doctrinal truth and of the Church's interests. His first Encyclical, *E supremi apostolatus cathedra*, announced that he would 'take the utmost care to see that members of the clergy are not ensnared by the cunning of a certain new science which is endeavouring to pave the way for rationalism'. The warning had been given, and effective measures were not slow to follow.

On 4th December 1903, by decree of the Holy Office, five of Loisy's works and two of Houtin's were placed on the Index. That decree was followed by others directed against Laberthonnière, Le Roy and Fogazzaro, as well as against some of the lesser fry, e.g. the Abbé Dimnet, who had described Loisy's criticism as 'so useful for those who understand it, so dangerous for those who do not'. Most of those concerned submitted, including Loisy, who abandoned his course at the Hautes Études.

[1] *Soixante ans de sacerdoce*, p. 54. He was at that time at the French Seminary in Rome.

But that counter-stroke in 'open order' was not enough. If Modernism were indeed the agglomeration of heresies it was claimed to be, the Pope had a clear duty as guardian of the faith to make known the evil in all its fullness. Pius X, under the expert guidance of Cardinals Merry del Val and De Laï, was keeping a watchful eye upon events, and he resolved to strike at once. In accordance with the method employed by Pius IX to condemn liberalism, he had two documents prepared [1]—an Encyclical and a catalogue of errors.

This catalogue was the first to appear. It was published (3rd July 1907) as a decree of the Holy Office, *Lamentabili sane exitu*, which replied to the Modernist thesis that criticism should be independent of theology. Independent? Yes, said the Holy Office in effect, upon condition that it does not fall into error; but here are some errors found in Modernist writings. There followed sixty-five propositions which were declared inadmissible. No author was mentioned by name, but it was easy to recognize most of those propositions as having been taken from Loisy, a few from Tyrrell and one from Le Roy.

Two months later, on 8th December 1907, appeared the Encyclical *Pascendi*,[2] a complete and systematic exposition of all errors that could be ranked under the heading 'Modernism', a word used officially now for the first time. It drew a portrait of the typical Modernist, as philosopher and theologian, as historian and critic, as apologist and reformer. It also showed that Modernist attitudes derived from the single error of twisting unalterable truth to suit modern thought, and explained how hypercriticism and immanentism led inevitably to the emptying of faith and the denial of revelation. The picture was so comprehensive that some, Bishop Dadolle of Dijon among them, took the view that this 'encyclopaedic description of Modernism' was only theoretical, that in practice no Modernist 'ever had a wing span equal to the enormous spread outlined by Pius X'. But the very purpose of the Encyclical was to leave no loopholes.

Pascendi included also a number of remedies likely to check the evil, notably certain bans upon teaching and the publication of books and reviews, as well as the setting up in every diocese of a supervisory council. Between 1903 and 1913 many works by Loisy, Le Roy, Turmel, Saint-Yves, Laberthonnière and others less notorious were placed on the Index. Several journals, knowing themselves to be affected by the condemnation, ceased to appear. The most notable of these were *Demain*, *Annales de philosophie chrétienne* and *Revue d'histoire et de littérature religieuse*, the last of which declared that

[1] By Cardinal Billot and Father Matiussi, according to some; according to others, by Father Joseph Lemius, O.M.I., a personal friend of Merry del Val. See J. Rivière, 'Qui redigea l'encyclique "Pascendi"?' in *Bulletin de littérature ecclésiastique de Toulouse*, Nos. 1 and 2, 1946.

[2] Its official title is *Pascendi Dominici Gregis*.

there was no longer room for it in the 'inquisitorial system set up in the Church'.

Pius X's stern measures fell upon the Modernist movement like a hammer-blow. The great majority of Catholics received the Pope's admonitions with unqualified obedience. The general public, in so far as they understood the issues at stake, acknowledged that the infallible magisterium was using its right and fulfilling its duty in denouncing errors. Neutral papers such as *Le Temps*, *Giornale d'Italia* and *Critica* approved what had been done. In the Modernist camp reaction varied. The most general attitude was one of unreserved submission, as in the case of Père Laberthonnière, of Édouard Le Roy and of Fogazzaro; but there were also instances of bogus submission, where the subject had recourse to mental reservation or other subterfuge. Some friends of the Modernists hinted that the Pope had gone too far, and Mgr Duchesne was credited with two sayings current at that date in Rome: 'St Peter's barque steered *à la gaffe*' and 'the Encyclical *Digitus in oculo*'. There was even stronger resistance in the form of books and pamphlets that appeared in various countries; the most sensational were *Ce que l'on à fait de l'Église* and *Il programma dei modernisti*, published respectively in Paris and Rome. Loisy maintained that no Modernist would recognize himself in the portrait drawn by the Encyclical. Buonaiutti wrote that the Pope had 'condemned a mere dummy or phantom', which did not prevent him a little later from accusing Pius of having 'destroyed a life in embryo'. Tyrrell spoke of 'the cruel document forced by cowardly or cunning hands from the ingenuous and timid simplicity of Pius X', and described it as 'a millstone round the neck of the Church'. Open revolt, however, was rare; some thirty priests at most left the Church. Loisy, called upon to make an act of full and complete submission, refused and was formally excommunicated in 1908. The Government then secured his election to the Collège de France. Tyrrell's defiance of the Pope in a letter to *The Times* entailed his excommunication (1907). In Italy, Buonaiutti adopted a more pliant attitude, which enabled him to remain in the Church until 1921. In Germany, Schnitzer, Wahrmund and Kraus left of their own accord. By and large the losses were small, considering the magnitude of the operation.

It is none the less true that there remained some fear for the future: if priests continued to foster Modernism in secret, the poison would gradually spread. Nor was that fear illusory, for three years after the condemnation Pius X felt obliged to take precautionary measures. The *Giornale d'Italia* had just printed a statement that critical theologians were continuing their studies and that Rome ignored them. A decree of the Holy Office directed all bishops to exclude from the teaching staff of their seminaries anyone 'notoriously suspect of

adhering to the errors condemned', and to refuse ordination to young men who shared such errors. By way of example, the superior of the seminary at Perugia was dismissed for having allowed his students to read Loisy and Fogazzaro. On 1st September 1910 a document emanating from the Pope himself went further still: the Motu Proprio *Sacrarum antistitum* obliged every priest to sign an anti-Modernist oath,[1] the form of which is extremely detailed, occupying no fewer than twenty-six octavo pages. Anyone violating this oath was to be reported to the Holy Office at once. The obligation to take this oath gave rise to a certain amount of agitation. In France a pamphlet claiming to have been written by a group of priests from various dioceses recommended 'external submission in silence'; but there were only six or seven refusals to swear. Resistance was stronger in Germany, particularly in the universities, so strong in fact that Rome agreed to dispense those professors who exercised no parochial ministry. Nevertheless, when all was said and done, Pius X had triumphed.

8. Excessive Reaction: 'Integrism'

Despite the energy with which he sought to destroy the Modernist error, the saintly Pope took pains to avoid any decision that might have wounded justice or charity. Thus Maurice Blondel was not ranked with the dangerous Modernists and suffered no censure.[2] Towards true believers who had gone astray Pius acted with exquisite gentleness; for example, he had Fogazzaro assured of his paternal affection immediately after he had been obliged to condemn *Il Santo*. 'While it is Our duty', he wrote, 'to do battle on behalf of truth, We lovingly embrace the enemies of truth, for whom We feel great compassion; with tears in Our eyes We commend them to God's goodness.' When Romolo Murri, having left the Church, fell upon hard times, Pius X granted him a monthly allowance. And in 1908, the year of Loisy's excommunication, the Pope wrote to the bishop of the diocese in which the rebel priest was living: 'Treat him kindly, and if he takes one step towards you, take two towards him.'

Unfortunately that truly evangelical way of understanding the conflict is supernatural; it is the way of a saint. One could not hope to find it in the common run of mortals. Throughout the history of the Church all periods that have witnessed great doctrinal disputes have also been marked by sordid incidents, by intrigues in which perfidy

[1] All candidates for the priesthood are still obliged to do so before ordination.

[2] His correspondence, published in 1960 under the title *Au cœur de la crise moderniste, le dossier d'une controverse*, has shown how clearly Blondel discerned from the very outset the grave philosophical and theological errors of a Loisy.

was often more prominent than zeal for truth. Every age has its heresy-hunters. Fifty years earlier such well-respected Catholics as Ozanam and Lacordaire had been the target of extremist calumny; so too, later, had Veuillot himself. The Modernist crisis provided many an opportunity for the unleashing of partisan fury, and the necessary intervention of ecclesiastical authority too often had its counterpart in less pacific dealings. Men who had no authority to do so took it upon themselves to track down the 'heretics' and denounce them in high places. The situation grew much worse when censures began to fall; the spirit of delation became rampant, in many cases seeking to hide personal vengeance beneath the cloak of godliness. And so it was that another crisis, interlocking with but more prolonged than that of Modernism, disturbed the Christian conscience. It is known today as the crisis of Integrism.

That crisis took the form both of campaigns waged orally or in print, and also of denunciations to Rome against more or less distinguished Catholic personalities, who were accused of sharing the errors of Modernism but were in fact hounded for quite different reasons. The number of such victims was enormous. Some had been indiscreet, e.g. the Abbé Bremond who had attended Tyrrell's funeral. But many others were denounced whose loyalty to the Church and to the Pope was indisputable. Among them were scholars such as Père Lagrange, the great Dominican who had founded the Biblical School at Jerusalem, and Canon Ulysse Chevalier, whose principal offence was that he did not believe in the authenticity of the 'Holy Shroud' or in the transport by angels of the 'Holy House' of Loreto. Among them, too, were writers, orators and statesmen: Ferdinand Brunetière, a fervent apologist for the faith ever since his conversion; Georges Goyau, a truly apostolic soul; even Albert de Mun. The highest members of the hierarchy, and indeed the very noblest figures, were the object of those calumnies: in France Mgr Mignot, Mgr Chapon, Mgr Gibier and Cardinal Richard himself; in Italy Mgr Radini-Tedeschi, Don Orione and many others. Mgr Amette, at that time coadjutor of Paris, had to go and give an account of himself in Rome. Mgr Baudrillart, whose stout resistance to Modernism was perfectly well known, was denounced to Merry del Val by an individual who urged his dismissal from the rectorship of the Institut Catholique. 'No, never,' replied the cardinal. Mgr Battifol, less fortunate, succumbed. Two incidents among many others showed how great was the power of the heresy-hunters. Mgr Duchesne, director of the French School in Rome and a member of the Académie Française, saw his *Histoire ancienne de l'Église* clapped on the Index—armed though it was with an *imprimatur* from the Master of the Sacred Palace—simply because it showed some 'flexibility' in arguing the transcendence of Christianity!

Finally, to complete this disgusting scene, Père Anizan, a saint if ever there was one, had to leave the Brothers of St Vincent de Paul, of which he was their noblest representative, simply because of odious calumny; and Leo XIII himself was spat upon by men who sank so low as to call him an accomplice of the Modernists.

And who were responsible for such vile insinuations? A little group of men no larger than the spearhead of Modernism, men of unequal worth both intellectually and morally: Père Le Floch of the Congregation of the Holy Ghost and long superior of the French Seminary in Rome; Canon Delassus of Cambrai; the Abbé Charles Maignen; Mgr Delmont, professor in the Facultés Catholiques at Lyons; the Abbé Emmanuel Barbier, an ex-Jesuit and able polemist, who saw red at the very mention of Liberalism, Modernism, democracy or Social Catholicism; the Abbé Boulin, alias Roger Duguet, a dubious character, a priest suspended by his own bishop and one who claimed to see the hand of freemasonry at every turn. The ringleader in France appears to have been a petty provincial academic, one Rocafort, whose very name would be unknown but for his involvement in this affair. The reviews that specialized in this detestable business were *La Vigie*, *La critique du Libéralisme*, *La foi catholique* and *La Revue internationale des Sociétés Secrètes*. France had the singular privilege of being the country most directly affected by this morbid agitation, no doubt because of the too logical character of her people, who always tend to carry an idea to its extreme. But no land was unaffected by the crisis. In Italy a number of little papers were remarkable for their violence: *Riscossa* and *Liguria del Popolo* at Milan, *Difesa* at Venice, *Unita cattolica* at Florence.

That horde of zealots who professed to champion the integrity of Catholic faith are generally known as 'integrists', and the erroneous element in the principles of their conduct as 'integrism'. The terms are comprehensive to the point of vagueness, and unfortunately no antonyms have been found. Their use, moreover, is more recent than the persons and events to which they refer: as late as 1910 Eugène Duthoit applied the word 'integrist' to Christians who, 'so far from reducing to a strict minimum the demands of religious truth, look to it for their principles of aspiration and action'. About 1923 it was often employed in its present sense by the review *Le Mouvement*. But it was not until 1947, in the famous letter *Essor ou déclin de l'Église* by Cardinal Suhard, Archbishop of Paris, that the term appeared in an official ecclesiastical document. Since then it has been used frequently in the press and in books, relatively seldom by the bishops,[1] but never so far by a pope.

[1] One notable instance of its use is the Doctrinal Report (1957) by Mgr (later Cardinal) Lefebvre, Archbishop of Bourges.

The extremists whom we have just seen at work called themselves 'integral Catholics'. The phrase is revealing: they were not only intransigent Catholics battling to defend their faith, like Louis Veuillot or Léon Bloy; they considered that they alone were in possession of truth; that they alone were faithful to the letter and to the spirit of the Catholic message, as well as to the teaching and wishes of the Sovereign Pontiff; in brief, that only their concept of religion was valid. It has been nicely said that they 'established a form of orthodoxy the limits of which were co-terminous with the prejudices of its founders'.[1]

This new orthodoxy had three basic flaws. First there was horror of all novelty, all modernity, identified purposely or not with Modernism. Secondly, the cult of integrity and purity of faith led to serious confusion between revealed truths and academic theories, between the constituent elements of the Church and customs or traditions whose value lay in their antiquity alone. Thirdly, in every field there was a taste for authoritarianism and forceful methods, which explains the frequent recourse to the Holy Office and the reprobation of democracy in any shape or form. 'Integrism' undoubtedly masked grave errors of attitude, but was it a heresy in the strict sense of that word? Opinions differ.[2] Its adherents certainly overvalued the external data of faith, but without harming its intrinsic content; they set too high a price upon dogmas, but never claimed that dogmas should be altered. Their attitude of mind, radically opposed to that of the Modernists, did not lead to subversion in the doctrinal sphere. It was nevertheless extremely dangerous for the Church; it tied her hand and foot, rendering her absolutely incapable of keeping contact with the changing world of men, and it delivered her up to be rent interminably by mutual denunciations and reprisals in defiance of that precept which stands first in Christ's teaching—Charity.

Attacks by self-styled integral Catholics followed one another uninterruptedly from the beginning of the Modernist affair until the death of Pius X. They were often so clearly the outcome of concerted effort that there was reason to suspect them of following a systematic plan. Attacks upon an individual were launched from all directions simultaneously; the same wording is found over and over again in anti-Modernist articles and pamphlets. The same sort of procedure had already been familiar within the Modernist camp, but it was now more clearly defined. Well-informed people were convinced that there existed a secret band-leader who directed the whole integrist concert, and Mgr Mignot actually named him in a memorandum, of which more

[1] J. Rivière, *Histoire du Modernisme*, p. 514.

[2] Père Auguste Valensin (*La Vie intérieure d'un Jesuite*, p. 25) says: 'Over against Modernism there stood its adversary, the opposite heresy of Integrism.' So far as I am aware Integrism has been the subject of no theological study which would enable me to approve or reject such a judgment.

presently. During the First World War a chance occurrence revealed that a clandestine organization of 'integral Catholics' did in fact exist. While searching the house of a lawyer name Jonckx, at Ghent, Father Höner, an officer of the German reserve, came upon several hundred letters, memoranda, etc., most of which were marked 'Confidential, to be burned'. Summoned by the German authorities, Jonckx handed over a dictionary of pseudonyms and coded formulae used in those documents. Father Höner, realizing the importance of his discovery, made arrangements to secure photostats. Although the 'Jonckx Papers' have never been published in full, from 1920 onwards they were made accessible to the press in sufficient numbers to publicize all that was known about a few initiates.

The attacks of the 'integral Catholics' were skilfully directed by a secret society, or rather by a federation of secret societies with headquarters in Rome, at the house of Mgr Umberto Benigni. This prelate, upon whom the most contradictory judgments have been passed—a 'strange and unscrupulous fellow' according to some, 'an ardent and sincere champion of the faith' according to others—had joined the secretariat of state in 1906 as an under-secretary of extraordinary affairs. Two years later he had founded *La Correspondenza di Roma*, and then a General Bureau of Information. But side by side with his press activity he had formed also an organization for 'defence of papal teaching', the *Sodalitium Pianum* (League of St Pius V). It was this organization, functioning in the manner of secret societies, with its own peculiar means of correspondence, its signs of recognition and its secret code, that controlled the 'integral Catholics'. The code name of the central nucleus was 'the Fir-grove', which was known only to the higher initiates, from whom came all directives. The rank and file were divided into three groups: clandestine members, ordinary secret members, and public members who were intended to serve the others as a screen. Some have maintained that the secret league had a thousand active members; but the diversity and even the hierarchy of its formations make such an estimate extremely hazardous.

How far did Pius X approve this undertaking? The report of the process of beatification (1950) shows clearly that he knew of the existence in various countries of groups of 'Catholics sharing the same sentiments of entire and unconditional loyalty to the directives of the Holy See', and that he approved the *Sodalitium Pianum* inasmuch as it sought to defend papal teaching and make war upon Modernism, though his approval in each case appears somewhat vague. Despite repeated requests from Cardinal de Laï, canonical approbation was never granted. And it is equally certain that Pius X was ignorant of the league's rapid turning aside from its original aims to become an organ of suspicion and delation; still less was he aware of the details of its

activity. Cardinal Merry del Val undoubtedly knew a great deal more about the whole matter, since his relations with Mgr Benigni were frequent and familiar; and it is clear from the documents of the Paris nunciature published by Clemenceau[1] that he received from the Firgrove information which might prove useful. We know, however, both from Mgr Benigni's own letters and from Father Antonelli's report of the process of beatification, that the secretary of state often restrained the excessive zeal of his subordinates even before placing the business under control of the Consistorial Congregation.

Nevertheless the activity of the 'integral Catholics' had some extremely unfortunate results. A heavy atmosphere prevailed within the Church, full of mutual suspicion and acrimonious polemic. The religious authorities felt embarrassed, pushed and pulled by men with no official warrant who strove to force their hand and prevented them making in full freedom those decisions for which they alone bore responsibility. Scholars and research workers were discouraged, losing confidence both in themselves and in their leaders. Non-Catholics enjoyed these disputes, and delighted in spreading abroad so singular an image of Christian charity. While Modernism had risked compromising the Catholic intellect, the very air which Catholics breathed was now poisoned.

Protests were not wanting. Some Italian and French bishops told Rome plainly that this system of finical and spiteful supervision was more than inopportune. On the accession of Benedict XV it was learned that the new Pope had informed Cardinal Billot, a friend if not protector of the 'integral Catholics', that their conduct filled him with mistrust. In January 1914 an article in *Les Études* had caused a great stir, and one French bishop resolved to take action. Mgr Mignot, Archbishop of Albi, whose sympathy with the progress of ideas had long been known, drew up a Memorial on the subject, and in October 1914 sent it to Cardinal Ferrata, the new secretary of state.[2] In it he drew a complete and vivid picture of the Integrist movement; spoke sarcastically of those readerless newspapers that had sprung up simultaneously in Paris, Vienna, Brussels, Milan, Cologne and Berlin, all seeming to obey a single inspiration; and denounced those 'condottieri of the pen' who 'under cover of intransigent and ferocious orthodoxy do nothing but satisfy personal grudges and seem to have taken it upon themselves to discredit the most able, most serious and most active workers'. He evoked 'the discouragement of intellectual toilers, denounced, hunted down or vilified by the printing presses of an occult power', and referred to the 'uneasiness' noticeable 'in many seminaries, in the scholasticates of religious orders and in university

[1] See Chapter V, section 2.

[2] It was published by the review *Le Mouvement* in 1923.

circles'. He even had the courage to say: 'The Church has lost a little of the prestige she enjoyed under Leo XIII.'

Benedict XV was waiting for just such a signal to act and put an end to a situation the perils of which he saw quite clearly. On 1st November 1914 appeared an Encyclical, *Ad beatissimi*, devoted to this matter. 'Let no individual,' said the Pope, 'through books, journals or the spoken word, set himself up as a teacher in the Church. With regard to questions upon which the Holy See has as yet given no ruling, and which can therefore be argued for and against, no one is forbidden to put forward and defend his own opinion; but in such discussions let there be no extravagance of language which might be a grave offence against charity. . . .' No Catholic could any longer reject this appeal to charity, which had now been formally expressed. 'We desire also', added Benedict, 'that all should refrain from employing certain terms which have lately been used to distinguish Catholics from Catholics'; an unambiguous statement which Père Yves de la Brière was able, without fear of error, to interpret as condemnation of the phrase '"integral Catholic", adopted by many as the symbol of a more rigorous orthodoxy'.[1] It need hardly be said that in no respect whatever did the admonitions of Benedict XV go back upon the condemnation of Modernism by his predecessor, which indeed he renewed in solemn fashion, denouncing the 'monstrous errors'. What Benedict did was to lead back the Church into that *via media* which is her true path, remote alike from either extreme. The reaction against Modernism had gone too far, and the infallible magisterium reduced it to just proportions. The crisis which had opened with the rash doctrines of Loisy and his rivals was truly at an end.[2]

9. The Balance Sheet

It is true that Pius X's vigour had saved the Church from a great peril, 'the most serious that had threatened her since the Protestant revolt', said Mgr Baudrillart; a peril, according to Père Rouquette,[3] such that 'no danger more radical, no catastrophe more complete' had ever menaced Christianity from within. Pius had played to the full that part of defender of the faith which is, whatever may be said, the first and foremost duty of the Vicar of Christ. Even though his intervention had also brought about the excessive counter-stroke of Integrism, its

[1] *Lettres de l'Église et de la patrie*, Paris, 1916.

[2] The *Sodalitium*, which Mgr Benigni himself had dissolved on the death of Pius X, was revived in 1915, under more restricted conditions. In 1921, when some of the Jonckx Papers were sent to Rome, the cardinal prefect of the Congregation of the Council asked Mgr Benigni for an explanation, and the organization was suppressed.

[3] 'Bilan du Modernisme', *Études*, June 1956.

happy results far outweighed the harm done by private passion, noble or ignoble. The readiness with which Rome was obeyed is a sign of the undisputed authority enjoyed by the Pope; and this latest triumph greatly enhanced that authority. Modernism 'in full flight', said Loisy, had offered very little resistance. When we remember the upheaval caused by the Bull *Unigenitus* condemning Jansenism, we can estimate the progress made and conclude that neither Pius IX nor Leo XIII had laboured in vain.

It is equally true, on the other hand, that the condemnation of Modernism had not dismantled the entire Modernist apparatus. We have seen that the original aims of the Modernists were justifiable. What could not be tolerated was the manner in which they sought to achieve their ends. 'I believe', said Mgr Lacroix, Bishop of Tarentaise, 'that by wanting to go too fast and too far the Modernists compromised all that was perfectly legitimate in their aspirations.'[1] That tactical error, which degenerated into doctrinal error, was, of course, no reason for rejecting what was useful and necessary in the desire to enable Christianity to resist her enemies by adopting their own weapons and methods. The condemnation fixed the limits beyond which a Catholic cannot go without falling into error; it did not forbid Catholics to tread the road along which the Modernists had gone too far. So true is this that it would be easy to show how certain currents of thought, which can be reasonably said to be more or less descended from Modernism, are today accepted by the Church, shorn of error and expressing themselves in language less disturbing and more precise. There is much sense, for example, in asking to what extent the 'personalism' of Emmanuel Mounier does or does not derive from that of Père Laberthonnière, and in seeking to determine at what point Teilhard de Chardin, friend and, in a sense, continuator of Édouard Le Roy, parts company from and even contradicts him.

One of the positive results of the Modernist crisis, followed by that of Integrism, and of the complementary papal decisions which put an end to both, has been to show Catholics the necessity and fruitfulness of dialogue. The attitudes of mind which lay respectively at the roots of those two errors are so fundamental that they were bound to survive; they are found today as yesterday in individuals and in groups whom it would be easy to name. The inescapable conclusion is that while Modernism and Integrism are equally to be avoided, the tension resulting from their opposition is creative, forcing the Church to be faithful to her vocation.

Oportet haereses esse. . . . Once the crisis had been overcome the Church understood more clearly that she faced a fundamental problem

[1] Cf. Chateaubriand's warning to the young Abbé Félicité de La Mennais: 'Do not go too far; do not go too fast.'

which the Modernists had failed to solve, but to which, notwithstanding the opposition of extremists on the other bank, she herself must find a solution. Charles Guignebert claimed that the Encyclical *Pascendi* had imposed upon Catholicism a regime of intellectual inertia; yet now, after fifty years, that judgment appears so unjust as to be absurd. Undoubtedly the Integrist scheme of delation had deplorable consequences which seemed sometimes to confirm Guignebert's opinion. The removal (though for one year only) of Père Lagrange from his Biblical School at Jerusalem was utterly disgraceful; so too was the treatment of Father Semeria, apostle of southern Italy. It was just such excesses that Benedict XV determined to end. But similar errors did not prevent the Church from drawing an obvious conclusion: 'Official rejection of baneful solutions entails an obligation to replace them with one more adequate. In other words, the sole effective means of successfully combating Modernism is an attempt to do better in the task which it failed to accomplish.' Those words of Jean Rivière are very much to the point. But it is exactly that need which the Church has been trying to satisfy ever since. The decisive answer was to be given by Pope Pius XI. An *élite* of scholars and Catholic philosophers, born among the ashes of Modernism, set to work with absolute loyalty to the Church, resolved to carry out their task strictly within her folds and according to her instruction. And their efforts have proved so fruitful that only half a century after the end of the crisis Modernism can be regarded as 'a completely outmoded phenomenon'.[1]

[1] J. Rouquette, op. cit. There is a tendency nowadays to identify modern 'progressism' with Modernism. That is a matter requiring some careful distinctions, and will be discussed in a later volume (*L'Église des Nouveaux Apôtres*). The same remark applies to certain attacks upon the theories of Père Teilhard de Chardin; one can be by no means an 'integrist' and yet not accept the whole of 'Teilhardism', just as one can be a 'Teilhardian' and yet be neither a Modernist nor a Progressist.

CHAPTER VII

WAR AND PEACE

1. 'Il Guerrone'

On 2nd August 1914 the Vatican newspaper *Osservatore Romano* printed an 'Exhortation to Catholics everywhere' in which Pope Pius X, who had only eighteen days to live, appealed for the last time to a world in the grip of suicidal madness. The aged Pope implored his sons to do all they could to avert the divine wrath, to pray and continue striving for peace. Then came these prophetic words: 'Almost the whole of Europe has become involved in a disastrous war of which none can envisage the perils, the carnage and the consequences without overwhelming grief and fear. . . .'

No one indeed could guess whither the world was to be dragged by the bloody machine which the war lords were even then setting in motion. For four years Europe would live in a blood-bath; then, for years afterwards, she would bear within her living flesh the wounds she had received. She would emerge from the tragedy broken, exhausted, diminished, threatened with new perils. It is not surprising that the Common Father contemplated the future with a nameless dread. The Church also was going to be rocked by the war, and Pius X knew it.

He had foreseen that war. Some mysterious gift had enabled him to look into the future while statesmen continued to disbelieve what it held in store. 'In 1906,' wrote Cardinal Luçon, 'when translating me from the See of Belley to that of Rheims, he made direct mention of the bloody cross I should have to bear in my new diocese'—a prophecy which ten years later proved to have been remarkably well founded. From 1911 or 1912 the thought became an obsession with the Pope. To those who enjoyed his confidence he would say: 'I see a great war approaching.' *Il guerrone*: the word was often on his lips. Cardinal Merry del Val relates that on several occasions, arriving for his morning audience, he was greeted with these words: 'Things are going very badly.' On one occasion, when he replied that in his opinion neither the Italo-Turkish conflict in Tripolitania nor the Balkan wars seemed capable of bringing about a general conflagration, the Pope gazed at him for a long time in silence, and then, lifting his hand in sign of warning: 'Eminence, you are wrong; the year 1914 will not end in peace.' In 1913 he told the Brazilian ambassador, who had come to pay

his farewell visit: 'You are lucky to be returning home; you will not see the coming war.' One day when walking with his chaplain Mgr Brossan in the Vatican Gardens he stopped and said very quietly: 'I'm sorry for my successor'; then, alluding to the famous maxims of the prophet Malachy—'*Religio depopulata*,' he murmured; 'it is true that Christendom is going to be depopulated.'

His sorrow and anguish became so intense that he could no longer hide them. Many who saw him enter St Peter's for a ceremony were amazed. Borne on the *sedia*, he seemed lost in a dream, blessing mechanically to right and left, but with no smile lighting up his immobile and gentle countenance. Again, on 25th May 1914, in a consistory that was to be the last of his pontificate, he delivered a poignant allocution upon the text 'O crux ave, spes unica', which men murmur in their darkest hours.

Since the Vatican archives for this period are inaccessible, very little is known about the Pope's activity on the eve of the war, and it is therefore impossible to say whether he confined himself to silent suffering or tried to halt the marching horsemen of the Apocalypse. There are, however, a few indications of his inmost thoughts. One of the most striking, which nevertheless appears to have attracted the attention of no historian, was his decision to hasten the current negotiations for a concordat with Serbia and to have the protocol signed by the cardinal secretary of state on 24th June 1914, that is to say at a moment when it was clear that the Serbian kingdom, victorious in the two Balkan wars and secret promoter of an irredentism now rife in the Croat and Slovene provinces of the Austrian Empire, had become enemy number one of the Central Powers. Did Pius X mean thereby to show that he was not uninterested in her future? Four days later occurred the crime at Sarajevo, followed quickly by the ultimatum from Vienna to Belgrade.

Various witnesses assert that other steps were taken. It is said that the Pope sent a personal letter to the Emperor Franz Josef, but that it remained unanswered. It is said that the Austrian ambassador was summoned to the Vatican to receive a message: 'The Emperor is approaching his last day,' the Pope is alleged to have urged; 'let him not dishonour the end of his life with a star of blood.' But all in vain. Finally, it is said that on the morrow of the declaration of war on Serbia the nuncio at Vienna asked for, and was refused, an audience with the aged monarch, at which he had intended to make yet one more appeal. When the Pope was asked by the Austrian ambassador to bless the arms of the Double Monarchy he replied: 'I do not bless arms, but peace.'

It was all to no avail, as Pius X was undoubtedly well aware. Having no more confidence in the things of earth, he said time and again to

those around him: 'I offer my poor life to the Lord that He may suspend the scourge . . .' Finally he penned the 'Exhortation' to all his sons, without exception. His last public act was to receive in audience the foreign seminarists who were leaving Rome for their respective countries in order to fight one another: Frenchmen, Germans, Belgians, Austrians, Englishmen, Slavs. The Church was being rent before his very eyes. . . . He asked them all not to forget the great law of mercy, even in the fury of war; and as he blessed them he was seen to be in tears.[1]

2. Benedict XV and the First World War

The tragedy which caused Pius X to die of grief weighed heavily on the pontificate of his successor. For four years, while Europe flamed, while men died by millions, while countries of ancient civilization became fields of ruins, the Vicar of Christ found himself confronted with problems the gravity and complexity of which appeared to exceed human strength. Benedict XV, however, faced the sphinx of history with an admirable vigour, courage and depth of view which are not forgotten despite the unfair silence that surrounds his memory. Misunderstood and calumniated, he followed the road dictated by his conscience, knowing well that the interests of God cannot be reconciled with the horrors of war, but are identical with the interests of peace.

Immediately after his election he made a solemn protest, declaring himself 'stricken with inexpressible horror and anguish before the monstrous spectacle of this war with its streams of Christian blood'. On many occasions, so long as the 'horrible butchery' endured, his voice proclaimed that Europe was committing suicide, that she was disgracing herself in 'the most sombre tragedy of human madness'.

But he did more than utter cries of indignation. He determined to act. One of his sayings defines exactly the attitude he resolved to take: 'The Pope is not neutral, he is impartial.' He did not intend to set himself above the turmoil, i.e. to consider himself as a mere unhappy spectator. And indeed he was no neutral; he even sought to intervene directly in the conflict. Why? Undoubtedly first and foremost through charity, because he was harrowed by his position as Pope of the *religio*

[1] Jean de Bonnefon, a journalist, declares that Pius died of the grief he felt at being unable to publish a letter he had written with his own hand, protesting against the violation of Belgian neutrality, a letter which his *entourage* held back in order not to commit the Church in favour of one side. And a Roman prelate, Mgr De Luca, told the author in 1947 that he believed, on unimpeachable authority, that Pius X took steps through intermediaries to prevent Italy from entering the war on the side of the Central Empires, her allies.

depopulata; he dreamed of putting an end to the massacre and of bringing back peace upon an earth restored to men of goodwill. Nor is it possible to see how the representative of Christ could have refused such a role. Again there was nothing wrong in his obeying an urge to enhance the prestige of the Holy See by giving it a part in the historic drama; and the belligerents themselves, by indiscreetly soliciting the Pope's spiritual authority with a view to their own interests, were in effect giving him a moral position of the first order.

But simultaneously with the motive of charity another reason—his far-sighted anxiety for the interests of the Church—prompted Benedict XV to attempt some definite action on behalf of peace. The conflict was a considerable embarrassment to the functioning of the ecclesiastical machine, so much so as to render it impossible. Once Italy had entered the war against the Central Empires, the German, Austrian and other ambassadors accredited to the Holy See were obliged to withdraw to Lugano, in Switzerland, and communications were interrupted between the Roman Congregations and the bishops in those countries.

Much more serious, the war was imperilling Catholic unity: the faithful were fighting one another not only on the field of battle, but also on that of lying propaganda. For in both camps Catholics adopted almost unanimously the spirit of the most feverish nationalism. In France the 'Sacred Union' reconciled Catholics and their adversaries: 25,000 priests served with the colours, 12,000 of them as combatants, and 4,608 fell on the field of honour. That sacrifice, laudable in itself, was destined to bear abundant fruit in the post-war religious field. But how many Catholics, indeed how many priests, accepted without demur the vilest outpourings of propaganda, disseminated the most dreadful calumnies and demanded the most pitiless revenge! It was the same in Germany, where the *Zentrum*, steadfast behind the imperial government, did not hesitate to support the worst forms of imperialism and pan-Germanism, and where a manifesto of seventy-six leading Catholics echoed that of ninety-three intellectuals in exalting the war as 'the new springtime of religion'. All that, having regard to the circumstances, was explicable, and even excusable; but it is no less understandable that the Pope should have wished to put an end to a situation so incompatible with the Catholic spirit, and one moreover (as was proved by a wealth of experience) in which the supranational character of the papacy was at stake.

Such were the reasons that led Benedict XV during the early months of the conflict not only to work for peace through numerous appeals, and requests for prayer, but also to suggest means for its restoration. What he sought was a 'stable and equitable' peace achieved through negotiation, 'weighing the rights and just aspirations of peoples', not a

punitive peace imposed by the victors on the vanquished 'who will prepare for revenge and transmit hatred from generation to generation'. This purpose, the nobility and sound sense of which none can deny, was revealed in a large number of public declarations and in more or less secret approaches about which little is known. The Pope's intentions had been made perfectly clear in the inaugural Encyclical of his pontificate (September 1914), in the Encyclical *Ad beatissimi* (November) and in the decree of January 1915, ordering prayers for peace. In September 1915 a special committee was appointed at the Vatican to give effect to those intentions and to bring about an end of the conflict. Negotiations began at once, the Pope using every means at his disposal to plead the cause of peace. Mgr Baudrillart, rector of the Institut Catholique at Paris, was instructed by Cardinal Gasparri, secretary of state, to offer France and her allies certain 'honourable conditions', which the Vatican believed Germany ready to accept. These included the evacuation of Belgium and northern France, and the restitution of Alsace-Lorraine in return for 'a good colony'. The German general staff, however, had much more grandiose designs. When a new emperor, Karl, succeeded the aged Franz Josef, Benedict XV and his nuncio at Munich, Mgr Eugenio Pacelli (later Pope Pius XII), did their best to further negotiations begun by the young Hapsburg and his minister Czernin. Additional feelers were put out: a letter to Cardinal Pompili, messages to various French bishops. But none of those intiatives bore fruit.

The most vigorous attempt was made in 1917. The situation seemed to favour a compromise peace: symptoms of lassitude were noticeable in both camps; in the Central Empires 120 million human beings had been reduced to famine through blockade by sea, but the submarine campaign was working havoc among the Allies. Russia was in a state of revolution; the French army itself was in the throes of a grave crisis; and, despite the intervention of the U.S.A., many people feared for the future. On 14th August 1917 all belligerent governments received a papal note inviting them to make peace and suggesting basses of negotiation. The note contained two tiers of proposals. (1) In order to re-establish peace, it suggested evacuation of all occupied territories, return to freedom of the seas, mutual abandonment of all claims in respect of war damage (except in clearly defined cases of devastation), and the opening of discussions on litigious questions. But (2), looking beyond the immediate present, Benedict indicated the foundations upon which alone a just and stable peace could be built: legal obligation to settle international disputes by arbitration; a general and proportional reduction of armaments; international sanctions against any power guilty of aggression. The famous Fourteen Points of Woodrow Wilson offered no more.

The initiative by itself did honour to him who took it. Moreover none of the governments which received the note disputed the Pope's right to issue such an appeal. In fact, however, the response was disappointing. The German and Austrian emperors thanked Benedict for his move and expressed a hope that his counsels would be followed; but no steps were taken or even promised that gave grounds for thinking that the plan would be carried out. The Allies let it be known that they would make no official reply.

Not only was the failure of Benedict's undertaking complete, but it had the singular and iniquitous consequence of rousing against him a flood of rage and bitterness which half a century has not sufficed to stem. Each of the two camps considered that the Pope had violated equity by not denouncing the other. With a degree of ingenuousness bordering on the absurd, each nation expected Rome to take a hand in the quarrels between States and to adopt its own views upon the origins of the war. To which Benedict XV replied: 'We reprove all violations of right, wherever committed, but to involve the papal authority in the disputes of belligerents would be neither useful nor appropriate.' He also told the French journalist Latapie: 'Every one of your accusations brings a retort from the Germans, and I do not wish to start a permanent debate or to hold inquests just at present. It is not yet time to disentangle the truth from all the contradictory accusations; the Vatican is not a court of law.'

It is astonishing to find how completely those words of wisdom were misunderstood. Later studies on the origins of the First World War make one more cautious in assigning guilt; while neither camp was wholly responsible, neither was wholly innocent. Alfred Fabre-Luce has summed up the case in this lapidary formula: 'Germany and Austria did things that made war possible; the Triple Alliance did things that made it certain.' But in 1914 and 1918 men were far from ready to accept such propositions. . . . The most deplorable result was a torrent of abuse unleashed against Benedict XV. In France, Clemenceau was credited with the phrase 'Boche Pope'. Léon Bloy referred to him as Pilate. Senior prelates and even bishops announced their disapproval of the Roman plan for peace, and from the pulpit of La Madelaine an illustrious Dominican orator, Père Sertillanges, pronounced in otherwise respectful terms a categorical *non possumus* to the papal scheme.[1]

[1] Cf. A. D. Sertillanges, '*La Paix française*', *discours prononcé en l'église Sainte-Madeleine le lundi 10 décembre 1917, en la cérémonie religieuse et patriotique prédisée par S.E. le Cardinal Archevêque de Paris* (Bloud et Gay, Paris, 1917). The operative words of that sermon (delivered to urge Frenchmen to give their gold for national defence) were as follows: 'Most Holy Father, we cannot for an instant entertain your appeals for peace.' It was rumoured at the time, and seems to be confirmed by reliable witnesses, that while Père Sertillanges *delivered* the sermon, he did so at the direct instigation of Cardinal

Nor indeed had Germany more cause for satisfaction; the creation of an eighth French cardinal, the celebration at Rome of the taking of Jerusalem by the Allies, and the condemnation of such crimes as the sinking of the *Lusitania* were looked upon as so many indications of partiality.

One question, however, must be faced. Did not the Pope's impartiality hide secret preferences, and was not the proposal of a 'white peace' an attempt to save the Central Empires? The Abbé Brugerette went so far as to say that 'Benedict XV served the interests of France's enemies in opposition to our own.' As to the second part of the question, all that we know of the state of mind prevailing at the Vatican in 1917 points to belief in an Austro-German victory; so it was not in order to prevent the defeat of those empires that Benedict took the initiative of proposing negotiations.

It is more difficult to decide whether the sympathies of the Pope and his *entourage* lay with the Central Empires. It must not, however, be forgotten that France had long since broken off diplomatic relations with the Vatican and had no ambassador there; to the letter in which Benedict informed the French president of his election Poincaré had replied with cold politeness, and Barrère, the French ambassador to Italy, had successfully opposed the appointment of a colleague to the Vatican for fear of offending the Quirinal. England and Russia were each represented by a simple minister of no great influence, while the Belgian ambassador received nothing but kind words of consolation. The enemy diplomats therefore had a clear field. It would be ingenuous to suppose that they did not, or to be surprised that they did, make use of their opportunity. One sensational incident, however, revealed some quite unpardonable conduct in the Holy Father's immediate circle: Mgr Gerlach, a German prelate and member of the Pope's household, was convicted of belonging to a network of secret agents whose activity resulted in the blowing up of the Italian cruiser *Leonardo da Vinci*.

On the other hand, once might ask whether Rome had not good reason to dislike the prospect of an Allied victory, which would mean the triumph of agnostic France and Protestant England, the advance of Russia to the Dardanelles and her eventual seizure of Catholic Poland. Later, in 1918, the Pope had little cause for satisfaction with the peace

---

Amette. At all events the printed text bears the archbishop's *imprimatur* dated 5th December 1917. The cardinal was said to have played his part in this matter at the express wish of President Poincaré. It was only at the death of Cardinal Amette that Père Sertillanges went into exile until 1939, when Pius XII reinstated him. Sertillanges always maintained a dignified silence. The affair was particularly painful to him, because in *La Vie héroïque* (3rd series, 1916, especially pp. 166–84), he had justified the attitude of Benedict XV.

that loomed on the horizon. Catholic Austria-Hungary was to be dismembered upon express demand of the Czech freemasons, and by Article XV of the London Agreement Italy had exacted as the price of her entry into the war the Pope's exclusion from the negotiations of the peace treaty.

All those factors must be taken into consideration when judging Vatican diplomacy. None can say whether the attempts made by the secretariat of state to deter Italy and the United States from coming into the war on the side of the Allies were dictated by the sole desire to prevent extension of the conflict. Nevertheless it must be emphasized that Benedict's plan for peace made provision for the restitution to France of Alsace-Lorraine; that the Pope on several occasions expressed keen sympathy for martyred Belgium; that despite pressure from the Irish at the Vatican he refused to patronize their struggle for independence, which would have weakened Britain at the height of the war; and that he more than once personally rebuked Wilhelm II in no uncertain terms, especially for the use of poison gas. Today, in fact, there are no grounds whatever for doubting that Benedict's declaration of impartiality was sincere.

One thing is quite certain: but for his impartiality, Benedict XV would have been in no position to carry out the task of humanizing war and alleviating its cruel effects. His efforts in that direction were numerous: a general exchange of seriously wounded prisoners of war, which was agreed by all belligerents; liberation of many civilian captives—women, children and the sick; internment in a neutral country of disabled prisoners of war; regulation of reprisals by preliminary declaration of motives. Nor, of course, was the strictly religious point of view ignored. Agreements were signed to ensure religious services in prison camps. These were also inspected by neutral apostolic visitors, who saw to the carrying out of those agreements and watched over the material condition of their inmates. Two measures undertaken by the Vatican during the war were more unusual. Collections on behalf of devastated territories were organized in all countries on both sides, including the Balkans; and Benedict XV managed to secure effective disbursement of the money received. Secondly, an office was set up to collaborate with the International Red Cross in searching for missing persons, tracing prisoners and forwarding mail to them. It is estimated that Benedict XV contributed 82 million gold lire towards those various undertakings or by way of direct assistance to those in distress.

That vast work of charity, which alone should suffice to win respect for Benedict's name, was acknowledged by only one sovereign ruler, who in one of the squares of his capital erected a statue 'To the great Pontiff of the world tragedy, benefactor of peoples without distinction

of race or creed'. But alas, the capital where stands that image of Benedict XV is Constantinople, and the sovereign who saluted in those very words his noble memory was the Sultan.[1]

3. The Peace Treaty

'We have won the war,' declared Clemenceau on 11th November 1918; 'now we shall have to win the peace, and that will perhaps be even more difficult.' So difficult indeed that the 'victory of right and civilization' hallowed the abandonment of those traditional Western values for which centuries of Christianity and humanism had vouched, and opened the gates to Communism, Fascism and National Socialism—systems diametrically opposed to the old traditions. The victory, moreover, was so insecure that peace was very quickly doomed and another war soon lowered on the horizon. The Holy See had no part in the series of treaties which followed hard upon the armistice. Sonnino had made Italy's entry into the war on the side of the Allies strictly conditional upon the Vatican's exclusion from any subsequent negotiations, fearing that the Pope might take such an opportunity to raise the Roman Question. Accordingly the Sovereign Pontiff could not make his voice heard at Versailles, at the Trianon, at Neuilly, at Sèvres, those Parisian suburbs where the terms of peace were evolved. Barred from the commissions which prepared the diplomatic instruments, he nevertheless had at Paris, in the person of Mgr Cerretti, a tireless and able representative who succeeded in making many contacts and whose activity behind the scenes was far from negligible. Furthermore the Pope's exclusion was advantageous inasmuch as the Holy See had no responsibility in the drawing up of the treaties; it remained aloof from the often sordid bargaining and underhand agreements which inspired many clauses. It cannot, however, be denied that those treaties were devised in opposition to Catholic interests, to the Church and to all that seemed likely to assure her power or her influence. Hostility towards the Church indeed begat at least a tacit understanding among statesmen who disagreed on many other points: Sonnino, president of the Italian Council and a passionate anticlerical, the ultra-radical Clemenceau, the Presbyterian Lloyd George, the Puritan Wilson, and Masaryk, high in the councils of freemasonry.

It would no doubt be unfair to attribute the unfortunate results of

[1] In 1962 a congress was held at Spoleto to study the policy of Benedict XV and the attitude of Catholics during the war. The most important addresses were those delivered by the president, Maurice Vaussard, by Mgr Leflon and by Father Angelo Martini. The congress as a whole did justice to the Pope of *religio depopulata*.

the 1919 agreements to the sole determination of a few men. It is clear, for example, that the collapse of the fragile edifice that had been the Austro-Hungarian Empire was inevitable from the moment when Franz Josef foolishly embarked on his tragic adventure. Even so, the peace which left Germany intact and overthrew the Catholic empire of the Habsburgs, so as to leave Austria 'a mere miserable stump' and Hungary a state that could not live, bore the stamp of Protestantism and freemasonry. 'Clemenceau's imbecile peace', said Aristide Briand to a friend, 'is a Protestant peace directed against Rome. . . . You'll never know to what extent hatred of the Pope inspired that gang.' [1]

The world situation that resulted from the peace treaties appeared by no means favourable to the Church; and, to make matters worse, she suffered terrible losses in various parts of the globe. In Mexico the persecution had taken a disastrous turn: the enemy seemed bent upon destroying Christianity root and branch. In the Near East, Asia Minor and Persia a wave of atrocities burst upon all the Christian communities, a wave so terrible that when it became possible to estimate losses more than 3 million Christians were found to have been removed by massacre or deportation.

In spite of that situation, however, Benedict XV did all that was possible towards enabling the Church to regain her position everywhere. Moreover there were certain aspects of the treaties signed at Versailles which the Holy See found no reason to deplore, particularly the resurrection of Catholic Poland on 14th November 1918. Benedict XV immediately recognized the new State and sent Mgr Achille Ratti as apostolic visitor. The latter's task, however, was no bed of roses. He had to undertake delicate negotiations with the Poles in the matter of German bishoprics in Silesia which the Vatican refused to make Polish. Above all, he was in Warsaw when the Red counter-offensive, led by Tukhachevsky, came within an ace of occupying the capital. But Mgr Ratti did a great deal to re-establish the Church in Poland, which was quickly strengthened by the touching loyalty of the masses. Appointed nuncio in 1919, the future Pope Pius XI was to leave his mark as a capable administrator on the newly born Catholic Poland.

Outside the scope of the treaties another Catholic nation, Ireland, achieved independence three years later. On 6th December 1921 an agreement was signed in London recognizing Ireland as independent, but excluding Ulster, which was to remain British. Opposed by Eamon de Valera, the treaty did not come into force until ten months after the death of Benedict XV; but none could doubt the victory of the Irish Catholics.

There was even one point in the diplomatic construction of the peace treaties which somewhat surprisingly confirmed the presence and

[1] Quoted by the Abbé Renaud. See p. 62, footnote 4.

authority of the Holy See. When the negotiators came to decide the fate of the German colonies, there was question as to future ownership of the property of Catholic missions in those territories. Some talked of transferring it to the Protestant missions. Finally, by Article 438 of the Treaty of Versailles, it was granted to the Holy See. That grant was confirmed by a letter from Balfour; it recognized in effect the supranational authority of the Pope in the entire missionary field, and is therefore important though seldom quoted.

Benedict XV, however, suffered one great disappointment during that period when the new Europe was trying to establish herself upon lasting foundations. Despite all its acknowledged defects, the Treaty of Versailles was none the less, in Clemenceau's words, 'an attempt at permanent pacification', seeking for the first time in history 'the bases on which to secure justice between peoples'. But its clauses had still to be applied, and, above all, victory had still to be won for the spirit of equity wherewith its authors claimed to have been inspired. A 'continuous creation', said Poincaré, would be necessary, and in order to provide for such the Allies resolved to set up a supranational organism.

Now Benedict XV had been the first—in 1917, too early perhaps—to advocate an authority whose duty it would be to prevent armed conflict by obliging all nations to submit their differences to arbitration, by imposing progressive and controlled disarmament, and even by punishing those who violated the pact. A scheme on those lines had been worked out in considerable detail by the Catholic Union of International Studies, which had held its sessions in Switzerland during the war. It is hard to see what other principles underlay President Wilson's subsequent Fourteen Points, especially the fourteenth point, which provided for the setting up of an international organism closely akin to that envisaged by the Pope. At the time very few people made the comparison and gave the Pontiff his due. But on 3rd October 1924, addressing the League of Nations, Joseph Motta, President of the Helvetic Confederation, paid the dead Pope this tribute: 'If mankind manages one day to get rid of war—and that day is perhaps as yet far distant—it will owe that priceless achievement to the principle of arbitration as proposed by Benedict XV.'

At Versailles, despite resistance, Wilson successfully advocated a League of Nations to which all free states might belong. Its aim would be to impose upon all governments respect for one another's rights, recourse to arbitration in case of dispute, as well as renunciation of excessive armaments and secret diplomacy. Aggressors would be punished with economic and (if necessary) military sanctions. With its Assembly, in which each member State, large or small, was represented by one delegate, its Council sitting three times a year, its permanent

Secretariat, its permanent Court of International Justice, its International Bureau of Labour and so on, Wilson's organization was certainly impressive, and before long it was to have its own Palace at Geneva. But since it had had no force of international police, and since the United States by vote of Congress refused to join the League of Nations, this latter represented no real source of strength.

It might have been expected that the highest spiritual power would have been associated with an undertaking founded upon the primacy of justice. But that power was carefully excluded from the League by the same hostility shown towards it from the very outset of negotiations. Looking back, one might ask whether it would have been desirable for the Holy See, as a member of the League of Nations, to become involved in purely temporal questions, in an atmosphere of intrigue where, as events quickly showed, the moral law was sometimes treated in the most curious fashion. At the time, however, Catholics were gravely offended by that exclusion, and consequently tended to show a systematic distrust of the 'Protestant and Masonic' institution at Geneva. Benedict XV, though at first grieved by his ostracism, soon adopted a generous attitude. Not only did he declare his approval of and confer his blessing upon the League, but he also instructed the Catholic Union of International Studies to establish a permanent link with it, and even managed to bring about collaboration between the Church and the new organization on a number of specific points. It was thus with pleasure that the Holy See saw Catholics take an important place in the International Bureau of Labour and the Office of Intellectual Co-operation. The Vatican was consulted when there was a question of determining the future of missions in mandated territories, and also in the debate as to the legal status of the Holy Places. It likewise took part in discussions on the reform of the calendar, about which there was a great deal of talk in the immediate post-war years. Upon certain very grave matters it was, indeed, the Vatican that took the initiative. Benedict XV, for example, denounced the continuance of slavery in various parts of Africa and of the Moslem world; and one of his last acts was an appeal for aid for Soviet Russia, which was then in the throes of famine.[1]

And so, excluded though she was from official negotiations, the Church found herself, thanks to the skill of Benedict XV, closely concerned with the restoration of peace. The Pope judged that peace with a lucidity far removed from the rather silly enthusiasm to which so many statesmen gave vent. While numerous voices echoed Wilson in proclaiming that an era of everlasting peace had just begun

[1] See Yves de la Brière, *l'Organisation international du monde et du Saint-Siège*, Paris, 1924. See also Mgr Bertoli's article 'Le Saint-Siège et l'Organisation internationale' in *Revue des Deux Mondes*, 15th May 1961.

under the aegis of the League, the Common Father, attentive to the protests that rose on all sides against what the Germans called the *Diktat* of Versailles, put the problem in its rightful setting. He reminded a party of French journalists whom he had received in audience that their most urgent duty was to labour for the reconciliation of hearts by avoiding all that might foster hate and the spirit of revenge. And in 1920, in his Encyclical *Pacem Dei Munus* on the same topic, he made this melancholy observation: 'Though treaties of peace have been signed, the germ of ancient discords has not been destroyed.' The future fully justified his words.

4. Re-establishment of Relations with France

When the Treaty of Versailles was signed Benedict had fewer than three years to live. During that brief period he did his utmost not only to bring about a general reconciliation, but also to re-establish the presence of the Church wherever possible. A new policy was introduced which was to be that of succeeding pontificates, an open-minded policy intended to broaden the Church's outlook, and one that was destined to have important consequences.

A first spectacular and significant gesture was made at the beginning of 1919, when President Wilson came to Europe. Among the capitals he proposed to visit was Rome; but it remained to be seen whether the Pope would uphold the principle laid down by Pius X, whether, that is to say, the doors of the Vatican would be closed to the illustrious visitor in the event of his calling upon the King of Italy.[1] Benedict XV very sensibly decided that the question should not arise. He received Wilson in his study and talked with him for twenty minutes—a gesture all the more remarkable inasmuch as a gathering of representatives of all the Protestant sects in Italy had arranged to welcome the President on the afternoon of the same day. Next year it was officially announced that the Pope, without forgoing his historical rights, was abrogating the protocol of his predecessor, in order 'not to prevent meetings so useful to peace by making it virtually impossible for Catholic heads of state to visit Rome'.

There was no more decisive proof of this widening of outlook, so characteristic of the Pope's entire attitude, than his spectacular reconciliation with France. The situation in that country was much altered. The virulent anticlericalism of 1905 had been replaced in popular opinion by sentiments of a very different kind. The sacred

[1] See Chapter V, section 2.

union of war-time had helped the adversaries towards a better understanding of one another. Catholics and anticlericals had formed many a friendship in the trenches. It seemed hard, moreover, to treat as second-rate citizens those priests and religious who had given unanimous proof of their patriotism; more than five thousand had died for France, while many others, led by Cardinal Amette and Mgr Baudrillart, had helped the civil authorities to strengthen the determination of the masses or had undertaken delicate missions. Politicians known as convinced *laïcs*, notably Aristide Briand and Anatole de Monzie, urged that France should re-establish diplomatic relations with the Vatican and that the Law of Separation should be modified.

Benedict XV was informed of this altered outlook by Mgr Cerretti, his representative in Paris during the peace negotiations. He immediately grasped the importance of the fact and foresaw the consequences that could be derived from it. The collapse of Catholic Austria-Hungary made it imperative that France should resume her ancient role as a great Catholic power. She alone could now give substantial help to the missions and protect the Catholics of the Near East. Mgr Cerretti accordingly made contact with various French politicians, and was often seen at Monzie's house in the Rue Férou.

Unequivocal signs of goodwill were given by the Vatican to the French Government, especially in the matter of Alsace-Lorraine, where the clergy were asked not to impede the functioning of the Concordat and where bishops were appointed in accordance with the wishes of Paris. In Morocco, too, Rome showed her readiness to oblige by nominating a French vicar-apostolic. Finally, French Catholics were delighted by the canonization of Margaret Mary Alacoque and Joan of Arc. At the ceremony, which took place on 16th May 1920, the Government of the Third Republic was represented by the historian Gabriel Hanoteux, a distinguished member of the Académie Française.

Reconciliation was in sight. The foundations of an agreement had already been laid by Mgr Touchet, Bishop of Orleans, who had missed no opportunity of assuring Rome that Paris was full of goodwill, and of proclaiming in France that Benedict was not the 'Boche Pope' he had been said to be. Negotiations were therefore opened, handled on the French side by the *chargé d'affaires* Doulcet and on behalf of the Vatican by Mgr Eugenio Pacelli. Re-establishment of diplomatic relations was decided without difficulty, notwithstanding some resistance in the Chamber and the Senate; and in 1922 Jonnart went to Rome as ambassador, Mgr Maglione to Paris as nuncio.

Once that first step had been taken, another followed without much delay. It was necessary to give the Church in France a legal standing. Since Pius X had rejected the *Associations cultuelles*, the position of

religious buildings was quite uncertain. Public opinion, however, supported by the *Association des Religieux anciens combattants*, favoured revision of the statute affecting religious congregations. The Abbé Renaud,[1] an able diplomat, was entrusted by Benedict XV with the negotiation of new arrangements. After discussions with leading French politicians and jurists, agreement was reached. The republican legislation was to be retained—'I certainly don't want to bring the French Republic to Canossa,' said Benedict—and the Pope was to recognize the French Government as having some say in the appointment of bishops as though a concordat existed. The French, on their part, would tacitly allow the return of religious, both men and women, and the reopening of many schools run by the teaching congregations. As for the *Cultuelles*, Rome would have no more to do with them than she had in the days of Pius X. But thanks to the perseverance of Mgr Cerretti, something was devised rather similar to the 'canonico-legal *cultuelles*' which the bishops of France had once been prepared to accept; and in due course the Conseil d'État gave legal status to these new bodies which were known as *Associations Diocésaines*. A fresh regime was thus established in France,[2] one that put an end to an ambiguous situation. Some Catholics judged it inadequate and wanted a regular concordat; but the proof of its worth lies in the fact that, despite the instability of French politics and the anticlerical scheming of the Bloc des Gauches and the Front Populaire, it continues to work.

5. Benedict XV and Italian Affairs

In Italy likewise Benedict XV sought to take advantage of the new post-war climate with a view to strengthening the Holy See's authority and increasing the influence of the Church. Two problems remained to be solved: that of the papacy's relations with the Italian State, and that of Catholic participation in the country's political life. At the time of his election to the papal throne Benedict's attitude towards the 'despoilers' had been no different from that of his two predecessors. He had not given the blessing *Urbi et Orbi* from the exterior balcony of St Peter's; nor since that date had he once left the Vatican, indicating thus that he considered himself still a prisoner, though he was usually careful to avoid any reference to his position as such. But the difficulties which the war had caused him in his relations with Catholic

[1] See p. 248, footnote 1.

[2] Benedict did not live to see it function; he died very soon after the agreements had been signed.

States had convinced him of the advantages his spiritual mission would derive from a reconciliation with the Quirinal. Even during the period of hostilities a commission of cardinals had looked into the question of what conditions might be made the basis of a *modus vivendi*; and secret contacts had already been made between emissaries of the two powers when the Italian Government managed to exclude the Holy See from any part in framing the peace treaties. Those contacts were renewed after the war, first in Paris, where Mgr Cerretti had talks with Italian diplomats, then in Rome, where the consistorial advocate Pacelli, brother of the future Pope, undertook discussions the details of which have never been revealed. In 1921 *Il Messagero*, the leading journal of the left, made reference to the subject and expressed a hope that formal negotiations would soon begin; and *Tempo*, a liberal governmental paper, wrote: 'A solution must be found to this old and embarrassing Roman Question.'

As regards the second problem, Benedict was able to make a decision. Pius X had already modified the *non expedit*, which since the days of Pius IX had forbidden Italian Catholics to take part in political life except within the narrow municipal sphere.[1] The bishops had made frequent use of the permission by virtue of which they might authorize Catholics to offer themselves for election and electors to vote for them. The 'Gentiloni Pact' had even made it possible to win seats for numerous 'Catholic deputies' in Parliament. On this point also wartime experience showed Benedict XV the impossibility of remaining for ever in an ambiguous situation: when there was question of Italy entering the war on the Allied side, the Catholics, who, like the Pope himself, disapproved of such a step, were powerless to prevent it. After the armistice, therefore, when new elections were to take place, the Sacred Penitentiary announced officially that the *non expedit* was abrogated.

It was immediately suggested that the Catholics of Italy should coalesce into a solid party with a view to strengthening their influence. Leo XIII and Pius X, as we have seen,[2] mistrusted Catholic parties, especially those which took their stand on the principles of Christian Democracy. Benedict XV felt differently: it was within the framework of a democratic regime that Catholics would have to play their part, and to forbid their recourse to democratic principles would have been to paralyse them.

During the final stages of the war a number of men, most of whom had belonged to the *Opera dei Congressi*, decided to lay the foundations of a Christian democratic party destined to unite Catholics not only at the religious and apostolic level, like the *Unione Popolare*, but also with a view to political activity. The leaders of this group were Count

[1] See Chapter V, section 5. [2] Chapter V, section 6.

Grosoli, former president of the *Opera dei Congressi*; the journalist Montini (father of Paul VI), who was head of the electoral union; Count Santucci; and, above all, Don Sturzo, who since the suppression of the *Opera* had occupied a key post in the general secretariat of one of the great Catholic organizations,[1] and was indeed the real life and soul of this new undertaking.

Don Sturzo and his friends asked the secretary of state and then the Pope himself whether their project would be accepted in high places. The answer was favourable. On 17th November 1918, thirteen days after the Austro-Italian armistice, Don Sturzo announced the birth of the Italian Popular Party (P.P.I.), and on 18th January 1919 its constitution was officially proclaimed. The new party would draw its inspiration from the principles of Catholic teaching, particularly (as regards social questions) from *Rerum Novarum*; but it would not be confessional. Shortly afterwards a twelve-point programme was published; it was perhaps a little too extensive, but it set before this newly created body the noblest ideals in respect of social justice, international morality and administrative organization. On certain points its theories were so audacious that even now, after forty years, some of them have not yet passed into the realm of fact—those, for example, concerning agrarian reform and the partitioning of great estates. Victorious at the 1919 elections, at which it obtained a hundred seats, P.P.I. entered upon a period of three years that were the most brilliant in its history. It won another seven seats in April 1921; it secured the passage, if not the successful application, of the Bills it had most at heart; and it was represented in more than one government, though threatened from within by friction between its two constituent elements (advanced democrats and bourgeois conservatives) and accused by reactionaries of fostering 'white Bolshevism'.

Benedict behaved with the utmost tact in face of P.P.I. He recognized the faith and sincerity of its leaders; but he was not unaware that as regards the Roman Question many people felt acutely embarrassed, not wishing to condemn the regime which had effected the unity of Italy, but equally unwilling to disapprove the official attitude of the papacy. Furthermore, he realized that P.P.I. must not on any account appear as subject to directives from the Holy See. Thus, when asked what he thought of the members of the new party, he replied: 'They have never entered the Vatican, and they never will.' His words were a statement of fact, but not a disavowal of P.P.I., such as would have belittled his personal relations with some of its leaders, notably Santucci and Grosoli.

This cautious attitude later bore good fruit, when the Italian democratic regime was superseded by Fascism. Benedict did not live to see

[1] Ibid., section 7 *ad fin.*

the triumph of Fascism; but one fact[1] proves beyond doubt that he foresaw it. During the summer of 1921, when the situation was deteriorating throughout Italy—while the value of money fell and the cost of living rose, while strikers seized the factories, while Communist squads attacked their officers and proclaimed the imminent sovietization of the country—Benito Mussolini made a speech in which he called upon Italians for a return to their greatness and declared that the universality of Rome was due in large measure to the radiance of the papacy. This was clearly an indirect appeal to the Holy See. Rumour said he had been advised by his friend Father Tacchi-Venturi, S.J. Soon afterwards Mussolini asked Count Santucci—who was already disturbed by the leftward swing of a part of P.P.I.—to put him in touch with someone in authority at the Vatican. Cardinal Gasparri and the future Duce met in close secrecy at Santucci's house on the Piazza delle Pigna. Mussolini asked the cardinal upon what conditions the Holy See would be prepared to settle the Roman Question if the Fascist movement were one day in a position to control Italian politics. That was the first step towards the *conciliazione* which Gasparri negotiated eight years later with the Fascist Government, and it is only fair to acknowledge the part played therein by Benedict XV.

6. Universal Presence of the Church

In the early 1920's the new Europe, whose structure was soon to prove so fragile, continued to be haloed with promise. Young Catholic forces were at work, ready to share in the task of building what seemed to be a brilliant future. Benedict XV was fully aware of the chances afforded by that situation, and in order to exploit them he acted on a scale that suffices to make him an outstanding figure in the recent history of the papacy.

In several countries no serious problems awaited him. Belgium recovered quickly from the disasters of war; the Church, under Cardinal Mercier's leadership, had been one of the bastions of resistance to the occupying power, and was therefore naturally associated with that recovery. The Belgian Catholic Party, though it no longer possessed an absolute majority in Parliament, managed to keep a Catholic at the head of the government. The years 1919–22 witnessed the passing of social and financial laws in the spirit of *Rerum Novarum*. As yet there was no sign of those difficulties—formation of a democratic left within the Catholic Party, and the growth of *flamingantisme*—which would later disturb the kingdom.

[1] Related by Fernand Hayward in *Benoît XV*, p. 133.

In Switzerland, where Benedict had found a good deal of support for his charitable undertakings during the war, Catholicism began to make progress which has since continued without interruption, gradually outstripping Protestantism; and that flowering was partly due to the appointment of Mgr Besson as Bishop of Lausanne and Geneva in 1920.

In Spain, where the political situation was by no means peaceful, with the Reds resuming terrorist activity against the clergy, King Alfonso XIII desired to show clearly that his country was still a Catholic kingdom. In order, therefore, to thank God for having preserved Spain from the sufferings of war, he dedicated it to the Sacred Heart. The same policy of reconciliation was pursued in Portugal, which had lately received the mysterious message of Fatima on 13th May 1917. Elections had returned a strong Catholic majority, and the presidency of Sidonio Paes opened a new era. Benedict XV seized the opportunity to re-establish diplomatic relations with Lisbon: the Law of Separation was shelved, priests were released from prison, ecclesiastical property was restored and public worship again became normal. All this, however, was only a brief rift in the clouds. Trouble soon began once more to rock the fragile republic; President Paes was assassinated, and a succession of *coups d'état* brought back political instability from which the country did not recover until 1926.

Germany at first gave grounds for similar and even worse anxiety: military defeat was followed by a revolutionary movement that seemed likely to engulf the whole country. Led by Liebknecht and Rosa Luxembourg, the 'Spartakus' movement roused the Baltic sailor and the workers of Berlin. Bolshevism loomed very near. The army, however, remained loyal, and in mid January 1919 Noske crushed the revolutionaries, who had failed to exploit their opportunity. A national assembly, meeting at Weimar, established the liberal democratic Weimar Republic, which Benedict XV did his best to support. The transfer of the nunciature from Munich to Berlin, the old imperial capital, was a significant step. That nunciature remained in charge of Mgr Eugenio Pacelli, a great diplomat who had held the office since 1917 and continued to do so for the next twelve years. Vatican diplomacy worked to prevent the conquerors from crushing Germany and to secure her readmission to the concert of powers.

Moreover splendid possibilities lay open to Catholicism in the new Germany. The *Zentrum*, with ninety deputies, represented one-fifth of the Constituent Assembly. Its leader, Erzberger, was one of the most outstanding figures in German political life. In the constitution voted on 11th April 1919 the Catholics won for themselves, under the heading 'Fundamental Rights', that complete freedom and equality

which they had been demanding for more than a hundred years, while some of the laws passed bore the stamp of Social Catholicism. Actually, however, the situation was less favourable than it appeared. The Germans, stung by defeat and resenting the presence at their head of a conventional bourgeois rather than a general in spiked helmet, chose as their scapegoat Erzberger, who had signed the armistice at Rethondes instead of imposing that task on the vanquished generals, and feeling against him ran so high that he was assassinated. His successor, Wirth, was also a Catholic, but the warning was serious. Another came from Catholic Bavaria: alleging that the leaders of the *Zentrum* were enlarging the party by the admission of Protestants, and that by allying themselves with the Socialists they were opening the door to revolution, the Bavarian deputies seceded and formed the *Bayerische Volkspartei*, which quickly showed itself remarkably well disposed towards the most violent theories of nationalism.

Benedict XV could not fail to take a keen interest in the affairs of central Europe, where the disappearance of the Habsburg Empire had resulted in a mosaic of smaller States whose future seemed altogether uncertain. As soon as the treaties of Saint-Germain and the Trianon were signed separating Austria and Hungary, the Pope made no secret of what he thought about the 'Balkanization' of the Danubian world. Relations had not always been good between the Vatican and Vienna, but the annihilation of a great Catholic power was a setback for Catholicism. To Austria, now a 'dwarfish deformity' of 80,000 square kilometres and with fewer than 7 million inhabitants, the Pope showed his sympathy in every way he could, receiving the Chancellor Renner with pointed solemnity and benevolence, handing him a large sum of money for the relief of distress among his people, and referring, in his address, to Burgomaster Lueger and to the work accomplished by his Social Christian Party,[1] which continued to play the leading part in Austrian politics.

In Hungary events took at first a more terrible turn. Exasperated by penury, wounded in her pride by the situation forced upon her, and delivered to the arrogant mastery of peoples whom in the past she herself had conquered, Hungary deluded herself with the dream that Communism could save the territorial integrity of the land of St Stephen. But her eyes were opened by one hundred and thirty-three days of Red dictatorship under Bela Kun, and a reign of terror which struck down many of the clergy. When Rumanian troops entered Budapest and swept away the Bolshevist regime, the Allies banned the Archduke Joseph; so Admiral Horthy came to power, and Hungary found herself in a still more hapless plight. Benedict XV sent as nuncio Mgr Schioffa, a skilful diplomat, a capable organizer and a tireless

[1] See Chapter V, section 9.

apostle of charity, who did much to build the Hungarian Social-Christian Party, which was destined to occupy an important place in the country's political life until the Second World War.

Benedict also managed to place on a firm footing relations between the Church and the new-born states. Czechoslovakia soon received official recognition from the Holy See, and the Archbishop of Prague was given primatial rank. A Catholic popular party was formed, and it enjoyed the support of many associations run by groups of enthusiastic young people. Despite the presence in the government of several freemasons, Beneš among them, the rising tide of Catholicism appeared irresistible; campaigns for *Los vom Rom* and propaganda in favour of a 'National Church' made little or no headway. Diplomatic relations were established with Rumania, and the nuncio attended the coronation of King Carol. The government at Belgrade also desired full relationship with the Apostolic See; Yugoslavia included powerful masses of Croat and Slovene Catholics, and a mission was sent to study the problems created by the new situation.

Nor did Benedict XV despair of establishing relations even with Soviet Russia. The Vatican's share in the international campaign against famine in that country was only one aspect of a long-term policy. Preliminary study of this matter was conducted at the Vatican and by observers sent to Russia, with a view to eventual resumption of diplomatic relations. At the same time attempts were made to reorganize the Russian Catholic Church, a task that seemed not altogether impossible now that Orthodoxy was no longer recognized as the official religion. But this did not prevent Benedict from answering an appeal from some high dignitaries of the Russian Orthodox Church, who told him of the terrible persecution to which that Church was victim and begged him to intervene. An approach was made to Lenin by the secretariat of state, to which Chicherin, people's commissar for foreign affairs, replied in a long memorial which the Vatican had the courtesy to publish in the *Osservatore Romano*.

Thus in the three years following the return of peace the Church revealed her presence throughout Europe. When one recalls that Benedict at the same time gave fresh impulse to her activity in the Near East by creating the Congregation for the Oriental Churches and the Institute for Oriental Studies,[1] that with *Maximum illud* he opened a new field to the missions,[2] and that he welcomed the Knights of St Columbus who were in process of becoming the militant wing of American Catholicism,[3] it is not hard to recognize in the frail figure of Della Chiesa the heir of Leo XIII and the forerunner of Pius XI. The prestige of the Apostolic See emerged greatly enhanced from this

[1] See Chapter X, section 10. [2] See Chapter XI, section 8.
[3] See Chapter X, sections 3 and 4.

pontificate which some have described as spiritless. When announcing the appointment of a Netherlands ambassador to the Vatican, the Dutch prime minister Van der Linden, a Protestant, declared in parliament: 'Today no political centre wields more influence in the cause of peace than does the Vatican. The Pope is truly one of the great powers.'

7. Diplomatic Achievements of Pius XI

The road pioneered by Benedict XV was followed by his successor, Pius XI, whose policy was foreshadowed by his first public act. Early in the afternoon of 6th February 1922, immediately after his election, the new Pope gave his blessing *Urbi et Orbi* from the exterior balcony of St Peter's, instead of from the interior gallery as his three predecessors had done, and his gesture caused a worldwide sensation. Like Benedict XV, Pius laboured to reassert the Church's presence everywhere, profiting by the situation that had resulted from the war. Inspired, however, by a clear-sighted empiricism, he had yet another and much wider end in view, one that arose from his splendid concept of the Church's mission and to which his nuncio in France, Mgr Ceretti, referred when he spoke of 'spiritual sovereignty'.[1] As well, therefore, as concluding the immediate post-war period of stabilization and reorganization, he prepared the ground upon which he foresaw the Church would have to fight other battles, in which the sovereignty of the spiritual would be at stake.

Nothing is more significant in the twofold design followed by Pius XI than the policy of diplomatic agreements which he practised during the first half of his pontificate, and which may have been suggested to him by an historical precedent. Immediately after the crisis of the French Revolution and the Napoleonic wars Cardinal Consalvi, a great churchman who was also a great statesman, had made systematic use of a convenient diplomatic instrument, the concordat,[2] with a view to restoring the rights and the authority of the Holy See. The lesson appeared sound to Pius XI and to Cardinal Gasparri, his secretary of state. The condition of Europe was not unlike that of a hundred years before; just as on the morrow of the Treaty of Vienna, men were now looking for a new equilibrium, and it was in the interests of every government to be on good terms with the Vatican. Moreover many of the new States were concerned with the organization of the Church

[1] See Chapter II, section 6.
[2] *The Church in an Age of Revolution*, Index, *s.v.* 'Consalvi'.

within their boundaries, for which purpose they had need of Rome. The papacy thus had an opportunity to achieve certain ends which it had very much at heart. In various parts of Europe, Benedict XV had obtained promising results; Pius XI went further.

A systematic policy of concordats was therefore undertaken, and with remarkable success. During the seventeen years of the pontificate fifteen agreements were signed; a sixteenth, with Portugal, was negotiated by Pius XI but not signed until shortly after his death. No other sovereign pontiff has concluded so many of such treaties: Latvia, Bavaria, Poland, Lithuania, Czechoslovakia, Italy, Rumania, Prussia, Baden, Austria, the German Reich and so on; the very list gives an idea of the work accomplished, and to it must still be added the names of some non-European countries, e.g. Ecuador. Each of those treaties raised particular problems, calling for different solutions. The most satisfactory was that signed with Austria. Some left a few difficulties unsolved, e.g. the Polish Concordat of 1925, which did not altogether allay the tension caused by the affair of the Uniates of Ruthenia and the Ukraine. There was even one failure: the Yugoslav Concordat, signed in 1935, could not be ratified, because the Orthodox Church excommunicated those who had drafted it.

One of the most astonishing successes was obtained in Czechoslovakia. The new republic was strongly 'secularist', and most of its rulers (freemasons and anticlerical) were hostile to any concordat with the Apostolic See. But Prague had need of the Vatican in order to settle various matters arising from the former administrative regime of the Church in Bohemia and Slovakia. Accordingly, in 1928, an agreement was signed, establishing a *modus vivendi* and laying down principles for the delimitation of dioceses, for the conduct of religious orders with headquarters at Vienna and for the selection of bishops. Its application was not easy; but Pius XI remained on good terms with the government at Prague until his death, agreeing in 1930 to replace the notoriously pro-German archbishop and forbidding Slovak priests to help the autonomists. In exchange the government quickly put an end to the confiscation of ecclesiastical property, withdrew its support from the 'Hussite' Church and even encouraged the meeting at Prague in 1931 of the first international Catholic congress.

That policy of diplomatic agreements was remarkable for its boldness, its pliancy and the scope of its results. It was even more so on account of the novel characteristics of those agreements, revealing a concern for matters to which Pius VII and Consalvi had scarcely given a thought, showing also how greatly the authority of the Holy See had increased and against what perils it meant to take precautions. Not only did the new agreements stipulate unqualified acceptance of freedom of worship, the exclusive right of the Holy See to appoint bishops (so

long as the government concerned offered no objection on political grounds) and the legal recognition of religious congregations, but the Holy See also endeavoured in every case to make the government accept very strict rules concerning Catholic Action, religious schools, seminaries and legislation on marriage. In several countries special immunities were granted to members of the clergy in respect of military service and even of appearance before the courts. The aim was not only to settle relations between one power and another, but also to enable the Church to check the operation of hostile forces in the field of morals and of institutions, and thus confirm her 'spiritual sovereignty'.

Pius XI's firmness of purpose was accompanied by a profound understanding of the aspirations of those states with which he negotiated. As soon as he had obtained what he wanted as regards essentials, he did not mind altering ecclesiastical boundaries so as to make them coincide with the new frontiers, allowing the clergy to take an oath of loyalty to the government if such were required, accepting (e.g. in Poland) partition of lands belonging to the Church, forbidding priests to militate in a political party, and even agreeing (e.g. in Rumania) that the whole hierarchy should be nationals of the country concerned. Such decisions were certainly bold, and were not always understood at the time; but they bore the stamp of a very great mind.

Three of those agreements appear to have roused a certain uneasiness on the part of 'liberals', especially of 'liberals' who most admire Pius XI for having so vigorously denounced the errors of various totalitarian regimes. Why, they ask, was he ready to make a pact with governments whose principles were far from democratic? The question was raised in respect of (*a*) the Italian Concordat following the Lateran treaties which settled the Roman question, (*b*) the Concordat concluded with Hitler's Third Reich, and even (*c*) the Concordat which, pioneered by the agreements of 1928 and 1929, then negotiated during the last seven years of Pius XI, was signed by his successor with Salazar's Portugal on 7th May 1940.

In this last case the manner in which the agreement was reached and afterwards given effect reveals clearly the inmost intentions of the great Pope. It is quite wrong to rank as totalitarian the regime which in 1926, at the end of a bloody upheaval leading to the collapse of parliamentary government, was inaugurated by a military *coup d'état* at Lisbon. The *Estado novo*, enlivened since April 1928 by a very great statesman, Professor Oliveira Salazar, who became President of the Council in 1932, was expressly opposed to democratic and parliamentary ideologies, but it accepted none of the principles of Fascism or of Nazism. Salazar is a fervent Catholic, a disciple of *La Tour du Pin* and the French Social Catholics. He came to power in the flood-time of a

veritable Catholic renascence which was not unconnected with the apparitions at Fatima in 1917; and the regime directed by him took its stand upon Christian principles, aiming to restore the institutions which Christianity has always defended—the family, a man's trade and the fatherland. The Concordat might therefore have hallowed an intimate union between the two powers, but in fact it did nothing of the kind. Pius XI and the President agreed to the separation of Church and State, and proclaimed the complete independence of each. Co-operation between them was achieved, though not without difficulty in some cases; but there was no submission of one to the other. And Cardinal Cerejeira, who was appointed Patriarch of Lisbon simultaneously with the accession to power of his old friend Salazar,[1] used often to repeat (and always embodied in his own behaviour [2]) some words which expressed the basic attitude of the Church in signing the Concordat: 'Separation and freedom'.

The agreement signed with Hitler's government by the Pope who wrote *Mit brennender Sorge* is more surprising; but it was not the result of an error, nor did it mark approval of the Hitlerian regime. Under the Weimar Republic Catholic influence was strong: the *Zentrum* produced several chancellors of the Reich—Fehrenbach, Wirth, Brüning, Marx—while the 'political prelates' Lauscher and Kaas wielded an authority that was not always to the liking of the hierarchy. It was natural for the Holy See to take advantage of a favourable situation by negotiating agreements with several of the 'countries' that constituted Germany—Bavaria, Baden and, above all, Prussia, which last enabled it to create the diocese of Berlin.

In January 1933 the Weimar Republic, undermined from within, collapsed under the blows of Hitler. Pius XI, however, though he knew the peril to which National Socialist doctrine exposed the Church, did not reject outright the offers of negotiation made on behalf of the new regime by Vice-Chancellor von Papen, himself a prominent Catholic. Many German Catholics hoped for a *modus vivendi* with National Socialism, in order to check the activity of elements hostile to the Church; but they did not, perhaps, take sufficient account of the fact that such an accord was likely to drive the Catholic masses, already inclined to nationalism and militarism, into the ranks of the Brownshirts. Pius XI was wide awake to the danger of the operation, but, as he said, 'when there is question of saving souls We feel brave enough to deal even with the Devil'. The negotiations begun under the Weimar Republic, but delayed by the combined opposition of the left and the Protestants, were now carried a stage

[1] They had been fellow students at the University of Coimbra.

[2] In order that their friendship might not expose the regime to anticlerical criticism, the Cardinal and Salazar never saw one another except in public and officially.

further and completed in July 1937. On paper the German Concordat is among the most satisfactory of the whole pontificate. It not only proclaimed the full liberty of the Church, but also recognized certain rights and prerogatives; the Catholic religion became part of the curriculum in public establishments, and religious congregations were authorized. This agreement, of course, earned the National Socialist regime international prestige, recognized as it now was by the highest spiritual authority. But the Church profited still more: the Concordat might be violated, as Pius was well aware, but it would enable Catholics to do battle from the strongest possible positions. At the height of the struggle which soon began between the Third Reich and the Church, Cardinal Faulhaber declared: 'The Concordat of 1937 was signed freely and in complete agreement; no one therefore can tear it up or violate its stipulations without forfeiting his honour.' For that reason Hitler subsequently avowed that he regretted having signed the pact; but Cardinal Pacelli, one of its architects, told the French ambassador, Charles-Roux, that he had no such regrets: 'Without it', he said, 'we should have had no juridical grounds for our protests.'

8. 'Conciliazione'

Of all the agreements signed by Pius XI, the most important were those concluded with the Italian Government on 11th February 1929. They solved the problem which for sixty years had formed a serious impediment to the Holy See's activity, the problem of Rome and the temporal sovereignty of the Pope; and at the same time a concordat settled the manner of the Church's life in Italy.

Though he had given his first blessing from the outside balcony of St Peter's after his election, Pius XI gave no sign during the early days of his pontificate that he wished to abandon the rigorous attitude of his predecessors. Indeed he declared that he too would defend 'the inviolable prerogatives of the Church and of the Holy See', and he left the Vatican only to visit Castel Gandolfo. But his purpose was not to leave matters where they stood. Public opinion throughout the world was beginning to take the view that the splinter should be removed from the new Europe; when congratulating Cardinal Ratti on his elevation to the tiara, Aristide Briand expressed outright his hope that a solution to the Roman Question might be found. Moreover Pius XI, born in northern Italy, did not cherish the same feelings of devotion to the papal territories as his predecessors who had seen the light of day in those parts. Cardinal Gasparri, whom he retained as secretary of state, was already convinced that the prestige and authority of the Apostolic See were not dependent on the size of its territorial domain.

The secret contacts made earlier with Italian statesmen were accordingly resumed, and President Netti had a meeting with Cardinal Gasparri. But the accession of Pius XI coincided exactly with those portentous happenings which swept away the democratic regime. Following the prolonged ministerial crisis of February 1922, power (if one may call it such) was in the hands of Facta, a good-natured fellow 'who possessed nothing but a ridiculous little police force and a superb white moustache', and who did not believe in the Fascist danger. The Socialists, who did believe in it, added to the disorder by launching a general strike. As for the Popular Party, it was already in decline: there was increasing tension between the left wing, led by Don Sturzo, and the right, under Santucci and Grosoli. Pius XI, though personally sympathetic towards Don Sturzo, felt uneasy about his manifest desire to reach an understanding with the Socialists and to establish normal relations with the Soviets—those Soviets whom the ex-nuncio had regarded with horror since his period of duty in Warsaw. In these circumstances the Pope was in no hurry to continue negotiations on the Roman Question with political groups which would also have been unable to make a reasonable solution acceptable to the public at large.

The situation changed when, on 30th October 1922, the Blackshirt columns entered Rome and Mussolini, called to power by King Victor Emmanuel, seemed to be welcomed by the great majority of people including some of the 'Populars' who received portfolios in his government. The new master of Italian destinies used often to quote Crispi's words: 'The greatest statesman will be he who solves the Roman Question.' There were secret conversations, in which Father Tacchi-Venturi took part. They continued even when, after the assassination of Mateotti (June 1924), Mussolini had established his dictatorship and rid the political stage of all democrats, including those of the Popular Party.

The Duce himself did not lose sight of the Roman Question. In February 1926 he published in his newspaper *Il Popolo d'Italia* an article declaring his intention to do all he could with a view to its settlement. If he wished to reorganize Italy, it was absolutely necessary that the ancient Catholic nation should be given a religious status; but the Vatican would never agree to this unless its sovereignty were recognized. Besides, Mussolini was much too subtle a politician to overlook the international prestige he would earn from a reconciliation with the Vatican. Pius XI was likewise well disposed, because he realized that he now had a unique opportunity to negotiate with a man who was able to make decisions on his own and impose them without fear of contradiction.

No sooner was Mussolini in sole command than he took steps which

were eminently satisfactory to the Church.[1] Official negotiations began in a new climate, and lasted for three years. On the Italian side they were conducted by Barone, a counsellor of state; on the papal side by the consistorial lawyer Francesco Pacelli, elder brother of the nuncio in Germany. Two hundred conferences of three or four hours were necessary, after each of which Pacelli went and gave the Pope an account of progress, at interviews which also lasted three or four hours. Few treaties have been so carefully prepared.[2]

The Lateran Agreements, which officially sealed the reconciliation between the two Romes, consisted of two diplomatic instruments: the treaty in twenty-seven articles and four subsidiary documents, and the Concordat in forty-five articles. Pius XI had required that both should be signed simultaneously. The treaty settled the question of Rome and the Pope's temporal authority. It did so by way of bilateral accord between the two powers, without reference to that international guarantee which Pius IX and Leo XIII had demanded, but which Benedict XV had categorically refused to envisage. The Pope recognized the House of Savoy as sovereign of Italy and renounced all claims upon the kingdom's territory. The Italian Government in turn acknowledged the Pope as having sovereign rights and prerogatives, together with everything implied thereby: autonomous government, legislative power, a police force, civil status, a flag, coinage, public services, postage stamps, a broadcasting station and even a railway. Financial clauses guaranteed the Holy See immediate payment of 750 million lire and the permanent interest on 1,000 million lire of Italian Government stock. The right of 'active and passive legation' was also specified: papal nuncios and diplomats accredited to the Pope were to have free passage through Italian territory.

Sovereignty without a territorial base would have been merely theoretical. And so the Lateran Treaty provided for the creation of a Papal State; there was some hesitation as to what it should be called, but 'Vatican City' was eventually agreed upon. In fact it was minute, including the basilica and piazza of St Peter, together with the museums, library, palace, gardens and dependencies of the Vatican—a total of 356 acres. To this were added the apostolic palaces of the Lateran, Holy Office, Chancellery, Dataria, Propaganda, Vicariat and Oriental Congregation, as well as the estate of Castel Gandolfo, the

[1] See Chapter IX, section 4.

[2] After the agreements had been signed, the Pope created Pacelli a marquess, and King Victor Emmanuel gave him the hereditary title of prince. Barone died shortly before full agreement had been reached. In the final months Mussolini himself conducted negotiations on the government side. Pacelli had kept an interesting diary, which was published in 1959 as *Diaro della Conciliazione*. Negotiations took place in the utmost secrecy, Mussolini having declared that any indiscretion would be considered as an attempt upon State security and that the guilty party would be sent to the Lipari Islands.

three other great Roman basilicas and the sanctuaries of Assisi, Loreto and Padua—all of which were granted the privileges of extraterritoriality. The Vatican City was not large enough even to house the services of a worldwide administration. Ambassadors accredited to the Pope could not reside there; no 'corridor' was provided to give direct access to the sea; the Italian police were to be responsible for keeping order in the piazza of St Peter's up to the bronze door of the basilica and the palace, where the Swiss Guard would be stationed. The sacrifices made by Pius XI for the sake of *conciliazione* were thus considerable. None but a pope with the energy of Achille Ratti could have accepted 'the minimum of body to contain the maximum of spirit: a territory of such minute proportions that it could be and had to be animated by the immense spiritual, sublime and truly divine power it was intended to uphold and to serve'. No more peremptory assertion of the Church's spiritual sovereignty was possible.

Meanwhile the Concordat satisfied the Church on all points.[1] It not only declared Catholicism the official religion of the State and nation, but also laid down in principle that all matters in which politics and religion might become involved should be settled in accordance with the laws of the Church. Dioceses were re-mapped to fit the new Italy. The Pope alone was to appoint bishops, subject to governmental objection on political grounds. The religious congregations were granted juridical recognition. Facilities were promised for Catholic Action. Religious marriage obtained full legal validity, and divorce became almost impossible. Feasts of obligation were proclaimed public holidays, and Catholic education was made obligatory at all levels.

The signing of the Lateran Agreements caused a great sensation. At Rome it was greeted with tremendous enthusiasm. On 25th July 1929, when Pius came out for the first time, carrying the monstrance, to be borne on the *sedia* around the piazza of St Peter's, preceded by a procession of several thousand prelates, priests and seminarists, fifteen thousand Italian soldiers and all the papal troops were only just sufficient to contain a crowd that filled not only the vast esplanade but the whole Borghi quarter—those Borghi which were soon to be pulled down to make way for the monumental avenue known as the Via della Conciliazione. Shortly afterwards the official visit of the Italian sovereigns to the Vatican crowned the triumph of Pius XI. Many people throughout the world realized the importance of this diplomatic success, and understood that, by contenting himself with a

[1] A visitor who congratulated Pius XI on the success of a 'great diplomatic act' was given this vigorous reply: 'It's not a diplomatic act, but an act of Our priestly magisterium.'

territory so small that it might be be considered merely symbolic, the Pope had opted finally for spiritual sovereignty and had done much to ensure it.

In some political circles, however, and even in some Catholic circles, there was more reserve. The democrats were indignant that Pius had done nothing to save the P.P.I., that party which had given grounds for so much hope but now found itself swept from the political stage, with part of its members reduced to exile or driven underground, while the remainder rallied to the Fascist regime and even accepted decorative posts therein. It was asked whether Pius XI, though gaining as head of the Italian Church, were not losing as head of the universal Church; and some left-wing polemists went so far as to say that the Vatican had become a mere organ of Fascist propaganda. A statement by Pius XI on the war in Ethiopia [1] and his decision concerning the French weekly *Sept* [2] were interpreted in the most tendentious way as proofs of his enfeoffment to Fascism. But in reality the conflict between the Vatican and the Palazzo Venezia, which broke out very soon after the signing of the Lateran Agreements, showed beyond doubt that when essentials, the true interests of the spiritual, were at stake Pius XI could prove himself a formidable warrior, and that the Church's independence had in no way been sacrificed.

9. Pius XI and France

There were some countries in which the Church met with no difficulties. Such was Belgium, where a special form of Catholic Action had just started with the Abbé Cardijn's J.O.C.[3] The Catholic Party remained powerful in the cabinet; and though it was perhaps a little inclined to confuse the political interests of Catholics with those of the Faith, it nevertheless exerted a Christian influence on public life, especially from the social point of view. In other respects, however, it gradually altered under the twofold thrust of the Fleming movement and of its more advanced elements, until at length in 1937 it split into two parties, the Katholicke Vlaamsche Volkspartij and the Social Catholic Party, which together formed the Catholic bloc. Devoted to the Holy See, Belgium appeared as one of the bastions of Catholicism; but certain Catholic elements of the right set up a 'Party of Christ the King', which advocated authoritarian methods in the service of Christian ideals, and *Rexisme*, under the guidance of Léon Degrelle, moved quickly towards a disturbing alignment with Hitlerian ideology.

[1] See Chapter IX, section 4. [2] Ibid., section 2.
[3] Ibid., section 6.

The position of the Church was actually strengthened in France and Britain, two countries whose victory had earned them the leadership of Europe. Tension between London and the Vatican in the matter of Ireland ceased with the creation of an Irish Free State; and in 1923 King George V and Queen Mary, on a visit to Rome, were received in audience by the Pope. Henceforward the British could make no objection to the very special affection shown by the Sovereign Pontiff for the Catholic nation whose existence they had just recognized. Re-establishment of friendly relations made it possible to surmount the difficulties resulting from (*a*) the Greco-Turkish War, in which the Vatican considered Britain as too Islamophil; (*b*) the situation in Malta, where London suspected Rome of secretly fostering Italian irredentism; (*c*) the creation in Palestine of a 'Jewish National Home', which caused the secretariat of state some anxiety as to the fate of the Holy Places. These, however, were minor incidents. Britain, where Catholicism was gaining ground in both numbers and influence, preserved a deferential esteem for the Pope, while Pius XI expressed his goodwill by entrusting to a British prelate[1] a new apostolic delegation with authority over the whole of East Africa.

Progress in France was even more satisfactory. No concordat, however, was signed. Following the resumption of diplomatic relations, many had regarded such a treaty as belonging in the natural sequence of events. It may be that the French episcopate, now accustomed to complete freedom in their dealings with the republican authorities, were apprehensive of fresh impediments. Perhaps, too, even such moderates as Poincaré, Barthou and Laval feared having to discuss once again the matter of secularism. No diplomatic instrument, therefore, was employed to alter the status of the Church in France. But this fact did not prevent good relations between the two Powers, except for a brief crisis; and the work of appeasement begun by Benedict XV was continued.

The single crisis which appeared to compromise relations between Paris and the Vatican occurred shortly after their official resumption. The Chamber responsible for the latter was that of the *Bloc National*, elected in 1922 and including 433 right-wing deputies in a total membership of 613. But at the end of four years, exhausted by the tremendous labour and the unpopular measures entailed by the duty of restoring order in the country, the moderates were ousted in 1924 by the *Cartel des gauches*, and power passed to the radical Édouard Herriot. Secularism occupied a prominent place in the *Cartel*'s electoral programme. Some of its leaders were ardent disciples of Combes. Herriot, who said he wanted to 'give the country peace', and declared himself as much an admirer of 'catacomb Catholicism' as an enemy of

[1] Mgr Arthur Hinsley, later Cardinal Archbishop of Westminster.—TRANSLATOR.

'bankers' Catholicism', yielded to the clamour for a revival of anticlericalism in the style of 1900.

It was therefore announced that measures would be taken to end the concordatory regime in Alsace and Lorraine; whence a violent conflict with the Catholics of those two provinces, who were so well organized and so determined that the government was obliged to retreat. Then it was proposed to apply strictly the law of 1901 affecting religious congregations, by expelling once again those which had taken advantage of the tranquil post-war climate to re-install themselves. The result was a stiff reaction conducted by Père Doncœur's *Ligue de Défense des Religieux anciens combattants*, with the result that Herriot thought it best to diasvow the project in a letter to the French cardinals. The sole product of this anticlerical renascence was the *Fédération nationale catholique*, which, under the direction of General Castelnau, rallied 1,800,000 Frenchmen in defence of their Church.

A more sensational episode now occurred. Contrary to the wishes of Herriot, who was nevertheless obliged to follow suit, the most violent leaders of the *Cartel* started a campaign for the closing of the French embassy at the Holy See. It was useless, they said, since it had not been able to prevent the transfer from Lyon to Rome of the *Œuvre de la Propagation de la Foi*, or the appointment in China of an apostolic delegate in defiance of the acknowledged rights of France. In 1925 the Bill passed by 314 votes to 230; but since the Senate refused to follow the Chamber, no steps could be taken to give it effect, and eighteen months later the *Cartel* foundered in the cyclone of an economic crisis which had been purposely contrived.

That brief French crisis was not regarded by the Church as serious. In the worst days of the *Cartel*, Cardinal Dubois, Archbishop of Paris, remained on good terms with French political circles, while Pius XI viewed the whole affair with unruffled calm. So far from perpetuating the dispute, the Vatican's behaviour was altogether conciliatory. In 1924 a confidential note was sent to all the bishops, recommending that all Catholics should accept *de facto* the secularist laws, and the new *ralliement* thus inaugurated was supported by the nuncio, Mgr Maglione, and the Assumptionist newspaper *La Croix*. The simultaneous condemnation of *Action française*, though its motives were doctrinal, formed part of the same picture. In 1928 Cardinal Gasparri made an express declaration asking Catholics to 'lay aside their personal preferences for such-or-such a form of government, in order the better to defend the interests of the Church'.

Pius XI, anxious though he was for good relations with the French democrats, and despite his eirenic policies mentioned above, never urged Catholics to enrol as such in the ranks of a democratic party. Soon after the war, however, there was talk of founding in France a

Christian democratic party similar to the Italian P.P.I. Marc Sangnier was approached, and was even encouraged by Cardinal Gasparri; but he declined the invitation. A link was then forged between the *Ligue de la Jeune République* and the *Fédération des chrétiens démocrates*. In 1924 various splinter groups from *Jeunesse catholique*, the *Semaines sociales* and the *Confédération des Travailleurs chrétiens* combined to form the Popular Democratic Party (P.D.P.) under the direction of Champetier de Ribes. This new formation was not a great success: its weekly *Petit Démocrate* never exceeded twenty thousand copies; nor, later, did its kindred daily *l'Aube* enjoy more than a small circulation, despite the talent of its editor Georges Bidault. The political role of P.D.P. remained limited; its sole leader, Champetier, was invited to join the government, and his influence on public opinion was small. France was so sharply divided into two blocs—a division further accentuated by the electoral system—as to prevent the emergence of a current of political thought which either the right or the left could claim as its own. Pius XI may not have been fully aware of the situation; he may have thought that a party too openly Catholic would be likely to hamper his relations with the government in power. At all events, while never disowning the Popular Democrats, he never lent them his support.

Whichever bloc was in power, relations with the Church remained excellent. Poincaré's National Union government, which included Herriot, put an end to the crisis and re-established the most friendly contacts with Rome. Nothing was to disturb the atmosphere until the Second World War, not even the return to power in 1932 of the *Bloc des Gauches*, with the government of Herriot, Daladier and Blum. In 1937, under a Popular Front ministry, Cardinal Pacelli, papal legate to the celebrations at Lisieux, was received with the utmost respect and preached a sermon in Notre-Dame on 'the Christian Vocation of France'. Understanding was now assured, officially at least, between the Republic and the Church.

10. End of the 'Post-War' Period

About 1930 it seemed that the restless and confused period known as the 'post-war' years was almost at an end. The fashionable quirks of that period were slipping into oblivion: no one now indulged in absurd practical jokes or wrote 'dada' poems. Some of the problems raised by the conflict had been more or less solved; others were about to take on a different hue. There were many signs that a new turning-point had been reached in human history.

The Church appeared to enter this second pre-war period with

splendid opportunities. In many lands she was firmly established, and even giving proof of quite remarkable vitality. Her official relations with nearly all States were good. The prestige of the Sovereign Pontiff was considerable, as was clear from a large increase in the number of ambassadors accredited to the Holy See.[1] There existed, however, grave reasons for disquiet, and Pius XI knew it better than anyone else. One day, long before the cataclysm was seen to be inevitable, he told the French ambassador Charles-Roux: 'The powers of evil are unleashed.'

He had three serious grounds for anxiety. First of these was the threat of war, which he felt to be increasing. Ever since his election he had done all in his power to set peace on the sure foundations of humanity and justice. In the delicate matter of the reparations imposed on Germany he had supported those who, like Lloyd George and Bonar Law, believed that Germany was in no position to pay the millions of marks demanded of her. When Poincaré occupied the Ruhr he wrote to Cardinal Gasparri a letter intended for publication, in which he expressed disapproval of the military operation, and then sent a prelate to make inquiries on the spot and distribute relief. When Upper Silesia was under discussion he told a Polish diplomat: 'Believe me, you will absorb too many Germans.' His courageous attitude on behalf of the vanquished was not always properly understood, and earned him some caustic criticism.[2] He strove for peace in other fields as well: at the Geneva Conference on the question of Russia; in Asia Minor, where the Turkish dictator Kemal Ataturk then ruled. In every way and on every possible occasion he supported the League of Nations and the international institutions attached to it. The reconciliation of victors and vanquished at Locarno earned for its authors the warmest papal congratulations, and Pius XI publicly approved the Briand-Kellog Pact, signed by sixty nations in 1928 in order to 'outlaw war'. It was even rumoured that he hoped for the election of Aristide Briand, the pilgrim of peace, as president of the French Republic.

And yet, despite the omens that seemed to indicate a peaceful future, e.g. the evacuation of the Rhineland in 1930, Pius XI felt the peace to be fragile and in danger. On Christmas Eve that year he addressed the Sacred College on the subject of peace. Comparing the 'sentimental, muddled and undiscerning pacifism' of some with 'the true peace of Christ that comes from God', he reminded his hearers that peace cannot be established by diplomatic instruments alone, but that it must be graven in the heart of man by the elimination of those passions which

[1] See Chapter II, section 7.

[2] A Cologne newspaper did not improve matters by thanking him for efforts on behalf of the vanquished with these words: 'He is the most German pope in history . . .'

seek to destroy it. He condemned 'unruly nationalism which forgets that other nations have a right to live and prosper'.

Such words sounded a strange warning at a time of peaceful euphoria; but that euphoria was relative, rather it was on the way to disappearance. After three years of unparalleled prosperity, the entire Western world was shaken by an economic crisis which, having started in the United States, was destined to affect the whole of Europe. 'Cyclical', as described by the economists, it assumed proportions and a degree of seriousness hitherto unknown. There was bankruptcy, unemployment—indeed the whole world, or at any rate all those countries which lived under the liberal-capitalist system, appeared on the verge of collapse.

Pius XI did not hide his anguish in presence of that unhappy spectacle; much of the Encyclical *Nova impendet* (2nd October 1931) was devoted to 'the very severe economic crisis' and to the 'lamentable situation of a host of unemployed'. Without in any way attempting to propose technical solutions, the Pope appealed to the principles of equity and charity, insisting once again on the rights of man in face of economic requirements and speaking with the voice of prophecy.

But the Pope's most terrible anxiety was due to the consequences which he saw resulting from the errors he denounced. Inspired by 'unruly nationalism', ideologies were emerging that were manifestly hostile to the Faith, to the Church and to God; and the anger stirred by the economic crisis was bound to render them more virulent. In Italy the regime established by Mussolini was moving quickly towards forms and methods which no Christian could accept. In Germany the foolish dissolution of Parliament by Chancellor Brüning, a Catholic, revealed to an astonished world the power of National Socialism, a movement toward pagan philosophy. Meanwhile in Russia, free now from the vain counter-attacks of the 'Whites' and indifferent to the *cordon sanitaire* by means of which it had been thought possible to isolate the Marxist regime, the Bolsheviks had liquidated the extremist opposition of Trotsky in 1929 and seemed determined, under the iron fist of Stalin, to impose their materialist and atheistic doctrines.

To those three threats Pius XI gave answer during the second half of his pontificate. Apostle of peace amid the increasingly dire omens of war, advocate of social justice, defender of the faith against totalitarian heresies: such was the triple role which he took upon himself.

CHAPTER VIII

FROM SOCIAL ACTION TO CATHOLIC ACTION

1. Social Catholicism after the First World War

'Social Catholicism'[1] entered the post-war period in the most favourable circumstances. The different classes of society had drawn closer to one another in the trenches, often in an atmosphere of fraternal unity. Men of the upper and middle classes had discovered the problems and anxieties of the proletariat, and had understood the need for radical reforms. The working class, on the other hand, had bettered its lot, thanks to higher war-time wages; it was now demanding further improvements, as was evident from the mounting frequency of strikes. The triumph of Bolshevism in Russia, the foundation in 1919 of the Third International[2] and the emergence almost everywhere of Marxist parties were so many signs of warning. But it was not good enough merely to tremble before terrifying posters of 'the man with a knife between his teeth'. It was necessary to oppose Communism with something other than liberal capitalism, especially in view of the fact that from 1929 onwards many intelligent people thought the latter system to be in mortal danger.

All these reasons explain why the Social Catholic movement flourished exceedingly during the twenty years between the two wars, a period no longer of invention and burgeoning, but of expansion and organization. Initiatives were fewer and less original, but achievements were more lasting. There was now hardly a single outstanding figure, except Don Sturzo in Italy; and even his activity was chiefly political. Albert de Mun, La Tour du Pin, Harmel, Toniolo and Verhaegen were dead; Marius Gonin alone survived. Nevertheless there were numerous men capable of effecting the advance of Social Catholicism at the twin levels of theory and practice; and in any case the movement had less need of distinguished leaders than of a sound framework, which it certainly possessed.

The influence of Social Catholicism was discernible in many fields. As early as 1919, Part XIII of the Versailles Treaty, concerning the foundations of a true social peace, appeared to have been extracted

[1] See Chapter IV.

[2] Distinct from the Second, which had been founded in 1884.

lock, stock and barrel from a Social Catholic manifesto. Labour, it declared, must not be 'considered as a piece of merchandise'; the wage-earners' right of association must be recognized equally with that of their employers; the worker is entitled to a 'living wage'. Leo XIII had taught just that. The forty-eight-hour week, the obligatory rest day once a week, the abolition of child labour and the inspection of working conditions were all ideas which Social Catholics had made familiar and which derived from the Leonine Encyclical.

The presence of Social Catholicism was manifested in another and no less official manner, by the part which Catholics played in the international institutions set up at that time with social ends in view. Christian syndicalists worked in the International Labour Office at Geneva alongside its first director, the Socialist Albert Thomas, who, when the Encyclical *Quadragesimo anno* appeared, declared in an official message to the Pope that the international organization of labour was not a spontaneous growth, but the fruit of earlier initiative. 'The seed', he continued, 'was sown in fertile soil that has been carefully tended over the years by tireless workers, including those inspired by the Encyclical *Rerum Novarum*.' [1] In 1926 a priest was admitted as an official of the I.L.O., and in the great hall used for plenary sessions the fresco exalting the 'dignity of labour' represents Jesus the Worker; it is the work of a Catholic artist, Maurice Denis.

One may go further still, and discover the increasing influence of Social Catholicism on political parties and indeed on whole regimes. It reached the world of politics by various and even contradictory paths. From it the leaders both of Austria and of the Weimar Republic drew their inspiration: in the former, Mgr Seipel, Schuschnigg and Dolfuss; in the latter, Brüning and Father Brauns, minister of labour. In Portugal, too, Oliveira Salazar appealed officially to the social teaching of Leo XIII and quoted La Tour du Pin. In France there were Social Catholics outside the little Popular Democratic Party, as there were in Italy outside Don Sturzo's P.P.I. In Belgium the powerful Catholic Party was so 'social' that its enemies accused it of being no more than a badly camouflaged representative of Socialism. This political commitment, however, which Rome accepted because of the increasing threat from the dictatorships,[2] was not without its dangers. By too often identifying Social Catholicism with Christian democracy, it brought about the eclipse of the former when Mussolini and then Hitler came to settle scores with the latter.

Now as to the legislative achievements of Social Catholicism. In

[1] Quoted by Mgr Bertoli, apostolic nuncio at Paris, in his article 'Le Saint-Siège et les relations internationales', *Revue des Deux Mondes*, 15th May 1961. See also Yves de la Brière, *L'Organisation internationale du monde contemporain et la Papauté*, Paris, 1924, and Albert Le Roy, *Catholicisme social et l'organisation internationale du travail*, Paris, 1937.

[2] See Chapter IX.

France we find Social Catholics behind the laws which established the eight-hour working day, holidays with pay and the first measures of social security; and in 1936, when employers and syndicalists met at the Hôtel Malignon, in order to seek a basis of agreement and thereby put an end to the crisis resulting from a long series of strikes, it was Social Catholicism that provided them with a solution in the form of collective contracts and committees of arbitration on which workers and employers would be equally represented. In Germany, under Chancellor Brüning and at the instigation of Brauns, six social laws were passed. In Italy, Don Sturzo secured the passing of a law on partition of the Sicilian *latifundia*; he also introduced a Bill for the establishment in agriculture of the obligatory contract with guarantee of security, and thus earned himself the nickname 'White Bolshevik'.

The influence of Social Catholicism was likewise apparent in the intellectual sphere. The press began to notice its activities, and many newspapers and reviews of all nationalities were favourable to the movement. In France these ranged from the *Chronique sociale* and *Dossiers de l'Action populaire* to such organs as the Assumptionist *La Croix*, the *Vie catholique*, the Jesuit *Études*, the Dominican *Vie intellectuelle* and *Sept*. At the crossroads of Social Catholic ideas stood distinguished literary figures: Blondel, Maritain, Gilson, Chevalier, as well as Chesterton and Papini. It is also worth remarking that 'personalism', which in the early thirties inspired youth movements such as *Ordre nouveau* and *Esprit*, owed more than its adherents realized to the social teaching of the Church.

Finally, we must not forget the practical achievements of that time. Catholic men and women of unbounded generosity were found in every sector: popular education, the relief of poverty, social service, loan societies. Two saintly figures were Marie-Jeanne Bassot, directress of the *Residence sociale* at Levallois, and the Abbé Hardman, founder of the *Missionnaires du travail.* Robert Garric too was inspired by the ideals of Social Catholicism when in 1919 he founded his *Équipes sociales*, groups of students and others who went out to help workers to improve their education. In 1934, when Cardinal Verdier, Archbishop of Paris, launched his campaign for the building of new churches in the suburbs of the French capital, his purpose was social as well as apostolic: by building these houses of God, Catholics would provide work for 500,000 unemployed who were on the borders of destitution. So too in other countries: Belgium, where the University of Louvain became a great centre of Social Catholic Action; Italy, where Don Orione's Sons of Divine Providence and Cardinal Ferrari's Company of St Paul were hard at work in similar fields.

In the United States the evolution of social theory among Catholics

was rather curious. The programme elaborated during the First World War by the National Catholic Committee[1] was approved and expanded after 1918 by the National Catholic Welfare Conference. But amid the material prosperity and craving for pleasure, which were characteristic of America in those years, its schemes were regarded as absurd, and Catholics settled down into the tranquillity of liberalism. Only one small group proclaimed that reforms would one day, sooner or later, be indispensable. This was the 'Catholic Worker', founded by Dorothy Day, an extraordinary woman who had come from anarchism to the Catholic faith without abandoning her indignation against injustice. Helped by Pierre Maurin, she waged throughout the U.S.A. a campaign of social conferences which were highly effective, thanks to her remarkable gifts as a speaker and the example of her austere life, and she stirred complacent Americans to an awareness of the misery that lay round about them. The 'Catholic Worker's' influence was lessened by the fact that it preached 'return to the land' as a panacea, but its adherents were responsible for the birth of Catholic trade unionism. And when the crisis of 1929 broke out, and twelve million unemployed demanded the right to live, Dorothy Day and her little group seemed justified. Roosevelt's 'New Deal' was in many respects closely akin to the Catholic social programme; and when well-to-do Catholics criticized the President's courageous measures, Mgr Ryan and his friend Mgr Haas told them in no uncertain terms: 'What you are rejecting are the ideas of the popes.'

2. Growth of Christian Social Science

In this complex history two facts call for special notice: (i) Christian social science was growing and at the same time strengthening its foundations; (ii) a serious effort was made to develop Catholic workers' organizations. Neither fact was anything new; both were a sequel to what had been begun during the war; but promises were kept and new paths were opened.

Social Weeks[2] were resumed in France in 1919, and were held each year until 1939 under the guidance of Eugène Duthoit (1869–1944), founder of the Institute of Social and Political Sciences attached to the Faculty of Law at Lille. They were continued also in Italy, Spain and Belgium. In England, Father O'Hea's 'Social Courses' began in 1920, linked with the trade unions and the workers' movement. Canada followed the French pattern, starting with a Week at Montreal in the

[1] See Chapter X, section 5. [2] See Chapter IV, section 15.

same year. Other countries followed suit: Chile in 1924, Czechoslovakia in 1932, Yugoslavia in 1933. In this latter year a group of French Catholics, led by Pasquier-Gronde, organized a Week at Algiers, to discuss the problems of the Mahgreb; and in 1935 the Catholics of Rhodesia devoted one to those of South Africa. In Latin America a number of such gatherings were held in Uruguay, and in 1937 a very successful one took place in Argentina. On the outbreak of the Second World War there were Social Weeks in twenty-one countries; Portugal and the Lebanon had just announced their plans for similar meetings, which were held in 1940.

Until 1913 there had been no unity of subject-matter for each Week. After 1919 all Weeks in every country concentrated upon a single important theme. The first phase had been devoted to clarification of the main principles of Christian social teaching. In the second, more importance was attached to the embodiment of those principles in institutions; among the subjects considered were the role of the State in economic and social life, the altered circumstances of industrial life and the social problem in the colonies. The result was a continuous elaboration of the social teaching of the Church in its application to concrete facts.

During those immediate post-war years initial steps were taken to link social doctrine with sociology. Hitherto there had been no such relations, excepting perhaps some half-hearted contact with the disciples of the Abbé de Tourville's *Science sociale*, who were distrusted by the democratic Social Catholics because of their 'counter-revolutionary' ideas. Moreover the direction taken by Émile Durkheim's sociological theories, which completely ignored religion, had increased the distrust of Catholics for that science, though its methods might have done them good service. It was during the years 1918–39 that Social Catholics discovered the importance of sociology. A Brazilian thinker, Tristan de Athayde, in his *Fragments of Christian Sociology*, drew their attention to the fact that it was not enough to have a 'social philosophy' without an empirical knowledge and a 'social art'. It would be an exaggeration to say that all Social Catholics were convinced by his argument and devoted themselves to the necessary positive research. But one of the ablest of such students was already at work in their midst: Gabriel Le Bras, who later showed them that Christian sociology is at the root of all constructive social endeavour as of every form of apostolate. It is regrettable that the 'Social Secretariats' (which came into existence before the Social Weeks and of which by 1922 there were thirty-two in France alone) were less successful than the Weeks,[1] and that even where they existed Catholics did not provide them with the means of becoming a great instrument both of documentation and of concrete achievement.

[1] Except in the U.S.A., where similar organizations exerted considerable influence.

3. Advance of Christian Syndicalism

In France, at the beginning of 1919, the *Fédération des Syndicats féminins* asked the powerful Parisian *Syndicat des Employés du Commerce et de l'Industrie* (S.E.C.I.) to organize a national gathering of all the Catholic syndical forces in the country. The invitation was accepted, and preparatory discussions were held during the spring and summer. On 1st November the representatives of 350 syndicates met in Paris. After only two days of debate a national organization was formed and called itself *Confédération française des travailleurs chrétiens* (C.F.T.C.). Though 'Christian' was chosen in preference to 'Catholic', the first article of the statutes declared that 'the Confederation intends to act in accordance with the social teaching of the Encyclical *Rerum Novarum.* It considers that the social peace necessary for the country's prosperity, and the professional organization which is the indispensable basis of that peace, cannot be achieved except by applying the principles of Christian justice and charity.' By 1920, 578 syndicates had joined the confederation, representing 156,000 members.

The success of C.F.T.C. was considerable; it recruited about fifteen thousand new members a year. This pleased neither the syndicalists of C.G.T., who resented the competition, nor the employers, who were furious at the sight of Catholic workers demanding their rights with so much vigour and sometimes with the same means as were used by C.G.T. The first clash was with the employers.

From 1920 onwards the new-born C.F.T.C. took part in the bank strike. Letters of protest were sent to Rome; but these complaints were rejected, and the syndical action of the French was more than once commended. The Halluin affair had very different echoes; in fact it revealed the fundamental divergence between the two currents which had always existed within the stream of Social Catholicism, that of more or less corporatist paternalism and that of the workers' movement. In 1920 the *Association catholique des patrons du Nord* was reconstituted; its avowed aim was to apply the social teaching of the Church, particularly as regards the existence of Christian workers' syndicates and collaboration with them in order to secure just conditions of labour. Indeed the association practised an undeniably generous social policy in the shape of housing, cheap restaurants and family allowances. It lay open to criticism, however, on the grounds that everything was done without the workers having a say in the matter; and tension was increased by the foundation of an employers' organization, the *Consortium du textile de Roubaix-Turcoing*, whose president Mathon and his manager Désiré Ley viewed the Christian

syndicalists with grave suspicion, ranking them with the popular democrats.

In 1924 the Consortium complained to Rome that C.F.T.C. had gone over to Communism. While Pius XI made a most careful and detailed inquiry, which lasted five years, strikes broke out in the textile industry. Halluin became what the employers called 'the red citadel'. But C.F.T.C., disapproving of the violent methods advocated by C.G.T., refused to form a 'single front' with it. In order to settle the dispute it suggested recourse to the prefect's arbitration, to which the employers no less than C.G.T. were strongly opposed. The strike continued, and the Catholic syndicalists opened a subscription to enable the workers and their families to live.

An event now occurred which was to have enormous repercussions. Mgr Achille Liénart, Bishop of Lille, subscribed to the strike fund 'on behalf of those', he said, 'who have shown their Christian spirit by seeking arbitration, and to help them in their distress'. There followed an explosion of fury. 'The Red Bishop' was insulted by the right-wing press and reported to Rome as having embraced Marxism. Pius XI retorted in spectacular fashion by giving him the red hat. Liénart meanwhile kept contact with the more moderate elements among the employers, and after seven months of uninterrupted strike managed to re-establish relations between them and the workers. The Pope wrote him a letter which put an end to the inquiry that had begun five years before. In it he affirmed the workers' right, no less than that of the employers, to form syndicates; he also advised the setting up of mixed committees to prevent conflict, and even agreed that wherever strictly Christian syndicates could not be formed, Catholics might share in the syndicalist activities of other groups.

This gesture had important consequences. Christian syndicalism in France made such strides that C.G.T. took umbrage, and a veritable trial of strength began in various parts of the country between Christians and *cétégistes*. These clashes, however, proved indecisive; if anything, they strengthened Christian syndicalism whose pugnacity had made a deep impression. On the eve of 1939 C.F.T.C. had 500,000 members in 2,384 syndicates, with affiliations in North Africa, Madagascar and New Caledonia. The peasants, whose more prominent syndical organizations still retained their 'corporatist' characters,[1] now started to follow the movement towards a purely workers' Christian syndicalism. There was a similar expansion of Christian syndicalism in Belgium, Holland, Luxemburg, Spain, Italy and Germany.

This story of the growth of Christian syndicalism and its struggle on two fronts, against the employers and against C.G.T., reveals the

[1] See Chapter IV, section 16.

attitude of the Church. It cannot be said that she sided against the employers, but she did show marked sympathy with the labouring classes.

Despite errors and inadequacies, Christian syndicalism remained influential. In 1920 all the movements in the various countries had decided to combine, and a congress at The Hague, attended by delegates from fourteen nations, had founded the International Confederation of Christian Syndicates. Though it did not include only Catholics, it acted in accordance with papal doctrine, rejecting class warfare and relying upon collaboration and arbitration. But the emergence of totalitarian regimes in various countries deprived it of the development which the enthusiasm that greeted its beginnings had seemed to promise.

The story of Christian syndicalism in the United States was quite different. There, as in Britain, Catholics saw no need to form themselves into separate syndical organizations, because political and religious questions did not arise in the existing syndicates. They belonged therefore to the American Federation of Labor (A.F.L.) or the Congress of Industrial Organisation (C.I.O.). But during the great economic crisis, and before Marxist theories had begun to make progress, some thought it would be useful to gather Catholic workers into a separate association where they could study the doctrinal and practical problems resulting from their faith. At first they were supported by the *Catholic Worker*, but afterwards held aloof, believing that improvement of industrial civilization from within was more profitable and more practical than return to the land. Thus was born the Association of Catholic Trade Unionists (A.C.T.U.). Its newspaper, *Labor Leader*, published a programme of reform inspired by the Encyclicals, and spoke for the first time of a 'guaranteed annual wage'.

Thus, through Christian syndicalism, the Church succeeded to some extent in re-establishing contact with the working class. That was not the only means at her disposal; we shall find her in an altogether different field creating institutions whose task was to replant the Cross in the heart of the Christian masses. But there was a link between those new undertakings and Christian syndicalism, a link that was fundamental in the rebuilding of Christendom.

4. Pius XI and the Encyclical 'Quadragesimo anno'

The powerful movement which henceforward led so many Catholics to become active in the social sphere, could never have achieved

what it did unless approved by the teaching Church. Times have changed since it was possible to count on the fingers of one hand the number of bishops interested in this class of problems. Since *Rerum novarum* the situation has altered almost beyond recognition, and there is scarcely one member of the hierarchy who swims against the stream.

What of the popes? Benedict XV, it is alleged, stood for outmoded paternalism; indeed one of his documents (March 1920) refers to 'inequality consistent with the order established by God', to the resignation with which we ought to endure 'inevitable misfortune'. Yet if we recall that at that time the danger of seeing 'the masses driven to the overthrow of society' was not pure hypothesis, the Pope's caution becomes understandable; so too does that of Cardinal Merry del Val, who insisted that all undertakings should have a specifically Catholic character, and pointed to the confusion that might arise from certain inter-confessional tendencies. On the other hand Benedict XV witnessed the birth of C.F.T.C. and of the Italian Workers' Federation, which was backed by Don Sturzo's Popular Party, and he was favourable to both. He also resumed the custom of sending a message to the presidents of the various Social Weeks.

Pius XI was still more encouraging, having had personal experience of social problems as a young priest in Milan. Both in conversation and in his correspondence he often expressed admiration for Leo XIII and *Rerum novarum*. Elected to the papacy, he thanked C.F.T.C. for its congratulations in a letter which praised that body for its effort 'to better the life of the working classes by putting into practice the principles of the Gospel, which the Church has always applied in solving social problems'. And when, three years later, employers in the Département du Nord complained to Rome about Christian syndicalism, he behaved with a degree of caution and reached conclusions which have already been mentioned. Don Sturzo, who came to talk to him about the Italian Confederation of Workers, likewise under attack, was given this reply: 'We know that the work it does is useful.'

This view was confirmed and strengthened in Pius XI by his gift of being able, like Leo XIII, to understand the signs of the times and to grasp the needs of the future. He was well aware that the old liberalism was dead and that the evolution of industrial techniques was leading to the degradation of the worker.

On 24th October 1929 the economic crisis began in New York, and the capitalist regime appeared doomed. There was no longer a balance of supply and demand, and millions of unemployed besieged the gates of bankrupt factories. The international monetary system fell to pieces, and the different countries took refuge behind insurmountable customs barriers. Crisis fostered crisis, and the economic landscape

became tragic: industry came to a halt, agriculture was faced with disaster, trade was paralysed and the banks were in danger. Yet while wheat was burned in the Middle West and coffee was used in Brazil to fire locomotives, millions of human beings were driven to penury and famine. Pius XI felt the situation keenly and told those nearest to him that the thought of it caused him sleepless nights. Then, at the very height of the crisis, he spoke.

The occasion he chose was the fortieth anniversary of *Rerum novarum*, 15th May 1931, and the new Encyclical began with the words *Quadragesimo anno*. Pius XI intended to do what Leo XIII had done earlier, by sounding an alarm and signposting new positions with like firmness and unwonted courage. His tone was even more abrupt than that of the Leonine text. Some of his phrases were monumental and quickly became famous: 'Inert matter comes ennobled from the workshop while the men there are degraded'; 'work is not a piece of merchandise'; 'the whole of economic life has become implacably hard and cruel'; 'the worker should not receive as charity what belongs to him in justice'.

The Encyclical included three elements. Pius began by listing the fruits of *Rerum novarum*: 'In the doctrinal sphere a Catholic social science had come into being and was growing richer day by day; in the practical sphere statesmen, ever more conscious of their duty, had devoted themselves to the carrying out of a large-scale social policy; and thus a new branch of law has been created, unknown to the previous century, which guaranteed workers respect for the sacred rights belonging to them as men and Christians.' The Pope thus set his seal on the efforts of Social Catholics and recognized their influence upon the legislation in many lands. The workers' associations themselves received formal encouragement; and though Pius would have preferred 'specifically Catholic syndicates', he allowed Catholic workers to join neutral organizations provided that these latter respected justice and equity, and allowed the faithful 'complete liberty to obey their conscience and the voice of the Church'.

Other elements of *Quadragesimo anno* were reminders of the principles which underlie all Catholic social activity. For example, the Encyclical repeats Leo XIII's doctrine on the right to private property and its twofold character, individual and social. It repeats that the fruits of production should be shared according to the requirements of the common welfare, and in such a way that every worker may have the opportunity of ownership. Like *Rerum novarum* it does not declare unlawful the wage-earning system, so long as the contract of work is fair, i.e. that the wage is just. Pius XI condemns both economic liberalism and Socialism. With this latter Catholics must not compromise in any way, not even with its more moderate elements,

because its concept of society and of man's social character is contrary to Christian truth.[1]

The most important sections of *Quadragesimo anno* had still to come. While continuing to give moral considerations pride of place, Pius XI went much further than Leo in his denunciation of the prevailing regime; his criticism passed from the social to the economic level. The most striking passages of the whole Encyclical are perhaps those which denounce the unfair distribution of this world's goods—'on the one hand a vast multitude of proletarians, on the other a small number of rich men with enormous fortunes'; and those which condemn not the principles of capitalism as a system, but the consequences of its abuse—'concentration of wealth, accumulation of discretionary power in the hands of a few'; those in which the Pope shows that this economic dictatorship makes even political power subserve its ends; and those, finally, in which he declares that capital 'hires the proletariat with the sole purpose of exploiting industry and the economic regime for its own benefit, regardless of the human dignity of the workers, of the social character of economic activity, and even of social justice and the common good'.

Pius goes on to suggest means for replacing, or at least for reforming, the unacceptable elements of that system. He advocates a professional organization reminiscent in some respects of the Corporation as conceived by La Tour du Pin, with its groups, its co-ordinated 'States', disciplined and subject to the requirements of the common good, but with more autonomy allowed to the workers in organizing themselves and defending their rights. The formula, in short, is 'The free syndicate within the organized profession'. The State should guarantee and protect that organization, so as to ensure good order throughout, but it should be careful not 'to withdraw from the lower groups the functions they are capable of performing themselves'. At a moment when totalitarianism was fastening its stronghold upon Europe, *Quadragesimo anno* was resolutely anti-State. It was also anti-bureaucratic, opposed to the triumphant bureaucracy which seemed to Pius one of the most dangerous forms of collective domination. Within the framework of this harmonious organization of society, founded on the reconstruction of 'professional bodies' and recognition of man's immediate realities—family, locality, trade—Pius XI went very far, though his language was on the whole cautious. He demanded a wage adequate to family needs, participation of the workers in the control of businesses and their access to capital ownership. He also insisted that the grievous disorder of society could be healed only by abandoning the confines of egotistic nationalism, by recognizing that all nations are 'closely linked together and

[1] For the Encyclical *Divini Redemptoris* on Communism, *see* Chapter IX, section 9.

interdependent', and by establishing 'obligations and institutions' at the international level. Summing up *Quadragesimo anno* in his great Encyclical *Mater et Magistra* (1961), John XXIII said rightly that the two fundamental themes of Pius XI's document are (i) the need to outlaw interest as the supreme rule governing the activities and institutions of the economic world, be it in the interest of an individual, of a group or of a nation in quest of prestige or power; (ii) the need to create a juridical order, national and international, endowed with stable institutions both public and private.

Social Catholics understood *Quadragesimo anno* as an act calling for further action. It was the subject of innumerable commentaries in their study circles and in their press, and to it henceforward they made frequent reference. One may safely say that until 1961, the year in which a third impulse was given by a third 'social' Encyclical, Social Catholicism lived by *Quadragesimo anno*. It would, however, be an exaggeration to maintain that *Quadragesimo anno* was a determining influence outside the circles already favourable to its teaching. A glance at the contemporary bourgeois press shows clearly that the papal document was often received with some annoyance. In France, the most widely read daily was content to summarize the Encyclical in thirty lines; *La Croix* alone printed the complete text.

5. Social Catholicism: Achievements and Problems

On the eve of the Second World War, when the factors of the social problem were about to undergo radical alteration, the balance of results achieved by Social Catholicism was largely positive. True, the picture included large areas of shadow. Fascist Italy and Hitler's Germany had eliminated all Social Catholic works, movements and syndicates for the benefit of their own totalitarian organisms. In Austria the Social Catholic Dollfus had been murdered by the Nazis. In Spain Social Catholics were divided, some accepting Franco's regime while others preferred exile. In Latin America the movement was still in its infancy. Even in those countries where it was most vigorous it was far from commanding unanimous support; the great majority of the proletariat, more and more favourable to the idea of class warfare, ignored or mistrusted it. It no longer confused—or did so far less often—the duty of justice and that of charity. It understood more clearly its obligation to grapple with the iniquity and disorder of the world.

Even the very character of Social Catholicism had changed. That which less than a hundred years earlier had existed only as a vague aspiration, a generous intention, had become a doctrine in both senses

of the word—the object of magisterial teaching to which no Catholic could refuse to listen, and a system of thought determining action. It was, moreover, an extremely pliant doctrine, applicable to all the circumstances of life. Its influence was clearly discernible in the realm of ideas as in the field of legislation. The notion of a 'living wage' had been imposed by Social Catholics, who had also been closely associated with efforts to limit the working day, to ban the excessive labour of women and children, to guarantee workers against the difficulties of life and assure them the indispensable rest from toil. But Social Catholicism had become something quite different from a mere method of improving the proletarian lot; it was now a complete concept of society. Moreover it had spread abroad the grand idea of 'the common good', inseparable from and complementary to that of the dignity of the human person; while the economic and social system which it sought to achieve was as far removed from inhuman liberalism as it was from State totalitarianism. Finally, by holding aloof from all forms of Socialism it bore witness to a constant care for moral as well as institutional reform. That is why Social Catholics were found in the front line of the battle against alcoholism, prostitution and pornography. That also is why they attached so much importance to the task of education.

And yet the balance was not wholly satisfactory. The most resolute partisans of Social Catholicism in 1939 criticized the movement on two grounds, one theoretical and the other practical. (1) Despite the efforts made to give the doctrine firm foundations, that doctrine could not as yet be said to have attained the breadth and exactness of certain hostile doctrines, particularly Marxism. Social Catholicism, says Joseph Folliet, 'thought more about the application of its principles than about those principles themselves: starting from initial postulates, it did not always subject them to preliminary criticism'. A social theology, a theology of property and money had still to be constructed. And Canon Leclercq admits frankly: 'The Christian social movement possessed the principles needed for correcting the abuses of economic liberalism and for purifying social life. But it failed to present them as a whole with a firmness and precision sufficient to impose them on society at large; it lacked a great theorist.' A new effort would be made to understand fully the reality to which Christian principles should apply, using the positive findings of sociology and the economic sciences.

(2) Though wonderfully creative, knowing how to adapt its activity to all circumstances, Social Catholicism showed more of the spirit of enterprise than of organization. In all truth, one has often an impression of disorderly and chaotic action: 'quasi-feudal independence of religious orders, dioceses, parishes and movements; rivalry

of political tendencies; petty quarrels between individuals, groups or traditions; opposition from intellectual coteries'. Such vagaries were harmful to efficiency, but nothing was done to stop them.

With those reservations, it is impossible to overrate the importance of the part played henceforward by Social Catholicism in the life of the Church. At a moment when revolutionary Marxism was trying to impose itself as a total concept of man and society, a doctrine inseparably linked with action, Christians were able to declare that they too were working to fashion the world of tomorrow. The problem of Christianity's attitude vis-à-vis the modern world was thereby solved. To the suffering masses Social Catholicism presented itself as inspired by so vehement a longing for justice, and so determined to end the scandal of inequality and oppression, that it deprived the enemy of some of his most powerful weapons. Lastly, and perhaps above all, having been born in the conscience of laymen and owing its development principally to men who were not members of the clergy, it strove to associate the laity with the fulfilment of Christ's message. It was no mere accident that in *Quadragesimo anno* Pius XI had spoken enthusiastically of certain apostolic methods which had been introduced during his pontificate and which invited the laity to advance the Church's cause. It was consciousness of the social problem that underlay the vocation of the great inaugurator of this new crusade. It was within the framework of Christian syndicalism, a notable manifestation of Social Catholicism, that the Abbé Cardijn conceived a plan destined to effect a veritable revolution in the life of the Church.

6. The Abbé Cardijn's Experiment

At Brussels on 10th July 1924 the Abbé Joseph Cardijn, to whom Cardinal Mercier had entrusted the social work of his diocese, welcomed a hundred Walloon priests, most of them directors of social undertakings and parish priests of industrial centres, whom he had invited to the Belgian capital. At his side stood three laymen: Fernand Tonnet, his secretary, a man of extremely humble origin but highly intelligent and self-educated; Paul Garcet, a junior bank clerk and son of a workman; and Jacques Meert, a Brussels metal worker. Cardijn spent several hours laying before his hearers a programme that had evidently been thought out in great detail. It was based on personal experience, and the warmth of conviction with which he expounded his views, cited his evidence and answered objections made a deep impression. The presence of three laymen, moreover, was sufficient to prove that his proposals were far from chimerical. Substantially his

scheme was to entrust the laity with the task of replanting the Cross in those places where the faith seemed to have been uprooted, and especially to give the workers themselves the responsibility of re-christianizing the proletariat.

Here was an idea that seemed altogether new—it stemmed in fact directly from the teaching of St Paul—and was calculated to astonish an audience of priests. At the end of the meeting, however, the programme was adopted with enthusiasm, and it was decided to organize a movement on a national scale: *La Jeunesse ouvrière chrétienne* (J.O.C.).[1]

At that date the abbé was in his forty-second year. His working-class background was immediately recognizable in his outward appearance and in that simple dignity characteristic of craftsmen who love and respect their work. His father, a small tradesman at Hal, had been practically illiterate but full of good sense and Christian faith. The mother, a domestic servant in a middle-class household, had possessed an unwonted share of intelligence and refinement. Life had not been easy in that home, where five children were born, and at the age of twelve young Joseph was ready to begin his apprenticeship. But when he told his parents of his wish to become a priest, they readily agreed in a spirit of unhesitating self-sacrifice, and sent him to the junior seminary at Malines. Since God willed it so, they would work a little harder for a few more years in order that their son might follow his vocation.

It was this direct and personal experience that determined Joseph Cardijn, even before his ordination, to devote himself entirely to the working class. He had shared its sorrows and anxieties, but while still a youth he had also discovered its apostasy. He has told how, as a young seminarist, he went home for the holidays and found his former playmates strangely distant; they regarded him as an enemy because he was studying for the priesthood, whereas they had months ago ceased to perform their religious duties and were, so it seemed to him, lost for ever to the Church. In Belgium at that time there were about 600,000 working-class boys, many of whom on leaving school took jobs in corrupt surroundings, where they generally became hostile to Christianity. Two facts in particular struck Cardijn: it was the working-class environment itself that led young people astray from their faith, and it was therefore within that same environment that action would have to be taken. But the clergy had no means of access. In 1903, at his father's deathbed, the young theological student had sworn to find a solution to this problem. J.O.C., in fact, was the sequel to that oath he had taken twenty-two years earlier.

[1] Its members are often called collectively *Jocistes* in the following pages.—TRANSLATOR.

Those years had been years of useful training in various ways. All the circumstances in which he found himself had helped to mature his apostolic vocation in the social field and to prepare for its fulfilment. As a master in the junior seminary at Basse-Wavre he had devised a successful method of teaching, which he remembered afterwards when he had to talk to young people. He remembered, too, his conversations in England with Baden-Powell, founder of the Boy Scout movement. He had also made a careful study of the spirit and functioning of the English trade unions. Appointed in 1910 curate of Laeken, a working-class suburb of Brussels, he had kept his eyes and ears wide open, and had learned a good deal with the help of his mother who kept house for him until her death. He had visited many a worker's home, talking their language and even attracting worse than lukewarm Catholics to attend his sermons. Often, too, he managed as if by accident to be passing by when the factory gates opened, so as to be seen by the workers, to make their acquaintance, to be recognized by them and to become their friend.

It was at Laeken that he had achieved his first success. Horrified by the sight of little girls put to work at the age of twelve, many of them unable to read or write, and virtually uncared for, he established what might be described as a combination of syndicate and study circle in order to save them from foundering in the degrading atmosphere of the workshops. He had no thought of starting a 'movement'; but he was soon suggesting to this little group of children activities and methods that were later to be those of J.O.C. He explained to them in simple terms that they must 'practise the truth of their faith in the concrete reality of their lives'. And he devised for them what he called *l'enquête*, a survey of the environment in which they worked and of the problems facing religion there. The children took it all with the utmost seriousness and their number grew quickly. The ideas of the Abbé Cardijn were spreading beyond the parish of Notre-Dame de Laeken.

Reaction was varied. One day, he tells us, when he asked a few wealthy ladies to help with their pennies the work he had undertaken 'for girls of the working class, who have souls exactly the same as have your daughters, Mesdames', some of them took umbrage and walked out! In the workshops the young militants were often beaten up, dragged by the hair or, at best, insulted and bullied. Many Catholics took Cardijn for a fanatic, a madman, a dangerous fellow who ought to be locked up.[1] But nothing could prevent the work from thriving; and a few weeks later, in 1912, a seventeen-year-old worker complained to the curate of Laeken that he had done nothing for the boys. This was

[1] See Van de Meersch's touching account in his novel *Pêcheurs d'hommes*, which tells of the beginnings of J.O.C.

Fernand Tonnet, who offered to help. Shortly afterwards another lad, Paul Garcet, joined Tonnet. Finally, in 1919, Jacques Meert joined the pioneer group and formed with them the first national secretariat.

The arrival of those three was a matter of some consequence. It transpired that Tonnet, despite his youth, had thought a good deal about the social problem and the difficulties of the Christian worker. He had observed much in Borinage, the rough district where he spent his childhood. At Quiévrain he had attended a mass demonstration at which a representative of A.C.J.F. had explained the principles of Social Catholicism. From that date he had been a regular reader of the association's journal *Vie nouvelle*, in the pages of which he had been thrilled by Henri Bazire's watchword 'Social because Catholic'.[1] Consequently he brought the Abbé Cardijn something more than goodwill and earnest purpose.[2]

On the eve of the First World War the stream which was to produce J.O.C. ten years later had already begun to flow, though not without all sorts of difficulties. Appointed in 1915, during the German occupation, director of social work in Brussels and chaplain to the Christian syndicates, Cardijn obtained from his twofold sphere of duty new light upon the problems he had most at heart. Twice imprisoned by the Germans, once for having protested against the arrest of young workers, and again on a charge of espionage, he used those months of enforced solitude to write down the substance of his thoughts during the previous years—a document which was to be later the manual of J.O.C.—for he was absolutely sure that the work he planned would flourish when peace returned. And when it did, he was ready to carry out the programme matured in the long silences of captivity.

In 1919 he formed the young workers of Brussels into an association called *Jeunesse syndicaliste*, which expressed its views in a journal of the same name. In the pre-war years he had studied social work in Germany, Britain and Holland, and by 1924 he felt prepared for an operation on a national scale under a less exclusive title than *Jeunesse syndicaliste*, which seemed to restrict activity to the defence of material interests. The workers must be apostles of the workers. They must regain for Christ their own social environment by permeating it with the Christian spirit. Their work must be a mission, their family life an example. Here was an entirely new concept of the apostolate, an almost revolutionary orientation given to what was already known as Catholic Action. In the words of Canon Tiberghien, one of the J.O.C.'s earliest friends, what was proposed was 'neither angling nor dragging, but a change of water in the fishpond'.

[1] See Chapter IV, section 12.

[2] See F. Tonnet, *Les sources boraines de la J.O.C.*, Louvain, 1947. Tonnet and Garcet died during the Second World War in the concentration camp at Dachau.

7. Catholic Action

The Abbé Cardijn's initial idea, to associate the laity with the apostolate, was not altogether new. 'Catholic Action' was already a familiar phrase and was destined to a glorious future. As early as 1903 Pius X had written: 'In order to bring about the return and consolidation of Christian life, we in our age have no more opportune means than the fostering of Catholic action.'[1] Catholic action[2] was already well established, understood not only in its literal sense of 'Christian conduct' but as denoting also the sum total of apostolic work distinct from spiritual undertakings and the associations set up to promote them.

Indeed if Catholic action is, as Pius XI described it, 'witness of charity, seeking to communicate the treasures of the Redemption to other souls', it is as old as the Church herself. Christ's words 'You shall be my witness . . . Go and preach the Gospel' were addressed to all the baptized, not only to the successors of the Apostles. 'The apostolate', says Pius again, 'is simply the exercise of Christian charity, which is binding upon all Christians.' In the wide sense good example, prayer and sacrifice are notable forms of apostolate, 'Catholic actions'; but the strict sense of 'Catholic action' refers to something different—to a special effort to spread Christian faith wherever it is unknown. And laymen have always been found engaged in that effort since the earliest days of the Church.

Without going back to medieval Christendom, in which the laity occupied a prominent place, one can find antecedents of Catholic action in the last four centuries: the Company of the Blessed Sacrament in seventeenth-century France; the *Compagnie della dottrina cristiana* in Italy; Ozanam's Conferences of St Vincent de Paul in the early nineteenth century; Father Diesbach and Bruno Lantieri's *Amicizie cattolice*. Later still, under Pius IX, we have the *Ligue catholique pour la défense de l'Église* in France; the *Union catholique* in Belgium; the *Katholischer Verein* in Germany; the *Piusverein* in Switzerland; the Catholic Union in Britain; the *Associacion de catolicos* in Spain. And international links were forged between the various movements, links of which the famous Congress of Malines in 1863 was one striking manifestation.

The pontificate of Leo XIII pioneered the development of Catholic action. While insisting above all on the duty of laymen 'to defend their faith and show it forth publicly', the great Pope realized that in

[1] Brief addressed to Count Grosoli, 6th November 1903.

[2] 'action' with lower-case initial; upper case was not used until the Church created a regular organization with that name.

order to be effective such activity on the part of Catholics 'must be placed under the control of a single authority which would give the whole movement its initial impulse'.[1] In other words the Church herself, through the medium of the hierarchy, must take the enterprise in hand. This was the first hint of an organized lay apostolate.

But the true begetter of Catholic Action, in the modern sense of the term, was Pius X, who more than once declared that 'Catholic action of the laity' was 'a most praiseworthy and even necessary undertaking in the present situation of the Church and of society'. His Encyclical *Il fermo proposito* may be considered as the charter of Catholic Action. He spoke of 'those select Catholic troops who intend to combine all their forces in order to fight antichristian civilization with all the just and legal weapons at their disposal by repairing the grave disorders that flow from it, by replacing Jesus Christ in the family, the schools and society at large . . . and by taking to heart in a very special way the interests of the people, especially of the industrial and agricultural workers'. His words gave Catholic Action a threefold end: polemical, social and apostolic. The last was naturally the most important in the eyes of the Pope whose motto was *Omnia instaurare in Christo.*

During his pontificate therefore great movements were set on foot or gained added strength: in Germany the *Volksverein*; in Italy the *Unione Popolare*; in France the *Association catholique de la Jeunesse française*. Under Benedict XV this manifold movement continued to progress, and the Pope himself took a keen interest in it. Accordingly when Pius XI ascended Peter's throne he found the ground well prepared, though imperfectly organized. As Archbishop of Milan, Cardinal Ratti had done much to foster Catholic Action, and in November 1921, shortly before his election, he had published a 'Letter on the Rules to be followed in Catholic Action'. In his first Encyclical *Ubi Arcano* he spoke of Catholic Action as very dear to his heart; and year by year until his death he repeatedly emphasized the need to spread the movement, to persuade all the faithful to take part in it and to organize its functions with a view to greater effectiveness.

His concern for the development and direction of Catholic Action was due to three facts: the numerical insufficiency of the clergy, the steady paganization of society and the increasing number of associations, etc., all with similar objectives and employing similar means, but weakened by their own rivalry. He decided therefore that the laity must be entrusted with part of the apostolic task reserved until now to the clergy; that such lay activity must be considered henceforward as a normal, indeed an essential, element in the constitution of the Church; and that centralized organisms must be set up to give it authority. 'Catholic Action', he wrote, 'is the organized participation of the

[1] Encyclical *Graves de Communi.*

laity in the hierarchical apostolate of the Church, transcending party politics, for the establishment of Christ's reign throughout the world.' And again: 'Catholic Action is nothing else than the apostolate of the faithful, who, under the guidance of the bishops, place themselves at the service of the Church and help her to carry out her pastoral ministry to the full.'

Thus in 1925, when the Abbé Cardijn appeared upon the scene, Catholic Action already existed in substance. It existed, however, as only a general movement, admitting to its works laymen of all social classes and of all conditions, acting (within the hierarchical framework of the Church) in particular parishes or dioceses, and consequently unable to adapt its apostolic methods to the various circumstances of class and position. The originality of Cardijn's new movement lay in the fact that it perceived the reality of differing social environments and applied that concept to the apostolate in order to diversify it and adapt it to the particular conditions of each social category.

8. Pius XI and J.O.C.

The Abbé Cardijn's J.O.C. was successful from the outset. Within six months one hundred and fifty local sections had been founded in Belgium; more than six hundred gatherings had been held, and a national secretariat set up. It had also met for the first time serious opposition, chiefly from the *Association catholique de la jeunesse belge*. This latter, a fundamentally middle-class and student group like A.C.J.F., had first of all embraced a section of working-class youth, but had then become scared of it and looked upon it with grave suspicion. Accused of dividing Catholics and urging class warfare, Cardijn went to see Cardinal Mercier. 'I don't quite understand your point of view,' said the Archbishop, 'but go and see the Pope; he will enlighten you.'

That visit to the Pope marked a date in the history of the Church whose importance cannot be overestimated. Arriving in Rome at the beginning of 1925, Cardijn managed with some difficulty to obtain a private audience. 'What do you want?' asked Pius. 'Most Holy Father, I want to kill myself in order to save the working class.' 'At last!' exclaimed the Pope. 'At last someone has come to talk to me about saving the rank and file. I'm forever hearing about an *élite*; but what we need is an *élite* among the rank and file—a leaven in the lump. The greatest service you can do the Church is to restore to her the working class she has lost. The common people have need of the Church, and the Church has need of them. Yes, in order to fulfil her mission the Church has urgent need of the working class. A Church

consisting only of the rich is no longer Our Lord's Church. It was mainly for the poor that He founded His Church. That is why the working class must be restored to Him.'

The founder of J.O.C., though he did not know it, shared one of Pius XI's major preoccupations, one that caused him ten years later to promulgate the Encyclical *Quadragesimo anno*—a resolve to re-establish the Church's presence among the poorest social classes. 'The great scandal of our time', declared Pius, 'is that the Church has lost the working class'; and ended that first audience with these words: 'Not only do I bless your undertaking . . . I make it my own.' He kept his word.

This new form of Catholic Action was therefore linked directly with the Holy See, its development watched closely by the Pope himself. Henceforward all papal documents referring to Catholic Action spoke of the new orientation it had received. The objectives proclaimed in *Quadragesimo anno* were exactly those of the Abbé Cardijn. 'In order to bring back to Christ the various classes of men who have denied Him it is necessary above all to recruit and train within their midst auxiliaries of the Church who understand their mentality and aspirations, and who can speak to their hearts in a brotherly spirit. The first apostles of the workers will be workers.' Elsewhere, addressing the representatives of A.C.J.F., he praised this new form of apostolate and likened it to that which he extolled in the mission fields—establishment of a native clergy capable of penetrating the native masses. 'Industrial workers, agricultural workers, sailors and students, each working as apostles among their fellows': such was the programme of what was soon to be called 'specialized Catholic Action'. And Pius XI said more than once that 'of all the signs of renewal' which made him optimistic about the Church's future the most splendid was the raising up of 'those serried ranks of young Christian labourers inspired with the noble ambition to regain the souls of their brethren'.

Protected now, and indeed officially patronized by Rome, the Abbé Cardijn's modest movement quickly assumed a most important place in the Belgian Church. Cardinal Mercier made clear that he approved it, and all the bishops followed suit. The first national congress, attended by five hundred delegates, was held in Brussels at Easter 1925. A banner was designed, a manual published and a female branch formed. Membership increased year by year; but resistance continued, and in 1928 Cardijn told the Pope so during an audience. 'Come to Rome with your workers,' answered Pius; 'the Pope will show the whole world what he thinks of your movement.' In September 1929, therefore, led by Cardinal van Roey, the new Archbishop of Malines, twelve hundred *jocistes*, all in working dress, were received at the

Vatican in an audience which lasted for three hours. Contrary to protocol an address was read to the Pope, who replied in a speech full of admiration and encouragement.

Other countries soon followed the example of Belgium, notably France under the leadership of the Abbé Georges Guérin and Père Anizan. Meanwhile the movement spread beyond Belgium and France. By 1939 J.O.C. existed also in Holland, Canada, Switzerland, Hungary, Yugoslavia, Spain, Portugal, Slovakia, Syria, Colombia, Britain, Ireland, Poland, North Africa, Indo-China, Luxemburg and China. In 1953 it had branches in sixty-five lands.

Among similar movements were *Jeunesse agricole chrétienne* (France, 1929), which spread to twelve other countries; *Jeunesse étudiante chrétienne* (Belgium, 1928), adopted in ten countries, including Canada; *Jeunesse maritime chrétienne* (France, 1930); and *Jeunesse indépendante chrétienne* (France, 1935).

CHAPTER IX

THE GREAT BATTLES OF POPE PIUS XI

1. 'Defensor fidei'

If Pius XI had died in 1930 instead of in 1939, he would have bequeathed an image of himself quite different from the one we know. He would have been celebrated, of course, not only as a successful follower of Benedict XV in his policy of concordats, but also as the Pope of Catholic Action, of Social Catholicism, of intellectual revival; as Pope of the coloured Churches and of the first effort towards ecumenism. He would not, however, have been recognized as possessing those characteristics which struck his contemporaries with such force and which seem today the outstanding features of his personality.

Achille Ratti's temperament was never in doubt; it was not he that changed after 1930. Those who knew him at the various stages of his life are unanimous in representing him as history depicts him: strict in matters of principle, imperious and often abrupt, but coldly resolute and never hesitating in face of responsibility or a risk once he had decided it must be taken. Before 1930 there had been very few occasions upon which he needed to display those gifts; afterwards there were all too many. Whenever he believed that the sacred deposit entrusted to him was gravely imperilled, he gave no thought to temporization or diplomatic accommodation, but struck at once and hard. Defence of the Faith was the ultimate purpose of all he did. It is manifestly the foremost duty incumbent upon the Vicar of Christ, and in this respect Pius XI's mind worked no differently from that of his namesakes—of Pius IX who had published the *Syllabus*, or of Pius X who had condemned Modernism. No other motive need be sought for any of his decisions, even when they were taken in a political climate which appeared to explain them, even when by taking them he happened at the same time to be defending human or cultural values. It is as *defensor fidei* that Achille Ratti must be represented amid the great events which give his pontificate its special significance and which were destined to earn for the papacy a worldwide authority and for his own memory an undying radiance.

2. The Condemnation of 'Action Française'

One affair, however, dates from before 1930. Compared with

subsequent events it is of minor importance, in the sense that (*a*) it involved no sovereign State, and (*b*) the errors which determined the Pope to intervene were nothing like so serious or widespread as those against which he was to fulminate his more celebrated anathemas. Nor in this case did he have recourse to the solemnity of an Encyclical, but pronounced his censure in a manner less sensational, after showing a good deal of patience. I refer to the matter of *Action française*, an affair indicative of the doctrinal firmness and the severity with which he was resolved to strike at those who impaired truth or compromised the Church.

At the time of his accession, 1922, the title *Action française* was borne by a daily paper and also by a movement of thought of which that journal was the mouthpiece. Charles Maurras (1868–1952), leading spirit of the movement and editor of the paper, was a gaunt little bearded man, whose sparkling eyes and voluble eloquence made one forget that he was stone deaf. A profound thinker, a first-class writer and a formidable dialectician, he had for more than twenty years been propounding a political theory directly linked with those of Bonald and Joseph de Maistre—the doctrine of traditionalist monarchism, with which was associated an intransigent nationalism. Served by a wealth of talent—Maurras himself, Léon Daudet, Jacques Bainville and others—the journal wielded enormous influence far beyond royalist circles. As for the movement, which started in 1908, its ranks had been swelled not only by professed royalists, but also by numerous enemies of the Republic: men with nostalgia for the *ancien régime*, patriots who had moved steadily in the direction of nationalism ever since the Dreyfus affair, 'integrists' who had survived the disapproval of Benedict XV, and a large number of those conservatives who, in all circumstances, advocate authoritarian methods. Among them were many Catholics.

Criticism had long been directed against *Action française* or, more exactly, against the principles on which Charles Maurras claimed to base his political doctrine. In 1908 *Le Correspondant* through Étienne Lamy's pen, and then two years later the Oratorian Père Laberthonnière in a book entitled *Positivisme et Catholicisme*, showed that *maurrasisme* was hardly compatible with Christian faith. Other polemists followed suit, and the French bishops asked that Maurras's works be placed on the Index. On 26th January 1914 the consultors announced that seven of those works stood condemned; and their decision was confirmed by the General Congregation, which added the paper *Action française*.

Pius X, however, delayed publication of the verdict. When it was reported to him on 29th January, by the secretary of the Congregation, he replied that the works in question were certainly prohibited, that the

condemnation would be promulgated as from that date, but that the decree was not published until such time as he personally thought fit. 'Maurras', he declared, 'is a good champion of the Church and of the Holy See.' Other reasons for this clemency were his unwillingness to disturb Catholicism in France on the eve of a war which he regarded as certain, and his anxiety not to offend the many distinguished Frenchmen, religious and secular, who had begged him to deal gently with the culprit. Benedict XV adopted the same attitude: in 1915, after careful consideration, he decided that if the decree were published during the war, 'political passions would prevent a fair assessment of such an act on the part of the Holy See'. So there the matter lay, as expressed by Pius X: *Damnabilis sed non damnandus*—condemnable but not to be condemned.

The affair took a new turn after the accession of Pius XI in 1922. The new Pope had not the same reasons as Pius X for showing indulgence towards Maurras and his supporters. On the contrary, he could derive small satisfaction from news that *Action française* was opposing his policy of *nouveau ralliement*; denouncing the resumption of diplomatic relations between the Vatican and Paris as the Church's acceptance of servitude; insulting the ambassador to the Holy See, who had dared to compete (and to compete successfully) with Maurras for a seat in the *Académie française*; criticizing the diocesan bishops; waging a violent campaign against international institutions and against those men who were advocating Franco-German reconciliation; and suggesting that the nuncio was a man of questionable morals. However, it would be false to suppose that Pius was moved in the last resort by political considerations. While it is true that the political enemies of *Action française*—liberal Catholics, Christian Democrats, supporters of the League of Nations—were loud in protest, it is equally certain that Pius XI was not the man to suffer dictation from anyone.

In 1923 there occurred a very strange incident, about which little is known but which was to have great importance in leading Pius to take a close personal interest in the affair. One day the Pope asked to be shown the file dealing with Maurras's consignment to the Index. That, he was informed, was quite impossible: the file had disappeared. Some maintained that its loss was due merely to disturbance of the archives of the Index when the latter was transferred to the Holy Office under Benedict XV. Others whispered that Roman friends of Maurras knew more than they cared to say, and even mentioned names. Whatever the truth, the manœuvre (if such it was) had an effect exactly opposite to what *Action française* expected; for the Pope himself decided to re-examine the whole question. He had spent forty years handling documents of all kinds, and, as he later revealed, he conducted his inquiry in great detail, 'at the risk of arriving late', and with absolute impar-

tiality, 'desiring only the truth', moved solely by the urge 'to prevent evil and procure good, apart from and above party politics'.

Pius was still studying the works of Maurras, Daudet and Bainville, as well as the pages of *Action française* itself, when alarming reports reached the Vatican of the movement's rapid progress among Catholic youth. A quarter, if not one-third, of French seminarists were adherents of Maurras, while A.C.J.F. complained that *Action française* was drawing off the most active elements of right-wing Catholic youth. The *Camelots du Roi*, a royalist organization for propaganda used by *Action française* for public demonstrations and acts of violence, was recruiting more and more Catholic members. One piece of news in particular struck Pius XI. In May 1925 the *Cahiers de la Jeunesse catholique belge* organized a referendum on this question: 'Among writers of the past twenty-five years, whom do you consider as your masters?' Maurras headed the list with 174 votes; Cardinal Mercier came last with six. The Belgian episcopate took fright; a group of distinguished Belgian Catholics published a warning, and Pius XI resolved to stand no more nonsense.

With what could he charge Maurras and *Action française*? In what respect could their doctrine be regarded by the Church as meriting condemnation? Criticism turned on two points: 'positivist naturalism' and 'excessive nationalism'. Maurras was certainly a positivist, and did not hide the fact. He often referred to Auguste Comte, author of the *Catéchisme positiviste* and one of the leaders of atheistic humanism.[1] According to Comte and his school, man, as a political animal, is governed exclusively, like all other living things, by his physical and biological environment—a view diametrically opposed to the Christian thesis that the political must be subject to the moral order. This, however, did not mean the elimination of religion, which indeed forms part of the framework of man's existence and helps him to live. Thus, while thinking that the Christian religion was 'irrevocably outmoded' and due for replacement by the religion of man, Auguste Comte had often expressed his admiration for the Catholic Church as an institution, notably because of the logic and solidity of her organization. Charles Maurras thought likewise. According to him the Church should not interfere in social life, where man is ruled by a 'physics of manners', and by infrangible political law. But as a principle of authority, an organism of social discipline, she deserved of admiration and must be defended, by unbelievers as well as by Catholics. Now that was nothing less than to empty the Church of her spiritual substance, to deprive her of her true *raison d'être*, which is not to organize society but to save souls. It was, in the words of Mgr Ricard, Bishop of Nice, 'to dechristianize Catholicism'.

[1] *The Church in an Age of Revolution*, pp. 308 ff.

In 1925 Maurras no longer professed this heresy in the extravagant form he had given it in his pagan youth, when he opposed to the 'Hebrew Christ', sower of anarchy, the tradition of the Church, which, as he said, had managed to 'truncate, remould and transform the turbulent oriental scriptures', so as to make of them an orderly system capable of lasting throughout the ages. But this error underlay all that he wrote, and all that his disciples wrote. With it he combined additional errors deriving from it, notably the subjection of man to society and the exaltation of national values to the detriment of all others. The Christian notion of the 'common good' was radically denied by the 'integral nationalism' which placed 'the motherland above all else' and could not agree that in the international order there might be, in Christian eyes, interests higher even than those of the motherland.

These grave errors of *Action française*—primacy of the political over the moral, denial of the spiritual element of Christianity, exaltation of national egoism—were easily discovered by Pius XI in the works of Maurras and the columns of *Action française*. One can imagine his feelings when he read an article in which Maurras, at the height of the Dreyfus affair, had approved Colonel Henry's forgery. In another the journal gave this advice: 'Let us buy the women, let us buy consciences, let us buy treason.' And in yet another (1923) he heard Léon Daudet exclaim: 'I'm delighted about the German famine!' The Church of Christ could hardly accept such allies; still less could she allow Catholics to be associated with an undertaking so expressly antagonistic to her principles.

The Pope, however, refrained from immediate recourse to stern measures. The *Action française* movement included so many excellent Catholics who did not share all Maurras's philosophical ideas—although they were more or less contaminated by the 'pernicious atmosphere' of positivist naturalism—that he thought it more useful to enlighten them before striking a final blow. After vain approaches to various members of the French hierarchy, he delegated this task to the aged Cardinal Andrieu, Archbishop of Bordeaux. On 27th October 1926 there appeared in *Aquitaine*, the diocesan bulletin, a declaration by that prelate. Having had to reply to a group of young Catholics 'on the subject of *Action française* and the attitude they should adopt towards it', he advised them to break away from it as quickly as possible. The wording of the archiepiscopal declaration was extremely harsh, describing the directors of the movement all together as 'atheists or agnostics', as 'Catholics by profession but not by conviction', as 'amoralists', and so on. The document, however, made the whole problem absolutely clear by denouncing in the plainest terms the Maurrasian heresy. Its only faults were a lack of serenity, the attribution to *Action française* as a whole the philosophical ideas of its

leader, and even the attribution to Maurras himself of opinions he had never taught, e.g. the need to re-introduce slavery. The stroke was therefore excessive and not very skilful; but it was an important warning, exceeding in importance that of the tired old man who had delivered it. There could be no more room for doubt when, on 5th September, a letter from Pius XI to Cardinal Andrieu was published, congratulating him upon having denounced 'a rebirth of paganism'.

It may be that Pius XI thought that sufficient, that the Catholics of *Action française* would listen to his appeal and abandon the movement. There appears, however, to have been some hesitation in the ranks of *Action française* as to what attitude should be adopted. Some, e.g. Jacques Maritain,[1] believed it would be possible for Catholics to remain within the political movement while eschewing doctrinal errors. Others protested that the papal condemnation was only a political and even a police measure inspired by politicians of the Briand type, and that if they had to choose between their two loyalties they would prefer *Action française*. Many ecclesiastical authorities, with Cardinal Maurin, Archbishop of Lyons, at their head, advised a course of 'wait and see'. Why did the directors of the monarchist movement suddenly favour a more stubborn attitude? On 15th December, in reply to various notes in *Osservatore Romano* and under the title 'Rome et la France', Charles Maurras's journal published an article of astonishing vehemence, accusing a 'small gang of simoniacal agents' of insulting good Frenchmen 'in their conscience as believers and in their honour as men'. Five days afterwards, in Consistory, Pius XI retorted by expressly forbidding all Catholics to belong to the undertakings, to remain in the school or to read the journal 'of men whose writings set aside our dogma and our morality'.

Just then an event occurred the immediate result of which was to harden the Pope's attitude: the lost file was providentially discovered. Pius himself, an experienced archivist, had given detailed instructions for the search. Moreover the turn taken by the affair was such that certain tendencies towards resistance were beginning to lose impetus. Now that the condemnation of 1914 was known, *Action française* could no longer enjoy itself by contrasting the wise and saintly Pius X with his deplorable successor. But, on 24th December, in answer to the consistorial allocution, Maurras's journal published a *non possumus* on the grounds that 'the question is not one of faith or morals, but of politics', and that what the Roman censor had had in mind was 'France herself, the true France'. Rome replied on 29th December 1926 by publishing the decree of the Holy Office as drawn up in 1914. To it was added an explicit condemnation of the journal *Action française*.

Action française, however, did not yield, finding a good deal of

[1] In his pamphlet *Une opinion sur Charles Maurras et le devoir des catholiques*.

support or at least of tacit encouragement, even among persons from whom a very different attitude might have been expected. Priests, religious, bishops, archbishops (eleven out of seventeen) and even Billot, a cardinal in curia, did not hide their sympathy with the condemned movement. The anticlerical press joyfully seized their opportunity to accuse the Pope of restricting freedom, while the Catholic press itself—excepting Francisque Gay's *Vie catholique*—appeared little anxious to defend the papal position. There were, nevertheless, a great many submissions, marked by a drop in the sales of *Action française*; some were sensational, e.g. that of Jacques Maritain who loyally abandoned for ever the Maurrasian camp, explained himself in a wonderful book entitled *Primauté du Spirituel* and inspired two collective works, *Pourquoi Rome a parlé* and *Clairvoyance de Rome*.

But Pius was coldly resolved upon victory. At his request 116 French bishops signed a manifesto approving and explaining the condemnation; those who believed they ought not to sign paid dearly for their refusal. Cardinal Billot was obliged to resign and retired as a simple Jesuit to a house of the Society. Several religious also, some of them notorious, were punished; among these was Père Le Floch, whose name had been mentioned in connection with the disappearance of that celebrated file. Meanwhile the Sacred Penitentiary decreed that any priest who gave absolution to supporters of *Action française* would be suspended from hearing confessions, that seminarists faithful to the movement would be dismissed, and that the faithful who remained stubborn in rebellion would be regarded as public sinners and refused the sacraments.

France became at once a tragic stage upon which friendships were destroyed and families divided among themselves, as in the days of the Dreyfus affair. Good Catholics were seen carried to a civil grave because of their allegiance to *Action française*; priests censured for having taken the last sacraments to their fathers who stood condemned; marriages and baptisms performed as in the worst days of the Terror. . . . It must be added that certain bishops devoted to the cause of repression a degree of energy more than equivalent to their erstwhile reluctance to enter the lists. Their severity astonished even Roman circles, which thought it quite natural that the excommunicated King of Italy should perform his Easter duties and have his chaplain.

Charles Maurras and his friends were now fully committed to rebellion. Their journal reached unparalleled heights of insult. Against 'the liar' (the Pope), against the *Diffamatore* (meaning *Osservatore*) *Romano*, against the nuncios Cerretti and Maglione, against all who talked of submission, the wretched rag screamed month after month with unimaginable fury. A paper which paraded as the mouthpiece of French culture at its highest carried articles on the

Bartholomew massacres, on Bishop Cauchon who sentenced Joan of Arc, on the Galileo affair, on the Borgias—articles which the most rabid freemason would not have disavowed.

Where did it all lead? 'One does not say *Non possumus* to the Pope,' said Mussolini to a friend of Maurras. Many Catholics deplored the revolt. The heads of the royal house of France themselves, the Duc de Guise and his son the Comte de Paris, did not hide their disapproval: in November 1937 they let it be known that they categorically rejected 'integral nationalism'. Ten years after the condemnation it was becoming more and more apparent that this unhappy situation could not last for ever. War now seemed inevitable, and many Catholics were unhappy about these divisions in the Church of France. Among those who intervened were Cardinal Pacelli, secretary of state; Cardinal Verdier; Mgr Grente, Bishop of Mans and a member of the Académie Française; the Carmelites of Lisieux; Père Gillet, master-general of the Dominicans; the Canadian Cardinal Villeneuve; and Georges Goyau himself, whom *Action française* frequently described as 'little green monkey'. Thus was made straight the way to submission and pardon. In 1937 Maurras wrote Pius XI a most noble letter in which he did homage to 'the motherhood of the Church', and in reply he received a three-page autograph letter full of kindness. A whole series of moves followed during the next two years, and a document was ultimately drafted which the governing committee of *Action française* sent to the Holy See.

Negotiations were already far advanced when Pius XI died. They were concluded soon afterwards under his successor Pius XII. After a visit to Paris by Mgr Ottaviani, assessor of the Holy Office, a new letter was sent to Rome, in which the committee expressed its 'sincere grief' for what had been 'disrespectful, offensive and even unjust' in their attitude, and rejected 'every principle and every theory opposed to the teaching of the Church'.[1] The Holy Office replied on 5th July by lifting the condemnation of *Action française*, but without mentioning that of Pius X against Maurras's philosophy.

3. 'Defensor Hominis'

No matter how grave the doctrinal errors of a movement to which, after all, only a small minority of Frenchmen adhered, they were as nothing in comparison with those upon which sovereign States, political regimes and whole peoples took their stand.

From 1930 onward Pius XI was at war with the various totalitarian

[1] In his book on Pius X (p. 218) Maurras expressly acknowledged that 'insubordination was a grave mistake'.

systems, which embodied the major heresies of the age. They were, as we have seen,[1] the end product and in some sense the compendium of forces that had long been urging man against God. Pius entered upon the struggle not for political reasons, as his enemies claimed, but for strictly religious motives, because he wished to defend the Church and the sacred deposit of faith. It was nothing less than a fight for God.

The radical antagonism of Christianity to the new regimes was obvious in certain cases, since those regimes themselves proclaimed it. In the case of Russian Communism, it could be doubted by no one who had read Karl Marx, for dialectical materialism is incompatible with the Christian faith. So also as regards National Socialism in Germany, which took its stand upon a kind of Nietzschean paganism. But was the same true everywhere? Italian Fascism, at least in its early days, did not appear so manifestly open to criticism; it respected the Church and showed itself anxious not to alienate the moral force she represented. Moreover it appealed to the principles of order and hierarchy, which are dear to the Church; and the corporatism which it promised to introduce, in order to solve the social problem, seemed at first altogether acceptable.

It might appear natural for the Church to ally herself with those authoritarian regimes which were likewise opposed to atheistic Communism. But in fact it was nothing of the kind, and Pius XI quickly showed that he intended to fight on both fronts. Above and beyond political interests, religious interests were at stake—those Christian values which it was his duty to defend; and here we see his unfailing clarity of mind. In all the new regimes that had come into existence since the war he recognized fundamental errors which must lead to their condemnation.

First among those errors was the intolerant nationalism which he had already denounced among the adherents of *Action française*. It was no less virulent in Italy and Germany, and even in Soviet Russia where it assumed other forms. In each case the Pope would repeat what he had so often before declared: 'The opposition between exaggerated nationalism and Catholic doctrine is manifest.'

But there was something much more serious. Whatever their respective ideologies, all those new regimes were *totalitarian*. According to them the State, the collectivity, was the sole legitimate reality. Under State direction all living forces must be united in order to ensure growth of the collectivity. The State therefore had a right to dominate man from his birth until his death, to impose upon him the

[1] Chapter I, section 9. It is worth noticing that all the totalitarian regimes took the form of personal dictatorship. The reason is made quite clear by Hans Hesse, a Nazi theorist, who wrote of the *Führerprinzip* as follows: 'The age of the masses in which we live has an imperious need of men to subdue and direct those masses. The leaders born of their womb are the incarnation of their will.'

principles, activities, ways of life and even opinions which it considered useful. In such a system man is nothing: the State alone counts. That doctrine was characteristic of the Soviets no less than of National Socialism, and indeed of Fascism, whose theorists coined the very word 'totalitarian'.

It was against this subversion of values that the Pope prepared to do battle. Strictly faithful to the teaching of the Church—the *Syllabus* had long since condemned the cult of the State—he denounced totalitarian 'statolatry'. This determined attitude involved the Church in dramatic, sometimes bloody, conflicts and had far-reaching consequences. Adopting it in the name of faith, because the totalitarian concept is unacceptable to Christianity which insists upon man's freedom and responsibility before God, Pius XI took his stand against the worst tyranny that has menaced the twentieth century. 'The Church', he said, 'rejects the theory, all too common nowadays, that the collectivity is all and the individual nothing. She does not accept the deification of the collective, which is a kind of social pantheism.' And he added these words, which represent the doctrinal basis of his attitude throughout the conflict: 'Man, as a person, has rights which he holds from God and which must remain inviolate. Society is made for man, not man for society.'

Here we have a striking (if only apparent) reversal of an earlier situation. Pius IX had been misunderstood when he condemned 'liberalism', which in his day had been the cause of so much error, disorder and violence. Pius XI, because the terms of the problems had altered, placed the word in a different light. One day after quoting a passage from Lactantius, 'In religion alone hath freedom elected to dwell', he exclaimed: 'The Church has always been and still is the champion of true liberty.' He sought to defend the human person against those 'cold monsters' of which Nietzsche had spoken. His anathemas, unlike those of the previous century, seem in no way opposed to human values; they defend what constitutes the greatness, and indeed the sole chance, of mankind.

4. Pius XI against Fascist 'Statolatry'

On the morrow of the *Conciliazione* an amusing story was current in Rome. Returning from the Lateran after the treaties had been signed, Cardinal Gasparri's car was halted by a crowd: two burly fellows were fighting like dogs in the street. 'I wonder', said His Eminence, turning to his companion, 'how long ago they signed a concordat.' *Se non è vero, è ben trovato*; for the ink was scarcely dry on the diplomatic

instruments when conflict began between the Vatican and the Fascist State, and seemed on the point of undoing all that had been achieved.

During the negotiations which had led to the agreements of 1929, care had been taken to avoid raising the doctrinal question as to whether or not the Fascist system was compatible with Christian principles. Besides the answer might have been ambiguous. It seemed beyond doubt that Mussolini himself had very little faith. His deepest convictions derived from a simplified form of Nietzsche's doctrine, which he voiced in a speech to the Garibaldians returning from the Argonne in 1919: 'I would like a pagan people, eager for strife, life and progress, without blind belief in revealed truths, and contemptuous even of miraculous panaceas.' Nor is there any reason to doubt that he persisted in the same way of thinking until his death.

This does not mean that he based his attitude on such principles, once committed to action; one might indeed ask whether Mussolini had any political philosophy at all. In 1921, when questioned as to the aim of his Blackshirts, he replied: 'What do we want? To govern Italy.' While Bolshevism had its 'doctrine for action' formulated in the works of Karl Marx and Lenin, and while National Socialism possessed its Koran in *Mein Kampf* and its 'Summa Theologica' in Rosenberg's *Myth of the Twentieth Century*, Italian Fascism never had any such thing. The religious thought of the regime, therefore, was inevitably vague. Mussolini showed a good deal of fellow feeling for the philosopher Giovanni Gentile, whom he appointed minister of public education in 1922; but he would not admit that Hegelian idealism was the regime's sole philosophy. He even permitted one extremist of the party to declare: 'Fascism seems the necessary foe of Christianity. . . . The new Roman Empire cannot be born unless it proclaims man God and ensures the domination everywhere of the strong and the initiates. Our God is the hero of Greek myths, or Mithra, or Siva!' [1] That, however, did not prevent Mussolini himself from writing in the Italian Encyclopaedia: 'The Fascist State is not indifferent vis-à-vis the Church. It does not create for itself a peculiar "God", as did Robespierre at the height of the Convention; nor does it seek to exclude God from the souls of men, as does Bolshevism; no, it respects the God of the ascetics, the saints and the heroes, and even the God acknowledged and prayed to by the primitive and ingenuous hearts of the people.' Like everything else, the religious attitude of the Fascist regime was, and remained until the end, dictated by the sole consideration of its immediate interests.

Pius XI had watched the rise of Mussolini and his *fasces* with some degree of satisfaction. Italy, threatened with anarchy and Bolshevism, manifestly needed the restoration of order, which the democratic

[1] Evola in *Critica fascista*.

parties were apparently unable to accomplish. When the Fascists marched on Rome, the Pope had told Count Dominioni, president of Catholic Action at Milan: 'I believe it will be possible to do much with Mussolini.' And some weeks earlier Mussolini had declared: 'The Latin and imperial tradition of Rome is represented today by Catholicism. If, as Mommsen said, one cannot live in Rome without a universal idea, I think and affirm that the only universal idea existing today in Rome is that which flows from the Vatican.' A year after assuming power he was able to assert: 'We promised not to touch the Church, one of the pillars of society. Well, the Church has not been touched or impaired. Nay more: we have actually enhanced her prestige.' There was some truth in his words: the crucifix had reappeared in schools and law courts; religious instruction had been declared obligatory; the army had recovered its chaplains; much religious property had been restored; the masonic lodges had been closed; the University of the Sacred Heart at Milan had received official recognition; the magnificent Chigi library had been offered to the Vatican; and the legalization of divorce, which had been so often mooted during the past sixty years, was finally rejected.

Nevertheless that honeymoon had been a troubled period. The violence of the Blackshirts had not left Pius unmoved, particularly when directed against priests. The Fascists systematically identified Catholic organizations with those of the 'Popular Party', whose democratic spirit they detested. On several occasions the Pope protested against these 'punitive expeditions', going so far as to speak (20th December 1926) of persecution so audacious, so wicked, that it respects neither the sanctity of churches, nor the dignity of bishops, nor the priestly character. Other incidents, though less grave, had likewise earned his rebuke: the issue of a 'Catechism of the National Fascist Party'; the erection of 'altars' to that strange idol; the publication at State expense of the complete works of Gabriele d'Annunzio, which are extremely immoral and had been placed on the Index.

But above all, as the Fascist regime became more firmly established its totalitarian character became more apparent and more pronounced. In 1925, at Milan, Mussolini himself uttered some words that were destined to fame: 'Everything in the State, nothing apart from the State, nothing against the State.' Successive measures taken by the regime accentuated the pressure of the State, which quickly developed into tyranny. Independent (including Christian) syndicalism was swept away and replaced by State-controlled Fascist syndicalism. The official 'corporatism', though it used the vocabulary of Vogelsang or La Tour du Pin,[1] was nothing but a massive State system, in which the real control lay with the minister. A decree of 1927 virtually suppressed

[1] See Chapter IV, section 7.

the Catholic scout movement and replaced it with the *balilla*. The Church could not accept this all-devouring brand of State socialism. Antagonism of principles became more and more apparent. 'By refusing the State God', said Evola, 'Christianity declares itself our enemy.' In the other camp Father Bevilaqua, a well-known Oratorian, wrote in 1926: 'There is an abyss between the end proposed to itself by the Fascist State and the supernatural end assigned to man by Christianity; one might say that here we have two religions.' And Pius XI declared in the same year: 'The current notion of a State is in formal contradiction with Catholic doctrine. A State which is its own end, a citizen wholly at the disposition of the State, a State to which everything must be related and which must absorb everything—no, that is not Catholic.'

It is tempting to ask why, in those circumstances, Pius XI agreed to sign the Lateran Agreements. 'It is commonly but quite mistakenly believed', writes a great Catholic historian, 'that the Catholic Church by signing a concordat with a government shows some kind of sympathy with that government, that she assents to an agreement only because of a certain identity of principles with the other contracting party. In reality the Church, either from desire for peace or as a matter of prudence, tries to establish political contact with all governments, whatever the ideological principles of the regime, though she is aware that in most cases the articles subscribed offer her a very poor guarantee against difficulties.' [1]

In the event, Pius XI considered a solution of the Roman Question so important for the Church that he had to set aside his own view of Mussolini's principles. In the case of minor shocks he admitted that silence was best in order to avoid worse evils. But when the Fascist attacked what he considered essential to the Church, he reacted with force and violence equal to the calm and patience he had hitherto shown.

The first incidents occurred even before the treaties had been ratified. Wishing to explain to Parliament his reasons for negotiating with the Vatican, Mussolini laid strong emphasis on the Church's character as a power conducive to good order. In the familiar style of Maurras [2] he contrasted 'the petty Jewish sect born like so many others in that feverish climate, similar to that of the Essenes', with the powerful organization of the Church which had not been able to develop until Rome had re-thought the Sermon on the Mount. A fortnight later, in

[1] André Latreille, in Latreille and Siegfried, *Les Forces religieuses et la vie politique*, p. 136.

[2] On a visit to Rome at Easter, 1929, I met Giuseppe Bottai, who had been in turn minister of corporations, governor of Rome and minister of public education. This well-known Fascist personality told me: 'The Duce has followed the *Action française* affair with close attention. He has read Maurras.'

a public letter, Cardinal Gasparri described these expressions as 'heretical and worse than heretical', mistaking 'the very essence of Christianity'. Nor, it was said, did Pius much like the phrase 'a truly Italian pope' with which Mussolini referred to him, or the Duce's assurance to the applauding deputies: 'We have not resurrected the temporal power of the popes; we have buried it.'

The real conflict, however, began when the Fascists attacked Catholic Action, especially its youth groups. In the usual manner of all totalitarian States, a press campaign was launched against Catholic institutions, whose offices were sacked in various places. The Fascist newspapers declared that while the political Lateran Treaty was final, the Concordat could be revoked. Catholic journals which protested were suppressed. Was Mussolini, in adopting this attitude, merely trying to show that he was not under the thumb of the Church, as the anticlerical wing of Fascism was insinuating? No, there was more to it than that; for he himself, as well as his press, insisted on the right of the State to take charge of the education of youth. Pius XI replied to these various attacks, first by placing on the Index a book entitled *Date a Cesar* (*Render unto Caesar*) by Misseroli, one of the regime's official theorists. Next he declared that since the treaty and the Concordat formed a single entity, they would endure or disappear together. Finally, he published an important Encyclical on the education of youth, *Divini illius Magistri*, in which, having claimed 'the independence of the Church as against the terrestrial power', he formally condemned 'all monopoly of teaching and education'. And, in order to make sure that there should be no mistake as to those for whom this warning was intended, the document appeared first in Italian.

During the winter of 1930–1 the situation became more tense. The Fascist press resumed and extended its attack upon the undertakings run by Catholic Action, accusing them of being centres of opposition to the regime and directed by ex-members of the Popular Party—a charge that was not entirely false as to their general spirit, but was literally true in very few cases. Accusation led to insult, to arbitrary and vexatious measures, and finally to blows. Catholic meeting places were closed by the police, and youth groups were declared disbanded, although authorized by law. The secretary of the Fascist Party had the imprudence to state that the Pope, when signing the Concordat, knew perfectly well that he was dealing with a totalitarian State, and that Fascism was behaving quite normally in eliminating those things of which it disapproved. Pius XI answered with a public letter to Cardinal Schuster, Archbishop of Milan, declaring that he would never abandon Catholic Action and that 'a totalitarian regime which sought to control the spiritual life was an absurdity in the intellectual order and a veritable monstrosity in the practical sphere'.

The sequel was a storm of defamation and terrorism against Catholic Action. Not only in Rome, but throughout Italy, boys and girls were assaulted and beaten. Buildings owned by Catholic bodies were pillaged; so too were episcopal palaces, e.g. at Verona and Priverno; so too, again, were a number of churches, among them San Lorenzo in Damaso at Rome. Fascist squads burned copies of *Osservatore Romano* in the newspaper kiosks, while others ransacked the offices of the great Jesuit review *Civiltà cattolica*. The *bête noire* of the Fascists was Mgr (afterwards Cardinal) Pizzardo, chaplain-general of Catholic Action. But demonstrators also paraded the streets, howing 'Down with the Pope! Down with Ratti!'

Pius reacted at first with moderation. Despite the gravity of events, he was loath to break with his co-signatory of the Lateran Agreements. Several of his speeches, however, voiced his indignation and his fears. He likened the persecution which afflicted 'the fairest region of the Church' to those then raging in Bolshevik Russia and Mexico. Once again he insisted that violence done to Catholic Action or Catholic youth was violence done to the Church herself and to the Pope. The real battle had not as yet begun. But now Mussolini, in an interview with a foreign journalist, repeated his celebrated formula: 'Everything in the State, nothing apart from the State, nothing against the State.' And he ended with these words: 'The child, as soon as he is old enough to learn, belongs entirely to the State, to it alone.' This time the Pope resolved to strike hard.

At the beginning of July 1931 the world was surprised by the publication of an Encyclical on Fascism, and even more so by the circumstances of its publication. It was not from Rome, but from abroad, and especially from France, that the documents was distributed to Catholics and even to the Italian bishops. Drafted by the Pope himself, *proprio pugno* [1] and in great secrecy, it was dated 29th June but not published by *Osservatore Romano* until 5th July. Written in Italian, it began with the words *Non abbiamo bisogno*. Starting with the Fascist attack upon Catholic Action, it proceeded to answer calumnious accusations point by point, proclaimed once more the Church's right to educate her youth. The Encyclical was a frontal assault on Fascism, 'that pagan statolatry' whose doctrine it declared inadmissible, and the oath exacted by the party from its members unlawful. Without expressly condemning the regime, or even the party, Pius XI put Catholics on their guard against all that was unacceptable in the ideology of Fascism and the conduct of its adherents.

Public opinion in Italy and far beyond was highly amused at seeing the Duce, who, in the endlessly repeated phrase, was 'always right',

[1] Mgr Fontenelle testifies to having seen seventy-five pages of text in the Pope's own handwriting.

called to order by the Vatican, like a schoolboy caught out of bounds. At Rome Trilussa, a popular story-teller, was credited with epigrams worthy of the old pasquinades; while the sales of *Osservatore Romano* soared from 4,000 to 100,000 copies. The retort of the Fascist press was feeble. In the name of the party it rejected 'with indignation the assertions of a recent Encyclical' and protested against 'its lies'; to which the *Osservatore* replied by printing a number of embarrassing documents. In various places Catholic members of the party were required to take the Fascist oath a second time; but nothing more was done, and, to the general amazement, the recent wave of terrorism was not resumed. Mussolini, of course, realized the enormous harm done to his prestige by conflict with the Pope. Counsels of moderation reached him from all over the world, particularly from America where 20 million Catholics were likely to upset current economic negotiations between Rome and Washington. Nor was the Pope willing to press matters too far, because (*a*) he still felt some gratitude and even some sympathy towards Mussolini, and (*b*) at a time when Germany was falling into National Socialism it was undesirable to exasperate the Italian dictator and thus drive him into the arms of his German counterpart, with whom he was for the time being on bad terms.

Secret negotiations were therefore opened; among those who took part was Father Tacchi-Venturi, an influential Jesuit and friend of Mussolini. In August 1931 the government announced that Catholic centres which had been illegally closed would reopen forthwith; and on 2nd September the text of a compromise was published. It contained three fundamental articles. The first declared that 'conformably with its religious and supernatural aims, Catholic Action does not concern itself in any way with politics'; its various sections, under direct control of the bishops, would limit themselves strictly to works of a spiritual kind. The second was concerned with professional and syndical associations, to which members of Catholic Action were quite free to belong. Finally, Catholic youth groups would 'abstain from all athletic or sporting activity and confine themselves to recreational and educative activity for religious ends'. Pointing the lesson of the crisis, Pius XI observed in his Christmas message that it had been 'an incredible advertisement, a worldwide advertisement' for Catholic Action. The final touch was given by Mussolini himself, who visited the Pope in great state on 11th February 1932.

This agreement, after the categorical terms of *Non abbiamo bisogno*, was variously judged. The left-wing press, and even some Catholic writers, were of opinion that His Holiness had thereby subjected Italy to Fascism; and indeed outward appearances might have seemed to justify their charge, for the great majority of Italian Catholics rallied to the Duce's regime. Pius XI no doubt considered that what he had

done was simply a choice of the lesser evil; that since the all-powerful Fascist State was in a position to do the Church a great deal of harm, it was better to compromise. Moreover one must take account of a certain irony in the Italian character, which has a way of observing shades of difference in seemingly clear-cut attitudes. Besides many Catholics, when asked why they belonged to the National Fascist Party, pointed to the P.N.F. badge and answered with a smile: 'Per necessità familiale.' In any case, Pius XI's feelings had not altered. Time and again the *Osservatore Romano* printed warnings against Fascist newspaper articles or books guilty of 'pagan statolatry'. In 1934 all the works of Giovanni Gentile were placed on the Index. The Pope took every opportunity to repeat that Catholic Action was 'the apple of his eye'. He sometimes deplored, in presence of witnesses, the disappearance of his 'beloved scouts' and his inability to create in Italy a 'J.O.C.' similar to those of Belgium and France. In August 1935, without openly criticizing Mussolini's hypernationalist and militaristic policy, he expressed his disapproval by arranging a huge peace pilgrimage to Lourdes, just before the outbreak of the Ethiopian war.

When that war began in the same month, backed by public opinion which had not forgotten the disaster of Adowa (1896) and which not unreasonably considered as a grave injustice the allied refusal to give Italy colonial territories, Pius XI intervened. True, he did not employ his usual vehemence in protesting against an act of aggression which violated the rules of humanity and struck a mortal blow at the concept of international co-operation. Nevertheless on 22nd August 1935 the *Osservatore Romano* published a brief communiqué rejecting the official thesis of 'living room'; and in September, when receiving the members of a congress of Catholic hospital workers, he told them of his 'unutterable grief'. 'A war that is simply one of conquest', he said, 'is an unjust war. . . .' Nor could some untimely words about the people's joy at Badoglio's lightning success obscure the memory of that declaration.

Later, in February 1938, when Austria was directly threatened by Hitler, the Holy See used all its authority in supporting the unfortunate Chancellor Schuschnigg, successor of the heroic Döllfuss who had been assassinated four years earlier. Pius XI prophesied to the French ambassador the terrible consequences that would follow from the abstention of the great Powers, and suggested to him the immediate dispatch of 200,000 men. The nuncio to the Italian Government asked the Fascists what they proposed to do; the most influential circles were mobilized to bring pressure on Mussolini; and the *Osservatore Romano* printed some outspoken articles. Too late, however, for the Berlin-Rome 'Pact of Steel' had been signed two years before, and the

Duce, who in 1934 had prevented an invasion of Austria by the Nazis, was now in the other camp.

This reversal of international policy marked the renewal of conflict between the Church and Fascism. Hitler's influence weighed more and more heavily upon Fascism, and Mussolini, for all his unwillingness, was compelled to align his regime with that of his German ally. In particular, he found it impossible to exclude from Italy those racist doctrines which three years earlier he had declared to be 'absurd, monstrous, stupid as only a German can be',[1] and 'just what one might expect from that part of Europe where not a single man could read or write at a time when Rome already had Caesar'.[2] The Italian press began to carry articles, and Italian publishing houses to issue books, advocating racism. The Holy Office condemned the most dangerous of such works; but it seemed that the campaign was well under way and that elements hostile to the Church would seize the opportunity to resume their violence. Fresh calumnies were launched against Catholic Action, which was accused of studying the problem of racism and condemning it. Worse still, marriage laws were announced, obviously inspired by German laws and intended to safeguard 'purity of race' in Italy.

Here was something unquestionably fundamental, and Pius XI, now an old and ailing man, but vigorous as ever in the field of morals, renewed the fight. His first gesture was symbolic. When Hitler paid an official visit to Rome on 3rd May 1938, the Pope left the city, in order, as he said, not to be present at the 'apotheosis of a cross inimical to the Cross of Christ'. 'The air here makes me feel sick,' he told those who watched him leave for Castelgandolfo. And during the whole period of Hitler's presence in Italy the Pope was seen to spend long hours in prayer.

Then the *Giornale d'Italia* published a 'racist creed' in ten points, and the *Difesa della Razza* invited Italians to embrace anti-Semitism, which had never yet struck root among them. 'It is nothing but apostasy,' answered Pius; 'it is the spirit of racist doctrine, contrary to the Faith of Christ.' When the Fascist Grand Council accepted the principle of the new matrimonial laws, Pius XI wrote in person to Mussolini and King Victor Emmanuel. The latter replied at once, promising to try to 'reconcile the two points of view'; the former never replied at all. Pius XI's last Christmas message was again devoted partly to denouncing the new peril, to exalting the Christian concept of marriage and to condemning violence in any shape or form.

The worst was expected. Mussolini had taken little part in the conflict since its renewal, except to say that Italian racism would not

[1] The author heard these words from the lips of the Duce himself.

[2] Speech of 17th August 1934.

resemble its German counterpart. But surely now his indignation would lead him to undertake a persecution of the Church such as Catholic Germany had already experienced. Yet nothing of the kind happened. Aggression against Catholics was not continued. Burning of the *Osservatore Romano*, which had been revived during the past few months, now ceased. During the winter of 1938–9 there was a lull. War was approaching, and Mussolini was not anxious to embark thereon with the thorn of Catholic resistance in his side. The aged Pontiff, too, was nearing the end of his life. . . . Appeasement of the conflict would fall to his successor. . . .

5. Pius XI against National Socialist Racism

For many months Pius XI had been at open war with Hitler's National Socialism; and it was really against this that his last heroic efforts were directed, for latter-day Fascism was dragged more and more forcibly by the logic of the Rome-Berlin alliance towards adhesion to German ideology. The conflict was much more serious and more violent than that between the Vatican and the Palazzo Venezia. Leader of a people almost entirely Catholic, the Duce knew well the boundaries he might not overstep. The rulers of Germany had not the same reasons for moderation in a land where Catholicism was the faith of a minority. Besides, the German temperament was quite different from that of the Italian people, which had long since learned from two thousand years of experience to exhaust in words its reserves of violence before giving them vent in the shape of deeds.

The first half of Pius XI's pontificate coincided exactly with the troubled but finally irresistible ascent to power of 'National Socialism'. This term denoted a movement which, inaugurated in 1918 by Anton Drexel, a mechanic, as the 'Workers' National-Socialist Party' (N.S.D.A.P.), began to attract some notice with the advent of its seventh member, Adolf Hitler, an ex-corporal of the Austrian infantry who had been earning his livelihood as a house painter. At the time of Cardinal Ratti's elevation to the papacy that movement was insignificant, so much so that in 1923, when Hitler, electrified by Mussolini's march on Rome, attempted a *putsch* which proved abortive, it was thought sufficient to send the silly little man to cool his heels in a fortress for less than twelve months. But the number of National Socialists grew very quickly. Already in 1925 they formed a by no means negligible party; Hitler already dominated his companions, and the Brownshirt adventure was now closely linked with the future of that extraordinary man whose 'gaze made one shudder', whose rugged eloquence exercised a sort of magnetic spell upon the crowds,

who had a 'marvellous gift of being able to express in lapidary phrases what the German people wanted to be told', but of whom none could say (or, perhaps, will ever be able to say) whether he was a genius or a madman, a genuine statesman or a dreamer of wild dreams.

'Promising bread and glory to the Germans humiliated by defeat and embittered by poverty',[1] Hitler appeared to millions of them as a man of destiny. Since 1929 the economic crisis had worked in his favour. The collapse of industrial production and a terrifying increase of unemployment had done much to swell his ranks. His Brown Front, open to malcontents of all sorts but extremely well organized, was far more active and more effective than the communist Red Front, the democratic Iron Front or the conservative and militarist Grey Front. Although many such distinguished politicians as Léon Blum saw fit periodically to diagnose the collapse of 'Nazism', it was clear to anyone with eyes to see that Hitler and his gang were very close to sovereign power.

Their rise was observed with anxiety by Pius XI, and perhaps even more so by Cardinal Pacelli, who had been nuncio first in Munich, then in Berlin, from 1917 until 1930, when he was appointed secretary of state. The Pope and his adjutant watched helpless as the German Catholics of the *Zentrum* slid gradually down the fatal slope, following an unpopular international policy, showing themselves incapable of solving the nation's grave economic problems, and taking no advantage of the miraculous financial recovery effected by Dr Schacht. Indeed, torn between the right-wing elements, which had been seduced by nationalism, and those of the left, which tended to confine themselves to social action, the *Zentrum* had in ten years lost much of its real strength. Its leader, Chancellor Brüning, a saintly man but head of a spineless government, played time and again into Hitler's hands. In September 1930 the dissolution of Parliament opened the flood-gates to the tide of National Socialism. Supported now by the army, big business and the banks, all of whom hoped to make use of him and then discard him, Hitler was about to fasten his hold on Germany. Field-Marshal Hindenburg himself, though re-elected president of the republic in 1932 thanks to Catholic votes contributed by Brüning, dismissed the chancellor, whom the Junkers regarded as a 'Red'. On 30th January 1933 Hitler formed a government with two of his friends, but also with some liberals and Catholics. A month later he had filled all posts with his own supporters, broken the opposition of the Communists after the Reichstag fire, won a parliamentary majority with

[1] The foregoing passages in inverted commas are quoted from André François-Poncet, French ambassador to Germany. His *Doctrine d'Adolf Hitler* and his diplomatic dispatches published in *Le Livre jaune* are among the most lucid analyses of the Hitlerian phenomenon.

17 million votes for his Brown Front, and obtained in full conformity with the law plenary powers that made him dictator of Germany.

From the very beginning National Socialism had clashed with the Christian Churches. The movement's earliest publications had revealed it as fundamentally antichristian. Arthur Dinter, one of the triumvirate which had directed the party during Hitler's imprisonment, had launched his *Hundred and ninety-seven Theses for the completion of the Reformation*. Rosenberg's entirely pagan *Myth of the Twentieth Century* had been issued by the Hoheneighen-Verlag Press, which was owned by Hitler. In *Deutscher Tag* (1922) an advocate of 'The League for a German Church' had written in glowing terms of a 'neo-Germanic cult'. Hitler's first biographer, Schott, had presented him as 'a genuine foe of the papacy and the Jesuits'. And year by year the Nazi press had printed articles demanding in the name of national unity the suppression of all Christian schools.

The Church had not remained inattentive or indifferent to these attacks. In 1923 Cardinal Faulhaber of Munich, who later occupied a foremost place in the resistance to National Socialism, warned his flock against the perils to which this still obscure movement might expose them. In 1925, 1926 and 1927 several bishops and Catholic publicists spoke in similar terms. In 1920, when the N.S.D.A.P. became the second party in Germany, formal warnings appeared in several dioceses, e.g. that of Münster, whose bishop went so far as to declare that the National Socialist programme contained ideas 'which no Catholic could accept without denying his faith upon cardinal points of belief'. Mgr von Galen's conclusion resounded throughout Germany: 'Can a Catholic join Hitler's party? Can a priest admit members of that party, as such, to religious ceremonies? We answer negatively.' In February 1931, in a joint letter, the Bavarian episcopate repeated the condemnation, and actually used the word 'heresy'. And when the Nazi Gauleiter of Hesse died the honours of Catholic burial were refused. Pius XI approved all those declarations and measures on several occasions.

When Hitler became master of Germany, the Church was confronted with a legal problem. As is well known, she counsels obedience to the lawful authorities, so long as the latter do not openly violate her rights and the precepts of religion. A month after his assumption of power Hitler delivered a pacific speech before the Reichstag, which was almost entirely National Socialist: 'The national government considers the two Christian confessions as the most important factors conducing to the moral preservation of our ethnic personality. It will respect the contracts made between them and the various German countries; in no case will there be any attack upon their rights.' To this the German bishops, meeting at Fulda, replied with a friendly (perhaps

a little too friendly) declaration, in which it was stated that 'without going back upon the earlier condemnations', they believed it 'possible to think with confidence that their general ban need no longer be regarded as necessary'. In other words, Catholics were no longer forbidden to join the Nazi Party.

It was in this new and temporarily favourable climate that the Concordat [1] was negotiated, a concordat desired by the German Government and agreed to by the Pope, 'despite many grave preoccupations', in hope of 'sparing German Catholics the anxiety and tribulations which might have been expected', and to 'make clear that he refused to none the hand of Mother Church'. In this case, even more than in that of Italian Fascism, it is necessary to repeat that when the Church signs an agreement with a government, she does not thereby intend to signify special sympathy towards that government, let alone to approve its principles. On the face of it this German concordat was most favourable to the Church. Although she agreed that one article should forbid all ecclesiastics and religious to belong to a political party (meaning the *Zentrum*), she obtained in return guarantees for Christian marriage, education and Catholic undertakings. She could now, moreover, for the first time since the Reformation, move freely into the whole of Germany, particularly into strongly Protestant regions such as Saxony and Württemberg. The creation of the bishopric of Berlin was among the most notable results of this diplomatic agreement, which, from the legal point of view, would have constituted a victory for the Church—if only it had been carried out.

Neither the conciliatory words of the Führer and the bishops, nor the very general formulae of the treaty signed in July 1933 by von Papen and Cardinal Pacelli, did anything to modify the absolute doctrinal opposition between National Socialism and Christianity. That opposition became still more evident when the theories of National Socialism took the form of simple maxims intended for the whole people and taught like a catechism. Their complete exposition was to be found in Hitler's *Mein Kampf* (*My Struggle*), begun while he was in prison. This bulky tome was regarded by all National Socialists as their Bible; it was presented to newly married couples on their wedding day, and its sales in Germany were so large that Hitler was able to renounce his salary as chancellor and live on its royalties alone. Other documents helped to complete the ideological foundations of Nazism, notably Rosenberg's *Myth of the Twentieth Century* and various works by Ley, Baldur von Schirach and others.

In one respect, that of 'statolatry', the opposition between Christianity and National Socialism was the same as between Christianity and Fascism. For Hitler, as for Mussolini, every man existed 'only by

[1] See Chapter VII, section 7.

the State and for the State', with this difference, however, that according to National Socialism the totalitarian State was a mere instrument of power belonging, like a Marxist-Communist system, to the people, who express their will through the party, which in turn directs them to the State—*Die Partei befehlt dem Staat.*

But in many other respects National Socialism, more ideological and less pragmatic than Fascism, opposed the principles of Christianity in a still more flagrant manner. Steeped in the thought of Nietzsche, of which they had not read much, but which, like many Germans, they breathed with the very air of their country, the theorists of National Socialism were all initiates of that extreme form of atheistic humanism which had been taught in such striking phrases by the prophet of Zarathustra. They were particularly familiar with the notion of Superman, together with themes derived more or less from oriental philosophy and from Schopenhauer on the Cosmos, the sole living being, of which all that exists, man included, is only the formal expression. This pantheism was naturally linked with the exasperated nationalism which had given Hitler and his gang their earliest opportunities, and which, swept along by the stormy blast of the great Wagnerian myths, expressed itself in a German neo-paganism, the old Teutonic gods being resurrected and adapted by Professor Ernst Bergmann to the scientific needs of the age.

The end product of this National Socialist philosophy was racism, a doctrine originating from the ideas of Gobineau, a French novelist, and developed by Houston Stewart Chamberlain, son of a British admiral who had married Wagner's daughter, and author of *The Aryan Concept of the World.* The individual, it was held, existed not in himself but as a product and element of the race, i.e. of the ethnic group into which he has been born. It is from the blood, seat of the racial characteristics, that all a man's intellectual and moral qualities derive. The primary source and supreme rule of all social organization and of all juridical order is the racial instinct. The only unforgivable sin is to betray, to bastardize, the race. 'The State must therefore take steps,' said Hitler, 'in the shape of law and all the resources of modern medicine,' to protect the race. The races of mankind are not all equal, the lowest of them being further from the highest than from the highest brute species. Superior to all others is the Aryan race, whose physical type is the tall, dolichocephalic, blue-eyed blond, the Wagnerian hero Parsifal. 'The Aryan alone has created the most advanced human civilization.' Wherever the Aryans have allowed themselves to interbreed, 'they have lost their creative faculty'. This race, which the Nazis declared to be specifically German—a rather surprising fact when one considers Hitler himself and such of his companions as Goebbels!—must dominate the world in right of its pre-eminence. 'The solution

of all problems lies in the vocation of a supreme race, of a masterly people disposing of the resources and potentialities of the entire world.'

Such opinions were voiced in all Nazi publications, and Pius XI had only to read them in order to appreciate how antagonistic they were to Christian doctrine. National Socialist thought, it is true, had some good features—a sense of community, an appeal to effort, courage and sacrifice; yet even these had been perverted by racist ideology. Hostile to individualism, Nazism tended to destroy the human person, sacrificing it to the Moloch of race as it had been sacrificed elsewhere to the Moloch of the State or of Society. More clearly still, racism, with its contempt of inferior races, was the very negation of the great precept of charity, upon which the Christian religion is founded. Hate instead of charity was proposed to millions of men; for Hitler and his doctrinaires were careful to name the enemies who would have to be destroyed—all those who 'sullied their race', who 'propagate dissolvent ideas', both capitalists and intellectuals, communists and internationalists. One category in particular was doomed to annihilation—the Jews, because they favoured the critical spirit, unrestricted freedom, capitalism and internationalism. To them Hitler and Rosenberg had devoted many vehement pages. By marrying German women the Jews were irretrievably defiling the Aryan race. The Church, of course, could not tolerate such theories, and in 1928 a decree of the Holy Office reminded Catholics that the Church 'condemns in the most unqualified manner hatred of God's chosen people, that hatred which is known as anti-Semitism'.

No one therefore could have any doubt as to the abiding opposition between the religion of the Cross of Christ and that of racism with its crooked cross—the swastika. The Nazi doctrinaires certainly entertained no such doubt. Rosenberg fumed against Christianity, and especially against Catholicism, which he described as 'judaized and asianized'. Hitler himself declared: 'A German Church is a mockery; one is Christian or German, not both together.' Rosenberg, again, denounced St Boniface, the apostle of Germany, as guilty of crime against the Aryan race. And one of the songs of the *Hitlerjugend* contained these words: 'The autumn wind scours the stubble; the age of the Cross is past. What has the son of a German mother in common with Pope and priests?'

In the circumstances it was evident that the National Socialists would regard the Concordat as a mere scrap of paper. No sooner had Von Papen congratulated himself upon the agreement, proclaiming the Pope 'ready to uphold National Socialism as part of his struggle with Bolshevism', than numerous incidents occurred, similar to those which had preceded the Concordat and in flagrant violation of its terms. The Association of German Youth was dissolved; members of a Catholic

Union congress were manhandled by Nazi storm-troopers; the *Katholikentag*, at which Von Papen himself had intended to deliver an address on the Concordat, could not take place. Meanwhile the first concentration camp for Jews, Communists and Catholics was opened at Dachau; the faithful throughout Germany were subjected to insult and injury; members of Catholic Action were assaulted; the headquarters of Catholic societies were invaded by the Brownshirts without interference from the police. This was the beginning of a veritable persecution which lasted until the fall of the regime.

Catholic schools were closed, or transformed into 'common schools'. Catholic newspapers were either suppressed or turned into Nazi journals by Catholics who supported the regime. 'Brown sisters' replaced nuns in the hospitals. At the same time the whole apparatus of the National Socialist State was devoted to propaganda in Christian circles on behalf of the neo-pagan movement.

Violence followed, and was carried even to the point of bloodshed. In the spring of 1934 Hitler found himself at grips with opposition from two quarters: (1) the advanced elements of his own party, who thought him too slow in accomplishing the true revolution, and (2) the reactionary elements, of whom Von Papen was spokesman. But the dictator confronted both adversaries. On the night of 30th June, acting in person, he struck down Roehm, head of the storm-troopers, while seventy-seven Nazi military leaders were put against the wall. Von Papen's collaborators were liquidated at the same time. Hitler also took this opportunity to vent an old grudge against General von Schleicher, the Nazi theorist Gregor Strasser and the Catholic leaders of whose feelings he was well aware. Erich Klausener, president of Catholic Action at Berlin, was shot. Adalbert Probst, president of the Sporting Association of German Catholics, was summoned to Berlin under some pretext, and a few days later his wife received his ashes by parcel post. Friedrich Beck, a distinguished member of Munich University, was 'accidentally' killed, and Fritz Gerlich, editor of the largest Catholic newspaper, was found dead in prison.

This was the signal for a grand assault. More than five hundred priests and religious were arrested, several of whom died in gaol. Much damage was done to ecclesiastical buildings, and more than one member of the hierarchy suffered violence. The bishops' palaces at Würzburg, Rottenburg and Mainz were sacked. At Paderborn the bishop's car was overturned and himself covered with spittle. Priests were haled before the courts under pretext of having broken the regulations on exchange control; others were charged with immorality. Year by year, almost month by month, Hitler's regime became more heavy, more oppressive, more antichristian. In 1935, reviving and developing a 'eugenic' law first published in 1933, a series of laws introduced

sterilization of the physically weak and persons of unsound mind. Anti-Semitic measures increased, among the most spectacular and most odious of which was the obligation upon Jews to wear a yellow star. A decree of 1936 compelled girls as well as boys to belong to the *Hitlerjugend*.

The Catholic Church has the honour of having stood, almost alone for several years, in the front rank of the battle against tyranny. While Protestant resistance to Hitlerism was the work of a few outstanding individuals such as Pastor Niemöller, the members of the Catholic hierarchy withstood the threat, if not unanimously, at least in very large numbers. Led by Cardinal Faulhaber of Munich and Bishops von Preysing, von Galen and Frings,[1] the episcopate launched a bold counter-offensive. Mgr von Galen, for example, answered the official thesis of unconditional obedience to the State as follows: 'An obedience which imprisons the soul, which violates conscience, the inmost sanctuary of freedom, is slavery—the most degrading form of slavery. It is worse than murder, for it crushes the very person of man; it attempts to destroy his resemblance to God.' From Fulda the government received continual and vehement protests against the violations of the Concordat. In January 1937 all the German bishops signed a joint letter declaring that they were 'ready to give the State what belonged to it and to support the Führer in his struggle', but that they demanded respect for the rights of the Church. Resistance came also from the great religious orders, Jesuit, Dominican and Benedictine, many of whose members were arrested or driven into exile.

Pius XI naturally supported this heroic stand with all the means at his disposal. It has been estimated that between 25th September 1933 and 26th June 1936 alone the Holy See sent to the government of the Reich more than fifty notes in one form or another, all protesting against violations of the Concordat. Hardly a day passed without the *Osservatore Romano* and the Vatican Radio denouncing the doctrines of Nazism and its violence, with the result that the Roman newspaper was seized by the Gestapo and listening to the broadcasts was prohibited. The principal National Socialist works, notably those of Rosenberg and Bergmann, were condemned by the Holy Office. Pius XI played a personal part in the struggle. He took every opportunity—a ceremony of canonization, a message to Cardinal Schulte of Cologne, general audiences granted to German pilgrims—to repeat his protests with untiring regularity. 'They want to dechristianize Germany', he would say, 'and lead her back to barbarian paganism.' In the spring of 1936, when opening the World Exhibition of the Catholic Press, he went still further, likening National Socialism to

[1] All three were friends of Cardinal Pacelli, who raised them to the purple after his accession to the Apostolic throne as Pius XII.

Bolshevism and describing them as 'enemies of all truth and of all justice'. In his Christmas address that year he repeated the same theme: 'The self-styled champions of civilization against Bolshevism use the very means employed by their adversaries.'

This firm attitude caused a worldwide sensation. Catholic resistance to Nazism was the first witness of the free world against the Brown dictator. Echoing the Pope's words, Cardinal Mundelein, Archbishop of Chicago, spoke freely of Nazi 'persecution', 'scandalous violation of justice', and expressed his astonishment that 'a whole nation should be willing to bow down before a handful of hooligans'. A joint letter of the American episcopate denounced Hitlerian paganism as 'an undertaking directed against the honour of the Church'. The German ambassador protested officially but in vain to Cardinal Pacelli against this philippic; His Eminence replied by taking from his desk an up-to-date record of Nazi violence. The event no doubt influenced the attitude adopted by President Roosevelt, who declared soon afterwards that it would be a good thing to 'quarantine the regime of terror and unlawfulness to which the dictators wish to subject the world'.

But Pius XI was determined to do more. After summoning the German cardinals to Rome for consultation he decided to promulgate a formal condemnation of National Socialism. He prepared it secretly and in person, as he had done in the case of the Encyclical *Non abbiamo bisogno* on Fascism. The manner in which he published it was lacking neither in irony nor in political adroitness. He had at the same time prepared another great Encyclical, *Divini Redemptoris*, dealing with Communism, in order to show that the Church was equally hostile to both forms of totalitarianism. This anti-Marxist document he published on 19th March 1937, so that the German press had time for brief rejoicing. At last the Pope had understood! He had rallied to the German fight against Bolshevism! But four days later, on Palm Sunday, 21st March, the parish priests of Germany read from their pulpits the text of *Mit brennender Sorge*, which secret messengers had delivered in roneotype, defying Himmler and the entire Gestapo.

The long papal document, written in great detail to avoid any tactical evasion, listed all the doctrinal errors of National Socialism. It recalled that the Church has never needed lessons in heroism from anyone, and that she was resolved not to be intimidated. One passage referred to the 'national God', a caricature of the true God 'before whom all nations are, as the psalmist says, drops of water hanging from a pail'—a prophetic warning of the doom awaiting Germany. It ended with an epitome of the Church's doctrine in face of collective oppression: 'Man, as a person, has inalienable rights which he holds from God.' And in order to make his thought still more clear, Pius XI published, on 13th April 1938, a regular *Syllabus* of National Socialist

errors, summarizing in eight points 'the pernicious doctrines masquerading under the name of science, which have no other aim than to pervert men's minds and deprive them of true religion'.

A new wave of violence followed against the Church, the hierarchy and religious edifices. Cardinal Faulhaber was publicly insulted. The campaign of defamation against priests and monks was intensified: fresh trials for immorality were publicized by the Nazi press. Hundreds of the faithful were sent to concentration camps. Many of the remaining Catholic offices were requisitioned; thus the great *Volksverein* building at München-Gladbach became the headquarters of a Hitlerian organization. The Bishop of Rottenburg saw his palace ransacked for the second time, while the Archbishop of Fribourg's private chapel was invaded and defiled. The Gestapo seized the banners of Catholic associations, depicting Christ or the Blessed Virgin. While Hitler's press gave vent to insult and calumny, *Das Schwarze Korps* published a caricature showing Pius XI between two naked girls, a white and a Negress, with the caption 'Catholic Race'. And Rosenberg, in Hitler's presence, answered the Encyclical and *Syllabus* with a speech of unsurpassable violence.

The aged Pontiff, however, was not to be silenced. During the twenty-three months that elapsed between the publication of *Mit brennender Sorge* and his death, twenty-three allocutions repeated the same warnings and the same condemnations; and his anguish increased as he watched the infiltration into Italy of the National Socialist heresy and even of racism. In 1938 three great speeches furnished him with an opportunity to speak still more loudly and extend the scope of the dispute, reminding his hearers that the Church of Christ is open to all men without exception, without distinction of race, and that there is 'only one, universal Catholic race'. It was in this year also that he spoke some words which echoed round the world and are now famous: 'It is not possible for Christians to embrace anti-Semitism: *spiritually we are Semites.*' His departure from Rome on the day of Hitler's official visit was a form of protest which the whole world could understand; his last Christmas allocution, delivered a few weeks before his death, voiced the same indignation, likening Hitler to the Emperor Nero.[1]

[1] One other episode illustrates Pius XI's determination not to give ground before the Nazi tyranny. Following the *Anschluss* and the occupation of Vienna by Hitler's troops (19th March 1938) Cardinal Innitzer agreed to an understanding with the conqueror, and the Austrian episcopate published a manifesto of adherence to the new regime. Pius immediately had the cardinal summoned to Rome, where he was received by Cardinal Pacelli, secretary of state, with overwhelming anger. Innitzer realized his mistake and, returning to Vienna, adopted the attitude commanded by the Holy See. The result was a 'spontaneous' demonstration of 200,000 people: his palace was attacked, pillaged and partly burned, while his secretary was thrown from a window and broke both legs. 'Now at last the purple showed in its true colour,' wrote Nazareno Padellaro, who gives an account of the whole episode in his *Pio XII*.

6. The 'Red Triangle': I. Soviet Russia

Grievous as were his clashes with Fascism and National Socialism, Pius XI knew well that 'the first, most serious and most widespread peril' was still the threat of Communist totalitarianism. It is plain to anyone who understands Marxism that conflict between it and the Church was inevitable. Long before the theories of *Das Kapital* had been read in the West, the popes had condemned Communism in a form that was not yet Marxist: Pius IX, for example, in 1846, ignorant that two years earlier Marx had written his celebrated phrase 'religion, opium of the people'. Thirty-two years later, in 1878, Leo XIII had condemned Communism as 'this fatal pest which attacks the marrow of human society and may destroy it'; yet he too seems to have had no precise knowledge of dialectical materialism and its consequences. After 1917 the situation changed. Marxism had in fact eliminated all other forms of Socialism, Collectivism and Communism, and had taken shape in a militant regime whose totalitarian nature was becoming more pronounced year by year. A formal condemnation of the Marxist heresy, therefore, had seemed to be due since the triumph of Communism in Holy Russia and the manifest danger to the world from its propaganda. Such condemnation, however, was delayed until the end of Pius XI's pontificate, after a number of tragic events in the U.S.S.R., Mexico and Spain, three countries which the Pope himself described as constituting a 'Red Triangle of terror and blood'.

On his accession to the See of Peter, Pius XI found a situation which, though at first glance peculiar, was nevertheless explained by the charitable vocation of the Church and by Benedict XV's anxiety to ensure her presence throughout the new Europe. Without recognizing the Communist regime *de jure*, the Vatican had established relations with the Moscow government with a view to offering help in the struggle against a dreadful famine raging at that time; and Benedict had decided to send a Mission of twelve priests for the purpose of organizing relief. Achille Ratti himself, moreover, was already interested in Russia: during his residence in Poland one of his tasks had been to assist Catholics living in Soviet territory; and in the course of his duties he made contacts which enabled him in 1919 to secure the release of Mgr Edward von der Ropp, Catholic Archbishop of Mohilev, who had been sentenced to death by the Bolsheviks. As Sovereign Pontiff he continued the generous undertaking of his predecessor. An agreement was reached whereby members of the Mission would refrain from any display of Christian faith or apostolic work, and would celebrate Mass only behind closed doors. Within twenty-three months of its arrival in Russia at the end of September 1922, the

Mission established 10 provision depots, 500 public kitchens, 500 centres for child relief, and eventually supplied food for 158,000 starving people daily. The persecution of Russian Catholics which began about this time did not prevent continuance of the Mission, which remained until the Soviet authorities demanded its withdrawal. 'They prefer', said the Pope, 'to doom thousands of innocent people to death rather than see them fed by Christian charity.'

He would certainly have liked to do more. Faithful to his policy of relations with all States, determined 'to refuse the Church's hand to no one', and even, as we have seen, resolved to treat 'with the Devil in person' if the interests of God so required, he envisaged an agreement with the Soviets. Such an agreement appeared all the more desirable in view of the fact that Orthodoxy had ceased to be the religion of the State and it therefore seemed *a priori* possible that Catholicism might now have a chance. In April 1922 an international conference was held at Geneva for the purpose of reorganizing the world's economy and terminating the diplomatic isolation of Germany and Russia, both of which were represented. Pius XI backed the efforts of the conference with a public letter, in which he declared among other things that 'the best guarantee of tranquillity is not a forest of bayonets, but mutual conference and friendship'. In another message he spoke of Russia with great benevolence, not overlooking, however, the anti-religious persecution in progress there. Contact was made between the secretariat of state and the Russian delegation. The Holy See offered to buy the icons and other religious objects confiscated by the Soviets, the money to be spent on the purchase of food. According to one story some of the Roman negotiators went a good deal further—a little too far in the Pope's opinion. At all events, nothing was achieved. The only tangible result was the Pope's intervention, by agreement with Moscow, on behalf of the Patriarch Tykhon, who had been arrested but whose trial did not take place.[1] But these negotiations at the diplomatic level, like the charitable work of the Mission, did not signify willingness on the part of Pius XI to show sympathy or indulgence toward the Communist regime. That much he made quite clear at a consistory in December 1924.

The Bolsheviks, in fact, had started to carry out the anti-religious articles of their programme as soon as they were firmly in power. Without waiting for the final establishment of Marxist society to eliminate religion, they had taken legislative steps to ruin it as an institution and to enfeeble it in the realm of conscience. Separation of Church and State had been proclaimed in January 1918, followed by

[1] A year later Tykhon made a declaration of total submission to the Soviet regime and was authorized to resume his patriarchal functions, though of course under strict surveillance.

many decrees of every kind: abolition of the post of religious teacher, subjection of all sermons to censorship, confiscation and sale of sacred vessels and icons, ban on religious youth groups. At the same time an ideological campaign had been started, to spread the principles of atheism and to breach the walls of religion by every possible means. Those measures and that propaganda had provoked resistance, but in 1918 the Soviets had quickly unleashed a persecution which affected the whole Orthodox Church.[1]

The Catholic Church naturally found herself involved in the operation, though she counted for very little in Soviet Russia. Whereas the Czarist empire had included 13 million Catholics, there remained only 1,600,000 after the separation of Poland, Lithuania and Latvia. They were distributed in nine districts (of which the archdiocese of Mohilev was by far the most important) and an exarchate for Catholics of the Byzantine rite. The legal situation of Catholicism, moreover, was peculiar—recognized in fact but ignored in law. Catholicism obviously constituted no danger to the Soviet regime, and yet it fell victim to the same persecution as did Orthodoxy, a persecution not entirely systematic and more or less sporadic, but ultimately most harmful to the little flock.

Hostile measures began in 1923 when Mgr Cieplak, apostolic administrator of Mohilev, and his vicar-general Mgr Budkiewiecz, together with thirteen priests and a layman, were arrested on a charge of having 'fostered the counter-revolution by pernicious usages'. They showed admirable courage, declaring that 'the idea of counter-revolution had never entered their heads', but that 'if they were called upon to betray their faith, nothing would make them yield'. The trial ended as had been foreseen. Mgr Budkiewiecz was executed on Good Friday, 1923, in appalling circumstances: tortured until he could no longer stand, one ear torn off, stripped to his shirt and mercilessly beaten—the mere remnant of a man. Mgr Cieplak, however, though likewise sentenced to death, was reprieved through 'the intervention of the Pope and several foreign governments'. Shortly afterwards Mgr Feodorof, exarch of the Byzantine Catholics, was condemned to life imprisonment. This was the signal for a series of attacks against the hierarchy, clergy and laity, many of whom were sent to the icy prisons of Solowki on the Black Sea, where a concentration camp was specially assigned for Christians; others died in prison, some of them reduced to madness by the torments they had endured.

Pius XI, however, did not despair of the future of Catholicism in Russia. To make good the disappearance of the hierarchy, he sent Mgr d'Herbigny, S.J., to confer episcopal consecration on a certain number of priests. At the same time he reorganized the Russian Church, in

[1] It will be studied in the next volume of this series.

order to adapt it to present-day conditions. Dioceses were redrawn and aspostolic administrators were appointed. As things turned out the majority were new victims of persecution—arrested only to be released and arrested once again. In 1932 there were no more than 300 priests in Soviet Russia, as against 963 in 1921; and of those 300 one-third were in prison. Even when the paroxysm of violence had died down, when the constitution of 1936 had—in principle!—allowed freedom of worship, and when the approach of war had decided the regime to avoid making martyrs, incidents continued to occur. In 1937, for example, a storm of persecution swept over Russia, and Mgr Frizon, apostolic administrator of Odessa, was shot.

Pius XI did not remain silent in presence of such events. Words were his only weapons; but he used them time and again to denounce the violence to which Christians of all confessions were subject, naming those responsible and proclaiming the shameful iniquities of Moscow. The most solemn manifestation of protest against the Russian persecution was a ceremony of expiation at which the Pope himself presided on 19th March 1930. In the basilica of St Peter, which was filled to overflowing by a crowd that included many Russian refugees, a special liturgy mingled the Slavonic and the Latin chant, invoked in the litanies the great saints of Holy Russia, and ended with the *De profundis* in memory of all the victims of Communism. This demonstration provoked in Moscow an outburst of fury against the Pope. *Pravda* showed him ringing a bell in the shape of a German helmet adorned with the swastika, while a pamphlet was distributed to millions of people assuring them that the Holy See was controlled by 'Georgian coiners, members of all the European general staffs, Washington senators, Swedish dukes, university professors, prostitutes and killer-police, all united in preaching the crusade of so-called civilization'.

But Pius XI did not confine himself to protesting against Communist violence and asking prayers for Russia. He took every opportunity to oppose the Soviet teaching with positive criticism, e.g. in the Encyclical *Quadragesimo anno* (1931). Several of his Christmas messages too, and speeches such as that to the International Catholic Press Congress in 1936, repeated and developed the criticism of 'that denial of all the rights of man and God'. They heralded the solemn condemnation of Communism in 1938.[1]

7. The 'Red Triangle': II. Mexico

On the other side of the world, in Mexico, the Church suffered an ordeal similar to that of Christianity in Russia. The Land of the

[1] See section 9 of the present chapter.

Plumed Serpent indeed had enjoyed few respites from religious persecution since its separation from Spain in 1821. That persecution had turned to violence after the coming to power in 1857 of the Indians Comonfort and Benito Juarez, and again after the collapse of Maximilian's empire in 1867. The regime of Porfirio Diaz had given the Church a breathing space; but the advent of the dictator Carranza, with underhand support from President Wilson, began a fresh era of persecution. A very large number of priests and religious were expelled, while others were tortured to death. Bishops were hounded like game through the wastes of cactus land. One priest was nailed up in a coffin and buried alive. Profanation was frequent, consecrated hosts being fed to dogs and horses, crucifixes used for target practice. Hundreds of nuns were raped. The Church had to lead a clandestine life. 'We are paying for the faults of our fathers,' said the Archbishop of Guadalajaea to Benedict XV in 1915. 'For the cruelty of the Conquistadors?' asked the Pope. 'Not so much that', replied the archbishop, 'as the mistake of having barred the natives from the priesthood.'

So far this antichristian outburst of revolutionary forces had retained a more or less traditional character; it was in fact the heritage of French Jacobinism. But after the triumph of Marxist Communism in 1917 the style of the persecution gradually altered as the rulers of Mexico adopted the methods employed by Moscow. Steps were taken first to drive out foreign priests, then to suppress the religious orders and forbid the taking of vows, then to reduce the national clergy to ridiculously small numbers. Catholic resistance was organized in the shape of refusal to buy goods, withdrawal of bank deposits and the systematic paralysis of social life. At the beginning of 1920 the ousting of Carranza by Obregon, a pure-bred Indian, aggravated the crisis: episcopal palaces and even the shrine of Our Lady of Guadalupe were blown up. When Catholics retorted by erecting a colossal statue of Christ on a mountain, Obregon revenged himself by expelling the nuncio.

All these, however, were only premonitory signs of a much more thoroughgoing persecution launched in 1924 by the new president, Calles, a half-caste ex-schoolmaster. For years on end everything possible was done to eradicate Catholicism from Mexico: arrest, expulsion and execution of priests and distinguished laymen; dismissal of religious of both sexes from hospitals—and even from lunatic asylums, the inmates of which were driven on to the streets. In the schools courses on atheism were provided, as well as lessons in sex; these latter included 'practical work' in the shape of visits by the pupils to maternity wards. The most curious part of this anti-religious campaign was the institution in 1925, by an apostate priest named Perez, of a 'National Church' separated from Rome and allied with the

secular regime. This 'Church' pretended to adapt the liturgy to the Mexican character by celebrating Mass with maize wafers, fermented agave juice and prayers translated into Indian dialect. Perez, however, found only two priests and a few hundred layfolk to join him. Police intervention was necessary before their ceremonies could take place; and even so they usually ended in attack by loyal Catholics armed with cudgels.

This persecution had tragic results for the Church in Mexico. Bishops and priests who were not thrown into prison, to die there of 'cardiac trouble', were expelled. Their mere presence in the country was a capital crime.[1] Hundreds of priests and religious defied the threat of death, and, disguised as workmen, as hawkers and even as policemen, went about the country saying Mass in barns or stables. Most famous of these clandestine priests was the Jesuit Miguel Pro, who was ordained in Belgium and returned to Mexico a few days after the edict banishing all priests. Month after month, repeatedly altering his disguise, he hoodwinked the police, managing even to celebrate Mass in houses watched by 'coppers'[2] and minister to prisoners awaiting execution. Arrested after more than a year, he in turn was led to the *patio de la muerte* and was shot together with his brother. He was allowed to die unbound, arms extended crosswise, holding a crucifix in one hand and a rosary in the other. His last words were: 'Long live Christ the King!' When Calles resigned, his victims were said to number 5,300.

Pius XI raised an indignant voice against those acts of violence. 'In Mexico', he said in 1926, 'anything called God, anything resembling public worship, is proscribed and trampled underfoot.' He spoke on the same note in his Encyclical *Iniques afflictusque*, where he drew a remarkable picture of all the Mexican Church had suffered. A lull appeared to set in, following the interdict laid on the whole country by the episcopate; complete suspension of all religious ceremonies caused so much unrest that the government feared mass insurrection. Pius XI took this opportunity to negotiate a *modus vivendi*—another 'pact with the devil'. But the persecution revived in a more subtle and insidious form. The Constitution authorized each state of the Mexican federation to fix the number of priests who might exercise their functions within its boundaries. But the result was quite ridiculous: 293 priests were 'recognized' for a total population of 17 millions; in the most favoured states there was one priest for 100,000 inhabitants. This manœuvre was denounced by the Encyclical *Acerbo nimis* (1932).

Pius XI, however, did not want rupture. He believed that Mexico was so old a Catholic country that religion could never be completely

[1] Cf. Graham Greene, *The Power and the Glory*.
[2] Fr. *argousins*.—TRANSLATOR.

uprooted from its soil. Resistance stiffened, particularly among the youth. In 1934, for example, the girls of a boarding-school which the authorities wished to close defended their house with such vigour that the police were obliged to use tear gas. Clandestine schools were opened almost everywhere. More important still were the efforts of the Catholic workers' movement, which won places in the syndicates, frequently ousting Communists and even arranging for Mass to be said in factories. The pilgrimages to Our Lady of Guadalupe proved, if proof were needed, that the Catholic faith was not dead. On the eve of the Second World War a change was noticeable: new men, less tainted with Marxism, were coming to power, and the religious laws were less rigidly enforced. An apostolic delegate was able to set out for Mexico, and the papal letter *Nos es muy* prepared the ground for reorganization of the Mexican Church. It was now plain that Christians could withstand Communism, if they had the resolution and the courage.

8. The 'Red Triangle': III. The War in Spain

It was perhaps the third side of the 'red triangle' which revealed most clearly the bloody nature of the struggle waged against the Church by Marxism and its allies. After the collapse of General Berengner's dictatorship (14th April 1931) and the departure of King Alfonso XIII into exile,[1] a new page of Spanish history seemed to open, with no suggestion of the tragedy that was to follow. The revolution had been effected quite peacefully, and the outlook was so optimistic that the new republic was nicknamed *Niña bonita*—'pretty girl'.

That charming title was not long deserved. But Catholics meanwhile gave the new regime a hearty welcome; some of them even appeared to forget rather quickly the historical role of the Spanish monarchy in defence of the faith. There were, too, some distinguished Catholics, e.g. Alcala Zamora, among the new rulers. *Te Deum* was sung in many places to celebrate the victory of the Republic; bishops and Catholic Action groups saluted the regime, which moreover began by showing marked respect for the Church. The nuncio, Mgr Tedeschini, had cordial conversations with representatives of the government.

Disenchantment followed very soon. All sorts of tendencies mingled or opposed one another in the republican ranks. They ranged from conservatives to avowed partisans of a communist regime under the leadership of Largo Caballero, 'the Spanish Lenin'. Many of these

[1] See Chapter VII, section 6.

latter were anticlerical; they found no difficulty in exploiting the age-old feeling of certain popular elements against the Church and the clergy, who were now accused of being allies of the monarchy, affronting with their wealth the misery of the lower classes, and obstructing social progress. The republic was not a year old when mobs began to attack convents and churches, pillaging and burning, without the slightest opposition from the government. Madrid, Murcia, Malaga, Granada, Barcelona, Seville—in all four corners of Spain the anti-religious fire blazed up with a simultaneity that cannot have been accidental: fifty-five churches or convents were burned in three days! Meanwhile, in the Cortés, Manuel Azana, president of the council, spoke these absurd but terrible words: 'Spain has ceased to be Christian.' In vain the liberal Catholics tried to stem the anticlerical flood; the atheist left carried all before it and the new constitution sanctioned not only the separation of Church and State, but also a regular process of dechristianization which caused the Catholic republicans to resign from the government. Religious orders were barred from 'trade, industry and teaching'; the crucifix was removed from schools; the Society of Jesus was suppressed and its property confiscated; divorce was introduced, and henceforth only civil marriage was to be recognized by the law. Against those measures Pius XI protested on 3rd June 1933 in the Encyclical *Dilectissima nobis*. That Catholic Spain should intend to get rid of God was surely the scandal of scandals.

The left had miscalculated their blow. They must have little understood the Spanish people if they thought it would meekly accept this semi-apostasy. Among Catholics there was a renewal of fervour which benefited Catholic Action; and all those hostile to Communism, which was making alarming progress, rallied to the defence of religion. Thus the election in December 1933 returned to power a right-wing majority, the basic elements of which were Popular Catholic Action, founded by Professor Gil Robles of Salamanca, and Calvo Sotelo's National Action. The crisis might perhaps have been ended at this juncture if solutions inspired by Catholicism had been given effect. Unfortunately nothing of the kind was done. The conservatives paralysed Robles's plan of reform, and the Church obtained only minor compensation. In the summer of 1934 a bloody insurrection broke out in the Asturias—at Oviedo priests and religious were butchered by the 'workers' militia—and it was clear that Spain was entering upon an ordeal worse than any she had yet experienced.

The left had pulled itself together, and with a view to the 1936 elections all left-wing parties combined to form a *Frente popular*, which was quickly dominated by the contradictory forces of Communism and anarchy. Elements hostile to those ideologies, including the old monarchist groups and Robles's republican party, rallied to the

Falange, which had been founded three years earlier by José Antonio, son of Primo de Rivera. Spain was now split in two, soon to become the scene of battle between two mutually hostile concepts of totalitarianism. And the Church, which had never sought this division in any way, found herself exposed by a tragic inevitability to the worst repercussions of the conflict.

The victory of the *Frente popular* was the signal for an outburst of anticlericalism that beggars imagination. Not only were legal steps taken immediately to expel the religious congregations, close the Catholic schools and forbid public worship, but monstrous cruelty too was given free rein. One hundred and sixty churches and convents were destroyed by fire; [1] priests and religious were hunted through the streets like wild beasts; at Madrid five nuns were lynched. Largo Caballero announced 'the near approach of total victory for the red flag'. Demonstrators, parading in red shirts and with red flags flying, alternated their howls of 'Viva Russia! Viva Thälmann!' [2] with vociferations against the priests. During the first five weeks 269 persons were killed and 1,287 wounded, all of them Catholics. 'We are solving the religious problem completely', declared the Catalan leader Andreu Mini, 'by getting rid of the lot—priests, churches, worship.' And when the monarchist deputy Calvo Sotelo protested in the Cortés against the impunity allowed to incendiaries and murderers, the communist Dolores Ibarruri, called 'la Pasionaria', shouted at him: 'This will be your last speech!'

The murder of Sotelo on the following night, 14th July 1936, precipitated civil war. General Franco, leaving Tetuan with Spanish-Moroccan troops, landed in Andalusia, and most of the army joined his movement. For thirty months Spain endured the horrors of war, divided both territorially and spiritually. Franco, as *caudillo* of the Falange, sought to rally the whole of faithful Spain; but in order to carry on the struggle he was obliged to accept military aid from Fascist Italy and Nazi Germany, both of them antichristian. Meanwhile the republican forces, which included many good men who desired only the social renovation of their country, were controlled by people's commissars directed by the Soviet ambassador, or by anarchists with neither faith nor law.

Unspeakable atrocities were committed during that appalling conflict.[3] In the provinces controlled by republican troops Catholics were the target of a persecution the cruelty and vileness of which equalled, and sometimes surpassed, the worst episodes of the Terror in

[1] The newspaper *El liberal* claimed that the nuns themselves had applied the torch!

[2] Communist hero of the anti-Hitler resistance.

[3] The most complete account in Spanish is *Historia de la persecusion religiosa en España*, Madrid, 1961. In French, see the collection of documents entitled *L'Espagne sanglante*, Paris, 1937; also Francisque Gay, *Dans les flammes et dans le sang*, Paris, 1936.

France: arson and pillage of religious buildings, with the loss of many priceless works of art; massacre of priests, monks and nuns. But even that woeful demonstration of anticlericalism was as nothing in comparison with what happened in various parts of Spain: priests hanging from butchers' hooks, corpses of nuns disinterred and subjected to every kind of profanation. The more moderate statistics give a figure of 7,534 priests and religious killed. But others suggest 16,750, including twelve bishops.

Such figures, and the mere mention of such horrors, suffice to explain why Pius XI adopted an attitude for which he was sometimes blamed. He was perfectly aware that atrocities were being committed on Franco's side also, notably in Basque territory, where many of the clergy were punished with frightful severity for their autonomist views as well as for their alliance with the republicans, and where the 'holy city' of Guernica was razed to the ground by aerial bombardment. He knew likewise the danger to which the national movement was exposed by its links with the Axis powers. Moreover in several parts of the Christian world voices were raised, notably that of the great novelist Bernanos in France, reproaching Franco and his allies for the use of means so manifestly opposed to Christian principles. But if it were necessary to choose, the Pope's choice was a foregone conclusion. In the one camp churches were burned and priests murdered. In the other, not only were Catholics respected, but the Caudillo even declared that 'Spain shall be an empire turned towards God', and his ministers took oath upon the Gospel. As early as September 1936, receiving a group of Spanish refugees, Pius XI denounced 'the satanic enterprise' which had lit the fire of hatred, and blessed those who were defending 'the rights and honour of God against a wild explosion of forces so savage and so cruel as to be wellnigh incredible'. In August 1928 diplomatic relations were renewed between the Vatican and Franco's Spain. While exhorting the victors to moderation and justice, the Pope expressed a wish to see the re-establishment in Catholic Spain of a regime whose foundations would be cemented by Catholicism. It was his influence too that prevented the Spanish Government from linking its destiny with that of the German and Italian dictatorships—a step which, as is well known, General Franco firmly refused to take during the Second World War—and which dissuaded the Spanish Church from tying itself to the regime. Herein lay the real problem of the future. Restored as a State institution, and finding herself entrusted with the keys of culture and morality, would the Church be able to resist the lure of power? Would she be able to ensure that her social teaching was not forgotten by those who would lead the country towards its new destinies? The attitude of certain members of the hierarchy, notably Cardinal Segura, and that of

Catholic Action later proved that the lessons of Pius XI would not be ignored.

9. The Doctrinal Condemnation of Communism: 'Divini Redemptoris'

Events in Russia, Mexico and Spain bore fruit identical with that of Fascist vexations in Italy and of Hitler's persecution in Germany: Pius XI reacted with his usual vigour. In 1936–7 the situation in the countries of the 'red triangle' convinced him that something must be done. He was urged also by what he saw elsewhere, particularly in France. The elections of May 1936 completed the triumph of the *Front populaire*, in which communist influence was strong. That same influence was predominant among the five million members of C.G.T.; processions, revolutionary songs, the communist salute and industrial strikes were all ominous signs. But there was something even more serious. A certain number of left-wing Catholics, impressed by the rise of National Socialism and Fascism, anxious too to bring about with all possible speed a social order more just than that of liberal capitalism, were advocating collaboration with the Communists. These latter did their best to further the scheme. Communist posters appeared on many a wall in Paris: 'Catholic, shake hands!' And that theme was developed in numerous speeches by the party leaders. Here plainly was grave danger; where would collaboration stop? The Church could not allow her members to make common cause with Marxist atheism in order to oppose Hitlerian paganism. In 1936 Pius denounced the manœuvre, whose only purpose, he said, was 'to provoke unthinkable connivance or, at the very least, a silence and toleration which present an untold advantage to the cause of evil'. It was necessary to cut short that campaign of 'the outstretched hand', and Pius XI spoke.

In point of fact His Holiness had already condemned Communism on many occasions. Almost every one of his thirty Encyclicals made some reference to the communist peril. This was true not only of *Quadragesimo anno* and *Caritate Christi* where it was natural, while speaking of social questions, to refute the Marxist theories, but also of documents whose subject-matter seemed remote from such problems, e.g. *Rite expiatis* on St Francis of Assisi and *Divini illius Magistri* on the education of youth. None of those Encyclicals, however, constituted a complete, systematic refutation of Marxist doctrine or a detailed analysis of its threat to religion.

At the end of winter 1936–7 the octogenarian Pope had just recovered from a long and serious illness, which some had thought he would never survive. During those weeks of fever and insomnia he had spent hours in meditation upon the present state of the world and the

duties it imposed on the Vicar of Christ. The result was the almost simultaneous publication of three Encyclicals: *Mit brennender Sorge* (14th March) on the religious situation in Germany, *Nos es muy* (28th March) on the situation in Mexico, and *Divini Redemptoris* (19th March) 'on atheistic Communism'. This near-simultaneity, it must be emphasized, was intentional and significant. At a moment when the outbreak of war in Spain threatened to engulf the whole of Europe, Pius XI meant to show that the Church would not allow herself to be enrolled by any of the mutually hostile blocs. But the Encyclical against Communism had a wider significance than that against Nazism. Faced with a doctrine much more carefully constructed than that of *Mein Kampf*, it replied with a correspondingly stronger critique and made fewer references to current events. True, it mentioned the religious persecutions in Russia and stigmatized the 'horrors of Communism' in Spain, which the Pope considered as resulting from a systematic plan of revolution; but his true purpose was not so much to preach a crusade as to show Catholics that no agreement, not even a tactical agreement, was permissible between Christianity and Communism.

For the first time in history, therefore, the Church made use of her infallible *magisterium* to attack the mighty war machine of Marxism. Pius XI, in the plenitude of his spiritual authority, came to grips with the most serious and most important problem of the age. Skilfully designed and revealing a firmness of exposition characteristic of Achille Ratti's gifts as a logician, *Divini Redemptoris* is a veritable charter of the attitude, both ideological and practical, which Catholics should possess in face of Communism.

After an exordium in which the Pope speaks of the 'frightful barbarism' into which whole peoples are in danger of falling, names the enemy, 'atheistic Communism which is undermining the foundations of Christian civilization', and recalls previous condemnations on the part of both his predecessors and himself, the first part of the document is devoted to a complete and lucid account of Marxism. Naturally enough, the Pope's criticism has nothing in common with the arguments of politicians and economists. When he declares Communism 'intrinsically perverse' he does so because it rests upon a false concept of man, of the world, of life. Dialectical materialism, which the Encyclical describes with great exactness, is unacceptable to a Christian because it admits only one reality, matter with its blind forces of which man, like the plant and the animal, is simply a result. The Marxist concept of society, governed in its evolution by the same materialistic determinism, is likewise unacceptable. It is thus the very essence of Marxism that Pius XI condemns. To this condemnation he adds another, censuring the method

employed by Communism to impose itself, i.e. totalitarianism, a method which 'strips man of his freedom', 'allowing to the individual as against the collectivity none of the rights natural to the human person', reducing him to the state of 'a mere cog in the system'. He shows lastly how Communism is 'anti-religious of its very nature' by recalling the Marxist analyses of religion, especially the celebrated formula 'opium of the people'.

The second part is a simple but powerful reminder of the Christian concept of man and of society. 'This little world that we call man is of greater worth than the vast inanimate universe.' 'Society is made for man, not man for society.' 'Society cannot deprive man of the rights which the Creator has granted him as a person.' Those lapidary phrases are opposed not to Communism alone, but to all the 'cold monsters' that threaten man's freedom and his very being.

More limited in its design, seeking mainly to give Catholics practical guidance, the third part of *Divini Redemptoris* nevertheless contains equally important and striking maxims. 'The means of saving the world from the ruin into which amoral liberalism has plunged us consist neither in the class struggle nor in terror, much less still in the autocratic abuse of the power of the State, but in the establishment of an economic order inspired by social justice and the sentiments of Christian charity. . . . There would be no such thing as Socialism or Communism if rulers had not spurned the warnings and lessons of the Church.' Nor does the Pope hesitate to speak of 'those Catholic industrialists who have ceaselessly opposed the workers' movement' which he himself had commended, and to deplore 'the occasional abuse of the right of ownership in order to defraud the worker of his just wage and of his legitimate social rights'.

Divini Redemptoris is surely one of the most important documents in the recent history of the Church. Yet a glance at the contemporary press inclines one to the view that it was not understood as it should have been. Its anti-communist sections were quoted at length in the bourgeois newspapers, and even in National Socialist and Fascist journals, but the rest was almost everywhere ignored. In France only *La Croix* printed the whole text.

10. The Last Fight of Pius XI

Such were the last eight years of Pius XI's pontificate—eight years of struggle. 'Not for a long time had the voice of a pope been raised so loudly or reached so large an audience.' [1] By his vigorous stand against

[1] Marc-Bonnet, *La Papauté contemporaine*, p. 119.

the monstrous idols of the age, by his defence of the human person threatened with annihilation, Achille Ratti gave back to the Church her age-long role as the living conscience of peoples and as guardian of the true values of civilization. But he fought for God on yet another field, as arbiter of international disputes. Here he lost.

The period through which the Church had just lived, and which forms the subject-matter of this volume, began with a war and, for the Church, a blaze of revolutionary persecution. It ended with another blaze of revolutionary persecution, worse than that of the Commune, soon to be followed by another war infinitely more extensive and more terrible than that which had been rendered famous by the charge of Reichshoffen's cavalry and the capitulation of Sedan. The world had driven deep into darkness during those seventy years.

Anguish at the thought of impending war had scarcely left the soul of Pius XI since his accession to the apostolic throne. We have seen [1] how few illusions he had as to the value of 'an artificial peace founded only upon paper', and how pertinently he remarked in 1923: 'The spirit of rancour and revenge has become swollen and almost legitimated.' From 1930 onwards the growth of Fascism, the rise of National Socialism, the steady reinforcement of Communism, together with the weakness and incoherence of democratic policies, left him in no doubt as to the chances of peace. Thenceforward peace was one of his constant themes. It had been the subject of *Pax Christi*, one of his earliest Encyclicals, and it recurred during the last eight years of his reign in more than thirty utterances. He backed Aristide Briand's efforts for peace and did his best to support the League of Nations, which officially ignored him. Ten or twelve times he alluded to the need for general disarmament—'A forest of bayonets is certainly not the best means of guaranteeing peace'—and denounced the expenditure upon armaments of enormous sums which might have contributed to the general welfare of mankind. He repeated his advice to every head of state, politician and diplomat whom he received in audience. Haunted by the spectre of war, he took every opportunity to proclaim his fear to the world.

At certain points his intervention was even more positive. Early in his pontificate he had helped to moderate the territorial claims of Poland upon Germany, and had tried to restrain Mustapha Kemel's attack upon Greece. Later, in 1937, we find him upholding China against Japanese aggression, and encouraging the French Government in its effort to find grounds for an understanding with Mussolini's Italy. Still more remarkable, he was called upon to play the part of international arbiter as Leo XIII had done between Germany and Spain [2]: when dispute arose between Haiti and Santo Domingo, the

[1] Chapter VII, section 10. [2] See Chapter III, section 11.

agreement which avoided fatal consequences was signed in the nunciature at Port-au-Prince.

As the clouds gathered the voice of Pius XI became louder and more pathetic. In 1934, at a moment when peace seemed threatened as much by the consequences of the economic crisis as by the revival of German militarism, the clamour over the Saar and Mussolini's ambitions, a vehement allocution in Consistory denounced once again the criminal folly of the arms race and prophesied that whose who precipitated war would deliver 'to massacre, ruin and death not only their own nations but the whole of human society'—a prophecy which none can read thirty years later without anguish of heart.

But the dread machine set in motion by men could not be halted by words, as Pius himself realized. One day when a friend suggested that he should once more raise his voice in denunciation of yet another threat to peace, he replied: 'Instead of talking about peace and goodwill to men who are not disposed to listen, I prefer now to talk about them to God alone.' When he fell seriously ill in 1936 he told his *entourage* that he offered his life for the preservation of peace. The powers of evil seemed triumphant everywhere. After Austria it was the Sudeten Germans whose annexation to the Third Reich Hitler demanded; at Munich the Western democracies capitulated; the whole of Czechoslovakia was threatened; the German press was already talking of wresting from Poland the absurd 'Danzig Corridor'; Fascist Italy was fuming with impatience, ready to rival in violence her ally in the Pact of Steel. Although he had none but supernatural hope of avoiding the worldwide catastrophe which he foresaw, Pius continued stubbornly and to the very last his struggle to check the Horsemen of the Apocalypse. At the end of September 1938, in the worst hours of the Munich crisis, being then a very sick man, he broadcast a moving appeal for peace. In January 1939 he received Chamberlain and Halifax, whom he warned against the tragic consequences of British hesitation. Finally, distressed by the spectacle of Mussolini's madness, which was steering Italy closer and closer in the wake of Germany, he summoned the whole Italian hierarchy to the Vatican for 11th February 1939, intending to deliver an allocution which he had already prepared.[1] 'Keep me alive until 12th February,' he told his doctor.

He died on the 10th, without beholding the fulfilment of what he had foreseen—the appalling spectacle of mankind's mad rush to the

[1] Published by John XXIII. It was both an appeal for peace and a stern warning addressed to the Fascist regime. Pius XII's biographer, Nazareno Padellaro, has stated on first-hand information that Pius XI possessed genuinely prophetic gifts during his last days. Receiving two Italian politicians, he told them that Italy would go to war on the side of Germany and that she would be beaten; he even declared that the peninsula would be invaded from Sicily and the south, that the Fascist regime would collapse and that many of its leaders would die a violent death.

abyss in those spring days of 1939. He did not witness that episode which remains the most indelible disgrace in the career of Mussolini: the invasion of Albania by the troops of Catholic Italy *on Good Friday*. But at least his voice had been raised so loudly that amid the frightful tumult of the ensuing years men could be certain that the Word of Christ would not pass away.

CHAPTER X

THE CHURCH CO-EXTENSIVE WITH THE WORLD

A. In Christian Lands

1. 'Co-extensive with the World'

The courage and vigour of the Church in her struggle with hostile States and atheistic ideologies are only one aspect of her task. Her activity was equally strong and equally effective in many other fields, where she had not only to guard the deposit of faith, but also to take the offensive with a view to conquest or reconquest. The work accomplished by Social Catholicism and Catholic Action was a manifestation of her resolve to win back for Christ those classes which had abandoned Him. During the period with which we are now concerned a similar effort was made to sow the grain of truth in ever widening acres; and here again splendid results were obtained, results that are among the most convincing proofs of the vitality of the Church.

At a time when she might have been thought wholly preoccupied with defence of the ancient fortress against a host of assailants, or overwhelmed with grief at the sight of so many of her children yielding to the temptations of apostasy, she was in fact everywhere at work regaining lost positions; achieving a spectacular recovery in territories where she appeared to have suffered eclipse; flowering in new countries with remarkable speed; elsewhere again making dispositions that would prove useful in the future; or, finally, seizing the opportunity afforded by colonial expansion. All this forms another and most important chapter in the history of the Church.

Mgr Grente, Bishop of Le Mans and now a cardinal, told me that one day he was walking along a corridor in the Vatican with Cardinal Pacelli, Pius XI's secretary of state, when His Eminence stopped suddenly before the *Mappa Mundi*, which Pope Pius IV commissioned from Giovanni da Udine *c.* 1560. Pointing to the huge fresco, the future 'Pope of the Coloured Churches' said in a loud voice: 'Excellency, we must be co-extensive with *that*. . . .'

2. In Protestant Europe

Reconquest of lost territory was a scheme of which no Pope had lost sight ever since the Protestant Reformation deprived the Church of large areas in the West. But until the French Revolution that scheme had scarcely been given effect; it was difficult to point to any sector where the Catholic faith had regained a firm foothold. It was otherwise in the nineteenth century. While an altered outlook led the governments of various countries to lower the legislative barriers erected against Catholics, these latter had given proof of more vitality and initiative, getting to grips with the Protestants and even managing to restore their Church in lands where it seemed ruined beyond hope of recovery. This process of restoration has continued uninterruptedly since 1870, and has produced some interesting results.

The most striking example, beyond any doubt, is furnished by Great Britain. Here a Catholic community which at the beginning of the nineteenth century numbered less than 100,000 increased during the next 150 years until it represented one-tenth of the total population. This astonishing change took place simultaneously with an alteration in the legal status of those who had been for so long nothing but contemptible 'papists'. The Catholic Emancipation Act (1829)[1] marked the beginning of the Catholic revival; and as that revival proceeded, it brought about new modifications in the arsenal of laws which had humiliated Catholics for three hundred years. Public offices and the universities were gradually reopened to 'Romans'. In 1910 Parliament dispensed George V and his successors from that part of the coronation oath which was offensive to Catholics but which all sovereigns had taken since 1688, to 'repudiate eucharistic transubstantiation, to condemn all worship or invocation of the Virgin Mary, and all other practices of superstition and idolatry such as exist in the Church of Rome'. The renewal of diplomatic relations with the Vatican in 1914 was not only an adroit diplomatic gesture, but also an acknowledgment of the loyalty of His Majesty's Catholic subjects. Finally, in 1927, Parliament passed the Catholic Relief Act repealing all remaining laws against Catholics and granting them full juridical parity with the faithful of other confessions. Excepting the Crown and the lord chancellorship,[2] Catholics could now aspire to the highest offices in the kingdom.

These changes revealed a manifest increase of Catholic weight in the

[1] *The Church in an Age of Revolution*, Chapter III, section 15.

[2] The sovereign continues to swear to be a 'loyal Protestant', and the lord chancellor is officially 'keeper of the sovereign's conscience'.

scales of British policy, but to what was that increase due? About 1850 Catholicism in Britain was limited to a few hundred old families; a very small middle class living mainly in the ports and consisting largely of traders in wine and foodstuffs, whose business brought them into contact with continental Europe; and above all, in the north, a proletariat reinforced with Irish elements. That did not constitute a very vigorous body, and Newman afterwards declared: 'There was no Catholic Church, not even a Catholic community.'

It was indeed the historic role of Newman, Manning and others of the Oxford Movement,[1] who believed themselves at first the heralds of an Anglican reawakening, to set in motion the great Catholic revival. Their conversion brought new blood to the Catholic faith. Intellectuals, theologians and clergymen of the Anglican Church took the road back to the ancient Catholic fold, and their example was infectious. Conversions continued to take place in the universities and the social strata whence the latter drew their members. Contrary, however, to the hopes fostered by Newman's conversion, there was no mass return; but, despite the lack of a ground swell, there was, and there remains, a steady flow. Nor was that flow impeded by the failure of the Halifax-Portal talks in 1889 and that of the Malines conferences under the aegis of Cardinal Mercier from 1920 onwards.[2] The number of conversions actually increased from 6,500 in 1900 to 7,500 in 1910; it reached a figure of 121,793 for the period 1920–30—an annual average of more than 12,000, which remained constant until the eve of the Second World War.

But the stream of conversions did not alone account for the rise in the Catholic population. Another factor was Irish immigration. It seems that Ireland, adopting in some sort though in a different way the role she had played in the West at the time of St Columba, formed a reservoir of Catholics in all Anglo-Saxon countries. The Irish tide had begun to reach Britain about 1850, after the potato famine; within ten years 800,000 Irish arrived and found jobs in the mills or mines. Then it turned towards the United States, and by 1910 there were more Irish in North America than in Britain. But the easterly trend was resumed after the world crisis of 1929, and in ten years more than 200,000 Irishmen landed, not to mention the temporary immigration (mostly feminine) of nurses and domestic servants. In England and Wales Catholics numbered about 1,300,000 by 1870, 1,800,000 by 1900, 2,375,000 by 1939. In Scotland the figure rose from 300,000 in 1870 to 700,000 in 1939. It should also be noted, in accordance with the Newman Demographic Survey, that many Catholics did little to distinguish themselves from their Anglican or Nonconformist

[1] *The Church in an Age of Revolution*, pp. 430–8.
[2] This matter is studied in the next volume.

neighbours, so that the number of 'baptized Catholics' was certainly higher; in 1939 it stood at very nearly 4,500,000.

Statistics, however, are not the sole evidence of the progress of Catholicism in Britain during the sixty-six years of our period. Other signs were the building of Westminster Cathedral at the beginning of the present century, during the episcopate of Cardinal Vaughan; the eucharistic congress held in London in 1908; the permission given by the hierarchy, after some hesitation, for Catholic students to attend the universities;[1] the increasing number of Catholics occupying diplomatic posts all over the world; the fame acquired by writers such as Gerard Manley Hopkins, G. K. Chesterton and Hilaire Belloc, all of them militant Catholics; and lastly, in 1913, the conversion of the entire Anglican Benedictine community of Caldey.

The Catholic Church in Britain, too, gave evidence in many ways of great spiritual vigour. The clergy, which in the middle of the nineteenth century consisted of only 1,000 members, counted 2,900 in 1900, 4,000 in 1911, 5,600 in 1939. The number of churches and chapels increased from 780 to 2,500. By 1939 there were half a dozen seminaries. Seventy-three orders and congregations of men, including 2,000 priests, had houses in various parts of the country, ranging from Benedictines, Cistercians and Carthusians to the Society of Jesus, Don Bosco's Salesians and the Fathers of the Divine Word. Up and down the land there were 1,300 convents of women belonging to 150 orders and congregations. The Catholic press was represented by the *Tablet*, the *Catholic Herald*, the *Catholic Times*, the *Universe* and the *Dublin Review*. Like all human groups which recognize themselves as a minority, the Catholics of Britain were on the whole more active in the fulfilment of their religious duties than those, say, of a country such as France. Apostolic zeal was kept alive by the Knights of St Columba, by the Archconfraternity of Our Lady of Compassion, founded in 1897 by Saint-Sulpice, and by the Cardinal Vaughan Society which was formed in 1903. The Beda College in Rome welcomed converts who desired to become priests, and the Catholic Young Men's Society was extremely active. The Church in Great Britain was, as it had always been since the days of persecution, bound to Rome by the strongest ties. The social teaching of the popes was familiar to very large numbers of the younger generation, and an Association of Catholic Trade Unionists had been formed, though it met with small support from Irish workers. Social Weeks had been inaugurated, and a Catholic Workers' Youth movement had made a promising start.

Thus on the eve of the Second World War Catholicism in Britain, though far from predominant, represented a body of opinion with which the authorities had to reckon. Moreover, compared with the

[1] At Oxford their number rose from 150 in 1914 to 700 in 1939.

religion both of the Established Church and of the various Nonconformist sects, which has been emptied by Modernism of all theology and reduced to a kind of practical moralism, it appeared as a bastion of genuine spiritual life. Rome had acknowledged this extraordinary reversal of fortune by restoring the English hierarchy in 1850[1] and the Scottish in 1878. In Great Britain by 1939 there were six ecclesiastical provinces with twenty-five dioceses, and every archbishop of Westminster has been raised sooner or later to the purple.

In 1871 *Germany* had 14,800,000 Catholics in a total population of 41,000,000—a proportion of 36·2 per cent; but though their number had increased by 1939 to 22,000,000, the proportion had fallen to 32·8 per cent, the total population at that date being 68,000,000. One may, however, say that during this period the Catholic Church in Germany made steady progress. One phrase which recurs frequently in the observations of German Catholics upon themselves is a fair summary of their situation: they felt they were 'leaving the ghetto'. Incorporated with Protestant Prussia by the treaties of 1815, the predominantly Catholic territories had at first but one idea, to live in loyalty to their faith, to stress their confessional identity and to regain their freedom. Hence the political character of their religion, with which, before 1870 and under the influence of Mgr von Ketteler, were associated distinctively 'social' features. The Kulturkampf, which ended in a victory for the Catholics, favoured their outlook: they suffered less from their inferiority complex. They continued their two-fold political and social activity, of which a young and fervent clergy took advantage in its effort to begin a thoroughgoing revival. Between 1900 and 1914 this social advance was accompanied by an attempt to raise Catholic life to a higher level. Here again they had to 'leave the ghetto', a task accomplished with some difficulty.

It was indeed in the intellectual sphere that the Catholic revival took place on the morrow of the First World War. While the *Zentrum* became bogged down in governmental tasks, concentrating almost exclusively upon defence of federalism, and while Catholic movements among the lower classes confined themselves to the useful but inadequate work of education and mutual aid, the achievements of Romano Guardini and Theodor Haecker roused enthusiasm of young Germans; and the influence of Mgr Münch, of the Benedictine abbey of Maria Laach and of the review *Hochland* brought about a spiritual reawakening of which liturgy and architecture provided additional evidence in their respective ways.

After 1933 the Catholic Church asserted her authority in quite a

[1] *The Church in an Age of Revolution*, p. 260.

different manner. The firm resistance of her bishops to totalitarian dictatorship and racism [1] made her a symbol of courage and freedom. After expansion came a period of deepening. The apostolate of the twenties bore its fruit; those years had witnessed the training of a Catholic *élite* which now managed to stand firm in time of persecution. And the bishops, ceasing to be the temporal princes of their dioceses, became in the fullest sense their pastors. In 1945, when the collapse of National Socialism opened up new paths for Germany, the Catholic Church, at any rate in the Federal Republic, was ready to play the important part that is hers today.

The situation of the *Netherlands* was altogether different from that of Britain. Dutch Catholics had remained numerous after the Reformation crisis; on the eve of the French Revolution they represented 38 per cent of the population. But they tended to diminish, so much so that in 1870 they were no more than 36·5 per cent. Worst of all, they were virtually second-class citizens, despised by the haughty and powerful Calvinists of the islands and the coast. Their cathedrals and parish churches had been confiscated by the Protestants; it was only with great difficulty that they were able to maintain schools and seminaries. They felt humiliated. It is from this standpoint that one must view developments in order to appreciate the Catholic recovery in Holland. Though they obtained juridical freedom in 1880, some time elapsed before Catholics really found their feet; but from 1870 onwards every ten-year period marked another stage of progress. Numerical increase was not spectacular. By 1939 they had regained no more than the 38 per cent representation they had enjoyed 150 years earlier. But even this indicates a slightly faster rate of increase than that of the population as a whole; the birth-rate, too, was higher among Catholics than among Protestants. More important was a change in the attitude of Catholics, and also their standing in the nation. The Netherlands Church, whose hierarchy had been re-established in 1853, to the great indignation of the Protestants, made a tremendous effort to secure her position in the country. The foundation of a Catholic syndical association (1889),[2] and of Mgr Schaepmann's Catholic Party (1897) did much to bring about that recovery. After 1914 the Dutch Catholics got rid of their inferiority complex; the more able of them occupied an increasing number of official positions, and a Catholic university was established at Nijmegen in 1923. More surprising, by 1939 they were represented in the administration of the State Radio. Finally, Catholic Holland could claim to be one of two countries [3] with more priests than any other—9,000

[1] See Chapter IX, section 5. [2] See Chapter IV, section 16.

[3] The other was Switzerland or, rather, its Catholic cantons. See page 346.

(secular and regular in about equal proportion), not to mention 1,000 to 1,500 brothers and 25,000 nuns, as well as 3,000 Dutch religious on the foreign missions.

The growing importance of Catholics in *Switzerland* is not to be reckoned by statistics; census records show that their increase was exactly proportionate to the general demographic rise. What the figures do not show is the psychological position taken by Catholics in the period 1870–1939. By 1870 the armed struggle between Protestants and Catholics [1] had almost faded from memory. But conflict had revived in the cantons of Berne, Zürich, Saint-Gall, Thurgau, Tessin and, above all, Geneva, where Carteret's radical party was engaged in what is called the Little Kulturkampf.[2] It was the stubborn resistance of Mgr Mermillod at Geneva, and of the mountaineers in the canton of Berne, that made the Catholics aware of their strength and helped to earn for them the respect of their Protestant compatriots. Mermillod's authority, enhanced in 1890 by the Roman purple, strengthened that of the Catholics as a whole. The foundation in 1889 of the University of Fribourg,[3] and the celebrity it soon acquired by the excellence of its teaching staff, counted for not a little in the growth of Catholic prestige. In the twentieth century Swiss Catholics could claim to have won the day. Their statesmen occupied the highest federal positions; their newspapers were widely read; their institutions, e.g. the Catholic Mission to Prisoners of War, played an international role during the world conflict of 1914–18. Rivalling the Netherlands in the number of priestly vocations, the Catholic Church in Switzerland was on the flood-tide of prosperity.

More surprising is the history of Catholicism in Scandinavia, where it had been practically wiped out by the Reformation. At the beginning of the nineteenth century there were only a few dozen widely scattered 'Romans', deprived of all legal rights. *Denmark* had been the first Scandinavian country to play fair by granting freedom of worship in 1849. The faithful at that time numbered 500. By 1939 they had increased to nearly 20,000; the most sensational conversion was that of the great writer Joergensen in 1896. Separated from the diocese of Osnabrück in 1868, Denmark formed a separate ecclesiastical district; it was an apostolic prefecture until 1892, when it was raised to the status of an apostolic vicariate. The Danish Church gave proof of

[1] *The Church in an Age of Revolution*, pp. 222, 242, 263.

[2] See Chapter III, section 4.

[3] Georges Python had the good sense to make it a State University instead of a Catholic Institute dependent on the hierarchy.

extraordinary vitality. This was due in large measure to its first modern bishop, Mgr Johannes von Euch (1834–1922), who became prefect apostolic in 1882, a man of great energy and unfailing tact in dealing with the authorities. He organized pilgrimages and processions, increased the number of parishes by ten, raised that of his priests from eighteen to sixty-seven (twelve of them Danes), introduced male and female representatives of sixteen different religious orders, as well as founding twenty-one schools and fifteen hospitals. He was assisted by Jesuits who had been driven from Germany by the Kulturkampf and whose college at Copenhagen exerted a profound influence on the young; also by the Sisters of Saint-Joseph de Chambéry, who entered the country in 1856 as teachers and hospital nurses. In 1939 the first bishop of Danish nationality was consecrated—Mgr Suhr, a Benedictine.

The process in *Norway* was similar, though less rapid. One of the first steps taken by the new Norwegian king, Oscar I, in 1845 was the grant of freedom to all Christian Churches. Thereafter the Catholic Church had the status of 'nonconformist Churches recognized by the State'. Catholic marriages were valid without a previous civil ceremony. Schools remained Lutheran, but Catholic children were exempted from religious instruction classes. Only one restriction remained: a paragraph of the Constitution forbade the entry of Jesuits into the kingdom, and it was not repealed until 1956. Within this new legal framework the Catholic Church was able to regain a foothold on Norwegian soil. In 1871 there were only 350 Catholics, many of them foreigners; in 1939 there were at least 3,000 served by forty-five priests, six of whom were Norwegians. The man responsible for much of this achievement was a Frenchman, Mgr Fallize, who became head of the Norwegian Church in 1887. In 1931 the apostolic vicariate of Norway was divided into three parts: Oslo remained a vicariate, while two apostolic prefectures were instituted, one for the north and another for the south. Some twenty orders or congregations were at work, chief among whom were the Sisters of Saint-Joseph de Chambéry in the hospitals. The number of female religious was estimated at 450, including twenty-five Norwegians.

Sweden reopened her gates to Catholicism more grudgingly. Although the Roman faith had regained a very small foothold at the beginning of the nineteenth century, thanks to the influence of Princess Joséphine de Beauharnais-Leuchtenberg and her spiritual director Mgr Studach, Lutheranism prevented Catholic expansion in any shape or form: no Swedish citizen might be received into the Church, and the children of Catholics were obliged to receive a Lutheran education. In 1858, however, six women were exiled for conversion to Catholicism, and the affair provoked such indignation

throughout Europe that in 1860 a law was promulgated abolishing sanctions against the papists. The situation of Catholics was further improved by royal decrees in 1870 and 1873, though religious freedom remained heavily restricted.

Between the latter date, however, and 1939 a change was gradually brought about by a succession of zealous vicars apostolic: after Studach came Mgr Huber, a Bavarian, then Mgr Bitter, a Hanoverian, then another Bavarian, Mgr J. Eric Muller, who was chosen and consecrated by Mgr Pacelli, nuncio at Munich. The rate of progress is rather difficult to determine, because statistics are vague until about 1910. At all events, in 1939 there were 3,750 Catholics in Sweden. During the same period, 1873–1939, the number of priests rose from eight to twenty-nine (five of them Swedish). There had been a Catholic cathedral at Upsala since 1923; 'stations', that is to say parishes, had been formed throughout the country, even in the north where that of Sörforsa, dating from 1924, covered half the kingdom! Not all of this was accomplished without opposition; Mgr Bitter, for example, had a hard struggle in his attempt to obtain a ban on the defamation of Catholicism by official teaching. Congregations of men were excluded from Sweden; but members of several female congregations came—Germans, Poles and, above all once again, the French Sisters of Saint-Joseph de Chambéry.[1] The foundation by these last of a 'French School' at Stockholm (1862) was the beginning of a remarkable story. Born in the humblest circumstances, this school, directed by a succession of extremely able women, eventually had 500 pupils and enjoyed such a reputation that in 1950 it was entrusted with the education of royalty.

Notwithstanding these welcome results the apostolic vicariate of Sweden met with serious difficulties, some geographical, others economic, on the eve of 1939: the vast distances were a severe handicap to a clergy that was far from numerous and relatively poor. But there were also legal difficulties, particularly surprising in a country looked upon as the very homeland of democratic freedom: contemplative convents were still forbidden; a Protestant intending to become a Catholic was obliged to notify his pastor, who then called and tried to prevent him from taking the final step; while counsellors of state and primary school-teachers had to take an oath to profess the 'pure doctrine' of Luther. And since the State Church had charge of the registers, Catholics had to apply to the Lutheran pastors in order to obtain a birth certificate.[2]

[1] A Swedish congregation of Brigittines, too, was founded.

[2] In 1951 most of these restrictions were abolished. Besides, the spiritual climate has completely changed since the Second World War. When the centenary of the French School was celebrated in 1962 the Catholic Archbishop of Chambéry preached in the Lutheran church of St John, in presence of the Lutheran Bishop Ljunberg of Stockholm.

The imposition of Protestantism upon *Iceland* by Denmark excluded Catholicism from that country until 1859, when Père Baudoin of Rheims converted one family and built a chapel. Work was resumed in 1892 and led to the formation of the first parish, then to the opening of a school and a hospital by the Sisters of Saint-Joseph de Chambéry. In 1939 there were 350 Catholics in Iceland, and the third Icelandic priest was about to be ordained.

In *Finland*, where the Fathers of Saint-Quentin took up residence in 1906, the vicariate apostolic was entrusted to them in 1926. Within ten years they had charge of 1,500 Catholics, and eighteen priests from France and Holland reinforced the two who had already begun their apostolate, one speaking Swedish, the other Finnish.

3. U.S.A.: A Church on the March

Among the numerous presents received by Leo XIII on 1st January 1888, the fiftieth anniversary of his first Mass, the most unexpected was a richly bound copy of the American Constitution. To President Cleveland's message of goodwill the Pope replied: 'Religion in your country is free to extend ever further the empire of Christianity, and the Church to develop her salutary influence. A great future awaits you. . . .'

This exchange of diplomatic compliments revealed Catholicism as occupying a foremost place in the Union. One hundred years earlier 300,000 wretched papists, living for the most part in Maryland, were hardly tolerated by the haughty crowds of Protestant colonists. Now they had increased to 7½ million, and their manifest influence in the political arena was earning them more and more respect. Thanks to the courage of her members, to the energy and intelligence of her leaders, as well as to circumstances that brought her an unceasing flow of immigrants, the Catholic Church in the United States was clearly on the march towards a most splendid future.[1]

The prodigious flowering of American Catholicism, which had been one of the most important features of the preceding period, had not been long slowed down by the Civil War. It was to continue at the same rate for a long time yet to come. The situation, indeed, did not change until after 1917, when steps were taken to limit immigration. But by that time the position of the Catholic Church was such that her prestige and influence were unassailable, and she was able to make progress in other fields.

That flowering was apparent, first, in the realm of statistics. In 1870 there were 3½ million Catholics; by 1914 they numbered 16 million.

[1] *The Church in an Age of Revolution*, pp. 362–9.

The principal factor of this increase was the steady flow of Catholic newcomers—Irish, Germans, Poles, Italians and subjects of the Austro-Hungarian Empire. Many of these immigrants crowded into the cities. In 1914 the total population of New York was about 2 million, among whom were 200,000 Irish, 150,000 Poles and more than 350,000 Italians. Boston, once exclusively Protestant, became 75 per cent Catholic. But the tide overflowed the eastern cities as German Catholics, together with many Poles, settled as farmers in the Middle West. The Catholic advance, therefore, was apparent also from the growing number of apostolic vicariates. Pius IX created thirteen, Leo XIII thirty and Pius X fifteen. To the six archdioceses already existing there were added Boston, Chicago, Dubuque, Milwaukee, Philadelphia, St Louis, St Paul and Santa Fe, until on the eve of the First World War the Catholic Church was present in every state.

Counting for much in the Union because of the number and wide distribution of her members, the Church was strong and thoroughly well organized. Her clergy increased at about the same rate as her laity: from 3,780 on the morrow of the Civil War the number of priests had risen to nearly 19,000 by 1914, while the proliferation of religious orders and congregations continued unabated.

Another element of her strength was the solid virtues of the hierarchy. Many of the earlier French bishops were succeeded by Irishmen, either direct from the Emerald Isle or descended from Irish immigrants, endowed with that admixture of realism and mysticism, that vigour and even that pugnacity which are characteristic of their race. Such, for example, were Cardinal Gibbons, Mgr Ireland, Mgr Corrigan and a host of others. They did not always agree with one another, but all left their mark upon their dioceses. In 1852, encouraged by Rome, they met for the first time in a 'national' or 'plenary' council, at which they discussed freely all questions of interest to the American Church. Two others were held at Baltimore (1866 and 1884), when crucial decisions were made, particularly on the subject of Catholic schools.

Indeed one of the most admirable features and most valuable assets of the Church in the United States is her educational system, which is perhaps more efficient than any other in the Catholic world. The parochial schools form the basis of the whole Church; in 1914 there were nearly six thousand, with two million children. Next there are teacher training schools, then secondary schools. These last date from the years after 1885 when a new effort was made to improve the standard of education as the tide of Catholic immigration rose. At the same time some of the older colleges were given university status; new universities, too, came into being, e.g. Georgetown, Notre Dame in Indiana and, above all, Washington, which was founded through the generosity of Mary Caldwell in 1889.

The extraordinary advance of Catholicism naturally provoked opposition. Violence was a thing of the past; there was no more burning Catholic churches or badgering nuns. Antagonism, however, showed itself in more insidious ways, e.g. hindering Catholic missionaries when they sought to make contact with the Indians. The American Protective Association, founded to defend Anglo-Saxon Americans against the Negroes and all 'foreigners', did its best to thwart Catholicism, which it accused of conniving at the Italian and Polish 'invasions'. In 1893, on the eve of a Catholic congress at Chicago, the association distinguished itself by distributing a forged Encyclical which represented the Pope as ordering a massacre of all heretics on the feast of St Ignatius of Loyola! In various states, moreover, a few attempts were made to interfere with the Catholic schools by way of legislation, but they failed. One result of these attacks was the foundation (1882), by Father Michael McGivney, of the Knights of Columbus, for the defence of the Church and the practice of charity. By 1914 it had 400,000 members.

Rome of course took a keen interest in that lightning advance; Leo XIII kept himself fully informed on American affairs, to the extent of making a personal study of the delicate problems that arose, e.g. the Knights of Labor [1] and Americanism.[2] By 1924 the United States had four cardinals. Two events crowned the successes of the American Church. One was the appointment of an apostolic delegate to the U.S.A.; but this was taken as a backhanded compliment by the bishops, who feared that the presence of such a dignitary might restrict the independence of which some had managed to take advantage. The other, which fulfilled the hopes of all, took place in 1908, when Pius X withdrew the Church in the United States from the authority of Propaganda and placed it, like old Christian Europe, under the Consistorial Congregation, thereby proclaiming that the U.S.A. were no longer to be reckoned as a missionary land.

4. Cardinal Gibbons and the Problem of Nationalism

Meanwhile two very awkward questions had arisen. During most of the nineteenth century the average American regarded Catholicism as an aggregate of disparate religious groups deposited on the soil of the Union by successive waves of immigration, unrelated to one another and having no contact with the mass of 'true Americans'. If that situation had lasted, Catholicism could have lost all chance of one day really counting in American society and of becoming one of the 'great

[1] See Chapter IV, section 6 *ad fin.* [2] See Chapter VI, section 2.

American religions'—today the most powerful of them all. The twofold transformation of a body socially and spiritually alien to the American organism into a united community fully integrated with the nation was effected between 1870 and 1914.

The Irish, whose arrival in the middle of the nineteenth century had completely altered the appearance and destiny of Catholicism in the United States, had not spread throughout the Union so as to mix with the English, Dutch and French elements already settled in the country. Arriving in large steamers under the guidance of their priests, they had kept strictly to themselves, hostile by principle to Englishmen and Protestants, and little inclined to rub shoulders with their brethren in the faith, Catholics of the old stock more socially developed than themselves. They tended therefore to stand aloof. The Irish Benevolent Union, founded in 1869, dreamed of absolute autonomy, with its own bank and its own shipping line to bring immigrants from Ireland. This attitude, on the other hand, did not prevent the Irish from stepping outside their ghetto and claiming rights by virtue of their numbers. It was thus not long before they occupied the most important episcopal sees. The position adopted by the Irish community in the affair of Trusteeism,[1] a position diametrically opposed to the laicizing and more or less autonomist tendencies in certain Catholic circles, helped to convince them that they alone embodied the faith and strength of the Church in their new homeland.[2]

Other Catholic groups looked upon this phenomenon with disapproval, particularly the Germans, who held second place in the scale of immigration. Excepting their common faith, everything divided them from the Irish: language, way of life, social and cultural attainments. Settled in the prairies, they too regarded themselves as a close community, with its own priests, bishops, schools and language. They mistrusted the Irish far more than other immigrant groups, e.g. the Poles and Hungarians, because the Irish seemed to them akin by language to the Americans and on the way to asserting their primacy. Tension arose, even within the national and provincial councils; and the situation was aggravated by the arrival of numerous Slavs and Italians, who felt themselves foreigners in the Irish churches and sought in turn to establish themselves as an autonomous community. About 1890 the tension reached breaking-point.

There existed in Europe a society named after the Archangel Gabriel; flourishing mainly in Germany and Italy, its purpose was to provide material and spiritual help to Catholics emigrating to the United States. Its president was the Marchese Volpe-Landi, its secretary general a German named Peter Paul Cahensly. At the Congress of

[1] *The Church in an Age of Revolution*, p. 363.
[2] See G. Shaughnessy, *Has the Immigrant kept the Faith?*, New York, 1925.

Luzern in April 1891 these two men presented a report, warning Rome that every year large numbers of the faithful were abandoning Catholicism because they did not find in the Irish American Church the religious climate they had expected. The solution proposed was questionable, to say the least. It would have meant granting a kind of autonomy to each of the ethnic groups, each with its own clergy. 'Cahenslyism', carried to its logical extreme, would have established within a given territorial area an Irish diocese, a German diocese, an Italian diocese and so on. If the Church had adopted such a scheme she would inevitably have been split into four or five national Churches whose influence would have been narrowly restricted.

A few bishops recognized the danger: Mgr Ireland of St Paul, Mgr Spalding of Peoria and, above all, Mgr Gibbons (1834–1921), who was to be until his death the true guide of the American Church. Born at Baltimore of Irish parentage, Gibbons was a skinny little man with wrinkled face, whose Roman hat always looked too large for him and whose profile no caricaturist could resist. But his far-sightedness, his unfailing judgment and his energy impressed all who met him. Broad-minded too, zealous but utterly human, and conceiving the Church as open to the whole world, he had the undeniable characteristics of a shepherd of souls. Vicar apostolic in North Carolina, then Bishop of Richmond and finally Cardinal Archbishop of Baltimore, he possessed a unique understanding of all American problems, and proved himself the most determined adversary of ethnical 'separatism', which could lead only to 'Cahenslyism'.

Leo XIII, struck by the report of the Society of St Gabriel, consulted Cardinal Gibbons, whom he knew well. Meanwhile an acrimonious dispute began in the United States between the American element of Catholicism and those who supported the immigrants. Cardinal Rampolla, Leo's secretary of state, wrote congratulating the society on its good intentions, but saying that the plan drawn up by the Germans 'to procure for each group of immigrants a bishop of its own nationality' was 'neither expedient nor necessary'. Then, as the conflict continued, Cardinal Ledochowski, prefect of Propaganda, sent the American episcopate an outspoken circular condemning the Luzern plan; and President Harrison thanked Gibbons warmly when the latter informed him that Rome would not do Cahensly's bidding.

Cardinal Gibbons, however, did not stop there. Taking a firm stand against certain bishops, e.g. Corrigan of New York and McQuaid of Rochester, who favoured some sort of division with a view to preserving their people's faith, he conceived the role of the Irish in a perfectly new way. Were they not, in the eyes of their fellow citizens, the least 'foreign' of all immigrants on account of their language as well as of the austere but popular and activist character of their faith? Ought

they not to form a kind of bridge between the various brands of Catholics from Europe and the great mass of the American people? The solution to the problem raised by diversity of origin could not be found in a pluralist system, but only in the complete adhesion of all Catholic elements to the American community through the medium of the Irish and their descendants.

Such then was the role assumed by the Irish at the great cardinal's instigation. In performing it they showed remarkable political sense, managing to accomplish both the fusion and the Americanization of the various Catholic groups, but without losing *de facto* pre-eminence in the American Church, which they continue to enjoy.

Meanwhile the Catholic Church was faced with further problems, less serious but far from negligible. It was her duty, for example, to integrate ethnical groups other than those of immigrants, and here she met with grave difficulties. Continuing the work begun by Père de Smedt,[1] she devoted herself to work among the surviving Indians; but results were slender, for reasons that are no discredit to the zeal of the missionaries.[2] As regards the Negroes, her opportunities were few; in the past she had had little to do with them, and they had come under the influence of various Protestant sects. In 1866, after the Civil War had secured freedom for the Negroes, only 300,000 out of 7 million declared themselves Catholics. The seriousness of the problem did not escape the American hierarchy; the Catholic Committee for Coloured Peoples was invited to study it, and several religious congregations of both sexes devoted themselves to the task of preaching among the blacks; but on the eve of the First World War there were only about 400,000 Catholic Negroes, including some fifty priests.

More disappointing still was the situation in the Philippines, which became American in 1898. The Philippine Church, dating from the sixteenth century and consisting of about 12 million Catholics, had been afflicted during the past hundred years by politico-religious disturbances. The native clergy had struggled to put an end to the predominance of Spanish religious orders,[3] and had then led a number of rebellions against Spain herself. Many priests had been executed. The American annexation raised grave problems. All Spanish members of the secular and of the regular clergy left the island, leaving gaps which it was difficult to fill, while a veritable invasion of Protestant missionaries began. To make matters worse, in 1901 a native priest, Gregorio Aglipay, started a schism, because he objected to the Church's 'alliance with the Yankee occupants'. His little Church, rather like that of the Old Catholics and hostile both to Rome and to Washington, was regarded by the people as the incarnation of national

[1] *The Church in an Age of Revolution*, p. 321. [2] See Chapter XI, section 11.
[3] *The Church in an Age of Revolution* ,pp. 401–2.

liberty, and soon had about 2 million adherents.[1] In presence of this difficult situation the American Church found herself taken at short notice and unprepared. Cardinal Gibbons, too, had been opposed from the outset to the annexation of the Philippines; nor was there any question of sending out American priests, who would have been ill received. Small groups of German, French and Canadian missionaries took the risk, but the shortage of priests continues to this very day.

5. The First 'Denomination'

The First World War was indirectly a source of additional strength for the Catholic Church in America. The episcopate disliked the prospect of intervention by the United States; but once the step had been taken they did all they could to guarantee the absolute loyalty of their flocks. And in fact the German-Americans, forgetting their ties with Germany, and the Irish-Americans, lulling their rancour against Britain, remembered only that they were Americans. The solid organization of the hierarchy made it possible to combine the efforts of Catholics by the creation of a National Catholic War Committee strictly subject to the episcopate; while the educational and charitable activity of the Knights of Columbus counterbalanced that of the Young Men's Christian Association, a Protestant body. And a thousand Catholic chaplains accompanied American units to the front.

Meanwhile a new factor seemed likely to check the spectacular progress of Catholicism: the United States virtually stopped all immigration from Europe. A law of 1917, by excluding illiterates, reduced the influx of Italians, Spaniards, Orientals and Slavs. Then, in 1921 and 1924, further measures limited the admission of foreigners to about 150,000 a year, with a strong bias in favour of Anglo-Saxons. Catholicism's external source of nourishment was thus dried up. But another phenomenon came into play: many more children were born to Catholic (especially Irish and Italian) families than to their Protestant counterparts, where conjugal morality was less strict. Consequently the Catholic fold continued to increase: it numbered 17,886,000 in 1920; 19,540,000 in 1930; 22,000,000 in 1939.

Thus the 'Roman Catholic Church', considered officially as one religious 'denomination' among a host of others [2] recognized by the authorities, was far ahead of the Methodists and Baptists, those two most flourishing varieties of Protestantism. Nor did she lead in point of numbers only. The prestige of American Catholicism was explained

[1] Today it accounts for no more than 7·5 per cent of the population. Moreover it is split into two parts; one is virtually Protestant, while the other, though true to the spirit of its founder, has many members who are thinking of a return to Rome.

[2] The figure varies almost from year to year. In 1939 it was about 280; in 1950, 250.

by the Protestant historian André Siegfried.[1] More affable than any other, more broad-minded than any of the Nonconformist sects, set within the framework of an infallible authority and more firmly welded by fraternal bonds, it appeared to him as an oasis of mystery where men of the twentieth century could breathe an air different from that of materialistic rationalism.

Resistance to Catholicism continued throughout the period. On two or three occasions various states, notably Oregon, attempted to alter their educational laws to get rid of the Catholic schools; but on each occasion the Supreme Court overruled their decisions. A virulent campaign was conducted by the Ku Klux Klan, a secret society founded on a small scale in the South after the Civil War, in order to repress the Negroes. Officially banned in 1877, it was revived in 1915, thanks to the efforts of W. J. Simmons, a Methodist parson, and quickly flourished under the leadership of its 'Eagles' and 'Dragons'; by 1922 it had a million members. Then it took a violently anti-Catholic turn. The Klan was behind the immigration laws and certain others on birth control. It also launched anti-papist campaigns, during which the most unbelievable stories found credence, those for example of secret artillery trained on the White House by Catholics, and of a mansion ready to receive the Pope when he arrived to govern the United States! Resistance to Catholicism, therefore, was still alive, and sufficiently strong to bar Alfred Smith's way to the presidency; but it achieved very little more.

Despite this masked opposition the Catholic Church continued the process of Americanization and unification during the inter-war years. Men and women of different national origins married in increasing numbers, and the bishops took every opportunity to assert the genuinely American character of the Catholic Church in their country, as well as her unqualified loyalty to the State and the ideals of the Union. The most important event of the period was the foundation in 1919 of the National Catholic Welfare Council, which was to form as it were a ministry of Catholicism with eight main services (Education, Immigration, Press, Social Action, Youth, etc.), each entrusted to a bishop and a permanent director.

As for recruitment of the clergy, vocations had always been plentiful among the Irish and Italian immigrants, and they remained so among their descendants. The number of priests reached 21,600 in 1920, 27,900 in 1930, nearly 36,000 in 1939, at which last date there were 17,000 seminarists. The influx of religious orders and congregations also continued, so that by the end of our period American Catholicism presented a sample of almost every habit and every rule that ever was.

Another characteristic of the Church in the United States was, and

[1] *États-Unis d'aujourd'hui* ,1927.

still is, her use of the most up-to-date means of communication, especially the press and radio. Even during the nineteenth century many bishops had founded journals of various kinds. The Catholic Press Association had been established in 1889, and by 1900 the American Church had at her disposal ten dailies, one hundred and fifty-eight weeklies, sixty-seven monthlies and six high-class reviews. After 1918 every diocese had its own newspaper, and in 1939 it was estimated that there were nearly six hundred Catholic journals and periodicals in the U.S.A. The coming of radio, about 1925, was at once recognized by the Church as opening up new fields for her apostolate. Her two most successful broadcasters were Father Coughlin, who talked on social matters, and Father Fulton Sheen of Illinois,[1] who dealt with dogmatic and moral subjects.

A marked change took place in two neighbouring sectors. In the nineteenth century American Catholicism had paid little attention to the social problem; the episcopate as a whole had been preoccupied with other questions. The average priest, moreover, was highly suspicious of the new social ideas, as indeed he was of everything imported from Europe. Only a few far-sighted prelates, such as Mgr Gibbons, stressed the urgency of the question and insisted that the spirit of *Rerum novarum* must permeate the Church. By taking the Knights of Labor [2] under his protection the Archbishop of Baltimore had shown the road that should be followed, but until 1914 few listened when he reminded his flock that 'the Church's greatest claim to glory lies in her being the soul of the people'. Things changed, however, after the First World War and the crisis of 1929. The growth of Catholic Action found a choice field in the United States. The American Catholic had always considered himself as entitled to a voice in the affairs of the Church, so that the Pope's appeal for 'lay participation in the hierarchical apostolate' fell on willing ears. It was in the form of 'general' Catholic Action, directly linked with the N.C.W.C., that the movement spread; 'specialized' Catholic Action hardly existed in the U.S.A. in 1939. But its success was rapid and remarkable; by securing decency in the cinema, collecting money for the missions and in several other ways Catholic Action declared itself with increasing confidence the motive element of American Catholicism.

The shadows in this brilliant picture of extraordinary achievement are few, but none the less real. The Negro problem remained unsolved and caused the Church serious concern during the inter-war years. There was also the diplomatic situation between the American Government and the Holy See. Since 1867, when Congress broke off relations in order to express its sympathy with Italian nationalism, a demand for their resumption had often been considered in the Catholic camp; but

[1] He is now auxiliary bishop of New York. [2] See Chapter IV, section 6.

nothing had been achieved. Neither the Democrats nor the Republicans, who succeeded one another in power, had dared to take the initiative of sending an ambassador to the Vatican.

Nevertheless, though she was not strong enough to secure the renewal of diplomatic relations with the Vatican, and though she seemed to fail with the Negroes, the Catholic Church in the United States was a power, and a power that would increase during and after the Second World War. One can re-read with amusement the peremptory words with which in 1900 Theodore Roosevelt dared to predict her future: 'The Catholic Church could never succeed in this country; she does not suit it; she is radically opposed to the idea which dominates the United States, our institutions, the temperament of our people.' A candidate for the presidency would have been careful not to express himself thus in 1939.

6. The 'American Way of Faith'

The American Church, centralized under the N.C.W.C., has assumed characteristics which differentiate her from all others. One might perhaps describe her as the most independent in the entire Catholic world. In 1884, for example, she was granted direct participation in the choice of bishops, Rome agreeing to appoint the titular of a see from a list of six names chosen by the clergy of the ecclesiastical province—three by the bishops and three by the parish priests—an arrangement which still left the Holy See more freedom of selection than in concordatory countries. But this tendency towards relative independence went hand in hand with a deep attachment to the Apostolic See and to the person of the Sovereign Pontiff. The number of American pilgrims to Rome increased year by year; distinguished men in all walks of life solicited and obtained the flattering title Privy Chamberlain of the Sword and Cape, while others dreamed of admission to the Order of St Gregory the Great. Countless American priests were made Prelates of His Holiness or Protonotaries Apostolic.

The very religion of American Catholics has several peculiarities. But some care is necessary when speaking of 'American Catholics': well marked differences are noticeable between the different parts of the Catholic community. Old states such as Maryland, Louisiana and New Mexico present quite a different appearance from the German-American or Polish-American groups; unification has not been carried to the point of absolute uniformity. It is none the less true that American Catholicism, considered as a whole, has its own special features. One might say that there exists an 'American way of faith' not unconnected with the famous 'American way of life'. Most striking of

these characteristics are as follows: (1) The prestige of the clergy. Priests live in contact with the nation, 'among the people, who recognize them as their protectors and their friends',[1] and concern themselves with all the interests of the country. In this way they have acquired considerable authority. The discipline they impose is very similar to that found in Ireland, whence so many American priests derive. The clergy indeed enjoy a measure of respect far greater than in the most Catholic countries of Europe; it is quite common to see the faithful kneel on the sidewalks when a cardinal or even a bishop passes by. (2) The great charity of American Catholics has led to the foundation of no fewer than 600 hospitals, 420 orphanages, 85 sanatoria and assistance centres of all kinds. They are keenly interested, too, in the foreign missions, supplying half the income of the *Œuvre de la Propagation de la foi* in 1939, and 66·5 per cent in 1951 under the direction of Mgr Fulton Sheen. (3) An extraordinary care for the education of youth; in 1939 the Church had 7,500 primary schools with 2½ million pupils, 2,000 secondary schools with 350,000 pupils, and 190 universities with 100,000 students. Catholic learning counts for much in the national life, but it is directed more to the practical sciences and research than to pure speculation. For this reason Modernism never ravaged the United States.

One may ask whether the emergence of those qualities was not accompanied by the simultaneous progress of serious faults. It has often been said that American Catholics, like all their compatriots of other creeds, yielded to activism and pragmatism, and that their Church, like all other religious societies in the United States, aimed less at fostering spiritual life than at regimenting and organizing the energies of her members. Under Leo XIII the crisis of Americanism[2] had undoubtedly revealed the presence of danger. But that crisis was by no means disastrous; for although the error threatened to mislead certain American Catholics, the papal letter proved a salutary warning, and since then observers have noted a sustained effort to stress the importance of the passive no less than of the active virtues. Here we have one of the most impressive features of American Catholicism during the inter-war years. Many European visitors to the Catholic universities expressed surprise at the number of communicants every Sunday. The eucharistic congress at Chicago in 1926 was a triumph. Numerous houses of retreat were opened. But the most striking symptom of this spiritual awakening was undoubtedly the prodigious growth of the contemplative orders—Cistercians, Visitandines, Poor Clares, Carmelites. Such factors help to improve the image, all too common in Europe, of American Catholicism as 'Christianity without the Cross'.

[1] Paul Bourget, op. cit. [2] See Chapter VI, section 2.

It is, however, true that in 1939 Catholicism in the United States, as also in Europe, was in danger of becoming entangled in that worldly prosperity that leads so readily to smugness. Not that the average American is more 'materialistic' than the average European; but it is difficult for him to resist the almost universal tendency to gradual loss of the substance of his faith. Many an ecclesiastical voice or pen has given warning of this danger, which has resulted in a slowing down, if not a halting, of the prodigious ascent of the American Church.[1]

7. Canada: the Decisive Stage

After the British North America Act of 1867, the French Canadians could consider themselves as having won the stern fight they had waged for a hundred years. The federal system granted equal rights to the four constituent provinces, New Brunswick, Nova Scotia, Quebec and Ontario. The two languages, English and French, were admitted, though English remained 'official'. Religion too enjoyed the benefit of clearly defined rights and guarantees; for this reason the Church had supported the federal system, which alone she believed capable of defending the country against American Protestant encroachment. A future of great promise seemed to lie before the heirs of Champlain, and that promise was amply fulfilled.

In sixty-six years the dominion attained the status of a world power. The French element assumed a place without which the Canada of today would be inconceivable, and the Catholic Church, of which that element remained the corner-stone, witnessed the steady increase of her influence and her prestige. Figures are eloquent in this respect:

Year	*Total population of the four provinces*	*Catholics*	*French Canadians*
1867	3,500,000	1,250,000	1,000,000
1901	5,375,000	2,300,000	1,700,000
1939	10,375,000	4,500,000	3,200,000

Two factors accounted for these impressive figures. First was the demographic fecundity of French Canadians, of which Catholic morality was the vigilant guardian: their families of thirteen, fifteen and sometimes twenty children ensured a fine future.[2] The second factor was immigration. Slow at first, the rate increased, especially

[1] In 1962 the proportion of Catholics in relation to the total population of the U.S.A. was almost stationary.

[2] About 500,000 (some say a million) French Canadians too have emigrated to the United States, especially to New England, forming entire cities and serving as strong Catholic bastions.

from 1900, when the construction of the Canadian Pacific Railway and the subsidies granted by the federal government for the transport and settlement of newcomers brought a flow of English, Germans, Irish and Ukrainians, many of whom were Catholics.

The French Canadians never lost their pride of place in the Canadian Church, of which they formed 67 per cent in 1939. Their political outlook, moreover, continued to be dominated by the urgent call to defend their national traditions, their liberties, their originality and their faith. All the great French Canadians obeyed that urge; the differences and even the opposition between them, which have been noted by Canadian historians, were in fact little more than shades of opinion. Some laid more stress on the need for anti-British resistance, others on the need to secure for French Canadians a fair place within the federal framework; but all were agreed that they must at any cost remain French. In this respect Honoré Mercier thought no differently from Sir Wilfrid Laurier or Henri Bourassa, founder of the Nationalist League, or, later, from Duplessis, who formed the National Union. With this traditional attitude the Catholic faith was quite naturally associated; it had always been the buckler of the Canadian soul. Harmony was therefore constant between the Church and the statesmen who directed the policies of French Canada, no matter to what party they belonged; but the hierarchy took care not to allow the Church to commit herself in favour of any single party. Thus, on the threshold of our period, when the Bishop of Three Rivers, Mgr Laflèche, advocated an ultra-conservative 'Catholic Programme', Mgr Taschereau, Archbishop of Quebec, at once made clear that the programme had been drawn up quite independently of the episcopate. Again Sir Wilfrid Laurier, while proclaiming himself 'liberal', was careful to explain that he had nothing in common with the 'revolutionary' liberals of Europe and that he would avoid any form of social excess or fanaticism.

The French Canadians, as champions of the Catholic cause, were confronted with adversaries determined to bar their way and to check all expansion. These were the Orangemen, named after William III, Prince of Orange, whose principal merit in their eyes was the ousting of James II in order to re-establish Protestantism on the throne. Partisans of a united English Canada, intransigent Protestants and active agents in the struggle against 'French and Catholic domination', they organized themselves into lodges, on the model of freemasonry, with headquarters at Toronto.

Thus all events, great or small, in the political life of Canada had religious implications. First there was the affair of Louis Riel, leader of the prairie half-castes, who twice rebelled in order to resist the penetration of his lands by colonists. On the first occasion (1870), thanks to

the great missionary Mgr Taché, the matter was settled peacefully. But in 1885 trouble broke out again, and the rioting ended in bloodshed; Riel was captured, hurriedly tried and hanged. Although the half-caste insurrection had involved the death of two missionaries, and although Riel had proclaimed himself prophet of an independent sect, a wave of wrath swept the entire French Catholic population. Next it was the indignation of French Canadians that caused the fall of Macdonald's federal government, following revelations of bribery connected with the building of the Canadian Pacific Railway. Again when Ottawa inaugurated its policy of subsidizing immigration in order to populate the western prairies, the Quebec newspapers protested against an operation which seemed likely to drown the French Canadians in a human flood from Europe; they complained also that it would cost less for a family to reach Edmonton or Winnipeg from London than from Quebec or Montreal. Then the Boer War naturally afforded French Canadians an opportunity to voice their sympathy with yet another small people which had fallen victim to British imperialism. Finally, the First World War provoked serious reactions. Having ignored appeals for voluntary enlistment, the French Canadians of Quebec actively opposed the conscription ordered by the federal government in 1917; and after the war the Nationalist League demanded and obtained submission of the peace treaty to Parliament.

The field, however, in which Catholic French Canadians put forth their main efforts was that of education. They were well aware that upon the French upbringing of their children depended their whole future, and the bishops reminded them time and again that the defence of their schools was the most imperative of their duties. The problem arose, of course, not in Quebec, but in those provinces where French Canadians formed a minority. The challenge was offered first in New Brunswick. Here the parliament cancelled all subsidies to Catholic schools, and so doomed them to virtual annihilation. But the uproar was such that a *modus vivendi* was found, the application of which was entrusted to two committees, one English and the other French. Next, in Manitoba, a law of 1890 abolished the educational rights of the minority and forbade the teaching of French. Despite a violent campaign by the Orangemen, this measure was overruled by the Privy Council in London. Fifteen years later, after an uneasy truce, a similar move in Saskatchewan and Alberta very nearly brought down Laurier's government, and one of his ministers resigned. Then (1910) the crisis was renewed in Ontario, where the British, supported curiously enough by the English-speaking Catholic bishops, sought to abolish bilingualism in the schools. The ensuing struggle lasted for seventeen years, ending with victory for the French Ontarians in 1917.

Those struggles were not the only proof given by Catholic French Canadians of their energy and determination. Realizing that the demographic fecundity of their race was their most valuable asset, they had started in the mid nineteenth century to move outwards into territory as yet uninhabited, the region of the Saguenay and of Lake St John. From about 1885, when the exodus southward became more rapid, colonists were often accompanied by their priests, who erected a wooden church wherever the settlers built their huts. Free grants of land were assigned to families with more than twelve children,[1] and this gave French Canadians a distinctively rural character which they were destined to preserve until the Second World War. Quebec, however, was not the only scene of this expansion. In the new western provinces, throughout the prairies to the foot of the Rockies, there were formed large groups which a visitor may still discover in the middle of Protestant and Anglo-Saxon Canada, rugged islets of French and Catholic loyalty.

Associated with this Catholic expansion on Canadian soil were the Oblates of Mary Immaculate,[2] a missionary congregation which in Canada gradually became pastoral as immigrants flowed in, and whose activities extended to all the Indian tribes.[3] Their apostolic drive continued in all directions: westward, but also towards Hudson Bay, the Keewatin, Labrador and even the Eskimo far north.

These numerous evidences of her vitality afforded by the Church in Canada received official recognition in Rome. The first French Canadian cardinal, Archbishop Taschereau of Quebec, was created in 1887 by Leo XIII, who also conferred the purple on the English-speaking Archbishop of Toronto. In 1899 a permanent Apostolic Delegation was erected at Ottawa. Finally, in 1908, the Canadian Church was withdrawn from the jurisdiction of Propaganda and placed under that of the Consistorial Congregation. Furthermore the establishment of a regular hierarchy in new circumscriptions kept pace with the progress of Catholicism. After Quebec, which had been made a metropolitan see by Gregory XVI in 1844, six other provinces were created by Pius IX and Leo XIII; in 1900 Canada possessed seven, together with twenty-one bishoprics, three vicariates and one apostolic prefecture. By 1939 there were twelve, with forty-three episcopal sees and seven apostolic vicariates.

[1] Beneficiaries numbered as many as 1,500 a year.
[2] *The Church in an Age of Revolution*, p. 392.
[3] See Chapter XI, section 11.

8. A Land of Faith

In order to give an idea of the strength of the Church in Canada it is not sufficient to describe her struggles and her territorial expansion. More impressive still is her strictly religious vitality which has never flagged and which, after all, is the ultimate reason for her success. At a time when so many countries were suffering from a dearth of vocations the number of Canadian priests rose at a steady rate. In 1867 there were 2,200 priests (regular and secular) among a million Catholics; in 1901, 4,600 among 2,300,000; in 1939, nearly 10,000[1] among 4,500,000. It was rare to find a family that had not given at least one son to the Church. Every diocese, even the most recent, had its own seminary. The bishops took a close interest in their future priests, and a Canadian college was founded at Rome by the Sulpicians in 1888.

Among that numerous clergy the religious occupied a most important place: in 1939 they numbered 3,500 out of about 10,000. The tide which had earlier brought so many orders and congregations from Europe to make foundations in Canada continued unabated. By 1939 all the great religious institutes of both sexes were represented and flourishing in the country, including some which had failed to take firm root in their native lands.

Nor had the clergy ceased to maintain firm control over most of the population. In 1939 its pristine authority and prestige were almost intact. Dispensed from nearly all taxes and disposing of fairly large material means, the priest was (and is) the notable respected by everyone throughout the countryside and in the smaller towns. Usually devoted moreover to his people, from among whom he himself had come, and knowing them intimately, he was the counsellor, guide and man of God to whom they looked not only for administration of the sacraments, but also for the direction of their lives. His authority might seem to some a little heavy, but it was justified by history and seldom disputed.

With great far-sightedness the Canadian Church had been careful to keep a firm hold on education in Quebec. She controlled seven thousand primary schools, as well as the teacher training colleges. The junior seminaries (at least one to each diocese) and fifty secondary colleges were dependent upon her, not to mention fifty schools of domestic economy and many others besides. In Quebec the bishops belonged by right to the Provincial Council of Public Instruction, assisted by an equal number of laymen appointed by themselves.[2] Together with the illustrious Laval University, founded at Quebec in

[1] This figure does not include more than 2,500 missionaries in distant lands.
[2] A similar committee supervised Protestant teaching.

1852, four other Catholic universities were recognized: Montreal (1878), Ottawa (1885), Antigonish and Memramcook (both later). In each case the metropolitan of the archdiocese was chancellor, a prelate rector, while many professors were priests or religious. It is easy to imagine the Church's influence upon the young in those circumstances.

Nor is it surprising that the Canadian people remained a faithful people into the mid twentieth century. Fundamentally rural, they retained certain peasant characteristics. Wherever the traveller landed on the banks of the St Lawrence he would find marks of solid faith: a church in every village, numerous convents, a crucifix at innumerable crossroads. Canadian families, too, preserved the Christian habits of their ancestors: grace before and after meals, prayer in common morning and evening. Divorce was not obtainable. Popular manifestations of piety were many, and brought together large numbers of people; such were the pilgrimages to Our Lady of the Cape and to St Anne of Beaupré.

It need hardly be said that that mainly rural Church, so firmly controlled by its priests, never experienced the crises precipitated in Europe first by Lamennais and then by the Modernists. Indeed a glance through contemporary newspapers and reviews almost makes one wonder whether such names as Loisy and Tyrrell were ever heard in Canada. Even 'Americanism' appears to have affected very few French Canadians. The Canadian Church, however, had its own problems. The clerical or, if preferred, theocratic aspect of Catholicism in Canada provoked a certain amount of criticism. But the anticlericals were not invariably irreligious; some declared themselves believers even while criticizing the excessive wealth of the clergy and its narrow-mindedness. On the eve of the Second World War, however, when contacts with Europe and the United States were more numerous and the standard of scientific knowledge was tending to rise among the intelligentsia, the problem of faith began to be felt, though official conformism makes it very difficult to determine its range.

The principal elements of renovation which the Church had adopted three-quarters of a century earlier were certainly not absent from Canadian religious life. Neither Catholic social doctrine nor Catholic Action was unknown, but they had been understood by Canada in a rather special way. The leaders of Canadian Catholicism had perhaps paid too little attention to the new problems raised by increasing industrialization. *Rerum Novarum* and *Quadragesimo anno* were read; Social Weeks were started; a national and Catholic form of trade unionism was introduced, in opposition to the American-type neutral trade unionism that was spreading. But the Catholic community does not impress one as having become more socially minded for all that. A

co-operative movement flourished throughout French Canada; but it retained a markedly confessional character, and when Père Georges-Henri Levesque, a Dominican, attempted to change that character just before the Second World War, he met with stiff resistance from the Jesuits, who took their stand on the attitude of Pius XI.

As for Catholic Action, it existed in Canada as early as the 1920's, as a replica of the French A.C.J.F., but more strongly marked with patriotic purposes than the latter. The appearance of specialized movements from 1935 onwards reduced the Catholic Association of Canadian Youth to little more than the A.C.Y., a merely patriotic and national organization. However, the growth of specialized Catholic Action raised for Canada, as nowhere else, the problem of relations between clergy and laity. The first great congresses and the work undertaken during the years preceding 1939 proved the admirable fervour of the laity in the service of the Church; but it remained to be seen whether long-standing customs would allow the clergy to grant the laity that freedom of action which was so desirable and which Pius XI intended them to have.

In spite of difficulties, which as yet were not serious, the Canadian Church at the end of our period was a powerful force in the land. In 1931 the Statute of Westminster had made Canada an independent State, in which the French Canadians accepted Bourassa's formula: 'Intellectual and moral loyalty to France, political loyalty to Britain, both subordinate to our exclusively Canadian patriotism.'

9. Opportunities and Perils of Latin America

Figures alone might lead one to conclude that the progress of Catholicism in Latin America had been as great as, if not greater than, in the United States and Canada; for in 1939 Catholics formed at least 90 per cent of a total population which had risen since 1830 from 18 million to 72 million. But the truth is very different.

The year 1870 found Latin America hardly recovered from the upheaval caused by the collapse of Spanish and Portuguese domination.[1] With few exceptions the Church was in more or less serious difficulties with the governments of the various states. Generally speaking that situation continued, varying in accordance with the political instability of those states, in most of which secularist ideology, supported by freemasonry, was extremely influential. In Brazil and Uruguay the positivism of Auguste Comte was virtually a religion. Then Marxism arrived to swell the anti-religious current leading to the

[1] *The Church in an Age of Revolution*, pp. 369–73.

tragic events of the new Mexican persecution.[1] In Ecuador the assassination of President Garcia Moreno (1875) was followed soon afterwards by the execution of Mgr Checa, Archbishop of Quito. In Colombia, on the other hand, Catholicism became once more the official religion in 1886; in 1900 the country was dedicated by law to the Sacred Heart; and in 1913 freemasonry was banned. On the whole, however, the situation was most confused and difficult so far as the Church was concerned; nor had it been altogether clarified and eased by 1939.

In order to improve this unhappy state of affairs, Pius IX had followed a systematic policy of concordats. His successors did likewise, taking every opportunity to negotiate an agreement or at least to start negotiations. Leo XIII, for example, succeeded in renewing the Concordat with Ecuador in 1881, and concluded one with Colombia in 1887, while a *modus vivendi* was established with Peru, Chile and Argentina.

Another proof of the Church's solicitude was the multiplication of ecclesiastical circumscriptions. In 1830 there were only 51 for the whole of Latin America; by 1900 there were 120 bishoprics and apostolic vicariates; at the death of Pius XI there were 268. The number of parishes, too, increased at the same rate; in Argentina it rose from about 300 in 1870 to 450 in 1914, to 563 in 1929 and to 722 in 1939. While that multiplication was insufficient, assigning to bishops and priests areas with which no one man could cope, it was at least a beginning, and the situation has since been further improved.

One innovation indicated clearly the Church's resolve to share in the expansion of Latin America. In 1899, at the invitation of Leo XIII, thirteen archbishops and forty-one bishops held a plenary Latin-American council in Rome. Under the presidency of Cardinal di Pietro the prelates spent nearly two months studying all the problems that affected the Church in their countries. Drawing inspiration from the canons of Trent and Vatican I, and anticipating in several respects the Code of Canon Law which was published eighteen years later, they formulated a number of decrees which the Pope confirmed in January 1900. That meeting foreshadowed the Latin-American Episcopal Council formed in 1958. At the same time, because of the great distances to be covered, Leo granted certain facilities touching administration of the sacraments.

A number of other grave problems confronted the Church in Latin America, apart from that raised by the presence in certain areas of pagan groups the task of whose conversion belonged, strictly speaking, to the missions.[2] What was the true level of faith among the baptized, who included the descendants of the *conquistadores*, those of the

[1] See Chapter IX, section 7. [2] See Chapter XI, section 11.

conquered aborigines, those also of the Negroes brought from Africa, not forgetting innumerable metis and mulattos? We need not here repeat in detail the criticisms to which the Latin-American Church was exposed, and which indeed many of her leaders did not hesitate to voice. Mediocrity among the clergy too often went hand in hand with a low level of morality among their people; concubinage among priests was accompanied by an enormous increase of illegitimate births among the faithful. Alcoholism, too, was widespread. Above all, and in a way more serious than the moral degradation, was the fact that Holy Church appeared too often as an institution alien to the real life of men. Ritualism and formalism clogged the true life of the soul.

Those manifest defects of Catholicism in Latin America, however, must not be allowed to hide its better qualities. While the faith in those countries often appeared too external and spectacular in the eyes of an English, French or German Catholic—though much less so in those of a Spaniard or an Italian—in countless souls it was sincere and deep-rooted. Significant in this respect is the example of Mexican Catholics resisting even unto death the attempt to dechristianize their native land.[1] It was not by way of flattery or propaganda that a succession of popes paid tribute to Latin America. Latin-American religion must be judged not by the erection of monumental statues of Christ in the highest pass of the Andes and on the summit of Corcovado in the Bay of Rio, nor by huge mass demonstrations such as took place in 1895 at the crowning of the Virgin of Guadalupe, but by the modest virtues found in a large part of the clergy and in large sectors of the faithful, a 'fervent piety whose value is not diminished by the fact of its expression through great traditional practices; a profound awareness of sin, which can make alliance with the worst vagaries of conduct and yet survive; an unfailing obedience and devotion to the Holy See and to the Pope; the refusal of any compromise with the enemy'.[2]

The Latin-American Church has improved steadily since 1870. The foundation (1858) of the Collegio Pio in Rome by Pius IX infused new blood into the Christian communities of Latin America by training an *élite* of bishops and priests, while the decisions taken by the plenary council of 1899 gave a fresh impulse. An effort was made to open seminaries, of which there were 223 in 1939; and if that seems little in so vast a territory, it does at least indicate considerable progress. Colleges for boys and girls were opened in very many places; and finally, strung out from Mexico to Chile, seventeen Catholic universities were training a Catholic intellectual class whose influence would one day be felt in public life.

[1] Graham Greene's *The Power and the Glory* shows how faith carried to the point of martyrdom can co-exist with a certain moral weakness.

[2] Robert Ricard, *Rythmes du monde*, 1961.

One agonizing problem, meanwhile, confronted (as it still confronts) the whole Latin-American Church throughout our period: a shortage of priests, due to various historical and sociological causes, particularly to the disappearance of the Jesuit 'reductions', to persecution and secularism, and to the Church's own delay in forming a native clergy. Statistics for 1939 provided some distressing figures: on average, Latin America had one priest per 5,000 Catholics;[1] but if account is taken of priests engaged in administration or those too old to exercise their ministry, the true average works out at about one per 10,000 or 12,000. Even so these figures do not tell the whole truth; for the enormous distances to be covered, and the widely scattered populations, made the apostolic task infinitely harder than in Europe. Little could be done to counteract those difficulties; illiteracy and the high rate of illegitimacy did not create a climate favourable to the flowering of vocations.

The situation therefore opened a wide field of action to the laity. Nothing was done before the First World War; the first steps were taken in 1917. In that year, under the auspices of the *Institucion Teresiana*, a female secular institute of Spanish origin, groups were formed with a view to establishing the Catholic presence in university circles. Catholic Action properly so called started in Latin America in the 1930's, though somewhat haphazardly; Colombia and Argentina led the way. J.O.C. had its groups in several countries. But rural Catholic Action, so necessary in regions where two-thirds of the population consisted of peasants, was as yet non-existent.

Besides the grave shortage of priests, some new problems had to be faced. The worst of these resulted from a profound change which began in about 1925 and which has continued since at an ever increasing rate, the change from a rural to an urban structure. Here, as elsewhere, the massive influx into the cities was accompanied by the process of dechristianization. It is true that the Church was not called upon to grapple with the racial question, which did not exist in Latin America; but the social situation was exceedingly grave. Excessive inequality between the classes, an inheritance from colonial days, reached stupefying proportions: in Chile, for example, 62 per cent of the population received only 24 per cent of the national income.

A minority of rich men, an underdeveloped and often underfed proletariat and, between them, a tiny middle-class fringe of no great means; a situation of that kind might well augur an alarming future, and the Church was directly concerned therein, first on the material plane. Deprived in several countries of her former resources, obliged to be in large measure self-supporting, and lacking a large well-to-do class whose gifts would have supplied her with a livelihood, she was

[1] France at that date had one per 750 and Canada one per 480.

driven either to sell her services or to obtain assistance from the wealthy, in either of which cases she risked alienating the people. What would happen when modern means of information, which were beginning to spread, drew the attention of the wretched proletariat to the injustice of their lot? Hostile propaganda, moreover, was already exploiting the facile argument of the Church's attachment to money. Marxism had its centre in Mexico, with Lombardo Toledano; but it was penetrating also into Guatemala and Brazil. Protestantism too, in its various forms, launched a full-scale offensive against 'decadent Catholicism'. This followed the International Missionary Conference at Edinburgh in 1910, and, above all, that held at New York in 1913, which set up a permanent Latino-American Committee. By 1924 six countries of Latin America each had a Protestant seminary, while seven had offices of information. In 1938, at Madras, representatives of all Protestant churches decided to regard Latin America as 'the sector of first importance'. At that date Protestantism had about 13,000 places of worship and 2½ million adherents in the South American continent. The peril was manifestly extreme.

10. Looking Eastward

Over against the Catholic Church stood the eastern half of the Christian world, separated from, suspicious of and often hostile towards her. It included those oriental groups which derived either (1) from the early heresies of Nestorianism and Monophysitism—the Chaldaean, Syriac (or Jacobite), Armenian and Coptic Churches; or (2) from the Byzantine schism—the Eastern Orthodox Church; or (3) from more recent break-aways, e.g. that of part of the Syro-Malabar Church in the seventeenth century. All these together represented about one-quarter of the Christian world.

In czarist Russia, since Orthodoxy was the State religion, Catholicism, like other creeds, could exist only in so far as it was tolerated by the Government. Though not continuously persecuted, it had suffered greatly, during the first two-thirds of the nineteenth century, from the imperial policy of Russianization, a policy which had been partly responsible for the breach of diplomatic relations between Russia and the Vatican in 1866.[1] Czar Nicholas II followed the same road as Alexander III, showing himself more understanding towards Catholics of oriental rites in Poland. Then, in 1903, he granted a constitution which guaranteed freedom of conscience: the penalties hitherto incurred by those who abandoned the State religion, and by priests

[1] They were resumed in 1882, thanks to the diplomatic skill of Leo XIII.

who administered the sacraments to converts, were abolished. Thus on the eve of the Bolshevik revolution 1,600,000 Catholics lived more or less peacefully within the borders of Russia properly so called,[1] where they formed heterogeneous groups: Poles, Byelorussians, Lithuanians and Germans in the north and west; in the centre and south, Poles and also Ruthenians, Armenians and Georgians of oriental rites. The clergy numbered 900 priests and controlled 1,200 places of worship. On the whole those groups were staunch and fervent, careful to resist Orthodox encroachment. While Catholicism seemed to make no progress in the Orthodox world, there were individual conversions, especially among the nobility and intelligentsia. Most important of these was that of the great philosopher Vladimir Soloviev (1850–1903), whose thought on the place of Orthodoxy in the bosom of the Universal Church was to prove one of the major elements of modern ecumenism, and who, under the twofold influence of Mgr Strossmayer and Anatole Leroy-Beaulieu, secretly embraced Catholicism in 1896.

In other countries where Orthodoxy was predominant the situation was more variable. It was fairly good in *Rumania*, where in 1939 Catholics numbered 2,300,000.[2] The Concordat of 1927 had granted them their rights and even salaries for the priests, and several congregations were opening schools. In the kingdom of *Yugoslavia*, 5 million Catholics formed two powerful groups, that of the Slovenes and that of the Croats and Dalmatians. The vitality of their faith was remarkable, thanks largely to the activities during more than half a century (1849–1905) of Mgr Strossmayer,[3] Bishop of Diakovar, who had embodied the national resistance of the Croats to Hungary, the intellectual and theological revival in that region, and the desire for union of the Churches. In the rest of the kingdom there were only a few ten thousands of Catholics. Serbia as a monarchy had been hostile towards them, particularly in the matter of education, and continued to be so as part of the Yugoslav federation. On more than one occasion that hostility led to bloodshed, the memory of which is preserved by bullet marks on the walls of Split Cathedral. In *Bulgaria*, reduced in size after the First World War, 35,000 Catholics (5,600 of the oriental rite) formed the diocese of Nicopolis and the vicariate of Sofia. In *Greece* the situation was better: although the Catholics numbered only 40,000, most of them belonging to the Latin rite, the work accomplished by the Jesuits since 1661 was bearing fruit. On the island of Syra, where they had their headquarters, there were no fewer than 10,000 Catholics with their own cathedral of Hagia Sophia on the summit of Frontado. Moreover, since 1890, the Jesuits had laboured systematically

[1] i.e. excluding the Russian part of Poland.
[2] Belonging either to the Latin or to the oriental rite.
[3] See the Index to *The Church in an Age of Revolution*.

to form a native clergy; it was still quite small, but was already preparing to produce some of its own bishops. There was also a Catholic cathedral at Athens; and the prestige of Catholicism was rising steadily, thanks to the teaching orders of both sexes, to whom Orthodox families gladly entrusted their children.

The most important elements in the history of the Christian East are to be found within the framework of those Churches whose most obvious characteristic is the use of liturgical rites other than the Latin. Together they form a huge sector extending from the Russian steppe to the extreme south of India, and from the highlands of Abyssinia to the American middle west; an extremely complex whole, containing sixteen or seventeen different Churches which follow at least six different rites—Maronites, Byzantine, Armenian, Syrian, Nestorian and Coptic. Excepting the Maronites, these oriental Catholic Churches are offshoots of separated Churches, offshoots which at one time or another returned to the Roman faith and obedience. Age-old traditions have endowed each with customs, rules and even spiritual characteristics which differentiate them from one another almost as much as from the Latin Church.

In 1870 the total number of oriental Catholics was only about 6 million. They could not, therefore, claim to carry much weight in the Universal Church. The Holy See did not, of course, ignore them, but the manner in which it treated them was not always commendable. In theory Propaganda maintained that each Church was entitled to remain faithful to its traditions. But in this matter we find the same tendency as has already been noticed in connection with the missions—the tendency to seek uniformity with a view to strengthening the authority of Rome.[1] At one session of the Vatican Council the Melchite patriarch, Gregory Youssef, warned the Church against the danger of trying to reduce the venerable Churches of the East to uniformity. But it seemed that the centralizing current was the stronger. The re-establishment of the Latin patriarchate in 1869 had been yet another symptom of the same tendency.

In 1878 this attitude towards the oriental Churches began to disappear. Soon after his election Leo XIII called for two reports, one from Mgr Vanutelli, apostolic delegate at Constantinople, the other from the Turkish consul in Rome, who was an Italian and a friend of the Pope's secretary. Both concluded that the Catholic Churches of the East could do much for the apostolate in their countries, if only they were respected and asked for their assistance. Leo therefore decided upon a eucharistic congress to be held at Jerusalem in 1893, which would show the East the true Catholic faith. Cardinal Langénieux,

[1] For the affair of the Armenian schism see *The Church in an Age of Revolution*, p. 292; for that of the Chaldaeans, ibid. pp. 388–9.

papal legate at the congress, brought back a detailed account of the spirit he had found among oriental Catholics, their fears and their hopes. This was followed in 1894 by two Encyclicals, *Praeclara gratulationis* and *Orientali dignitas*, which were supplemented by a number of decrees the application of which was entrusted to a committee of cardinals. Praising 'the august antiquity which ennobled the rites of their Churches', he remarked that that very diversity 'proclaimed the divine unity of the Catholic faith, and revealed an apostolic origin'. He showed that 'ritual differences and traditional ecclesiastical autonomies' could prepare the way for a reconciliation with schismatic Orthodoxy. He also insisted upon the great respect that apostolic delegates must show towards the patriarchs, and forbade Latin priests and missionaries to bring an oriental Catholic into the Latin rite.[1]

Other steps taken by Leo in this field were the healing of the Armenian schism, restoration of the Coptic patriarchate of Alexandria and the removal of Latin interpolations from various rites. He also inaugurated patriarchal conferences at the Vatican, for the study of questions relative to the East and its Christian peoples. Moreover he went so far as to allow Latin priests working in the East, e.g. the Assumptionists at Constantinople, to transfer to the Byzantine rite.

Pius X did not accelerate this movement, but neither did he check it. He gave the Ruthenian Catholics a bishop of their own rite; and the celebration at Rome in 1908 of a Byzantine pontifical High Mass, to mark the fifteenth centenary of the death of St John Chrysostom, showed that the path had not been abandoned, even though it were not followed with quite the same buoyant step.

The second stage was cleared by Benedict XV. On 1st May 1917 he created the Congregation for the Oriental Church, with jurisdiction over all matters concerning the persons, discipline and rites of the Eastern Churches in communion with Rome. Autumn of the same year saw the opening of the Pontifical Institute of Oriental Studies. Run by the Jesuits, its purpose was to train Latin priests desirous of exercising their ministry in the East, but it also welcomed oriental priests who wished to pursue higher studies. Finally it was Benedict XV who proclaimed St Ephraem of Syria a Doctor of the Church.

The work was completed, so far as concerns our period, by Pius XI. Several times during his pontificate he reminded Catholics of their duty to understand their oriental brethren, and thus gave new impulse to the achievements of his predecessor. He was clearly looking beyond the communities united with Rome to the much greater mass of separated Christians whom he longed to win for the Church. That was plain from his Encyclical on the third centenary of the death of St

[1] Later he even abolished the title (but not the office of) 'prefect apostolic' in territories where there was a patriarch.

Josaphat, Archbishop of Polotsk, as well as from another commemorating the Council of Nicaea and from his letter on SS. Cyril and Methodius. The addition of a course on oriental rites to the programme of seminary studies was an even more significant measure. In 1929 the Encyclical *Rerum Orientalium* recapitulated all that Rome had done for the Christian East. Also under Pius XI the jurisdiction of the Congregation for the Oriental Church was extended to include even Latin Catholics throughout the Near East; and in 1930 a Commission for Russia was set up to deal with the special problems raised by that country. The Oriental Institute received fresh vigour; in 1925 it was given the right to confer the doctorate, enlarged its field of teaching and had its library enriched with books assembled by Mgr Tisserant and Father Karakevski from all over the East. Hard by the Institute, the 'Russicum' was training priests to know and understand the Slav world. Two of the most important acts due to the Pope's oriental policy were (*a*) the preliminary steps towards an oriental code of canon law, and (*b*) the elevation to the Sacred College of Mgr Tappouni, patriarch of the Syrians, in 1935.

The results of an effort extending over three pontificates were apparent by 1939. All oriental communities of any importance had regained their own hierarchy. A good deal had likewise been done to provide seminaries and schools for those Churches. Among several such institutions in Rome were the Greek College of St Athanasius, founded in the seventeenth century for seminarists of the Byzantine rite, and the Ethiopian College founded by Benedict XV in 1919; in the East itself were the famous seminary of St Anne at Jerusalem, the Institute of St Leo at Athens and a college at Adrianople for the Bulgarians. In several respects a thorough reform had been achieved, particularly that of the Ruthenian Church under Leo XIII. Nor should it be forgotten that in all those undertakings the popes had received invaluable assistance from many religious congregations—Jesuits, Redemptorists, Assumptionists, Lazarists—who gave some of their members special training and made them adopt the rites and usages of the Orientals.

During the period with which we are concerned some of the Eastern Churches endured terrible ordeals. The Uniat Church of Ruthenia and White Russia, dismembered since the partition of Poland, was subjected to appalling treatment by the Russians: prison, the knout and Siberia claimed thousands of martyrs; its rites were brought into line with those of schismatic Orthodoxy; the last Apostolic See, that of Chelm, was suppressed in 1875, and the faithful incorporated by force into the State Church. Such, however, was the loyalty of the Ruthenians that in 1905, when Czar Nicholas II introduced some degree of tolerance, 500,000 of them asked to return to communion with Rome, though they were obliged to adopt the Latin rite because

Russian law forbade Catholics to use the Byzantine. During the First World War Ruthenians in Habsburg territory had much to endure, now interned by the Hungarians as Russophils, now persecuted by the Russian occupants who wanted to set up a National Church. And when the war was over, conflict between the Ruthenians and the Poles, then the police persecution waged by Warsaw, inflicted new trials upon those unfortunates. It is understandable that many of them emigrated to the United States.

Still worse sufferings were the lot of several communities in the Near East. In 1895 the Catholic Armenians shared the fate of their compatriots when Abdul Hamid, 'the Red Sultan', ordered massacres which claimed 300,000 victims. And when the Ottoman terror swooped again upon the Christians (1915–22), the Armenians and the Chaldaeans in northern Mesopotamia perished in large numbers. So too with the Melchites, whose Church emerged from the war, and then from famine, bloodstained and disorganized. So too, again, with the Syrian Catholics, whose three dioceses vanished in the whirlwind. So too, finally, with the Maronites, age-old champions of the Catholic cause in the Near East, who in 1860 had been victims of the Druse terror and who were now once again arrested, assassinated or starved to death by thousands.

Despite these and other ordeals, most of the Catholic Churches of the Orient continued to show amazing vitality; many of them experienced an impressive numerical increase. The Syro-Malabars of India rose in sixty-six years from 225,000 to 750,000. The Copts of Egypt doubled in twenty-five years. And in 1935 the Maronites, with 355,000 members, 600 priests and 700 monks, were the most important religious group in the Lebanon.

CHAPTER XI

THE CHURCH CO-EXTENSIVE WITH THE WORLD

B. Apogee and Reform of the Missions

1. A Leper among Lepers

ONE day in May 1873, on the island of Mani, in the centre of the Hawaiian Archipelago, a new church had just been consecrated, and after the ceremony six priests sat down to table with the vicar apostolic, Mgr Maigret. All belonged to the Congregation of the Sacred Hearts of Jesus and Mary, ordinarily known as Picpucians.[1] During the meal they discussed the state of the Pacific missions. It seemed good: fine churches were being built on many of the islands: the number of baptisms was rising steadily; the field had been tilled and the harvest was ripening. But one of them spoke a single word, 'Molokaï', and the others understood. Molokaï was only one among a host of lovely islands, by climate and landscape a veritable paradise. But twenty-five years earlier the dreadful scourge of leprosy had fallen upon the archipelago and was still wreaking havoc among the native population. A panic-stricken government had been unable to think of anything better than to round up the lepers and confine them to the peninsula of Kalawao on the north of Molokaï. More than a thousand of these miserable folk were there, deprived of contact with the outside world, reduced almost to the condition of brutes, and indeed treating one another like wild beasts. The mere mention of leprosy was enough to trouble the missionaries. The same thought had occurred to all seven: a priest was needed in that hell. But who would go? There are some orders that no religious superior dare give, some appointments that he cannot make.

Into the silence fell another word: *Moi.* One of them had volunteered—Joseph de Veuster, in religion Father Damien. He was thirty-three years old. 'Like Jesus Christ . . .', whispered Mgr Maigret. Like Jesus Christ . . .; and the bishop accepted.

There then began one of the noblest of all human ventures. Landing in the autumn of 1873 from the little steamboat *Kilauea*, which served the islands, Father Damien found himself immediately in what seemed

[1] *The Church in an Age of Revolution*, pp. 89 and 404.

to be truly hell. The essential horror was not his isolation among those leonine muzzles, those walking skeletons, those bodies with purulent extremities; nor was it the pestilential odour that hung about the place. More painful to a priest was the moral degradation of those dying outcasts, the sight of mothers abandoning their children, the revolting orgies. 'Here there is no law and no morality,' they said ever and again; 'what is the use?' In that world of utter desolation Father Damien stood alone and destitute, so lonely and so destitute that on the first night, since no hut awaited him, he had no resting-place but the foot of a great tree, no food but some bread he had brought with him from the ship. He was alone, healthy, amid lepers. He was to remain with them for sixteen years, until his death.

Confronted with such horror and such misery, others had lost heart. If Father Damien was sometimes tempted to despair, none knew it. From that scum he had to refashion men, and he set to work without delay. Son of Flemish peasants, he was familiar with all a farmer's tasks, and his strength was equal to every challenge. An extensive programme of cultivation was put in hand, and all the lepers who were strong enough had to do their bit. Water was brought from the mountains, first by lines of carriers with Damien always at their head, and later by canal. The old, infected huts were burnt and replaced by new ones, for the missionary was a good carpenter. Roads leading to the villages were cleaned, and cemeteries laid out. The happiest day was that on which a brand new church was opened, with a ceremony attended by all who could stand.

More important than this material renascence was the moral resurrection accomplished by Father Damien in the hell of Molokaï. Where violence, hate and the worst disorders had prevailed there grew up a new spirit, a spirit of charity. The Kanakas were simple creatures, somewhat ingenuous, driven by instinct, but responsive to good. None of the Protestant missionaries who worked in the archipelago had ever gone to live among them. Father Damien had made himself so much one of themselves that he would sometimes say from the pulpit, 'We lepers'. His very presence sufficed to spread friendship, and broken families came together once again. Burglary and attacks on the person ceased. Girls formed themselves into societies dedicated to Our Lady, and learned to sing; for the boys Damien arranged athletic competitions. Even the insane, the most hideous of all leper groups, were calmed. Nor did Father Damien hesitate to use vigorous methods in his determination to secure order; the big stick helped to get rid of alcoholism and hooliganism. In five or six years Molokaï was changed.

Before long there was talk among the islands about this unusual missionary; it was seldom that the *Kilauea* failed to bring food,

clothing and medicine. The nuns of Honolulu, unable to join Damien, organized collections, and even managed to buy a bell for the church. With success came jealousy; Protestant missionaries, alarmed by the number of conversions, tried to obstruct his work. Father Damien was advised to take a rest, but he refused. He was then subjected to an unspeakable outrage: under pretext of avoiding contagion, and though still uncontaminated by the disease, he was forbidden to leave the leper colony, and thus condemned to a living death. In order to make his confession he had now to go alone in his boat to within hailing distance of the steamer, from whose deck one of his brethren heard him in Latin and gave him absolution.

This dreadful doom ended as might have been foreseen. Father Damien had never taken precautions against leprosy, and one day, while taking a foot-bath in water that was much too hot, he felt nothing. The symptom was all too clear: for twelve years his robust constitution had resisted, but now the ghastly virus had proved too strong. Father Damien had long since foreseen and accepted this eventuality; now he was to be in very truth 'a leper among lepers'.

Four years he took to die. The disease was merciful in his case, to the extent that it did not attack his eyes until the very end; it also spared him the abominable rotting of his members. But his face, that handsome peasant face, became bloated and deformed. Who would have recognized in that leonine mask the fine fellow who had come among the living dead so many years ago?

As he drew towards the goal of life a cry of wonder echoed through Europe and America. 'Ye who pass the cliffs of Molokaï, bow low!' exclaimed one German newspaper. A Kanaka princess, regent of the isles, went to see him and confer a decoration. Japan sent a doctor and medical supplies. But Damien's supreme consolation was the certitude that his achievement would survive. An auxiliary had been sent, one of his old schoolfellows also had arrived, his own brothers spoke of joining him, and some nuns had offered to go and look after his orphanage. He died on 15th April 1889, at the age of forty-nine, and was buried as he had wished at the foot of the great pandanus tree where he spent his first night in the island. A cross was erected near by, upon which were inscribed the words: 'Greater love than this no man hath than to lay down his life for those he loves.' The lesson of that life, and of others like it, was drawn long afterwards by Mahatma Gandhi[1] in words that no Catholic reads without a thrill of pride: 'Care of the lepers is so dear to missionaries, and above all to Catholic missionaries, because there is no other service that demands a greater spirit of self-sacrifice. A leper colony requires the highest ideal and the most perfect abnegation. The world of politics and of journalism can

[1] In a speech to students at Lahore.

boast few heroes comparable with Father Damien. But the Catholic Church possesses thousands of men and women who, like Father Damien, have dedicated themselves to the service of lepers. It is worth while trying to discover the source of such heroism.'

2. A Great Missionary Epoch

The first half of the nineteenth century, it will be remembered,[1] had witnessed the resurrection of the missions. The movement continued and even accelerated, especially (*a*) during the last quarter of that century, when growth of the missions ran parallel with the extension of colonialism, and (*b*) on the morrow of the First World War, when the Catholic apostolate adapted itself to new conditions and so made fresh progress at a time when white supremacy was about to be challenged. One must not, however, imagine that those results were obtained without difficulty. It has often been said that the facilities offered to missionaries by technical advances made their task much easier; but that is true only to a certain point. True, the days were long since gone when to embark for Asia or Africa was in itself a dangerous undertaking, but missionaries had still to face numerous perils. Many died of the so-called colonial diseases, about which so little was known. Many were the victims of xenophobia inflamed by stronger and stronger nationalist currents among colonial peoples; in sixty-six years more than two hundred and fifty missionaries died violent deaths.

Throughout our period one of the most serious difficulties other than those inherent in missionary life was the rivalry of non-Catholic missions. The missionary activity of Orthodox Russia, organized since 1898 by the Kazar Institute in Korea, China, Japan, Syria and Abyssinia, was of small importance, and it ended altogether in 1917. But the Protestant missions made constant progress. All Churches deriving from the Reformation sprang to the apostolate; the United States alone had 300 Protestant missionary societies, Britain 160, Germany 45, not to mention the Bible Societies, which had been federated since 1920 in an International Council of the Missions. While there was no open opposition, Catholic missionaries often ran foul of Protestant enterprises—at the Cape, for instance, in Madagascar, in Togoland and in certain Pacific archipelagos, which were for long firmly closed against Catholicism.

Other more formidable adversaries emerged with the years. After 1917 Marxist Communism waged relentless warfare wherever possible against the Christian missions, which Lenin himself had likened to the

[1] *The Church in an Age of Revolution*, pp. 379 ff.

colonial enterprises of capitalism. Then, in the years immediately before the Second World War, there was a rebirth of Islam, slow at first but soon gaining impetus at an ever faster rate. Islam had always opposed an almost invincible resistance to Christian penetration, so much so that in North Africa, for example, it would have been easy to count the number of conversions made since the French conquest of Algeria. Henceforward the missionaries would no longer have to face a kind of inert mass, but an organism conscious of its strength and of its opportunities.

3. Rome, Capital of the Missions

Each of the four popes who succeeded one another on the Apostolic throne between 1878 and 1922 was wide awake to the needs of the missions, and strove to strengthen, encourage, organize and even to reform them. Leo XIII, whose pontificate coincided with the most impressive phase of colonial expansion, understood and repeatedly emphasized that the Church alone, mother of civilization, could endow the colonial venture with the soul it so manifestly lacked. The missionary movement had no more spirited protector than he. He personally followed its course, urged the religious institutes to become more and more missionary, took a close interest in the progress of the existing *œuvres missionaires* and witnessed the birth of a third—that of *Saint-Pierre-l'Apôtre*. It was at his request that the White Fathers and the Fathers of the Holy Ghost undertook the penetration of black Africa. More important still, he realized fully the urgent need to form autochthonous Churches in Asia and Africa, and therefore to enlarge the native clergy. His apostolic letter *Ad extremas* (1893), on the clergy in the Indies, foreshadowed the grand designs carried out thirty years later by Benedict XV and Pius XI.

It has been said of Pius X that he was so preoccupied with restoring the interior life of the Church that he cared little about her expansion. That simply is not true. Though his measures were not comparable with those of his successors, one of his major achievements was the reform of Propaganda with a view to giving it greater freedom of action. He also created forty-one missionary circumscriptions, and devoted some of his diplomatic activity to support of missionary work, e.g. in a letter to the Mikado Mutsohito.

Benedict XV, whose care for the oriental Churches we have already noticed, could not but be interested in the missions. During the war he granted audiences and spent hours of labour on behalf of the Missionary Union of the Clergy. When the peace treaties were negotiated he found means of intervening to prevent the German missions from

passing into any but Catholic hands. In eight years he created no fewer than forty-five apostolic vicariates and prefectures. The great act of his pontificate, however, was the publication of the Encyclical *Maximum illud*, in which, laying down the duties of the hierarchy, and indicating the attitude that missionaries should adopt, he proclaimed the supra-national character of the Church and set the apostolate on that road along which it was to move into the future.[1] There can be no doubt whatever that the expansion of Catholicism could not have taken place as it did but for the Pontiff whose last words were 'The missions ...'

Pius XI used frequently to say that the thought of there being on earth a thousand million souls who knew not Christ literally prevented him from sleep. Indeed scarcely a month of his pontificate went by without his concerning himself in one way or another with the missions. The Encyclical *Rerum Ecclesiae*, resuming earlier papal teaching, finally determined the method to be employed in the Catholic apostolate, and thus proposed a radical reform of the whole missionary field. His sensational gesture in consecrating the first six Chinese bishops showed his resolve to translate that proposal into reality. Moreover it was he who created the largest number of apostolic circumscriptions; who decided to entrust the missionary territories to most of the orders and congregations, even to those which had never before done such work, in order to beget missionary vocations; who greatly enlarged the College of Propaganda on the Janiculum, near St Peter's; who conceived the idea of a missionary exhibition in 1925, and on the eve of his death ordered another to be held in 1940.

The direct and personal action of the popes on behalf of the missions was helped by the Congregation *de Propaganda Fidei*. Re-organized by Pius X, Propaganda played an enormous part in the development and organization of the missionary movement. The palazzo on the Piazza di Spagna was the centre from which the whole immense missionary task was accomplished all around the earth. The Congregation of Propaganda appointed vicars and prefects apostolic, assigned territories to the various religious orders; took charge of and disbursed the large sums of money collected by the *œuvres missionaires*; and controlled the training of missionaries, for which the Scientific Missionary Institute was formed in 1935. It was thus, throughout the four pontificates, the indispensable auxiliary of the popes in all that concerned the great work of Catholic expansion.

Rome was capital of the missions not only because she issued doctrinal instructions and made administrative decisions. She now managed the powerful associations which linked the entire Church with the missionary endeavour. The first half of the nineteenth century had produced two *œuvres missionaires*: Pauline Jaricot's *Propagation de*

[1] See section 8 of the present chapter.

la Foi and Mgr Forbin-Janson's *Œuvre de la Sainte-Enfance*, which had contributed much to the revival of the missions. A third, the *Œuvre de Saint-Pierre-l'Apôtre*, was founded in 1889 by Jeanne Bégard, a rich but saintly young woman, for the maintenance of coloured seminarists and the building of churches in Asia. When she became seriously ill, Pius X entrusted her foundation to the Institute of Franciscan Missionaries of Mary. Benedict XV commended it to the whole Christian world, and in 1929 Pius XI gave it its final statutes.

There were many other undertakings concerned with the material welfare of the missions, but all did not possess the means and the range proportionate to their generosity of heart. This dispersion of effort did not serve the common cause, and Pius XI, soon after his accession, took steps to deal with the situation. He did not suppress the three existing *œuvres*, but he forbade the creation of new ones. Henceforward the offerings of the faithful were to be administered according to 'a rational and methodical plan'. In 1922 the *Propagation de la Foi* was transferred from France to Rome. Between that date and 1929 a series of *motu proprio* perfected the new arrangement. Attached directly to the Congregation of Propaganda, the *Œuvre de la Propagation* became the central organism, its directors being at the same time those of *Saint-Pierre-l'Apôtre*. *Sainte-Enfance* remained apart, entrusted with the training of youth in missionary lands, but it too was controlled from the Piazza di Spagna.

Besides this vast undertaking for the provision of material assistance there was another of a quite different character; its purpose was not the collection of funds, but one that was in a sense even more important. In 1915 Father Paolo Manna, of the Milan Foreign Missions, decided to start a movement that would rouse among a hitherto indifferent clergy more interest in the missionary problem. This was the Missionary Union of the Clergy, which asked priests to pray and obtain prayers for the missions. Cardinal van Rossum, prefect of Propaganda, was enthusiastic, and in 1919 he secured its approval by Benedict XV in a passage of *Maximum illud*, which gave it worldwide status. Pius XI took it under his protection and by 1939 the Union numbered 160,000 priests.

4. Public Opinion and the Missions

Since the beginning of the nineteenth century the current hostile to the missionaries, unleashed by Voltaire and the *Encyclopédistes*, had been reversed.

Missionary reviews, whose success was already well established, made still further progress, thanks to the impulse given by the *Annales*

de la Propagation de la Foi. But numerous other missionary organs were founded, addressing themselves to readers at various levels. The *Annales de la Sainte-Enfance* (1868) 'aimed at giving an account, day by day, of the work accomplished by apostolic labourers', and indeed comprised a rich quarry of information. All countries soon had their missionary reviews: in Spain, for example, *El Siglio de las Misiones*; in Ireland, *The World.* More scientific were the French *Revue d'histoire des Missions* and the German *Zeitschrift für Missionswissenschaft.* Propaganda, of course, had its own, as did most if not all of the missionary religious institutes.

To make known the missions was now among the principal designs of the Papacy and of the Church. The *Fides* agency, established by Pius XI, supplied the press with news concerning them. 'Missionary chairs' were founded in several Catholic universities, often in association with chairs of ethnology, a field in which missionaries had much to learn. Modern means, too, were employed to foster goodwill towards the missions; the Church devoted several 'universal exhibitions' to missionary work, such as that held in the Vatican gardens in 1925. In 1931 the colonial exhibition at Paris included a missionary pavilion, which proved a great attraction. Permanent missionary museums collected documents on the history of the missions, which have proved to be invaluable for the study of ethnology; the most important was established at the Lateran and endowed with the most up-to-date apparatus. Films also were early used to help missionary propaganda.

Thus the whole Church was invited to share in the missionary task. In 1926 'Missionary Sunday' was instituted, on which Catholics throughout the world would be informed of the work accomplished, and of the need for men and money. The numerous canonizations and beatifications of missionary martyrs, often of quite recent date, showed the importance attached by the Church to the work for which those saintly men and women had laid down their lives. And in 1925 Pius XI made a gesture of great significance when he gave the missions as their heavenly patron the celebrated young saint of the age, Thérèse of Lisieux, who during her short life had suffered and prayed for them.

5. In the Service of the Missions

The previous epoch (1789–1870) had witnessed a veritable torrent of missionary institutes, and that phenomenon continued unabated. The old congregations—Jesuits, Lazarists, Redemptorists, Franciscans—showed amazing vigour. Institutes born in the nineteenth century followed in their footsteps: Fathers of the Holy Ghost, Picpucians,

Fathers of the Holy Cross, Oblates of Mary Immaculate, Congregation of the Immaculate Heart of Mary, Marists, Marianists, the Society of St Joseph of Mill Hill, Salesians, Pallotines, White Fathers and many more.

But that was still inadequate; the harvest awaited other reapers, and new institutes arose: in Italy the Fathers of the Consolata at Turin; in Austria the Benedictines of St Odilon; in Spain the Fathers of Mary Immaculate; in Holland the Fathers of the Divine Word; in Ireland the Society of St Columban, better known as the Maynooth Missions; in France the Fathers of La Salette, the Oblates of St Francis de Sales, the St Quentin Priests of the Sacred Heart. Nor was America far behind, with the Priests of Maryknoll in the U.S.A., and the priests of the seminary of St Francis Xavier in Canada. In 1939 there were more than eighty such institutes that could be considered of real importance.

Nuns were twice as numerous as priests. In many places they prepared the way for those who would preach the Gospel; elsewhere, particularly in Moslem countries, they formed the only possible link, through women and children, with native populations. In 1959 there were no fewer than 180 female missionary institutes. Besides the Sisters of Charity, there were others dating only from the nineteenth century. Some of these, e.g. the White Sisters, were associated with male institutes; others, e.g. the Blue Sisters of Castres and the Chartres Sisters of St Paul, were autonomous. Some, like Mère d'Youville's Grey Sisters in Canada, played an important part from the outset.

In order to prepare for, or to support, their apostolic task, religious of both sexes made increasing use of orphanages, dispensaries, hospices, hospitals, leper colonies and schools. Although the more wealthy Protestants outdistanced the Catholics as regards the number of their hospitals, from 1920 onwards a great effort was made to build Catholic hospitals wherever possible. The American Fathers of Maryknoll attracted a fair number of doctors; medical training was provided by the missionary seminary of Galway in Ireland and by the Association of Würzburg in Germany. A scheme for a missionary order of female doctors was suggested by two Scotswomen, Agnes McLaren and Margaret Lamont, both converts from Puritanism who had done medical work in India. The plan was carried out in the United States by Anna Dangel, a Tyrolean, who in 1925 founded the Medical Mission Sisters. Just before the Second World War Father Gemelli, rector of the University of the Sacred Heart, established medical training centres for missionaries at Milan, Bologna and Parma.

The second means of action, schools, became the normal and indeed obligatory annexe of the missions. Thereby it was possible to transform the younger generations and to baptize children whose parents were still pagan but who later followed their example. In 1890 China had

5,000 missionary schools teaching 100,000 children; in 1939 there were more than 9,000 teaching 300,000. Nor was education confined to elementary schools. Several religious orders opened secondary colleges, many of which welcomed non-Christians, while the Jesuits ran regional seminaries, colleges, universities and scientific institutes.

This twofold charitable and educational activity became increasingly part and parcel of social work closely allied with the apostolate. In many areas the missionaries found themselves obliged to serve as guides, as technical advisers and almost as guardians of their converts. In the name of Christian morality they fought such social scourges as alcoholism, and, notably in black Africa, opposed certain customs which degraded the human person, e.g. the 'dowry', which led to the sale of girls like cattle. In China and Indo-China they fought against the introduction of concubines into the home, and in the East Indies against the horrible practice of suttee. In the long and often shameful chapter of white colonization the missionaries invariably took upon themselves the task of social advancement, complementary in some respects to their strictly apostolic labours.

Two other features must be noted in the missionary movement, and first the growing importance of the part played by the laity. This was indeed nothing new: missionaries had long been enlisting lay support in the East Indies, China and Indo-China. But such recruitment became systematic, particularly after the First World War, with the introduction, particularly in Africa, of native catechists. The same period saw the beginnings of another form of lay collaboration in the shape of Catholic Action. In Europe itself a number of organizations were set up to prepare men and women for work alongside the missionaries. Undoubtedly the most important of these was *Ad Lucem*, a French institution formed in 1931 at Lille by seven students who hoped to effect a synthesis of the missionary vocation and the desire to share in the lay apostolate. *Ad Lucem* quickly attracted doctors, nurses, teachers and social helpers; its first foundation was made in 1936 by Dr Aujoulat, at Efok in the Cameroon, and was an immediate success. The poor village was rebuilt of locally made brick, while Aujoulat himself served as joiner, metal-worker, farmer and stockman, as well as medical officer. Even the Second World War did not halt the progress of that undertaking, and by 1945 the clinic had 170 beds and was giving 150,000 consultations a year.

The second feature was no less important. Within the general framework of the missions we find men and women whose primary vocation was not strictly missionary but contemplative. Settling in Asia or Africa, they aimed not so much at converting the natives as at bearing witness among them to the most purely spiritual element of the Christian faith. Thus a Trappist monastery, Our Lady of Consolation,

was founded (1883) near Peking; others followed in various parts of the world. The Benedictines of Monte Cassino, Belgium and Pierre-qui-Vire made foundations in Africa as well as in Korea and Cambodia. The Strict and the Common Observance of Cîteaux did likewise in Indo-China and South Africa respectively. Nor did the female orders lag behind: Poor Clares and Carmelites both opened houses in missionary lands; but the most extraordinary achievement was that of the Trappistines in Japan. They made a foundation there in 1898, and on the eve of the Second World War there were nearly two hundred Japanese Trappistines.

6. Colonialism and the Missions

The last part of the nineteenth century and the beginning of the twentieth witnessed the apogee of white domination of the world. Exploration reduced the zones of *terra incognita* almost to the point of disappearance. Behind the explorers came soldiers, then colonists and traders, to form new 'colonial empires'. It might have seemed at that time that the whole planet would be partitioned among the conquering whites.

White ambitions did not halt even at the boundaries of Far Eastern countries which had remained closed to white penetration and white commerce. Japan, under the far-sighted emperor Mutsohito, had managed in 1868 to adapt herself to Western civilization; but China retained much less independence. After the scandalous Opium War of 1842, she failed to modernize herself sufficiently to withstand foreign ambitions, or to neutralize them by setting one against another. Every circumstance served to increase the pressure of the whites. The European chancelleries divided 'zones of influence' among themselves; and the outburst of xenophobia known as the Boxer Rising (1900) led only to severe repression and an increased weight of coercive measures. Even after the overthrow of the Celestial Empire, in 1912, China remained for the whites a field of exploitation.

This is no place to argue the merits and demerits of Western 'colonialism' and 'imperialism', to ask whether they brought more happiness than suffering, more progress than vice, to subject peoples. It is, however, undeniable that the missions were to a very large extent associated with them, as they had been long ago with Spanish and Portuguese colonization. The missionaries made their way into conquered countries in order to evangelize them, and not seldom placed themselves under armed protection. There was nothing reprehensible about that: in barbarian territories, where the most elementary law of nations was unknown, it was natural that the missionary should seek

military protection. Conversely, the colonizing powers appointed themselves protectors of the missions; the murder of a white missionary meant 'loss of face' for all whites and must be avenged. In China the link between the Western powers and the missions was actually given official standing. All treaties imposed by the victors had contained clauses acknowledging that link, and in 1862 Napoleon III had secured recognition of France's general protectorate of all Catholic missions. That situation—which the Holy See accepted by the decree *Acerbo nimio* in 1888—lasted until about 1922, and it would be pharisaical to deny that it favoured the missionary cause. But what about the other side of the coin?

It is quite clear that the bond between the missions and European expansion tended to identify the man of God with the conqueror, the designs of the former with those of the latter, Christianity with European civilization, sometimes even the interests of the Church with those of the protecting power. Certain missionaries, too, believed in all good faith that to serve their earthly motherland was to serve the Church; they saw nothing wrong in celebrating their national festivals or hoisting national flags on their steeples.

And so the missionaries found themselves, in the eyes of non-Christians, ranked with the conquerors, obeyed because they were stronger, feared and sometimes hated. This fact explains why, whenever the European powers seemed to lack strength, Christians paid the price of popular fury, e.g. in the Boxer Rising. Even when the situation took no such tragic turn, the 'protected' missions were inevitably isolated from the masses whom they had hoped to baptize. Occasionally such isolation assumed concrete form, as at Peking where the missions occupied a separate quarter surrounded by a defensive wall. Some understandable but none the less clumsy measures emphasized that isolation still further; in 1899 Mgr Favier, auxiliary of Peking, obtained the signature of an agreement which gave to missionaries the Chinese dignity of mandarin, and to bishops that of viceroy together with a right to the ritual prostrations enforced by Chinese etiquette. It was not thus that the apostles and their disciples had converted the pagan world; neither St Peter nor St Paul had entered Rome wearing the senatorial toga and preceded by lictors.

Herein lay the most serious danger of a situation which, we must repeat, appeared to be dictated by circumstance; it prevented that process of conversion which the history of the Church shows to be normal. In order to make headway in a pagan world, the earliest missionaries mixed with the various peoples, became Greek among Greeks, Gentile among Gentiles; and thus they formed around themselves little groups of Christians whom they trained in the faith. After a while they chose priests and deacons from the young community.

Then, a good deal later, when the community was sufficiently well developed and organized, it received a native bishop. The goal was always the same: to constitute indigenous Churches as integral parts of the Church Universal and equal in all respects with those of older Christian countries. The Church indeed was not regarded as truly established in any region until this final stage had been reached.

Mutatis mutandis, one might ask whether the paucity of results obtained by the missions in modern times was not due to the fact that they had departed too far from the example of their great predecessors; whether it were not time to break the bond that seemed to tie the missions to colonialism, and to implant the Church firmly among the colonial peoples themselves by trusting them with responsibility for their own spiritual destinies and treating them on an equal footing with the whites. The problem of coloured Churches, therefore, had now arisen in a manner linked with that of colonialism. It had, of course, been faced long ago in another connection. In the sixteenth century Father Matteo Ricci, then the vicars-apostolic sent out by Propaganda, and later still Father de Nobili in India, had championed the cause of native clergy in autochthonous Churches. Some of the popes, notably Paul V in 1615 and Gregory XV in 1622, had expressed their views on this matter, often with rare foresight. Native seminaries, too, had been opened. But all those undertakings had failed to achieve the hoped-for results, because of dogmatic disputes (e.g. the famous Quarrel of Rites) and customs that took root under the Spanish and Portuguese 'patronates'. The coloured clergy were subsequently involved in the ruin of the missions; in 1820 they numbered only 275 priests. The mid nineteenth century witnessed a splendid revival. At the call of Gregory XVI and Leo XIII, and thanks to the initiative of Mère Javouhey, Father Libermann and Jeanne Bégard, a serious effort was made to recruit native priests, and by about 1900 there were nearly seven thousand of them, mostly in the Indies and the Far East. Even so there was not one coloured vicar or prefect apostolic, let alone a coloured bishop. The stage had thus not been reached at which the Church could be considered as established in accordance with the traditional process. Was it not high time that she should be so?

Events were about to render such a step absolutely indispensable. Before the end of the nineteenth century there were signs of a phenomenon that would dominate the twentieth: the ascendant star of colonial peoples and coloured races. As early as 1885 the Congress Party in India was agitating for independence. In China the Boxer Rising, encouraged behind the scenes by the emperor himself, was more than a banal crisis of xenophobia. The defeat of the Italians by the Ethiopians at Adowa (1896), and that of the Russians by the Japanese at Mukden and Tsushima (1905) revealed to subject peoples that the

whites were not invincible. The process was accelerated by the First World War, after which there were anti-European movements almost everywhere: the Tien-tsin riots, revolt against France in Syria and the Moroccan Rif, the anti-British Wafd campaign in Egypt, Gandhi's policy of 'non-violence' in India, and anti-Dutch agitation in Indonesia. The 'Decline of the West' prophesied by Spengler seemed no longer a mere hypothesis in a philosophy of history.

7. Benedict XV and Pius XI Establish the Coloured Churches

In November 1919 there appeared a great Encyclical, *Maximum illud*, on the missionary problem. After so many centuries of effort and sacrifice, said the Pope, it was clear that the objective of the missions had not been attained. The pagans still numbered a thousand millions; many more than the Christians. Surely it was necessary to revise the methods and introduce new means. The Encyclical was particularly emphatic on two essential points. (1) It declared the danger of nationalism, which had done such harm to the missions during the recent conflict. The missionary should do the bidding of Scripture: 'Forget thy people and thy father's house.' 'The mission entrusted to you', said the Pope, 'transcends by far all human interests. Remember that you work not for an earthly homeland, but for the kingdom of Christ.' The warning was plain, and the tone forthright: 'What a pity it would be if missionaries ignored their dignity to the extent of placing national interests before those of heaven. It would mean a dreadful loss. . . . The missionary would thereby lose all influence over the peoples in his charge.'

This critical section was followed by (2) another more constructive. 'The Church of God is catholic; nowhere, among no people, can she be a foreigner.' It was therefore indispensable that missionaries should have a thorough knowledge of the language and customs of the countries to which they were sent. Furthermore it was desirable that 'all peoples should be able to provide their own sacred ministers'. Benedict then voiced his indignation that, 'despite the wishes of the sovereign pontiffs, regions introduced centuries ago to the faith were still without a native clergy worthy of the name . . . even those whose populations enjoy a high level of culture and had produced some distinguished men'. Something had been wrong or lacking, he said bluntly, in the methods hitherto employed; and *Maximum illud* ended with these decisive words: 'Only where there functions completely a clergy properly trained and worthy of its holy vocation has the missionary crowned his work.'

The programme was thus laid down more clearly than ever before: no time must be lost in developing a native clergy and preparing for the introduction of an autochthonous hierarchy. To the fulfilment of that programme Benedict XV devoted the three years that remained to him. Of this there is abundant proof in his numerous messages, e.g. to the Missionary Union of the Clergy; in his instructions to vicars and prefects apostolic; in his negotiations with Peking for the appointment of an apostolic delegate to China. Though he had no time to create a native episcopate, there is no doubt that he had such a step in mind.

The Pope's instructions, however, met with some resistance in missionary circles. An anonymous writer declared in the *Journal de Pékin*: 'The creation of a native episcopate and the institution of a native clergy are errors of judgment,' and one religious went so far as to assert that 'in certain cases disobedience is legitimate and necessary'. Moreover during the eight years following *Maximum illud* Propaganda had to intervene on five occasions to deal with various errors.

Fortunately Benedict's successor, Pius XI, proved himself straightway a determined partisan of missionary reform. Information reached him from India, where a Belgian Jesuit, Père Gille, a zealous advocate of native promotion, had been sent back to Europe by his superiors; and the *Revue catholique des idées et des faits*, which was well known to enjoy the favour of Cardinal Mercier, had sided with him. A press controversy had followed, during which the *Bulletin catholique international* gave statistics showing that the growth of a native clergy went hand in hand with the increase of conversions.

The result was a new Encyclical, *Rerum Ecclesiae* (February 1926). Achille Ratti, as we have seen, was never a man to mince his words. 'Why', he asked, 'should the native clergy be prevented from governing its own people? What are the missions for, except to establish the Church on firm and regular foundations? And how can the Church take root among the pagans by means other than those whereby she did so long ago among ourselves?' His Holiness then proceeded to some thinly veiled criticism, and even to positive threat; religious congregations which had perhaps boasted a little too much of the results obtained by their missions were reminded that they held the territories entrusted to them by the Holy See in virtue of 'an act that is always revocable'. Going into detail, Pius regretted that in certain missions the native priests, even those of a mature age and great experience, had been reduced to subaltern tasks, 'placed at the bottom of the table', and that insufficient effort had been made to raise them to a high level of Christian culture, even while men of their several races were proving themselves of first-rate quality in the Roman universities. These criticisms, the Encyclical made clear, were directed only against certain mistakes, and did not detract from the admiration due

to the missionaries as a whole for their devotion, their generosity and their spirit of self-sacrifice; but it was obvious that changes were on the way.

The Pope's first gesture was the appointment of a native priest, and a low-caste priest at that, to the bishopric of Tuticorin—the first non-European bishop of the Latin rite in India. Then, on 28th October 1926, six Chinese priests received episcopal consecration from the hands of Pius himself at a magnificent ceremony in St Peter's.

A new chapter had begun in the history of the missions. While it shocked some, it was generally welcomed as the logical term of the course set by recent popes. Without misjudging the agelong work accomplished by white missionaries, the Pope indicated that it was time to get rid of a view which tended to 'represent Catholic preaching as foreign merchandise or as an instrument of domination in the hands of European Powers'. The movement thus inaugurated has proceeded steadily ever since. Pius XI himself continued to appoint autochthonous bishops; there were twenty-eight at the time of his death.[1]

Pius XI did more than effect a formal change in the distribution of dignities and functions; he started a development which is not yet complete. The theology of the missions has been revived, based upon a deeper concept of the equality of men before God, that is to say of the universality of the Redemption. Such obstacles to progress as those of the Chinese and Malabar rites have been removed. Missionaries have become more attentive to the spiritual values contained in non-Christian religions; as Gregory the Great advised those whom he was sending to England, they seek to 'baptize' rather than to destroy those realities. Art itself has taken a turn in the same direction: instead of bogus Gothic or bogus Byzantine missionary churches, one finds Christian edifices built in the style characteristic of native temples, while painting and sculpture offer to the piety of coloured peoples images with the features of their own respective races.

8. Asia Opened to Christ

No complete historical picture of the missions since 1870 is possible within the limits of this volume; space allows only a rapid bird's-eye view. It was in the *Near East* that the missionary revival began during the nineteenth century. Schools had been one of the most successful means of establishing the Catholic presence in territories which Islam

[1] One of the first acts of his successor, Pius XII, was to confer the mitre and crozier on a Negro priest; more, he admitted a Chinese and an Indian to the Sacred College, and when he died the coloured Churches had 116 bishops. John XXIII created a Japanese and a black cardinal, and in three years appointed thirty-four native bishops.

rendered almost impenetrable, and the effort in this direction was continued. The years following 1878, when the Conference of Berlin recognized the protectorate of France over the Catholics of the Levant, witnessed an extraordinary flowering of education, in which Lazarists, Dominicans, Jesuits and Assumptionists rivalled the Marist Brothers and those of Ploërmel, not to mention the female congregations. The college at Antura, founded by Père Leroy, became the training centre for the intellectual *élite* of Syria, the Lebanon and Egypt. In 1882 the Jesuits founded the University of St Joseph at Beirut, which has produced so many doctors, chemists and engineers. The Assumptionists at Constantinople, where they settled in 1881, extended their influence throughout Asia Minor and Palestine. In Persia the Lazarist mission had secured so firm a foothold that it was made an apostolic delegation. All that surge was halted by the terrible flood of antichristian passion which broke out in 1914 and lasted for ten years, a flood whose ravages we have seen [1] among the oriental Catholic Churches. In Asia Minor, while the ancient communities were decimated, the mission stations were swept away; that of the Capuchins at Trebizond was reduced literally to a heap of cinders. In Persia the apostolic delegate was murdered. Even in Syria and Palestine the influence of the missions was affected. But as soon as the whirlwind had passed an effort was made everywhere to restore the situation, and the congregations sent out fresh teams. In Syria and the Lebanon, by 1939, there were no fewer than thirty-one Latin congregations as well as fifteen of the oriental rite; in Egypt there were about twenty, and in Palestine twenty-five; while the University of St Joseph and the college of Antura were more flourishing than ever. The Lazarists returned to Persia and Armenia; the Barnabites set out for Afghanistan. Numerically the results seemed insignificant: a few hundreds, a few thousands, at best a few ten thousand Latin Catholics. But the influence of those small nuclei was out of all proportion to their numbers.

In *India* also the nineteenth-century revival was impressive, especially in view of the fact that it began more nearly from scratch. By the restrictions imposed by Gregory XVI on the rights of the Portuguese *padroado*, and by the regular dispatch of vicars-apostolic, Rome had taken the situation firmly in hand; several of those vicars, e.g. Mgr Bonnand, had infused new blood into the Indian Church.[2] Serious problems remained, notably that of the 'Goanese Schism'.[3] In 1886 Leo XIII restored peace by granting the Archbishop of Goa the honorary title 'Patriarch of the Indies', but confining his authority to Portuguese possessions; in the rest of the country the regular hierarchy

[1] Chapter X, section 10.
[2] *The Church in an Age of Revolution*, pp. 391, 392. [3] Ibid., p. 390.

was established, with twenty-nine dioceses. This system of twofold jurisdiction lasted until 1928, when it was superseded by a new agreement. Having a clear field, the missions set to work with renewed earnestness. There was an influx of numerous orders and congregations, male and female, whose members were of many different nationalities. One of their principal achievements, as in the Levant, was the founding of schools. In 1900 Catholic education was represented by no fewer than 12 university colleges, 128 high schools and 1,247 ordinary schools; by 1939 those figures had trebled. The results of all that effort were visible: in 1871 Catholics numbered less than 800,000; they were 1,200,000 in 1891, 2,400,000 in 1920, 3,800,000 in 1939. Those figures must not deceive; they represented less than 1 per cent of the total population, but provided evidence of a remarkable vitality. Some delicate problems, however, remained outstanding, e.g. the Hindu caste system. To this the Church replied by founding the pontifical inter-caste seminary at Kandy (1893), by admitting all castes to her clergy and, as we have seen, appointing a bishop of low caste. By 1939 her main sources of anxiety were (*a*) the shortage of priests, and (*b*) the unequal distribution of the faith, the northern half of India having no more than 750,000 Catholics.

A similar effort was made in outlying countries. In 1886, thanks to the Oratorians and the Oblates of Mary Immaculate, *Ceylon* was given a regular hierarchy; Jesuits, Benedictines and Sylvestrines followed, so that in 1939 Catholics numbered 800,000, one-tenth of the population.

Baluchistan was reached for the first time in 1880 by the Mill Hill Fathers, and thereafter by Jesuits and Dutch Franciscans.

In *Burma*, where the persecution of 1830 had virtually eliminated all hope, the Parisian and then the Milanese Foreign Mission regained a foothold; several apostolic vicariates were formed, and by 1939 they included a total of 160,000 Catholics.

Daring ventures were undertaken even in *Tibet*, where such slender results had been obtained; the Parisian Foreign Missions had martyrs as late as 1931, with Père Nussbaum; and the Canons Regular of the Great St Bernard established hospices in the Himalayan passes, while the Franciscan Missionaries of Mary founded leper colonies.

Indo-China[1] had already a long Christian history. The missions had flourished there until the eighteenth century. After a period of eclipse they had revived at the beginning of the nineteenth century; but a savage persecution had followed, destroying three-quarters of the Catholic communities.[2] In *Cochin-China* and *Tonking* the year 1885 witnessed a hecatomb of Christians; but Christianity remained

[1] This name is applied to the whole area between China and India, excluding Burma but including the Malay peninsula.

[2] *The Church in an Age of Revolution*, p. 394.

vigorous, and developed rapidly under French protection. Growth of the native clergy kept pace with that of the Church herself; there was also a steady influx of missionaries representing many different congregations; among them were Sulpicians, who opened a successful inter-racial seminary at Hanoi, while Cistercians, Benedictines and Carmelites founded contemplative houses. In 1939, 1,500,000 Catholics formed only 8 per cent of the population; but their influence and prestige were considerable, even though threatened by Communism and the Buddhist renascence. Progress was slower in *Cambodia*, a great centre of Buddhism, but Catholicism had reached *Laos*. In *Siam*, where persecution had halted expansion, Catholicism began slowly to regain ground, thanks especially to the foundation of schools, which, though few at first, were sufficient to alarm the Buddhists, who in 1940 unleashed another persecution. As for *Malaysia*, which in 1807 had afforded shelter to the famous Central Seminary of the Foreign Missions driven from Siam, the mission, long confined to the principal cities and to groups of Chinese and Indian emigrants, tried to penetrate the aborigines rather than the Malays, among whom Islam was, as everywhere, an insurmountable barrier.

It was perhaps in *China*, which today weighs so heavy upon the Christian soul, that the most spectacular progress was made. Indeed, when one recalls the sacrifices made on her behalf, one is tempted to ask whether China were not the favourite daughter of the missions. Catastrophic about 1800, the situation had greatly improved by 1870; but it was still far from satisfactory.[1] In the latter year, despite the Treaty of Tientsin (1818), and that of Peking (1860) which entrusted protection of the missions to France, odious calumnies arising from the saving of abandoned Chinese babies by the *Œuvre de la Sainte-Enfance* resulted in a riot at Tientsin, during which some Sisters of Charity and two missionary priests lost their lives. Thirteen years later, in Szechwan, three other missionaries died under hideous torture. In 1888 the Holy See placed missionaries of all nationalities under the French protectorate. In view of the repeated antichristian incidents, France brought strong pressure to bear with a view to defending the rights of missionaries, and these were guaranteed by the so-called Favier Treaty of 1899. Peace, however, was not thereby secured. In 1900, encouraged by the dowager empress, there occurred the Boxer Rising, the most violent explosion of xenophobia that China had ever experienced. At Peking the Europeans endured two months of terror, confined to the legations and the missionary quarters. Five bishops, thirty European priests, ten nuns, four brothers, one hundred Chinese priests and thirty thousand of the faithful perished. That ghastly tragedy was followed by a no less horrible repression; but in

[1] *The Church in an Age of Revolution*, pp. 395–8.

spite of the prevailing religious calm, which was not affected by the revolution of 1912, there were occasional outbursts until the very end, involving the death of both missionaries and nuns. In 1939 it was officially estimated that over a period of one hundred years 162 missionaries had been killed in China.

It is remarkable that that disturbing situation did not slow down the apostolate. The example of the martyrs [1] seems to have inflamed the courage of the others, and after 1901 the messengers of the Gospel were able to reap the harvest sown by them. During the preceding period many orders and congregations had rivalled one another in zeal for China; now they came afresh, and by 1939 the missionary personnel numbered 4,500 priests belonging to ten institutes. There were also sixty native congregations. Rome accompanied the territorial progress by creating apostolic vicariates and prefectures as soon as possible; in 1939 there were more than a hundred. That progress was made in all directions, even in the most distant regions such as Inner Mongolia, where the Scheutists used methods not unlike the Jesuit 'reductions' in Paraguay.[2] Extraordinary results, too, were obtained in the educational sphere; by 1939 there were more than 16,000 schools with 500,000 pupils. There were also the Aurora University at Shanghai, founded by the Jesuits in 1903; the School of Higher Studies at Tientsin, opened in 1922; and the Catholic University of Peking, established in 1925 by American Benedictines and taken over in 1932 by German Fathers of the Divine Word. Faithful to their most ancient traditions, the Jesuits occupied a distinguished place in the field of science, notably with their famous observatory at Zi-ka-Wei. The welfare services run by women included 700 dispensaries, 250 orphanages and more than 200 hospitals. On the eve of the Second World War the Catholic Church in China seemed destined to the most glorious of futures. The number of baptized had risen from 370,000 in 1870, to 750,000 in 1900, to 1,300,000 in 1910, to 3,200,000 in 1939—one Catholic in every 165 Chinese. China, with her six native bishops, afforded the most striking example of missionary reform; and that immense capital of experience was about to be imperilled indefinitely by the advent of Communism.

The bloody ordeal had been more terrible in *Korea* than in China, and the recovery there was also more remarkable.[3] In 1885, as soon as France had obtained religious freedom for those subject to her jurisdiction, conversions followed rapidly one upon another, extending even to the royal family. In 1899 there were 17,000 baptized Catholics; 44,000 in 1900; 77,000 in 1910. The annexation of the country by

[1] Thirty-three had been canonized by 1939.
[2] *The Church in the Eighteenth Century*, Index.
[3] *The Church in an Age of Revolution*, pp. 398–400.

Japan, which tried to foster Shintoism there, did not slow down the forward surge. The Foreign Missions were joined by Bavarian Benedictines, Maryknoll Fathers, Missionaries of St Columban and many female communities, including Carmelites. In 1939 the Korean Church numbered about 150,000 souls.

Japan too felt a change of climate in the missionary zone. Mutsohito's 'Meiji' revolution of 1868 had set her on the road to Europeanization. In 1873 the Mikado promised appeasement, and Pius IX took the opportunity to create two apostolic vicariates. In 1889, when the monarchy became constitutional and granted freedom of belief, Leo XIII at once established Tokyo as an archbishopric with three suffragan sees. Finally, in 1899, missionaries were allowed unrestricted freedom of activity, and the Catholic renascence began apace. In dark times the little flock had given proof of amazing loyalty; Catholic communities had survived for two centuries, without priests, fathers baptizing their children, and defying all risks. As peace returned, the small nuclei grew. In 1870 there were scarcely 15,000 Japanese Catholics; by 1899 there were 50,000, thanks to the labours of the Missions Étrangères de Paris, who were assisted by Marianists, Spanish Dominicans, German Jesuits and a dozen female congregations. A special effort was made to form a Catholic intellectual *élite*. Five Marianists who arrived in 1888 opened colleges at Tokyo, Nagasaki and Osaka. In 1913 the German Jesuits founded a high school that afterwards became the Sophia University. A Catholic review was established. The missionaries organized learned congresses and regular conferences. Along with that striving for intellectual penetration there went an earnest endeavour in the purely spiritual field, one result of which was the astounding increase of the Trappistines.[1] Benefiting, like China, from the missionary reforms of Benedict XV and Pius XI, the Catholics of Japan had a bishop of their own race by 1927; by 1941 all their bishops were Japanese. Though the numerical increase had been less rapid in the final years, because of a nationalist reaction in favour of Shintoism, the 100,000 Japanese Catholics enjoyed a prestige that had been made known to all the world by the presence among them as French ambassador of Paul Claudel, the great Christian poet.[2]

9. Grandeur and Suffering in the Islands

It was perhaps to Oceania that the most sensational episodes of the missionary epic belong. There, with much difficulty,[3] the Church had

[1] See section 5 above, *ad fin.*

[2] The Second World War was a severe trial to the Church in Japan. The atomic bomb at Nagasaki killed 7,000 out of 10,000 Catholics in the city.

[3] *The Church in an Age of Revolution*, Chapter VII, section 13.

obtained a firm foothold during the first seventy years of the nineteenth century. The same courage and devotion were manifested during our period. The penetration of New Guinea and the evangelization of Papua by the Issoudun Fathers of the Sacred Heart alone form an astonishing chapter. The surprises that awaited the missionaries in those parts were sometimes remarkably odd; Père Verjus, for example, discovered with horror that a friendly dish he had just shared with an apparently peaceful tribe was actually a stew of human flesh.

In eastern Oceania, i.e. the Sandwich, Society, Gambier and Marquesas islands, the Picpucians made rapid progress which took them as far as Tuamotu and Easter Island. By 1939 all those peoples were Christian, either Catholic or Protestant. More difficult was the penetration of central Oceania—Wallis, Futuna, New Caledonia, Samoa, Fiji—where the Marists met with resistance from the natives, and also with such strong Protestant opposition that the kingdom of Tonga was long closed to them; some progress, however, was made in New Caledonia. As for western Oceania, it was not only in New Guinea that the Picpucians and Milan Missionaries met with difficulties, but also in the Marianas, the Carolines, the Solomons and New Hebrides. Nevertheless the Church took root; by 1939 there was scarcely an island of any importance that had not its Catholic community, and Rome had been able to form twenty apostolic vicariates. There as elsewhere the Church had played her civilizing role, opening schools, hospices, leper hospitals, and raising the one-time cannibals to the dignity of men.

Circumstances were of course different in the great land masses of the extreme South Pacific, Australia and New Zealand, where the population consisted mostly of European immigrants. Australia, where Irish missionaries had begun work among the convicts as early as 1820, had later welcomed English secular priests as well as French Marists and Benedictines, and the movement spread to New Zealand. Opening the eucharistic congress at Sydney in 1928, the archbishop remarked with pride that without a shadow of official help the Catholic Church had reached the figure of 1,200,000 souls. Though a minority, that Church gave evidence of uncommon vigour, founding charitable institutions, fostering Catholic Action, financing missions to the few thousand boomerang handlers who were slowly dying out in their mountains. Australia was divided into six archbishoprics, seven bishoprics and two vicariates; New Zealand into four bishoprics. But that rapid growth does not belong, strictly speaking, within the missionary framework.

10. From the Eskimos to the Indians

In America substantial results had been obtained; but in 1870 there was still much to do in many fields. In Canada, after the epic westward and northward drives, in which the Oblates of Mary Immaculate and the Grey Sisters of Montreal had distinguished themselves, there were loose ends to be tidied up and a work of consolidation to be carried out. The Church was well established among the Indian fur hunters, but it had to be organized. This was done by other Oblates, among whom were Mgr Breynat, the 'flying bishop', and Mgr Grouard, apostle of Athabaska, who died in 1931 at the age of ninety-one after sixty-nine years of work in the far north. Within sixty years that task was fulfilled, and Rome was able to create a regular hierarchy in five ecclesiastical provinces with fifteen dioceses, leaving all the regions farthest north to the care of vicars-apostolic.

But the labour of consolidation did not prevent further advances wherever necessary. In the very highest latitudes of the continent lived a few thousand Eskimos, among whom the first mission was established in Alaska, which had been sold to the United States by Russia in 1867; and to this apostolate a young Italian Jesuit, Father Tosi, dedicated himself with superhuman energy. In fifteen years he obtained such results that in 1894 Rome appointed him vicar-apostolic. Only two thousand of the fifteen thousand Eskimos were Catholics, but the Church had taken root in what was to become the forty-ninth state of America.

Things were more difficult in the extreme north of Canada, i.e. in the future vicariates of Mackenzie, Keewatin and Hudson Bay, to which the Oblates of Mary Immaculate devoted their efforts. The first ventures, *c.* 1870–80, ended in failure; it was not until 1912 that Père Turquetil managed to erect the first mission, the cost of which may be judged by recalling the martyrdom in 1913 of Pères Le Roux and Rouvière, whose livers the Eskimos tore out and ate. Other missionaries died of cold, sickness or accident. Results were so disappointing—years and years without a single conversion—that there was question of abandoning the field. Quite suddenly, however, the situation improved; and Père Turquetil, who had prayed St Teresa of Lisieux to intercede for his mission, attributed the miracle to her intervention. There was soon a 'cathedral' under her patronage, and in twelve years, 1928–39, five Eskimo missions were founded, including one built by Père Roger Buliard on Victoria Island at 92 degrees north. Grey Sisters of Nicolet arrived in 1931 and opened a hospital at Chesterfield. Three Eskimo apostolic vicariates were created. One can understand some words addressed by Pope Pius XI to Mgr Turquetil

on the subject of his mission: 'It is the finest, the most arduous and the most meritorious. If We could visit a single mission, yours is the one We would choose.'

Catholic missions in the U.S.A. were less hazardous, but encountered other difficulties. In the Indian territory Père de Smet, S.J., had earned for the Society such prestige that in 1868 the federal authorities had entrusted him with negotiations for the submission of the Sioux. But when General Grant signed peace with all the 'redskin' tribes (1869–70) and it was decided to replace the government 'agencies' with religious stations, only eight out of seventy-two were assigned to the Catholics, who had a right to thirty-eight. Even the protests of the Indians themselves, who sent envoys to Washington, failed to make the President reconsider his decision. The Church then formed a Catholic Office of the Indian Missions, and a little later the Catholic Association of Missions to the Indians, which financed them. From 1886 the Catholic forces were in position, but results were disappointing. In 1907 there were only 40,000 Catholic American Indians; most of the remainder belonged to Protestant sects. Furthermore, since their admission to American citizenship, and the extravagant enrichment of some by the discovery of oil on their lands, the old Redskins were moving in ever greater numbers from their reserves and merging with their white and Negro compatriots.

In Latin America, where the populations of the various States consisted largely of a heterogeneous mass—Indians, half-castes and Negroes—the missions began to revive in 1870, after having been ruined first by the suppression of the Jesuit Reductions in Paraguay and then by the upheavals resulting from the winning of independence. Teams of missionaries from Europe were at work. The effort was continued and amplified throughout our period, mostly by European religious of a dozen or so orders and congregations; but after the First World War Catholics of various Latin-American countries themselves took an increasing share in the work. As a rule those countries, even when anticlerical, helped the missions or at least refrained from interfering with their work, in the knowledge that evangelization was one means of integrating the non-civilized into the national life.

The missionary history of Latin America during this period produced some outstanding men, such as Mgr (later Cardinal) Cagliero, apostle of Tierra del Fuego, and the French Redemptorist Père Chouvène, who worked among the Indians of Peru. It was marked no less by some tragic episodes, in the form not only of official persecution but also of natural catastrophe or epidemic, e.g. tuberculosis, which in ten years killed 95 per cent of the Catholics in Tierra del Fuego. But the results obtained were impressive: in Colombia Catholicism included practically the whole population; in Patagonia,

between 1875 and 1925, the Salesians baptized all the Indians. On the eve of the Second World War, however, much remained to be done: there were still vast areas not yet reached, often in very difficult and dangerous regions; but even among the frequently enormous masses whom the Church had already baptized there was the abiding shortage of priests.

11. Towards the Heart of Africa

Of all the continents it was undoubtedly Africa that afforded the missions most satisfaction. In 1870 they were well established on the periphery of Africa, but had not penetrated far into the interior.[1] There were also large areas of *terra incognita*, and, as the explorers opened them up, missionaries followed. In 1876 the International Association for the Exploration of Africa officially declared that missionaries of all denominations would have full freedom of activity in the newly discovered territories. The Protestants prepared at once to seize this opportunity, and the Catholics could not lag behind.

The man who embodied that determination to introduce Catholic missions into the heart of Africa was Cardinal Lavigerie, Archbishop of Algiers and founder of the White Fathers.[2] Rome naturally adopted his views, entrusting to him first an apostolic delegation for Equatorial Africa, thus empowering him to act in at least one-fourth of the continent.

The epic of the White Fathers began in 1873, and to their endeavours for the conquest of Africa there was added almost at once a tremendous effort in the service of a humanitarian cause—the abolition of slavery. Though forbidden in principle, there was still a flourishing trade in Negroes destined for petty African potentates, Arabian despots and even South American landowners; and it was carried on in the same abominable conditions characteristic of earlier days. Informed of the gravity of that scourge by the first White Fathers whom he had sent into the interior, Lavigerie undertook the struggle against slavery with his accustomed energy. While he personally conducted the campaign throughout the West, and won Leo XIII's support for the crusade, his White Fathers were the most active opponents of the slave traders and their iniquitous practices. Liberation and evangelization must go hand in hand—a profound idea and one of great significance.

In 1873 three White Fathers started for Timbuktu, their purpose being to buy young Negro slaves whom they would train as doctors. But they never reached their objective; the Tuaregs massacred all

[1] *The Church in an Age of Revolution*, pp. 408–15.
[2] Ibid., Chapter VII, sections 8, 10, 16.

three. This initial failure did not discourage the cardinal; while preparing for new Saharan expeditions he turned also in another direction, that of the Great Lakes, for which some White Fathers set out from Zanzibar in 1878. The lakes lay on one of the slave-trade routes, and difficulties were not long delayed. One group reached Tanganyika at the cost of two lives; another advanced towards Lake Victoria at the cost of three. Lavigerie had to admit failure a second time; but his imagination was never at a loss, and a new beginning was made. Since the missionaries were exposed to such danger, why not send them under armed escort? So he went to Belgium and enlisted some retired papal zouaves for the task. One mission left for the Upper Nile, another left from Zanzibar, others moved into the Sahara. Still there were losses; still bloodshed. Once again the Tuaregs murdered three Fathers; eight others died of fever; d'Hoop, one of the zouaves, was murdered while trying to snatch a little slave girl from a trader. Even where the situation appeared satisfactory, a mere puff of wind was sufficient to unleash violence, as in Uganda.[1] But all those efforts and sacrifices ultimately bore fruit. Thirty years after the White Fathers' entry upon the scene there were substantial Catholic communities in Black Africa, foreshadowing the yet larger and more vigorous Christian groups of today.

Nor, meanwhile, did Lavigerie forget North Africa, where he had dreamed of reviving the old Christian loyalties submerged by Islam. There too his White Fathers achieved wonders. In the venerable archiepiscopal see of Carthage, which the Pope re-created for him, he bore the title 'Primate of Africa'; and no title had ever been more deserved.

The White Fathers, however, were by no means the only congregation to devote themselves to the African continent. Others were the Fathers of the Holy Ghost, the Fathers of the African Missions, the Scheutists, the Jesuits, the Mill Hill Fathers and several more, both male and female. In 1939 there were twenty-eight congregations or institutes of men and some forty of women at work in Africa; among them dark skins were becoming more and more numerous.

The penetration of Africa was carried out in face of frequent and formidable difficulties: the murderous climate; the hostility of local chiefs, witch-doctors and slave traders; the native mentality, which was often unstable and, after rapid conversion, inclined to fall back into the old pagan errors; and also such customs as polygamy which the Africans did not readily abandon. Finally there was Islam, which was gaining strength year by year at the end of our period.

But while the obstacles were numerous, Africa offered also great opportunities to the Christian apostolate. The African soul frequently

[1] For the martyrs of Uganda, see p. 402.

proved more open to the faith than many European souls. The most famous episode in the Catholic history of Africa is that of the Uganda martyrs, who have since been canonized. In 1882 the White Fathers, who had established the small Christian community, had to leave under threat from the Moslems. When they returned four years later they learned that their first converts had baptized 177 others and were training 600 catechumens. But at that moment the local princeling, alarmed by the progress of the whites, unleashed a savage persecution. Christianity had made its way among his own *entourage*; he had his chief page put to death, and with his own hand killed a Christian whom he caught catechizing one of his companions. Eighty victims perished, including thirteen of the ruler's pages, amid frightful tortures, many being burned alive. Yet in face of that ordeal the young Church proved itself equal to that of the catacombs. None of the condemned apostatized; all encouraged one another to remain firm, and it was due to that sowing of blood that Uganda soon afterwards became one of the most vigorous centres of African Catholicism.

Thus was Lavigerie's hope fulfilled, 'to transform Africa by means of the Africans'. But it was fulfilled in another way also, for one of the most active instruments of Catholic penetration was furnished by native catechists. Chosen from among the best Christians and sent to the still pagan villages to open a small school where they would provide the rudiments of education and of religion, they sowed the Christian grain in many places; and catechists remain one of the basic elements of the African Church.

By 1939 the situation was as follows. In three main sectors the Church could boast of having obtained extraordinary results: in the region of the Great Lakes, in the Belgian Congo and in the Cameroon. In the first of these the White Fathers had worked to such good effect that there were nearly 1,500,000 Catholics in Uganda, 800,000 in Tanganyika, 1,200,000 in Ruanda Urundi; in all, 18 per cent of the population. In the Belgian Congo, first entrusted to the Scheutists but later shared among all the congregations represented in Belgium, the number of Catholics had risen from a few thousands in 1900 to 800,000. In the Cameroon, where the German Pallotine Fathers and the Saint-Quentin Fathers of the Sacred Heart had settled just before 1914, the latter, together with the Spiritans and the Mill Hill Fathers, now had charge of 500,000 faithful.

Those three regions, however, were by no means the only ones in which the Church had obtained a firm foothold. In Algeria, Tunisia and Morocco, all Moslem countries, conversions were rare; but the secular clergy and numerous congregations of both sexes had made many contacts and wielded considerable influence through their schools, orphanages and charitable institutions. In the Sahara the

White Fathers had stations in a number of oases, and Ghardaia was the centre of a missionary circumscription four times the size of France. Italian missions were at work in Libya and Cyrenaica. Meanwhile in Egypt, where the Coptic Church had been restored in 1895 and was growing stronger, Jesuits, Carmelites, Salesians, Lazarists and others had care of about 800,000 souls. The whole coastline of Africa was studded with missionary outposts. Senegal had its cathedral at Dakar. Progress had been made also in the Sudan, despite opposition from certain French administrators, and there was a flourishing Catholic community in Upper Volta; so too in Guinea and Sierra Leone, where the Lyons Missionaries had suffered so heavily from the climate. As in Liberia, their tenacity had succeeded in creating Catholic groups of a few thousand souls. In Angola the Fathers of the Holy Spirit and their congregations had converted about 40 per cent of the population. Considerable advances had been made among the Negroes of South Africa and Rhodesia, to the number of about one million. In Madagascar the French occupation had opened a fertile field to the apostolate by putting an end to slavery as well as to the vexations of the Hovas, and by 1939 there were 700,000 Catholics in the island. On the east coast, Bagamayo was now the starting-point of missions to the lakes, while in Mozambique the zeal and enterprise of the Portuguese clergy were already bearing fruit.

The Catholic missions had thus laid solid foundations throughout most of the continent. The situation, of course, was far from perfect: in some sectors there were only a few thousand baptized; in others the missionaries were killing themselves with work; the native clergy was still very small—less than 1,200 priests; and the Catholic Church had no more than 15,000 members in a total population of 140 million. But the impulse already given was destined to take Christian Africa to a very high level after the Second World War.[1]

12. Provisional Balance Sheet. Prospects for the Future

Considering as a whole the results obtained by the missions during the period with which we are concerned, one is entitled to regard the balance sheet as satisfactory. In 1870 approximate estimates put the number of faithful in missionary territories at about 7,000,000; in 1927 there were 14,600,000, and in 1939 nearly 23,000,000, a figure that

[1] In Africa, as elsewhere, administrative organization had followed the progress of the missions. In 1939 there were two archdioceses, seventeen dioceses, seventy-eight apostolic vicariates, thirty-three prefectures, one mission and one abbey *nullius*. Twenty-five years later, almost the whole continent was divided into dioceses.

doubled between that year and 1962. The Church had taken root all over the world, covering the planet with a strongly centralized organization which comprised more than five hundred apostolic circumscriptions. Here are the statistics of personnel dependent on the Congregation of Propaganda at 30th June 1939:

Priests		*Brothers*		*Sisters*		*Cate-chists*	*School-masters*
Western	15,505	Western	6,456	Western	34,433	91,716	76,135
Native	6,406	Native	2,176	Native	18,581		
	21,911		8,632		53,014	91,716	76,135

SUM TOTAL OF PERSONNEL: 251,408

Those figures, however, did not warrant unqualified optimism. Specialists on missionary problems frequently urged Catholics to face the facts and not to be carried away with excessive enthusiasm. The most disquieting truth in 1939 was that the Catholic flock in most countries was not increasing at a rate proportionate to that of the population. Again, in order to survive, the Catholic communities in care of the missions had to rely very largely upon help supplied by the ancient Churches of the West, and that help was inadequate. Huge areas suffered severely from lack of priests. In India and in China there was scarcely one to 700,000 inhabitants; in the most prosperous regions of Africa the missionaries were almost overwhelmed by the flood-tide of conversions, which raised more and more complex problems; in South America there were districts where, for lack of priests, the faithful never received more than the sacrament of baptism. Nor was the financial aid given to the missions equal to their needs, despite the efforts of various societies. Speaking frankly, the resources of the Catholic missions often seemed nugatory in comparison with those of their counterparts which the Anglo-Saxon countries financed much more liberally.

Another ground for anxiety was the existence of two great sectors of humanity which appeared as insuperable obstacles to any Catholic expansion. One of those sectors was the Communist world; by 1939 it looked ready to extend in the direction of China, where some provinces were already in Communist hands. The other was the Islamic world, containing at that date 267 million souls; it reached from Malaysia to Morocco, from Turkestan to the shores of Lake Chad, and was more firmly closed than ever to Christian penetration. Islam was awakening from its long torpor and beginning once again to proselytize, particularly among the African Negroes, where its success was due not only to the easy-going morality which it allowed, but also to the

readiness with which it harmonized elements of ancient fetishism with genuine religious pride and real greatness of soul.

Those difficulties, however, were no cause for pessimism. Let us repeat: in matter of religion statistics are far from providing the best means of judging results. A single conversion can be of capital importance, as was that of Lu Tse-tiang in 1926. Chinese minister of foreign affairs, he became not only a Catholic, but a Benedictine monk, and ended his life as Abbot of St Peter's at Ghent. In 1939, as had always been the case, the influence of the missions extended far beyond their own localities; over and beyond the visible benefits they conferred they diffused a spiritual radiance in the pagan environment and gradually drew it nearer to the Gospel. Even while remaining Moslems, the students of Beirut University and Antura College understood and respected Christianity, while the many pages in which Mahatma Gandhi spoke of Jesus Christ provided striking evidence of Christian forces.

Prospects for the future of Catholic expansion were by no means unfavourable. Everything presaged not so much a missionary springtide as a summer of bounteous harvests. More important still was the fact that the Church, thanks to Benedict XV and Pius XI, had revived her most ancient teaching while adapting it to modern techniques, and had accomplished a decisive reform both in her methods and in the personnel of her missionaries. At a moment when the upheavals caused by war and the rise of coloured peoples were about to call in question the supremacy of the white race, the missions found themselves detached from Western tutelage and ready to continue their task in new circumstances. The very concept of a mission, 'founded on the distinction of evangelizing and evangelized countries', was able to evolve until it 'denoted simply a stage in the spiritual impregnation of the universe'.[1] The Church herself, on the point of applying the term 'mission' to every effort of christianization in the sociological as well as in the geographical field, was prepared to run the risks of change.

'A spiritual impregnation of the universe . . .' Surely it was that which Cardinal Lavigerie sought when, in presence of the refractory bloc of Islam, he bade his sons and daughters not to try for individual conversions among the Moslems, but to influence whole masses by working among them as teachers and nurses, by simply bearing the witness of charity and prayer; that witness which was borne soon afterwards by the sacrifice even unto death of a man upon whom our own age would look as the lighthouse of tomorrow's apostolate—Charles de Foucauld.

[1] Père Naidenoff.

13. Charles de Foucauld, 'Universal Brother'

At the end of October 1901 the French officers who, with four companies of sharpshooters, held the outpost of Beni Abbes, on the borders of Morocco and Algeria, were not a little surprised to meet in the oasis, dressed as the most shabby of Bedouins, a man whom several of them had known in uniform—the Vicomte Charles de Foucauld (1885–1916), an ex-captain of cavalry. His behaviour, too, surprised them still more. Refusing to come and live in the fort, deliberately holding himself aloof from the palm trees and gardens, he went to reside in a lonely little dale, not far from the sandhill where, with a few palm trunks, random stones and earth mixed with straw and water, he soon built a kind of oratory, not unlike the poorest *zaouias* of the Islamic marabouts. What was he going to do, this priest who did not belong to the White Fathers, who lived more austerely than a Trappist and who seemed to be pursuing an altogether personal experiment directed to some great mystical purpose? At midnight his little bell rang out; then he sang the office, out of tune but with fervent voice. It was known that he fed on dates and ground corn, that he slept fully clothed on a bed of reeds in a cell so small that he could not lie flat.

This ascetic had come a long, long way. As a twenty-three-year-old sub-lieutenant of hussars at Pont-à-Mousson he had astonished the garrison with his extravagance and wild behaviour. Orphaned at the age of eight and badly brought up by an over-indulgent grandfather, he had reached manhood devoid of faith and with practically no moral sense. Military discipline and traditions, however, had saved him from the worst excesses. While serving in South Oran he had discovered Africa and experienced its purifying spell. Turning his irresistible longing for adventure to exploration, he had travelled through Morocco, which at that time was closed to Europeans, and had brought back information of some scientific value. But above all, those long meditations in the desert, and also his contact with Islam, his sense of being a *roumi*, a man of Rome, a Christian, whatever that might be, had led him to take a less simple view of the religious problem. In presence of the Abbé Huvelin, that soul of light in an ailing body, whom he had gone to see, Charles de Foucauld was vanquished and called to his vocation at a single stroke. 'Kneel down and confess your sins,' the priest commanded. In vain he stammered, 'I haven't the faith . . .'; he could not but obey the gently imperious voice. From the sacristy of Saint-Augustin in Paris there went forth a new man.

Years of uncertainty followed. He knew his goal: 'As soon as I believed there is a God', he said later, 'I understood that I could do

nothing else than live for Him.' But the way that would lead him to that goal was not at once clear. He spent some time as a Trappist at Notre-Dame-des-Neiges, then at Akbes, fulfilling with joy the sternest demands of the Rule, but failing to realize his dream in community life. So he left before having had time to become a priest, and went to the Holy Land in search of more isolation, more abjection. Thus it came about that the Poor Clares at Nazareth employed a mysterious gardener, whose rough clothing could not hide his aristocratic features, and whose long hours before the Blessed Sacrament in their chapel filled the nuns with astonished admiration. One day the abbess, enlightened by God as to the truth, bade him at length be faithful to his true destiny by receiving the priesthood and carrying Christ to the world. In October 1901, therefore, about four months after his ordination, he understood that he was not called to remain a Trappist. Should he be a missionary? Africa, with its vastness and its peoples that knew not Christ, attracted him more strongly than ever. 'That land,' he said, 'those souls, have been awaiting the Gospel for nineteen hundred years.' He would take it to them, but in a new way, simply by manifesting Christ. On arrival at Beni Abbes he knew the road he must follow.

'A small monastery of fervent and charitable monks, loving God whole-heartedly and their neighbour as themselves; a *zaouia* of prayer and hospitality, of such piety as to enlighten and warm the whole region; a little family imitating so perfectly the virtues of Jesus that all the folk around may begin to love Jesus.' Such was his grand design. There was no question of an apostolate in the usual sense of the word. He did not seek to convince by argument, or to make conversions. 'I am not a missionary but a hermit,' he would often say. He desired nothing else than to render Christ present and radiant, so that His grace might slowly and secretly penetrate those among whom His servant dwelt. The power of example would be worth a world of theological demonstrations.

Two parts of that programme were accomplished. The hermitage very soon became a place of prayer, known as such throughout the oasis and even beyond. The chapel was just 'a simple pillared corridor covered with reeds', said Lyautey (who visited the place), with a plank for an altar, tinplate candlesticks and, for sole decoration, a figure of the Sacred Heart with outstretched arms, which the Father himself had painted on a sheet of calico. But every day a number of French troops, officers and men, went to kneel there, and the Moslems, who are men of prayer, admired the *roumi* marabout whom they saw spend so many hours by night and day adoring his God. The very presence of the Oratory sufficed to alter many ideas about the irreligion of the French, the impiety of those Christians who were never seen at prayer.

The second part of the programme, to show forth the charity of Christ, was a remarkable success. In a very short time the hermitage became the centre as it were of a court of miracles, to which all who were in trouble, sick or indigent flocked for assistance. And the Father gave, gave inexhaustibly, even beyond his means, abandoning his own food to the hungry, distributing the money given him by his family, parting even with a length of cloth which a compassionate relative had sent him to replace his tattered habit. There was no physical or moral wretchedness that he failed to relieve. Slavery existed in that part of the world, and the French military authorities had not yet decided to abolish it. Foucauld received the slaves—as many as twenty at a time—bought them whenever his resources allowed, and restored them to free labour. The rumour of that unbounded generosity spread; from *douar* to *douar*, from oasis to oasis, men talked of the white hermit at Beni Abbas. His hermitage became commonly known as the *Khaoua*, the brotherhood, while the neighbourhood spoke of him as 'Khaouia Carlo', Brother Charles. It was a victory. With his white robe, on which he had sewn a heart of red material, he was able to go anywhere; even in Tafilalet, where the Moroccans were trigger-happy, no one would have dared attack him.

There was now but one dark cloud on his horizon. He was alone. No 'brother' had come to join him at the hermitage and found that special kind of institute of which he dreamed. Nevertheless he drew up its Rule in minute detail. He called it 'The Little Brothers of the Sacred Heart of Jesus', with whom he joined (on paper) 'Little Sisters', and even a larger association open to any man or woman who wished to share in the great task of making Christ present to the world. But as a matter of hard fact, the very few postulants who knocked at the hermitage door recoiled from the austerity and privation of the life proposed to them—a life which, for his part, Brother Charles still found too easy, too sheltered from the risks imposed by the paradox of the true life of faith. A visit from his former comrade Laperrine, now master and prophet of the desert, known as *Le Saharissime*, was a source of fresh inspiration to him. The Touat, the Gouara, the Tidikelt and, farther away still, Hoggar, that wildest heart of Africa, where the French Army had not yet occupied—it was toward those lands of greatest solitude that the Lord was calling him to bear his full testimony. Sadly, therefore, leaving his friends and his hermitage, he set out on his last stage, for his supreme achievement.

The difficulties were enormous, and the vicar-apostolic of the Sahara had not concealed them from him. But Foucauld had declared himself 'ready to go to the ends of the earth and live till the last judgment' in order to 'offer love' to those who knew not the God of love. Hoggar at that time was truly the end of the world. Its Tuareg inhabitants were

by no means an altogether peaceful folk. What would the white hermit do? 'I shall stay, I shall study the language and translate the Holy Gospel; I shall make contact with the Tuaregs.' That simple programme represented an entirely new concept of Christian expansion, a mysterious renewing of the apostolate.

Thus was born Tamanrasset, today one of the 'high places' of the Christian world. In the very heart of the massif, 1,500 kilometres from Beni Abbes, another hermitage arose, poor as the first, and the man who settled there led the same life of prayer and renunciation as before. The solitude, in fact, was much greater, and there were no French rifles to protect the hermit. He carried out faithfully the task he had set himself, to establish contact with the Tuaregs, win their confidence, 'tame' them and bring about the reign of peace between himself and them; not to talk to them directly of Christ, but to lead them to understand that the religion which obliges a man to be so good, so brotherly, must be a good religion. That was a sowing of the Gospel, sowing it in order that others yet to come might reap.

The Tuaregs watched him, and gradually learned to love this foreigner who spent his days visiting the poor and tending the sick, who helped the farmers and instructed them in new skills, who even taught the women to sew, knit and spin, and whom they heard at night chanting his prayers. Nine years passed thus, during which the Universal Brother made not one conversion; but those years were nevertheless wonderfully fruitful, since he attained the end he had had in view, and proved that his method was sound. He was still alone; no 'little brother' had come to join him, and he had even had to obtain permission to say Mass without a server. Perhaps he felt some disappointment; but he knew that unless the seed corn dies there can be no harvest, and he was the seed corn, destined to die that others might reap later. 'Our destruction', he wrote, 'is the most powerful means we have of uniting ourselves with Jesus and doing good to souls.' Our destruction . . .

On 1st December 1916 Foucauld was alone in the fort which the French troops had built when they first occupied Hoggar, and where he had agreed to live because the country's security had been threatened, since the outbreak of the First World War, by roving bands more or less subsidized by the enemy. The passage had been built in such a way that only one man at a time could pass. The voice on the other side of the door was familiar, that of a local half-caste whom the hermit had welcomed on more than one occasion. Without hesitation the Father opened the door and put out his hand. Betrayed, like Christ, by a friend, Charles de Foucauld was thrown to the ground, tied and questioned by the *fellagas*: 'When does the convoy arrive? Are there French troops in the neighbourhood?' He answered not a word, but

prayed in silence. At the head of a personal notebook, under the two words 'Jesus Caritas' and the heart surmounted with a cross, he had written: 'The more we lack on earth, the more we shall find of that which can give us the best of earth: the Cross.' At that moment the Universal Brother lacked everything, but the Cross was near. A shot was fired by a nervous guard, a bullet penetrated behind the right ear and came out through the left eye. The white hermit of Tamanrasset lay dead upon that earth to which he had brought the message of Christ's love. It was the first Friday of December, a day which the liturgy devoted to the Sacred Heart.

Twelve years later, in 1928, Albert Peyriguère, another white hermit, settled in a Berber village of the Moroccan High Atlas, and for thirty years lived as an embodiment of faith and charity. Later a priest from Versailles, Père Voillaume, carried Foucauld's message a stage further by founding the Little Brothers and Little Sisters, for whom Brother Charles had paved the way.[1] Later still, some European priests would go to India, in order to bear the same testimony of renunciation, prayer and love. Who knows whither the road pioneered by Charles de Foucauld will lead? Maybe the Church has received from him a fresh opportunity and a method which will render her apostolate fruitful in the world of tomorrow.

[1] See M. Carrouges, *Le Père de Foucauld et les Fraternités d'aujourd'hui*, Paris, 1963.

CHAPTER XII

SAINT TERESA OF LISIEUX

1. A Saint among Us

This is the strange story of a girl who managed, at the age of fifteen, to enter a lowly Carmelite convent in Normandy. There she took her vows. There for little more than nine years she lived the life of prayer, silence and austerity which is everywhere that of the daughters of Avila's saint, whose name this humble religious bore. There she was attacked by tuberculosis. There she died, and was buried in a deal coffin, as the Rule prescribed, accompanied by a small group of priests and relatives to the local cemetery, where her community had a concession. During the short period which that little nun spent in the cloister, nothing distinguished her from her fellows—no remarkable act, no supernatural manifestation, no miracle. Even her virtues had none of the striking 'colour' which at once marks out an unusual religious destiny. Her monastic sisters, three of whom were also her sisters according to the flesh, failed to recognize those virtues; everything about her was so reserved, one might almost say ordinary and even banal. They were certainly far from recognizing that this frail child was made of the stuff from which God forms the souls He has reserved unto Himself. It might be said that this Carmelite lived solely in order to obey the precept of the *Imitation*: 'Love to be unknown and accounted as nothing.'

Very soon after her death, however, a rumour was heard and quickly spread. Borne by none knows what prescience, what gratitude, report reached the town from Carmel, and thence to many parts of the Christian world: Was not the little nun of Lisieux a saint? Next year a book was published: *The Story of a Soul.*[1] Only two thousand copies

[1] When Teresa of Lisieux died she left three writings of unequal importance in which she set down the facts of her life, all three composed at the request of her religious superiors. She knew that from those documents would be extracted her obituary notice. Thinking that the pages of the modest exercise books could not be used as they stood, she had explicitly authorized her own sister Pauline, a nun of the same convent and for some time her prioress, to cut and complete her draft. After Teresa's death Mother Agnes of Jesus set to work. She fused the three documents into a single narrative, modifying the order and recasting the style. Thus was established the text of *The Story of a Soul*, the only one in circulation during the period with which the present volume is concerned. In 1947 plans were made for a complete and strictly faithful edition of the *Autobiographical Manuscripts of St Teresa of the Child Jesus*. The work was carried out by Père François de Sainte-Marie, a learned Carmelite, assisted by teams of Carmelites and Dominicans. It appeared first in 1956 in the form of a photographic reproduction of the notebooks, accompanied by three volumes of an introduction, notes and tables. Printed editions followed.

were printed; but within a few months hundreds of thousands more were required, and the work has since been translated into thirty-five languages. A new jewel had been added to the crown of Christian mystical literature.

At once the 'little saint of Lisieux', as she was commonly called, became famous. Preachers quoted her from the pulpit, articles were devoted to her in newspapers and reviews and she was made the subject of more than one book. A popular and spontaneous cult developed. There was talk of miracles obtained through her intercession. In the trenches during the First World War countless men liked to keep a picture of her in their pockets; chaplains distributed pamphlets which gave the facts of her life and summarized her teaching; and hardened soldiers began to feel a deep affection for the cloistered nun who had suffered like themselves, who had felt cold like themselves, who had been confronted like themselves with death, and whose words no less than her example came to them as a promise of peace and a hope of eternity. 'There will still be saints canonized by Rome,' Renan had sneered; 'there will never be another canonized by the people.'[1] He was wrong; it was the popular voice that first canonized Teresa, not only in France, but also in Canada, Brazil and Britain.

On 23rd April 1923 Pius XI declared her blessed. Two years later, 17th May 1925, he inscribed her in the catalogue of the saints, at a magnificent ceremony in St Peter's which was attended by a crowd so vast that the Pope himself expressed his amazement. Finally, in 1927, by a decision whose profound significance was not understood at the time, Pius XI proclaimed the young Carmelite, who had never left the enclosure of her convent, Patroness of the Missions.

The glory that followed is unparalleled by that of any other modern saint. Books about her flowed from the press. Grave theologians studied her autobiography. All subsequent popes spoke of her with admiration; for them she is 'the darling child of the world', but she brings an *omen novum*, a new message. Her name re-echoed on all sides, and many towns desired to have a church called after her. Lisieux, the city where she had lived so unknown, was now her city and a place of pilgrimage. Crowds that grew year by year thronged to venerate the reliquary in which her body lies.[2] The basilica subsequently built to contain it was consecrated in 1937 by no less a person than the papal secretary of state, Cardinal Pacelli, whom the Pope had sent as his legate. The renown of the Carmelite saint has spread even beyond the Catholic Church; some Protestants study her doctrine of grace; some

[1] *Études d'histoire religieuse*, p. 162.

[2] It was exhumed and brought back to the convent on 26th March 1923, two months before the beatification.

Orthodox place her image alongside the icon of the Mother of God; and a story is told of a Moslem under sentence of death, who asked that he might have before his eyes at the moment of execution a picture of the Christian virgin. It seems that in this girl, who died quite unknown at the age of twenty-four, twentieth-century man recognizes one of his guides, a messenger of God bidden to reveal to him the words he waits to hear.

What words? The answer is far from simple. We are not here concerned with the influence of a living person, and it is therefore difficult to grasp Teresa's providential role. The greatest saint of modern times seems to have had no relations with those times. Not only did she never leave her convent to denounce the errors of the world, but her book itself makes hardly an allusion to the problems confronting that world. She who knew that she would 'enlighten souls as did the prophets' is utterly remote from the style of the prophets. For Teresa all is secret, all is interior. *The Story of a Soul* is nothing else than the story of her soul, but that personal experience, so genuinely set in the light of the God-Man's infinite love, includes within itself all the anguish, all the suffering of her contemporaries. From that cloistered life, so simple in appearance, there rises a song so pure that it has given peace to millions. The mission of St Teresa of Lisieux cannot be understood except in the supernatural order, by virtue of which she occupies a place of paramount importance in the history of our age.

2. A Little Norman Girl of Fifteen Years

A general audience granted by Leo XIII was proceeding as usual. A French pilgrimage had attended his Mass, and was now filing past him according to protocol. Each pilgrim in turn knelt, kissed the Pope's foot and hand, received his blessing, rose at a signal from one of the Noble Guards and moved on. Suddenly the regular procedure of the ceremony was interrupted. A fifteen-year-old girl, kneeling before the throne, had just kissed the papal slipper. Leo XIII put out his right hand; but instead of kissing it the young pilgrim joined her own, and then, raising tear-filled eyes to the Pontiff, she cried: 'Most Holy Father, I want to ask you a great favour.' A shudder of amazement ran through the crowd of prelates, chamberlains and pilgrims; the gesture was unthinkable. The Pope lowered his head to the girl until their faces almost touched, and his deep, dark eyes looked into hers. Agitated but determined, she continued: 'Most Holy Father, in honour of your jubilee allow me to enter Carmel at fifteen.' Emotion must have caused her voice to tremble, for Leo raised his head and murmured: 'I do not understand . . .' The horrified French priest directing the

pilgrimage intervened: 'Most Holy Father, she is a child who wishes to enter Carmel at the age of fifteen, but the superiors are at present considering her request.' What he did *not* say was that the superiors in question were strongly opposed to her wish, and none more so than himself. 'Well, my child,' said the Pope kindly, 'do whatever the superiors tell you.' The incident seemed closed, but the little girl was not to be discouraged. Laying her hands on the Pope's knee, she implored him once again: 'Most Holy Father, if you say yes, everyone will agree.' Surprised, no doubt, by such childlike audacity, Leo answered slowly and firmly: 'Come, come! You will enter if God so wills.' The two Noble Guards touched her on the shoulder, and then, as she made no move, took hold of her arms. But she remained kneeling, her hands joined and still resting on the Pope's knees. She had at length to be forcibly removed. As she was lifted up Leo placed his hand on her lips, then gave her a final blessing. Next moment she was at the door, in tears.

That child whom the Vatican ceremonial had not daunted was Thérèse, fifth surviving daughter of Louis Stanislaus Martin, a small tradesman, by his wife Zélie Guérin. Both parents were models of piety. The mother died in 1877, when Thérèse was only four, and Martin moved with his children from their original house at Alençon to Lisieux, where his brother-in-law was in business as a chemist. Thérèse had thus spent her childhood in a house called 'Les Buissonets', at Lisieux. She was a pensive little thing, idolized by her father and indulged by her older sisters. Her life would have followed the course normal at that time for little girls of her environment—five years' education at a Benedictine boarding-school, holidays with her family at home or at the seaside—had not the peaceful succession of years been thrice disturbed by the entry into religion of three sisters. Pauline and Marie had become Carmelites; Léonie had tried her vocation with the Poor Clares. Those events had not failed to impress the youngest.

Thérèse was an endearing, attractive child, but liable to outbursts of temper which left her confused and full of amiable remorse. She was highly—almost too highly—sensitive; nor was the excessive tenderness of a doting father calculated to render her less emotional, less vulnerable to the ups and downs of life. But that child had inherited from her mother a remarkable degree of strength, which enabled her very early to control the unduly sensitive side of her character. At once reserved and candid, frank with others and yet able to conceal a whole world of feelings, ideas, dreams and fears—such was Thérèse Martin, whom Les Buissonets treated as a little girl.

However, on at least one occasion in her youth those nearest to her had cause to recognize that not everything about her was as simple as

it appeared. Thérèse was ten years old. Her eldest sister Pauline had just entered Carmel. A few weeks later, after a talk with her uncle Guérin, who spoke to her about her deceased mother, she fell victim to a strange malady in which both the psychological and the physical seemed to play a part: violent fevers, headaches, long fainting fits and delirium, during which latter the child, over-excited and downcast by turns, seemed prey to inexplicable terrors. The whole thing had been attributed to some unknown disease; but today, in the light of her own testimony, there is reason to believe that such an explanation is inadequate.

The authentic portraits of Thérèse at thirteen or fourteen, that is to say just as her life was about to take a decisive turn, leave a curious impression. The face is pleasant, attractive, not with mere prettiness but with a mysterious beauty. Beneath the magnificent fair hair, which was praised by all who saw it, the features are clean cut; the prominent brow is slightly arched, the nose straight, the chin rather broad and rounded, the mouth large. More remarkable still—and this is apparent even in the badly touched-up photographs that were reproduced by the thousand after her beatification—are the eyes; deep, serious and penetrating eyes that seem to gaze beyond the here and now. They are said to have been greenish-blue and wonderfully bright. But as one looks at them even in a mere picture, one feels that they opened upon unknown depths and that the smiling beauty of that girl concealed great interior struggles.

Herein lies the abnormal element of that childhood, as revealed by *The Story of a Soul* together with the evidence of her sisters on one or two points. 'Interior life' is a commonplace term, but all the best of what it can convey is applicable to the invisible reality of that destiny. At an age when other children think only of playing with their dolls, at an age when adolescent girls hear within themselves the first stirring of their hearts, Thérèse had already travelled stages along the road that leads to Carmel, and undergone a mystical experience so rich in discovery and learning that one would hesitate to believe it possible but for the saint's own testimony, in which there was no shadow of falsehood or illusion.

At the age of four, when Thérèse learnt that one of her sisters was entering Carmel, she said: 'I'm going to be a nun too.' Whether or not she fully understood the significance of those words, it is certain that henceforward her rich interior life unfolded on a level completely different from that of her outward existence. Charismata and signs were bestowed upon her, some of them terrifying and painful. Thus at the age of six or seven she had a vision—incomprehensible at the time, the meaning of which later became clear—of her beloved father, afflicted in mind as well as in body, a veiled figure passing before her to

death. Other visions were more consoling. At the height of the ordeal which disturbed her teenage years she received the most wonderful of consolations. While her sisters knelt praying by her bed, where she lay delirious, a statue came to life; the Blessed Virgin came towards her and smiled.... And that was the end of her trial; a sickness which she herself, when she came to set down the facts, did not hesitate to ascribe to the Devil had been turned by the Queen of Heaven into a source of grace and light. That simultaneous march as it were in two worlds was to continue to the end.

More admirable, however, than the mysterious side of her interior life was the continuous progress towards full discovery of the highest truths of Christian faith. It is certain that at the age of eleven Thérèse spent many an hour in her room thinking about God, the shortness of life, eternity, and that she knew herself, without any boasting, destined to glory. But it is equally certain that no hint of that glory was ever revealed to mortal eyes; certain likewise that in early childhood she found what was to become the most decisive maxim of her conduct, namely, that human strength alone would not suffice to reach the appointed goal, that only Christ could realize in her His plan and stamp her with His image. At the moment of her first communion she rediscovered the great law of the mystics, that one must give all to Christ, that one must, in St Paul's words, make Him live within one.

That journey was no easy matter. It is quite false to believe that on her road to sanctity Thérèse walked always on a path of rose petals. 'In that girl of flesh and blood, of nerves and soul, the perfect interior unity was not achieved without struggle and suffering.' [1] A first-hand witness of her interior life [2] has felt entitled to assure us that from the age of four and a half years, until 1886, i.e. until her fourteenth year, Thérèse passed through 'a time of obscurity'.

At all events, after the ecstasy of Our Lady's smile, she had to endure a period of scruples, of profound unrest, of doubt about herself and the orientation of her life. Many saints have passed through a similar ordeal—though generally not in such tender years—and God usually delivers them from it stronger and more firmly rooted in their determination. So it was with Thérèse Martin. On Christmas Day 1886, in a moment of time, the New-born Babe rescued her from darkness. All that she had been unable for several years to do, Jesus did at a stroke, and so magnificently that Thérèse would later speak of that hour as that of her final 'conversion'. The 'night of her soul' was changed into 'torrents of light'. What she then understood, because she had

[1] André Combes.

[2] Her sister Céline, Sœur Geneviève de la Sainte-Face, who entered Carmel later than St Teresa. See Père Plat, *Céline sœur et témoin de Sainte Thérèse de l'Enfant Jésus*, Lisieux, 1963.

remained submissive to the workings of grace, was that all she had suffered had a meaning through and in Christ, that by referring herself to Him even in the smallest details of life she would obtain from Him all she could desire. The twin pillars of what was later to be the spirituality of 'little Teresa' were already present in that soul designed by God for sublime greatness: the spirit of childhood and the supernaturalization of suffering.

Thus at the age of fourteen, when she set out on the Norman pilgrimage to Rome, Thérèse was something very different from the over-excited adolescent who vexed the priests by interrupting the papal audience with her unseemly request, something different from the enthusiastic little pilgrim who grovelled in the arena of the Colosseum in order to kiss the sacred earth hallowed with the blood of martyrs. Those things were mere externals. The interior of that soul was much richer, more extraordinary. That little girl had already advanced far along the mystic way. Face to face with the Crucified, gazing upon a commonplace picture of Him, she had experienced the same feeling of complete renewal as had the other Teresa before the 'Ecce Homo' in the convent chapel, or St Francis of Assisi before the crucifix in the church of St Damien. Better still, she had understood that the interior call she had heard was not addressed to herself alone, but that she would have to reveal it to the world, that her mission would be to save souls for Jesus.

A few weeks before the departure for Rome, indeed, she was given irrefutable proof of that vocation. She had heard talk about an item of news, a horrible murder followed by the criminal's arrest. Then an extraordinary and sublime idea occurred to her: she would spiritually adopt that grim murderer whom human justice was going to blot out from the roll of the living. Surely Christ in dying brought His grace to all men, even to the vilest sinner. For every man—Thérèse unconsciously was thinking like Pascal—He shed a drop of blood. Pranzini too had a right to salvation; so had Thérèse, 'devoured by thirst for souls', 'longing at all costs to rescue sinners from eternal fire', the right to start her career as mediatrix. Her prayers would obtain that conquest of souls which alone can comfort Jesus in His agony. So she prayed, imploring God to save that darkened soul. More, she offered to God, on Pranzini's behalf, the very blood of the Crucified. . . . And she received an answer: God made known to her that He had granted her request. For just as he was laid upon the guillotine, Pranzini, who had refused the aids of faith, suddenly turned and kissed the little crucifix which the chaplain held to his lips. That fact was reported by the newspaper *La Croix*. Thus while the wisdom of men hesitated to admit her to Carmel, Thérèse knew fully the significance for her of that contemplative life for which she longed.

3. The Little Flower

Thérèse Martin entered the Carmel at Lisieux on Monday, 9th April 1898, ten months after she had asked and received her father's consent. It was only right, she thought, that her happiness should have been purchased at a great price. Her happiness . . . but how different it was from that desired by the common run of men. To those who know it only from outside, monastic life appears so easy, sweet and uneventful. Anyone with experience of life in a Carmelite or Trappist house knows how false is that image . . . but Thérèse was not entering Carmel to seek worldly happiness; she was going in search of Christ's love and the joy of His Cross.

Carmel is a penitential order. The great saint who gave it its final form, Teresa of Avila, hoped that her daughters might by their continuous prayer and self-sacrifice take upon themselves the collective sin of the baptized and, by making expiation, reopen the gates of heaven to many an erring or ignorant Christian. Hence the austerity of the Rule. The cell is little better than that of a prisoner: seven or eight metres square; whitewashed walls; plain wooden cross; quilted mattress on a plank by way of bed; no linen or hempen sheets, but two rough serge blankets; a jug of water in one corner; a small bench, plain desk and workbasket: such were the material surroundings of Teresa's religious life. The fare was in keeping, less than modest throughout the year: fasting from 14th September to Ash Wednesday; abstinence from milk, butter and eggs during the whole of Lent, even on Sundays; dry bread and water on Good Friday. Teresa suffered from this regime. The cold particularly was a severe penance; she never got used to the icy dampness of her cell, to those sleepless nights of shivering beneath threadbare blankets, to that rising in the early hours, when her body, chilled and benumbed, found difficulty in adapting itself to the rhythm of liturgical life. 'I nearly died of cold,' she said; and indeed towards the end of her life she maintained that failure to take account of climatic differences in applying the Rule showed lack of common sense.

Those physical sufferings were accompanied by others of quite a different kind but equally hard to endure—those inseparable from community life as such. It is absolutely futile to expect twenty women (or men, for that matter) to live together day after day in a limited space without friction. Having entered Carmel 'under no illusion', to quote her own words, Teresa, observed Père François de Sainte-Marie, 'was not spoiled'. Reading her own testimony one feels that she was completely misunderstood. Mère Geneviève de Sainte-Thérèse, saintly founder of the Lisieux Carmel, considered her desire for

sanctity too ambitious, and tried to clip her wings. It was worse under Mère Marie de Gonzagne, who in nine years was twice her prioress, a woman of great gifts but prone to hypochondria. Time and again the young religious was subject to the acid comments and rebuffs of that disciplinarian. But contact with other members of the community was not much easier: the meddlesome goodwill of one led to the most understandable irritation, while the susceptibility of another seemed very much like spitefulness. Even with those who might have given her the compensations of affection, her two sisters according to the flesh who had preceded her into the convent—and the eldest of whom, Pauline, Mère Agnès de Jésus, was for three years prioress—her relations were few and far from intimate; they were rendered impossible not only by the Rule, but also by the determination of Teresa herself, who refused in advance any such consolation. 'Suffering', wrote the saint, 'opened its arms to me as soon as I entered Carmel'; and her words must be taken literally. But one must read also those which follow: '... and I embraced it with love.'

All the evidence goes to show that Teresa never let it be seen that she was affected by such trials. She appeared gay, smiling, sometimes even frolicsome, with 'heaven in her eyes'. She excelled in making her companions laugh in recreation time, and at organizing little sketches for their amusement. If she was sick and confined to the infirmary, the community seemed to lack something, to lack joy. From these facts one can only infer a deliberate attitude resulting from an effect of self upon self. On all the surviving portraits of St Teresa as a Carmelite [1] we find the same smile, a smile which at first glance suggests nothing but peace and gaiety, but which, when examined closely in its facial context, reveals a certain melancholy approaching sadness, even in the most heavily 'doctored' prints. One imagines the strength of character needed by that affectionate and over-sensitive girl in order thus to dominate her natural reactions and continually present to those around her that equable temperament, that smiling graciousness.

If only, amid those most human sufferings and those mortifications so bravely endured, she could have been consoled by Him whom she had come to seek on Carmel! In obeying the Lord's irresistible summons she had always known she would have none but Him to fulfil the longing of her soul. Other difficulties, however, and other trials awaited her. In her autobiography such phrases as the following often recur: 'I had nothing for my soul but the daily bread of a fearful dryness.' But Teresa conquered that suffering along with the rest. The only ordeal, in fact, which mattered in her eyes was not that inflicted by cold and hunger, any more than it was arising from human

[1] Her sister Céline, who entered after her, was a keen photographer, and, having received permission to bring her camera, she took numerous snapshots of the saint.

relationships, but that which God Himself sometimes imposes on the soul that seeks Him and which He alone can satisfy.

Thus the cloistered life of Sœur Thérèse, which appears from without as simple and untroubled, was really a time of almost uninterrupted trial supported by her with amazing fortitude. There is a widespread but wholly false image of 'the Little Flower'. Based upon a few of the saint's own words about the 'shower of roses' she would send from heaven, words perpetuated by the monstrosities of repository art, it has long distorted the true message of the heroic girl. Its early success was due perhaps to a misunderstanding. It was not roses that Teresa gathered on Carmel; or if she did so it was through a brake of thorns.

4. The 'Little Way of Childhood'

Teresa's spiritual drama was the uncertainty as to whether or not God loved her. She felt so weak, so wretched, incapable of accomplishing by herself the labour necessary for the attainment of her goal—'to be a saint'. For a long time a dreadful darkness hung over her soul; she felt abandoned by Him whom she had come to seek on Carmel. She waited anxiously for an answer through the words of her prioress or in the sermons of a preacher. At the start of her religious life the works of St Teresa of Avila and St John of the Cross helped her towards the light; later she abandoned them, wishing to receive that light only from her confrontation with infinite Love. Still, how difficult it was to grapple with the temptations slipped into her heart by the Enemy. Once he nearly succeeded. 'My vocation', Teresa admitted, 'seemed to me like a dream, a chimaera.' Who knows what havoc that searing doubt might have accomplished, but for some words of sound advice from the novice mistress, Mère Marie des Anges.

Yet in her quest for God Teresa was not abandoned. On several occasions she received mysteriously the answer, as she had received it as a child from the smiling Virgin or on Christmas Eve. Once again, while she was praying in the convent garden, the Mother of God wrapped her in her veil, placing her, as she herself said so simply, in 'a supernatural state'. Another time, during Stations of the Cross, she received the wound of love, and with it the sweet, piercing certitude that she was not forsaken. But here we have one of the most sublime elements of that soul's adventure: she never wished for those charismatic graces, those direct manifestations of God. One idea occurs often in her writings, expressed in different ways: 'I do not desire sensible love; provided Jesus feels it, that is enough for me.' And again: 'I prefer sacrifice to any ecstasy . . .' What sacrifice? The most obscure:

discovery of her own weakness and 'the heart-wounds that cause such suffering'.

There you have the starting-point of Teresa's spirituality, a point which makes her so close to every human being, so sisterly to sinners. She knows herself, she feels herself so much a thing of naught, incapable of reforming herself, of subduing the distractions which grip her during the divine office, of not experiencing irritation towards such-and-such a sister, or annoyance at the bitterly cold nights and that rising in the early hours of a new day. Of course those struggles of a soul marked by God belonged to a realm much higher than that attained by the majority of mortals whose consciences are clogged with sordid sins. But this feature of Teresa's psychology is fundamental. Can one say with the novelist Maxence van der Meersch, who has spoken of her with more fervour than truth, that 'knowing herself vanquished in advance' she simply baptized her failure? No; that would entitle the worst sinner to believe himself on the right road, since he would have failed completely in his efforts to progress. It would mean overlooking the fact that knowledge of her own weakness and wretchedness never prevented Teresa from making that effort of self against self without which no one advances along the way of light. For that heroic girl there was question never of legitimating failure, but of hallowing it.

She starts therefore from a clear knowledge of her weakness. She knows she is nothing in comparison with the great saints whose example she has studied and whom she dreams of imitating. She has understood her limitations, and realized that it is not within her power to surmount them. She is only a feeble child behind convent walls, barred from the heroic vocations upon which, she tells us in a moving passage, she had set her heart—the vocation of an apostle, of a crusader, of a missionary, of a martyr. But since the Lord has willed her so, He must intend to make use of this poor sustenance; He will manage to do something with her weakness. 'Since I cannot grow great', she says, 'I must endure myself as I am, with my countless imperfections.' It is therefore such as she is that she will seek the way to heaven, in her weakness, through that very weakness. This humble nun, who has been brought up on little more than the catechism and the Gospel, is thus in line with the most mysterious, the most paradoxical, teaching of St Paul: 'When I am weak, then am I strongest' (2 Cor. xii. 10).

Such is the way of St Teresa, the 'very straight little way, very short, a completely new little way'. She felt herself too small, quite small, hardly 'a grain of sand'; but she believed with all her soul that her very weakness could provide her with a means of reaching God. How could she doubt it, since Jesus Himself had often said so? 'Amen

I say unto you, unless ye be converted and become as little children, ye shall not enter into the kingdom of heaven.' 'Suffer little children to come unto me . . . for of such is the kingdom of heaven.' 'He who will become little as this child shall be great in the kingdom of heaven.' Here we have what theologians call 'the way of childhood'—the way of St Teresa. It was not for nothing that her name in religion placed her under the protection of the *Child* Jesus.

'This way', said Benedict XV, 'excludes the feeling of self-satisfaction, the presumption of thinking oneself able to attain a supernatural state by human means, and the mistaken idea that one can rely upon oneself in time of peril and temptation.' Easy? No indeed. Here one must not be misled by the adjective 'little' which Teresa employs. In order to follow the 'little way', unrelenting self-control, humility and complete abandonment to the divine will are required. Teresa's spirituality is not quietism; only at the cost of continual effort does the soul finish by being fully restored to God. Nor is it mere stoicism; for Teresa the little way is impossible for man alone.

Closely linked with her notion of the spiritual life is a definite method of progress therein, starting from the little things of everyday life. Teresa asks nothing more than acceptance with humility and simplicity of each difficulty as it comes; complete fulfilment of the duties of one's state, no matter how hard that may be; the taking of every opportunity to help one's neighbour; subjection of oneself to small sacrifices that will be known to God alone. And all in the full light of Christ's charity. But this sum total of day-to-day striving demands a degree of courage greater than that of certain heroic deeds, especially if that victory over self is to be accompanied by a smile and appear quite natural.

By supernaturalizing the whole of daily life, Teresa aspired to the complete liberation from egoism and the submission of all the faculties to supreme Love, i.e. to sanctity. That sanctity, as she herself so rightly said, consists not in any particular act, but in 'a disposition of the heart which renders us humble and little in the arms of God, conscious of our weakness and confident to the point of rashness in His fatherly goodness'.

5. Offered as a Holocaust

If Teresa's spiritual experience had stopped at this point it would, though worthy of admiration, have lacked its full significance. In order fully to appreciate the 'little' Carmelite, one must consider the sacrificial aspect of her vocation.

Here we enter a world to which, of course, those without the Christian faith have no access—the world which we call 'the communion of saints' and which the Church requires us to accept as a dogma. There sinners and saints form a single whole; all are elements of the Church, Christ's mystical Body. And since they are associated one with another by Christ's Blood, by the grace of baptism and by the common call to salutation, it is natural that the merits of the saints should overflow mysteriously upon the rest, that their sacrifices should compensate in the eyes of infallible Justice for all the wickedness and shortcomings of sinners. This fact it is that warrants the existence of contemplative orders.

When she entered Carmel, Thérèse Martin expressly declared that such would be her vocation. Her sister Céline tells us: 'She regarded religious life principally as a means of saving souls.' All the remainder of her life was spent in the certitude that her ultimate purpose was to labour in order to win souls for God by offering to divine Justice all that she was, all that she did. Thereby her 'little way' assumed a meaning much higher than that of a method of self-discipline; it led to a participation of the praying soul in the economy of salutation.

Since God loves men, he cannot be only a God who chastises. The 'waves of infinite tenderness' in Him must spread over the earth. His merciful love 'desires to embrace souls' and draw them to Him. If He is asked with sufficient confidence, He will be constrained to mercy. Only an offering of love is needed in order to ask Him....

Teresa reached that decisive stage on 9th June, feast of the Most Holy Trinity, 1895, when she resolved to offer herself entirely to 'Merciful Love', to the most loving God who wishes not to chastise men for their faults, but to burn them with love in order to purify them.

She had now reached the mystical summit; she had really climbed Mount Carmel. Between May and September 1896 she understood—or rather God made her understand—that it was her true road. As soon as the soul has delivered itself entire to Divine Love, all other purposes are nothing in comparison. Suffering itself finds its meaning, no longer in penitential acceptance, but in that whirlwind of love which carries away the soul by uniting her with the sufferings which Jesus Himself endured for the love of men.

Offered as a holocaust for the salvation of the world, Teresa of the Child Jesus knew henceforth that she had accomplished all that the Lord expected of her. And she had found peace. Sufferings might return, among them the very worst—divine abandonment and tormenting doubt; but Teresa was now established, far beyond such things, in the supernatural love which is that of Jesus dying, abandoned by all on Calvary.

6. 'There is no Greater Love than This . . .'

Since her early days in the convent there had been abundant evidence that Teresa's physique was not equal to the austerities of Carmel, which were aggravated by those to which she subjected herself. Her superiors and companions, however, failed to notice her increasing pallor or that she was growing thin; they were so accustomed to seeing her, and were no doubt also misled by her constant good humour, her smile and the complete absence of any complaining.

During the year 1895 the state of her health deteriorated more seriously. She suffered frequently from a little dry cough, and, as we now know from her book, she was feverish and felt increasingly tired. But she said nothing, even to the prioress, who at that time was Mère Agnès, her sister Pauline. January and February 1896 were terrible months—wet and bitterly cold. Tuberculosis had no difficulty in laying hold of so weakened an organism.

Lent came, and the invalid followed it as she had done for years: fasting and abstinence, the discipline for the space of a *Miserere* on Tuesday, Thursday and Friday in Holy Week. Still the community, seeing her fervour at the divine office, suspected nothing. On the night of Maundy Thursday Teresa received what she later described as her 'first summons, like a gentle and distant murmur . . .' Who would believe that this poetically mystical language referred to the frightful reality of a haemorrhage? But here we must let the saint herself speak.

'At midnight I returned to our cell, and had hardly laid my head on the pillow when I felt a stream bubbling up to my lips. . . . I thought I was going to die and my heart was overwhelmed with joy; however, as I had just extinguished our little lamp, I mortified my curiosity until morning and slept peacefully.' Only in the morning, when the bell called her to rise, did she go to the window and look at her handkerchief: it was dark red, full of blood and half dried.

Having taken part in the divine office as usual, and after chapter, Teresa knelt before her prioress and told her what had happened. The prioress was now Mère Marie de Gonzagne, that disciplinarian whose robust frame knew nothing of sickness and who was obsessed, both for herself and for others, with the desire for austerity. From her Teresa 'easily obtained' permission to complete the observance of Lent. She continued her life as usual, working like the others, though with a greater effort, and trying always to hide her condition.

But there was still that dry, obstinate cough which she could not hide, which finally alarmed the prioress. A doctor came to examine Teresa; he decided there was nothing seriously wrong and prescribed

some fashionable remedies, including a more adequate diet. This latter seemed to take effect, and the cough diminished.

The winter of 1896–7, however, left no doubt as to the true state of affairs. One day one of the novices, of whom she had charge, saw her almost fainting, obviously at the end of her endurance, and she told the prioress, whose eyes at last were opened. Pauline and Céline, too, now learned of last year's haemorrhage and tenderly rebuked Teresa for her silence. It was decided to forbid her to attend the offices, and the doctors were again called in. Too late. At the beginning of July, despite her protests, she was moved from her cell and given a proper bed in the infirmary.

From this time Teresa passed through the successive stages of advanced tuberculosis. About that there was nothing extraordinary; it was in a sense merely a continuation of her 'little way'. But she had to face another and more terrible ordeal. At Easter 1897 darkness again enveloped her soul, plunging her into a night more fearful than any she had yet experienced. This state of dereliction, except for momentary intervals when she was visited by the Venerable Anne of Jesus and even by Our Lady herself, was to endure until the very last moments of Teresa's life. Nevertheless she recognized here too the hand of God, accepted the ordeal with love, and died at about 7 p.m. on Thursday, 30th September 1897, with these words upon her lips: 'Oh, I love . . . My God . . . I love you.'

For anyone who understands its meaning and significance, the message of St Teresa of Lisieux is the most complete and relevant retort to that atheistic humanism, which we have seen to include all forms of contemporary apostasy. To the assertions of Nietzsche and Karl Marx the saint opposes the sole irrefutable answer, that which is given not only through the written word, but which springs from vital experience and is sealed with blood. 'God is dead,' said the prophet of Sils-Maria. For Teresa it was nothing to say that He lives; He is life, so manifestly that when everything might have persuaded her of His annihilation, she still knew that nothing could destroy Him, because He is the sole Reality.

CHRONOLOGICAL TABLE

DATE	HISTORY OF THE CHURCH	POLITICAL AND SOCIAL EVENTS	ART, LITERATURE AND SCIENCE
1871	Pius IX rejects the Law of Guarantees. Beginning of the *Kulturkampf*. Foundation of workers' clubs (Maignen, La Tour du Pin, Mun).	Proclamation of the German Empire. Treaty of Frankfort. Paris Commune. *Kulturkampf*. The trade unions.	Gramme presents the dynamo to the Paris Academy of Sciences. Pottier composes the 'Internationale'.
1872	Mgr Mermillod and the Swiss 'Little *Kulturkampf*'.		
1873	In Germany the May Laws. Birth of St Teresa of Lisieux.	Fall of Thiers: McMahon succeeds him.	
1874	Confessional Laws in Austria.	Windthorst, president of the German Centre.	
1875	Opening of Catholic universities in France.	Garcia Moreno assassinated.	
1876			Graham Bell invents the telephone.
1877		In France, crisis of 16th May. Gambetta's saying: 'Clericalism, there's the enemy!'	Charles Cros and the gramophone.
1878	Death of Pius IX (7th Feb.). Election of Leo XIII (20th Feb.).	Death of Victor Emmanuel II. Italian Catholics forbidden to take part in political elections. Treaty of Berlin.	The combustion engine (gas). Edison and the electric lamp.
1879	Encyclical *Aeterni Patris* (on Thomism).	End of the *Kulturkampf*.	
1880	French laws against the congregations.		Rodin's 'St John the Baptist'.
1881	Remains of Pius IX outraged in Rome. First eucharistic congress. Lavigerie vicar apostolic of Carthage (Tunis). Foundation of the *Union de Fribourg* (Social Catholics).	Assassination of Czar Alexander II. Treaty of Bardo (Tunisia).	Abbé de Broglie's *Positivisme et Science mentale.*
1882	The martyrs of Uganda.	Signing of the Triple Alliance. Death of Garibaldi and of Gambetta. In France, compulsory and secular education.	
1883		France in Annam and Tonking. Foundation of first Marxist group.	Death of Louis Veuillot. Papal Brief on historical studies, and opening of the Vatican archives. Foundation of the Biblical School (Jerusalem) and of the newspaper *La Croix* (Paris). Death of Karl Marx.

DATE	HISTORY OF THE CHURCH	POLITICAL AND SOCIAL EVENTS	ART, LITERATURE AND SCIENCE
1884	Encyclical *Nobilissima Gallorum* (to the French nation) and *Humanum genus* (against freemasonry). Giuseppe Sarto, Bishop of Mantua. Third national council of Baltimore.	French law on syndicates.	
1885	*Immortale Dei* (on Christian politics). Leo XIII arbitrates in the Carolines affair.	International measures against slavery.	Hertz discovers the principle of radio.
1886	The martyrs of Uganda.	'Boulangisme' in France. Drumont publishes *La France juive*. Crispi in power.	Linotype. Combustion engine (petrol).
1887	First Christian syndicates. Harmel's workers' pilgrimage.		Condemnation of Rosmini. The first skyscraper.
1888	Death of Father Hecker. Thérèse Martin enters Carmel.	Accession of Wilhelm II.	The pneumatic tyre.
1889	Foundation of Fribourg University. Institution of the feast of the Sacred Heart.		The Eiffel Tower. Chardonnet and artificial silk.
1890	Cardinal Lavigerie toasts the *Ralliement*. Loisy's thesis.	Conference on labour at Berlin.	Renan's *L'Avenir de la Science*. Branly discovers the principle of wireless telegraphy. Pithecanthropus.
1891	*Rerum Novarum*.	Franco-Russian alliance.	The motor-car.
1892	Encyclical *Au milieu des sollicitudes* (on the *Ralliement*). Circular on the nationality of American bishops.	Panama scandal in France.	Marcy presents the first 'cinematograph'. Death of Renan.
1893	*Providentissimus* (on Scripture). Mgr Sarto patriarch of Venice and cardinal. Loisy leaves the Institut Catholique.		Blondel's thesis, *L'Action*. Death of Taine.
1894	Constitution *Orientalium* for the Eastern Churches. Joan of Arc proclaimed Venerable.	Spueller's discourse on the new 'spirit'. Assassination of Carnot. Condemnation of Dreyfus. Foundation of *Le Sillon*. Massacre of the Armenians. Accession of Czar Nicholas II. Sino-Japanese war.	Conversion of Brunetière after an audience with Leo XIII. Lumière and the cinema.
1895	Opera dei Congressi in Italy.		Huysmans' *En Route*. Branly then Marconi accomplish radio. Röntgen: X-rays.
1896	Malines conferences (on unity).	Italian defeat at Adowa (Ethiopia). France in Madagascar.	
1897	*Divinum illud* on the Holy Ghost. Americanism. Death of St Teresa of Lisieux.	Greco-Turkish War.	Léon Bloy's *La Femme pauvre*.
1898		The Dreyfus Affair. Spanish-American War. Fashoda.	Death of Puvis de Chavannes.

DATE	HISTORY OF THE CHURCH	POLITICAL AND SOCIAL EVENTS	ART, LITERATURE AND SCIENCE
1899	Leo III's letter to Cardinal Gibbons on Americanism. Ordination of Eugenio Pacelli. Encyclical *Annum Sacrum* on the Sacred Heart.	Dreyfus pardoned. Marc Sangnier takes direction of *Le Sillon*. Transvaal War.	Planck and the Quantum theory. Taylor's system. Haeckel's *L'Enigme de l'Univers*.
1900	Foundation of Utrecht University.	Assassination of Umberto I. Boxer Rising in China.	Péguy founds *Cahiers de la Quinzaine*. Death of Nietzsche. Pierre and Marie Curie: radium.
1901	Encyclical *Graves de communi* on Christian democracy. In France, law of associations (against the teaching congregations).	Death of Queen Victoria and accession of Edward VII.	
1902	Combes launches attack on the congregations. Establishment of the Biblical Commission. Beginning of the Modernist crisis: Loisy's *L'Évangile et l'Église*.		
1903	Death of Leo XIII (20th July), election of Pius X (4th August); Merry del Val secretary of state.	Manchurian War (1904–5). Foundation of 'Bolshevism'.	The brothers Wright and the aeroplane. Pius X's *motu proprio* on sacred music.
1904	Decree on the codification of Canon Law. Suppression of the *veto*. President Loubet visits the King of Italy; diplomatic relations between France and the Vatican broken off. Charles de Foucauld settles in the Sahara. First Social Week (Lyons).	The Entente Cordiale.	
1905	Law of Separation (France). Growth of the Modernist crisis: Le Roy's *Qu'est-ce qu'un dogme?* and Fogazzaro's *Il Santo*. Decree on frequent communion. *Il fermo proposito* on Italian Catholic Action.	Russo-Japanese War. Russian revolution.	Discovery of the photo-electric effect (basis of the photo-electric cell). Einstein and relativity.
1906	*Vehementer nos* against the separation; inventories; rejection of *cultuelles*; Briand's conciliatory circular.	Dreyfus rehabilitated. Conference of Algeciras on Morocco.	Death of Brunetière.
1907	Condemnation of Modernism, decree *Lamentabili* and Encyclical *Pascendi*. Mgr Della Chiesa Archbishop of Bologna.		Death of Huysmans.
1908	Excommunication of Loisy; condemnation of 'democratic Christian' journals.		Death of Zola.

DATE	HISTORY OF THE CHURCH	POLITICAL AND SOCIAL EVENTS	ART, LITERATURE AND SCIENCE
1909	Foundation of the Biblical Institute. Joan of Arc beatified.	Massacre of Armenians.	
1910	Decree *Quam singulari* on the communion of children. Condemnation of *Le Sillon*. Roosevelt incident in Rome.	French law on workers' retreats. In Portugal, assassination of King Manuel, proclamation of republic.	Péguy's *Le Mystère de la charité de Jeanne d'Arc*.
1911	Constitution on the Breviary.	Agadir incident. Italo-Turkish War. Proclamation of the Chinese republic.	Rutherford analyses the atom.
1912	*Singulari quadrini* on the German syndicates.	French protectorate over Morocco. Balkan War.	Péguy's pilgrimage to Chartres. Claudel's *L'Annonce faite à Marie*.
1913		Poincaré president of France.	Deaths of Péguy and Psichari.
1914	Seven books by Maurras placed on the index, but publication of the fact suspended. Death of Pius X (20th Aug.), election of Benedict XV (3rd Sept.); Cardinal Gasparri secretary of state.	Outbreak of the First World War.	
1915	Missionary Union of the Clergy.		Einstein and relativity.
1916	Murder of Charles de Foucauld (1st Dec.).		
1917	Congregation of the Index attached to the Holy Office. Promulgation of the Code of Canon Law. The Pope's note to the belligerents. Mgr Pacelli nuncio at Munich. Foundation of the Congregation for the Oriental Churches.	Russian revolution (March–Nov.). In Mexico, abolition of ecclesiastical property.	Death of Léon Bloy.
1918	Mgr Ratti in Poland. *Maximum illud* on the missions. Foundation of the Institute of Oriental Studies.	11th Nov., Armistice.	Rutherford splits the atom.
1919	Raising of the ban for parliamentary elections in Italy.	Revolution of Bela Kun in Hungary (April). Treaties of Versailles, Saint-Germain, Trianon and Neuilly.	The Ford System.
1920	Mgr Pacelli nuncio at Berlin. Encyclical *Spiritus Paraclitus* on Scripture. Canonization of Joan of Arc.	Poland repels the Bolshevik invasion.	
1921	Mgr Ratti Archbishop of Milan and cardinal. Resumption of diplomatic relations with France. Malines Conversation. University of the Sacred Heart, Milan.	Ireland a Free State.	

DATE	HISTORY OF THE CHURCH	POLITICAL AND SOCIAL EVENTS	ART, LITERATURE AND SCIENCE
1922	Death of Benedict XV (22nd Jan.), election of Pius XI (6th Feb.); Gasparri remains secretary of state. Encyclical on peace. Foundation of J.O.C.	Mussolini takes power in Italy. Mustapha Kemal in Turkey.	Notre-Dame de Raincy, the first concrete church.
1923		Occupation of the Ruhr. Primo de Rivera dictator in Spain.	Louis de Broglie and wave mechanics.
1924		Death of Lenin.	
1925	Several concordats. Canonization of St Teresa of Lisieux. In France, formation of the Fédération Nationale Catholique. *Quas primas* (Christ the King). Death of Cardinal Mercier. The Abbé Cardijn with Pius XI (J.O.C.).	Treaty of Locarno.	
1926	Encyclical *Rerum Ecclesiae* on the native clergy, and (28th Oct.) consecration of the first six coloured bishops. Protests against the Mexican persecution. Creation of the French J.O.C.		
1927	Consecration of the first Japanese bishop. The affair of *Action française*.	Congress of Lausanne.	
1928	Concordats and *modus vivendi* (Portugal, Czechoslovakia). Rome condemns anti-semitism.		
1929	The Lateran Agreements (11th Feb.). Foundation of Vatican City.	Economic crisis in U.S.A., then in Europe. Dictatorship of Stalin in U.S.S.R.	J. Maritain's *Degrés du Savoir*.
1930	Encyclical *Casti connubii* on Christian marriage. Mgr Pacelli secretary of state.		Papini's *Vita di Cristo*.
1931	Social encyclical *Quadragesimo anno*. Encyclical *Non abbiamo bisogno* against Fascism.	The Spanish republic.	Death of Vincent d'Indy.
1932	Encyclical *Acerbo nimis* on the Mexican persecution. Creation of an Institute of the Missions.		First essays in television.
1933	Concordat with the German Reich.	Hitler chancellor of the Reich. Salazar draws up the Portuguese constitution.	Death of the Abbé Bremond.
1934	Condemnation of the chief German racist books.	Assassination of the Austrian Chancellor Dollfuss. Hitler 'Reichsführer'.	The Joliot-Curie discovery of artificial radioactivity.
1935		Italy invades Ethiopia.	

DATE	HISTORY OF THE CHURCH	POLITICAL AND SOCIAL EVENTS	ART, LITERATURE AND SCIENCE
1936	Cardinal Pacelli legate in S. America. *Vigilanti cura* on the cinema.	In France, Popular Front and Blum's ministry. In Spain, beginning of civil war.	F. Mauriac's *Vie de Jésus*.
1937	Encyclicals *Mit brennender Sorge* against National Socialism; *Divini Redemptoris* against Communism. Apostolic letter *Nos es muy* on the Mexican Church. Cardinal Pacelli legate at Lisieux.		
1938	Death of Père Lagrange.	Annexation of Austria by Germany; Czechoslovak crisis. Hitler in Rome. Conference of Munich.	Beginnings of electronics.
1939	Death of Pius XI (10th Feb.); election of Pius XII (2nd March); Cardinal Maglione secretary of state. July, raising of the ban on *Action française*. 29th Oct., consecration of twelve coloured bishops.	End of Czechoslovakia. Italy occupies Albania. German-Soviet Pact. 1st Sept., invasion of Poland, beginning of the Second World War.	

SELECT BIBLIOGRAPHY

THE following are the principal works cited by the author in his extensive bibliographical notes.

GENERAL HISTORY

Volumes xviii–xx in the 'Peuples et civilisations' series: M. Baumont, *L'Essor industriel et l'impérialisme économique* (1878–1904); P. Renouvin, *La Crise européenne et la première guerre mondiale*; M. Baumont, *La Faillite de la paix* (1918–39). R. Scherb, *Le XIXe siècle*, 1957, and C. Morazé, *Les Bourgeois conquérants*, 1957. *Bilan du monde* (1958–9).

RELIGIOUS HISTORY

Fr Heiler, *Der Katholizismus seine Idee und seine Erscheinung*, 1923; Dom Gaillard, *Histoire de l'Église*, 2 vols., 1962; C. Ledré, *Un siècle sous la tiare*, 1955; L. E. Halkin, 'Un Siècle d'histoire pontificale: de Pie IX à Pie XI' in *La Revue nouvelle* (Brussels), July–August, 1951; A. Latreille (ed.), *Histoire du Catholicisme en France*, vol. iii, 1962. See also *Enciclopedia cattolica.*

CHAPTER I. 'GOD IS DEAD!'

P. de Lubac, *Le Drame de l'humanisme athée*, 1944; E. Borne, *Dieu n'est pas mort*, 1959; J. Lacroix, *Le Sens de l'athéisme contemporain*, 1958; U. von Balthazar, *Dieu et l'homme d'aujourd'hui* (French trans.), 1958; R. Guardini *La Fin des temps modernes* (French trans.), 1952; I. Lepp, *Psychanalyse de l'athéisme moderne*, 1961; G. Combes, *L'Assaut contre le Christ*, 1948; G. Huard, *Essai sur l'histoire de la Franc-maçonnerie*, 1930; C. Andler: *Nietzsche* (*see also* lives and studies of Nietzsche by L. A. Salomé, 1904, L. Klager, 1930, and D. Halévy, 1909); Père H. Chambre, *Christianisme et Communisme*, 1959; J. V. Calvez, *La Pensée de Karl Marx*, 1956.

CHAPTER II. UPON THIS ROCK . . . MY CHURCH

Mgr T'Serclaes, *Le Pape Léon*, 1894–1906; B. O'Reilly, *Life of Leo XIII*, 1886; Mourret, *Histoire générale de l'Église*, vol. ix, 1933 (also lives and studies of Leo by Guillermin, 1902, F. Hayward, 1930, V. Mangano, 1931, E. Soderini, 1932). The most important works on Pius X are those by Mgr Marchesan (1910) and Père Dal-Gal (1953); *see also* Cardinal Merry del Val, *Impressions et souvenirs*, 1951, and lives of Pius by C. Ledré (1952), F. Hayward (1951). On Benedict XV *see* G. Goyau, *Papauté et chrétienté sous Benoît XV*, 1922; F. Hayward, *Un pape méconnu, Benoît XV*, 1955. Among numerous studies of Pius XI are Y. de la Brière, *Les Luttes présentes de l'Église*, six series, 1924–38; A Saint-Denis, *Pie XI contre les Idoles*, 1938; M. Pernot, *Le Saint-Siège, l'Église catholique et la politique mondiale*, 1932; also the memoirs of Mgr Confalonieri (1957), Mgr Arborio Mella de Sant' Elia (1956) and Cardinal Ruffini (1961).

CHAPTERS III (LEO XIII: OPTIONS ON THE FUTURE), V (PIUS X and 'THE INTERESTS OF GOD'), VII (WAR AND PEACE), IX (THE GREAT BATTLES OF POPE PIUS XI)

GENERAL: A. Latreille and A. Siegfried, *Les Forces religieuses de la vie politique*, 1951; Mgr Cristiani, *Le Vatican politique*, 1956. FRANCE: A Dansette, *Histoire religieuse de la France contemporaine*, 1951; Père Lecanuet, *Église de France sous la IIIe République*, vols. ii and iii, 1930, 1931; J. Brugerette, *Le Prêtre et la société contemporaine*, vols. ii and iii, 1935–6; M. Vaussard, *Histoire de la démocratie chrétienne*, vol. i, 1956; M. Darbon, *Le Conflit entre la droite et la gauche dans le Catholicisme français*, 1953; L. Capéran, *De l'avènement de Combes à la Séparation*, 1927; L. V. Méjan, *La Séparation*, 1959; L. Crouzil, *Quarante ans de séparation*, 1945. ITALY: G. Candeloro, *Il movimento cattolico in Italia*, 1953–61; G. Spadolini, *Opposizione cattolica*, 1956. BELGIUM: H. Pirenne, *Histoire de Belgique*, 1926, and Deharveng's *Histoire de la Belgique contemporaine*. GERMANY: J. Rovan, *Histoire de la démocratie chrétienne*, vol. ii, 1956; G. Goyau, *Bismarck et le Kulturkampf*, 1922; also study of Bismarck by H. Valloton, 1961. For the relations of Pius XI with Nazism and Communism: H. Mau, H. Krausnick and A. Grosser, *National-socialisme allemand*, 1963; A. Galter, *Le Communisme et l'Église catholique*, 1956; B. Féron, *Dieu en Russie soviétique*, 1961.

CHAPTER IV. THE TRIUMPHANT MARCH OF SOCIAL CATHOLICISM

R. Kothen, *La Pensée et l'action sociale des catholiques, 1759–1944*, 1958; G. Hoog, *Histoire du catholicisme social en France, 1871–1931*, 1946; H. Rollet, *L'Action sociale des catholiques en France*, 2 vols., 1948, 1950; J. Zamanski, *Nous, catholiques sociaux*, 1947; E. Barbier, *Histoire du catholicisme libéral et du catholicisme social en France*, 5 vols., 1922; X. Vallat, *La Croix, les lys et la peine des hommes*, 1960; E. Ritter, *Die Katholisch-Social Bewegung*, 1954; C. Massard, L'*Œuvre sociale du cardinal Mermillod*, 1914; R. Rezsohazy, *Origines et formation du catholicisme social en Belgique*, 1958; P. Gehin, *Le Catholicisme liègeois et la question sociale*, 1959; A. Gambasin, *Il movimento sociale nell' opera dei Congressi*, 1958; A. de Gasperi, *I cattolici dall' opposizione al governo*, 1955.

CHAPTER VI. MODERNISM: A SPIRITUAL AND INTELLECTUAL CRISIS

J. Rivière, *Le Modernisme dans l'Église*, 1929; E. Poulat, *Histoire, dogme et critique dans la crise moderniste*, 1962; Père Rouquette, 'Bilan du Modernisme' in *Études*, June 1956; J. Guilton, *Pensée moderne et le catholicisme*, 1937; Abbé Steinmann, *Friedrich von Hügel*, 1963; P. Scoppola, *Crisi modernista e rinnovamento cattolico in Italia*, 1962; 'N. Fontaine', *Saint-Siège, Action française et Catholiques intégraux*, 1928; J. Paliard, *Maurice Blondel et le dépassement chrétien*, 1950.

CHAPTER VIII. FROM SOCIAL ACTION TO CATHOLIC ACTION

G. Lévard, *Chances et périls du syndicalisme chrétien*, 1935; Mgr Guerry, *L'Action catholique*, 1936; Cardinal Richard, *Notions sommaires sur l'Action catholique*, 1958; E. Vauthier, *Initiation de l'Action catholique*, 1955; G. Nosengo, *L'Apostolato dei laici*, 1947; P. Bayart, *Action catholique spécialisée*, 1935; F. Klein, *Nouvelles croisades de jeunes travailleurs*, 1934; Abbé Cardijn, *Laïcs en première ligne*, 1963, and *Fiches de pastorale*, 1958; J. Rouzet, *Jocisme mondial*, 1935.

CHAPTER X. THE CHURCH CO-EXTENSIVE WITH THE WORLD

BRITAIN: D. Mathew, *Catholicism in England*, 1936; E. I. Watkin, *Roman*

Catholicism in England, 1957. U.S.A.: T. Roemer, *The Catholic Church in the United States*, 1950; L. Putz (ed.), *The Catholic Church in the U.S.A.*, 1956. Canada: G. de Québec, *L'Église catholique au Canada*, 1944; R. Blanchard, *Le Canada français*, 1960. Latin America: C. la Torre, *L'Église catholique en Amérique Latine*, 1910; A. Serrau and others, *Terres d'angoisse et d'espérance*, 1959. Eastern Churches: R. Janin, *Églises orientales et rites orientaux*, 1955; C. de Clercq, *Les Églises unies d'Orient*, 1930. N. Liesel, *Les Liturgies catholiques orientales*, 1959; J. Hajjar, *Les Chrétiens uniates du Proche Orient*, 1962.

Chapter XI. The Church Co-extensive with the World

Mgr Delacroix (ed.), *Histoire universelle des Missions*, vol. v, 1963; Missionary Union of the Clergy, *Le Siège apostolique et les Missions*, 1959; T. Ohm, *Les Principaux Faits de l'histoire des Missions*, 1962; B. de Vaulx, *Les Missions, leur histoire*, 1960; R. P. Millot, *Missions d'aujourd'hui*, 1960; O. Engelbert, *Père Damien*, 1963; Cardinal Constantine, *Réforme des Missions au XXe siècle*, 1960; B. de Vaulx, *Églises de couleur*, 1958; J. F. Six, *Itinéraire Spirituel de Charles de Foucauld*, 1958, and *Vie de Charles de Foucauld*, 1962.

Chapter XII. Saint Teresa of Lisieux

Père François de Sainte-Marie and others (ed.), *Manuscrits autobiographiques de sainte Thérèse de l'Enfant Jésus*, 1962; Mgr A. Combes, *Sainte Thérèse, contemplation et apostolat*, 1949; *Introduction à la spiritualité de sainte Thérèse*, 1948; *Sainte Thérèse et la souffrance*, 1948; *L'Amour de Jésus chez sainte Thérèse*, 1949; Père Piat, *Histoire d'une famille*, 1945; Père Petitot, *Vie intégrale de sainte Thérèse*, 1925.

INDEX

INDEX

D0124877